RISING SUN, FALLING SKIES

RISING SUN, FALLING SKIES

THE DISASTROUS JAVA SEA CAMPAIGN OF WORLD WAR II

JEFFREY R. COX

First published in Great Britain in 2014 by Osprey Publishing,
PO Box 883, Oxford, OX1 9PL, UK
PO Box 3985, New York, NY 10185-3985, USA
E-mail: info@ospreypublishing.com

Osprey Publishing is part of the Osprey Group

A CIP catalogue record for this book is available from the British Library

ISBN: 978 1 78096 726 4
E-pub ISBN: 978-1-4728-0834-9
PDF ISBN: 978-1-4728-0833-2

Page design by Ken Vail Graphic Design, Cambridge, UK
Index by Mark Swift
Cartography by Boundford
Typeset in Adobe Garamond Pro, Myriad Pro, Minion Pro & Trajan Pro
Originated by PDQ Digital Media Solutions, Suffolk, UK
Printed in China through World Print Ltd

14 15 16 17 18 19   12 11 10 9 8 7 6 5 4 3

Osprey Publishing is supporting the Woodland Trust, the UK's leading woodland
conservation charity, by funding the dedication of trees.

www.ospreypublishing.com

GLOSSARY

ABDA	American–British–Dutch–Australian
ABDACOM	American–British–Dutch–Australian Command
ABDAFLOAT	ABDA Navy Operational Command
ABDAIR	ABDA Air Operational Command
ABDARM	ABDA Army Operational Command (sometimes called ABDARMY)
asdic	European term for sonar sound detection equipment
HMS	His / Her Majesty's Ship – prefix used for ships of the Royal Navy
HR. MS.	*Harer Majesteits* (English: His Netherlands Majesty's Ship) – prefix used for ships of the Royal Netherlands Navy
kamikaze	relating to a suicide mission, e.g. a kamikaze pilot was trained to make a suicidal attack
Kido Butai	the primary Japanese air carrier attack force
Tokkeitai	the Imperial Japanese Navy's military police
US Navy	United States Navy
USS	United States Ship – prefix used for ships of the US Navy

CONTENTS

Prologue 7

Chapter 1. On the Day Before 11

Chapter 2. Just a Little More Time 29

Chapter 3. Breakdown 53

Chapter 4. Finding Trouble 69

Chapter 5. Shooting at Venus 113

Chapter 6. Slapped Together 127

Chapter 7. Luck – The Battle of Balikpapan 151

Chapter 8. Bloody Shambles 163

Chapter 9. Can't Catch a Break – The Battle of the Flores Sea 173

Chapter 10. A Thousand Cuts 191

Chapter 11. Too Clever by Half – The Battle of Badoeng Strait 223

Chapter 12. No Breath to Catch – Preliminaries to the Battle of the Java Sea 241

Chapter 13. Nerk Nerk Nerk – The Sinking of the *Langley* 265

Chapter 14. One Shell – Day Action of the Battle of the Java Sea 281

Chapter 15. A Turn Too Far – The Second Part of the Battle of the Java Sea 307

Chapter 16. A Hopeless Plan – The Escape from Java 325

Chapter 17.   Dancing in the Dark – The Battle of Soenda Strait   339

Chapter 18.   Nowhere to Run – The Second Battle of the Java Sea   353

Chapter 19.   To the Winds – Escape Attempts from Java   369

Chapter 20.   Aftermath – Not Quite Vanquished   401

    Notes   416

    Bibliography   474

    Index   480

PROLOGUE

Few events have ever shaken a country, or become part of the national consciousness, in the way that the Japanese attack on Pearl Harbor affected the United States. Even today, more than seven decades after that fateful Sunday, almost every American knows the date December 7, 1941. Everyone knows what happened on that date – the start of World War II in the Pacific.

It is common knowledge. It is also wrong.

For World War II in the Pacific did not begin at 7:55 am local time on December 7, 1941 with the massive surprise attack on the base of the United States Pacific Fleet at Pearl Harbor: an attack that sank virtually all the fleet's battleships and left it, in the word of one official message, "immobilized" and unable to help fight against the Japanese hell that was about to descend on Southeast Asia.

By 7:55 am on December 7, World War II in the Pacific had been in progress for more than eight hours.

The first act of the war was not nearly as spectacular as Pearl Harbor, but it was just as dramatic. And deadly. It took place over the South China Sea, off the coast of what is now Cambodia. There, an Australian pilot by the name of Patrick Bedell and his flight crew, operating a British Royal Air Force Consolidated PBY Catalina flying boat out of Singapore, was intercepted by Japanese fighters. Shot down in an exploding fireball, Bedell and his flight crew were killed, their bodies never found.

Their "crime?" They had gotten too close to the Japanese invasion fleet destined for British Malaya, now called Malaysia.

While Pearl Harbor attracted all the headlines, for obvious reasons, the deaths of Patrick Bedell and his crew were actually the more significant incident. For Pearl Harbor was only the means to an end. Bedell and his crew were standing in the way of the ultimate goal: the conquest of tin- and rubber-filled Malaya with its fortress of Singapore and the oil-rich islands around the Java Sea – Borneo, Sumatra, and Java.

In the time immediately after Pearl Harbor, the war in the Pacific became something of a blur, as the Japanese juggernaut quickly racked up conquest after conquest. Lost in that blur were the efforts of Patrick Bedell and small groups of British, Australians,

Americans, and Dutch, whom the attack on Pearl Harbor had left largely isolated in the Far East, to fight the Japanese advance alone.

The back of their resistance would be broken by their defeat at the hands of the Japanese at the Battle of the Java Sea. But by then the "Java Sea Campaign," as the US Navy would later call it, was largely decided. It had long since stopped being a test of arms and had become a test of character.

These Allied troops were thrown together by circumstances; cut off from reinforcement or in many cases retreat; operating with old, obsolete equipment and dwindling supplies; unable to get any rest, and, perhaps the most daunting feature of this campaign, enduring Japanese air attacks day after day after day. With few notable exceptions, their goal was not to win – that was impossible – but to delay the Japanese. Facing a relentless and thoroughly vicious enemy, these Americans, British, Dutch, and Australians responded not by running or surrendering, but by defiantly holding on, trying to buy weeks, days, hours. They were the modern "300" Spartans of Leonidas, a thin line of defenders sent forward to delay a thoroughly alien invader until a better line of defense – and offense – could be established.

But the knowledge that they were alone, cut off, outnumbered, outgunned, would take its toll. The certainty that every day with the rising sun would come Japanese bombs falling from the sky would eventually take its toll. This is evident from the titles of some of the relatively few books written about parts of this campaign: *The Fleet the Gods Forgot*; *The Lonely Ships*; *Every Day a Nightmare*; *Playing for Time*; *Another Six Hundred*.

These were the men of the US Asiatic Fleet, the British Eastern Fleet, the Royal Netherlands Navy's East Indies Squadron and the Royal Australian Navy – and their supporting units like Patrol Wing 10, the Royal Netherlands Naval Air Service, the US Army Air Force's 17th Pursuit Squadron (Provisional), and submarine crews from all these fine nations.

This is their story – the story of how they ended up in the Java Sea Campaign, and of how they fought, endured, and suffered, through those first months of the War in the Pacific. This book is for them, to them and to their memory. It aims to preserve their exploits, their sacrifices, and their accomplishments.

Many books have covered various parts of the Java Sea Campaign – commemorating fleets such as the US Asiatic Fleet, Force Z, and the East Indies Squadron, individual ships like the *Houston*, the *Perth*, and the *Exeter*, units such as Patrol Wing 10, the Far East Air Force, and the Royal Netherlands Naval Air Service. But few have covered the naval campaign in its entirety – from the hammer blows of the destruction of the Far East Air Force and Force Z in the first days of the war, which crippled Allied resistance in the Far East, to the attempted escape of the remnants of ABDACOM and its naval forces in the early days of March 1942. This book will attempt to fill that void so that, hopefully, the struggles of our servicemen in the early days of the Pacific War may be better understood and appreciated.

To preserve the memory of these men and their achievements, this book is written not just for historians and scholars (both amateur and professional), but also to people new to history, looking to explore for the first time our fascinating past and what it can teach us. It therefore tries to simplify. The use of military acronyms is kept to a minimum, time is presented in the civilian, 12-hour format (local unless otherwise noted), and military terms such as "crossing the T" or "line turn" are explained in either the text or the notes.

The reader is encouraged to check out the endnotes. Not only do they form the factual basis for this narrative, but they are also a concerted effort to acknowledge previous histories detailing various elements of the Java Sea Campaign. Those authors and researchers deserve credit for their efforts at preserving the memory of this overlooked World War II campaign.

Perhaps most importantly, the reader should be aware of one critical consideration: every word of this book, every conclusion, every praise, every criticism, is written from the perspective of an attorney sitting safe at a desk some seven decades removed from the events described herein, who will hopefully never be subject to the horrors experienced by the subjects of this book, writing not because the job requires it, but out of a love of and fascination with the Java Sea Campaign that has existed since childhood. It is in my capacity as an attorney that I made a shocking discovery. While writing this book, I was asked to provide legal assistance to a veteran of the Pacific War who had served in Iwo Jima and Okinawa, and his wife. After the matter was completed, I discussed the war with the veteran and heard some remarkable stories. I thanked him for his service in the Pacific War, in protecting the freedom of speech that allows the publication of this book. After that, I left.

A half hour later I received a call from his wife. She told me how meaningful my thanks had been to him, because, as he explained it to her, he had never been thanked for his World War II service.

To me this was both shocking and shameful.

So, in my own small way, *Rising Sun, Falling Skies* is an effort to say to these heroes of the Pacific who served in the Java Sea Campaign with little in the way of appreciation or even acknowledgment, and to all of our veterans and our current servicemembers who are deployed around the world protecting the freedoms we enjoy, though we may not fully appreciate them, these two words:

THANK YOU.

CHAPTER 1

ON THE DAY BEFORE

On the day before the attack on Pearl Harbor, Japanese Vice Admiral Ozawa Jisaburo stood on the spacious bridge of his flagship, the heavy cruiser *Chokai*, looking out over the South China Sea, preparing to carry out the invasion of Malaya.[1] Though the marquee event was to take place thousands of miles away at Pearl Harbor, Ozawa was in the real center of the action, the real objective of the Japanese war effort – the conquest of Malaya (now Malaysia) and the Netherlands East Indies (Indonesia): "Strike South," as the Japanese sometimes referred to this massive operation, or the "Centrifugal Offensive," as US military theorists would later call it.

This was the beginning of World War II in the Pacific, and Admiral Ozawa, as well as everyone on the naval general staff in Tokyo, knew it. It has often been said that World War II was actually a continuation or an extension of World War I. That may have been true in Europe. But not in the Pacific. While World War I did have some effect in East Asia and the Pacific, World War II in the Pacific, or the "Pacific War," was essentially unrelated to World War I or, for that matter, World War II in Europe. On the contrary, it has been argued that this Pacific War was a natural (some might say inevitable) outcome of the meteoric rise of Japan.

The seeds of the Pacific War were indeed many and varied, but probably the most direct route to the war was opened on July 8, 1853, when, propelled by the US annexation of California, the opening of Chinese ports, the shift from sail to steam, and the growth of the American whaling industry, Commodore Matthew Perry from the US Navy sailed into Tokyo Bay with his four ships to "re-establish trade and discourse between Japan and the western world," or at least to agree to open certain ports to American trade and to replenish coal and supplies for the US commercial whaling fleet. For America, it was the age of Manifest Destiny, and Japan was needed to help attain that destiny. For Japan, which had isolated itself from most foreigners since 1626, Perry's arrival and refusal to brook opposition to any aspect of America's request proved to be as traumatic as the Japanese response was ultimately dynamic – dynamic in a way few countries have ever

11

been able to achieve. On March 31, 1854, Japan signed the Treaty of Kanagawa signaling friendship between the two countries, opening two ports to American ships, agreeing to help American ships and their passengers and crews shipwrecked on the Japanese coast, and allowing American ships to buy supplies, coal, water, and other necessary provisions in Japanese ports.

This victory for the Americans, after a celebratory feast, ultimately precipitated a national upheaval for Japan, sowing the seeds that would later come to fruition in the Pacific War. In 1867, Japan's military dictatorship, known as the Tokugawa Shogunate, was removed from power and the archaic, feudal shogunate system for rule by generals was dismantled. Now Japan would be ruled by an emperor.[2] This was considered a major improvement. Starting in 1868 with the official fall of the Tokugawa, rule by an actual emperor who had real power was restored to Japan. This throne was occupied by a man who, during his lifetime, was known to the West by his given name of Mutsuhito; since according to Japanese tradition, the given name of the emperor was not referenced during his rule. However, like many royal families in Asia, he was given a second name to be used posthumously, especially in Japan. It was by this name that this emperor's rule would become known to history: Meiji.

The Meiji Restoration, as this era would eventually become known, would be marked by an amazingly swift change from an isolated, feudal, agricultural society to a modern, industrialized one with ties and influence the world over. Japan began a crash course in modernization that may be unrivaled in all of human history, in terms of both the scale of its effort and its phenomenal success.

The new powers of the emperor were enshrined in a "Constitution of the Empire of Japan," usually called the Meiji Constitution, a rather complicated and somewhat controversial blueprint for the new Japanese government. After the Meiji Constitution came into effect in 1890, Japan became a constitutional monarchy, of a sort. The emperor was constitutionally limited to absolute power. The civilian government was parliamentary in nature, but the national parliament, the Diet, had little real power. Historically, however, the Japanese emperor had not ruled directly. The emperor, who was also the chief priest of Japan's state religion, Shintoism, was believed to be the descendant of the sun goddess Amaterasu of the southern island of Kyushu so an element of divinity was always attached to the emperor's image. The emperor was separated from his subjects by concentric circles of advisors, courtiers, generals, ministers, and the imperial bureaucracy. This separation was an extensive and deliberate construct, intended to protect the emperor. It is in this context that the Meiji Constitution with its vague and sometimes contradictory terms must be understood.

Under Meiji, Japan moved relentlessly forward with modernization, industrialization, and Westernization. Meiji had seen what had happened to neighboring China, with the European powers using the weakness and corruption of the ruling Qing Dynasty to nibble away at its sovereignty – resulting in "concessions" that gave sovereignty to the French in part of Shanghai, to the British in Hong Kong, to the Germans in Tsingtao, and so forth. He was determined that this would not happen to Japan. And the Japanese, with an admirable determination, modernized within the space of a generation.

But that modernization, industrialization, and Westernization had a very dark thread running throughout, a subtle thread that went little noticed in the West. Japan had been isolated for more than 200 years as a response to initial visits by aggressive Christian missionaries starting in the 16th century who, the Tokugawa and the emperor felt, threatened Japan's Shinto religion. In 1626, Christianity was banned in Japan and the country closed its doors to outsiders. To the Japanese, the Americans and Europeans were "barbarians" – although that particular feeling was mutual – so Perry's entry into Tokyo Bay and his refusal to accept any compromise was offensive, intolerable, humiliating. It was a loss of "face," an always ephemeral concept that remains hugely important in Asia and imperfectly understood in the West.

Meiji and his advisors came up with a solution that would turn Westernization on its head. In essence, they would learn all they could about the Europeans and Americans, copy their industry, modernize the Japanese military, and then drive the barbarians out of the Japanese home islands. Japan would drive outward, conquering its neighbors to create a buffer zone that would prevent the Europeans and Americans from ever setting foot on Japanese soil again.[3]

Soon enough, Japan was indeed copying those European powers in helping itself to pieces of a corrupt and weakening empire. With a desperate need for resources and space for its exploding population, in 1894 Japan went to war with China for control of Korea, which both countries had been ruling as a co-protectorate. Using the pretext of Korea's Tonghak Rebellion, which both Japanese and Chinese troops had been sent to quell, the Japanese marched down the strategic Liaotung (Liaodong) Peninsula west of Korea and captured the strategic port of Port Arthur (now the Lüshunkou district of Dalian). China had been considered stronger than Japan up to this point, so Japan's rapid defeat of Chinese land and naval forces demonstrated to the world that Japan had become a military power to be reckoned with. Under the Treaty of Shimonoseki, signed on April 17, 1895, China recognized the "independence" of Korea, which was now ruled by a Japanese puppet government, and ceded Formosa (Taiwan), the Pescadores Islands, and the Liaotung Peninsula to Japan, including the forced leasehold of Kwantung, an area at the tip of the Liaotung Peninsula that included Port Arthur. Alarmed at the sudden Japanese aggression and expansion, Germany, France, and Russia under the terms of the Triple Intervention agreement – a direct response to the first Sino-Japanese conflict – threatened war with Japan if it did not give up Kwantung. The Japanese were outraged, but they could not very well fight three major powers at once – yet – and they returned Kwantung to China.

Having possessions on mainland Asia, however, put Tokyo on an imminent collision course with Russia and its eternal search for a warm-water port. In December 1897, the Russian Far East Fleet arrived up to occupy Port Arthur, essentially doing some base-shopping and counting on the guns of the fleet's battleships to smooth out any negotiations on price. Sure enough, shortly thereafter, having only just regained control of Kwantung, the Chinese agreed to lease it to the Russians for a pittance. The Russians immediately began fortifying the city and building a rail line to link Port Arthur to Mukden in Russian-controlled Manchuria, moving their Far East Fleet to Port Arthur.

The Japanese government in Tokyo was livid, but was also rapidly learning this game of international power politics. In 1902, Japan agreed to an alliance with Great Britain, its first with a Western power since the Meiji Restoration. It was another sign of the coming of age of Japan, and as such contained emotional significance to its people. From a practical standpoint, though, this alliance was clearly aimed at Russia, who now would have to worry about a two-front war and be unable to bring its full military power against Japan or Britain.

That nice piece of diplomatic maneuvering completed, what followed was the Russo-Japanese War, a seemingly small affair with large strategic implications. Tokyo declared war on Russia – *after* the Combined Fleet of the Imperial Japanese Navy[4] had found the Russian Far East Fleet off Port Arthur, sunk most of it, and bottled up the rest inside the harbor.[5] Once again, the Imperial Japanese Army marched down the Liaotung Peninsula and laid siege to Port Arthur. After several months of fighting with extremely heavy casualties, Japanese troops captured the city and destroyed the remnants of the Russian Far East Fleet. Meanwhile, the tsar had sent the Baltic Fleet halfway around the world to relieve Port Arthur. The Japanese destroyed that fleet, too, at the Battle of Tsushima in 1905. The United States brokered an end to the war through the Treaty of Portsmouth, which recognized Tokyo's gain of Kwantung, Port Arthur, and its railway, but, much to Japan's anger at the United States, failed to grant Japan the indemnity it wanted to pay off its huge war debts. Nevertheless, Japan had emerged from its first major war with a European power victorious.

Now Japan was acknowledged by all as a great power in its own right. Its interests, its wishes, its needs, its actions would have to be seriously considered in any foreign initiative in East Asia and the Pacific. But herein lay seeds of the Pacific War. East Asia was a crowded place (it still is), with Britain ruling Malaya, Singapore, and northwest Borneo; the Netherlands ruling the East Indies; the French ruling Indochina; the United States, through its victory in the 1898 Spanish–American War, holding the Philippines and Guam; China ruling whichever parts of China it had not yet conceded to Europeans; and Russia wanting to expand and control everything within its reach. If Japan's expansionist appetite continued, it was bound to bump against these other powers in its neighborhood, with unpredictable results.

Japan's wars with China and Russia, though not without significant cost, had been of immense benefit to the rising empire. Emperor Meiji died in 1912, having presided over the almost total transformation of Japan, at least outwardly.

Meiji was succeeded by his son the Crown Prince Yoshihito, who would eventually become known by his posthumous name as the Emperor Taisho. Taisho was physically weak and sickly and overcome with vanity; moreover, while highly intelligent, he had either no concern or no talent for politics. Meiji doesn't seem to have had much hope for Taisho, and had been grooming his grandson, Taisho's son Hirohito, for the throne.

Weak as the new emperor was, however, the eruption of World War I on the other side of the globe would provide Japan with more opportunities to expand its influence throughout the Far East and deep into the Pacific.

On August 23, 1914, Japan was one of the first countries to declare war on Germany in support of its ally Great Britain. It had offered this support in return for German lands in Asia, and Britain agreed, asking for Japan's help in destroying German raiders in Chinese waters. Germany held a lease on the Chinese port of Tsingtao (which the Germans called Tsingtau), at the end of the Shantung (Shandong) Peninsula across the Yellow Sea from Port Arthur. The German Navy kept a small fleet here that it used to patrol the German island holdings in the Pacific, which included Saipan and Tinian in the Marianas chain, the Caroline Islands (including a fine harbor at Truk), and the Marshall Islands. These German holdings now became immediate targets for Japanese attack. Germany recalled its warships to Tsingtao, but the Japanese Army moved down the Shantung Peninsula and took the city. Deprived of its principal base in the Far East, Germany had to abandon the Marianas, Carolines, and Marshalls to the Japanese. Quick, simple, and effective.

Elsewhere, things did not go as well for Japan, at least not politically. Japanese strategy always called for another Tsushima, or a "decisive battle," in which the Imperial Japanese Navy would commit its main battle fleet to destroy the enemy in a single big battle. This theme would later appear time and again in World War II. So when the British requested Japanese assistance in the Mediterranean, the imperial government did not see another Tsushima opportunity developing there – certainly not a situation that would directly benefit Japan. Consequently, Tokyo sent only four destroyers to help the Royal Navy. Unsurprisingly the British were underwhelmed.

Ultimately, World War I was officially ended by the Paris Peace Conference, of which the infamous Treaty of Versailles was only a part. Japan was allowed to keep Tsingtao (which it later relinquished), Saipan, Tinian, the Carolines, and the Marshalls. The Japanese thought their effort in the war merited more of a reward; the British, upset at receiving only four Japanese destroyers to help them in the Mediterranean, thought Japan was lucky to be getting that much.

And with that, another seed of the Pacific War was sown. Japan was now the only major potential rival to Britain and the United States for power in the Far East. Moreover, it would be able to use those same territorial gains to threaten US-held Guam and had the potential to cut off the Philippines from American support and supply. This new strategic reality was not lost on American and British military analysts. The likelihood of another war increased.

It would increase further through a series of arms control treaties that, like most arms control treaties, were well-meaning but deeply flawed. One of the causes of World War I had been a naval arms race between Britain and Germany that centered on the construction of the highly effective but expensive "dreadnought" class of warship. In reality, World War I did not terminate that contest; it just replaced Germany with Japan. The desire to end this expensive arms race was the impetus behind the Washington Naval Treaty of 1922. Signed by Britain, France, the United States, Italy, and Japan, the intent of the treaty was naval disarmament and limitations on future naval construction. "Capital ships" (which at this time meant "battleships and battlecruisers," the latter of which were essentially battleships without the armor) and aircraft carriers, that new type of fighting ship still in its infancy, were specifically limited in terms of the tonnage a country was allowed to have, as well as the size of each ship. In terms of total tonnage, the accepted ratio for Britain, the United States, Japan, France, and Italy was approximately 5:5:3:1.75:1.75.[6] No capital ship could have guns larger than 16in. Construction of new capital ships was prohibited. Cruisers were not limited in total tonnage, but could be no larger than 10,000 tons each. Destroyers were limited to 1,500 tons each.[7] Furthermore, in the Pacific no country was permitted to build new bases or fortify existing bases between Tokyo and Singapore.

Through the remainder of the roaring 1920s, battleships were scrapped or converted into aircraft carriers (which was allowed, since no one had any carriers yet) in order to comply with the Washington Treaty limitations. So, in terms of getting rid of "capital ships," the treaty was a success. But overall, both the Washington Naval Treaty of 1922 and its successor, the London Naval Treaty of 1930, were failures, inasmuch as, as a practical matter, they encouraged conversion of capital ships to aircraft carriers, which would be the main naval weapons of the next war. Moreover, more generally, they limited weapons only in countries that intended to abide by the treaty, not in those that either did not sign the treaty or else intended to break it. As an added complication, the Japanese were outraged that the treaty limited them to what they believed was a position of inferiority to Britain and the United States. That the United States required a two-ocean navy and Britain a three-ocean navy, whereas Japan needed only a one-ocean navy and could thus maintain superiority in the Pacific, mattered little to the Japanese. In Japan, the treaty was a national outrage, another loss of "face," and it was a key factor in the rising nationalism of the Japanese military establishment.

Japan would have other concerns in the immediate aftermath of the Washington Treaty, specifically the devastating 1923 Tokyo Earthquake. The enormous outpouring of support from the United States that followed this event helped reverse the downward trend in US-Japanese relations. However all that improvement was undone the following year by immigration legislation in the US that severely restricted Japanese immigration to the United States. The Japanese found the measure profoundly offensive and racist. The effect on US-Japanese relations was disastrous, and the slow-but-steady deterioration resumed.

That deterioration would provide the Japanese with yet more motivation to modernize their navy and think creatively in ways that would be detrimental to the long-term security interests of the Western powers. For example, the Imperial Japanese Navy refused to abandon its long-held idea of the "decisive battle" like Tsushima. But with the

Washington Treaty ostensibly forcing Japan into a set disadvantage against its likely rivals in such a battle, Japanese naval strategists looked for ways to gain a decisive edge.

Considering that, at least in the days before radar, darkness could hide its inferior numbers, the Combined Fleet trained relentlessly (and often ruthlessly) in night combat. It perfected high-quality optics for night spotting and developed illumination rounds, flares, and float lights that were more reliable and burned more brightly than their American counterparts.[8] It worked tirelessly on developing better torpedoes. It designed and, in 1928, launched the *Fubuki* class of destroyers, which featured enclosed dual 5in mounts, a steel bridge structure, a top speed of 38 knots, covered torpedo mounts, and one set of torpedo reloads; these were considered revolutionary developments.[9] Finally, the Imperial Japanese Navy's Naval Air Force became the world leader in naval aviation, both in its pursuit of carrier aviation – the aircraft carriers *Akagi* and *Kaga,* which would take part in the attack on Pearl Harbor, both came online during this period, converted from capital ship hulls due for scrapping under the 1922 treaty – and in its development of seaplanes and seaplane tactics.

The Washington Naval Treaty was arguably Japan's last attempt at outwardly restraining its expansionist ambitions in the name of "peace." As the treaty was concluded, Emperor Taisho's health began forcing him to withdraw from power and ultimately left him bed-ridden. His son, Crown Prince Hirohito, groomed by Meiji to be the next great emperor of Japan, became regent on November 29, 1921. Young Hirohito gained experience at the levers of power as Taisho's health continued to deteriorate. Finally, on December 25, 1926, Taisho died, and the Crown Prince became Emperor of Japan.

Upon Taisho's death, the new era of Showa ("enlightened peace") was proclaimed. The name Showa would turn out to be ironic, for Hirohito would start two wars in the course of his reign.[10]

And those wars were not long in coming. As before, China was the first target. Since the fall of the Qing Dynasty in 1911, China had lacked an effective central government. For all intents and purposes, the country was ruled by hundreds of warlords, each with their own little fiefdom.[11] Chiang Kai-shek, the recognized leader of China, was less a president than the most powerful of the warlords, less a Napoleon than an Agamemnon. In 1928, the same year that Hirohito was formally "enthroned" or confirmed as Emperor Showa, the second-most powerful Chinese warlord, Chang Tso-lin, was killed by a bomb planted by members of the Kwantung Army, the Japanese unit protecting the Japanese-held railway in Manchuria.[12] Soon, the Kwantung Army, full of fanatical officers pushing for Japanese militarism and expansionism, would become synonymous with intrigue and trouble. Many believe that their activities were conducted on secret orders of Hirohito and his closest advisors, but often without the permission or even the knowledge of Japan's civilian government.[13]

In 1931, Japan took another step towards war. The Kwantung Army was looking to expand Japanese holdings in China from the small area around the railway to all of Manchuria. It needed an excuse to invade. On the evening of September 18, an explosion hit the tracks of the railway near Mukden. That the explosion damaged neither the tracks nor the engine was a good tip off as to who had caused it, but the Kwantung Army blamed nearby Chinese troops for what would become known as the "Mukden Incident," or, later, the "Manchurian Incident." The Kwantung Army moved up the Liaotung Peninsula to take Mukden itself, and then expanded outward, including making a gratuitous strike at Shanghai, the center of Western investment in China, to coerce the Western powers to push Chiang for a settlement. After about five months of fighting, Japan had complete control over Manchuria.

Meanwhile, the advancement of the Showa agenda continued apace. Tokyo had been a signatory to the London Naval Treaty of 1930, a follow-on to the Washington Naval Treaty of 1922, but while the United States and Great Britain had complied with both the Washington and London treaties – much to their detriment in the subsequent Pacific War – the Japanese now had no intention of abiding by the London Treaty's terms. For instance, under the new treaty, cruisers were again limited to a maximum tonnage of 10,000. The cruiser *Mogami,* first in its class, was completed in 1935, loaded with armor, torpedo tubes, and five 6in triple turrets. The declared weight was 8,500 tons, though the true design weight was 9,500 and at trials it would displace 11,169 tons. Foreign naval observers saw the *Mogami* and were suspicious, but could not prove anything.[14] What they could not have even suspected was that the turret base rings for the cruiser were designed so that the 6in triple turrets could be easily replaced with 8in dual turrets, as would be done on the eve of the war.[15] Those 6in triple turrets ended up as secondary armament for another violation of the London Treaty, the gigantic superbattleship *Yamato*. As is often the case, an arms control treaty had proven to be utterly useless.

The advancement of Japanese naval aviation continued simultaneously. Admiral Yamamoto Isoroku, who would lead the Combined Fleet during the attack on Pearl Harbor, had convinced Hirohito of the utility of attack aircraft launched from aircraft carriers. Yamamoto trained carrier pilots relentlessly to fly and fight in all kinds of weather. The accident rate and the accompanying fatality rate were high, but all this training honed the Japanese Naval Air Force into the best naval aviation force in the world – long before it entered combat.

It was during this period that the Imperial Japanese Navy developed what was arguably the crown jewel and definitely the most dangerous weapon of its surface fleet – the Type 93 torpedo. By far the finest torpedo of its time, the Type 93 had a diameter of 24in and was unusually long at 29ft, 6in. It carried an explosive charge of 1,080lb, the largest of its kind. But what made the Type 93 so special was its range. At its high-speed setting of 48 knots, it had a range of 20,000m – more than 12 miles. At its slowest speed setting of 36 knots, it could go an incredible 40,000m – more than 24 miles. By comparison, the US Navy's Mark 15 torpedo, used by destroyers, had a maximum range of 5,500m (just over 3 miles) at its high-speed setting of 45 knots and a range of 13,700m (less than 9 miles) at 26 knots – a speed so slow that it could be outrun by Japanese warships. On top of that, the Mark 15 was powered by steam, which left a trail of bubbles that was easily spotted. The Type 93 was powered by oxygen, which left no bubbles and little visible wake. The Japanese went to great lengths to conceal the Type 93; its devastating power would be a rude shock to the US and Royal Navies in the Pacific.[16] Much later, the torpedo's extreme effectiveness and unusual length earned from noted historian Samuel Eliot Morison the title by which the Type 93 would become famous – "Long Lance."

As the advances in Japanese naval technology continued, the descent of Japan's political system into militarism, expansionism, and extreme nationalism continued apace. A provision of the Meiji Constitution by which the ministers representing the army and the navy had to be members of those services became the leverage for the army gradually to take control of the government. Paradoxically, the military dominance of the government came about at a time when the military itself was dominated not by its senior generals but by a cadre of younger, junior officers, many of whom had surreptitious connections to the emperor and the royal family, who were now pushing the government and their senior officers into more and more extreme positions.[17] With their strings allegedly being pulled by the Imperial Palace, these officers would become involved in assassination and murder.

On November 14, 1930, Prime Minister Hamaguchi Osachi, who had championed acceptance of the London Treaty and who had rammed through cuts to the navy budget, was wounded by an assassin; Hirohito himself later pardoned the assassin. On May 15, 1932, as part of a larger revolt that became known as the "May 15 Incident," a group of young navy officers, supported by army cadets and civilians, attempted a coup that resulted in the death of Prime Minister Inukai Tsuyoshi, who had demanded cuts to the military budget. The trial of the conspirators descended into a circus. The conspirators proclaimed their loyalty to the emperor while the courts received a petition containing some 350,000 signatures – and some 110,000 letters written in blood – pleading for leniency. Nine youths in Niigata pleaded to be allowed to be executed in place of the accused; to show their good faith, they each sent a severed finger. Unsurprisingly the conspirators received very light sentences.[18]

And so began the pattern later called "government by assassination" as civilian control of the military was effectively at an end. Opponents of the position of the emperor, including members of the cabinet, the army, and the navy, had an unfortunate habit of ending up dead. Meanwhile rival factions within the military developed ambitious plans of attack and conquest. A faction of mostly army officers, known as the "Strike North" faction, wanted to attack what they considered the true enemy of Japan, the Soviet Union. But Emperor Hirohito had been intent since the 1920s on striking south, where British-ruled Malaya and northwest Borneo, and the Netherlands East Indies (which the Japanese called the "Southern Resources Area,") could provide the oil, rubber, tin, and arable land that Japan needed for self sufficiency.

On February 26, 1936, another failed coup made an attempt on the life of yet another prime minister, Okada Keisuke. The coup, called the "February 26 Incident," was easily put down, which, given that the mutiny had in reality been encouraged and instigated by the royal family and the emperor's closest advisors as a pretext for eliminating the Strike North faction, was not surprising.

But Hirohito realized that the Strike North faction did indeed have a point: the Soviet Union *was* a threat. A Japan making its long-awaited advance south could easily find a knife in its back courtesy of the malevolent Marxists north of Manchuria. Such was the impetus for Japan entering the 1936 Anti-Comintern Pact with Nazi Germany and Fascist Italy. Now, if the Soviets attacked the Japanese in the north, they would have to watch their own backs from their western border.

With that matter settled, Hirohito proceeded with what had been his plan all along: to conquer China and move south along the coast all the way to Malaya and the East Indies. The phrase *hakko ichiu* – "bringing the eight corners of the world under one roof" – now became prominent in imperial propaganda. The phrase has been attributed to the mythical emperor Jimmu enthroned in *c.* 660 BC, but it had been a part of Japanese foreign policy ever since Meiji, with the aim of bringing all of East Asia under Japanese control. The military buildup now took place openly. Japan had renounced the Washington Naval Treaty in 1934, had withdrawn from the Second London Naval Disarmament Conference begun in December 1935, and was not a signatory to the Second London Naval Treaty of 1936.

The Kwantung Army, always with support from the imperial family, continued to nibble away at northeast China, bringing the Rising Sun to the outskirts of the ancient capital of China, Peking (now called Beijing). On July 7, 1937, elements of the Kwantung Army were on night maneuvers near Tientsin on the opposite side of the Marco Polo Bridge over the Hun River from Chinese forces, when gunfire erupted. Precisely what happened still is not clear. But Tokyo used this so-called "Marco Polo Bridge Incident" to leverage a full-scale invasion of China. The Japanese were very careful never to publicly acknowledge that what was happening in China was actually a "war," preferring to maintain the pretence of this being yet another "incident" such as had been occurring regularly since 1931.[19]

The emperor had been told by his army advisors that within a month Nanking (Nanjing), the Nationalist capital, would be conquered, forcing Chiang Kai-shek to surrender, reduced to, at best, a puppet ruler. So Hirohito authorized the deployment of the bulk of the army to mainland China. Peking was rapidly occupied. A large amphibious landing was staged in the area of Shanghai to quickly take China's largest city and port. But the Japanese had not anticipated that Chiang, dependent on the political support of Shanghai and counting on Western intervention, would send his best troops – troops trained by the Germans – into the city to contest the Japanese advance inch by inch. Three months later, when by Japanese projections China itself was to have fallen, they had yet to clear Shanghai.

However, with only limited Western support and after suffering massive losses among his best troops, Chiang's army was forced to retreat towards Nanking, some 70 miles to the west along the Yangtze River. Japanese troops, infuriated by their unexpectedly heavy losses in and around Shanghai, gave chase. In a pattern that would continue in the Pacific War, orders were sent out that the protocols governing the treatment of prisoners of war were not to be observed with Chinese troops.

The Japanese assumption that once they captured Nanking Chiang would surrender proved a catastrophic miscalculation. With his troops unable to defend his capital, Chiang evacuated his government and his remaining troops westward along the Yangtze, some 800,000 of Nanking's more than one million residents joining in this headlong flight.[20] The Imperial Japanese Army called on the navy to interdict this retreat from the air. One such raid, on December 12, 1937, was directed at fleeing transports moving west upriver from Nanking. A flight of navy bombers under Lieutenant Okumiya Masatake attacked and sank what the army had told them was a Chinese transport, but was actually the US Navy gunboat *Panay*. Understandably outraged, the United States now had grounds for war with Japan, a war neither country wanted or needed at that point in time. As a result the United States had to accept Tokyo's apology and some monetary compensation.[21]

But the massive flight of refugees from the doomed Chinese capital would prove entirely justified. The Japanese, the Chinese government would later charge, killed 390,000 in their advance on Nanking.[22] On December 13, 1937, units of the Imperial Japanese Army, led by a division under the command of a notorious sadist named Nakajima Kesago, entered Nanking.[23] No one – at least no one outside the Japanese military establishment – could have predicted what happened next.

After earning a reputation for "civility" in wartime conduct ever since the First Sino-Japanese War (1894–95), the behavior of the Imperial Japanese Army upon its occupation of Nanking reached the lowest depths of the worst, most depraved, most barbaric conduct of the 20th century. It would become known as the "Rape of Nanking," which indeed it was. Some 20,000 women were raped, most repeatedly, many in front of husbands, fathers, or children who were murdered when they attempted to intervene.[24] Iris Chang, the prominent scholar on the Rape of Nanking, would comment that "using numbers killed alone, the Rape of Nanking surpasses much of the worst barbarism of the ages," including the Roman destruction of Carthage and Tamerlane's sacks of New Delhi and Syria.[25] By some accounts, the massacre continued for six weeks, leaving some 260,000 dead, more than a third of the city in charred ruins, and everything of value shipped off to Japan.[26] The conduct of the troops was so ghastly that even local observers from Nazi Germany were horrified – calling the Imperial Japanese Army "bestial machinery" – and tried to take measures (that were ultimately ineffectual) to try to protect some of the Chinese population.[27]

World opinion increasingly turned against Japan as a result of the Rape of Nanking. Worse, Chiang Kai-shek refused to surrender, merely retreating to Chunking (Chonqing), far inland in the mountains of the upper Yangtze. Chinese public opinion hardened still more against their uninvited Japanese guests. Chinese in Japanese-occupied areas boycotted Japanese products, further fueling Japanese anger. So the terror continued, but Chiang refused to come out for decisive battle. When the Japanese struck, Chiang simply moved his army somewhere else. Tokyo kept committing more and more troops and materiel to the "China Incident," but no end was in sight. It was the proverbial quagmire; Japan had committed 1.5 million troops to China and suffered 600,000 casualties.[28] Yet Japan could not seem to win the war, nor could it pull out without losing "face" and ending its self-styled leadership of the Asian peoples and the imperial policy of *hakko ichiu* entirely, which was inconceivable.

On December 22, 1938, Japan's prime minister, Prince Konoye Fuminaro, gave a speech in which he proclaimed a "New Order in East Asia" with the Japanese united in a struggle to help the people of Asia – under Japanese leadership, of course – drive out the Western imperialists.[29] Two years later, Foreign Minister Matsuoka Yosuke would turn the "New Order" into the infamous "Greater East Asia Co-Prosperity Sphere." The rallying cry became "Asia for the Asians." The critical caveat, "So long as those Asians are Japanese," somehow did not become a part of imperial propaganda.

While the Soviet Union had been supplying Chinese communists with weapons during the course of the Chinese Civil War, the piecemeal support that the West had offered to Chinese Nationalist forces increased, motivated by growing international sympathy for the Chinese and rising anger at Japan's brutality. Japan countered by taking control of Chinese ports of entry for this material support, such as Canton (Guangzhou), Tsingtao, Fainan, and the Spratly Islands; and cutting off the British colony of Hong Kong and the Portuguese colony of Macau. The Western countries responded by going through British-ruled Burma and French Indochina. Claire Lee Chennault, a former US Army officer now serving as an air advisor for Chiang, would coordinate some air support from the United States and would, eventually, lead American volunteers in a squadron of Curtiss P-40 Warhawk fighters, famously emblazoned with shark mouths on their engine cowlings, to help the overmatched Chinese Air Force. But soon enough, Chennault's pilots would be just as overmatched as the Chinese they were helping, as the Japanese unleashed what became one of their most fearsome weapons of the war.

On June 29, 1940, a dozen new, rather strange-looking monoplane aircraft appeared at the airfield at Yokosuka Naval Air Station, some 70 miles south of Tokyo. Lieutenant Shimokawa Manbei briefed the 12 pilots before him on this new aircraft. Called the *shi* experimental carrier fighter, the plane was still in the test stage without a pilot's manual or anything else that explained how to handle it. Nevertheless, it was to be made operational as quickly as possible.[30]

Any troubling thoughts the pilots may have had as to Japanese procurement practices were lost when they actually tested the fighter. It was a dream to fly. It had a top speed of 330 miles per hour; an incredible rate of climb; unheard-of maneuverability; powerful 20mm cannons in the wings and two "backup" 7.7mm machine guns in the nose. It also had no armored cockpit – very little armor at all, in fact – and no self-sealing fuel tanks. But pilot protection had never been a concern for the Japanese.[31]

And so the new carrier fighter was made ready. Its official name became the Mitsubishi A6M Type 00 (*Reisen*) Carrier Fighter, Model 11. In designating the aircraft in reports, the Allies would eventually dispense with the confusing Japanese naming system and instead use people's names – females for bombers ("Nell," "Betty," etc.), males for fighters ("Claude," "Oscar," etc.). This fighter would ultimately have an official Allied reporting name of "Zeke," but few actually used that. Mitsubishi's Type 00 designation gave the new fighter the name by which it would become famous across the globe: the "Zero."[32]

The Zero literally chased Chiang Kai-shek's already overmatched air force out of the skies over China. On one occasion, September 13, 1940, the Zeros feigned retreat and doubled back, surprising the 27 Chinese fighters who had returned. The result was 27 Chinese fighters – the entire Chinese force – shot down; for no Japanese losses in return.[33] Okumiya Masatake would later admit that with all of Japan's early success in the Pacific War, "we could not possibly have achieved our sea, land, and air victories with a fighter plane of lesser performance than the Zero. Our entire strategy depended on the success of this aircraft."[34] Chennault observed the Zero's performance with awe. He had never seen, had never even heard of anything like it. He dutifully sent reports of his observations about the Zero's performance to Washington and London; his reports were deemed not credible and ignored.

But even the Zero could not tip the war in China decisively in Japan's favor. Japan had already conquered everything worth conquering in China – its ports, its industrial areas, the majority of its arable land, most of its navigable rivers. It meant nothing. Chiang would not surrender, could not be made to surrender. The "China Incident" kept eating more and more resources – $5 million a day, a staggering sum for that time – while the continuing Japanese atrocities were alienating the very countries on whom Japan depended for import of those resources, such as the United States. Only 10 percent of the oil Japan used was produced in the home islands. Another 10 percent came from the Netherlands East Indies. The remainder, 80 percent, came from the United States. And that flow of oil was in danger of being cut off. In 1939, the United States announced it was withdrawing from a 1911 trade agreement with Japan. In July 1940, the United States prohibited export of high-grade aviation fuel and steel scrap to Japan, crippling Japan's steel industry.[35] It was not so much that the Americans were tired of seeing their exports to Japan being turned against the Chinese, although they were, but that they strongly suspected that their exports to Japan were about to be turned back on themselves.

Thus, the deterioration of relations between Japan and the West continued as World War II in Europe began. In June 1940, a month after President Roosevelt had moved the Pacific Fleet from San Diego to Pearl Harbor, the US Congress authorized the Two-Ocean Navy Act, providing for a massive expansion of the US Navy. In a few years, the US Navy would achieve quantitative superiority to the Imperial Japanese Navy in the Pacific, and any chance of the Japanese assembling the East Asian hegemony that had been the goal of Meiji and now Hirohito – *hakko ichiu* – would be gone unless immediate action was taken.[36] Tokyo did its calculations. Based on the Two-Ocean Navy Act and Japan's own naval expansion, Japan's naval strength relative to the US would peak in late 1941.[37]

The next downgrade in relations came when Japan became a signatory with Nazi Germany and Fascist Italy to the Tripartite Pact on September 27, 1940. Theoretically, the pact was a supplement to the earlier Anti-Comintern Pact directed at the Soviet Union, but the purpose of this supplement was different – to discourage the United States from entering the war in Europe or from taking up arms against Japan, or, as Japanese Foreign Minister Matsuoka put it, "to prevent the United States from encircling us."[38]

In many respects things were falling into place much better than Emperor Hirohito could have hoped. The Wehrmacht's success in Europe would be Japan's opportunity. With France under Hitler's rule, Indochina was ready to fall into Japanese hands. Britain could barely defend itself against Hitler, so how could it defend Singapore, Malaya, and Burma? The Dutch government had fled the Nazi-occupied Netherlands and set itself up in London as a government-in-exile, but it could do little to support the defense of the East Indies. And the Imperial Japanese Navy had the quantitative advantage over the US Pacific Fleet and the British and Dutch naval forces in the Pacific combined. A policy paper from the Imperial Japanese Army declared, "Never in our history has there been a time like the present," while a former army minister said that Japan must "seize this golden opportunity! Don't let anything stand in the way!"[39] The naval general staff had been planning this operation for a long time and now Admiral Yamamoto, although an opponent of the war, fine-tuned those plans. In summer 1940, after the fall of France, Hirohito had approved the move to "Strike South." After a series of clashes with Red Army troops in Mongolia in 1939, Japan reached a peace agreement with the Soviet Union in fall of 1940, thereby securing its northern flank and cutting off the flow of Russian weapons to China. Slowly, quietly, personnel reserves were called up and the chess pieces were moved into place.

Tokyo requested that Vichy France "invite" Japanese troops into the northern part of Indochina. Some initial reluctance on the Vichy government's part was easily quelled by Nazi Germany. Japanese troops quickly occupied Hanoi. Privately Hirohito would call his Indochina policy "looting a store during a fire."[40] Its action brought protest, but not much else. The Allies rationalized that Japan was simply trying to cut Chiang's supply line through Indochina and did not suspect that a full-scale invasion of their Far East interests was in the offing. However, in July 1941, again at the "invitation" of Vichy France, Japan occupied Saigon with the 22nd Air Flotilla, part of Japan's 11th Air Fleet established at the Saigon air complex.

The Japanese now effectively surrounded the Philippines, with Saigon to the west; Formosa, where the 21st and 23rd Air Flotillas, also of the 11th Air Fleet, were based, to the north; and the Marshall Islands to the east. Saigon was in range of British Malaya and all-important Singapore, as well as northwest Borneo, which could serve as a gateway into the East Indies. Their intention was clear. The response from Washington was outrage – and, on August 1, 1941, Japanese assets were frozen and a total trade embargo on Japan put in place. The British and the Dutch quickly followed suit.

Emperor Hirohito and his advisors apparently had not anticipated such a strong response from the United States and its allies to the occupation of Saigon. The trade embargo meant that Japan would have to make do with only 10 percent of its normal oil supplies. Although there had been some buildup of Japanese domestic oil reserves in preparation for this day, it had not proceeded as quickly as they had hoped. By the most optimistic projections, without the United States, Japan had only enough oil for approximately one year of war.[41]

Japan and the United States were now at an impasse. Washington would not lift the trade embargo until Japan had withdrawn from both Indochina and China. Japan would not withdraw from China; in the eyes of Emperor Hirohito and his advisors, to do so would mean a loss of "face," the end of *hakko ichiu* and Japanese ambitions in East Asia, and Japan's reduction to a second-rate power. On this, the army and the navy, who generally despised each other, agreed. General Tojo Hideki, who became prime minister in October 1941, predicted, "America may be enraged for a while, but later she will come to understand [why we did what we did.]" To Tojo, like most of the other senior Japanese leaders, risking war with the United States was better than being ground down without doing anything.[42]

So the long-term plan of Emperor Hirohito and of the Japanese military, to seize the resources of Malaya and the Netherlands East Indies, was now a national imperative. Becoming self-sufficient through the seizure of Southeast Asia was now more than philosophical; it was essential for national survival. Now Japan would finally drive the Europeans and the Americans out of East Asia.[43]

That said, while the oil fields of Borneo, Sumatra, and Java were Japan's primary objective, there was some disagreement as to how its forces would get there. The major issue was the Philippines. The Japanese did not really need the archipelago during this phase, but their advance to the so-called "Southern Resources Area" would be threatened by the US forces centered on the Clark airbase complex north of Manila and the Cavite Navy Yard on Manila Bay, pointing like a dagger at the Japanese supply lines back to the home islands. Even if the United States remained neutral, their presence was still a major danger. Only by seizing control of the Philippines could Japan eliminate that threat. But, as Admiral Yamamoto Isoroku of the navy's Combined Fleet successfully argued, that danger would be eliminated only at the expense of adding a bigger one – a sortie of the US Pacific Fleet out of Pearl Harbor in Hawaii to relieve the US forces in the Philippines. So the concept of the Japanese attack on Pearl Harbor was born, out of the mind of Yamamoto Isoroku, who had lived in the United States, understood it, even liked it. Better than anyone around Emperor Hirohito and his political circle, Yamamoto knew what going to war with the United States would most likely mean – a catastrophic defeat for Japan.[44] As Yamamoto had famously told Prime Minister Konoye in August 1940, "In the first six to twelve months of war with the United States and Great Britain I will run wild and win victory upon victory. But then, if the war continues after that, I have no expectation of success."[45]

While the Japanese would have the advantage in the short term, they knew they could not match America's industrial and military might in the long term. What they were hoping for was a continuing manifestation of the American political weakness and isolationism that had kept it out of the war so far. Admiral Yamamoto's projection of six months was key. The Japanese hoped they could build up their East Asian empire during that timeframe – adding the Philippines, Malaya, the East Indies, Thailand (already an ally), and Burma, and building up a defensive web of islands including Guam and the Marianas, the Carolines, the Marshalls, the Gilberts, Wake, and New Guinea.[46] By the time the United States was mobilized, Japan hoped its new defensive network would make the American public question whether retaking far-away East Asia was worth the cost in lives and in materiel, opening the door to a political settlement that could allow Japan to keep its territorial gains. Yet that strategy relied on doing nothing to so outrage the American people that they would refuse to listen to any settlement short of an unconditional surrender.

And so plans that Admiral Yamamoto and the Japanese had developed were put into motion. Slowly, quietly, in ones and twos, the aircraft carriers whose names would become infamous – *Akagi, Kaga, Hiryu, Soryu, Shokaku, Zuikaku* – made their way to a rendezvous in a remote, isolated bay on Etorofu in the Kurile Islands north of Hokkaido variously called Hitokappu or Tankan Bay. The carriers, officially called the 1st Air Fleet, would be joined by a sizable escorting force: *Hiei* and *Kirishima,* two fast battleships that had been converted from battlecruisers; *Tone* and *Chikuma,* two bizarre-looking heavy cruisers capable of carrying an increased number of seaplanes; and the light cruiser *Abukuma,* leading a squadron of eight destroyers. Referred to as the Japanese Carrier Striking Force in US Navy circles, it was and is more commonly known by the informal name of *Kido Butai* – "Striking Force."

On November 26, *Kido Butai* departed Hitokappu Bay for its date with Pearl Harbor and history. Less well known are the other elements of the Japanese plan, or, as US military analysts would later call it, the "Centrifugal Offensive": simultaneous strikes designed to leave the Americans, British, Australians, and Dutch completely off-balance, all peripheral objectives but necessary to achieve Japan's overall strategic goal: final victory in China. The biggest strike, tasked with conquering the all-important "Southern Resources Area," would be led by the appropriately named Southern Expeditionary Force.

As it moved southward, the Southern Expeditionary Force and its component parts would have a bewildering series of temporary titles, titles like "Malaya Force," "Kuching Force," "Davao Force," "Invasion Force," "Escort Force," "Support Force," "Distant Support Force," all of which would change depending on the objectives. This in itself was typical of Imperial Japanese Navy doctrine. It could not put a force of ships together and just send it towards the objective; it always had to divide it up into parts.[47]

The Southern Expeditionary Force was generally made up of two pincers: an Eastern Force and a Western Force. No matter how many times the specific names of the forces changed throughout the war, each of these pincers generally had the same ships. With this pattern in mind, the Japanese forces dedicated to taking the Southern Resources Area looked generally as follows.

The Southern Expeditionary Force was under the command of Vice Admiral Kondo Nobutake, commander of the 2nd Fleet. Directly under his command were the battleships

Kongo and *Haruna* (sisters to the *Hiei* and *Kirishima*); three sister heavy cruisers *Atago* (his flagship), *Takao*, and *Maya*; and eight destroyers. These ships were to provide "distant support," a favorite designation of the Imperial Navy that in practice usually meant "just far enough away to be of no reasonable use." His ships were deployed at Mako, in the Pescadores, and, except for *Maya*, which was sidetracked to the invasion of the Philippines, set out to sea on December 4, 1941, just before the war started.[48]

The Eastern Force was commanded by Vice Admiral Takahashi Ibo, commander of the 3rd Fleet. His flagship was the heavy cruiser *Ashigara*. Under his command were the 5th Cruiser Division, consisting of the heavy cruisers *Myoko, Haguro,* and *Nachi*; the 2nd Destroyer Flotilla, with the light cruiser *Jintsu* and eight destroyers; the 4th Destroyer Flotilla, with the light cruiser *Naka* and six destroyers; the necessary transports; and the light aircraft carrier *Ryujo*. The *Ryujo* and a destroyer squadron led by the light cruiser *Natori* were about the only ships that would shift between the eastern and western pincers as needed. The Eastern Force started out deployed at Palau, in the Marshalls just east of Mindanao, to make a quick attack on the Philippines as the war started. Its job was to strike Mindanao, and then move southward to Jolo, Tarakan, Balikpapan, and Banjermasin in eastern and southern Borneo; Menado, Makassar, and Kendari in the Celebes; Ambon in the Moluccas; and Timor in the Lesser Soenda Islands.[49]

The Western Force was commanded by the aforementioned Vice Admiral Ozawa Jisaburo, in his flagship, the luxurious heavy cruiser *Chokai*. He had with him the 7th Cruiser Division, consisting of the heavy cruisers *Kumano, Suzuya, Mikuma,* and *Mogami*, and a screen of seven destroyers; the light cruiser *Sendai* leading the 3rd Destroyer Flotilla; the light cruisers *Yura* and *Kinu*, each of whom directing a flock of submarines; and the necessary transports. Ozawa's ships had left Samah, Hainan Island, setting up to operate off Cam Ranh Bay, French Indochina, so that as the Pearl Harbor attack was in progress he could land Imperial Japanese Army troops on the Malay Peninsula to move on Singapore. Then he would take Brunei, Sarawak, and Kuching in western Borneo and Sumatra, centering on the massive oil fields at Palembang. The Eastern and Western Forces would reunite for the final attack on Java.[50]

In support of these naval operations were the 11th Air Fleet of the Japanese Naval Air Force, headquartered on Formosa under the command of Vice Admiral Tsukahara Fushizo. The 11th Air Fleet consisted of 21st and 23rd Air Flotillas based on Formosa, whose objective was to neutralize US airpower in the Philippines, and the 22nd Air Flotilla based in and around Saigon, whose duty was to support the Malaya invasion. Their war activities started on December 2, when they began reconnaissance flights over British airfields in Malaya and US airfields in the Philippines.

And so on the day before Pearl Harbor, Imperial Japan was a maze of contradictions. An island nation run by the army. An emperor constitutionally limited to absolute power. An emperor with absolute power who would only use that power indirectly. An effort to end a war by starting a much larger war. Ending a war next door by starting another war 3,000 miles away. Starting a war they knew they would most probably lose.

CHAPTER 2

JUST A LITTLE MORE TIME

On the day before the attack on Pearl Harbor, Admiral Thomas C. Hart, commander of the tiny force of ships known as the US Asiatic Fleet and the senior US naval commander in the Far East, worked late into the night after taking the afternoon off to play golf.[1] His war preparations complete, or at least as complete as they could be, he thought it was time to get some relaxation; it might be the last he would get for a long time. As it was, the golf was not very relaxing.

Admiral Hart had taken command of the Asiatic Fleet on July 19, 1939. Tall, thin, white-haired, nearing retirement at age 65, Hart, it was probably hoped by the administration in Washington, would be more diplomatic, more malleable than the man he was replacing, Admiral Harry Yarnell.

The Asiatic Fleet was something of a holdover, the latest evolution of the force that Matthew Perry had led into Tokyo Bay. Its purpose now was as it was then – to "show the flag," to let everyone know that the United States was watching the Far East in general and China in particular. Its small force included a squadron of gunboats to patrol the Yangtze River and protect Americans living and working in the chaos that was China.

The United States had condemned Japan's actions in China and refused to recognize Japan's sovereignty in the areas of China it had conquered. Japanese authorities told Admiral Yarnell that, to prevent any more unfortunate "accidents" like the *Panay*, he should cease having US gunboats sail the Yangtze. In no uncertain terms, Yarnell told them to go to hell. He gave a similar response when Japanese authorities in Shanghai told Yarnell that foreign warships would have to get clearance from Japanese port officials when they left port.[2]

This approach did not go down well with the State Department. It preferred the approach taken by Yarnell's subordinate and commander of the Yangtze River Patrol,

Admiral William A. Glassford, who was more political than martial. He believed that, like it or not, the Japanese were in charge and had to be respected even when the Japanese treatment of foreigners in Shanghai became outright harassment – verbal abuse, forcing them off the sidewalk to walk in the street, always looking to cause an incident that could be blamed on the Europeans and Americans.

Historian Edwin P. Hoyt, in one of his works on the early war in the Far East, put forward the view that if there had been more Americans who shared Admiral Yarnell's thinking, the Japanese takeover in Asia might still have been stopped, but there were simply too many who were like Admiral Glassford, who held the view that since the Japanese now controlled Shanghai, they had to be respected.[3] This is probably an overstatement, but the principle is nevertheless valid. The British military in Shanghai warned Glassford that his attitude only made the United States seem weak in Japanese eyes, but Glassford's opinion, with the backing of the State Department, prevailed. Yet he State Department had a method behind its weak responses. The United States was not ready for a war with Japan and the Roosevelt administration needed time to build up American forces in the Pacific. But while turning the other cheek may be virtuous in individual conduct, in affairs of state it is often more likely to worsen a conflict than to end it. Indeed, in trying to avoid a war, the State Department was actually making such a war more likely.

Naturally that war would most likely hit the US Asiatic Fleet first which made it Admiral Yarnell's problem. Except that, when his tour of duty ended and he indicated that he'd like another, the US Navy declined in accordance with the wishes of Secretary of State Cordell Hull. But if the US government thought Admiral Hart was going to be more of the type that they wanted for the Asiatic Fleet, they misjudged their man. He had little use for attitudes like that of his subordinate Admiral Glassford, or, for that matter, Glassford himself.

Admiral Hart took stock of the situation in Shanghai and did not like what he saw. He realized that the Asiatic Fleet must be readied for war but this in itself was a tall order. The US Navy had three major fleets: the Atlantic, the Pacific and – if you stretched the term "major" – the Asiatic. The Atlantic and Pacific Fleets were large, the Asiatic Fleet tiny. The commander-in-chief of the Pacific Fleet flew his flag in a battleship; so did his counterpart in the Atlantic Fleet. The Asiatic Fleet had no battleship; its flagship was a heavy cruiser, of which they had exactly one: the USS *Houston*. An old light cruiser, the USS *Marblehead*, and 13 ancient destroyers completed the Asiatic Fleet's seagoing surface warships.

In terms of numbers, it was not an impressive collection. Furthermore, the Asiatic Fleet was also caught in a sort of philosophical no-man's land. After Commodore Perry's social call on Tokugawa Japan, the fleet's big moment in the sun had come in 1898 when the US Navy defeated the Spanish in the Battle of Manila Bay, thus securing the Philippine Islands (and ultimately Guam) for the United States. The victory had its drawbacks. The Philippines are an archipelago of islands, the largest being Luzon in the north and

Mindanao in the south; in between were the countless islands of the Visayans. With so many islands and so much coastline, the Philippines were practically indefensible. The island of Luzon had at least two major prime landing beaches at Lingayen Gulf and Lingosari Gulf. An enemy such as Japan could easily land and gain a foothold.

Owing to these issues of defensibility, the United States had never quite figured out what to do with the Philippines. In its long-standing series of plans for fighting wars with potential enemies, with each enemy color-coded, the color for Japan was orange. "War Plan Orange" dealt with the issue of the Philippines by not even trying to defend them from a Japanese invasion, only, at best, maintaining a defensive foothold. According to the plan, upon an enemy invasion US Army forces would conduct a fighting withdrawal to the Bataan Peninsula and Corregidor and other islands in Manila Bay. With Manila as the main port for the Philippines, the idea here was to hold a blocking position sealing off Manila Bay, not so much denying the enemy the port of Manila, as denying them use of the port until either relief could arrive from Pearl Harbor in the form of the Pacific Fleet and army reinforcements or the army units could hold out no longer. In any event, once the reinforcements arrived, the islands could be retaken.

Some fortification was done in line with this plan, including turning Corregidor and various islands in Manila Bay into fortresses and constructing a small navy base at Mariveles Bay at the end of the Bataan Peninsula. Nevertheless, no one seems to have believed it would actually work. The full timetable for the plan called for holding onto the Bataan and Corregidor positions for some six months until the Pacific Fleet arrived. No one knew if the US troops cut off in the Philippines could hold out for that long, or if the Pacific Fleet would arrive in time. In any event War Plan Orange became something of a pipe dream after World War I when the Japanese acquired the Mariana, Caroline, and Marshall Islands from defeated Germany. Now the Japanese had a web of bases between Pearl Harbor and the Philippines. There was no way the Pacific Fleet could fight through in the given time-table.

Nevertheless, because of bureaucratic inertia as much as anything else, War Plan Orange remained in effect. It may not have been a good plan, or even a plan with a chance of success, but at least it was *a* plan, and that was good enough for the military establishment in Washington. The US Navy did make one concession to the plan's likelihood of failure: it refused to deploy significant forces to the Philippines. If these ships were likely to be lost or endangered early on, they wanted to limit the damage. This was not irrational, by any means, but the ships it did deploy there were going to feel very, very alone; hence Hoyt's description of the Asiatic Fleet in the title of his 1976 book as "the Lonely Ships."

This postwar bureaucratic inertia was, if anything, reinforced by a few major developments. The first was the 1922 Washington Treaty and the subsequent 1930 London Treaty, which prohibited construction or fortification of bases between Japan and Singapore. This left the United States unable to fortify its bases in the Philippines or Guam. When World War II struck in the Pacific, the true folly of these treaties would become apparent.

The second major development came in 1934, when US Congress set in motion a transition to independence for the Philippines to be completed in 1946. After this independence measure, the United States became exponentially more popular amongst Filipinos. General Douglas MacArthur, former US Army Chief of Staff, who had considerable experience in the islands, where his father had fought in the 1898 Spanish-American War, resigned his US Army commission to help the new Philippine president set up armed forces for the archipelago.

All of these events, however, were being overtaken by the aggressive behavior of the Japanese. Admiral Hart knew he had to get his fleet ready.

So, in short order, Hart moved the fleet and its headquarters out of Shanghai. The fleet would now operate out of its bases in the Philippines, of which it had several. The main base was Cavite Navy Yard, some 8 miles southeast of Manila on Manila Bay. It was not actually a navy yard in the true sense because it did not have permanent drydocks and was tiny – all its wooden and metal buildings (along with a sturdy old Spanish fort, for good measure) were crammed in an area of only 50 acres.[4] But it did have access to the nearby Sangley Point Naval Air Station, from which the Asiatic Fleet operated its seaplanes and which also housed the US Navy's main hospital in the Far East and three 600ft radio transmission towers called "Radio Cavite."[5] There was also a seaplane base at Davao on the Gulf of Davao on Mindanao. In addition to the small navy base at Mariveles, there was an older base at Olangapo, on Subic Bay north of Manila, where the navy placed a small floating drydock.

Admiral Hart did not move all the US Navy assets out of China. Admiral Glassford and his gunboats would stay, for now, but he moved most of them. Hart ordered the flagship USS *Houston* to the Philippines, and relocated his own headquarters onshore to the nondescript but air-conditioned Marsman Building on the Manila waterfront that was at the time safer than Shanghai. He also ordered dependants of US Navy personnel home. It was an extremely unpopular order but it was a prudent move, and the sailors of the Asiatic Fleet would later appreciate what Hart had done to save their families from the hell that was to come.

Since the winter of 1939–40, Admiral Hart had been candidly told that in the event of war his command was to be "As Is" – in other words, that he was going to get almost nothing in the way of reinforcements.[6] With that unpleasant knowledge, Hart tried to prepare his command by engaging in very intensive training. Day and night the ships and air crews trained. The US Asiatic Fleet was considered a prestigious posting and Hart knew his fleet traditionally took the best and the most motivated. His men were up to this challenge and were soon, from a training standpoint at least, the best US Navy force in the world.

And they had to be, because their ships were by no stretch of the imagination the best the US Navy had to offer. The strongest ship in the Asiatic Fleet was the USS *Houston*. Commissioned in 1930 as a light cruiser of the *Northampton* class, the *Houston* was converted into a heavy cruiser, carrying nine 8in guns. Like all the *Northampton*s, the *Houston* was a good, strong ship, and she also had a uniquely prestigious history: she had hosted President Roosevelt on four cruises. The president considered the *Houston* "his ship," an affection that the crew enthusiastically returned.

But there were issues associated with the *Houston*. She had recently received a new skipper, Captain Albert H. Rooks, so he and his crew were still getting to know each other. She was a so-called "treaty cruiser," built to comply with the 1922 Washington Navy Treaty and thus not quite of the caliber of her Japanese counterparts. Even worse, she carried no torpedoes. For reasons known only to the US Navy, it was decided that US cruisers should not carry torpedoes, the only cruisers in the Western navies not to carry torpedoes as a matter of policy. The *Houston*'s six torpedo tubes, like those of most US cruisers, had been removed. This left American cruisers at a severe disadvantage, especially in combat against enemy battleships with their stronger armor. In addition, the *Houston* was in dire need of maintenance in the form of a refit.

The Asiatic Fleet had one other cruiser, the light cruiser USS *Marblehead*, under the command of Captain Arthur G. Robinson. Her torpedo tubes had not yet been removed like those of the *Houston*, and she also carried 12 6in guns. However, as a member of the *Omaha* class commissioned in 1924, she was practically prehistoric. Despite her age, she was a very well-run ship; Admiral Hart said she always showed "high efficiency" and added "[S]he was an old ship but her personnel always made the best of what they had and this Cruiser could always be depended upon."[7] With her four smokestacks, she looked very similar, albeit larger, to the destroyers of her age, a similarity that would have some effect on the campaign to come.

All of the Asiatic Fleet's destroyers – USS *Alden, Barker, Bulmer, Edsall, John D. Edwards, John D. Ford, Parrott, Paul Jones, Peary, Pillsbury, Pope, Stewart,* and *Whipple* – were those mini-*Marblehead*s, members of a class of destroyers called the *Clemson* class, completed just after World War I. For most of the 1920s and 1930s these destroyers could be found everywhere throughout the US Navy, but by 1940 standards they looked rather strange. Their straight decks from bow to stern earned them the title "flush deckers," while their four smokestacks – just like the *Marblehead*'s – earned them the nicknames "four-stackers" or, more jocularly, "four-pipers." But they were poorly compartmentalized, underarmored, and underarmed. They carried four 4in guns in individual mounts behind large gun shields, not powerful enough to penetrate the armor of even an enemy destroyer. Their antiaircraft protection consisted of one 3in antiaircraft gun and several machine guns. Their most powerful weapons were their torpedo tubes, of which they carried 12, more than most ships of the upcoming war, although these tubes were not in rotating mounts midships as in the newer destroyers, but in four banks of three, two on each side. They also carried depth charges and sonar (known to the Europeans as asdic) for antisubmarine work, at which they were dependable. Although these ships were old, quirky, and needed constant care, they were loved by their crews. They were serviced by the destroyer tender USS *Black Hawk,* which provided supplies and limited repair services.

The most powerful element of the US Asiatic Fleet, and one on which both Admiral Hart and his bosses in Washington were counting, was the submarine force. Three submarine tenders – USS *Canopus, Holland,* and *Otus,* plus the submarine rescue vessel USS *Pigeon* taking care of 29 boats – USS *Perch, Permit, Pickerel, Pike, Porpoise, S-36, S-37, S-38, S-39, S-40, S-41, Sailfish, Salmon, Sargo, Saury, Sculpin, Seadragon, Seal, Shark, Skipjack, Snapper, Spearfish, Stingray, Sturgeon, Swordfish, Sealion, Searaven, Seawolf,* and *Tarpon.* It was hoped that they could at least make the Japanese invasion fleet pay a heavy price.

The units of the fleet in the Philippines were rounded out by the yacht *Isabel* (now technically Admiral Hart's flagship), six PT boats, six minesweepers – *Bittern, Finch, Lark, Quail, Tanager,* and *Whippoorwill* – the tug *Napa,* and the schooner *Lanikai.* The tankers *Pecos* and *Trinity* would serve as mobile gas stations to the fleet.

The air component of the Asiatic Fleet was Patrol Wing 10. Four seaplane tenders – USS *Childs, Langley* (which had been converted from the US Navy's first aircraft carrier to a seaplane tender), *Heron,* and *William B. Preston* – could turn any quiet cove into an instant airbase for the 28 Consolidated PBY-4 Catalina flying boats of Patrol Wing 10. Their job was to perform reconnaissance out to sea, monitor Japanese movements, and engage in very limited antiship activities; the Catalinas could carry two torpedoes or four bombs. But these slow, lightly armored flying boats were not designed to face aerial opposition.

Patrol Wing 10 and the float planes carried on the *Houston* and *Marblehead* were the only air units in the Asiatic Fleet, indeed the only air units at Admiral Hart's disposal. There were no fighters, dive bombers, or torpedo bombers. For fighter protection for his bases, his ships, and his seaplanes, Hart was dependent on his US Army counterpart, Major General Douglas MacArthur. It was not an ideal arrangement.

With the war clouds looming, in July 1941 President Roosevelt recalled MacArthur to service as a major general and incorporated his only partially finished Philippine army and air force into the defense the United States was preparing for the Philippines. All the army forces, American and Filipino, were organized under the US Army Forces in the Far East. The army air force units were organized into the Far East Air Force and placed under US Army Forces in the Far East.

General MacArthur had an infectious enthusiasm and optimism as well as tremendous political skills. But, as Admiral Hart would write in his diary, "Douglas knows a lot of things which are not so."[8] Hart biographer James Leutze would say, "With the eloquent MacArthur, public delusion and even self-delusion was always possible because he was, oh, so persuasive."[9] And with MacArthur, self-delusion was rampant, as well as his malice towards anyone who would try to disavow him of that delusion. He found the plan for defense of the Philippines as contemplated under War Plan Orange, now incorporated into the war plan called Rainbow 5, needlessly defeatist. MacArthur campaigned energetically for the Roosevelt administration to not consider the Philippines "indefensible." He claimed instead that he would turn the archipelago into a fortress, with 200,000 Philippine troops at his command that could be used for a counteroffensive against Japan. That is, he would do this if Washington sent him reinforcements, especially air reinforcements, and if he had until spring 1942 to train the Filipinos. Throwing away 20 years of belief that the islands were indefensible, Roosevelt and his senior army generals bought into MacArthur's thinking.[10] The US Navy did not, and continued to refuse to reinforce the Philippines, ultimately directing Admiral Hart to withdraw southward from Manila "at discretion" upon the outbreak of war.[11]

Meanwhile, the Americans, British, Chinese, and Dutch, or the "ABCD Powers," as they were sometimes called, were trying to come to some agreement as to a coordinated strategy for resisting the Japanese advance. Admiral Hart had championed such a unified strategy very, very hard, but so far the discussions were foundering on two major issues.

The first was the different status between the British and Dutch as combatants in the current war on the one side and the United States as a non-combatant prior to Pearl Harbor on the other. The British and Dutch wanted to know what it would take to get the United States into the war, the *casus belli*. President Roosevelt could not say; he probably did not know.[12]

The second was the apparent British obsession with the island of Singapore, the "Gibraltar of the Far East" and the cornerstone of British policy in the region, where Britain had built a major naval base. The British regarded Singapore as an impregnable fortress; the Americans regarded Singapore as all-too pregnable – virtually indefensible, in fact – and not worth a major commitment in any case. These differences of opinion on Singapore were irreconcilable.

For those reasons, the discussions produced only limited agreements that succeeded in creating a very confusing series of acronyms but little of the planning and coordination that would be needed in the event of war.

The first of these limited agreements came out of the so-called ADA ("Anglo–Dutch–Australian," with Australia also representing New Zealand) meeting in Singapore in late February 1941, when it was concluded that a large-scale Japanese attack on Australia and New Zealand could not be carried out so long as Singapore was operating as a British navy base and that Japan could not attack Malaya and the Netherlands East Indies simultaneously.[13] As a result, the Japanese would likely attack Malaya and Singapore first. Plans for mutual defense and coordination were drawn up.[14]

Next came a staff agreement executed on March 29, 1941 called "ABC-1" ("American–British Conference"). For purposes of the Pacific War, ABC-1 merely stated that if the United States went to war with both Japan and Nazi Germany, Germany would take top priority, with a commensurate commitment of US naval forces to the Atlantic. The most relevant portion of the agreement stated that American forces in the Far East would cooperate with the British and Dutch as much as possible, so long as it did not compromise the primary mission of US forces in the region in defending the Philippines.[15] The big stumbling blocks were the inability of the United States to state under what circumstances it would enter the war, and its refusal to provide a force to help the British defend Singapore.

A month later, in April 1941, the naval staffs had a week-long "ADB" (as in "American–Dutch–British") conference in Singapore, which took place at the same time as a "BD"

("British–Dutch") conference. These discussions focused on the defense of Singapore, on which they ultimately failed. The British wanted most naval forces to be committed to convoying troops and supplies to Singapore. They had somehow convinced the Dutch of the wisdom of this position, but not the Americans, who vehemently disagreed. Eventually, they reached the "ADB-1" protocol, under which the Americans, British, and Dutch ultimately agreed to coordinate local defense when war with Japan took place and that American naval forces retreating from the Philippines would head for Singapore. Washington was disgusted with the Singapore-centric nature of the agreement and with London's demand for American forces to defend British-ruled Singapore when the British were not willing to commit significant forces of their own.[16] Washington not just rejected it, but withdrew its earlier permission under ABC-1 to cooperate with the British and Dutch. In August, the British agreed to completely support the Netherlands in case of a Japanese attack on the East Indies, and the ADB-1 plan became "ADB-2." The Americans were underwhelmed by the changes.[17] American, British, and Dutch officers did eventually reach an agreement called the "Plans for the Employment of Naval and Air Forces of the Associated Powers in the Eastern Theater in the Event of War with Japan" (PLENAPS), but Washington disapproved of it.[18] For now, this confusing alphabet soup series of conferences and plans came to an end, as did Admiral Hart's hopes for a unified Allied strategy.

With no formal operating arrangements with the British and no coordinated plan for the defense of the Far East, the US Navy reiterated what had been its policy all along: once the Asiatic Fleet could do no more to defend the Philippines, Admiral Hart would have authority to retreat "at discretion."[19] Though he would make a futile effort at getting the navy to support a plan by which the Asiatic Fleet would fight in support of MacArthur, Hart began setting up a gradual retreat to Borneo, and, ultimately, the Dutch naval base at Soerabaja (Surabaya) on the island of Java.

So, while Admiral Hart was being directed to retreat, General MacArthur's efforts to convince Washington that the Philippines were not "indefensible" started to bear fruit, as the army began pumping air power into the Philippines to build up the dilapidated Far East Air Force. Up until now, the US Army Air Force in the Philippines had been almost nonexistent. Despite having a large, fairly well-equipped airbase complex at Clark Field, some 60 miles north of Manila, it had very few aircraft. Its few bombers were of the obsolete B-10 and B-18 variety, while its fighters were the P-35, classified as obsolete and "unsuitable for combat," and the almost laughable P-26 Peashooter.[20] Now, the US Army Air Force would rush its front-line fighter, the Curtiss P-40 Warhawk, and its all-world bomber, the Boeing B-17 Flying Fortress, which had just gone into production, into Clark Field almost as fast as they came off the assembly lines.[21] Those assembly lines had been gearing up for the war, but they were not there yet, and the first reinforcements came in slowly, in part because the Philippines were so far from the United States. The plan was ultimately to stage 100 B-17s and 200 P-40s into the Philippine airfields. Of course, this assumed that they had until spring 1942 to do so.

And so the Far East Air Force developed a network of bases. The biggest by far was Clark Field but in order to disperse the aircraft so that a single air attack would not destroy them all, there were others, although most were in fairly primitive condition. Two other fields, Nichols and Nielson, were located near Manila; the latter was home to the headquarters of both the Far East Air Force and the recently-organized V Interceptor Command (Provisional), which had charge of all the fighter squadrons in the Philippines. A fourth, also near Manila, was a tiny, recently-built airfield called Del Carmen.

A fifth airfield, Iba, was some 75 miles northwest of Manila, on the approach from Japanese-held Formosa, where it was known that the Japanese had large airfields. Iba was the only place in the Philippines with radar, still very new and something of a novelty, that was positioned to effectively detect incoming attackers.[22] A sixth, hastily-built airfield at a pineapple plantation at Del Monte was located 500 miles to the south on Mindanao. From these bases, it was planned that the P-40 Warhawks would provide air cover over the Philippines while the tough B-17s would strike at enemy warships and landing convoys that approached the islands. The Army Air Force had high hopes for the B-17. They said it could "hit a pickle barrel from 20,000 feet."[23] Perhaps, but what if that pickle barrel was moving?

These developments should have been comforting to Admiral Hart, but they were not. Hart tried to coordinate defense and reconnaissance efforts with General MacArthur, only to be met with indifference and even contempt. Hart and MacArthur had family connections and had dealt with each other pleasantly for a long time, but no longer. MacArthur referred to Hart and his command as "Small Fleet, big Admiral," and at one point the general sneeringly told Hart, "Get yourself a real fleet, Tommy. Then you will belong."[24] The admiral tried, not unreasonably, to get naval control over air operations over the waters surrounding the Philippines; MacArthur responded with what Hart described as a "perfectly rotten" letter that "went about as far as his active brain could take him toward being nasty to the Navy in general and me in particular."[25] Calling Hart's proposal "entirely objectionable," MacArthur would go on to note that "the term 'Fleet' cannot be applied to the two cruisers and the division of destroyers at your command," and to find "manifestly illogical" the idea of putting his air force, even just over water, under control of a naval force "of such combat inferiority as your Command …"[26] The insulting message got MacArthur admonished by US Army Chief of Staff General George C. Marshall; the Navy would have command over aircraft over water.[27]

However, the insults hardly ended there. Admiral Hart would initiate conversations with General MacArthur to formulate plans for the defense of the islands. The general responded "with boredom, disinterest, or strong indications of independence."[28] MacArthur would tell Hart that he was "not going to follow, or even be in any way bound by whatever war plans have been evolved, agreed upon and approved."[29] MacArthur said he did not care about, did not need the Asiatic Fleet; he could defeat the Japanese with his 200,000 troops and his air force in a "glorious land war."[30]

The arrogance and insanity of the commander of US Army Forces in the Far East toward the Asiatic Fleet continued for most of the summer and fall, right up to the outbreak of the war. On November 4, 1941, General Lewis Brereton arrived in Manila to take command of the Far East Air Force under General MacArthur. He brought with him written confirmation of the changes in Rainbow 5 that MacArthur had wanted. MacArthur was now authorized to defend all the Philippine Islands. The Far East Air Force now had specific orders under Rainbow 5: in the event of hostilities, the defending air forces were to carry out "air raids against Japanese forces and installations within tactical operating radius of available bases."[31]

The new aircraft kept coming, if only at a trickle. By December, the Far East Air Force had exactly 35 B-17s. For fighter cover, the Far East Air Force had 72 P-40Bs and Es, the only "modern" pursuits, in the islands. Clark Field was headquarters of the 24th Pursuit Group. The 24th Pursuit Group consisted of the 20th Pursuit Squadron, also at Clark, which by December 1941 had 18 P-40Bs; the 3rd Pursuit, with 18 P-40Es at Iba Field; and the 17th Pursuit with 18 P-40Es at Nichols Field. Also on Luzon was the 21st Pursuit, with 18 P-40Es at Nichols Field; and, based at Del Carmen, the 34th Pursuit Squadron, which was stuck using 22 of the badly underarmored and underarmed P-35As, so useless that their pilots had dubbed them "flying cordwood."[32] Technically, both the 21st and the 34th were part of the 35th Pursuit Group, but because its headquarters had not yet arrived they were under the command of the 24th Pursuit Group, which had the effect of making the V Interceptor Command (Provisional) superfluous, at least temporarily.[33]

Clark Field was also home to the entire inventory of B-17s in the Philippine Islands, under the rubric of the V Bomber Command. The V Bomber Command was also superfluous for the moment because it consisted of only the 19th Bombardment Group, which consisted of the 14th, 28th, 30th, and 93rd Bombardment Squadrons, totaling 35 B-17s. The Far East Air Force was uncomfortable basing all the B-17s at Clark, and the new airfield at Del Carmen was intended to help disperse the bombers. Also on hand were the pilots and ground crews of the 27th Bombardment Squadron (Light), intended to be based at Del Monte, but their aircraft, 52 A-24 Banshee dive bombers (the Army version of the Navy's famous SBD Dauntless) were being shipped in a convoy escorted by the heavy cruiser *Pensacola* and had yet to arrive.[34]

While Admiral Hart was busy running his ships through a vigorous training regimen, MacArthur remained supremely confident that "it would be impossible for the Japanese to attack the Philippines before the following April.[35] The United States had "plenty of time," he told Hart.[36]

US Navy intelligence felt otherwise, however. On the morning of November 27, 1941, as negotiations between the United States and Japan broke down for the final time, the Chief of Naval Operations sent out a war warning. It was now expected that, within the next few days, Japan would initiate some sort of aggressive action, either in the Philippines or Malaya. Admiral Hart did not want all his ships caught by an air attack at Cavite, so he prepared to disperse them across the islands. The timing of the warning was unfortunate for the *Houston*. The cruiser was at Cavite having radar installed. Her topmast had already been cut and cables run down her foremast in order to place the aerials for a radar set that was due to arrive from Pearl Harbor. But all work was stopped as crewmen were immediately recalled to their ships and preparations were made to leave.[37] The dispersal of the ships was necessary, as events would show, but the lack of that radar would prove to be a devastating blow to hopes for successful defense of the Allied positions in the Far East.

Not that the Asiatic Fleet was completely without radar, for Admiral Hart had received a very unexpected and indeed unintended reinforcement, the light cruiser USS *Boise*. The *Boise* had just escorted a convoy into Manila, but with the war warning, she was ordered to stay and put herself at the disposal of Hart. This was a significant reinforcement. Under the command of Captain Stephen B. Robinson, the *Boise* was a new light cruiser of the *Brooklyn* class. She was a light cruiser only because she had 6in guns instead of 8in guns. She had no torpedo tubes, but she did have 15 rapid-fire 6in guns, in five triple turrets. She also carried radar, the only ship available to Hart to do so since the work on the *Houston* had been suspended. As far as light cruisers go, the *Boise* was a monster. The admiral was elated.

So Hart took the final steps, dispersing his ships to make sure they were not caught together by air attack in port, and preparing the retreat to the Indies. The *Houston* was sent to Iloilo, the port of the Philippine Island of Panay. She would be the flagship of Task Force 5, the seagoing attack force of the Asiatic Fleet, under the command of Admiral Glassford, who was being recalled from Shanghai with his gunboats. The *Marblehead* and destroyers *Paul Jones, Stewart, Bulmer, Barker,* and *Parrott* were sent to Tarakan; the *Black Hawk* and destroyers *Whipple, Alden, John D. Edwards,* and *Edsall* were sent to Balikpapan, both on Borneo and both home to major oilfields. If the Dutch asked their commanders why they were there, they were to develop "difficulties" that would require them to stay there for the time being.[38] Two destroyers, *Peary* and *Pillsbury,* were at Cavite being repaired; another two, *Pope* and *John D. Ford,* were guarding Manila Bay from submarines. Seaplane tender *William B. Preston* was sent to Magalag Bay with three Catalinas, and the *Heron* was sent to the Gulf of Davao, both on Mindanao; they were sent for both dispersal and reconnaissance.[39]

And just in time, for on December 2, things started happening. Under the personal direction of Admiral Hart, Patrol Wing 10 had stepped up its patrols of the South China Sea, where they detected increased Japanese convoy activity.[40] On December 2, a PBY piloted by Lieutenant (j.g.) William Robinson flew over Cam Ranh Bay and found more than 30 Japanese freighters and transports in the harbor.[41] That same day, an unidentified aircraft over Clark Field was tracked by the Iba radar; no interception was ordered.

The next day another Catalina flew over Cam Ranh Bay and found that the number of ships had increased to more than 50, including several cruisers and destroyers. The following day another Catalina patrol reported that all of the ships were gone. They had left for parts unknown. The meaning was obvious.

If that was not evidence enough, the increasing number of aerial incidents over Luzon should have been. Early in the morning of December 4, the Iba radar tracked an unidentified plane over the Lingayen Gulf. During a dawn interception exercise, a flight of P-40s from the 20th Pursuit nearly collided with another unidentified aircraft. Later that morning, one of Patrol Wing 10's planes, patrolling around Manila, spotted a twin-engine Japanese bomber off the coast. The incidents continued on December 5, prompting General MacArthur finally to order any unidentified aircraft in Philippine airspace to be shot down.

What these incidents over Luzon portended was not lost on General Brereton, who had been anxious over the security of his aircraft for some time. About a week earlier, he had flown back from a conference in Australia to Clark Field and found his B-17s and P-40s all lined up by the runway, nice and neat and shiny, wingtip to wingtip, a beautiful picture of organization that could have been destroyed by just a few bombs. Upon landing Brereton chewed out the ground crew. "Fortunately ... I was not leading a hostile bombing fleet. If I had been, I could have blasted the entire heavy bombardment strength of the Philippines off the map in one smash. Do you call that dispersal? It's wrong." Now he would handle dispersal himself. On the night of December 5, 16 B-17s from the 14th and 93rd Bombardment Squadrons – approximately half the bomber strength in the Philippines – were sent to Del Monte, which at this point had a runway but little else, to be out of the range of Japanese air attacks from Formosa.[42] The plan was to stage them into Clark Field when necessary.[43]

In the meantime, General Brereton did all he could to get the Far East Air Force ready for the war they were about to face. The insane optimism of Douglas MacArthur was tempered in the Far East Air Force. During the morning of December 6, the pilots of the 17th and 21st Squadrons at Nichols Field were called in for a briefing by Colonel Harold George, chief of staff for the Far East Air Force's Interceptor Command. His opening words were not standard motivational-speaker material, but they were honest, "Men, you are not a suicide squadron yet, but you're damn close to it." The pilots listened in stunned silence.

In fact the situation was far worse as George and his pilots had not seen Chennault's reports on the Japanese Zero. Chennault had watched the Zero, even inspected the wreckage of a Zero that had been shot down; he had developed the specifications and even tactics for defeating the Zero with planes like the P-40. He had forwarded his reports to Washington and London. Those reports were deemed not credible, and, Chennault would later say, some of his reports to Washington were even deliberately destroyed.[44] For George and his pilots, ignorance would be not bliss, but fatal.

Colonel George tried to prepare bombing strikes against the Japanese bases on Formosa, especially around the port of Takao (Kaohsiung). At the request of Admiral Hart, the increasingly dangerous patrol routes near Formosa had been taken over by B-17s. But General MacArthur would not allow reconnaissance missions anywhere near Formosa. Since Formosa was home to the Japanese airbases from which any attack would most likely come this seemed illogical. After repeated protests by General Brereton, MacArthur relented somewhat, allowing patrols to come up to the international boundary of Formosa, where at high altitude they could photograph the Japanese airbases. Yet there appear to have been no photographs taken.

MacArthur seemed to remain in some sort of delusional state. Hart privately called MacArthur "erratic" and "no longer altogether sane ... he may not have been for a long time."[45] On December 5, 1941, in a meeting with Admiral Hart and British Admiral Tom Phillips, the commander of the Royal Navy detachment at Singapore, MacArthur spoke confidently: "The inability of an enemy to launch his air attack on these islands is our greatest security ... [N]othing would please me better than if they would give me three months and then attack here ... that would deliver the enemy into our hands."[46]

But what if they did not give him three months?

On December 2, 1941, to tremendous pomp and circumstance, the British battleship HMS *Prince of Wales* arrived in Singapore. What the powerful Royal Navy battleship was supposed to do next was anybody's guess.

Owing to the fact that Axis submarines had made the Mediterranean too dangerous for travel (as the Royal Navy carrier *Ark Royal* and battleship *Barham* had found out the hard way) to get from England to Singapore, the *Prince of Wales* had had to sail around Africa, with a well-publicized stop in Capetown, South Africa, and then a second stop in Colombo, Ceylon, before pulling into the Singapore Naval Base, a journey of some 12,000 miles.[47] The decision to send her to Singapore was even longer and far more meandering. The journey of the *Prince of Wales* was almost finished – in more ways than one, unfortunately – but the journey of the British decision makers in the Admiralty and Whitehall was still nowhere near a conclusion.

For some two decades, British defense policy in the Far East had been based on one word: Singapore. The British had a belief, not so much a postulate as an outright article of faith, that the island was the key to defense of their interests in the Far East – which consisted, largely, of Singapore.

This rather circular thinking was not exactly irrational. Singapore was and to this day remains one of the most valuable pieces of strategic real estate in the world. As the old adage holds, real estate value is based on three things: location, location, and location. And Singapore had all three.

An island at the tip of the Malay Peninsula, Singapore is right on the South China Sea, one of the heaviest areas for commercial shipping traffic in the world. The main avenue for transit from the South China Sea to the Indian Ocean, and then the Suez Canal and Europe, is the Strait of Malacca, between the Malay Peninsula and the Indonesian island of Sumatra – a strait to which access is controlled by Singapore. A less convenient alternative to the Strait of Malacca was the Soenda Strait (today the Sunda Strait) between Sumatra and Java – and Singapore is within striking distance of that, too. For all practical purposes, if you wanted to get from East Asia to India, the proverbial crown jewel of the British Empire, or even Europe, you had to go through Singapore, one way or another.[48]

Yet, while in possession of such a valuable strategic asset, the British never figured out what to do with Singapore or how it should fit into a coherent defense policy in the Far East. There were other British holdings in the area – Hong Kong, most famously, but also northern Borneo and Malaya proper, as well as its further-away Pacific Dominions Australia and New Zealand. But Hong Kong was regarded, accurately, as indefensible, and the British government displayed little concern for Malaya and Borneo, except to the extent that they could defend Singapore. Everything was about Singapore. It was an intense preoccupation that was both emotional and rational, but only vaguely rational, and the best minds in the British political and military establishment could never quite bring it into focus.

The central feature of the "Singapore Policy" as it became known was the aforementioned Singapore Naval Base. The British had recognized a need for a fleet base in the Far East since the end of World War I. The Royal Navy had controlled the seas for centuries because it could choke off its competition at the source. The French, the Dutch, the Germans, and the Spanish could not leave their ports without coming within striking distance of the British Isles. This enabled Britain to keep its maritime supremacy while maintaining short supply lines. With the dawn of the imperial age, the supply lines to British colonies became very, very long, but with their rivals located in Europe, the British could still choke them off at the source.

But after World War I, the British faced a new issue. Their latest rival for control of the sea was Japan. Unlike Britain's European rivals, Japan could not be choked off at the source from bases close by in the British Isles; she could only be fought at the end of a long and very tenuous supply line. The solution seemed obvious: the British wanted a base available for a Royal Navy fleet within the Far East which could approximate their bases in Britain proper, just in case they needed it, but without actually having a fleet based there on a permanent basis.

In 1921, the British decided that the fleet base they wanted should be at Singapore, much to the disgust of Australia and New Zealand, who felt that locating the base at Sydney would both be safer and better protect their own interests.[49] With that the question became where to put the base on Singapore Island. To do so, Royal Navy planners had to determine how such a base could be defended. Britain was well aware of Japan's typical strategy for taking enemy ports. In the Sino-Japanese War, to capture Port Arthur, located at the tip of the Kwantung Peninsula, the Japanese attacked down the peninsula from the city's landward side. In the Russo-Japanese War, to capture Port Arthur (again), in exactly the same way. During World War I, to capture Tsingtao, located at the tip of the Shantung Peninsula, the Japanese once again attacked down the peninsula from the city's landward side.

Based on this record of performance, British strategists determined that to capture Singapore, located at the tip of the Malay Peninsula, the Japanese would most likely attack from the sea.[50] While this conclusion may seem counterintuitive, there was in fact a certain logic to it. The Malay Peninsula was, for the most part, covered in dense jungle. The British considered that jungle impenetrable, so they believed that anyone attacking down the peninsula would be restricted to the roads, which could be easily defended.

As a result of this belief that Malaya was impenetrable, Singapore Naval Base was placed on the northern side of the island on the Johore Strait, at the mouth of the Sungei Sembawang (which had to be diverted) in the neighborhood known as Seletar (which gave the base its alternate name), within easy reach of the mainland. The base appeared to be a marvel:

> Singapore was the stuff of dreams: an anchorage capacious enough for the largest navy afloat; four square miles of shore facilities with docks and cranes to refit great ships; abundant stores of food and munitions; an excellent commercial seaport next door; and proximity to the oil wells and refineries of Sumatra. It was ringed with artillery, minefields, and aerodromes. To the north lay a jungle impenetrable, it was thought, to overland attack.[51]

A closer inspection would reveal that the naval base was not quite the stuff of dreams it was made out to be. The artillery was battleship-caliber – three 15in, six 9.2in, and 14 6in guns – but those guns were fitted on the seaward side of the island and could not command the landward approaches.[52] In fact, the base did not have the ability "to refit great ships," as the British sheepishly admitted; while it did have a very large graving dock and a floating drydock, it had neither the personnel nor the machine tools nor even the spare parts to handle major repairs to capital ships.[53] Moreover, the base was in artillery range of the mainland, but the mainland contained only supposedly impenetrable jungle. Yet military history has taught us that impenetrable features are all too easily penetrable if there is a skillful commander and a determined invading force. The Alps were impenetrable to an army until Hannibal crossed to make war on Rome. The Wilderness of Spotsylvania was impenetrable until Stonewall Jackson went through it to outflank the Union Army at Chancellorsville. And the Ardennes Forest was considered impenetrable until the German panzers streamed across it in 1940 to pierce a mortal hole in the Allied line defending France.

But for the moment at least, those were not concerns. When it opened, mostly, in 1938, after 15 years of debate, cancellations, cost overruns, and other construction issues, the British now had their fleet base.[54] For a fleet that did not yet exist. Basing a fleet so far away was (and is) expensive, and the tropical climate, with its heat, humidity, frequent storms and warm water were hard on the ships and their machinery. When and if the Japanese started causing trouble, the fleet could be in Singapore in 70 days to deal with them and protect jittery Australia and New Zealand. That strategy carried the catchphrase: "Main fleet to Singapore."

Everything changed when Hitler invaded Poland and World War II started in Europe. The "Main Fleet to Singapore" policy had naively assumed there would be no war in Europe that would keep Royal Navy assets committed in home waters (an assumption that was increasingly in doubt in Whitehall in the run-up to the war), but that is exactly what happened. The U-boat menace from World War I made an encore performance, to which the Kriegsmarine added convoy raiders such as the pocket battleship *Admiral Graf Spee*. Although the *Graf Spee* was ultimately sunk, in a tremendous victory for an always-skillful Royal Navy, that single German ship had put severe strain on the already massive Royal Navy commitment in the Atlantic.[55]

The Royal Navy also suffered some emotional body blows, such as a U-boat penetrating the main base at Scapa Flow to sink the battleship *Royal Oak,* and the sinking of the aircraft carrier HMS *Glorious* and her minimal escort of two destroyers by the German battlecruisers *Scharnhorst* and *Gneisenau*. Things quickly got even worse when France surrendered. The Royal Navy had counted on the French Navy to control the Mediterranean and guard the trade routes through the Suez Canal. With the French gone, Britain had to do the work itself, which stretched the Royal Navy even further. Then Italy entered the war. Now the Royal Navy had to fight to keep the Mediterranean, stretching its scarce assets further yet.

Perhaps the worst blow, from both a material and an emotional standpoint, had been the foray of the German battleship *Bismarck*.

The *Bismarck* had left Norway in May, 1941, with a single cruiser as escort to raid British shipping in the Atlantic. The British sent the battlecruiser HMS *Hood,* considered the most powerful ship in the Royal Navy as well as its spiritual heart, and this same *Prince of Wales* to intercept the German monster in the Denmark Strait between Iceland and Greenland. The resulting engagement did not go quite as the British had planned. The *Hood* took a 16in shell from the *Bismarck* in her magazine and exploded, leaving only four survivors. The *Prince of Wales* tried to avenge her lost comrade, and delivered a hit that punctured one of the *Bismarck*'s fuel bunkers. But, in an ominous sign, the new British battleship suffered a critical electrical breakdown that knocked her main guns offline. She was forced to withdraw and the *Bismarck* disappeared into the Atlantic.

This left the Admiralty in a virtual panic. A German battleship was roaming free to ambush supply convoys that Britain desperately needed, and they had no idea where she was. That is, until the German admiral in charge decided to send a long wireless telegraph message to Berlin describing their exploits and the hole in their fuel tank that was forcing the *Bismarck* to head to France for repairs. British intelligence, after a fashion, was able to track down the source of the transmission to the *Bismarck* in the Bay of Biscay, where British torpedo planes and battleships combined to put her under.

As an institution, the Royal Navy was (and is) extremely resilient and dependable, continuing a long tradition of being one of the best navies in the world. But holding out against Hitler alone, fighting in the Atlantic and the Mediterranean spread it extremely thin. Australia and New Zealand had to commit their own naval assets to help Britain in its hour of need. The war, in the words of Captain Charles S. Daniel, Director of Plans for the Admiralty, was placing "a greater strain on the Royal Navy than it has probably ever experienced before in its history."[56]

"Main fleet to Singapore" had not considered the possibility that Britain would be fighting a war in Europe at all, let alone a war in which the Royal Navy would be under such unprecedented strain. More and more assets had to be husbanded closer to home, which meant that fewer and fewer assets could be made available to Singapore, and none of what it could make available could be done so quickly. "Main fleet to Singapore" in 70 days soon became 80 then 90 then 180 before it was indefinitely postponed. Australia and New Zealand felt both angry and betrayed.

And so, when war seemed inevitable in the Far East, the pressure on Britain to do *something* was extremely high. Reinforcements for Singapore had to be found. Yet, for a strategic asset of such importance, Singapore always seemed to be the absolute last priority for reinforcement.

The Chief of Staff Far East determined that it needed no fewer than 336 aircraft to defend British interests, a number that was later increased to 556; they had just 182.[57] Their main fighter in Malaya was the Brewster Buffalo. Stubby and squat – their pilots derisively called it the "Peanut Special" – the Buffalo was perhaps the ugliest monoplane fighter ever conceived, as well as poorly designed and, by 1941, quite obsolete.[58] It did not inspire confidence and was generally hated by its pilots. Buffalos, however, were both cheap and available. Meanwhile Claire Chennault's reports regarding the Zero ended up buried on an intelligence officer's desk in Singapore. The racism that denigrated the potential performance of Japan, all too prevalent in the Allied countries, had clouded the judgment of the Royal Air Force.

With the Battle of Britain over, the Royal Air Force now had 99 fighter squadrons in Britain, all of which were well-stocked with modern front-line fighters like the Hawker Hurricane and the Supermarine Spitfire which had enjoyed much success during the Battle of Britain.[59] But at the end of August 1941, in a questionable decision that had grave implications for Singapore, Prime Minister Winston Churchill promised 200 Hawker Hurricanes and 200 Warhawks to Joseph Stalin.[60] A few weeks later, Air Chief Marshal Robert Brooke-Popham, who on November 14, 1940 had become British Commander-in-Chief, Far East, was told by London that because of these shipments to the Soviet Union, no modern fighters could be spared for Singapore. Heavy bomber production was at 5,000 annually; not one was sent to Singapore.[61]

Air Chief Marshal Brooke-Popham himself was something of another symptom of the low priority of Singapore. He had been called out of retirement to become the Far East commander; quite a few thought he should have stayed retired. Admiral Hart called him "rather muddle-headed" and noted that things in Malaya did not seem to be running smoothly under his leadership.[62] Sir Alfred Duff Cooper, sent by Churchill to assess civil–military cooperation in Singapore, called Brooke-Popham "damned near gaga."[63] Brooke-Popham's chief talents seemed to be consistently falling asleep at meetings and making injudicious statements to the press.[64]

Once he arrived, Brooke-Popham promptly declared Malaya "the easiest country in the world to defend" because, "There's one main road running roughly from north to south and a railway line. So long as we can hold these, the country stays ours." Amphibious landings were not a problem, he said, because of the "impenetrable jungle" between the coast and the road.[65] Therefore, the only question about the defense of Malaya was the matter of the naval forces, which had been conveniently left out of his command portfolio.

However, as an air marshal, Brooke-Popham did understand the needs of air power and set about constructing a network of airfields. Indeed, then-Captain John Collins, who was on the staff of the Royal Navy's China Force in Singapore, would later state that the marshal's statements were only to reassure the public, and that privately he was well aware of Singapore's limitations.[66] Singapore Island had four airfields: military airfields at Seletar, Sembawang, and Tengah, and the civilian airport at Kallang. Nevertheless, Brooke-Popham felt confident because he did not regard the Japanese as "air-minded, particularly against determined fighter opposition."[67] The air marshal would try to obtain modern aircraft, but would, in response to a question from a reporter as to why they had no modern aircraft in Malaya, explain his lack of such aircraft in terms infamous for their arrogance and stupidity: "We can get on all right with Buffalos out here, but they haven't got the speed for England; let England have the 'super' Spitfires and the 'hyper' Hurricanes. Buffalos are quite good enough for Malaya."[68]

Later, Member of Parliament Sir Archibald Southby would bitterly state, "One month's supply of the aircraft sent to Russia would have saved Malaya."[69] Indeed, it would potentially have saved the naval forces sent to the Far East as well.

The primary goal of Prime Minister Winston Churchill and the Admiralty was to deter rather than defend against a Japanese attack. Yet their efforts were warped by memories of the *Bismarck* incident, and in fact the possibility of a similar attack existed, for the *Bismarck* had a sister, an even larger beast called the *Tirpitz* then based in Norway. Terrified of a repeat of the *Bismarck* episode, the Admiralty kept three of their new battleships of the *King George V* class, of which the *Prince of Wales* was a member, watching her at all times.

The discussions between the Admiralty and Churchill, and the resulting controversy that continues to stem from those discussions today in hindsight, have been detailed in many other fine works. Those discussions are confusing but may be summarized as follows. The Admiralty saw the issue at Singapore as defensive, and wanted to send a big fleet – the aforementioned 48 ships from the ABD-1 plan, headed by the aircraft carrier HMS *Ark Royal*, the battleships HMS *Nelson* and *Rodney*; three old "R"-class battleships (which later became four); ten cruisers and 32 destroyers.[70] These ships would be gradually freed from Atlantic duties by the US Navy coming in to help in the Atlantic, but were also intended to address American concerns about the ABD arrangements. So, no modern battleships for Singapore. Yet, though the "R" class ships – HMS *Revenge, Royal Sovereign, Ramillies,* and *Resolution* – were old, slow, and unmodernized, they were big and had big guns. Basing them at Singapore was bound to cause the Imperial Navy to have second thoughts about attacking.

Churchill perceived things differently. He saw the *Tirpitz* as tying down British forces many times larger than she was. He envisioned doing the same thing to the

Japanese. He proposed sending a small, fast force of two fast battleships and one aircraft carrier to Singapore. There they could form a "fleet in being," threatening to raid Japanese supply lines before disappearing into the thousands of islands of the Netherlands East Indies.

Winston Churchill was undoubtedly one of the great leaders in world history and all Western civilization owes him a debt of gratitude. Brilliant, shrewd, insightful, witty, he was right the vast majority of the time but in this instance he was disastrously wrong.

The prime minister's flawed policy was the result of a very basic misunderstanding. The *Tirpitz* was tying down the Royal Navy because she was operating from a secure port. Singapore was not a secure port, but was instead a Japanese target for capture. Churchill mistakenly believed that the major Japanese threat was commerce raiding in the Indian Ocean; he could not understand that Singapore itself was a Japanese target.[71] His small force was not nearly big enough to deter the Japanese from attacking that target. One veteran admiral would later say, "British naval policy in Far Eastern waters was based on unrealistic threats and imaginary deterrents, conceived in Mr. Churchill's strategical cloud cuckoo land."[72]

Sir Dudley Pound, First Sea Lord of the Admiralty, eventually acquiesced in part to Churchill's proposal by agreeing to send one battlecruiser and one aircraft carrier out east together with a battleship. The aircraft carrier would ultimately be the HMS *Indomitable*. The battlecruiser would be the HMS *Repulse,* then escorting convoys in the Indian Ocean. Under the command of Captain William Tennant, this old veteran of World War I was nevertheless a fast ship and had been heavily modernized with new features including radar. The *Repulse* carried six 15in guns, but her antiaircraft armament was lacking.

That left the battleship. The arm wrestling between the Admiralty and Churchill still did not end. All they could agree to was sending the battleship HMS *Prince of Wales,* a member of the new *King George V* class and veteran of the *Bismarck* affair, to Capetown (with a stop en route in Freetown, Sierra Leone) and then determine where she should go from there.

The *Prince of Wales,* under the command of Captain John Leach, was a very new battleship – too new, perhaps. She carried ten 14-guns, in one dual turret and two unusual quadruple turrets. She also had 16 high-angle dual-purpose 5.25in guns in eight dual mounts. State-of-the-art radar, both warning and fire control, tied it all together. Some even applied to her the ominous cliché "unsinkable."[73] But there was something dark about her, something that had nothing to do with her terrible ventilation that often had crewmen sleeping on the deck to avoid the stifling cabins.

Those ten 14in guns, while modern and large in number, were also the smallest caliber for any major battleship, another legacy of the Washington and London Treaty era.[74] While still under construction in Liverpool she had been hit by a Luftwaffe bomb. The damage was repaired, but some would whisper that she had never felt quite right after that, as if she was the maritime equivalent of a "lemon." Then, when the battleship was being moved from the Liverpool docks she was run aground. She was still in her period of "working up" – that period of time when a new crew is operating a new ship for the first time and learning about its characteristics, handling, machinery, and layout – when the *Bismarck* emergency hit, so she was thrown into the breach, along with the *Hood*, in essence before her crew was fully trained. The *Prince of Wales* survived, but her ill-timed electrical issue had left her helpless. While some historians have denied it, the superstitious nature of sailors leaves little doubt that there were those who wondered if she was a "Jonah" – an unlucky ship.[75]

But, like most military officials, Churchill and the Admiralty did not consider a ship's luck when determining deployments. So, in the early afternoon of October 25, 1941, the *Prince of Wales*, still without working up, left Greenock naval base on the Clyde estuary, with the destroyers HMS *Electra* and *Express* as permanent escorts, and destroyer HMS *Hesperus* as a temporary escort.[76] They were designated "Force G." The atmosphere on board was generally "relaxed and cheerful," though there were notes of foreboding. On board that day was Royal Navy Midshipman D. G. Roome, who would later say:

> We were sailing into the unknown, with almost complete lack of information on what to expect in the way of opposition. We felt the operation was a gamble and that we were sticking our necks out and that we would be lucky if we got away with it. My belief at the time was that we should never have got ourselves in the situation we did.[77]

Royal Marine Maurice Edwards described the atmosphere aboard her as they left:

> It wasn't made clear to us that we'd be going to Singapore, and the first place I recall stopping at was Freetown. You must remember the lower decks weren't very well informed on what was going on, and I suppose the same could be said for all but the highest ranking of officers.[78]

The British sailors aboard the battleship did not know, but Franklin Roosevelt did. Churchill could not wait to tell him the news:

> As your naval people have already been informed we are sending that big ship you inspected into the Indian Ocean as part of a squadron we are forming there. This ought to serve as a deterrent to Japan.[79]

Precisely when the decision was made to send the *Prince of Wales* to Singapore is unknown; there is no record of it, nor is there a record of the discussions between Churchill and First Sea Lord Sir Dudley Pound on the subject.[80] This curious lack of documentation as to who said what when continues to be a source of suspicion and controversy in Great Britain, a permanent dead end in efforts to piece together the events leading up to disaster.[81] What is known is that on November 11, the Admiralty ordered the *Prince of Wales*, still en route to Freetown, Sierra Leone and onward to Capetown, to meet the *Repulse* in Ceylon for the final dash to Singapore.

Elsewhere, though, things were not going according to plan. While steering his new command into Kingston, Jamaica, the captain of the *Indomitable* steered the brand new aircraft carriers into a sandbar and soon the *Indomitable* was headed for Norfolk to repair a gash in her new hull, and the Admiralty was looking for a new captain.[82] There was no replacement carrier available for deployment to Singapore.

Meanwhile, the *Repulse* had docked in Durban, where the legendary Field Marshal Jan Smuts, now prime minister of South Africa, addressed the crew. He was perhaps unique among the British (and indeed American) military establishment in his consideration of Japan. His words were not so much of war, but of warning. As one sailor later remembered:

> We cleared lower decks just wanting Smutts [sic] to say his piece as quickly as possible so we'd begin our run ashore. I can recall not being in the least interested in what I was about to hear, until, that is, he began talking. From the onset he shattered our conceptions of the Japanese military stating in clear terms that if hostilities erupted we weren't going to be confronted by a race of inferiors. To the contrary he felt the Japs weren't in the least concerned by the possibility of conflict with Britain. He also made it clear despite what we'd been told in the past that they possessed a fully modern air force. Though the one comment that's never left me were the fatalistic words he feared many of us wouldn't be returning from this mission and he'd pray for our safety during the troubled times ahead.
>
> None of us could possibly have imagined the accuracy of this prophecy.[83]

After leaving the *Hesperus* behind, Force G sailed on, with the conditions below decks on the poorly ventilated *Prince of Wales* becoming nothing short of unbearable for the crew. At Colombo, in Ceylon (now Sri Lanka) the *Prince of Wales, Express,* and *Electra* met up with the *Repulse* and two destroyers arrived from the Mediterranean, HMS *Encounter* and *Jupiter.* The British commander in the Mediterranean had considered them useless. The *Jupiter* was a new, overstrength destroyer, but she had serious engine issues, though not as bad as those of the *Encounter,* which threatened to stop the destroyer at any time. The force entered the Singapore Naval Base on December 2 as Force G's commander watched from ashore.

That commander was Sir Thomas Spencer Vaughan Phillips. While the *Prince of Wales* was in Capetown he had flown to Pretoria to meet with Field Marshal Smuts. A few days after this meeting, Smuts sent a telegram to Churchill with his own prophetic take on Admiral Phillips and his mission:

> He has much impressed me and appears admirable choice for most important position … In particular, I am concerned over present disposition of two fleets, one based on Singapore and other on Hawaii, each separately inferior to Japanese navy which thus will have an opportunity to defeat them in turn. This matter is so vital that I would press for rearrangement of dispositions as soon as war appears imminent. If Japanese are really nippy there is here an opening for a first class disaster.[84]

When Force G arrived at Ceylon, Admiral Phillips had flown ahead to Singapore to confer with the local officers. On December 1, while he was there, he had been promoted to full admiral and appointed commander-in-chief of the Royal Navy's newly-formed Eastern Fleet.[85]

Admiral Phillips had been a vice admiral on the naval general staff during the *Bismarck* crisis and was a well-known staff officer. Nicknamed "Tom Thumb" due to his short stature, he was highly intelligent and well respected by his staff. Phillips also thought himself always right, had trouble delegating and was known for being difficult to work with. The respected British naval historian Arthur Marder would describe him as "a man of strong will and considerable obstinancy who seldom smiled and was often rude, though he usually had the grace to apologize afterwards."[86] Admiral Sir James Somerville, who would later command Royal Navy forces in the Indian Ocean, called the 53-year-old Phillips "the Pocket Napoleon" and said, "He always looks like death and tries to do far too much."[87] Phillips was by reputation a "battleship admiral," believing in the invincibility of battleships against aircraft. So wedded was he to this position that at one point an exasperated friend told Phillips, "[W]hen the first bomb hits, you'll say, 'My God, what a hell of a mine!'"[88] But reputations can be deceiving. During his time on the naval general staff, Phillips had specifically requested the deployment of Hawker Hurricane fighters to Malaya – and been rejected by Churchill, a decision that still rankled with the admiral.[89]

A few days later, while the *Prince of Wales* sat at the Singapore Naval Base undergoing some repairs and maintenance work, *Repulse* started on a trip to Australia ("largely for political considerations," as Admiral Phillips would tell Admiral Hart) with destroyers HMS *Vampire* and *Tenedos*.[90] Admiral Phillips himself went to Manila to confer with Admiral Hart and General MacArthur. After MacArthur made yet another of his soliloquies, Phillips and Hart got to work. Like Field Marshal Smuts, Hart was impressed by the British admiral: "Admiral Phillips showed himself to be a remarkably able officer – possessing very broad knowledge, with keen intuition and judgment. Even though our association with him was brief we sensed that he was the best man we had encountered.[91]

The meetings ran from December 5 into December 6. To summarize, Admiral Phillips and Admiral Hart agreed that Singapore was indefensible. Phillips stated that he believed his force was too small to accomplish anything and dangerously unbalanced, without a carrier or adequate destroyers. He requested help from Hart in the form of two destroyer divisions. Although Hart had been told to make informal arrangements for cooperation in the Far East, he demurred, trying to develop a sense of British commitment to the naval campaign, the lack of which had doomed ABC-1 and the confusing alphabet soup plans. During the meeting, Hart received word from the US naval liaison in Singapore that the US had agreed to enter the war in support of Britain in certain circumstances. Typical of the treatment Hart got from Washington, no one had told him.

By this time, it was obvious that something was going on in the South China Sea. Shortly after noon on December 6, a Royal Australian Air Force No. 1 Squadron Lockheed Hudson piloted by Flight Lieutenant John Ramshaw operating out of Kota Bharu, a city and major British air complex in northern Malaya near the Thai border, sighted three Japanese warships headed straight for Bangkok. Were the Japanese going to occupy Thailand and then move down to Malaya? The British had prepared for such a contingency. Continuing eastward for about 60 miles, Ramshaw spotted a massive convoy headed into the Gulf of Thailand. At 12:30 pm he reported it in – one battleship, five cruisers, seven destroyers and 22 transports. In actuality, this was Admiral Ozawa's invasion force destined for Malaya – flagship *Chokai*, light cruiser *Sendai*, 12 destroyers, a hospital ship, the seaplane tender *Kamikawa Maru*, and 18 transports carrying the Japanese 25th Army under General Yamashita Tomoyuki. Ramshaw ducked into a cloud to avoid a float plane launched by the *Kamikawa Maru*. He requested permission to shadow the convoy until relieved by another Hudson. Incredibly, it was denied.[92]

Fifteen minutes later, another Hudson, this one piloted by Flight Lieutenant James Emerton, spotted another convoy – two cruisers, ten destroyers, and 21 transports about 415 miles from Kota Bharu headed northwest – and reported it in. This was, in fact, Admiral Kondo's covering force (battleships *Kongo* and *Haruna*; cruisers *Atago* and *Takao*), the Japanese Cruiser Division 7 (*Kumano, Suzuya, Mikuma, Mogami*), and a nearby force of transports. Emerton requested permission to shadow the convoy. Once again, it was denied.[93]

Eventually at 4:20 pm Flight Lieutenant Ken Smith and his crew took off from Kota Bharu in yet another Hudson to try to find the convoys. But increasing darkness and inclement weather prevented him from finding anything.[94] Air Command's denial of Ramshaw's and Emerton's requests would prove a serious, inexplicable, and inexcusable mistake.

The sighting reports were met with extreme consternation in Manila. Not nearly as sanguine as his British colleagues back in Malaya and London, Phillips was ready to assume the worst – the Japanese were headed to the Isthmus of Kra or even Malaya itself.

Admiral Phillips' first reaction was to recall the *Repulse* and her escorting destroyers *Tenedos* and *Vampire* from their trip to Darwin. His second order of business was to return immediately to Singapore, which, oddly, turned out to be much more difficult than imagined. During the course of his meetings with Admiral Hart, his two Royal Air Force pilots had vanished. Guessing they had gone out for some "R and R" in the way that soldiers, sailors, and pilots usually did, the military police searched practically every bar, brothel, and strip club in Manila, but the pilots were nowhere to be found. Phillips was forced to use one of Patrol Wing 10's PBY Catalinas, piloted by Duke Campbell, to return to Singapore. On Phillips' way out, Hart told him that he had ordered the *Black Hawk* and Destroyer Divison 57, with the *Whipple, Alden, John D. Edwards,* and *Edsall* to head from Balikpapan for Batavia; ostensibly this was for rest and leave, but in actuality they were going to join Phillips in Singapore.[95]

As it turned out, Phillips' two Royal Air Force pilots had gone to a movie without telling anyone. Upon their return, the pilots received a royal dressing down, in what was one of the very few instances of being chewed out for *not* going to a bordello.

But this was one ray of humorous light in a sky of dark clouds, an ominous atmosphere that would soon turn tragic.

So concerned were the British commanders in Singapore that they ordered night searches of the South China Sea with long-range Catalina flying boats from the Royal Air Force's No. 205 Squadron. Accordingly, at 6:30 pm on December 6 a Royal Air Force Catalina under Flight Lieutenant R.A. Atkinson was dispatched from Seletar to try to find Japanese activity. At 2:00 am on December 7, after not hearing from the first PBY, a second, under the command of Australian Flying Officer Patrick Edwin Bedell, was sent up to take over the patrol.[96]

Eventually, Atkinson's Catalina returned reporting that nothing had been found. Meanwhile, Flying Officer Bedell, his crew, and his PBY simply vanished. Far East Air Command in Singapore had no hard evidence as to what had happened to Bedell's plane, but they had strong suspicions: suspicions that would have to wait until after the war for confirmation.

Bedell's Catalina had come very close to the Japanese convoy – far too close for the comfort of Japanese Admiral Ozawa. At 8:20 am on December 7, when Bedell was near Phu Quoc Island off the Cambodian coast, he was spotted by a floatplane from the seaplane tender *Kamikawa Maru*. The Japanese pilot Ensign Ogata Eiichi maneuvered onto the PBY's tail and opened fire. Whether the attack caused damage is uncertain, but the Catalina turned away from the convoy and neither pilot pursued the exchange further.[97]

But Flying Officer Bedell was persistent. At around 9:00 am, some 40 minutes later, Bedell and his Catalina apparently came so close to the convoy that they fell afoul of its air cover, a unit of five Nakajima Ki-27 fighters of the Japanese Army Air Service. Given the codename "Nate" by the Allies, the Ki-27 was a slightly older warplane with fixed landing gear, but against the Soviet Union it had proven to be a fast, maneuverable first-class fighter, certainly more than a match for a lumbering flying boat. Acting on orders from Admiral Ozawa to get rid of the Royal Air Force seaplane, Flight Leader Lieutenant Kubotani Toshiru had his Nates make individual passes at the PBY. The Catalina tried to defend itself, but when the fifth Nate took its shot, the flying boat exploded in midair.[98]

On the day before the attack on Pearl Harbor, Flying Officer Patrick Bedell and his seven crewmates gained the unwanted distinction of being the first fatalities in a vast conflagration that in the eyes of most was still to come.

CHAPTER 3
BREAKDOWN

JAPAN STARTED HOSTILITIES. GOVERN YOURSELVES ACCORDINGLY.

With this short and cryptic message sent out by Admiral Hart at 3:10 am on December 8, 1941 – December 7, 1941, in Hawaii – the Pacific War began for the United States Asiatic Fleet. Unlike his army counterpart in the Philippines, Hart was not one given to melodrama. The drama was in the substance of the message. Even more drama was in the reaction. Although everyone had anticipated war (except, apparently, Douglas MacArthur), it was still a shock nonetheless; certainly everyone still had more questions than Hart or anyone else had answers.

Back home in the United States, civilians were listening to their home radios while broadcasters announced the grim news out of Pearl Harbor and reported the news about the ominous silence coming from Guam. But American soldiers and sailors in the Far East generally had only sporadic access to this news. They had to rely on the unofficial rumor mill, and the official words of their superiors. And in the case of Admiral Hart, those words were few indeed.

For the men of the seaplane tender *William B. Preston*, anchored at Malalag Bay in the Philippines, the questions and uncertainty were magnified by isolation – not only from the US mainland, not only from the bulk of the US forces at Pearl Harbor, but even from their own Asiatic Fleet and their own Patrol Wing 10. Nestled in their hiding place in the western part of the Gulf of Davao on the southern coast of Mindanao, the crew of the *Preston* had no idea that the long-expected war had finally arrived.

Ever since Tommy Hart had taken its helm, the Asiatic Fleet had been preparing for war, and it was ready – or at least as ready for war as its limited resources would allow. And the *William B. Preston* was no exception. Deployed in Malalag Bay with a secret stash of aviation fuel ashore and three PBY-4 Catalina flying boats moored on the water, the *Preston* and her skipper, Lieutenant Commander Etheridge Grant had been given their orders. They had their plans. Now would be the time to execute.

The *Preston* received Admiral Hart's note that the war had broken out at 3:40 am. By 5:15 am, one Catalina, P-6, was already in the air on a scouting mission. The other two flying boats, P-4 and P-7, were moored to buoys close to the beach.[1] In the meantime, Commander Grant set the *Preston* at Condition Two, which meant that half her guns were manned. No Japanese forces had been reported in the area but, ominously, no one – or at least no one in the Asiatic Fleet – knew where the fearsome Japanese aircraft carriers were at present.

They would soon find out.

At 7:10 am, the air raid alarm on the *Preston* sounded. Nine Japanese fighters roared overhead beneath low cloud cover. Not the famous Japanese Zeros, but the older, fixed-landing gear Mitsubishi A5M4 fighters, to which the Allies would give the reporting name "Claude."[2] The *Preston* opened up with her considerable antiaircraft guns, but the fighters had no interest in her.

Cannons blazing, the Claudes made straight for the two moored Catalinas. The PBYs never had a chance. Lacking armor and self-sealing gas tanks, the flying boats were shredded by gunfire. Both Catalinas exploded, vomiting expanding pools of flaming gasoline into the bay. One crewman trying to escape was badly burned and had to be dragged to the beach. Another crewman, Ensign Robert G. Tills, was killed when a bullet went through his skull.[3] He was the first American killed in Asia in the Pacific War.[4]

The *William B. Preston* sent word to Patrol Wing 10 that she was under attack and got under way, moving toward the entrance to the bay for maneuvering room. In her former life, before her conversion to a seaplane tender, the *Preston* had been a flush-deck destroyer like those of the Asiatic Fleet. Whatever the shortcomings of the aged four-pipers as destroyers, they were good as seaplane tenders. Her conversion had cost her some speed, but she could still make 25 knots. She also still retained considerable weaponry. She would need every bit of her destroyer heritage because the Claudes had ignored her for a reason: she was to be the target of someone else. Specifically, 13 Nakajima B5N "carrier attack planes," as the Japanese called them; "torpedo bombers" as they were known in the West. These B5Ns would become famous by their reporting name "Kate" as very deadly torpedo bombers. On this day they emphasized the "bomber" part of that designation, as they circled to bomb the *Preston*. For some 30 minutes, the seaplane tender raced and twisted to avoid their munitions. She was surrounded and drenched by tall geysers of water from exploding bombs, all of which missed. With their bomb racks empty, the Kates followed the Claudes and turned away to fly back to their carrier.

The attack at least revealed to the Americans that one of the aircraft carriers was somewhere in the area. But which one? The small size of the attack, the use of older Claude fighters, and an ineffective bombing attack by Kates suggested that this was not the work of the Japanese Naval Air Force's "A Team."

And indeed it was not. Unbeknownst to virtually everyone in the Asiatic Fleet the primary Japanese carrier attack force – the *Kido Butai* – was away at Pearl Harbor, conducting the very business that had led to Admiral Hart's message.

The attack on the *Preston* and its PBYs had come from the light carrier *Ryujo*, under the command of Lieutenant Aioi Takahide. It had made an earlier sweep over Davao City but, having found nothing there (much to the disgust of Lieutenant Aioi), it proceeded to go after the *Preston*.[5] Davao City would get a second air raid from the *Ryujo* later that day, by two Kates escorted by three Claudes.[6] The city's few antiaircraft guns managed to damage one Claude sufficiently that it crashed in the Mindanao jungle. The pilot got out, burned the remnants of his aircraft so it would not fall into enemy hands, and killed himself "in the true Bushido spirit" to avoid capture.[7] This was the first taste the Americans had of the Japanese preference for suicide over surrender, and the news quickly made the rounds of the US forces in the Philippines.

The *Ryujo* was the tip of the spear, or at least the tip of one of the spears held by what would become known as the Japanese "Octopus" spreading its tentacles all over the Pacific and Southeast Asia. A large number of those tentacles were grouped together into Vice Admiral Kondo Nobutake's aforementioned Southern Expeditionary Force, of whose Eastern Force the *Ryujo*'s specific directives were to provide cover for the planned Japanese landings at Davao and Legaspi in the southern Philippines. In addition to the *Ryujo*, this covering force consisted of the destroyer *Shiokaze* directly attached to the carrier to retrieve any pilots with botched takeoffs or landings; the 5th Cruiser Division, consisting of the heavy cruisers *Myoko*, *Nachi*, and *Haguro* under the command of Rear Admiral Takagi Takeo; and the 2nd Destroyer Flotilla, with eight destroyers being led by the light cruiser *Jintsu* and Rear Admiral Tanaka Raizo.[8]

The Japanese had done their homework. They knew exactly where, when, and what they wanted to attack. The *Preston* and her flying boats had been spotted in the Malalag anchorage on December 6.[9] Like all the other Japanese pieces on the Pacific chessboard, the covering force had left Palau on December 6 in order to be close to its targets.[10] It was certainly much closer than Commander Grant or his sailors would have preferred. Two precious Catalinas had been lost, but his ship had survived unscathed and even shot up a Claude so badly that it had to ditch, though its pilot was rescued. The *Preston* turned back toward the beach and rescued survivors of the flying boats, but its efforts were cut short by the unexpected return of Catalina P-6 with unwelcome news: three unidentified destroyers had been sighted 15 miles south of the Gulf of Davao, headed toward the *Preston*.[11]

There were no other US forces in the area. The destroyers had to be Japanese, looking to trap the seaplane tender in the gulf. Even if she had retained her full destroyer weaponry, the *William B. Preston* could not expect to survive a bout with three Japanese destroyers.

Commander Grant ordered the *Preston* to get out before the trap closed, squeezing out all 25 knots her ancient engines would allow. P-6, completely unaware of the earlier attack, was left to make sense of all the messages from Patrol Wing 10 asking for updates on the status of the *Preston*.

Both tender and Catalina were ordered to Polloc Bay on the west coast of Mindanao.[12] They were on the run, hunted by an adversary that was more numerous, more powerful and relentless, with whom they had only barely survived their first encounter. The *William B. Preston* could not win; she could only hope to hold on until the Pacific Fleet arrived to assist her. The crew had no idea what had started all this, what that message from Admiral Hart meant, or when the Pacific Fleet would arrive to help them.

It was the first day of the war.

News of War – December 8, 1941

The outset of the Pacific War in the Philippines is almost a comparative case study in both how and how not to handle the start of a war.

In the pre-dawn darkness of December 8, Admiral Thomas Hart had been awakened in his room at the Manila Hotel by a phone call around 3:00 am from Lieutenant Colonel William T. Clement, the duty officer at the Marsman Building, who had told the admiral "[P]ut some cold water on your face. I'm coming over with a message."[13] The US Navy radio station at Cavite had picked up the general broadcast by Lieutenant Commander Logan Ramsey of Patrol Wing 2 all the way across the Pacific on Ford Island at Pearl Harbor: AIR RAID PEARL HARBOR. THIS IS NOT DRILL.[14] As the staff pondered the signal, another broadcast came in, this official notice from the US Pacific Fleet at Pearl Harbor: ENEMY AIR RAID, PEARL HARBOR. THIS IS NOT A DRILL.[15]

So Lieutenant Colonel Clement woke the admiral and went to the Manila Hotel to give him the news. Sitting on the edge of his bed, Hart quickly scrawled the message he had long prepared for this situation, "Japan started hostilities. Govern yourseles accordingly" on a piece of paper and handed it to his staff for broadcast to the Asiatic Fleet.[16] In so doing, Hart, a veteran of the Spanish–American War and World War I, was so nervous he left out the "v."[17]

That letter was not all he left out of the message, however, as the *William D. Preston* was to discover, and as Captain Frank B. Wagner, commander of Patrol Wing 10, found out when Hart's message reached Sangley Point at 3:15 am. Like everyone else, Wagner had no idea what Hart's message meant, but he did have a well-rehearsed plan for his aircraft and he put it into effect. He ordered the Catalinas to perform reconnaissance over the South China Sea, their wings holding deadly 250lb bombs but their machine guns filled with training ammunition – in another indictment of American prewar preparations in the Philippines, it was the only ammunition available. Wagner planned to disperse his seaplanes so they could not all be destroyed at the same time; he sent seven Catalinas to the tender *Childs* in Manila Bay, five to Cavite and four to Los Banos, on the coast of a lake called Laguna de Bay 80 miles southeast of Manila; seven remained at Olangapo to conduct reconnaissance over the South China Sea.[18]

Meanwhile, Admiral Hart was conferring with Admiral Glassford before sending him off to Iloilo to command Task Force 5. Given Hart's stated lack of confidence in Glassford, it was unsurprisingly not a pleasant meeting. Glassford was going off to war to command a force of ships, "'hoary with age, tradition and pride,' and strong in little else," with "his chances of success and even survival … limited," and yet, in his own words, "Needless to say, I was happy to get away from pessimistic and uncongenial Manila and on my own again."[19]

But Admiral Glassford would have to get there first. This would quickly prove to be not quite the routine matter everyone had hoped. Admiral Hart sent Glassford on a barge into Manila Harbor where, after a short visit to his old gunboat *Luzon*, he made his way to the *Langley* where he boarded the PBY that would fly him down to Iloilo. In the meantime, Captain Wagner of Patrol Wing 10 had been informed about the attack on the *William B. Preston* in Davao Gulf. He greeted the admiral wearing his helmet, a reminder to Glassford, as if he needed one, that they were at war and that he was about to go off to war in a slow, cumbersome, unarmored flying boat with no fighter escort.[20]

Admiral Glassford and his staff, together with a truckload of luggage, were loaded into Catalina P-3. While they were doing so, the crew were busy replacing a defective starter cable, normally a 15-minute repair. They were interrupted by the eerie, ominous wail of air raid sirens. With a large formation of Japanese bombers and fighters approaching, the crew aborted the repair; they would start the flying boat using a hand crank. As sirens continued and the bombers neared, a crewman got the crank, inserted it into the engine, and turned it. The crank promptly snapped off. Swallowing their mounting panic, the crew was able to jury-rig starter cables long enough to get the plane started. After what seemed like an interminably long run across the water, the overloaded Catalina scurried to take off, staying low in what would be a successful effort to avoid the notice of the Japanese aircraft.[21] Behind them, in the distance, they could see giant smoke plumes rising from the direction of Iba and Clark Fields.[22]

DESTRUCTION OF CLARK FIELD – DECEMBER 8

The events surrounding the Far East Air Force and its performance in the hours after Pearl Harbor on December 8, 1941, remain both disputed and controversial – in part a consequence of the chaos that marks the start of any war – with a very critical factual piece missing that will likely never be known. As official navy historian Samuel Eliot Morison put it, "If surprise at Pearl Harbor is hard to understand, surprise at Manila is completely incomprehensible."[23] William Manchester called it "one of the strangest episodes in American military history."[24] What can be noted at a minimum, however, is the stark contrast between Admiral Hart's relatively cool, well-planned response with his limited resources and the almost paralyzed response of General Douglas MacArthur with his sizable air forces.

A cook from the 20th Pursuit Squadron, Private Harry Seiff, was the first soldier at Clark Field to hear of the attack on Pearl Harbor, in this case from a commercial radio broadcast.[25] Rumors like that spread very quickly, and soon the news was all over the airbase complex; it eventually traveled to the other four major airfields of the Far East Air Force on Luzon: Nielson, Nichols, Iba, and Del Carmen. The Official Army History explains the reaction among the US troops:

By breakfast, the news of the attack on Pearl Harbor had reached all ranks. The men had for so long accepted the fact that war with Japan might come that the event itself was an anticlimax. There was no cheering and no demonstration, but "a grim, thoughtful silence." War with Japan was not, for the American and Philippine troops, a remote war across a wide ocean. It was close and immediate.[26]

When and how General MacArthur found out is disputed. Most likely, Admiral Hart's chief of staff, Admiral William R. Purnell, gave the news to Brigadier General Richard K. Sutherland, General MacArthur's chief of staff. At the same time, the signals section of MacArthur's headquarters had picked up the signal from Pearl Harbor and informed Sutherland. Either way, Sutherland telephoned MacArthur at his palatial penthouse on top of the Manila Hotel at about 3:30 am. MacArthur's response was said to be incredulous: "Pearl Harbor! Pearl Harbor! It should be our strongest point!"[27]

At 5:30 am came the first orders from Washington in response to Pearl Harbor, in the form of a radiogram from General George C. Marshall, US Army Chief of Staff. It read: HOSTILITIES BETWEEN JAPAN AND THE UNITED STATES ... HAVE COMMENCED ... CARRY OUT TASKS ASSIGNED IN RAINBOW FIVE ...[28] As a reminder, under Rainbow 5: "In the event of hostilities, the defending air forces were to carry out 'air raids against Japanese forces and installations within tactical operating radius of available bases.'"[29]

The outlying bases were notified of the Pearl Harbor attack, though once again rumors had already beaten the official word. All combat units were placed on alert. By around 4:30 am, the pilots of the 17th and 21st Pursuit Squadrons at Nichols Field, on the outskirts of Manila, were sitting in the cockpits or beneath the wings of their P-40Es. So was the 20th Pursuit Squadron at Clark in its P-40Bs. The 34th Pursuit Squadron, located at the much smaller Del Carmen Field, had not been alerted.

The 3rd Pursuit Squadron at Iba Field was also ready, even though it had already been through an eventful night. Around midnight, the radar at Iba Field radar had registered contacts flying in from the north; this was a flight of Japanese bombers on another probe such as they had been carrying out for the previous week. The commander of the 3rd Pursuit Squadron, First Lieutenant Hank Thorne, had ordered his squadron awakened from their sleep, which they were by a "reveille" from a bugle boy so excited he could only get one sour blast through his horn.[30] Thorne had ingeniously developed a rudimentary system for night interception. He led a flight of six P-40Es into the air, and, guided by the

Iba radar, attempted to catch the intruders. Unfortunately, the Iba radar only showed contacts, not numbers or altitude. The radar operators watched as the American pursuit intersected that of the Japanese. Thorne's pilots saw no aircraft; the Japanese had been at an altitude of 20,000ft, and Thorne's squadron had in fact flown under them. The squadron returned to Iba and made the first night landing at that field by the lights of cars and trucks as they shone on the runway.[31]

Meanwhile, the command of US Army Forces Far East was breaking down. General Brereton, commander of the Far East Air Force, drove from Nielson to General MacArthur's headquarters to speak to the general. Rainbow 5 required offensive action against the Japanese, and they already had their plan to bomb the Japanese airbase complex at Takao on Formosa. They wanted to get in the first strike and catch the Japanese aircraft on the ground. But Brereton needed MacArthur's permission to carry out the attack. He arrived around 5:00 am, but MacArthur's chief of staff General Sutherland prevented Brereton from seeing MacArthur. Why Brereton could not see the general, or, more precisely, what Sutherland said was the reason, is disputed but included the following: MacArthur was "in conference" with his senior generals and could not be disturbed; MacArthur was with Admiral Hart and could not be disturbed; MacArthur was with Philippine President Manuel Quezon and could not be disturbed.[32] But Sutherland told Brereton to proceed with his plans and that he would get MacArthur's permission for the attack.

Understanding that time was slipping away, General Brereton returned to see General MacArthur at about 7:15 am. Again, General Sutherland prevented him from seeing MacArthur and told Brereton that MacArthur had not responded to his request for permission to attack Formosa. After Brereton pressed him, Sutherland went into MacArthur's office, quickly returned, and said MacArthur had denied the request. "The General says no. Don't make the first overt act."[33]

The reasoning, at least as stated by General Sutherland, is bizarre and nonsensical. The phrase "first overt act" was a specific reference to the "war warning" of November 27, 1941: " … hostile actions possible at any moment … If hostilities cannot, repeat, cannot be avoided the United States desires that Japan commit the first overt act …" A furious Brereton made a fairly logical counterargument: "Damn it! Wasn't the bombing of Pearl Harbor an overt act? Can't the General acknowledge that we're at war?"[34] The answer would seem to be in the negative. Brereton returned to his headquarters in a fury, "his face pale, his jaw hard."[35]

The lunacy emanating out of General MacArthur's office by no means ended there. It has been alleged that MacArthur was deferring to the wishes of the Philippine President Manuel Quezon to remain neutral in any Pacific conflict. Quezon denied that, however, and reportedly told Major General Dwight Eisenhower in 1942: " … MacArthur was convinced for some strange reason that the Philippines would remain neutral and would not be attacked by the Japanese."[36] In any event, the Japanese had already violated Philippine neutrality and attacked the islands directly, with their earlier attack on the

William D. Preston in Davao Gulf. General Brereton had not been informed of this attack and so could not make the argument. Yet MacArthur's headquarters had been informed about the Davao attack at 6:15 am, and Sutherland and MacArthur still maintained that Japan needed to commit the "first overt act."

On top of these absurdities was the fact that General MacArthur was subject to orders from General Marshall to carry out attacks in accordance with Rainbow 5. MacArthur seems to have regarded the directives to attack the Japanese as more what might be called "guidelines" than actual orders. He was willfully ignoring them.

Additionally, it was apparently during this conversation that Sutherland is said to have complained to Brereton about an alleged lack of intelligence information about the Takao airbase complex.[37] Sutherland may have used this as another excuse to delay the attack on Formosa. Brereton returned to his office and told his staff that they could send three B-17s on a photoreconnaissance mission over Formosa – the same type of photoreconnaissance mission that General MacArthur had refused to allow the previous week. The staff were incredulous, pointing out that they had enough information to prepare target folders for the attacks, although without calibrated bomb target maps or aerial photographs.[38]

At 8:00 am, General Brereton called yet again. General Sutherland called him back at 8:50 am and told him to "Hold off bombing Formosa for the present." Incredibly, Sutherland also told Brereton not to call again about the planned attack.

At about the same time, Brigadier General Gerow in General Marshall's office called MacArthur to ask if he had received the cables that Marshall had sent earlier – the ones directing him to attack as directed in Rainbow 5. MacArthur said yes, but offered no explanation for his not having responded sooner.[39] Gerow said, "I wouldn't be surprised if you got an attack there in the near future," repeating it for emphasis, and told him not to get caught with his aircraft on the ground, as they had been at Pearl Harbor.[40] MacArthur responded, "[T]ell General Marshall that 'our tails are up in the air.'"[41]

This was indeed the truth, though not because of anything General MacArthur had done. A little before 8:00 am, the Iba radar informed the Aircraft Warning Service at Nielson Field that at least 30 Japanese aircraft were flying south over Luzon, apparently headed for Clark Field. The warning service teletyped that information to the Clark Field headquarters of the 24th Pursuit Group, where its commander, Major Orrin Grover, was responsible for coordinating all the interceptor squadrons on Luzon.

The B-17 Flying Fortresses of the 19th Bombardment Group, sitting at Clark Field, were immediately ordered into the air; they might not be bombing anything, but at least they would not be caught on the ground. Major Grover scrambled two squadrons of interceptors – the 20th at Clark and the 17th at Nichols Field – and sent them to patrol at 15,000ft over Tarlac, 21 miles north of Clark. Grover later claimed that he ordered the 34th to patrol over Clark to take care of any Japanese aircraft that broke through the 17th and 20th, but there is no record of such an order. The P-35As of the 34th might have been enough to take care of a few bombers but little else. The B-17s and P-40s at Clark Field took to the air with almost nothing in the way of air traffic control, with aircraft crisscrossing as they roared down the runways for takeoff. Miraculously there were no collisions.[42]

At 9:23 am, General Brereton received the discouraging news of Japanese air attacks on the US Army base at Camp John Hay near the town of Baguio, and a small airfield at Tuguegarao, all in northern Luzon.[43] Brereton ignored General Sutherland's instruction and called again at 10:00 am; Sutherland reiterated that no offensive mission was authorized. In the meantime, MacArthur's headquarters finally received confirmation of the attacks on Baguio and Tuguegarao and the second air attack on Davao City. Evidently considering these the "first overt act," at 10:14 am General MacArthur himself apparently called Brereton and authorized strikes on Formosa.[44]

Brereton's staff continued with preparations to launch a bombing attack over Formosa at last light in the afternoon. Charts for the attack and overlays pinpointing Japanese airfields were prepared for briefing the pilots and navigators. Meanwhile, for some reason, they decided to continue with the photoreconnaissance mission. In other words, a photoreconnaissance mission to gather information for a bombing strike was to take place at virtually the same time as the bombing strike itself. This, despite the fact that Clark Field did not have enough cameras, forcing an expedition to Nichols Field to pick up additional equipment.

While all this was going on, the Warhawks and Flying Fortresses that had been hurriedly ordered to take off from Clark Field were running out of fuel and had to land. The 17th and 20th Pursuit Squadrons and the 19th Bomb Group had flown back to Clark. The pilots went to lunch while their aircraft were fueled and serviced. The pursuit squadrons of the 3rd at Iba, the 21st at Nichols, and the 34th at Del Carmen remained on the ground the entire time.

By 11:30 am, in the words of the Army Air Force Official History, "[A]ll American aircraft in the Philippines, with the exception of one or two aircraft, were on the ground."[45]

At 11:27 am the Iba radar picked up a large flight of aircraft some 70 miles away over the Lingayen Gulf, off northwestern Luzon, heading southeast. Iba reported the sighting to the Aircraft Warning Service, where a second attack group heading south over central Luzon was being tracked as well. By 11:37 am, the Aircraft Warning Service teletyped the report to Major Grover. Within ten minutes, Major Grover issued orders to cover both of the major airfields. Iba Field would be patrolled by the 3rd Pursuit, which would also block the first flight of Japanese aircraft, flying southeast off Lingayen Gulf. The all-important Clark Field was going to be patrolled by 21st Pursuit, which would also serve to block the second flight of Japanese aircraft flying south over central Luzon.

These orders, sensible under the circumstances, would be changed within minutes because Major Grover apparently became convinced that the airfields were not the targets. At around 11:45 am, he changed his orders and repositioned both the 3rd and 21st Pursuit Squadrons over or near Manila Bay.[46] After urgings from Lieutenant Joe Wagner, commanding the 17th Pursuit Squadron, he ordered that squadron to take off from Clark

Field and patrol over Manila Bay. Now, the Far East Air Force would have a sky swarming with P-40 Warhawks, at multiple altitudes, ready to repulse any air attack – on Manila.

As a result of this change in orders, the biggest US airbase in the Philippines – the biggest Allied airbase in the Far East – and a major secondary base, containing the all-important radar set, were unguarded. An entire squadron of fighters, the 20th Pursuit Squadron, was left on the ground at Clark Field, without orders.

This did not please Colonel Harold George, chief of staff for the V Interceptor Command, who was watching the progress of the incoming enemy aircraft and the positioning of his own pursuit squadrons from the plotting room at Nielson Field.[47] With increasing apprehension over the safety of Clark Field in particular, he sent the code phrase KICKAPOO, which meant, as he explained it, "Go get 'em," to the 24th Pursuit Group's headquarters and Major Grover; whether he actually received it is unknown.[48] But shortly thereafter, Lieutenant Andrew Krieger, flying a Warhawk of the 3rd Pursuit near Manila, was tuned to the 24th Pursuit Group's command radio frequency, over which he heard someone yell, "Tally Ho, Clark Field! Tally Ho, Clark Field! All Pursuit to Clark! Messerschmitts over Clark!"[49] "Tally ho!" was the code calling the pursuits to converge on the airbase; "Messerschmitts" was an indicator of the latent racism still present in the American defenders who could not accept the threat presented by the non-white Japanese and assumed the attackers were white Germans in their famous Messerschmitt Bf-109 fighters. A dozen P-40s – eight from the 3rd and four from the 21st Pursuit Squadrons – arrived to protect the airbase at around 12:30 pm, but seeing no enemy aircraft, and having no orders, the P-40 pilots headed for Iba.[50]

With the Japanese attack group rapidly closing in on Clark Field, the Aircraft Warning Service in desperation sent last frantic warnings to Clark Field using every method at its disposal. But there was, as the Army Air Force history calls it, a "breakdown of communications."[51] One breakdown involved the radio call, which never got through; it may have been jammed by the Japanese. The Aircraft Warning Service sent a teletype, but, in another "breakdown of communications," the man at Clark Field responsible for monitoring the teletype was at lunch. The Aircraft Warning Service called twice. Here were two more "breakdown[s] of communications." The first time it left a message; the second time it was told the person responsible would get the message as soon as he came back from lunch.[52]

At 12:30 pm, the Clark Field radio room (which was located in a trailer) received a curious series of messages from Iba Field, home of the 3rd Pursuit. A message transmitted in Morse code reported a large flight of aircraft approaching. It was followed by a repeat of the same message by the voice of an increasingly alarmed radio operator at Iba. His frantic transmissions ended abruptly. At about the same time, a Manila radio broadcast had just reported that Clark Field was being bombed by the Japanese. In the mess hall at Clark Field, the report brought laughter.[53]

They were still laughing at 12:35 pm, when a member of the 20th Pursuit on the ground at Clark Field saw coming out of the northwest "two perfect V [sic] of Vs," totaling 53 twin-engine bombers, "one behind the other, their wings glistening in the sunlight" heading straight for them.[54] "Good God Almighty – yonder they come!"[55]

Upon seeing the aircraft, Sergeant Bill King fired his pistol three times into the air as a warning, then rushed to phone the 20th Pursuit operations room, where Major Grover was located. King told the man who answered, First Lieutenant Benny Putnam, to sound the air raid alarm. Upon hearing the message, Grover, who seems to have been in something of a daze, was skeptical, asking, "How does he know they are Japanese planes?" Overhearing the question, King yelled into the phone at Putnam, "We don't have so goddamn many!"[56]

Only now did the air raid sirens sound. Only now was First Lieutenant Joseph Moore, head of the 20th Pursuit, able to order the red warning flags signaling INTERCEPT raised. Only now did the 18 P-40 Warhawks of the 20th Pursuit jump into their cockpits and desperately start taxiing down the runways of Clark Field.[57]

It was too late.

The Japanese Naval Air Force's 21st Air Flotilla (consisting of the 1st and Kanoya Air Groups) and the 23rd Air Flotilla (consisting of the 3rd, Takao, and Tainan Air Groups), and the Japanese Army Air Force's 5th Air Force, all based on Formosa, had been preparing for this attack for approximately a month. [58] They had been scheduled to launch their own attack on the American airbases in the Philippines at dawn. But a particularly bad case of ground fog kept them on the ground until around 11:00 am. Now appearing over Clark Field were 27 Mitsubishi G4M bombers, which the Allies would call the "Betty," of the Takao Air Group and 26 G3M bombers, which the Allies would call the "Nell," of the 1st Air Group, their air crews apprehensive, fully expecting that now, eight hours after Pearl Harbor, American interceptors would be waiting for them.[59]

The Japanese had anticipated the possibility of resistance. Concerned about their bombers going into combat with American pursuit aircraft, they experimented with ways to extend the range of their new Zero fighters so they could escort the bombers throughout. By adjusting the fuel mixture and the speed, they were able to do so. So a flight of 34 Zeros of the Tainan and 3rd Air Groups, led by Lieutenant Sakai Saburo, who would become Japan's best fighter ace, escorted the bombers. Sakai too expected to see a sky filled with P-40 Warhawks. Instead the American pursuit aircraft and bombers were still on the airfield.

From an altitude of about 20,000ft, the first "V" of bombers dropped their munitions, followed by the second "V" some 15 minutes later. The attack was exceedingly well executed. At 20,000ft, the antiaircraft guns of Clark Field could not reach them, nor could the P-40s, just taking off. The Nell and Betty bombers lazily dropped their bombs in walking rows or "sticks." Hangars, shops, mess halls, barracks, and supply buildings were smashed. The radio room received a direct hit, knocking out communications completely.

Amazingly, no one had bothered to tell the 19th Bomb Group of the presence of enemy aircraft so they could disperse their bombers; the 19th's Flying Fortresses were sitting in nice, neat rows, their silver bodies shining in the sun. Two B-17s had managed to take off, as had Lieutenant Moore and two other Warhawks of the 20th Pursuit, all of which immediately went into maximum climbs, though this made no difference now. Another P-40, making its takeoff run, had its tires blown by bomb shrapnel and had to abort. Four more P-40s were destroyed by bombs as they attempted to take off.

And it would get worse. Lieutenant Sakai's Zeros shepherded their charges away from any possible American pursuit, then turned around and spent the next hour making repeated low-level strafing runs on Clark Field, specifically targeting the remaining aircraft. With few exceptions, the antiaircraft gunners of the US Army's 200th Coast Artillery Regiment (Anti-Aircraft) heroically stood by their guns in the face of the strafing. Ground and combat crews even turned the machine guns of grounded aircraft on low-flying Japanese aircraft, or undertook to rescue valuable equipment from the burning ground installations. Lieutenant Fred Crimmins received severe wounds in a vain attempt to save a B-17; Chaplain Joseph F. LaFleur repeatedly ignored low-flying strafers to minister to the wounded and dying; and Private First Class Greeley B. Williams, from a gunner's post in one of the B-17s, kept up a steady fire on Japanese aircraft until he was killed. But it was hopeless. With communications now cut off, there could be no reinforcements. No one could contact the 17th and 21st Pursuit Squadrons, now uselessly protecting the approaches to Manila.

But the 20th Pursuit did get those three P-40s into the air. There Lieutenant Randall B. Keator attacked a flight of three Zeros and acquired the distinction of shooting down the first Japanese aircraft over the Philippines; Squadron Commander Lieutenant Moore, in a series of dogfights, destroyed two others. At Del Carmen Field, some 15 miles away, pilots of the 34th Squadron, seeing great clouds of smoke and dust billowing from Clark some 20,000ft into the air, immediately scrambled their P-35s to try to help. Although the P-35s were consistently outmaneuvered and several of them were seriously damaged, their pilots claimed three of the enemy aircraft.

The results at Clark Field were devastating. Twelve B-17 Flying Fortresses were destroyed and three badly damaged, mostly by strafing – almost half the heavy bomber inventory of the Far East Air Force. Thirty-five fighters were destroyed on the ground or in the air.

And that was not all. Communications from Iba Field and its precious radar had ended abruptly for a reason. The second of the two air formations reported by the radar at Iba, consisting of 26 Bettys of the Kanoya Air Group and 27 Nells of the Takao Air Group, escorted by 51 Zeros, had in fact attacked Iba Field. The 3rd Pursuit Squadron had patrolled the South China Sea until their fuel was dangerously low, then headed back for Iba. Twelve had managed to land, with the remainder in the landing pattern, when the bomber force and its escort of Zeros struck. With their fuel almost gone, the remaining airborne P-40s had very limited options, but they tried to make the most of them. Lieutenant Jack Donaldson was credited with destroying two Japanese aircraft. They also managed to frustrate Japanese attempts to copy the devastating strafing runs made at Clark Field. But that was just about the only bright light in an otherwise very dark scene. Five P-40s were shot down and three others crash-landed when their fuel ran out. Of the 3rd Pursuit Squadron's P-40s, only two escaped destruction. Barracks and service buildings were smashed. Aircraft maintenance equipment and spare parts were lost.

Worst of all, the Iba radar installation was destroyed. No more would there be early warning of Japanese air attacks.

With one brilliantly planned and executed attack and one utterly incompetent, negligent defense by the Americans, the Japanese had destroyed half the Far East Air Force – the largest and most modern Allied air force in the East – and all of its offensive capability. The United States still had 18 B-17 Flying Fortresses and about 45 P-40 Warhawks remaining in the Philippines, but they no longer had anywhere near the numbers to be more than a nuisance to the enemy. The Japanese, with over 400 aircraft available, had almost total air superiority over the Philippines. Once the remnants of the Far East Air Force were ground down or forced to withdraw, the Japanese Naval Air Force's 11th Air Fleet would redeploy to points south to keep the momentum of the Japanese offensive. The Japanese Naval Air Force would use the control of the air gained at Clark Field to expand south. The Americans would never again get enough air replacements back into the Far East to challenge Japanese air superiority. From now on, American, British, Dutch, and Australian forces would have to operate in the constant fear of air attack.

Precisely what happened that morning of December 8, 1941, on Luzon has been the subject of considerable examination, analytical articles, and numerous books.[60] The issues boil down to two questions. First, why was the long-planned attack on Formosa delayed? Second, why were there no American pursuits positioned to defend Clark Field and Iba Field?

The second question is more easily addressed than the first. Major Grover's deployment of his pursuits to Manila was nothing short of abysmal and was arguably negligent. He left the biggest airbase and a major secondary airbase unguarded to protect Manila. Precisely why he felt the need to protect Manila instead of the airfields is unclear, but that is beside the point. Long term, Manila could not be protected without the airfields. Even worse, since the Japanese were coming from the north, it was possible to protect Manila from positions over Clark and Iba Fields, but not vice versa.

Major Grover did offer something of a defense in his after-action report on the engagement. Grover claims that he ordered the 34th Pursuit Squadron to deploy over Clark Field. His word is the only evidence that he actually did so, but claims that the 34th was given orders on two different occasions that morning but received neither should give pause for thought. Again, however, that is beside the point. Grover had therefore ordered his best interceptors, the P-40s, to protect Manila while ordering only the obsolete P-35s of the 34th Squadron to protect his largest and most important airbase, which goes back to the question of what was Grover thinking – or not thinking. Also unanswered is why Major Grover gave no orders for the 20th Pursuit Squadron to defend Clark Field, where its Warhawks remained on the ground to be shot to ribbons. It is hard to escape the conclusion, however improbable, that Grover simply forgot about the 20th. One historian called Grover's decisions here "hard to understand," "bewildering and fatal."[61]

Returning to the first major question about the events of December 8, 1941, and why the planned airstrike on Formosa was never launched, it becomes necessary to examine a second question intertwined with the first: what was going on in General Douglas MacArthur's office that morning?

The major feature of the first hours in the Philippines after the attack on Pearl Harbor is the disappearance of Douglas MacArthur. Precisely what MacArthur was doing all morning, between 3:30 am when he was informed of the Pearl Harbor attack, and 10:15 am, when he called Brereton, and why Sutherland continually blocked General Brereton's access to him, remains an enduring mystery. Those who did see MacArthur that morning disagree as to what he was doing, but the descriptions of the commander of US Army Forces in the Far East are disturbing.

Historian John Costello, author of *The Pacific War: 1941–1945*, states that MacArthur was in an "apparent cataleptic state," and that, "The shock of events seemed to have clouded his judgment."[62] Historian Eric Morris supports this when he relates that, "An air of unreality gripped MacArthur at his headquarters …"[63] MacArthur biographer William Manchester says the general was "[n]umbed," and reports that those around MacArthur described him as "gray, ill, and exhausted" that morning.[64] Historian Michael Gough says MacArthur simply "froze."[65] Historian Stanley Weintraub considered the possibility that General Sutherland was trying to shield a MacArthur in shock:

> Had he [Sutherland] been making decisions by reading MacArthur's mind rather than consulting him? Nothing of the sort fits MacArthur's own inglorious know-nothing account. One must return to the image of a stunned, pajama-clad figure, more proconsul than general, sitting on his bed in the predawn darkness and reaching for his Bible rather than rushing to action. A paralysis of will, in part concealed by loyal lieutenants.[66]

A comment to the official Air Force history states:

> Considering other events, and MacArthur's non-appearance throughout the morning of that critical day, this student believes that a plausible explanation is [that] MacArthur suffered at least a mild nervous breakdown upon receiving the news of Pearl Harbor – and realizing his inevitable defeat in the Philippines – and that Sutherland's primary task that morning was to get the "boss" to pull himself together and assume effective command. After the efforts that MacArthur had initiated to repudiate the long-standing strategy of "delay-and-defend until the fleet could arrive to reinforce", in favor of an aggressive forward defense relying largely on the striking power of the B-17s he demanded, it boggles the mind to discover another believable explanation for his failure to even meet face-to-face with his air force chief that morning. Further evidence of his tenuous response to events is his continued commitment to a forward defense of the beaches, until he precipitously abandoned those plans in favor of the retreat to Bataan immediately after the Japanese landing at Lingayen Gulf – too late to move the mountains of material needed to feed and support his army.[67]

The explanation that MacArthur suffered a nervous breakdown when he heard about Pearl Harbor seems to be the most likely and yet perhaps the most kind explanation for his behavior in those first few hours. For months MacArthur had been convinced and had publicly stated that the Japanese would not attack until March 1942, or "the warm season," as he called it. His defense plans for the Philippines depended on that time table. As the signs that war was imminent grew in number, he seemed uninterested in hearing about those signs or even in finding out whether those signs existed. A very plausible scenario would be that when the Japanese finally started the war by attacking Pearl Harbor, MacArthur at first refused to accept that the Japanese had attacked this quickly, that his own forces were not prepared for the war, and perhaps most importantly, that he, Douglas MacArthur, had been wrong. As the morning went on, and perhaps at General Sutherland's prodding, MacArthur shifted his belief that the Japanese had not started the war to a belief that the Japanese would not attack the Philippines, even though they already had. It may have been only the relentless reports of Japanese incursions and attacks that snapped MacArthur out of his state of unreality. At 10:15 am, he finally gave the order to proceed with the attack on Formosa.

It is difficult and unseemly to criticize someone who makes serious or even catastrophic mistakes because of a mental breakdown. Even the best and toughest of warriors can break under the mental pressures of war for which no training can prepare. MacArthur biographer William Manchester notes that even Napoleon, George Washington, and Stonewall Jackson suffered similar lapses.[68] But any sensitivity to MacArthur's all-too-human plight must be tempered with knowledge of the absolute viciousness and outright dishonesty that he would use to blame others – especially those such as Admiral Hart, who actually had done their jobs well – for the disaster unfolding in the Philippines.

As General Brereton bitterly put it, "'The first overt act' had been committed. The Japs had hit us and hurt us."[69] American air power in the Far East was in ruins. And from Pearl Harbor came this chilling message: THE PACIFIC FLEET HAS BEEN IMMOBILIZED.[70]

The Pacific War was eight hours old.

CHAPTER 4
FINDING TROUBLE

The British had not been able to determine exactly what happened to Flying Officer Bedell's Catalina off the coast of Cambodia, but even without hard evidence they had strong suspicions, suspicions that the Japanese would confirm shortly after midnight on December 8.

THE JAPANESE INVASION BEGINS – DECEMBER 8

A storm front over the South China Sea had prevented any effective aerial search, but the British Far East Command in Singapore had caught glimpses of what might be hiding behind that storm front. Those glimpses were not encouraging. At 3:45 pm a Royal Australian Air Force Hudson operating out of Kuantan spotted a Japanese ship with "a large number of men on deck in khaki" north of Kota Bharu, headed west.[1] Two Hudsons of No. 1 Squadron were sent out of the Kota Bharu airbase to investigate this report. Early in the evening they reported four unidentified ships approximately 60 miles from the coast. At 5:50 pm, one of the Hudsons sighted two ships 120 miles north of Kota Bharu, both headed toward Kota Bharu itself. One of the ships, which the Hudson judged to be a cruiser but was later identified as the destroyer *Uranami*, opened fire on the Hudson and drove it off. Because of nightfall and the storm, the British could carry out no further reconnaissance.[2]

Kota Bharu was part of a small network of British airdromes in northern Malaya. With the Malay peninsula divided longitudinally by a mountain range that in some places topped 7,000ft, the British Far East Command had placed pairs of airdromes on each side of the mountain range near the Thai border. To the west lay Alor Setar, just inland from the Andaman Sea coast, and, to its southeast, Sungei Patani. To the east, on the coast of the South China Sea, were Kota Bharu and, to its southeast, Gong Kedah. Positioned in and around these bases were British air and army assets to counter a Japanese invasion – of Thailand.

Although it was by no means certain, for some time London and the Far East Command had believed there was a strong possibility the Japanese would invade Thailand to secure their supply lines before moving on to Malaya. In fact, British military planners had hoped this would be the case. Operation *Matador*, by which British Army troops would cross the border from northern Malaya into Thailand and establish defensive positions at key beaches, airfields, ports, and roads, was designed to prevent any successful invasion. A less ambitious operation, called Operation *Krohcol*, had also been planned, to seize a defensive position 30 miles inside Thailand at a place called "The Ledge" – a road cut into the side of a mountain that led into Malaya. British and Dominion troops were positioned to execute either of these plans, waiting in the pouring rain for the orders to proceed.

But both of these plans had one major flaw: because of international political considerations, the British could not invade the nominally neutral Thailand until the Japanese did. This meant that the British needed clear warning of a Japanese invasion.

The storm was conveniently covering the Japanese Malaya Force (the current designation of the Western Force) under the command of Vice Admiral Ozawa, operating from the relatively luxurious heavy cruiser *Chokai*. Ozawa was trailing behind the invasion force's close escort, the Kota Bharu Invasion Force, under Rear Admiral Hashimoto Shintaro, consisting of his flagship light cruiser *Sendai*, the destroyers *Ayanami*, *Isonami*, *Shikinami*, and the aforementioned *Uranami*, minesweepers *W-2* and *W-3*, and subchaser *CH-9*. With them were the transports *Awagisan Maru*, *Ayatosan Maru*, and *Sakura Maru* carrying 5,300 army troops of the so-called Takumi Detachment, named after their commander Major General Takumi Hiroshi. These were troops of the 56th Regiment of the 18th Division, veterans of the war in China. Their destination was Sabak Beach, near Kota Bharu.[3]

The British knew the Japanese had something underneath the storm, but that same storm prevented them from learning exactly where the Japanese were headed. Air Chief Marshal Brooke-Popham had been given authority to begin Operation *Matador* and British troops had been positioned on the Thai–Malayan border, but he understandably could not bring himself to pull the trigger without more evidence.

In fact, the Japanese were about to conduct the very ambitious amphibious invasion of the Kra Isthmus – the narrowest part of the Malayan Peninsula in southern Thailand – that the British had feared. Landings on Kota Bharu, Singora, Tepha, and Patani were followed a few hours later on December 8 by landings at four ports further north – Nakhon Sri Tamaret, Bandon, Chumphon, and Prachuap.[4] So would start the first Japanese landing to drive out the Westerners. The irony that their first invasion to see Asia ruled by Asians was of Thailand, a part of Asia already ruled by Asians, seems to have been lost on the Japanese. After resistance that might generously be described as half-hearted, the Thai government surrendered.

Unfortunately for the British, their first indication of the Japanese objective came at approximately midnight on December 8, still a little more than an hour before Pearl

Harbor, when Indian troops patrolling the beach fronting Kota Bharu sighted the three Japanese transports in the gloom offshore. Moments later came the naval artillery: 5in shells that pounded the beach in advance of the landing craft that were now approaching.[5]

But the same storm that had covered the invasion force's approach also caused problems for the landing itself. High winds churned the water and capsized several landing craft, roughing up the invaders even before they had a chance to close with the enemy.

The British defenders of Kota Bharu may have been outnumbered and outgunned but their response to the Japanese attack was both swift and efficient. The area was defended by the 8th Indian Infantry Brigade of the 9th Indian Infantry Division, supported by four 3.7in Mountain Howitzers of the 21st Mountain Battery. Sabak Beach and the neighboring Badang Beach were the responsibility of the 3/17th Battalion, Dogra Regiment, supported by the 73rd Field Battery of the 5th Field Regiment, Royal Artillery, deployed adjacent to the Kota Bharu airbase just a mile and a half back from the beach. The British had fortified the narrow beaches and islands with land mines, barbed wire, and bunkers. The Imperial Japanese Army began to feel the full weight of those fortifications. The sounds of explosions and small arms fire reached the airbase and spurred a quick report. Air Vice Marshal Pulford reacted quickly to the news of the landing by immediately ordering an all-out attack on the invasion transports.[6]

In this context, an "all-out attack" was not much: only ten Lockheed Hudson bombers, all of the Royal Australian Air Force's No. 1 Squadron, were at Kota Bharu, of which only seven could be immediately armed with bombing loads. But the pilots were determined to make the most of what they had. At 2:08 am, to the sounds of explosions and the flicker of small arms fire in the darkness some 2 miles away, the Hudsons roared down the runway fully laden with 250lb bombs and soared into the air. Because it was night, coordination of the aircraft was deemed impossible so the pilots were instructed to make individual attacks.[7]

Their first counterattack resulted in at least two bomb hits on the 9,794-ton transport *Awagisan Maru*, setting it afire. One Hudson tried to strafe the Japanese infantry on the beach, but was shot up and crashed into a fully laden Japanese landing barge, killing the pilot, Flight Lieutenant John Leighton-Jones, his crew and some 60 Japanese soldiers and sailors. The first wave returned to the airbase to rearm. As they did so, the second wave of three Hudsons started their attacks. The only one to achieve results was Flight Lieutenant Ken Smith and his crew, placing two bombs in a cluster of ten landing barges, capsizing several and leaving the rest badly shaken.

Another Hudson, its bombs having failed to release from their bomb racks, was sent out over the South China Sea to scout out enemy ships. On its return leg it maneuvered for a low-level attack on a dark shape in the water. Unfortunately, the dark shape turned out to be not a relatively helpless transport, but the flagship *Sendai*, which launched an avalanche of antiaircraft fire in return. Lucky to escape, pilot Flight Lieutenant John O'Brien now targeted the Japanese transport closest to shore and scored at least one bomb hit on the *Awagisan Maru*.

Now the third wave of air attacks from the Royal Australian Air Force's No. 1 Squadron was under way. Flight Lieutenant Colin Verco scored at least one bomb hit on the *Sakura Maru*. Lieutenant Smith had a "stick" of four bombs straddle the *Ayatosan Maru*, damaging the thin-skinned transport. Another Hudson piloted by Flight Lieutenant Oscar Diamond dropped an additional bomb on the burning *Awagisan Maru*, exploding just forward of the bridge and starting yet another fire.

The Australian pilots continued this pattern of making low-level bombing runs, rearming and taking off again until 5:00 am, but Japanese antiaircraft fire took a severe toll, shooting down at least two Hudsons and badly damaging three others to the point where they had to be written off. Nevertheless Admiral Hashimoto had had enough of the pounding and ordered an immediate withdrawal. General Takumi convinced the harried Hashimoto to give him more time to reinforce his troops fighting on the beach. So at 6:00 am all the Japanese ships that could headed back out to sea with the exception of the *Awagisan Maru*, burning fiercely and with at least 110 killed or wounded.[8]

The Japanese were fortunate in heading out to sea as the plucky Royal Australian Air Force No. 1 Squadron had been joined by seven Vickers Vildebeest torpedo bombers of the Royal Air Force's No. 36 Squadron to continue the fight. Flying out of Gong Kedah they were sent out after the temporarily retreating transports, but the stormy conditions worsened, and the combination of wind, rain, and antiaircraft fire so battered these antiquated, fabric-covered biplanes that only four managed to release their torpedoes, scoring no hits.[9] At about 8:00 am, 12 Hudsons from the Royal Australian Air Force's No. 8 Squadron arrived overhead. Based in Kuantan, which would unwittingly have a decisive role in the days ahead, No. 8 had been informed at 2:00 am of the landings at Kota Bharu. It had taken off at 6:30 am and, after forming in four flights of three, sped to the battlefield. The Kota Bharu airbase had sent warnings that the Japanese ships were withdrawing, but the first flight missed the signal and bored in on the transport closest to shore, the luckless *Awagisan Maru*. They added at least another bomb to her collection, but it was for naught; the burning transport had already been abandoned. The remaining Hudsons pursued the retreating ships, but the invasion convoy had already disappeared under cover of the storm front. Despairing of finding the ships in the murk, Flight Lieutenant Charles "Spud" Spurgeon chose to make a low-level bombing run on the transport closest to shore, which was, once again, the *Awagisan Maru*. He added another bomb to her misery, but added to his own as well when shrapnel from his bomb's explosion tore into his Hudson and forced it to crash land at Kota Bharu. Of the 12 aircraft in this attack, five were damaged.[10]

The Far East Air Command in Singapore, in another example of commendable British efficiency in the early hours of the Pacific War, had ordered all hands on deck, trying to get every serviceable bomber in their inventory to strike at the Japanese off Kota Bharu, but they were outnumbered, outgunned, and uncoordinated. Worse, by this time, Japanese Zeros from the 22nd Air Flotilla were making their appearance after covering the other landings on the Kra Isthmus. They arrived just in time to foil a last effort by the No. 8 and depleted No. 1 Squadrons to provide air support to the hard-pressed British Army troops on the ground. Eight Bristol Blenheim bombers of the Royal Air Force's No. 60 Squadron came in to lend a hand, managing to obtain one bomb hit, once again on the *Awagisan Maru*, but were chewed up by antiaircraft fire, suffering two shot down and a third badly damaged.[11]

The *Awagisan Maru* would have the dubious distinction of being the first Japanese ship sunk in World War II. Precisely when and where is disputed. British and American sources indicate that the Blenheims achieved the very last hit on the hapless transport and finally put her under.[12] But on December 12 the Dutch submarine *K-XII*, under the command of Lieutenant Commander H. C. J. Coumou, torpedoed and sank an unidentified ship off Kota Bharu. The description of the ship given in Dutch logs precisely matches that of the *Awagisan Maru*.[13] Either way, the case of the *Awagisan Maru* was mostly but perhaps not entirely to the credit of the Royal Air Force. The unarmored transport had survived at least six bomb hits and possibly a seventh without sinking, which did not speak well of the effectiveness of the 250-pound bombs the British were using.[14] That was not the fault of the pilots, but their consistent choice to attack a burning, disabled, and later abandoned transport when other targets were available is open to question.

Nevertheless, the pilots of the Royal Air Force and the Royal Australian Air Force and the Indian infantry had ample reason to be proud. The defense of Kota Bharu was the first time a Japanese invasion fleet had been forced to turn back before it could fully complete its landing operations. It was the only time an invasion fleet had been repulsed by air power alone.[15] The Japanese planning for the invasion, which would go so well almost everywhere else, had been botched at Kota Bharu inasmuch as they had not first neutralized the airbase with naval artillery fire. Japanese infantry had suffered heavy losses. The performance of the British and Australian pilots and the Indian troops had been brave, determined, and resourceful. And, ultimately, for naught.

There were just too few British, Australians, and Indians and too many Japanese.

By midmorning, General Takumi had three full infantry battalions ashore. By 10:30 am they had reached Kota Bharu. Within a day the British would be forced to abandon the airbase. It would have a ripple effect down the Malay Peninsula and well into the South China Sea.

THE BRITISH DEFENSE: FORCE Z SETS SAIL – DECEMBER 8

Unfortunately for the British, their spirited and determined but ultimately futile defense of Kota Bharu would prove to be the high point of their defense of Malaya.

Some of that was the result of a bad call. Far East Command had guessed that the Japanese would take over northern Thailand before moving into the Kra Isthmus and Malaya. Army and air forces were positioned to block that move from Thailand into

Malaya. But the Japanese had instead invaded the Kra Isthmus (with help from the Thais) and Malaya itself. The British were now overextended. Their guess as to the Japanese objective had been educated and reasonable, but wrong.

On the evening of December 7, Admiral Phillips met with Air Chief Marshal Brooke-Popham and General Arthur Percival, the British Army commander in Malaya, to develop an operational plan that they would communicate with London. The Admiralty had asked Phillips about options for contesting the Japanese expedition given the forces he had. Phillips sent a message back to London saying that if his force was inferior to that of the Japanese, he would try a hit-and-run raid, but otherwise he would try to attack the invasion forces. His message received no response.[16] It seemed apparent by this time that Phillips' deterrent force was failing to deter, but London simply had no idea what to do next.

Shortly after midnight on December 8, Marshal Brooke-Popham told London he could not execute Operation *Matador*, the operation to take up defensive positions within Thai territory. But he did put into effect Operation *Krohcol*, the less ambitious plan that aimed to capture "The Ledge", 30 miles inside Thailand. Unfortunately, *Krohcol* would fail miserably; the British troops were stymied and driven back by the fierce resistance of Thai "police" who were likely disguised Japanese troops. Worse, because the British Army troops had been positioned to carry out *Matador* and *Krohcol*, they were now out of position to defend against the actual Japanese invasion.

It was at about 3:30 am that, apparently, a curious and rather mysterious meeting of the British leadership in Malaya took place in a darkened war room deep in the bowels of the Singapore Naval Base. The meeting included Admiral Phillips with his staff, Air Chief Marshal Brooke-Popham with members of his staff; Air Vice Marshal Conway Pulford, commander of the Royal Air Force in the Far East; and the British civilian leadership in Malaya. When and why the meeting was called remains unclear but the main topic for discussion was, in the appalling absence of direction from London, the course of action to be determined for Phillips and his naval forces – whether to flee the superior Japanese forces or fight them.[17]

The main reason for the meeting seems to have been Admiral Phillips' wish to secure some political backing for what he knew would be a risky sortie by the *Prince of Wales* and *Repulse* to attempt to derail the Japanese invasion. He preferred to fight rather than retreat to Ceylon, Australia, or the East Indies, but he was reluctant, at least outwardly, to risk his two capital ships – the only Royal Navy capital ships in the Far East – in an attack on the Japanese invasion convoys unless he got an authoritative statement that it was absolutely necessary for the defense of Malaya. This he secured from Brooke-Popham, although it has been alleged that Phillips maneuvered Brooke-Popham into making that statement.

Admiral Phillips spent considerable time and effort explaining his concern about air attacks, especially those from torpedo bombers, and trying to secure some form of air protection for his ships. Air Vice Marshal Pulford gave some disheartening information about the limitations of his aircraft and his pilots, who were not trained to fly over water, but agreed to provide air cover within those limitations.

The meeting is revealing inasmuch as, for someone allegedly deeply committed to the idea of battleship supremacy, the "battleship admiral" Phillips seemed determined to get some type of air protection. He stated that he did not fear high-level bombers or dive bombers – the former because of their relative inaccuracy, the latter because none were known to be nearby. But he also believed that an attack by Japanese torpedo bombers operating out of Saigon, though unlikely due to the weather conditions and what was believed to be their effective operating range, would be extremely dangerous.

The mysterious meeting was effectively ended at around 4:15 am, with an air raid warning, and yet another sign that the British had badly underestimated the Japanese.[18] The Far East Command had been convinced that the Japanese bombers based in Saigon did not have the range to reach Singapore. When 17 of those Japanese bombers – G3M Nells of the Mihoro Air Group – appeared over Singapore in the predawn darkness and began bombing the city, the British authorities began to reevaluate this belief. General Percival later said the bombing was "rather a surprise."[19]

The bombing itself was largely ineffectual – Singapore's main port at Keppel Harbor and the airfields at Seletar and Tengah suffered very minor damage – but it showed that British planning for the defense of Singapore and Malaya was far worse than had been originally thought.[20] For instance, when the bombers appeared at 4:15 am, Singapore was brilliantly lit, practically a beacon guiding the Japanese to their targets. Most of the antiaircraft positions were not manned, and antiaircraft fire from Singapore City was almost nonexistent; the most effective fire came from the antiaircraft batteries of the *Prince of Wales* and *Repulse* docked at the naval base. Finally, the bombing was almost over before the air raid sirens sounded. The Japanese had been ashore in Malaya for four hours, yet Singapore air defense was still woefully underprepared.

And it did not stop there. Flight Lieutenant Tim Vigors, acting commander of the Royal Air Force's No. 453 Squadron and a decorated Battle of Britain veteran with night fighting experience, asked for permission to take three Brewster Buffalos from the Sembawang Airfield up to intercept the bombers. His request was denied on the grounds that they did not want to expose the fighters to the friendly fire of the local antiaircraft gunners. Additionally, the Buffalo was not a night fighter.[21] The Royal Air Force did have night fighters – twin-engine Beauforts – but they were positioned in the north at Sungei Patani because they were designated ground attack aircraft. Sometimes, bureaucracy was almost as much of an enemy as the Japanese.[22]

Upon conclusion of the bombing-disrupted meeting, Admiral Phillips directed a message declaring his intentions to sail and try to disrupt the Japanese landing operations, to be transmitted to the Admiralty. London acknowledged receipt of the signal at 9:30 am, but otherwise gave no answer.[23] Admiral Phillips returned to the War Room at 6:30 am to work out the details of his operation with his chief of staff Admiral Arthur F. E. Palliser and Admiral Sir Geoffrey Layton, the commander of the Royal

Navy's China Station, which had been dissolved to be merged with Phillips' new Eastern Fleet. At this point, the seriousness of the situation off Kota Bharu became apparent and necessitated that Kota Bharu should become the objective rather than Singora. Phillips, apparently very concerned about having enough destroyers to give his capital ships decent antisubmarine protection, was heard to say, "I certainly can't go to sea until I have some more destroyers."[24] But that issue was apparently dealt with to his satisfaction, and at 9:34 am Phillips sent another signal to the Admiralty, stating in relevant part:

PROVIDED [THAT] AS I HOPE I CAN MAKE 4 DESTROYERS AVAILABLE INTEND TO PROCEED WITH *PRINCE OF WALES* AND *REPULSE* DUSK TONIGHT 8/12 TO ATTACK ENEMY FORCE OFF KOTA BHARU DAYLIGHT WEDNESDAY 10TH.[25]

Again, he was giving London a chance to tell him not to go. And once again, his message got no reaction from London.[26]

As December 8 wore on, it became apparent that the British Army and Royal Air Force units in northern Malaya were in trouble. The British Army units were simply overextended and could not resist effectively until they could reassemble. The Royal Air Force's aircraft were being chewed up by the Japanese. Combat was showing that, contrary to Air Marshal Brooke-Popham's assertions, the Buffalo was simply not good enough for Malaya, or for much else.

All of which put even more pressure on Admiral Phillips to do something. At around 12:30 pm, Phillips held a council-of-war in his cabin on the *Prince of Wales* with members of his staff, Captain Leach and Captain Tennant. Looking ill and damp from the sweltering conditions below decks on the flagship, Phillips, "concisely and in sharp tones," laid out the deteriorating situation in northern Malaya and their unhappy options in response: stay in harbor waiting for reinforcements and get bombed, retreat to the Indian Ocean, or counterattack.[27]

The first two options were non-starters, especially with British and Dominion troops fighting and dying in northern Malaya. Retreating in particular, while probably the smartest option, was almost profane given the fanfare with which the *Prince of Wales* and *Repulse* had arrived in Singapore. But the counterattack option was dangerous, as Phillips well knew. It was for that reason that he assembled a small, high-speed task force. The ships available at Singapore, in addition to the *Prince of Wales* and *Repulse*, were the light cruisers HMS *Durban, Danae, Dragon*, and *Mauritius*; and the destroyers HMS *Express, Electra, Tenedos, Stronghold, Encounter, Jupiter*, and the Australian HMAS *Vampire*. En route to Singapore and set to arrive within days were the 8in armed heavy cruiser HMS *Exeter*, the Dutch light cruiser *Java*, the World War I-era British destroyers HMS *Scout* and *Thanet* and the US Destroyer Division 57 with the destroyers USS *Whipple, John D. Edwards, Edsall*, and *Alden*, ordered over by Admiral Hart to support the British.

But Admiral Phillips knew he could not wait. *Danae*, *Dragon*, *Mauritius*, *Encounter*, and *Jupiter* were undergoing repairs and not ready. *Durban* and *Stronghold* were too slow for the fast task force that Phillips wanted. That left the battleship *Prince of Wales*, the battlecruiser *Repulse*, the Royal Navy destroyers *Express*, *Electra*, and the World War I-vintage *Tenedos* and *Vampire* for this raiding force.

The plan was a relatively simple hit-and-run operation based on surprise and speed. They would sail into the Gulf of Siam and let British air reconnaissance of Japanese movements determine their target as Singora or Kota Bharu. Admiral Phillips would wreak havoc on whatever invasion beaches the scout aircraft identified, then make a high-speed run back to Singapore. An exception was to be made for an opportunity to strike at the main elements of the Imperial Japanese Navy. Intelligence officials had reported that the invasion operations had a covering force of seven cruisers, 20 destroyers, and only one capital ship – a *Kongo*-class battleship. If they had a chance to engage and sink the *Kongo* with the *Prince of Wales'* superior gunpower, they would do so. Otherwise their target would be the invasion beaches and their supporting transports.[28]

Aside from the aforementioned *Kongo*, there were, in Admiral Phillips' view, two major dangers: submarines and aircraft. Phillips had been informed that on December 2 US Navy Catalinas had spotted 12 Japanese submarines off Indochina heading south, likely toward his capital ships, and that mines were a strong possibility along his transit route.[29] His hope was that his destroyers would keep the Japanese boats at bay; in any event, his ships could easily outrun submerged submarines.

A far bigger concern was Japanese air power. Admiral Phillips had termed the French cessation of Indochina to the Japanese as "France's most dastardly deed" and was well aware of the dangers posed by the Saigon airbase complex, especially aerial torpedo attacks.[30] The admiral apparently stated that no shore-based torpedo attack on ships at sea had been delivered at a range of greater than 200 miles – at least none that he knew of. Based on this experience, if they stayed outside a 200-mile radius of Ca Mau, Indochina, where the British believed the Japanese had an airbase, they would be outside the limit of the effective range of Japanese aerial torpedo attack. Apparently, however, Phillips was not entirely confident of this analysis. So he would time the return run to Singapore to minimize daylight exposure, and would try to obtain air cover.[31]

Admiral Phillips had called the meeting more as an affirmation of a decision he had already made than as a true council of war, but he did give everyone a chance to speak, asking, "Now what do you think of this plan?" The response he got was a long, thoughtful silence. It was the widely -respected Captain Tennant of the *Repulse* who first declared his support for the operation. "We've come to secure our communications. That was our purpose. Now that we're here, I don't see what possible alternative we have but to do as you proposed."[32]

At the end of his presentation the admiral asked, "Does anyone think we shouldn't go?" The response:

All were unanimous that it was impossible for the Navy to attempt nothing while the army and air force were being driven back, and that the plan for a sudden raid, though hazardous, was acceptable. There was also the psychological effect of the fleet putting to sea in this grave emergency.[33]

This meeting lasted about half an hour. Shortly thereafter, at about 1:30 pm, Admiral Phillips held a second, larger meeting with his staff and the skippers of his raiding force. It went much like the first meeting. "Gentlemen," Admiral Phillips bluntly declared, "this is an extremely hazardous expedition … Nevertheless, I feel that we have got to do something."[34] The admiral sought opinions, but the issue was never in doubt. He wanted to attack. His staff and his skippers wanted to attack. They did not want to abandon their comrades fighting in northern Malaya, and they wanted a chance to strike back at the Japanese aggressors.

After the discussion was over, Admiral Phillips concluded this second meeting with the summation, "We can stay in Singapore. We can sail away to the East – Australia. Or we can go out and fight. Gentlemen, we sail at 5 o'clock."

So, on a day when indecision and paralysis was seemingly the rule, Admiral Phillips, in whom "the spirit of Drake and Nelson burned with a fierce fire," was the exception and took the initiative.[35] For which he would ultimately pay with his life.

His was a logical plan, with three serious drawbacks.

The first Admiral Phillips could not control: the Japanese invasion would be largely completed by the end of the day on December 9. If he had wanted to stop the invasion at sea, he needed to have been at sea a few days before, but that option had been unavailable because of political considerations. It was already simply too late.

The second was the nature of the task force itself. With two capital ships and four destroyers – no cruisers, not many destroyers, and no air power – it was badly unbalanced. In reality, it was much the same problem Admiral Phillips had had since leaving the United Kingdom. This was just the best he could do.

The third problem, very much related to the second, was air cover. The Japanese were deploying significant air assets in their invasion of Malaya. Admiral Phillips' reputation as a "battleship admiral" preceded him, but, once again, for someone who allegedly believed firmly that aircraft could not sink battleships, he spent a lot of effort analyzing the threat from air attack and trying to get fighter protection for his ships. His estimate of the effective range of what he really feared, aerial torpedo attack, based on the British experience with the Germans and Italians, was logical. It was also wrong; the Japanese bombers based in Indochina in reality had a range of about 1,000 miles.

It was but one of a number of catastrophic miscalculations about Japanese aerial capabilities, but Phillips had tried to hedge his bets. Earlier that morning he had placed a request in to Air Vice Marshal Pulford for air support in the form of (1) aerial reconnaissance 100 miles north of Phillips' force during daylight on December 9; (2) reconnaissance off Singora at dawn on December 10; and (3) fighter protection off Singora during daylight on December 10.[36]

Air Vice Marshal Pulford could provide the reconnaissance, but with the heavy losses in northern Malaya, fighter protection was an increasing struggle. Lieutenant Vigors of the No. 453 Squadron proposed a plan to keep six aircraft over Phillips' force during daylight. The problem was that the squadron's Buffalos did not have the range to reach Singora and provide the necessary air cover; there was no other guarantee of any other fighter protection. Phillips rejected his plan, on the grounds it required him to stay within 60 miles of the coast, which restricted his freedom of movement too much.[37] Ultimately, it was arranged that Admiral Phillips could call on the No. 453 Squadron, which would be on standby at Sembawang if he needed them.

Regarding Phillips' decision to proceed, naval historian Samuel Eliot Morison wrote:

> Those who make the decisions in war are constantly weighing certain risks against possible gains. At the outset of hostilities Admiral Hart thought of sending his small striking force north of Luzon to challenge Japanese communications, but decided that the risk to his ships outweighed the possible gain because the enemy had won control of the air. Admiral Phillips had precisely the same problem in Malaya. Should he steam into the Gulf of Siam and expose his ships to air attack from Indochina in the hope of breaking enemy communications with their landing force? He decided to take the chance. With the Royal Air Force and the British Army fighting for their lives, the Royal Navy could not be true to its tradition by remaining idly at anchor.[38]

Arthur Nicholson, in his respected history of the operation, perhaps said it best: "Admiral Phillips' decision was one that was fully in accord with Royal Navy traditions of attacking the enemy, no matter what the odds, and of going to the assistance of the Army. The Royal Navy had not built its magnificent reputation over the centuries by avoiding battle."[39]

The admiral would leave behind his chief of staff, Admiral Palliser, to act as a liaison with the Royal Air Force in general and to try to arrange that fighter cover off Singora on December 10 in particular. Palliser would also provide Admiral Phillips with intelligence information and logistical assistance from shore.

Admiral Phillips had a few other issues involving his ships. Departure was delayed because the *Prince of Wales* had a boiler under repair; without it she could not go at full speed. Of greater concern was her state-of-the-art antiaircraft fire control radar. Like the battleship's ventilation system, the radar had been designed for the cold North Sea and north Atlantic, not the heat and humidity of the tropics. The radar had not taken too well to the tropics and had broken down en route to Singapore. On the afternoon of December 8, after the *Prince of Wales* had been in Singapore for almost a week and just hours before she was to sail, it finally occurred to someone that the radar should be fixed. Three Royal Air Force technicians were sent on board but could not fix it within the time frame. The *Prince of Wales* would have to sail without it.[40]

With that rather large oversight not taken care of, at 5:10 pm on December 8, 1941, the *Vampire* moved off from the Singapore Naval Base into the Johore Strait, followed by the *Tenedos*, then the *Repulse* and finally the flagship *Prince of Wales*. They would meet the *Express* and *Electra*, practicing their minesweeping, outside the harbor. It was this "puny force of six ships" that Admiral Phillips was taking into the South China Sea to fight the massive Japanese invasion.[41] Just before sailing, Phillips officially gave this task force the name that would, for all the wrong reasons, become famous: "Force Z."[42]

It was a somber procession, with more than a touch of dread. Admiral Layton called the procession "a pathetic sight" and did not expect to see the ships again.[43] One staff officer expected them to be "slaughtered."[44] Royal Marine Maurice Edwards from the *Prince of Wales* recalled: "As we left the Straits of Johore I had a terrible feeling of foreboding we just didn't know what we were going to encounter but one thing I do remember is being convinced that we'd never get back to the colony in one piece."[45]

As the force sailed through the Johore Strait, a message was flashed from Air Vice Marshal Pulford, a response to Admiral Phillips' last plea for air cover: REGRET FIGHTER PROTECTION IMPOSSIBLE.

"Well, we must get on without it," the admiral shrugged.[46]

On board the *Repulse*, her skipper, Captain William G. Tennant, addressed his crew on their newest mission. "We are off to look for trouble," Captain Tennant said. "I expect we shall find it …"[47]

SUBMARINES GO TO WAR – DECEMBER 8

Admiral Hart's laconic message to the Asiatic Fleet after Pearl Harbor announcing the start of the war had been followed at 3:45 am by a second, much less well-known message: SUBMARINES AND AIRCRAFT WILL WAGE UNRESTRICTED WARFARE.[48]

Captain John Wilkes, newly reappointed commander of the US Asiatic Fleet's submarine force, called all of his commanders in to his flagship, the submarine tender *Holland*. With his two submarine division commanders joining him, Captain Wilkes told the submarine skippers that this, the first war patrol, would be both "the most dangerous and the most informative as to enemy methods on formations, convoying, anti-submarine warfare."[49] His priority was getting this information. Each skipper was told to "use caution and feel his way."[50]

As Clark Field and Iba Field burned, Stuart Murray, one of the submarine division commanders who had earned the nickname "Sunshine," gave a speech that was anything but. "Listen, dammit. Don't try to go out there and win the Congressional Medal of Honor in one day. The submarines are all we have left. Your crews are more valuable than anything else. Bring them back."[51] As wartime motivational speeches went, it was not exactly Leonidas. And it was arguably not in line with US submarine doctrine.[52] The skippers were given their marching orders. First priority targets would be capital ships, followed by loaded transports. Then would come smaller combatants, including destroyers, transports, and supply ships. Merchantmen were to be sunk with one torpedo if possible. Shoot on sight at all times.[53]

FORCE Z AND THE BATTLE OFF MALAYA

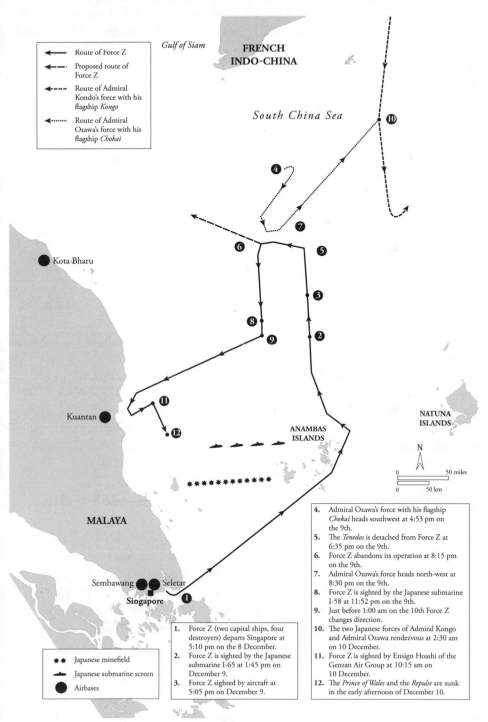

Route of Force Z

Proposed route of Force Z

Route of Admiral Kondo's force with his flagship *Kongo*

Route of Admiral Ozawa's force with his flagship *Chokai*

Gulf of Siam

FRENCH INDO-CHINA

South China Sea

⑩

④

⑦

⑥

⑤

Kota Bharu

③

⑧

②

⑨

⑪

Kuantan

⑫

ANAMBAS ISLANDS

NATUNA ISLANDS

N

0   50 miles

0   50 km

MALAYA

Sembawang   Seletar

Singapore

①

Japanese minefield

Japanese submarine screen

Airbases

1. Force Z (two capital ships, four destroyers) departs Singapore at 5:10 pm on the 8 December.
2. Force Z is sighted by the Japanese submarine I-65 at 1:45 pm on December 9.
3. Force Z sighted by aircraft at 5:05 pm on December 9.
4. Admiral Ozawa's force with his flagship *Chokai* heads southwest at 4:53 pm on the 9th.
5. The *Tenedos* is detached from Force Z at 6:35 pm on the 9th.
6. Force Z abandons its operation at 8:15 pm on the 9th.
7. Admiral Ozawa's force heads north-west at 8:30 pm on the 9th.
8. Force Z is sighted by the Japanese submarine I-58 at 11:52 pm on the 9th.
9. Just before 1:00 am on the 10th Force Z changes direction.
10. The two Japanese forces of Admiral Kongo and Admiral Ozawa rendezvous at 2:30 am on 10 December.
11. Force Z is sighted by Ensign Hoashi of the Genzan Air Group at 10:15 am on 10 December.
12. The *Prince of Wales* and the *Repulse* are sunk in the early afternoon of December 10.

Captain Wilkes informed them that, as the only remaining force, they should not take unnecessary risks. The fleet submarines – those submarines the US Navy usually named after fish or other sea creatures – had all been issued the Mark 14 torpedo that contained a new secret weapon: the Mark 6 exploder assembly, which included both contact and magnetic influence features. The concept behind the magnetic exploder was deceptively simple. A ship is built on a single beam called a keel. From the keel flow the interior girders that form a ship's skeleton. The hull is built around as the "skin" to this skeleton. The hull on the sides of a ship, since these areas expect combat, is usually armored. But the hull on the very bottom of the ship is not armored at all. If you can cause an explosion under a ship, you can snap the keel, which will serve as breaking its back. The keel can no longer support the weight of the ship, which will likely break in two.

This magnetic exploder was supposed to detonate when it entered a ship's magnetic field, which would in theory be directly under the ship's keel. This idea had been a sort of holy grail among torpedo developers. The British had tried it and found that it did not work. The Germans had tried it and found that it did not work. Nonetheless, the US Navy had complete confidence in it. Captain Wilkes optimistically stated that the Mark 6's magnetic exploder should produce "amazing" results.[54]

And with that, the submarines, except for the *Sealion* and the *Seadragon*, both of which were undergoing refit, were given their assigned patrol areas. By December 11, 22 submarines of the US Asiatic Fleet submarines were at sea to fight the Japanese. Two – *Permit* and *Perch* – were stationed off Subic Bay. Two – *Sailfish* and *Saury* – were off Vigan, Luzon. *S-36* was in Lingayen Gulf, with *Stingray* just outside it. Five – *Seawolf, Sculpin, Skipjack, Tarpon,* and *S-39* – headed east, four – *Shark, S-37, S-38,* and *S-40* – south of Luzon. Three – *Pickerel, Spearfish,* and *Sargo* – were assigned to patrol near Cam Ranh Bay. Two – *Sturgeon* and *Searaven* – headed to Formosa; *Pike* for Hong Kong; and *Swordfish* for Hainan Island.

DECISIONS NOT MADE IN LONDON – DECEMBER 9–10

In the surreality that surrounded the discussions, such as they were, about the deployment of the *Prince of Wales* and *Repulse* to Singapore, perhaps nothing captured just how backwards the entire process had been as much as the meeting called by Winston Churchill late on the evening of December 9.

It was 10:00 pm when the prime minister convened a meeting with First Sea Lord Sir Dudley Pound and about ten personnel in the Cabinet War Room. The agenda was the *Prince of Wales* and *Repulse*. As Churchill rather famously later described it:

> We had only one key weapon in our hands. The *Prince of Wales* and the *Repulse* had arrived at Singapore. They had been sent to these waters to exercise that kind of vague menace which capital ships of the highest quality whose whereabouts is [sic] unknown can impose on all hostile

naval calculations. How should we use them now? Obviously, they must go to sea and vanish among the innumerable islands. There was general agreement on that.[55]

How the ships were to "vanish" in the Indies, where the islands were filled with Japanese agents, he never made clear. Based on Admiral Phillips' earlier transmissions to the Admiralty, however, Churchill and the First Sea Lord had to be aware that the *Prince of Wales* and *Repulse* were already at sea in the midst of their counterattack.[56]

As the rather sketchy minutes of the meeting described it:

The Admiralty were invited to give careful attention to the following alternative plans; – (a) A plan to restore the command of the Pacific by concentrating a superior Anglo-American battle fleet at Hawaii with a view to offensive action against the Japanese mainland, and (b) A plan to employ "Prince of Wales," "Repulse" and "Centurion" (a former battleship now used as a target ship) as rogue elephants.[57]

Indeed, Churchill favored sending Force Z across the Pacific to join the shattered American battle line at Pearl Harbor as the nucleus of a new fleet. "We were all much attracted by this line of thought. But as the hour was late we decided to sleep on it, and settle the next morning what to do with the *Prince of Wales* and the *Repulse*."[58]

As historian Arthur Marder acidly commented:

It is an extraordinary fact that 48 hours after the Japanese attack on Pearl Harbor, the authorities in London seemed to be discussing in a leisurely way what the operational role of Force Z should be, and deciding to sleep on it, when that Force was already committed to a hazardous enterprise.[59]

So the *Prince of Wales* and *Repulse* sailed off to battle before Whitehall had even decided whether they should be in battle at all.

THE DESTRUCTION OF FORCE Z – DECEMBER 10

When Admiral Sir Tom Phillips led Force Z out of Singapore late in the afternoon of December 8, he did so with the understanding that, except in case of emergency, he would not use the voice radio or wireless telegraph. This was in keeping with the doctrine known as "radio silence." The use of radio or telegraph could enable the enemy to use High Frequency Direction Finders (HFDF or "Huff Duff" in the military shorthand) to locate a position. Just the previous spring, Admiral Phillips had seen how the Royal Navy had actually lost the German battleship *Bismarck* in the Atlantic Ocean until she transmitted a long message back to Germany. This allowed the Royal Navy to fix her position, track her down, and put her under.

Admiral Phillips was not going to allow that to happen to Force Z. At the same time, he knew he was setting out at a time when the situation was rapidly changing. He also was certain he would need help from shore at some point, especially air cover and air reconnaissance. As such he had left his chief of staff, Admiral Palliser, in Singapore to act as liaison, to keep him apprised of any new intelligence information, and to try to obtain air support (especially air support over Singora on December 10) and whatever other support Force Z might need. How Admiral Palliser would be able to achieve this when Force Z was operating on radio silence is unclear. Presumably, Palliser would have to anticipate – in other words, "guess" – what his admiral wanted and needed while all alone facing the Japanese. It was a tall order.

On the other side of the South China Sea was Admiral Phillips' primary opponent in this particular game, Japanese Vice Admiral Ozawa Jisaburo. Since his graduation from the Japanese naval academy in Etajima in 1909 the performance of Ozawa had been such that he was and continues to be regarded as one of the Imperial Japanese Navy's best admirals. Highly intelligent, a student of naval history, respectful of his opponents and considerate of the men under his command, his verbal commitment to command the Malaya Force had given even the army – when relations between the army and navy were generally antagonistic – confidence in the navy's desire to see the invasion concluded successfully. Ozawa had never met Admiral Phillips, but by reputation he highly respected him.[60]

Despite its small size, Force Z represented a serious threat to Japanese plans for Malaya and, indeed, for the entire Centrifugal Offensive. Thanks to Churchill's public announcement that it would act as a suitable deterrent and widespread newspaper coverage of its journey from the United Kingdom, the Japanese were well aware of the presence of the *Prince of Wales* in the region. Indeed, on December 3, a Japanese reconnaissance plane found the *Prince of Wales* and *Repulse* sitting at Seletar.[61]

But her presence did not derail Japanese invasion plans: instead Admiral Kondo's Southern Expeditionary Force was augmented with battleships and increased air power.

The Western Force, called the Malaya Force for the immediate mission, was under Admiral Ozawa, with his flag in the 8in armed cruiser *Chokai*. Nearby were the four 8in armed *Mogami*-class heavy cruisers of the 7th Cruiser Division, under the command of Rear Admiral Kurita Takeo, along with the light cruisers *Yura* and *Kinu* and a screen of four destroyers. Kondo himself would remain off the southeastern coast of Indochina in the *Chokai*'s luxurious sister ship *Atago*, his flagship, with her other sister *Takao* and, most importantly, the battleship *Kongo* and her sister ship *Haruna*. The basic plan was for Ozawa to lure Force Z well out into the South China Sea where the *Kongo*, *Haruna*, and the collection of cruisers could destroy it.

But as formidable as this arrangement of surface forces appeared, the Combined Fleet did not have complete confidence in it. The major problem was that the Combined Fleet currently had nothing available that could outclass the *Prince of Wales*. The Imperial

Japanese Navy's famous superbattleships *Yamato* and *Musashi*, the two biggest battleships ever to sail the face of the earth, were not yet operational. The rest of the navy's battleships were of roughly the same vintage as the *Repulse* and, in any case, the Combined Fleet was so committed to keeping them safe and using them only in the case of the "decisive battle" that these battleships mostly stayed in port. The *Kongo*-class ships were the best the Japanese had, and these were in fact converted battlecruisers of World War I vintage.[62] They were fast and armed with 14in guns, but with limited armor, essentially the Japanese equivalent of the *Repulse*. So despite their superior number of ships and effective torpedoes, they were still outgunned. And they knew it.

The obvious way to tip the scales in their favor was with air power.

Based in and around Saigon was the 22nd Air Flotilla, under the command of Admiral Matsunaga Sadaichi. Originally, the 22nd consisted of two air groups: the Genzan Air Group commanded by Lieutenant Commander Nakanishi Tsugumichi operating out of Saigon itself, and the Mihoro Air Group commanded by Lieutenant Hachiro Shōji operating out of Thú Dâu Môt, each group equipped with 36 Mitsubishi G3M "Nell" bombers. Attached to the 22nd was the so-called "Yamada Unit" of 25 Zero fighters and six C5M "Babs" reconnaissance aircraft based at Soc Trang, southwest of Saigon. All were under the command of the Japanese 11th Air Fleet based in Takao, Formosa.[63] This was a formidable force on its own, but with the news that the *Prince of Wales* and *Repulse* were en route to Singapore, Admiral Yamamoto gave his own response to Churchill's "deterrent" force by ordering elements of the Kanoya Air Group, with 27 more modern Mitsubishi G4M "Betty" bombers, to stage from Takao on Formosa to Thú Dâu Môt.[64]

These land-based elements, the "air flotillas," of the Japanese Naval Air Force had no real equivalent in the Allied or the other Axis countries. Although they were adequate as bombers, the Nells and Bettys were not in the same league as the B-17 Flying Fortress and the B-24/LB-30 Liberator. However, the B-17 would prove relatively ineffectual at attacking ships, largely because the bomb it carried was too small. And, unlike the Nell and Betty, neither the B-17 nor the B-24/LB-30 could carry torpedoes, which were far better ship-killers than bombs. The closest Allied equivalents to the Betty and the Nell were the American Martin B-26 Marauder, which many pilots found too dangerous to handle; and the British Bristol Beaufort, which pilots were still learning to use. Significantly, Admiral Phillips and the British had no idea the Nells and Bettys could carry torpedoes; for reasons unknown, British intelligence reports on the capabilities of both aircraft had never reached Phillips or even the naval general staff in London.[65]

Torpedoes could directly sink ships by opening holes in the sides, while bombs usually could only indirectly sink ships, by causing secondary damage like detonation of ammunition magazines or a loss of power. The Japanese air flotillas therefore specialized in killing ships. On November 30, Kanoya Air Group had been "unofficially" told to attack the *Prince of Wales* and *Repulse* using the newly arrived Bettys. Day and night-training was immediately put into place.[66]

As an additional "deterrent" force, the Japanese moved a fleet of submarines into scouting positions in the South China Sea, and ordered two minesweepers, the *Tatsumiya Maru* and the *Nagasa*, to mine the channel between Tioman and the Anambas, the most likely route of the new battleships. Some 1,000 mines were laid the night of December 6/7.[67]

Admiral Phillips had placed a very high priority on air cover and the element of surprise and had done everything he could to achieve both. It did not look like he would get the fighter cover he wanted off Singora on December 10, but the consequences would be mitigated if he could remain undiscovered, and he had maintained the strictest radio silence in order to achieve just that. But he knew his vanishing act would not last forever.

And any lingering hope Admiral Phillips may have had for getting fighter cover for that time when he was discovered was quashed at 1:25 am on December 9 with the following signal from his chief of staff Admiral Palliser in Singapore: FIGHTER PROTECTION ON WEDNESDAY 10TH WILL NOT, REPEAT NOT, BE POSSIBLE.[68]

The reason, as Admiral Palliser later clarified, was the loss of the Kota Bharu airbase, and, for that matter, most of the other airfields in northern Malaya. Palliser also reminded Admiral Phillips of the Japanese aircraft in Indochina and informed him of a request to General MacArthur to use his long-range B-17s to attack the Saigon airbase complex.[69] He had no way of knowing his request was a futile one: after MacArthur's sorry performance on December 8 he had hardly any B-17s left.

So without air cover but still with the element of surprise Force Z continued with the mission, although now Phillips headed more towards Kota Bharu than Singora. At 7:13 am Force Z passed east of the Anambas Islands. Passing west of or through the islands would have been much faster, but there were suspicions that the Japanese had mined the Anambas channel. After passing the Anambas, Force Z turned to a new course of 330 degrees True, later changing to 345 degrees True, still heading for Singora.[70]

But Force Z's luck was changing for the worse. At 1:45 pm Japanese submarine *I-65* spotted the battleships and reported: TWO *REPULSE* TYPE ENEMY BATTLESHIPS SPOTTED … COURSE 340 SPEED 14 KNOTS.[71] *I-65* shadowed Force Z for five hours, not registering on the Royal Navy destroyers' asdic, losing them once in a storm at 3:50 pm, finding them again at 4:52 pm, then losing them for good when the submarine was forced to dive by an approaching aircraft – which turned out to be a Japanese floatplane from the cruiser *Kinu*.[72] Admiral Phillips had no idea he had been found or was being followed.

I-65's report seemed to have bounced around for almost two hours before getting into the hands of someone in authority, but when it did, the reaction in the Malaya Force was electric.[73] Admiral Ozawa, who had incorrectly believed the Royal Navy battleships were still at Singapore, was shocked by the report and immediately ordered the transports, still only half-unloaded, northward back into the Gulf of Siam away from the British force.[74] At 4:00 pm the report reached 22nd Air Flotilla headquarters in Saigon. One of the C5M "Babs" reconnaissance aircraft operating out of Soctrang had flown over

Singapore on a photographing mission, and was diverted to Saigon to have its pictures developed. Its photographs revealed that there were no capital ships at Singapore.[75] *I-65*'s report was thus confirmed.

The 22nd's aircraft were in the process of loading bombs for another attack on Singapore, but after receiving this report they immediately began switching to torpedoes. Although it was getting dark, the threat Force Z posed to the Japanese plan was regarded as so serious that Ozawa ordered Admiral Matsunaga to attempt a night attack in stormy weather. At 6:00 pm 53 Nells and Bettys took off to look for Force Z.[76] But as is often the case in searching the open sea, finding an enemy surface force was easier said than done. The same storm that had prevented the British from finding the Japanese invasion convoy was hampering Japanese attempts at finding Force Z.

But the murky, drizzly conditions broke and the skies cleared at about 5:00 pm, revealing a typical beautiful South Asian sunset and an object that would become ubiquitous in the weeks and months ahead: a Japanese floatplane. This one was an Aichi E13A "Jake," a first-line floatplane. This particular Jake was from the light cruiser *Kinu*, but following behind it was another, from the *Suzuya*, and yet another, from the *Kumano*.[77] They would now play the role of stalking Japanese paparazzi to publicity-shy Force Z. Indeed, the *Kinu*'s floatplane had signaled Admiral Ozawa: FOUND 2 ENEMY BATTLESHIPS. POSITION WSM. COURSE 340 DEGREES. 13 KNOTS. 3 ESCORTING DESTROYERS.[78] The *Kinu*'s report was a surprise to the Japanese admiral, if only because he had no idea she had sent up a search plane.[79] Nevertheless, her report, quickly followed by similar reports from the *Suzuya* and the *Kumano* aircraft, was fortunate for Ozawa, as the earlier reports from *I-65* had been incorrect due to a mistake in her navigation calculations. But these reports came in at a surprisingly steep price. The *Kumano*'s floatplane apparently crashed, *Suzuya*'s crash-landed in the water and had to be rescued by the destroyer *Hamakaze* and the *Yura*'s suffered heavy damage when it hit a mountain on Procondor Island.[80]

At 6:35 pm the destroyer *Tenedos* was sent back to Singapore. This was all according to plan; like her namesake island off the coast of Troy, the *Tenedos* was the smallest of the escorting destroyers and, as expected, was now running low on fuel. *Tenedos* did have additional instructions. She was to contact Admiral Palliser the following morning at 8:00 am to arrange for a destroyer escort to meet Force Z at dawn on December 11 at a point north of the Anambas, where the British expected a Japanese submarine ambush; they were to escort the battleships back to Singapore.[81] What the message did not do was reveal what Phillips planned to do and where he planned to go before heading back to Singapore.

Admiral Phillips now knew he had gone from the hunter to the hunted. The floatplanes were just harbingers of doom, presaging attack from the surface or the air. Now, with surprise lost, he would need all his wits just to get home. Consequently, Phillips decided to give up on attacking Singora or Kota Bharu and to instead return to Singapore. However, at 6:50 pm he actually had Force Z change course to 320 degrees

True towards Singora.[82] This appears to have been a calculated move to throw off the pursuing Japanese floatplanes, with the notable drawback that it took him further away from Singapore.[83]

Just after this course change, however, the veteran destroyer *Electra*, operating off the starboard bow of the *Prince of Wales*, reportedly (at least according to some sources) sighted a flare estimated at 5 miles ahead. Force Z shortly thereafter turned to port away from the flare. The flare could have both illuminated the force and marked its position in the darkness for Japanese forces, thus turning away from it would make sense. However, neither the Admiralty Report nor *Electra* survivor T. J. Cain's respected book on the destroyer mentions it, and there is a question as to whether Admiral Phillips even knew about the flare, whether the *Electra* reported it, or whether the flare caused any reaction by the British.[84]

What is certain is that the flare caused a very definite reaction by the Japanese.

The pilots of the 22nd Air Flotilla were growing tired and dispirited flying over the dark waters of the South China Sea attempting to relocate Force Z, when Lieutenant Takeda Hachiro, whose three-plane group was scouting ahead of the main force, radioed that their quarry had finally been found. To illuminate the enemy battleships in the dark so the Japanese aircraft and warships could find them, his report continued, "We have dropped a flare."[85]

The report was picked up by Admiral Ozawa's flagship *Chokai*, where it also generated much excitement – which rapidly turned into something else when the *Chokai*'s lookouts reported that Lieutenant Takeda's flare had been sighted immediately over their ship.

Amidst rising horror on the bridge of the *Chokai*, Admiral Ozawa frantically flashed repeated messages to a disbelieving Lieutenant Takeda's aircraft: WE ARE CHOKAI. Ozawa then ordered an immediate turn to the north, while he sent to Admiral Matsunaga in Saigon a frantic message: THERE ARE THREE ATTACKING PLANES ABOVE *CHOKAI*. IT IS THE *CHOKAI* UNDER THE FLARE.[86]

With the officers on the *Chokai* in a near panic, Admiral Ozawa sent repeated messages to Saigon to try to forestall the attack. Admiral Matsunaga finally understood the mistake his aircrews were about to make and cancelled the attack and recalled all his aircraft. Obviously, there was too much danger of friendly fire in the dark. Still not believing the order, Lieutenant Takeda continued circling over the terrified *Chokai* until 8:30 pm. Grumbling, the pilots of the 22nd Air Flotilla then headed home, where they would arrive about midnight.

When the flare was dropped, Force Z (or at least the *Electra*) and the *Chokai* had been anywhere from 5 to 25 miles apart.[87] Neither side saw each other in the darkness, on the Japanese side in part because the flare disrupted night vision. The air warning radar on the *Prince of Wales*, which could have detected Lieutenant Takeda's aircraft, had been shut down so its active transmissions would not be detected. The *Prince of Wales'* surface search radar was apparently on, but did not detect the *Chokai*.[88] The near miss here tantalizes the mind with "what ifs" and speculation about the outcome of a night surface engagement, but it is all academic. The two surface forces would never come this close again.

At 8:15 pm, the ominous cruiser floatplanes had disappeared, the flare incident had passed, and Admiral Phillips turned south. Indeed, if his intent in continuing northward was to fool the Japanese, he had succeeded. Unfortunately, he had also fooled the Far East Command.

The appearance of the floatplanes and the change in course probably tipped off the skippers in Force Z that the mission was off, but Admiral Phillips used the flagship's blue Aldis blinker lamps to flash its confirmation at 8:55 pm:

I HAVE MOST REGRETTABLY CANCELLED THE OPERATION, BECAUSE HAVING BEEN LOCATED BY AIRCRAFT, SURPRISE WAS LOST AND OUR TARGET WOULD BE ALMOST CERTAIN TO BE GONE BY THE MORNING AND THE ENEMY FULLY PREPARED FOR US.[89]

This was the proper decision but a bitter disappointment for the British. Captain Tennant of the *Repulse* responded by signaling his agreement with the decision and encouragement to what must have been a dejected Admiral Phillips.[90]

Yet Phillips would be presented with another chance to fulfill his mission when, at 11:55 pm on December 9, he received the following message from his chief of staff:

ENEMY REPORTED LANDING KUANTAN, LATITUDE 03° 50' NORTH.[91]

Kuantan was on the east coast of Malaya, halfway between Singapore and Kota Bharu. If the Japanese were landing at Kuantan, there would be a grave danger that the still significant British forces to the north would be cut off. By this time Phillips must have been exhausted, operating on little sleep and even less food, and possibly suffering from that most insidious and dangerous of addictions: chocolate.[92] But Tom Phillips – little "Tom Thumb" Phillips – was every bit as brave, every bit as tough, every bit the warrior as Achilles. The report was worth checking out. Without signaling Singapore of his intentions – again – Admiral Phillips ordered Force Z to head to Kuantan.

But he was not heading there unnoticed. Sometime around midnight, the Japanese submarine *I-58*, under the command of Lieutenant Commander Kitamura Soshichi, sighted Force Z in the dark heading south. Operating on the surface only some 600yd from her prey – she may have been intermittently detected on the *Prince of Wales*' radar – the submarine got off a contact report, promptly submerged, and, after a fortuitous course change by the battleships, was positioned for an attack, only to be beset by a faulty torpedo tube hatch that left Kitamura and his crew fuming. The delay allowed the *Prince of Wales* to pass by unmolested. By the time she was able to get five torpedoes off at the *Repulse* – a sixth was stuck in the tube – the battlecruiser was headed away from the submarine and presenting a narrow, difficult-to-hit stern profile. Not surprisingly, the torpedoes missed. More than a little disgusted, *I-58* surfaced, reported the position to Saigon, and followed, but the British force was speeding along at 25 knots and finally pulled away out of sight at 3:05 am. *I-58* had gotten off four contact reports, but only two of them reached Saigon – one sent at 2:11 am showing that Force Z had turned away from the Japanese surface forcer, and the last one reporting that the battleships had escaped, but leaving off such minor details as the battleships' position, course, and speed.[93]

In the wee hours of December 10, Admiral Phillips received a cryptic message marked "Personal from First Sea Lord." It stated: AS TORPEDO ATTACK ON SHIPS AT ANCHOR IN JOHORE STRAIT CANNOT BE RULED OUT, I AM SURE YOU HAVE IN MIND M/LD. 02033/41, DATED 22 APRIL 1941, PARAGRAPH 18-(14), WHICH YOU TOOK SO MUCH INTEREST IN.[94]

The document to which Pound referred, "M/LD. 02033/41, Dated 22 April 1941," was titled "Defence of Harbours Against Special Craft." Paragraph 18-(14) stated that ships should be berthed at docks or in basins instead of in stream to avoid torpedo attack. Given that he was at sea, Phillips could not understand the relevance of the signal, muttering something about "the [F]irst Sea Lord going off at half-cock."[95] The precise meaning of the signal remains a mystery. It may indicate that London did not know Phillips had left Singapore, though that remains something of a stretch. It may indicate that the Admiralty had intelligence about the ability of the Japanese aircraft in Saigon to carry torpedoes, though the evidence strongly suggests otherwise.[96] If so, why such vital intelligence would be transmitted in such a vague manner is puzzling.

For that intelligence was indeed vital and very relevant to Admiral Phillips at this time. The reception of *I-58*'s 2:11 am report in Saigon at about 3:15 am spurred a flurry of activity. With Force Z headed south, the surface forces could not catch it and at 6:45 am they were ordered to return to Cam Ranh Bay.[97] Now the only way to stop the British battleships was air power. Admiral Matsunaga ordered ten bombers of the Genzan Air Group, armed with small 250kg (550lb) bombs to maximize their range, to take off at 6:00 am to conduct a sector search for the battleships. But they were just the beginning. Nine bombers and 18 torpedo aircraft of the Genzan Air Group took off at 7:55 am, followed by 18 bombers and 17 torpedo carriers of the Kanoya Air Group at 8:14 am, and then 26 torpedo bombers of the Mihoro Air Group at 8:20 am. After making their rendezvous and organizing into flights of about nine aircraft each, they proceeded independently southward along the 105th meridian. The plan was to have a continuous air attack. The Genzan Air Group would kick things off with a bombing attack from about 8,000ft, followed by its own torpedo aircraft. The Mihoro and Kanoya groups would attack in turn as they arrived.

Unaware that death was now literally in the air but with the sense of forboding that had accompanied this mission from the start, Force Z continued on its probe of Kuantan. At dawn they were 60 miles from the alleged invasion beach. They had thought they had spotted the invasion force at 5:15 am when they spotted black shapes on the horizon to the north, but the objects turned out to be a trawler towing barges. At 6:30 am, *Repulse* reported that they were being shadowed by an "enemy reconnaissance aircraft"; this particular aircraft was never identified and may have been a Royal Air Force Beaufort on a scouting mission out of the soon-to-be-abandoned Kuantan airbase.[98] Finally closing in on the reported landing site, the Royal Navy took a page out of the Japanese playbook and launched a floatplane, a Supermarine Walrus flown by Lieutenant C. R. "Dick" Bateman off the *Prince of Wales* at 7:18 am to scout Kuantan, under orders to not use his radio. The old biplane flew to Kuantan and saw nothing, flew back to the *Prince of Wales* to report NOTHING TO REPORT, and flew off to Singapore, landing at 11:30 am.[99]

Not satisfied with the Walrus's report, Admiral Phillips had Force Z steam close to shore to look at the Kuantan beach area for itself. Again, no activity. One humorous soul on the bridge of the *Repulse* tried to lighten the grim mood with a travelogue: "On the starboard beam, dear listeners, you can see some of the beauty spots of Malaya."[100] Still not satisfied, while the *Repulse* launched her Walrus, flown by Petty Officer William J. T. Crozer, to run an antisubmarine patrol, Phillips ordered the destroyer *Express* into one of the shallow coves to see what she could find.

The persistent feeling of dread intensified. As Reg Woods, manning one of the pom-poms on the *Repulse*, remembered it:

> Early in the morning we arrived off the coast of Kuantan and even though one of *Prince of Wales* Walrus seaplanes had conducted a thorough search of the area the destroyer *Express* was ordered into the cove to evaluate a situation we could see from onboard ship was devoid of all activity[.] [T]his was nothing more than a futile exercise wasting valuable time, and was most probably the final nail in the coffin of both our ships.
>
> As expected, HMS *Express* returned shortly afterwards, reporting "All is quiet as a wet Sunday afternoon." I began to feel uneasy about all this. We were now sitting ducks if an air attack was launched. And it was a relief to leave the area though on our way out we investigated a suspicious looking tug that'd been spotted on reaching Kuantan as it was towing, what looked like troop carrying barges, I think I'm correct in stating about this time our skipper gave orders for one of our Walrus sea planes to be launched.[101]

The text of Lieutenant Cartwright's report on *Express'* expedition into the cove, signaled at 8:45 am, is disputed. Some have the message as Woods relates it above, while another version has the message as COMPLETE PEACE.[102]

Complete peace was not the state of the little destroyer *Tenedos*. All alone off the Anambas – and on the course to Singapore that Force Z would have been using if not for the Kuantan interlude – she had reported in to Admiral Palliser as ordered, but she soon had far more immediate concerns. At 9:52 am one of the Genzan Air Group's scout aircraft found her and dropped its two 250kg (550lb) bombs. Both missed. Skipper Lieutenant Richard Dyer immediately reported the attack, and in short order made two more reports (at 10:05 am and 10:20 am) of a far more troubling sight: the massive Japanese air armada looking for Force Z. Because Admiral Phillips had turned toward Kuantan, the 22nd Air Flotilla was looking in the wrong place – for now. But the *Tenedos* did not escape their notice. One bombing wing of the Genzan Air Group, Lieutenant

Nikaido's squadron of Nells, mistook the little old destroyer for a big battleship and launched its attack with 500kg (1,100lb) bombs. Through skillful maneuvering by the old ship, all nine bombs missed. At 10:30 am Dyer signaled: ENEMY AIRCRAFT ARE DROPPING BOMBS. But *Tenedos* had survived, Dyer finding the experience "exciting rather than frightening."[103]

Lieutenant Dyer's radio warnings were heard on the *Electra* and the *Prince of Wales*, but apparently not in Singapore.[104] They should have told Admiral Phillips that there were now large numbers of heavily armed Japanese aircraft in the area south of his position – that is, between him and his base in Singapore – and they were looking for him. They should have told him that the clock was ticking and time was running out. But he was determined to find out just what was happening at Kuantan even if it killed him. After his floatplane had found nothing, his own flagship had found nothing, and his destroyer scout had found nothing, Phillips *still* was not satisfied that there was nothing at Kuantan, that the invasion report had been wrong. At the suggestion of Captain Tennant, Phillips turned the two battleships back to the east to investigate that menacing-looking trawler towing barges they had spotted earlier – as if the Japanese might be hiding the thousands of troops and hundreds of tons of equipment for an invasion of Kuantan inside this little trawler and her barges.[105] One history called this action, "a ludicrous risk to take on an errand that one destroyer could have performed."[106] As the hours had ticked down to minutes, the minutes ticked down to seconds, and those precious seconds ticked down to their fate, the only Allied capital ships for thousands of miles were checking out a trawler.

That fate was now at hand, over the ships in plain sight, in the form of a Mitsubishi G3M bomber piloted by Ensign Hoashi Masame of the Genzan Air Group, one of the ten Nells sent up to scout ahead of the main force. At 10:15 am Hoashi sent out the first of three messages that formed the death warrant for the *Prince of Wales* and *Repulse*:

ENEMY FLEET SPOTTED AT LAT 4N. LONG. 103.55E. COURSE 60 DEGREES.

ENEMY FORCE CHANGED COURSE TO 30 DEGREES.

ENEMY FORCE ESCORTED BY THREE DESTROYERS. ORDER OF FORMATION IS KING-TYPE BATTLESHIP, *REPULSE*.[107]

The other pilots had trouble deciphering his message, however, and Saigon directed him to broadcast in the clear, acting as a beacon for the air flotilla.[108] For their part, Force Z picked up Ensign Hoashi's signal, as did the *Tenedos*, which sped up to reach Singapore more quickly. Perhaps not unexpectedly, Air Command in Singapore, the only ones who could actually protect Force Z with aircraft, did not pick up the signal that would have alerted them that their capital ships were now in trouble. The *Prince of Wales* spotted Hoashi's aircraft, and the *Repulse* picked up more aircraft on radar bearing 220 degrees – to the southwest.[109]

After the intense shiphunt, its aircrews now tired, its aircraft low on fuel, the Japanese 22nd Air Flotilla had found their prey in the *Prince of Wales* and the *Repulse*. The long morning search had cost the Japanese aircraft most of their fuel, so they had no chance to coordinate their attack, but instead had to attack on arrival and then retire. But a fuel gauge nearing "E" did not reduce the deadliness of their attacks.

The Royal Navy had never been one to run from a fight. From the flagship came the general order: ASSUME FIRST DEGREE ANTIAIRCRAFT READINESS. On the *Prince of Wales*, the normally happy occasion of the distribution of the rum ration was ended by loudspeakers' amplification of the bugle call signifying, "Action stations. Repel aircraft."[110]

The *Prince of Wales* and *Repulse* both hoisted the giant White Ensign, used only in battle, on their masts; the White Ensign was an old tradition, like the Roman Eagle, signifying pride and power. By another flag, this one a signal in the form of a blue pendant, Admiral Phillips ordered SHIPS TURN TOGETHER 30 DEGREES TO STARBOARD, which brought them to 135 degrees True.[111] The *Prince of Wales* was now headed southeast, with the *Repulse* on her starboard quarter. At 11:13 am, the radar contacts came into visual range: eight Nell bombers of the Mihoro Air Group under the command of Lieutenant Shirai Yoshima approached off the starboard bow at an altitude of about 10,000ft. Antiaircraft fire control on both battleships had been hard at work on their calculations (involving factors like range, speed, and altitude) to feed to their gunners manning the antiaircraft guns, the state-of-the-art 5.25in high-angle dual purpose and the 40mm Bofors on the *Prince of Wales*, and the Norman Conquest-vintage 4in guns on the *Repulse*. Now all ships of Force Z, except the *Vampire*, which on the port side was outranged, opened fire to starboard,[112] completely ineffectively. Phillips' starboard turn was throwing off the calculations for the antiaircraft fire and even masked some of the guns. The British admiral realized his mistake and tried to correct it with another signal SHIPS TURN TOGETHER 50 DEGREES TO PORT.[113] Once again, the turn fouled the antiaircraft guns. The Japanese aircraft were taking no evasive action whatsoever but the violent maneuvering had ruined the antiaircraft guns' chance to turn back or even mildly inconvenience the Nells. They stayed in their tight formation "with complete disregard for anti-aircraft fire."[114] Now they were into their bombing runs.

These Nells each carried two 250kg (550lb) bombs. Because these were not large munitions, Lieutenant Shirai ignored the *Prince of Wales* and concentrated in a high-level attack on the *Repulse*, which, like a typical battlecruiser, was less heavily armored. Soon after, at 11:22 am, the old ship was surrounded by eight fingers of water – the Nells only dropped one bomb each on this first run – seemingly reaching up to grab her like the tentacles of a South China Sea Kraken. But the Kraken would have to wait; the splashes subsided revealing the *Repulse* with only a small curl of smoke to reward Shirai's efforts. One bomb had fallen to starboard, seven more to port. Only one had hit, going through the portside hangar to explode in the Marines' mess. This caused a small fire in the catapult deck and cracked a steam pipe, but the damage was negligible; it did not impair the *Repulse*'s combat effectiveness and was quickly repaired.

The Nells roared overhead and prepared to make another pass, but unknown to the British, disgusted that they had not brought down any of their tormenters, their antiaircraft guns were actually taking a toll. Five of Lieutenant Shirai's bombers had been hit, two so badly that they had to immediately return to base. The remaining six disappeared, apparently forming up for another attack.[115]

Now Force Z had time to breathe and take stock. The Japanese attack had drawn blood but it was merely a flesh wound. Admiral Phillips had not handled his ships well, and he knew it. His cumbersome fleet maneuvers had spoiled the antiaircraft targeting and left his gunners fuming. Willing to admit his mistakes, Phillips ordered an increase in speed to 25 knots and the ships to act independently in future attacks.[116]

The lull was short-lived, maybe ten minutes. The radar on the *Prince of Wales* picked up an even larger formation of aircraft approaching from the southeast. At 11:38 am they came into view low over the horizon: two formations totaling 17 Nells from the Genzan Air Group.[117] They crossed the bows of Force Z, continuing to lose altitude. Admiral Phillips watched from his chair on the *Prince of Wales*' captain's bridge, appearing "very composed, very calm," while Captain Leach and several other officers stood nearby, also watching the unfolding spectacle.

It was Lieutenant Commander R. F. Harland, the ship's torpedo specialist, who spoke the unspeakable: "I think they're going to do a torpedo attack."

Admiral Phillips' reply, to the extent Harland remembers it, was incredulous.

"No, they're not. There are no torpedo aircraft about."[118]

But making a fairly strong argument otherwise was the steadily decreasing altitude of these new attackers and, more importantly, the large, steel, cylindrical-type things mounted under the fuselages of the Nells. Destroyer *Express* noticed, signaling: PLANES APPROACHING HAVE TORPEDOES.[119] The bridge of the flagship filled with shock and dread.

As author Alan Matthews, historian for the Force Z Survivors Association, later described it, "They were torpedo bombers, the likes of which no British serviceman had ever seen before … In a few short minutes, Force Z was about to suffer the most horrific aerial onslaught at the hands of the Japanese war machine."[120]

These Japanese bombers were indeed carrying torpedoes, in this case the deadly Type 91 aerial torpedo, weighing about 800kg (1,763lb), with a warhead of approximately 150kg (330lb). They were set to run at a blazing 42 knots, which they could do for a full 2,000m (2,190yd). As it would prove throughout the war, the Type 91, like most of the excellent Japanese torpedoes, was a devastating weapon unmatched in Allied arsenals. The Nells, coordinated by Commander Nakanishi, sorted themselves off the port bow into groups of three and approached in a vast arc. One group of nine, commanded by Lieutenant Ishihara Kaoru, made for the *Prince of Wales*; Nakanishi was a passenger in this group, probably in Ishihara's plane. The other group of seven Nells (one had been forced to return to base by mechanical troubles), led by Lieutenant Takai Sadao, headed for the *Repulse*.[121]

The flagship braced for the incoming Mitsubishis. All eight high-angle 5.25in antiaircraft guns on the port side had perfect firing solutions, only to be delayed by a fire control slow to give the order to open fire, amid some indications that fire control was having technical difficulties. But open fire they did, firing salvoes at individual aircraft, none of which seemed to be hit.[122]

The British had never seen a torpedo attack like this, never seen torpedo-carrying aircraft like these Mitsubishis. The Japanese Naval Air Force had elevated torpedo attacks to a science with their pilots the best trained in the world while the aircraft and torpedoes themselves were also unrivalled.

The Royal Navy's own torpedo bomber, the Fairey Swordfish, was legendary, beloved and murderously effective, as the Italians had found out at Taranto, which the Japanese had used as a blueprint for Pearl Harbor. But the Swordfish was also an aged biplane with a ridiculously slow speed of less than 100 miles per hour, and had to drop its torpedo from an altitude of no higher than 50ft. The British gunners had spent a lot of time practicing how to shoot down torpedo bombers against the Swordfish, but all that practice was utterly useless against the blazing-fast Nell, coming in at a speed of 150 knots – about 180 miles per hour.[123]

The 5.25s switched to area fire, sending up a wall of shrapnel. Still the Japanese came. The 40mm Bofors, manned by Royal Marines, joined in. Still the Japanese came. The 40mm pom-poms joined in, spewing 2lb shells. Still the Japanese came. The Oerlikons and machine guns joined in. Still the Japanese came. All the *Prince of Wales'* antiaircraft armament that could be brought to bear to port was roaring, sending up a storm of white-hot metal, anything to stop the incoming Nells. Still the Japanese came. They were relentless.[124]

Now it was up to Captain Leach. He needed to present an inviting target – the large beam profile of the *Prince of Wales*, usually perpendicular to incoming torpedo pilots – long enough to get the Japanese pilots on their necessarily long approach to commit to dropping their torpedoes, but not so long that he could not turn his ship to parallel the course of the torpedoes and thus present a small bow or stern profile – a tactic called "combing the torpedo tracks" or some slight variation thereof – and thus reduce the chances of a hit to almost nothing. There was no science to it. It was all observation, gut, and practice. How long he held his course, when the enemy dropped their torpedoes, when he turned, how fast he turned – that would determine whether the *Prince of Wales* would escape unscathed.

Finally, Captain Leach ordered "hard-a-port." The wheel was thrown over. At 25 knots, the *Prince of Wales* heeled over to starboard as the hull began to turn to port.[125] The turn threw off the aim of one of Lieutenant Ishihara's Nells, which headed for the *Repulse*.[126] The destroyer *Express*, in the pilots' line of approach, apparently forced two of the Nells to drop too early; one of the torpedoes exploded on hitting the water, another seemed to pass under the destroyer.[127] But the remainder dropped their deadly fish from 650–1,650yd from the *Prince of Wales*. In a little more than two minutes, the torpedoes would reach the battleship's position which the Nells themselves would do in approximately 30 seconds.

Unable to turn away fast enough, the Mitsubishis roared low over the flagship, raking her decks with machine-gun fire in an effort to suppress her antiaircraft defenses. The indignant British gunners returned the favor, but now they began to have problems; the ammunition in the pom-poms was separating and causing the barrels to jam. After this exchange the Nells flew off to starboard and back to base, except for one, piloted by Petty Officer Kawada Katsujiro, which crashed into the sea with no survivors, a victim of the *Prince of Wales*' guns.[128] Of the remaining eight aircraft, three were damaged, but none seriously.

The two minutes finally ended. Captain Leach's "hard-a-port" had enabled the flagship to avoid the Japanese torpedoes.

All but one.

At 11:44 am, the *Prince of Wales* suffered an explosion on the starboard side near the giant aft quadruple "Y" turret, sending a column of water 200ft into the air. The battleship seemed to be lifted from the water, "bounc[ing]" or "whipp[ing]" several times according to some. Gunner's Mate Alan McIvor, manning one of the portside 5.25in gun turrets, described the terrifying noise caused by this explosion:

> A matter of seconds before being hit, we'd been training our gun on one of the planes that had taken part in this first attack. Suddenly there was a tremendous explosion. I can best describe the noise as tons of plate glass shattering on a pavement. Immediately, we lost all power to our gun which was stopped whilst training aft.[129]

Ominously, power was immediately lost throughout most of the ship. Most disturbingly, a massive shudder, "like a boy running a stick along a corrugated iron fence, only amplified," went through the ship for about thirty seconds.[130]

In all the annals of World War II, of all the torpedo attacks across the Pacific, the Atlantic, and the Mediterranean, it is difficult to find a single non-fatal torpedo hit on an undamaged capital ship or cruiser that was even remotely as catastrophic as this one.

The *Prince of Wales* had been hit right where her outer port propeller shaft – the farthest to port of the battleships' four screws – exited the hull. The engines delivered power to turn the ship's propellers through a long shaft contained in a passage that resembled a giant pipe. The shaft went through several bulkheads, with flexible glands maintaining water-tight seals between the shaft and each bulkhead. The shaft exited the hull and continued along outside and mostly under the hull, connected to it by two support struts that resembled the letter "A" (thus earning it the alternative name "A-bracket") just before terminating in the propeller itself. The torpedo had left a 4x6m hole by the shaft, badly weakened the support struts, and damaged the shaft itself, causing the shaft to spin off center and eventually to windmill. It was the propeller shaft spinning off center that had caused the giant tremor.[131]

It was a catastrophic injury. Before it could be shut down, the off-center shaft, turning at maximum revolutions to propel the flagship at 25 knots, destroyed the glands that prevented sea water from entering the ship through the shaft passage's interior bulkheads. The bulkheads themselves were severely damaged. Water rushed in through the damaged shaft passage. Pumps could not handle the flooding and forced the evacuation of "B" Engine Room. The flooding extended to the shaft passage itself and proceeded along the path of the shaft into the interior of the ship, including "Y" Action Machinery Room, the port Diesel Dynamo Room, "Y" Boiler Room, the Central Auxiliary Machinery Room, and a number of other compartments aft that provided the ship with power and propulsion.[132]

The effect was immediate. The *Prince of Wales* quickly took in 2,400 tons of water, her stern quickly settling by 5ft with an 11.5-degree list to port. And that was just the beginning.

Most of the *Prince of Wales'* stern compartments were now without power and auxiliary electrical power was offline, meaning no internal communications, ventilation, steering, and pumps, and no training and elevation of the 5.25in and 2lb gun mounts.[133] Two of those 5.25in turrets that were still able to fire were on the starboard side forward, but now the list to port meant that they could not depress low enough to engage torpedo aircraft.[134]

Loss of power to the pumps meant that she could not pump out the water rushing into her hull. Loss of power to the electrical steering gear meant that the battleship could only steer by using her engines; that is, varying the speed of her port and starboard propellers. But the torpedo had already made that almost impossible. At 11:50 am, much of the damaged outboard port propeller shaft shattered and broke off, carrying with it the struts and the propeller itself. The debris got caught in the inboard port propeller, damaging it and forcing its shutdown at 12:02 pm. Essentially the *Prince of Wales* could no longer steer and was left in a very slow port turn.

Loss of power to the internal communications also created chaos. Messages had to be hand-delivered by runners. Damage control could no longer quickly respond to the quickly deteriorating situation or properly allocate personnel and resources. Indeed, the crew of the *Prince of Wales* may never have been totally conscious of the damage done to their ship.

All this had been caused by one torpedo, one torpedo that had not even produced the massive explosion witnessed on the port side. As the torpedo had struck where the hull curved under the ship most of the explosion was under the ship, lifting it up and magnifying the damage. The explosion everyone had seen was a second torpedo detonated by the shockwaves through the water caused by the first.[135]

In short, the state-of-the-art battleship *Prince of Wales*, commissioned less than a year ago, was maimed, reduced to a crawl, and unable to defend herself, by a single torpedo. With armed enemy aircraft still inbound, her situation was grave. One survivor said of the crew, "Everyone had the same expression on their faces – wide-eyed and wondering what was going to happen next as the ship began to take a heavy list to port."[136] On the bridge, Admiral Phillips and Captain Leach seemed to say little about the damage caused by the torpedo hit and appeared "somewhat stunned."[137]

Meanwhile, the *Repulse* was by no means escaping Japanese attention. The six remaining Nells of Lieutenant Shirai's flight from the Mihoro Air Group now reappeared to drop their 250kg (550lb) bombs from 12,000ft on the *Repulse*. Although the bombs fell in a tight group around her, they all missed. Meanwhile, Lieutenant Takai's torpedo attack had been delayed because he, by his own admission, was caught in a momentary panic that he was about to attack the *Kongo* and needed his fellow pilots to convince him that the target was indeed the *Repulse*.[138] Finally, at 11:56 am, Takai's group of seven Nells, plus one from Lieutenant Ishihara's group, bored in on the port side of the *Repulse*.[139] It is believed that a second group of eight Nells, these under the command of Lieutenant Takahashi Katsusaki of the Mihoro Air Group, attacked at about the same time, probably immediately behind Takai. The battlecruiser trained her 4in antiaircraft guns – of which she had 20 – to port to engage the new attackers. However, they were much older than their counterparts on the *Prince of Wales* (many of them were hand-operated, which given her loss of power might have come in handy on the flagship) and simply could not put up the volume of fire of their stricken comrade, so the Nells just blasted through. The pom-poms joined in, but like their counterparts on the *Prince of Wales* they jammed owing to separated cartridges.[140] The battlecruiser's antiaircraft barrage here was hardly impressive.

However, Captain Tennant seems to have determined that maneuver was the best way to beat a torpedo attack. Tennant was a master of seamanship and remarkably cool under pressure. Saying nothing, he would simply stroll from side to side of the *Repulse*'s bridge, indicating with circular motions of his hands which way he wanted the wheel to be turned.[141] Like a bullfighter he held the red cape of the *Repulse*'s beam side just long enough to get the bullish Japanese pilots to commit. Then Tennant pulled the cape away by simply turning *Repulse* to port toward her attackers. Again, the Nells flew low over the battlecruiser and raked her decks with machine-gun fire, causing casualties, but thanks to Tennant's handling the *Repulse* combed all the torpedoes.

What followed Lieutenant Takai's attack was something of a lull in Force Z's midday nightmare. The situation on the *Prince of Wales* was indeed grim. The shaft passage was now a veritable pipe pumping thousands of tons of seawater into compartments that the battleship's designers had never thought to be so vulnerable and thus knocking out multiple redundant systems at once – especially those involving the electrical system.

The flooding, simply coming in through the shaft, had been so severe that counterflooding of the starboard voids ordered by Captain Leach only managed to knock 2.5 degrees off the list.[142] The ship's lights had gone out and now the interior had only dim illumination from blue emergency lights. The rudder was still intact, but electric steering was out and manual steering was almost impossible with internal communications offline; the *Prince of Wales* now could only plod forward at 15 knots in a slight port turn. The ventilation system was without power and the atmosphere below decks, which had not been good to begin with, was now unbearably, dangerously, hot and stifling, causing the damage control teams to suffer heat exhaustion and requiring their constant rotation.[143]

The damage control situation in the *Prince of Wales* was in a state of chaos. Damage control parties managed to connect electrical cables to some of the silent antiaircraft guns and they started in setting up a flooding boundary to confine the flooding to the stern area, but they seemed to accomplish little else. This was where the lack of a proper working-up period may have crippled damage control efforts. The working-up period is essential for getting the ship's parts and crews to operate effectively together, working out the ship's kinks, its procedures, any problems or defects. It involved training to the extent that duties became instinct, so much so that crews could perform them blindfolded – literally – which is precisely what was needed in the *Prince of Wales* at this point.

The loss of internal communication further prevented any effective coordination of damage control efforts. For example, those damage control teams connecting power cables to the guns might have been better utilized rerouting power from the three functioning dynamos running from the still-effective boiler rooms, which would have restored electrical power to most of the ship. The various officers and chiefs on the ship undoubtedly gave full effort to save the ship, but without adequate knowledge as to the *Prince of Wales* itself – where they were supposed to go, what they were supposed to do – they often ended up spinning their wheels. Survivors reported many, many crewmen on the *Prince of Wales* during this time simply standing around or even sleeping. As one survivor later described it, "There seemed to be lots of people with nothing to do and nowhere to go; many laid [sic] down and seemed to sleep on mess tables and stools."[144] They wanted to save their ship, but with no practice and no communications, no one could tell them what to do. The *Prince of Wales* was in a pitiful state, but she was not hopeless. Two of her four engines and their propeller shafts still functioned. Neither her guns nor, apparently, her rudder were damaged. There was still a chance to save her and get back to Singapore.

During this down time, Captain Tennant signaled Admiral Phillips that the *Repulse* had damage from her bomb hit under control. He also asked Phillips if his wireless was still in action, in case he wanted the *Repulse* to relay any reports to Singapore. For an ominously long time, there was no reply from the flagship. Finally, at 12:10 pm, the *Prince of Wales* responded by hoisting two black balls from a yardarm, signifying "not under control."[145] It was an "ominous portent of annihilation that was observed with dismay from the bridge of the *Repulse*," now some 3 miles away due to her wild maneuvering, who reduced speed to 20 knots and closed in on the maimed flagship to see if she could help.[146]

Worse, to Captain Tennant's horror, the flagship had not even sent out a signal informing Singapore of their plight. He had broken Admiral Phillips' precious radio silence at 11:58 am, to send a message: OEAB, the code for ENEMY AIRCRAFT BOMBING.[147]

This signal reached the operations room at Air Command, Singapore, at 12:19 pm, the first indication they had received of Force Z's location and status since its departure on December 8.[148] Air Command was prepared for this emergency, at least as prepared as it could be. Royal Air Force No. 453 Squadron was sitting at the Sembawang on Singapore Island waiting for just such a call to provide Force Z with air cover – and frustrated that they had not yet received it.[149] Given the rather vague instructions to "look after an important ship which was being bombed," 11 Brewster Buffalos under the command of Flight Lieutenant Vigors took off at 12:26 pm, just seven minutes after reception of Tennant's signal.[150] But could they get there in time?

By Aldis lamp, Admiral Phillips signaled the *Repulse*: HAVE YOU BEEN HIT BY TORPEDOES? Captain Tennant responded: THANKS TO PROVIDENCE HAVE SO FAR DODGED NINETEEN TORPEDOES.[151]

The Japanese were amazed that no British fighters had shown up; they would do everything they could to take advantage of this unexpected good fortune while it lasted. Saigon ordered Ensign Hoashi to remain in contact with Force Z and he did so, lurking over the battleships like an angel of death calling in more and more demons. At around 12:20 pm, just as the *Repulse* was approaching to assist the stricken *Prince of Wales*, and just as the Buffalos at Sembawang were preparing to take off, came yet another attack.

Low on the horizon off the starboard bow of the *Repulse* appeared more incoming aircraft. These were from the Kanoya Air Group, 26 torpedo-carrying Mitsubishi G4Ms under the command of Lieutenant Miyauchi Shichizo.[152] Miyauchi had almost missed Force Z entirely. They had trouble following Ensign Hoashi's beacon and were enclosed by clouds. Fuel running dangerously low, Miyauchi was about to give up and head back to base when the *Repulse*'s biplane was spotted on its antisubmarine patrol. Petty Officer Crozer had not found any submarines, but had spotted the tug they had seen earlier – again – and, because he had been ordered to not use his radio, was flying back to make a report. The Mitsubishis followed the Walrus, which was slow and lightly armed and thus of no use in combat, right back to Force Z.[153] This would not be the last time in the Pacific War that an antisubmarine patrol would actually lead an enemy airstrike to its target.[154]

The deadly Bettys of the Kanoya Air Group were divided into three squadrons under the command of Lieutenants Nabeta Yoshikichi, Iki Haruki, and Higashi Moritaka.[155] Lieutenant Commander Miyauchi was in one of Nabeta's aircraft. These aircraft were carrying an upgraded model of the Type 91 aerial torpedo, the Model 2 with a 205kg (450lb) warhead.[156]

About 3 miles away from the Force Z, they split into two formations: one with 17 Bettys from the squadrons of Lieutenants Nabeta and Higashi, which made for the *Prince of Wales*, the other with nine of Lieutenant Iki's aircraft seeming to hold back behind the first group. The approach of the Betty bombers in this attack was somewhat haphazard, although this lack of coordination proved to be effective. The fuel situation of Commander Miyauchi's pilots was so desperate that he may have ordered them simply to drop their torpedoes at will. The Mitsubishis of Nabeta's and Higashi's squadrons rocketed in towards the flagship's exposed starboard side.

The *Prince of Wales*, the Royal Navy's most powerful warship, was now a sitting target – dazed, battered, bleeding, shuffling along at 15 knots. Her engineers managed to coax a few more revolutions from the two of her engines that still functioned to get the waterlogged battleship moving a little faster, but she was still practically incapable of steering. The best that could be said of her plight was that at least this attack was coming on her starboard side, where she still had two of her 5.25in turrets under power. But even that was of limited value: due to the list, the guns could not depress enough to hit the attackers. The Royal Navy gunners, in desperation, tried to train the other two starboard turrets, still without power, with ropes and chains. It was no use; they were too heavy to move. Only some of the pom-poms had power, and these jammed, again, because of ammunition separation. The *Prince of Wales* was unable to fight.

With little in the way of antiaircraft fire to discourage or even mildly inconvenience them, the Japanese pilots held their torpedoes until what was considered point-blank range: 500m (nearly 550yd). Eleven of the Bettys actually broke off their attack and now made for the *Repulse*, but the remaining six dropped from a place where it was almost impossible to miss. The crew of the *Prince of Wales* could only watch helplessly as the torpedoes streaked ever closer; with her steering offline, the battleship could take no evasive action. They braced for impact.

At 12:23 pm the flagship was rocked by four explosions a few seconds apart. One was a torpedo tearing straight through the bow underneath the anchors, leaving a hole 7yd in diameter. The second was a torpedo planting itself in the hill near "B" turret, which, when combined with the previous flooding of the starboard voids to correct the list, drastically increased the flooding woes of the battleship. A third seems to have been another "sympathetic" detonation of a torpedo caused by the shockwaves from one of the earlier hits. The fourth, and perhaps the worst, was a torpedo detonation near the "Y" (aft main) turret; whether the torpedo struck the ship or just exploded close by is not clear, but it did add to the *Prince of Wales'* torment – it left an 12x4yd hole and bent the outboard starboard propeller shaft inward, wedging the propeller between the starboard inboard shaft and the hull, damaging the propellers again. Now the battleship was down to one screw – that one with a shaft already damaged by the outboard screw – and her speed was cut to 8 knots.[157] This hit also ruined damage control efforts to set up the flooding boundary to limit the flooding to the stern. Before the hit the stern trim had increased to more than 8ft; it was now only going to get worse as the stern began actually to sink. Whatever chances the *Prince of Wales* had had for survival were now gone.

And now *Repulse* was having serious problems. The flagship had been on the *Repulse's* port beam when the Kanoya attack had started. Eight of the Bettys that had broken off their attack on the *Prince of Wales* now joined Lieutenant Iki's bombers in a rather disorganized attack on the *Repulse*. They seemed to simply converge on the battlecruiser, with most coming from starboard, but Iki's flyers seemed to hold back. Once again, Captain Tennant held out the red cape and succeeded in getting eight Kanoya Bettys – probably three of Lieutenant Higashimori's and five of Lieutenant Nabeta's – to commit to attacking his starboard beam, dropping their torpedoes at a range of 2,500yd; then he pulled the red cape away and turned to starboard to present the narrow bow profile and comb their torpedoes.

Except that this time, in pulling the red cape away from these bombers, he was forced to hold it out for three others that had been making a torpedo run at the *Prince of Wales*. They pulled away at the last minute and made for the inviting target of the *Repulse's* port beam, also dropping their torpedoes at a range of 2,500yd.

Whether intentional or not, the Japanese had launched what was known as an "anvil" attack – dropping torpedoes from two different directions, usually the beam and the bow – and had executed it perfectly. The *Repulse* was trapped. If she turned to avoid these new torpedoes she would present her large beam for those that had been dropped earlier. Captain Tennant attempted some limited maneuvers but there was largely nothing he could do. "Stand by for torpedo!" he ordered over the loudspeakers.[158]

Shortly afterwards, the *Repulse* suffered a large explosion amidships on the port side. But the battlecruiser barely noticed it; it had struck the "torpedo blister," a steel bubble that extends outward from the main hull to absorb torpedo hits without causing structural damage. Captain Tennant's damage control teams were very efficient and limited the damage. She continued to move about at 25 knots.

The *Repulse* had been very fortunate that the torpedo had struck the blister, and that a second torpedo had just missed her, passing right under the overhang of her bow.[159] She could not have known that her luck had run out.

At 12:20 pm Admiral Phillips himself sent out a distress signal: EMERGENCY. HAVE BEEN STRUCK BY A TORPEDO ON PORT SIDE. NYT W 0222 R06 4 TORPEDOES. *REPULSE* HIT BY ONE TORPEDO. SEND DESTROYERS.[160]

Historians remain somewhat puzzled by this message; Phillips had maintained the all-important radio silence in order to ensure the Japanese did not know his position yet he had not broken it for a further two hours once his position had been discovered. Moreover, since Force Z was under air attack, conventional wisdom suggests that Admiral Phillips should have called for air cover instead of destroyers.

The nine Mitsubishi G4Ms of Lieutenant Iki remained to enter the fray. He had planned to attack the *Prince of Wales*, but since he noticed she had been hit by more torpedoes, he decided to target the plucky *Repulse*. He ordered his squadron to split up to make a pincer attack; he had not originally planned to make such an attack, but the battlecruiser's movements had forced him to change sides.[161] Six would work their way around to the starboard side, approaching in two groups of three aircraft each, each group approaching at a different angle, while Iki would lead three to attack the port side.[162]

While her crew had resented the publicity surrounding the *Prince of Wales* – sullenly dubbing their ship the "HMS Anonymous" – and equally resented playing second fiddle everywhere to this "Jonah," the *Repulse* was an unusually proud and happy ship.[163] They knew each other and they knew their ship. They had complete confidence in their captain and he in them. They firmly believed that, despite the age of the *Repulse*, they had the better ship and the better crew. In fact, they believed they had the best ship in the fleet. And now, in the last hour, the last minutes of her life and the lives of many of her crew, the *Repulse* and her crew would get their chance to prove it.

The *Repulse* was magnificent, running like a well-oiled, well-designed machine that belied her age. Spotters picked out the aircraft. Antiaircraft fire control called out the distance, range, and altitude to the battlecruiser's gunners. In a perfectly executed variation of the anvil attack, the six of Lieutenant Iki's pilots that had made for the *Repulse's* starboard side dropped at about 2,500yd and left, while Lieutenant Iki himself and his two wingmates made their high-speed torpedo run on the port side, closing to 600yd before dropping their deadly tin fish. The ancient 4in antiaircraft guns and the close-range 40mm pom-poms (and one particular 20mm Oerlikon manned with gusto by Australian Midshipman Robert Ian Davies) of the *Repulse* roared in defiance.[164] And they exacted a price. Iki was able to turn away from the battlecruiser after dropping his torpedo, but his wingmates tried to fly over the ship – and over the No. 2 pom-pom, an 8-barrelled gun near the stern commanded by Sub-Lieutenant R. A. W. Pool.[165] The aircraft of one, Petty Officer Momoi Stoshi, simply exploded. The gunners observed the pilot of the other, Petty Officer Taue Ryochi, with an astonished look on his face when he realized he had a fire in the rear of the fuselage – a preview of the Betty's later nickname, the "Lit Cigar," because of her propensity to catch fire.[166] The bomber crashed shortly thereafter.

Meanwhile, on the bridge of the *Repulse*, spotters pointed out the incoming torpedo wakes, six from starboard, three from port. The wily Captain Tennant, with the help of his navigation officer Lieutenant Commander H. B. C. Gill, used every maneuvering trick he had to avoid them. "I found dodging the torpedoes quite interesting and entertaining until in the end they started to come in from all directions and they were too much for me," Tennant would later say.[167] The *Repulse*, the old lady, pirouetted like a prima ballerina.

The loss of his wingmates had not been in vain for Lieutenant Iki. At least two of his flight's torpedoes struck. One hit near the engine room and one, believed to have been dropped by Lieutenant Iki himself, near the stern. Iki's torpedo was especially bad, jamming the rudder while the *Repulse* was in a starboard turn. The battlecruiser's damage control was efficient and she could still make 20 knots but was only able to steam in circles; she wasn't going anywhere. Almost as an afterthought, one torpedo struck the starboard side near Boiler Room "E."[168]

Very few ships can survive four torpedo hits. The *Repulse* was at an additional disadvantage because her aging design was lacking in watertight compartmentalization. She was disemboweled, quickly developing a 12-degree list to port that showed no signs of abating. No amount of pumping, no damage control, efficient or otherwise, could save her now. In five minutes, the *Repulse* had gone from dancing to dying.

Captain Tennant ordered over the ship's loudspeakers, "All hands on deck. Prepare to abandon ship, God be with you."[169] The Carley floats, a type of life boat, were released. The *Repulse* rolled heavily to port. Tennant described the end:

> Men were now pouring up on deck. They had all been warned 24 hours before to carry or wear their lifesaving apparatus. When the ship had a 30° list to port, I looked over the starboard side

of the bridge and saw the Commander and two or three hundred men collecting on the starboard side. I never saw the slightest sign of panic or ill discipline. I told them from the bridge how well they had fought [for] the ship, and wished them good luck. The ship hung for at least a minute and a half to two minutes with a list of about 60° or 70° to port and then rolled over at [12:33 pm].[170]

Men tried to slide down her starboard side into the sea; stepping off the sinking port side was not recommended, since they could get caught in the ship's superstructure or suction when she sank. Some had the misfortune of sliding down the starboard side and landing in the water in the torpedo hole, which brought them back into the ship. As the *Repulse* continued rolling, the holes made by the torpedoes appeared, followed by the torpedo bulge; both were hazards to crew sliding down the hull. Eventually she was completely on her port beam ends – her port side – and her remaining crew had to stand on the exposed starboard side.

The superstructure – her masts, smokestacks, and topside compartments – dragged the *Repulse* further to port until her stern was exposed, with her propellers still turning. The stern then slipped under, leaving the bow jutting into the air for a few more seconds until it disappeared as well. As one crewman described it, "She went down quite peacefully, as though glad it was over."[171] Another one said, "It was a sad end to a very happy and efficient commission; but it was also a clean and gallant end to a beautiful old lady."[172]

Captain Tennant was still on board. He had made it to "B" Deck, which he figured was a good place to enter the water. As the water swept over him, the *Repulse* took him down in one final embrace before, lungs bursting, he floated to the surface. If his crew had any say in the matter, they were not going to let him drown. As soon as he was spotted on the surface, he was pulled aboard one of the Carley floats and ended up on the *Vampire*. The gallant Midshipman Davies was never seen again.

Admiral Phillips had paid attention to the *Repulse*'s plight and at 12:28 pm had ordered the *Electra* and *Vampire* to her assistance. Now all they could do was pick up survivors. They found the surviving men of the *Repulse* in the water giving three cheers for their captain and their ship, "the Old Girl," and even singing "Roll Out the Barrel."[173]

Still remaining were two squadrons of Nells from the Mihoro Air Group, one of nine under Lieutenant Ohira Yoshiro, the other of eight under Lieutenant Takeda. Each aircraft was armed with a single 500kg (1,100lb) bomb, and all were about to take their turn. And now the agony of the *Prince of Wales* was about to end permanently.

Lieutenant Ohira was starting his bombing run on the battleship when his bombs suddenly dropped, apparently because his bombardier accidentally pressed the bomb release.[174] The remainder of his squadron followed and the bombs landed in the sea. That left the eight Nells under Lieutenant Takeda, probably wanting to redeem himself after the previous incident where he had almost bombed the *Chokai*. But the issue was largely academic; the *Prince of Wales* was a sinking corpse, plodding at 8 knots or so northward while being dragged down by 18,000 tons of seawater.[175] The Mitsubishis approached the battleship at 12:41 pm. Corpse or not, the battleship's few remaining gunners were determined to make a final stand and opened up on Takeda's bombers. Despite the Nells' altitude of 9,000ft and the paucity of the functioning guns, they managed to hit five of the Japanese aircraft.[176] It was futile, yet it was also very heroic. Nevertheless Takeda's aircraft ignored them, flying from the port bow to starboard and dropping their bombs on the helpless ship.

On the captain's bridge of the *Prince of Wales*, Admiral Phillips stood with his staff officers and Captain Leach, now wearing helmets, and counted the bombs as they fell from each aircraft. At the last moment Captain Leach shouted, "Now!" and they all fell flat to the deck.[177]

Lieutenant Takeda's seven bombs (the eighth failed to release) were very accurate even though they scored only one hit. Six bombs near-missed the hard-hit stern area, bashing the hull in and jolting the already fragile last propeller. The seventh hit amidships, penetrating the main deck and exploding in an emergency first aid station that had been treating 200–300 wounded. Shrapnel shredded the intakes for the last remaining functioning boiler room, and it was forced offline.[178] The *Prince of Wales'* limited movements now ground to a halt.

There are several stories of Japanese aircraft flashing messages to the British destroyers at this time, one version being: CEASE FIRING. PICK UP SURVIVORS, while another is WE HAVE FINISHED OUR TASK. NOW YOU MAY CARRY ON.[179] The stories are apocryphal; the Japanese had neither the fuel nor the time for such showmanship. In any event, it is clear that they had specific orders only to sink the capital ships.[180]

Now deathly silence descended on the *Prince of Wales* with the ominous exception of the sound of flowing water as it flooded into the hull. Some of that flow was intentional, as one of the gunners, for reasons known only to him, flooded a few of the magazines, doing nothing to help the battleship's rapidly decreasing buoyancy. Most of what sounds there were came from the cries and moans of the wounded, especially those newly hurt in the just-bombed first aid station. Officers and men still milled about, some talking, some dazed, some brooding, some in stunned silence. These men were every bit as brave, dedicated, and skilled as those on the *Repulse*, but they had been denied the chance to show it. The loss of internal communications had turned them into a confused, listless, leaderless mob. Even now, because of the communications breakdown, Captain Leach and his staff may not have entirely understood the extent of the battleship's injuries.

Seemingly the captain's bridge of the *Prince of Wales* was in some denial. At 12:52 pm Admiral Phillips sent another wireless transmission: EMERGENCY. SEND ALL AVAILABLE TUGS. MY POSITION 003° 40' N. 104° 30' E.[181] He was grasping at straws. Meanwhile, on his own initiative, Lieutenant Commander F. J. Cartwright had his destroyer *Express* approach the flagship. He was greeted by a blinkered signal from the bridge: WHAT ARE YOU COMING ALONGSIDE FOR?[182] Commander Cartwright hid his incredulity at their response: IT LOOKS AS THOUGH YOU REQUIRE

ASSISTANCE. Captain Leach reluctantly agreed to have wounded and non-essential personnel transfer to the *Express* and at 1:05 pm the destroyer pulled alongside and ran lines and gangplanks across for evacuation.

Now a desperate flurry of signals was sent to Singapore. First at 1:00 pm was the *Electra* with the grim news: MOST IMMEDIATE. H.M.S. *PRINCE OF WALES* HIT BY 4 TORPEDOES IN POSITION 003° 45' N. 104° 10' E. *REPULSE* SUNK. SEND DESTROYERS.[183]

At the same time that *Electra* sent her signal, Admiral Phillips sent one as well: MOST IMMEDIATE. H.M.S. *PRINCE OF WALES* DISABLED AND OUT OF CONTROL. Then one minute later: EMERGENCY. SEND ALL AVAILABLE TUGS. MY POSITION NOW IS EQTW 40 (?). Two more messages, both garbled, would go out from the flagship.[184]

But the admiral and Captain Leach were rapidly running out of straws to grasp. Leach went to the quarterdeck, where a large number of men had gathered, and asked for volunteers to stay and help save the ship. He got a few, but he looked sad and forlorn as he returned to the bridge.[185] Within a few minutes – precisely when and how is unclear – the order to Abandon Ship was given.

Once again the evacuation went calmly, though discipline became strained at times. One survivor said, "[I]t was done quietly and almost as if hands had been piped to bathe!" Wounded were placed in Carley floats and released into the water. Men tried to walk across the gangplanks or swing across on ropes to the *Express.*

But as the dying *Prince of Wales* continued her heel over to port, pulling her main deck away from the *Express*, keeping alongside the battleship became more and more of a problem for the destroyer. Lieutenant Commander Cartwright wanted to stay alongside as long as he could to evacuate as many as possible, but he had to pull away before the battleship took the *Express* with her on her final plunge. It was a difficult and dangerous call.

As the *Prince of Wales* finally completed her capsize and ended her agony, Lieutenant Commander Cartwright waited until the last possible second. Then he yelled, "Slip!" and the lines were cut (or, in one case, snapped). Then he yelled "Starboard ten! Full astern together!" Before the *Express* could clear, as the battleship tipped over, her bilge keel struck the bottom of the *Express*, lifting the destroyer up and nearly capsizing her to starboard. But the *Express* rolled back into place, with a 20ft gash in her hull plating. Admiral Phillips, leaning over the bridge of his flagship, gave Cartwright a calm wave, apparently in approval of his tremendous job of seamanship, one that saved hundreds of lives on this day – and, unwittingly, even more in the days ahead.

The final fate of Admiral Sir Tom Phillips is unknown. He was last seen by the *Express* on the bridge of the *Prince of Wales* as the battleship began to capsize, acting as if he was in no hurry to leave. Some survivors said that he wanted to leave only after all of the crew had been evacuated, but the ship sank before he could do so. Most dispute this story, however. One report has him asking someone to go to his cabin and retrieve his best cap. He was observed to dismiss his staff, telling them to save themselves. He was also heard muttering to himself, "I cannot survive this …" Admiral Phillips was never seen again. Captain John Leach was found floating face down, apparently fatally injured while trying to abandon ship. It was a body blow to the survivors of the *Prince of Wales*, who had loved their captain. Both Admiral Phillips and Captain Leach were tremendous losses for the Royal Navy.

At 1:24 pm the *Prince of Wales* completed her capsize and now was completely upturned, her keel exposed to the sky but still momentarily floating.[186] That was the sight that greeted the Brewster Buffalos rushed to the scene by Far East Command. The first to arrive were two from No. 243 Squadron, dispatched out of Kallang on receipt of Captain Tennant's original call for help. They apparently scared off Ensign Hoashi, who took his Nell into a cloud and disappeared. They were quickly joined by a third from the 4 Photographic Reconnaissance Unit, which took pictures of the scene. Just after these three fighters arrived on the scene came the ten Buffalos of Lieutenant Vigors' Royal Air Force No. 453 Squadron. Vigors first split up his aircraft to try to act as avenging angels on any remaining Japanese aircraft. They saw a few bombers in the distance but they could not catch them, as he related: "By the time I got my squadron on the scene the battle was over. I just saw the Prince of Wales sink on the horizon, and by the time I was over the remnants there was not a Japanese aircraft in sight."[187]

The only thing the Brewsters could do now was helplessly circle overhead as the *Prince of Wales* took her final plunge and the destroyers picked up the dirty, oily, half-drowned survivors. The next day, Lieutenant Vigors reported that he was heartened by what he saw of these survivors. Even though they had been through a terrible ordeal and were in desperate straits, he saw them continually giving him the thumbs up and cheering:

> It was obvious that the three destroyers were going to take hours to pick up those hundreds of men clinging to bits of wreckage and swimming around in the filthy, oily water. Above all this, the threat of another bombing and machine-gun attack was imminent. Every one of those men must have realized that. Yet as I flew around, every man waved and put up his thumb as I flew over him. After an hour, lack of petrol forced me to leave, but during that hour I had seen many men in dire danger waving, cheering and joking, as if they were holiday-makers at Brighton waving at a low-flying aircraft. It shook me, for here was something above human nature.[188]

Or so he thought. As one survivor of the *Prince of Wales* explained it, the Buffalos had become "the focal point of all the despair and frustration felt by the bulk of the survivors at the complete lack of support from the air."[189] Their fury, while understandable, was eminently unfair as they would come to know in less emotional moments. It was not the air crews' fault in the slightest. They had been waiting at Sembawang to provide air support to Force Z. When they finally got that call, they had taken off within 15 minutes, so quickly they had not even had time for a briefing. Lieutenant Vigors, himself livid at Admiral Phillips for not requesting air support, was winging it both literally and figuratively as he led his squadron out to sea to find the distressed ships.

At 1:18 pm, the *Electra* would send one last signal, one that would send shockwaves through Singapore all the way to London: MOST IMMEDIATE. H.M.S. *PRINCE OF WALES* SUNK.[190]

It was the last signal sent by Force Z during this engagement, the last of nine signals – none of which asked for air support. In Singapore, Captain John Collins was still trying to arrange for tugs for the *Prince of Wales* and *Repulse* when Admiral Palliser took a signal from the tray, turned to him, and said, "You need not worry about the tugs. They are both sunk." Collins was stunned.[191]

A force of capital ships was being blasted to oblivion by enemy bombers simply due to a lack of air cover. In the years since the destruction of Force Z, the actions of Admiral Phillips and in particular his apparent refusal to ask for air cover have been closely examined and largely excoriated. One history even went so far as to say: "[T]wo great ships and many good men were lost because one stubborn old sea dog refused to acknowledge that he had been wrong."[192] Phillips never had a chance to defend himself or explain his actions, the precise reasons for which will forever remain a mystery. Most histories examining the destruction of Force Z offer their own theories. It is worth a short digression to briefly consider some of the main points.

The two major questions surrounding Admiral Phillips' handling of Force Z are: Why did he not tell Singapore on December 9 that he had cancelled the operation to Singora and was returning? And, secondly: Why did he never request air support, even after having been discovered by Ensign Hoashi's plane?

The failure to alert Singapore that he had cancelled the operation is understandable inasmuch as Admiral Phillips was maintaining radio silence. This was a judgment call, both questionable and understandable, yet it came with a price: Singapore and most importantly his chief of staff and air liaison Admiral Palliser did not know he was returning. They thought Force Z was still headed north to Singora when instead it was headed south for home.

The second question is much more difficult to understand. Admiral Phillips had spent so much time and effort before he set sail trying to get air cover for Force Z, especially off Singora on December 10. Yet, when he very obviously needed it most because he was under air attack, he never asked for it.

Lieutenant Vigors, whose plan to provide air cover Admiral Phillips had rejected, was bitter:

> I reckon this must have been the last battle in which the Navy reckoned they could get along without the RAF. A pretty damned costly way of learning … Phillips had known that he was being shadowed the night before, and also at dawn that day. He did not call for air support. He was attacked and still did not call for help.[193]

But the idea that Admiral Phillips was too arrogant and proud to call for air cover should be rejected. After the *Bismarck* incident Phillips was well aware that his battleships might be vulnerable to air power, and he took steps to minimize that vulnerability. Additionally,

Phillips does seem to have been one who was able to admit mistakes and correct them; specifically he allowed his ships to operate independently after his botched handling of the first Japanese attack. These are indicators of a serious, thoughtful officer willing to reexamine his own beliefs in the face of contrary evidence, not one consumed by pride to the point where he puts those under his command at risk.

And Admiral Phillips does seem to have had a change of heart in the middle of this mission on the subject of air support. On December 8, Admiral Phillips was trying desperately hard to get air cover. On December 10, when he needed it the most, he did not even attempt to do so. What happened in the interim was the December 9, 1:25 am, message from Admiral Palliser that included the very relevant line: "Fighter protection on Wednesday 10th will not, repeat not, be possible." Admiral Phillips and Admiral Palliser had discussed extensively getting fighter protection off Singora on December 10. If understood in this context, it is possible to interpret the sentence as, "Fighter protection *off Singora* on Wednesday 10th will not, repeat not, be possible." And that is undoubtedly what Palliser meant. But is that how Phillips understood it?

Most historians seem to think it is, on the basis of those conversations on December 8 (less than 24 hours before) between Admiral Phillips and Admiral Palliser. Yet, it must be remembered that as Force Z left Singapore, Air Vice Marshal Pulford had signaled Admiral Phillips REGRET FIGHTER PROTECTION IMPOSSIBLE. Furthermore, by dawn on December 10, Phillips had received multiple messages from Admiral Palliser that gave a picture of collapsing British airpower in Malaya.

Given the context of those messages and Admiral Phillips' subsequent actions, it seems likely that he did interpret Admiral Palliser's message as that fighter protection was impossible not just off Singora, but *anywhere*; that the air cover he had previously arranged with Lieutenant Vigors was no longer available; and, thus, there was no point in calling for it. Nor can Palliser be blamed; his was an understandable mistake. It is the way of war. Every battle perched on a knife edge, often depending on the smallest of margins. From a single torpedo permanently disabling the *Prince of Wales* to the two missing words *off Singora* that spelled the difference between life and death for Admiral Phillips and many of the crews of the *Prince of Wales* and *Repulse*.

All told, 840 sailors were lost, 513 on the *Repulse* and 327 on the *Prince of Wales*.[194] The survivors were disembarked in Singapore that night in a rainstorm. Some of the wounded were taken to Alexandra Hospital, some to the sick bay of the newly arrived cruiser *Exeter*. Everyone was in shock. Lieutenant Henry Leach of the *Mauritius* was on the dock looking for his father, Captain John Leach of the *Prince of Wales*.[195] His was one more in a sea of heartbreak.

En route to Singapore with the survivors, *Express* passed the HMS *Stronghold* and USS *Whipple*, *John D. Edwards*, *Edsall*, and *Alden*, who had responded to Admiral Phillips' call for destroyers, heading in the opposite direction. *Express* signaled that the action was over, but the ships proceeded to search the area for more survivors. None were found. While returning to Singapore, *Edsall* found the fishing trawler that had so obsessed

Admiral Phillips that morning. The trawler, identified as *Shofu Fu Maru*, was taken to Singapore where the Japanese crew was interned. The barges she had been towing had been full of grain.

The air attack had forced the *Repulse*'s Walrus seaplane to race back for Singapore, but, desperately short of fuel, Petty Officer Crozer had to force land between Tioman Island and mainland Malaya – in a minefield. His maydays brought help from Singapore in the form of two flying boats and the destroyer *Stronghold*, who managed to tow the Walrus out of the minefield and through a storm back to Singapore safely on December 11.[196]

Captain Tennant came ashore to be greeted by a stunned and deeply troubled Air Vice Marshal Pulford. Pulford's words were, in their own way, a fitting epitaph for Force Z: "My God, I hope you don't blame me for this. I had no idea where you were."[197]

In London, Churchill and the Admiralty were still deliberating on their Far East policy. Nevertheless, although Churchill's plan may have been nonsensical and his advocacy of it arrogant, although the Admiralty's plan had been flawed and its decision-making lethargic, none of them had wanted this. The reaction in London was emotional devastation and though told many, many times, is worth telling again.

The next morning after the battle, Prime Minister Winston Churchill received a phone call at his bedside from First Sea Lord Sir Dudley Pound. He was choked with emotion, so much so that Churchill had trouble understanding him. Finally, Pound broke the news:

> "Prime Minister, I have to report to you that the *Prince of Wales* and the *Repulse* have both been sunk by the Japanese – we think by aircraft. Tom Phillips is drowned."
>
> "Are you sure it's true?"
>
> "There is no doubt at all."

The Prime Minister hung up the phone and lay back down in bed.

> In all the war, I never received a more direct shock ... As I turned over and twisted in bed the full horror of the news sank in upon me. There were no British or American ships in the Indian Ocean or the Pacific except the American survivors of Pearl Harbor, who were hastening back to California. Over all this vast expanse of waters Japan was supreme, and we everywhere were weak and naked.[198]

Back in Saigon, there was celebration among the pilots of the 22nd Air Flotilla. They knew they had accomplished something historic, something even greater than the "Sea Eagles" of *Kido Butai* had at Pearl Harbor. For the first time, they had sunk two battleships under way at sea in fighting trim with nothing but air power.

Yet that same sense of accomplishment tempered their celebration. They were on the cutting edge of a new era, yet it is instinctive for the end of the old era to give one pause. Admiral Ozawa tempered it further by reminding them that their victory would not have been possible without the submarines who reported Force Z's position. Additionally, though Great Britain was now an enemy, the Imperial Japanese Navy as an institution was very conscious that Britain had been the first great power to befriend Japan after its arrival on the international scene; the Royal Navy had been the model after which the Imperial Japanese Navy had patterned itself.

And there was more than a little sympathy for the plight of Force Z. One of Lieutenant Iki's pilots who had attacked the *Repulse* told him wistfully, "I did not want to drop the torpedo. She was such a beautiful ship … such a beautiful ship …"[199]

On December 18, 1941, Lieutenant Iki commanded a reconnaissance flight over the Anambas Islands. The course took him near the battle site. Once his mission was completed, he went to the graves of the *Prince of Wales* and *Repulse*; when the weather is clear and the water calm, the sunken wrecks can be seen from the air. As his Betty passed over the grave of the sunken *Repulse*, he dropped a bouquet of mixed flowers. He dropped a second bouquet over the *Prince of Wales*. He later explained that one was for his wingmates from the Kanoya Air Group who had been brought down by the gunners of the *Repulse*. The other wreath was for all British sailors who had died in the battle. Their display of bravery in defense of the ships had gained them the utmost admiration from all pilots in his squadron.[200]

CHAPTER 5
SHOOTING AT VENUS

For the British it had certainly been a disastrous December 10, 1941. They would take no comfort in the knowledge that their allies' war efforts were progressing disastrously as well. For at almost precisely the same time as the death knell tolled on the *Prince of Wales* and the *Repulse* off Singapore, some 1,500 miles away the American military presence around Manila was reeling.

Admiral Hart was in the Marsman Building, with its view of the F-shaped Cavite Peninsula and its US Navy installations, when the air raid sirens sounded just after 12:40 pm.[1] A message had come in: MANY ENEMY PLANES APPROACHING FROM THE NORTH. ETA MANILA 1255. While most would set off to shelters, many in the military had no such luxury. Admiral Hart certainly did not believe that he did, as he headed to the roof to see what was going on. Patrol Wing 10's Captain Wagner stood on the balcony of his office.[2] What they saw were 26 Nells, these of the Imperial Japanese Navy's 1st Air Group under the command of Lieutenant Commander Ozaki Takeo.[3] Ozaki's bombers, each carrying 12 132lb general purpose bombs, broke off from a large group of Japanese aircraft targeting the Manila area, and began approaching Cavite from the east.[4]

As the sirens wailed, US Navy ships in the harbor tried to get under way to gain maneuvering room for evasive action, with the destroyer *John D. Ford* having to free herself up from refueling operations at Sangley Point, on the tip of the northern horizontal of the peninsula.[5] Four Catalinas of Patrol Wing 10 attempted to get airborne. With some Zeros of the 3rd Air Group as escorts, the Japanese bombers, operating at an altitude of about 24,000ft in waves of nine, flew over the narrow Cavite peninsula at around 1:00 pm without bombing, most likely picking out their targets.[6] As the bombers finished their pass at 1:02 pm, four 3in antiaircraft guns at Sangley Point manned by the 1st Separate Marine Battalion opened up on the aircraft overhead.[7]

But neither the guns of Sangley Point nor the 3in guns at Cavite Navy Yard itself could reach the Japanese attackers, who were flying too high.[8] The Marine gunners might as well have been shooting at Venus. The guns of Sangley Point did manage to shoot down one aircraft – unfortunately, one of their own, a P-40 that had been trying to protect the seaplanes desperately trying to take off. The pilot, Lieutenant Jim Phillips, was fished out of Manila Bay unharmed.[9]

The Japanese were ruthlessly and effectively exploiting the air superiority so easily gained at Clark Field. Lieutenant Commander Ozaki's bombers circled around Manila Bay to begin another pass at Cavite. It was at 1:14 pm that the Nells finally dropped their first bombs.[10]

Most of the bombs struck Canacao Bay, the water between Sangley Point and Cavite, near Machina Wharf, sending up a "solid curtain of water, over one hundred feet high and a half-mile long."[11] But this first attack was accurate enough. It seems to have been a bomb from this strike that knocked out Cavite Navy Yard's power plant.[12] With it went the electricity to the yard, rendering the firefighting mains unable to pump water to fight the fires caused by bomb hits.

"[L]ike a flock of well-disciplined buzzards," according to one witness, Lieutenant Commander Ozaki's bombers circled Cavite Navy Yard.[13] With almost no aerial opposition and with limited antiaircraft fire, the Nells continued the bombing, apparently consisting of four separate runs, that the US Navy itself would call "leisurely and accurate."[14]

At a very crowded Machina Wharf, submarine tender *Otus*, loading supplies, was straddled by two sticks that miraculously missed. She got under way and was not hit again.[15] But berthed next to her were submarines *Sealion* and *Seadragon*, undergoing refits: *Sealion* with her engines disassembled, and *Seadragon* being painted, with loads of paint cans on her deck. *Sealion* took two direct bomb hits from the second pass, one on her stern that wrecked her engines, the other just aft of her conning tower. *Seadragon*, berthed right next to her, had shrapnel cut into her own conning tower. Minesweeper *Bittern*, also berthed at Machina, was set ablaze.[16]

Destroyers *Peary* and *Pillsbury* were also moored, this time at the neighboring Central Wharf, undergoing repairs after sharing a near-fatal collision a few days earlier. *Pillsbury* was able to get under way and escape. But after several near misses, *Peary* took a bomb hit that wounded her skipper, Lieutenant Commander Harry H. Keith. *Pillsbury* was on the receiving end of a near miss. Ferry launch *Santa Rita* took a direct hit and was instantly vaporized.[17]

But the ships of the Asiatic Fleet were not the intended targets of this attack. Lieutenant Commander Ozaki was not going to make the mistakes that Admiral Nagumo had made at Pearl Harbor in ignoring the shore facilities. Their main target was the Cavite Navy Yard itself: its machine shops, storage yards, industrial facilities, ammunition dumps, and dockyards. The base, its facilities all cramped together on the peninsula, took an absolute pounding, one that was horrific even by the standards of World War II. The third attack seems to have been particularly damaging, detonating most of the Asiatic Fleet's torpedo supply and starting a large fire in the closely packed wooden buildings of the base's industrial area. The early bomb hit to the power plant proved decisive. With the firefighting mains unable to pump water and thus nothing to stop them, the fires increased in intensity and spread quickly, turning Cavite Navy Yard and parts of neighboring Cavite City into a raging inferno threatening everything and everyone on shore or close to shore.

The Central Wharf was particularly dangerous. Blazing oil from nearby leaking fuel storage tanks had reached the wharf and detonated air storage flasks in the nearby torpedo workshop. Destroyer *Peary* was in danger of being incinerated when the minesweeper *Whippoorwill*, under the direction of Lieutenant Commander Charles A. Ferriter, moved in between the Central and Machina wharves and nudged her bow against the *Peary's* stern. A 6in hawser was tied to the destroyer and the *Whippoorwill* backed to pull the *Peary* free, but the line snapped. They tried it again. The line parted again. Realizing that the *Peary* still had two mooring lines tying her to the Central Wharf, the *Whippoorwill* managed to pull the destroyer clear once the lines were removed.[18]

Over at the Machina Wharf, *Seadragon*, wounded by the attack on her sister *Sealion*, was in an almost identical danger to the *Peary*. The heat blistered and melted the paint on her hull, and the approaching blazing oil threatened to detonate torpedoes on the wharf and incinerate the submarine. Minesweeper *Bittern*, right next to her, was already ablaze, her magazines threatening to detonate. *Seadragon's* skipper, Lieutenant Commander William Edward "Pete" Ferrall, initially abandoned the submarine as hopeless, but quickly thought better of it and brought the crew back. Lieutenant Richard E. Hawes sent in his ship, the appropriately-designated submarine rescue vessel *Pigeon*. With the *Pigeon* suffering from a faulty rudder that had to be worked by hand, Lieutenant Hawes ignored the safety of his own ship to sail in with a tow line and, helped by the engines of the *Seadragon*, pull the submarine clear. As they moved off, a large fuel tank on the wharf exploded, sending blazing oil into the bay and scorching their hulls.[19]

Admiral Hart continued watching the inferno from the roof of the Marsman Building, oblivious to his own safety. "At least one group of airmen were performing well," he acidly remarked.[20] The admiral's anger at the Far East Air Force swelled, as did that of most Navy personnel. One man angrily complained: "Where the hell is our fighter protection? If the damn AA can't reach them why can't we get a little help from the army guys? They been roasting us about our waddling ducks, and where are they now? Yeah, where?"[21]

Unfortunately most were twisted, blackened wreckages on the runways of Clark and Iba Fields. But it had already been a very busy day, and indeed a very miserable day for the Far East Air Force.

That morning, the Japanese had landed army troops at Vigan and Aparri, with the objectives of securing the airfield at each location. Upon being informed of the landings, the Far East Air Force – B-17s, P-40s of the 17th Pursuit Squadron and P-35s of the 34th Pursuit – and Patrol Wing 10 began bombing and strafing runs on the Japanese, opposed by a few Ki-27 Nate fighters of the Japanese Army Air Force.[22] Five Catalinas of Patrol Wing 10 attacked the heavy cruisers *Ashigara* and *Maya*, light cruiser *Kuma*, and destroyers *Asakaze* and *Matsukaze* without scoring a hit.[23] The Far East Air Force was more effective. Off Vigan, minesweeper *W-10* was sunk by P-35s of the 34th Pursuit, who also strafed transport *Oigawa Maru*, setting it afire and forcing its beaching. Strafing P-40s damaged the light cruiser *Naka* while B-17s hit the transport *Takao Maru*; which was also beached. Off Aparri, three B-17s bombed minesweeper *W-19*, forcing her to run aground, a total loss. While trying to help the *W-19*, light cruiser *Natori* was damaged by a near miss, as was the destroyer *Harukaze*.[24] However, these were only minor inconveniences for the Japanese as opposed to major losses.

Meanwhile, the Japanese Naval Air Force was conducting a massive attack on the Manila area that included the 1st Air Group's raid on Cavite and raids by the Takao Air Group on the Nichols and Del Carmen airfields, which had largely escaped the devastating air raids of December 8. At 11:15 am, the 5th Pursuit Command had received warning of enemy aircraft approaching from the north. The 17th and 21st Pursuit Squadrons had been brought up to strength from the remnants of the other squadrons destroyed on December 8, and they now tried to do what they had not been allowed to do two days earlier. The 17th covered Manila Bay, the 21st covered the port of Manila and Cavite, and the 34th covered Bataan.[25]

But the attacking bombers had an escort of 56 Zero fighters of the 3rd and Tainan Air Groups. The 17th and 21st Pursuits took on the 3rd Air Group's escorts and made superhuman efforts to break through the escorts, but there were too many Japanese fighters. In all 11 Warhawks failed to return, either shot down or running out of fuel. The American pursuits were simply overwhelmed.[26]

Not overwhelmed, amazingly enough, was a single Patrol Wing 10 Catalina flying boat, P-5, flown by Lieutenant Harmon T. Utter. Flying to safety, Utter's slow, unarmored PBY was attacked by three Japanese Zeros of the 3rd Air Group. Utter's bow gunner, Chief Boatswain Earl D. Payne, sitting in a compartment underneath the cockpit, managed to shoot down one of the deadly Zeros, head on, no less. In so doing, he scored the US Navy's first verifiable air-to-air "kill" of a Japanese aircraft in the Pacific War.[27] Utter's PBY was badly shot up with the starboard engine out, but he was able to land on the sea near Corregidor and taxi to shore for repairs. He was fortunate; Catalina P-12, piloted by Ensigns Robert Snyder and William Jones, returning from an attack on the invasion beaches, was ambushed by a Zero as the flying boat tried to land at Laguna de Bay. It exploded in midair with no survivors.[28]

Nichols Field was hit by a punishing bombardment by the Takao Air Group. Del Carmen was covered by dense clouds and so avoided bombing, but the Zeros of the Tainan Air Group went in for low-level strafing runs, catching many of the 34th Pursuit's P-35s just after they had landed from their earlier counterattack. Antiaircraft defenses for Del Carmen, like Nichols, were pathetic, and some officers resorted to shooting their .45cal pistols at the strafing aircraft. Oil tanks and 18 P-35s were destroyed, and the field was temporarily abandoned.[29]

As the Japanese aircraft flew off after "two hellish hours," Cavite Navy Yard was not so much a navy base as a lake of fire worthy of Milton, a colossal conflagration.[30] With no power to pump the firefighting equipment, the massive fires burned deep into the night, giving the sky over Manila and Manila Bay an orange glow. Almost the entire base was literally turned into molten slag.[31] The Asiatic Fleet suffered a massive loss of some 230 torpedoes, which would cripple its destroyers later on.[32] One of the giant radio towers at Sangley Point was knocked down.[33] The low-frequency transmitter used to communicate with submerged submarines was destroyed, meaning that submarines could only communicate with the base on the surface, usually only at night.[34] There is simply no way to overstate the devastation at Cavite Navy Yard. PT Boat skipper Lieutenant John Buckley described the base as "flattened."[35] The US Navy Official Chronology would describe it as "practically obliterated." Admiral Hart called it "utterly ruined."[36] Author Dr John Gordon, defense analyst and retired US Army officer put it in appalling perspective: "The Japanese bombing of the Cavite Navy Yard was the most devastating attack on a US naval installation since the British burned the Washington Navy Yard in 1814."[37]

It was while standing on the roof of the Marsman Building, watching with anger, horror, and helplessness as Cavite burned, much as Priam watched burning Troy from Pergamon, that a Navy yeoman gave Admiral Hart the latest breaking news, which seems to have arrived at light speed from Singapore: the *Prince of Wales* and the *Repulse* were sunk.[38] Admiral Phillips, whose one meeting with Hart had left the American admiral very impressed (no mean feat), was gone, as was the backbone of any Allied naval resistance in the Far East.

Gone, too, was the backbone of Allied air resistance. After its failed attempt to stop this Japanese attack, the V Interceptor Command was left with only 30 pursuit aircraft – 22 P-40s and eight near-useless P-35s. They could no longer offer hope for even a semblance of adequate protection for the air and navy bases on Luzon, and would be limited to reconnaissance work only.[39] The 18 remaining B-17s were withdrawn to Del Monte, and eventually Australia.[40]

That night, Admiral Hart informed Washington that the US Navy's position in Manila – and the Philippines – was untenable.[41]

US NAVY HEADS SOUTH – DECEMBER 8–14

Although the heavy cruiser USS *Houston* was in Iloilo and not in Cavite, she went through her own narrow escape. Admiral Glassford had arrived in his PBY Catalina late in the afternoon of December 8. The cruiser immediately got under way. An hour later her lookouts spotted antiaircraft fire from Iloilo and a ship on fire in the harbor. Once again, Japanese intelligence had been very good. They had known about the cruiser's presence on Panay and had come for her, taking out a helpless freighter instead. They had missed her by only an hour.[42]

Later that night, Radio Tokyo broadcasted news of Imperial Japan's victories that day, including Pearl Harbor, Clark Field – and the sinking of the USS *Houston*. The crew found the propagandist's claims amusing; the cruiser would be reported sunk so many times that later on in the Java Sea Campaign she would earn the nickname "Galloping Ghost of the Java Coast."[43] That night *Houston* also received orders to join up with the light cruiser *Boise* and the destroyers *Paul Jones* and *Barker* for her first mission of the war: to escort the seaplane tender *Langley* and the tankers *Trinity* and *Pecos* out of Philippine waters to the Netherlands East Indies.[44]

On the morning of December 9, the *Houston* made her rendezvous with the *Boise* and the destroyers. Even though the *Houston* was designated as the heavier ship and had bigger guns, the crew felt much more comfortable having the *Boise* with her 15 rapid-fire 6in guns and radar alongside. Shortly thereafter, the *Langley*, the *Trinity*, and the *Pecos* were spotted heading southward at their best speed of 10 knots. They had been ordered by Admiral Hart to flee Manila for the Indies on December 8, given that there was no longer any air cover to be had.

Three lightly armed ships packed with flammable bunker and aviation fuel traveling unescorted through a war zone were bound to make the crews nervous. That day the *Langley* sighted a shining object in the sky. Determining that it was an attacking aircraft, the seaplane tender's 3in antiaircraft guns fired 250 shells at the target. Watching the confrontation were the crew of the *Pecos*, including their skipper Commander E. Paul Abernethy – that is, until the Filipino mess attendant, after bringing Abernethy a sandwich, asked, "Why for *Langley* shoot at Venus?" Sure enough, the *Langley* had been shooting at the second planet from the sun. Watching the exchange from the *Houston*, Lieutenant Lee Rogers commented, "They're really protecting us."[45] Abernethy would say the incident was a good pointer drill even though there was no ammunition "for interplanetary target practice." The crew of the *Langley* would respond that they "had brought Venus down." The incident became a running, good-natured joke in the Asiatic Fleet, especially on the *Langley*.[46] They were grateful to have the *Houston*, the *Boise*, and the four-pipers here to guard them from threats both international and interplanetary.

Throughout the night and into the next morning, the crews of Admiral Glassford's little force kept receiving bad news. The US Navy now acknowledged that two battleships had been sunk at Pearl Harbor. Commercial radio out of the Philippines reported that US forces were being heavily hit. Not so, according to one solitary broadcaster out of Manila, who during his noon newscast on December 10 said that the Americans were actually doing quite well. His station immediately went off the air. At the same time, the US Navy radio station at Sangley Point reported Japanese bombers over Manila; then it, too, went dead. It did not take long to figure out Cavite had been bombed.[47]

Admiral Glassford would be tested during this voyage. The officers of the *Houston* were not impressed with their new flag officer. As pilot Lieutenant Thomas B. Payne explained, "We just didn't have the same confidence in Admiral Glassford as we did in Admiral Hart. He didn't have any fleet experience. That wasn't his fault, but that was the situation."[48]

And, in the eyes of many, Admiral Glassford would fail that test. At sunset the lookouts on the *Houston* reported funnel smoke to the west. The *Houston*, *Boise*, *Paul Jones*, and

Barker immediately headed toward the contacts. Silhouetted by the setting sun, they were identified as a cruiser and two destroyers, all Japanese. At a range of 28,000yd, the *Houston* and *Boise* trained their guns on these men-of-war.[49] But that was all they did. The bemused crews watched as Glassford seemed unable to make up his mind as to what to do, first slowing to 10 knots, then speeding up to 20 knots, then slowing once again. Finally, the admiral gave the order to turn away from the enemy ships. The admiral never gave the order to fire and the opposing forces went their separate ways.[50]

The crews of the US warships were outraged at Admiral Glassford. *Houston* pilot Walter Winslow was "thoroughly disgusted" and "silently cursed the admiral for being a coward."[51] Gunnery officer Al Maher said Glassford did not know what he was supposed to be doing with the task force.[52] Here he had three Japanese targets dead to rights and with an apparent massive advantage in firepower. Already not popular with the men, Glassford was viewed more as a politician than as a fighting sailor, and this incident played into that image.

While that view would prove to be largely correct, in terms of this incident it was largely unfair. Admiral Glassford's orders were to escort the convoy, not engage the enemy. Additionally, the accuracy of the sighting is questionable. Postwar research of Japanese records revealed no Imperial Japanese Navy warships in the area. The closest unit was the 2nd Destroyer Flotilla, commanded by Admiral Tanaka in the flagship light cruiser *Jintsu*, leading several destroyers. But this flotilla was far off to the east.[53] Precisely what the lookouts saw is unknown.[54] In any event, it was dusk and any combat action would have dragged on into the night, which would have hindered the American chances of success.

The next day, December 11, saw Admiral Glassford's fleet make a hair-raising transit through the Sibutu Passage, where they expected to find Japanese submarines lying in wait. Fortunately there were none, but any relief at that thought came crashing down with the news about the *Prince of Wales* and the *Repulse*. As Winslow put it, "These two ships were to have been the backbone of our naval strength for the defense of Southeast Asia, especially since reinforcements from our crippled Pacific Fleet were not available. It seemed to us that every damned break of the game was going against the Allies."[55]

The new backbones of the Allied defense of Southeast Asia were now the *Houston* and the *Boise*, who led the convoy safely into Balikpapan on December 14.

TORPEDO TROUBLES OF US SUBMARINES – DECEMBER 1941

By far the strongest arm of the US Asiatic Fleet was its submarine force. They were, in effect, the guerilla fighters of the US Navy, able to sneak behind enemy lines and wreak havoc. High hopes had been placed in their ability to disrupt the operations of the currently numerically superior Japanese, especially since most of them were armed with the Mark 6 magnetic exploder.

The submarine *Seawolf*, under the command of Lieutenant Commander Frederick Burdette Warder, headed to Aparri, where the Japanese had landed on December 10. Sneaking around a destroyer that was, for some reason, running its sonar, Warder got into the harbor and found a Japanese seaplane tender sitting at anchor. Warder lined up a shot, with a range of 3,800yd, and fired four torpedoes from his bow tubes. Two torpedoes were set to run at a depth of 40ft and two were set to run at 30ft so they would detonate under the ship's keel and actuate the Mark 6 magnetic exploder.

Yet no explosion resulted. Warder turned the *Seawolf* around to run quickly out of the harbor, but managed to fire his four stern tubes at a range of 4,500yd at the still-anchored target. He watched through his periscope and saw a plume of water, but no explosion. The exploder must have failed. Furious at having wasted eight precious torpedoes, Warder led the *Seawolf* out of Aparri into the Pacific.[56]

The *Seawolf* was not alone in her experience. For example, on Christmas Day, submarine *Skipjack*, under the command of Lieutenant Commander Charles Lawrence Freeman, operating in the Palaus, came across a Japanese aircraft carrier, apparently the *Ryujo*, and a destroyer. She fired three torpedoes at a range of 2,200yd. All missed; the sonarman later decided that he had underestimated the range by 1,000yd or so.[57] That same day the submarine *Perch* under Lieutenant Commander David Albert Hunt fired four torpedoes at a steamer off Hong Kong. Three torpedoes missed; one circled around and headed back for the *Perch*, exploding off the submarine's beam.[58]

The worst miss came off Lingayen Gulf, on the northwest corner of Luzon. For decades the Lingayen Gulf had been considered the gateway to Manila and the most likely site of an enemy invasion. For reasons known only to Admiral Hart and Captain Wilkes, the US Navy had placed no mines or other static defenses in the gulf and stationed only one submarine, Lieutenant Commander John Roland McKnight, Jr's *S-36*, inside it. Perhaps not surprisingly, this, the only American defense for the gulf, was pulled out in a communications mixup. Wilkes tried to replace the *S-36* with the *Stingray*, under the command of Lieutenant Commander Ray Lamb, but the Stingray was suffering from leaky pipes that could give away her position to enemy destroyers on the surface. At 5:13 pm on December 21, while *Stingray* was returning to Manila to have the pipes replaced, she sighted funnel smoke. Turning his submarine to investigate, Lamb found multiple smoke columns – an invasion convoy – headed into Lingayen. He immediately sent out a contact report. Due to the lack of aerial reconnaissance because of Japanese control of the skies, this was the first indication that the Japanese were now making their long-expected, main invasion into Lingayen Gulf. In response he was ordered to attack the convoy and he was in perfect position to do so. But Lamb's efforts were at best half-hearted. The *Stingray* returned to Manila without having fired a single shot and Lamb was immediately relieved of command.

To counter the convoy, Captain Wilkes rushed six submarines – *S-38*, *S-40*, *Salmon*, *Permit*, *Porpoise*, and *Saury* – to the scene. But it was too late; the Japanese had already set up an antisubmarine perimeter in the shallow waters of Lingayen Gulf. The only Asiatic

Fleet submarine to get through was *S-38*, under the command of Lieutenant Commander Wreford Goss "Moon" Chapple. Chapple's boat came upon a line of four transports coming in. Waiting until they closed to about 1,000yd, Chapple fired four torpedoes. No hits. This was becoming a pattern, and a disturbing one at that. A destroyer had apparently seen the torpedo wakes but could not find *S-38*. Chapple reloaded his bow tubes, reset the torpedoes for a shallower depth, and launched two torpedoes at an anchored transport. One explosion later, the 5,445-ton transport *Hayo Maru* went to the shallow bottom.[59] In evading a destroyer counter attack, *S-38* ran aground. Chapple was able to work his boat free and eventually came back to attack again, only to be foiled when a Japanese plane dropped a stick of bombs on his submerged boat. All missed. Surfacing that night, the *S-38* suffered a battery explosion and was forced to withdraw.[60]

The other submarines fared miserably. The *Hayo Maru* was the only ship sunk out of more than 80 the Japanese had sent into Lingayen Gulf.[61] Lieutenant Commander John Burnside, commanding the *Saury*, rounded San Fernando on the night of December 23 to enter the gulf and ran into a flotilla of destroyers. He found one stopped and fired a torpedo at it. It missed. *Saury* was ordered out and *Salmon* in. *Salmon* was commanded by Lieutenant Commander Eugene Bradley McKinney. Running on the surface on the night of December 23, he tried to penetrate the gulf but ended up boxed in. Two torpedo attacks on Japanese destroyers registered no hits. Lieutenant Commander Nicholas Lucker Jr, commanding the *S-40*, tried to get into the gulf on a submerged run just after dawn. He launched four torpedoes at a ship at a range of 1,000yd without any hits. Mechanical problems gave away the submarine's position to the escorting destroyers and *S-40* was treated to a whipping counterattack, but survived. *Porpoise*, under Lieutenant Commander Joseph Anthony Callaghan, could not get in at all and was turned away by a destroyer dropping 18 depth charges. *Permit*, under the command of Lieutenant Commander Adrian Hurst, was the last to try. On a daytime submerged approach to the gulf, Hurst fired two torpedoes from his stern tubes at two destroyers from a distance of 1,500yd. Both missed. As he was diving to avoid a counterattack, he was told that the main induction – the main air line to the engines – had flooded. The boat became difficult to control and he was forced to withdraw.[62] Submarine historian Theodore Roscoe later called the Lingayen Gulf "a crucible of frustration."[63]

But that crucible had begun before Lingayen Gulf and extended well outside it, and the disturbing pattern was everywhere. On December 14, the *Sargo*, under the command of Lieutenant Commander Tyrell Dwight Jacobs, had been vectored to intercept three Japanese cruisers. He did so but was unable to close range. Guessing they were escorting a convoy, Jacobs kept tailing them and was proven right, coming upon a freighter. He launched a torpedo; it exploded prematurely. Was something wrong with the Mark 6 magnetic exploder? Or perhaps even the Mark 14 torpedo itself? Had the Japanese found a way to make it explode prematurely? As an experiment, Commander Jacobs and his executive and torpedo officers decided to deactivate the exploder. On December 24, Jacobs sighted two cargo vessels through his periscope at a range of 1,000yd. He launched two torpedoes at the lead ship and one at the trailing ship. No hits. As the merchantmen fled, he launched two more torpedoes at the lead ship from his stern tubes, range 1,800yd. No hits. Later, two more merchantmen came into the *Sargo*'s sights. Two torpedoes emerged from the stern tubes at a range of 900yd. No hits. An hour later, two more freighters came into sight. Jacobs decided to take his time and confirm every aspect of the attack with his executive officer, doing all in his power to ensure a hit; 57 minutes later, he fired two torpedoes at the lead ship and two torpedoes at the rear ship, range 1,000yd. No hits.[64]

Furious, exasperated, and mystified, Jacobs again discussed the attacks with his executive and torpedo officers. They guessed that the torpedo was running deeper than set; the depth setting had been calibrated under peacetime conditions, with a dummy warhead that was lighter than an actual warhead. At the next opportunity, making a submerged daylight attack so he could be sure of the range and confirm everything with his executive, he fired one torpedo at a range of 1,200yd at a slow-moving tanker. In spite of the tanker's explosive cargo, there was no earth-shattering explosion. Commander Jacobs broke radio silence to report to the Asiatic Fleet Submarine Command. He had fired 13 torpedoes in six different attacks.[65] He had deactivated the Mark 6 magnetic exploder. He had adjusted the torpedoes' depth setting. Even so, he had recorded no hits.

These results led Commander Jacobs to question the reliability of not just the Mark 6 magnetic exploder, but the Mark 14 torpedo itself.[66]

WITHDRAWAL FROM THE PHILIPPINES – DECEMBER 11–25

Although the fall of the Philippines may have been inevitable, the destruction of the Far East Air Force had made it almost effortless, at least for Japanese air assets. With no fighters to oppose them, Japanese bombers appeared over Manila every day at noon. "You could set your watch by them," remarked Captain Wilkes.[67]

The destruction of the Far East Air Force had also stretched the US Asiatic Fleet to breaking point. Admiral Hart had counted on General MacArthur's B-17s to provide reconnaissance information for submarine attacks, but now Hart had to use his own PBY Catalina flying boats – slow, unarmored aircraft – to provide that information, invariably without fighter escort, usually in skies controlled by the Japanese. Worse, owing to the loss of MacArthur's B-17s, Hart's PBYs now had to be used for suicidal bombing attacks. They had indeed been designed for bomb and even torpedo attacks, but not in contested skies, and now the flying boats were derided as "flying coffins."[68] The plight of the Catalina's flight crews was best summarized by a message, made famous in a later battle and said to be from a PBY on reconnaissance duty: HAVE SIGHTED ENEMY PLANES … PLEASE NOTIFY NEXT OF KIN.[69]

Through all this – the complete destruction of their base and the continued bombing – Admiral Hart tried to keep the Asiatic Fleet operating in some semblance of support for the defense of the Philippines. Missions continued as usual as far as possible; Catalinas were sent on reconnaissance missions; submarines were sent on war patrols; even the battered destroyer *Peary*, having gotten some emergency repairs and a new commander in Lieutenant Commander John M. Bermingham, was sent out for her first war mission, an antisubmarine patrol between Luzon and the Philippine island of Mindoro.[70]

But almost nothing went according to plan. The Japanese had landed at Legaspi on December 11. Some of the Far East Air Force's few remaining B-17s bombed the invasion convoy to little effect while submarines achieved little in the way of results. On December 12, seven of Patrol Wing 10's Catalinas operating out of Olangapo were sent up to attack a force of Japanese warships reported off Subic Bay. The report was false, which left Admiral Hart outraged – and understandably so.[71] Nine Zeros of the Tainan Air Group, led by Lieutenant Seto Masuzo, found the seven sitting in a line in the waters of Subic Bay refueling. The Catalinas tried to fight back with their machine guns, but their tracers were observed bouncing off the Zeros – the practice ammunition they had been issued had little piercing power.[72] All seven were destroyed on the water. An hour later, three Zeros of the 3rd Air Group made another strafing attack.[73] The Catalinas were so shot up – ten out of the original 28 flying boats were now gone – that Hart ordered their withdrawal the next day.[74]

But the worst performance seemed to be that of General Douglas MacArthur. Whereas before the war he had shown no interest in the affairs of the Asiatic Fleet and had even denigrated its status as a fleet, now he wanted to know every day what Admiral Hart was doing to defend the Philippines. Nothing was ever enough. Lack of numbers or air cover meant nothing to him. The disaster taking place before his eyes required a scapegoat and MacArthur would make sure that scapegoat was Admiral Thomas C. Hart. Well aware of this Hart opined, "[MacArthur] is inclined to cut my throat and perhaps [that] of the Navy in general."[75] The general's messages back to Washington continually referenced Hart's "inactivity."[76] As the Philippine situation got worse, so did MacArthur.

The general had two major complaints. One was the almost total ineffectiveness of US Navy submarines in opposing the Japanese landing convoys. It was a legitimate complaint, to which Admiral Hart, just as frustrated as MacArthur with the submarines, had no answer. Only slowly were Hart and his crews coming to recognize the problems with the Mark 14 torpedo and Mark 6 magnetic exploder.[77]

The second, greater complaint was centered on Convoy No. 4002, which consisted of eight transports and freighters escorted by the heavy cruiser USS *Pensacola*, and therefore known as the *Pensacola* Convoy. This convoy, originally intended to reinforce MacArthur's forces, carried the ground crews of the 7th Bombardment Group and other air combat and service personnel with a total of 4,690 officers and men; 18 P-40 Warhawks intended for the 34th Pursuit Squadron to replace its obsolete P-35s; 52 disassembled A-24 Banshee dive bombers for the 27th Bombardment Group (Light); artillery, machine guns, and large supplies of aviation fuel and ammunition.[78] This convoy had originally been intended to reinforce MacArthur's forces.

Though the *Pensacola* Convoy had left Honolulu for Manila on November 29, two days after the "war warning" of November 27, the transports and freighters had not had their defenses augmented, nor had their cargo been loaded with thought of immediate usage or fast unloading. When word of the Pearl Harbor attack came, Washington became anxious for the safety of the convoy and its valuable supplies – and was not exactly sure what to do with it. Between December 7 and December 12, the *Pensacola* Convoy's orders were changed six times, which included redirecting the convoy to Sydney, then back to the Philippines, then to Honolulu, then to Brisbane, then back to Honolulu, before finally, by order of President Roosevelt on December 12, sending it back to Brisbane.[79]

The turn to Brisbane took place against a background of a political tug-of-war between the US Army, as directed by General MacArthur, and the US Navy. Essentially, MacArthur wanted the convoy to push through to the Philippines. Admiral Hart, with what might be termed lukewarm backing from the US Navy, believed that Japanese control of the air meant that any reinforcement efforts by sea were doomed and he did not want to have his few ships committed to a suicide mission. MacArthur termed this Japanese blockade as only a "paper blockade."[80] The general's belief may have been "delusional" and "out of touch with reality," as one author described it, but it was fully supported by MacArthur's superiors in Washington.[81] Considering that the US Navy had tried to get the *Pensacola* Convoy recalled to Honolulu, just getting it directed to Brisbane was a political victory for MacArthur. But the convoy never did reach the Philippines; Washington came to its senses and ultimately directed most of the *Pensacola* Convoy's supplies to Australia and the East Indies.

For events had overtaken the convoy. On December 22, the Japanese had made their biggest landing – 43,000 troops of General Homma Masaharu's 14th Army – at Lingayen Gulf. On December 24, 7,000 more Japanese troops landed at Lamon Bay, southeast of Manila. With the Japanese advancing everywhere, at 9:00 am on December 24, one of MacArthur's staffers told Admiral Hart that Manila was to be evacuated within 24 hours because it was to be declared an "open city," meaning that MacArthur would not defend it.[82] In a belated accordance with Rainbow 5, he ordered all his army forces on Luzon to abandon Manila and withdraw to the Bataan Peninsula and the islands in Manila Bay. The withdrawal might have been palatable if Manila had been immediately threatened, which it was not, or if Bataan had been stockpiled with supplies in accordance with Rainbow 5, which MacArthur had not done because that would have been "defeatist."[83] Declaration of Manila as an open city meant that it could not be attacked under international law. But the Japanese continued to bomb Manila.

Admiral Hart was furious with the lack of notice, but could do nothing about it. He scrambled to move Asiatic Fleet supplies stored in the city, including most of the submarines' spare parts and a large stockpile of Mark 14 torpedoes, but found they mostly had to be abandoned.[84] Where he personally would go was another question. After consulting with his staff in the Marsman Building, Hart decided to leave the Philippines and head to Soerabaja, in the Netherlands East Indies, where the Asiatic Fleet could regroup. As if to endorse his decision, three Japanese air attacks shook the building.[85] The disastrous air situation had already prompted General MacArthur to order General Brereton to head to the Netherlands East Indies and Australia to rebuild the devastated Far East Air Force.[86]

So, on Christmas morning, Admiral Hart turned over the naval command in the Philippines to Rear Admiral Francis Rockwell, commandant of the 16th Naval District. Rockwell would fight from the island of Corregidor in Manila Bay with a few PT boats and other small remaining naval assets. The submarines were to stay and fight as long as possible, then join the rest of the Asiatic Fleet at Soerabaja.[87]

Admiral Hart had planned for his withdrawal, and had ordered two PBY Catalina flying boats reserved in Laguna de Bay so that he and his staff could use them. Things were getting worse by the hour. Hong Kong surrendered to the Japanese on Christmas Day, as did the island of Jolo, west of Mindanao. The fall of Jolo threatened Hart's route of escape; he needed to leave immediately. But just as the Catalinas were uncovered and he was heading for them, so was a Japanese air attack. Both PBYs were strafed and exploded on the water.[88]

If Admiral Hart wanted to escape the Philippines and continue the war in the Netherlands East Indies, he would have to get creative.

CHAPTER 6

SLAPPED TOGETHER

On the drizzly evening of January 1, 1942, a periscope popped out of the water outside the northern entrance to the Dutch port of Soerabaja, on the north coast of Java.[1] The periscope turned around a few times, checking the area, then it popped back into the water from whence it came. Shortly thereafter, the periscope popped out of the water again, this time taking the rest of its submarine with it. This was the USS *Shark*, which had more than usual panache for a submarine – she was flying the four-star flag of a full US Navy admiral, Admiral Thomas Hart of the Asiatic Fleet, and was technically serving as his flagship. As a mode of transport for a full admiral the submarine was, to say the least, atypical, but it was a necessity brought on by the destruction of Hart's Catalina just minutes before he was to board.

The five-day trip from the Philippines had been anything but comfortable. Jammed aboard were Hart and his staff, a Dutch liaison officer, and other personnel, totaling 66 passengers in addition to the submarine's usual crew. For obvious security reasons the *Shark* tried to stay submerged as much as possible, but the mass of people crammed aboard needed oxygen. Temperatures inside the *Shark* rose to more than 100 degrees; tempers rose even higher.[2] Skipper Lieutenant Commander Louis Shane Jr did a good job simply keeping the boat from exploding.

A Dutch patrol boat went out to investigate the *Shark*, eventually leading her in to the roadstead and letting her discharge her high-ranking personnel. Admiral Hart was able to establish his headquarters on Soerabaja's waterfront in the Oranje Hotel, the same building that Task Force 5 had been using since Admiral Glassford had arrived a few weeks earlier. Lieutenant Commander Shane then took his *Shark* out for her war patrol.

Admiral Hart spent about a day in Soerabaja setting up his new headquarters and going over his messages after being unable to communicate for five days on the submarine. Now he was finding out just how bad the situation was with an unchecked Japanese advance and mounting US losses. And tucked into those messages was one even more disturbing to the admiral:

STEPS ARE IN HAND TO CREATE SUPREME COMMAND IN SOUTHWEST PACIFIC UNDER WHICH WILL BE UNIFIED COMMAND NAVAL FORCES UNDER US ADMIRAL PROBABLY YOURSELF.[3]

Admiral Hart cabled back suggesting they choose someone else, citing health concerns, though that was likely just an excuse to turn down the command. Hart had long believed that such an organization could not operate effectively unless the Allies developed a unified strategy.[4]

But with impressive speed the Asiatic Fleet was setting up for action in the Indies. The Dutch had commandeered the Oranje Hotel for its use. Captain Wilkes and the submarine command had also made the trip down, on the submarine *Swordfish*, traveling very light, carrying only themselves, the submarine force's payroll records, a radio, and a typewriter, which they treated as a mascot.[5] They also set up shop in the Oranje Hotel. Meanwhile, as of December 20, Patrol Wing 10 had also arrived – to a welcome of an air raid alarm and antiaircraft fire; the Dutch had not known they were coming.[6] By the time Hart disembarked they were already deploying for reconnaissance operations. Captain Wagner was in Ambon, at the far eastern end of the Indies, with the *Childs*, its Catalinas patrolling the Molucca Strait out of Ambon, which they shared with some Australian Lockheed Hudson bombers of the Royal Australian Air Force's No. 2 Squadron.[7] The two seaplane tenders the *William D. Preston* and *Heron* were still in Soerabaja, with the *Heron* about to leave. The *Langley*, considered too slow for front-line operations in a combat zone, had been sent to Darwin, the small port in the extreme north northwest of Australia about 1,200 miles from Java.[8]

Shortly after arriving in Soerabaja, Admiral Hart received a request from Vice Admiral Conrad E. L. Helfrich, the Commander of Dutch naval forces in the East Indies, to meet him in Batavia, the capital of the Netherlands East Indies, at the other end of Java. It was a good idea and, in any case, a necessary diplomatic courtesy, so Hart made the all-night train ride from Soerabaja to Batavia. The next morning, January 4, Helfrich met him at the station and accompanied him to the mansion of Dutch Governor General Tjarda van Starkenborgh Stachouwer, making small talk on the way.[9]

Admiral Helfrich ushered Admiral Hart into the large office in which the Dutch Governor General and the Deputy Governor General, Hubertus Johannes van Mook, were waiting. Helfrich then handed Hart a press release announcing the formation of ABDACOM. It was to be a unified command (in theory, anyway) of all the American, British, Dutch, and Australian forces in Southeast Asia, combining in an effort to stop the Japanese. British Army Lieutenant General Sir Archibald P. Wavell, a veteran and respected British commander who had expertly handled the British forces in Egypt, would be its head.

Admiral Hart was struck by one particular facet of the press release: against his express wishes, Hart was to be the head of ABDA naval forces. Before Hart had even finished reading it, the governor general asked him what his plan was for stopping the Japanese.

Admiral Hart had been set up, and he knew it. Admiral Helfrich had known about the new ABDA formation and had said nothing. Helfrich, angry that he himself had not been named ADBA naval commander, wanted Hart to look weak and incompetent before the governor general. In this he succeeded. Hart deflected all questions as to his strategy, saying that such discussions were premature until General Wavell could arrive. He stated that he had not asked for this job and wondered whether he might be too old for it. These were words of diplomacy, out of consideration for the obviously bruised sensibilities of the Dutch and the feelings of Helfrich. His consideration would not be returned.

Destined to become another central figure in the unfolding disaster in Southeast Asia, Conrad Emil Lambert Helfrich was a Dutch native of the Indies, born in 1886 in Semarang. He had worked his way up through the ranks of the Royal Netherlands Navy, mostly as an instructor at the High Naval Military School (essentially the Dutch command school), before returning to the Netherlands East Indies in 1931 as chief of staff for its naval forces. In 1935 Helfrich was promoted to rear admiral and took command of the East Indies Squadron, becoming commander of the East Indies Naval Forces in 1939. A promotion to vice admiral followed in 1940.[10]

Fat, balding, having the look of an aging barroom brawler and the bullying streak to match, Admiral Helfrich posed a striking contrast to the dapper, almost debonair Admiral Hart. The highly intelligent Helfrich was an accomplished hydrographer and had theoretical knowledge from his days as an instructor at the command school, but he had never commanded a ship, his seagoing experience consisting entirely of his four years as head of the East Indies Squadron.[11]

And, as the incident with Admiral Hart indicates, Admiral Helfrich had plenty of tools for bureaucratic and political mischief in his arsenal, and he was very happy to use them. Soon enough, van Mook would begin a campaign to replace Hart, complaining about him to the Dutch government-in-exile, the British government in London, and the Americans in Washington.

SURVIVING COMBAT – DECEMBER 26, 1941–JANUARY 3, 1942

The formation of ABDA on paper was only one of a number of actions demonstrating how the war had progressed while Admiral Hart had been out of contact, and the war was not waiting for the new organization to get itself sorted out.

On December 26, the Dutch naval command in Soerabaja had received a report of two Japanese cruisers, two destroyers, and three transports at the island of Jolo, at the extreme southern end of the Philippine chain and the far northern end of the Makassar Strait, the freeway into the Netherlands East Indies. Soerabaja ordered the Dutch commander on Ambon to attack with all forces available. For the Dutch commander on Ambon, this consisted of two Brewster Buffalos, so he had to ask the Australians and the Americans for help. The Australians were happy to supply their Lockheed Hudson bombers, of which they had three from the Royal Australian Air Force No. 2 Squadron at the Laha airfield on Ambon, but those bombers lacked the range. Captain Wagner of Patrol Wing 10 had just established itself in Ambon, so the Dutch, who were almost as aggressive in using seaplanes as the Japanese, asked him to launch an airstrike with his long-range PBY Catalina flying boats.[12]

It was an idea that could be called creative, desperate, or both. Catalinas could indeed be very useful as bombers and as torpedo carriers, but not against fighter opposition. Intelligence information about the mission was scanty, as the pilots were told their target "was in the vicinity of the island of Jolo."[13]

Six PBYs of Squadron VP-101 took off around midnight, timed to arrive over Jolo at dawn. They separated into two three-aircraft groups. But timing never seemed to be with the Allies during this phase of the war, and it was not with them now. Both groups managed to lose each other in the predawn darkness, and both groups arrived over Jolo while it was still too dark to bomb. Independently, with little knowledge of what the other group was doing, each headed for TuTu Harbor on Jolo's southern coast, expecting to find the reported ships. But there was nothing there; Jolo had two harbors, and intelligence had picked the wrong one. The frustrated Catalina pilots headed for Jolo Harbor on the northern coast.

Unfortunately this harbor was heavily fortified with antiaircraft guns.[14] Under their vicious barrage, the PBYs tried to set up their bombing approaches, only to discover the last piece of information missed by intelligence: Jolo was protected by 24 Zero fighters.[15]

The fighters swarmed around the Catalinas, turning the bombing attack into an unmitigated disaster. Four Catalinas were shot down and the remaining two were damaged, with no hits to show for their effort. The attack temporarily destroyed Patrol Wing 10 as a fighting unit.

Later that morning a Dutch Dornier Do-24K flying boat operating out of Tarakan made a second attack on Jolo. This was also unsuccessful, but at least the aircraft, though mauled by antiaircraft fire, was able to escape before the Zeros could scramble.[16] As was frequently the case in this budding American–British–Dutch–Australian partnership, the left hand had not known what the right hand was doing.

Meanwhile, that same day, the submarine *Perch* had torpedoed the Japanese supply ship *Nojima* in the South China Sea southwest of Hong Kong, but the *Nojima* did not sink.[17] At least the torpedoes had not turned around and headed back for the *Perch*, as had happened to her on Christmas Day.[18]

Perhaps the most frustrating of these developments to Admiral Hart was the experience of the destroyer USS *Peary*. If Hart's journey from the Philippines had been less than comfortable, it was a pleasure cruise compared to that of the *Peary*. It will be recalled that the *Peary* was being repaired at Cavite when the Japanese performed their pulverizing air raid. The helpless destroyer took a bomb hit that badly injured her skipper and killed her executive officer. Lucky to survive the attack in any semblance of working order, the *Peary* had received some emergency repairs and was assigned a new skipper, Lieutenant

Commander John M. Bermingham. Bermingham, whose tour of duty had ended and who was waiting for a trip back to the United States, had been chosen for this command on December 14 by virtue of the Asiatic Fleet's personnel commander running into him as he stood on a dock watching the repairs to the *Peary*.[19] This was a curious vetting, but Bermingham, a former executive officer of the *Stewart*, proved himself up to the challenge and quickly earned the respect of the crew.[20]

With Hart's departure from the Philippines Admiral Rockwell was now in charge, and he took the opportunity of the *Peary* and *Pillsbury* being assigned wartime duties off Corregidor to call their skippers in to discuss releasing them to join Hart in the Indies. While they were at this conference, the Japanese subjected the *Peary* to two hours of bombing while Bermingham, Rockwell, and *Pillsbury* captain Lieutenant Commander Harold Clay Pound watched from shore and her new executive officer, Lieutenant Martin M. Koivisto, desperately maneuvered the destroyer through Manila Bay. Though she suffered a few near misses, the *Peary* survived largely unscathed.[21] Her crew was more than happy at 8:30 pm on December 26 to be ordered to clear out of the Philippines and join Task Force 5 at Soerabaja.[22]

But under skies now controlled by the Japanese, this would prove to be complicated. The *Peary* and the *Pillsbury* were separated, under the theory that at least one would get through.[23] *Pillsbury* succeeded, but the *Peary* was another story entirely. Not taking any chances, the astute Bermingham had the *Peary* head south under cover of night, and by dawn the next morning, December 27, the destroyer was hidden in remote Campomanes Bay on the west coast of Negros Island. Since the cove was especially deep, Bermingham was able to pull the destroyer very tight with the shore, tied to some trees. He then ordered his crew to cover her with palm fronds and green paint. Several flights of Japanese bombers passed over throughout the day, hunting fugitive US ships, but they mistook her for part of the island. As soon as the sun was down, the *Peary* was under way again.

Commander Bermingham had received notice of the Japanese concentration at Jolo, the subject of the disastrous bombing attempt by Patrol Wing 10, with cruisers now patrolling the area and Japanese submarines now mining the ever-dangerous entrance to the Makassar Strait, her shortest route to Soerabaja. The *Peary* would have to shift her route to the east. Only 30 miles north of Jolo, she went through the Pilas Strait into the Celebes Sea. Now, she was out of the Philippines and away from Jolo. However, at 8:10 am the next morning, December 28, they found a four-engine Japanese seaplane, a big Kawanishi HK6 "Mavis" flying boat, shadowing them from 8 miles off the port quarter. Battle stations ordered, the crew manned their guns – guns which would be useless against high-flying aircraft. So began nine hours of psychological torment. The flying boat, joined two hours later by a second one, made repeated bombing runs without dropping any bombs, forcing the *Peary* into evasive maneuvers, keeping her crew tense and draining their energy. Commander Bermingham tried to radio for help, but he could not raise any Allied ship or base. The destroyer's lookouts spotted two Catalinas flying to the west but could not contact them either. Then, the Japanese seaplanes were joined by two twin-engine Nell bombers armed with torpedoes and pressed their attacks in earnest. Only by some incredible seamanship by Bermingham was the *Peary* able to escape without suffering any damage. Their munitions expended, the Japanese tormentors departed, leaving the exhausted crew in peace. Darkness would arrive shortly, and when the morning came the *Peary* would be in friendly territory under the protection of Allied aircraft.

At 6:05 pm, with the *Peary* off Kema, Celebes, those friendly aircraft finally came – three Lockheed Hudson bombers from the Royal Australian Air Force. Maybe now things would get easier for the *Peary*. The destroyer flashed the recognition signals from her searchlight and the crew saw one of the pilots wave back. Many of the *Peary*'s crew waved at the Hudsons, others cheered, relieved their day of torment was over, until one of the Hudsons entered a bombing approach from astern.

Incredulous at this turn of events, Commander Bermingham initially held his antiaircraft fire, but again took no chances. He swung the *Peary* to starboard and a 250lb bomb exploded 100yd off the port beam. Her port heel as she rapidly turned threw a crewman, Seaman First Class Billy E. Green, overboard; he was last seen swimming for a nearby island. The Hudsons made two more bombing and strafing attacks. The first bomb missed, but the second exploded near the port propeller shaft – a very dangerous place for Allied ships during this campaign. Shrapnel killed Seaman First Class K. E. Quinaux, who had been manning a .50cal machine gun. The engine room was shredded, cutting the steam line to the steering engine and forcing a change to hand steering. The angry seamen of the *Peary* fired back, badly damaging one of the Hudsons. Only at dusk did the Hudsons depart, leaving the *Peary* to deal with the damage.

And the damage was extensive. The starboard engine was overheating, so only the port engine could be used. All the maneuvering had left them short of fuel and feed water. Steering the destroyer himself from the after deckhouse, Commander Bermingham put in to Maitara, in the Molucca Islands, at dawn on December 29, for temporary repairs and a new covering of palm fronds and green paint. He went to a small Dutch military installation in nearby Ternate to get help and, he hoped, some fuel. He could not get the latter, but the Dutch warmly greeted the *Peary* and gave them as much of the former as they could spare, especially food. In the meantime, the destroyer was finally able to get a message through to Task Force 5, detailing the day's events, the attacks, and the condition of his ship. He received an acknowledgment, but nothing else from Soerabaja.

Back in Ambon, Captain Wagner of Patrol Wing 10 had received a report of an UNKNOWN SHIP BELIEVED TO BE A JAPANESE CRUISER off Kina from veteran PBY pilot Duke Campbell, who had been rescuing airmen from Patrol Wing 10 shot down in the disastrous Jolo mission.[24] Wagner had conferred with the Australians and Dutch, who, excited that they finally had a chance to strike back at the Japanese aggressors, sent aloft three Australian Lockheed Hudsons to attack it. Now Wagner received a report from the Dutch at Ternate of a US destroyer that had been bombed by "British planes." Putting two and two together here made for a terrible answer.

The attack had been nothing more than an honest, tragic mistake. Ambon had been told that two US destroyers were coming down from the Philippines together through Makassar Strait. No one had known that any US ships were still that far north, and with the green paint covering her, the four-piper *Peary* bore more than a passing resemblance to a Japanese light cruiser. Campbell "felt terrible about it." The Australian pilots had only followed their orders, though how they had managed to miss the American flag on the *Peary*'s mast is unclear.

Captain Wagner took immediate steps to help the battered *Peary*. He sent messages to the destroyer to come down to Ambon. But like a pet just beaten by an abusive owner, the *Peary* cowered in her little corner of the Indies. Commander Bermingham did not completely trust Wagner's messages and in any case did not want to reveal his position to the Japanese by responding. Captain Wagner, apprehensive about the destroyer's fate when his messages were met with silence, directed the seaplane tender USS *Heron*, the closest available ship, to go to Ternate and find the destroyer. Catalinas on patrol were told to keep a watch out for the *Peary*.

It was one of those seaplanes, P-8, piloted by Tom McCabe and Gordon Ebbe, that finally found her. After a fruitless search for more survivors of the disastrous Jolo raid, P-8 received the message to look for the *Peary* near Ternate, so she headed there. So well had the *Peary* been camouflaged that it took P-8 three passes over the small cove on Maitara to find her. They landed and flashed a message to the *Peary*. A launch carrying Bermingham came out from the destroyer to meet the PBY. As McCabe later recalled, the exchange was far from pleasant:

> The skipper came out by boat and we talked. I told him that Pat-Wing-10 thought he should come to Ambon. He told me what had already happened to his ship since the war started. He didn't know if he wanted to come down. He said, "I've been bombed by everyone else and I'm not about to let you guys have a shot at me, too!

Unfortunately, the *Peary* could not spend the war hiding in Maitara, nor could she find any fuel in Ternate, but if she carefully husbanded her remaining 19,000 gallons, she had barely enough to reach the Dutch base at Ambon. By dusk on December 30, the temporary repairs were complete, if ultimately ineffectual, and on the evening of December 31 the *Peary* pulled into Ambon. However, frantic messages flashed from the tender *Childs* forced the destroyer to stop as she entered the harbor; she had been about to sail into the base's protective minefield. The skipper of the *Childs*, Doc Pratt, went over to pilot the *Peary* through the minefield. As he conned the destroyer, Pratt noticed that the bridge crew looked "very shaky."

With the *Peary* in port, the *Heron* now faced a similarly hazardous journey. The *Heron* pulled into Ternate and her skipper, Lieutenant William L. Kabler, went ashore for four hours. At 9:30 am the seaplane tender spotted another giant Mavis flying boat, of the Toko Air Group.[25] With a top speed of 11 knots, the tiny *Heron* would struggle with speed and maneuvering, but she did have one secret weapon: skipper Kabler was a trained naval aviator and a qualified bomber and torpedo-plane pilot. His piloting skills would be needed as never before.[26]

On its initial run, the Japanese aircraft got too close and took fire from the *Heron*'s four .50cal machine guns and two 3in antiaircraft guns. The Mavis then began another, mainly psychological, game where it would make both real and fake bombing runs. Using his experience as a bomber pilot to judge when the bomber would release its payload, Lieutenant Kabler was able to maneuver the *Heron* to avoid every bomb. At 3:20 pm, six more four-engine Mavis flying boats appeared, making bombing runs in two waves of three. The bombs of the first wave were avoided completely. One bomber of the second wave was forced to abort and withdraw by a 3in shell hit to one of his engines. The remaining two made their attack. Their bombs also missed. Then at 4:00 pm, five deadly Nell bombers appeared and dropped 20 100lb bombs from 5,000ft. The little *Heron* was straddled. Almost all the bombs missed, but three detonated about 15yd off the port bow and a fourth miraculously detonated not on the ship itself, but on top of the mast. The result was 28 casualties, including one seaman killed, one mortally wounded, and considerable damage topside. But it could have been far worse.

And for a while it looked as if it might be. At 4:47 pm, as those bombers finally withdrew, three more four-engine Mavis flying boats came armed with torpedoes. They attacked off both bows and from the port quarter, in a version of the anvil attack. But the attack was poorly coordinated and Lieutenant Kabler was able to avoid the torpedoes and even shoot down one of the Mavises, whose crew refused rescue.

After her eight-hour ordeal, in which she had survived ten attacks by 15 aircraft who had used 46 bombs and three torpedoes against her, in which she had shot down one aircraft and damaged another, the *Heron* welcomed the curtain of darkness to fall on what had been an amazing performance by her crew and her commanding officer, William Kabler. She made best speed for Ambon.

Meanwhile, with the Japanese pressing ever harder, ever further to the south, the battered destroyer *Peary* was quickly ordered away from Ambon to Darwin, Australia. She arrived at the northern Australian port on January 3, 1942. After a collision, three bombings by the Japanese, one bombing by Allies, and three nights disguised as a grove of palm trees, the destroyer *Peary* was temporarily safe.

ESTABLISHMENT OF ABDACOM – JANUARY 10

On January 10, General Wavell arrived in Batavia to assume command of the joint Allied command that he would name ABDACOM.

Deputy ABDACOM: Lieutenant General George H. Brett, US Army;
Chief of Staff: Major General Sir Henry R. Pownall, British Army;
Intelligence: Colonel Leonard F. Field, British Army;

Navy Operational Command: Admiral Thomas C. Hart, US Navy
(ABDAFLOAT);

Chief of Staff: Rear Admiral Arthur P. E. Palliser, Royal Navy;

Air Operational Command: Air Chief Marshal Sir Richard E. C. Peirse,
Royal Air Force (ABDAIR);

Army Operational Command: Lieutenant General Hein ter Poorten,
Netherlands East Indies Army; (ABDARM); and

Chief of Staff: Major General Sir Ian S. Playfair, British Army.

The idea behind ABDACOM was to throw all the resources in the area from the United States, Britain, the Netherlands, and Australia into a joint command to defend the area. And what an area it was, too – from Burma in the west to Darwin in the east (added at the demand of Australia's prime minister), a distance of some 3,100 miles; from the Philippines in the north to Java in the south, a distance of some 2,600 miles. Covering those distances with the slim forces on hand was almost asking the impossible. Even just supplying those forces over those distances was a problem. Darwin was to be the main logistics base for ABDACOM, but it was 1,200 miles from Java. Getting supplies to Darwin from the US and Britain would be extremely difficult; forwarding those supplies to the front would complicate things further.

While ABDACOM may have been a unified command, it was never unified in strategy. Before the war, Admiral Hart had pressed for such a unified strategy in dealing with the Japanese, but it never developed. Britain was focused on Singapore and largely dealt with Malaya and Burma on its own. The Philippines were technically part of the ABDA area but were now effectively in isolation. The Dutch were more interested in defending the Indies, while the Australians were focused on protecting their homeland. Perhaps to take advantage of that divergence in interest, ABDACOM was divided into three zones – the British handled affairs in the western end, the Dutch in the center, and the Americans in the east. National interest often trumped group interest in ABDACOM.

Multinational forces have always been part of warfare, not the norm but not uncommon either, dating back as far as warfare can be traced; even the Bronze Age Greeks in their attack on Troy consisted of armies from multiple kingdoms.

But these multinational forces were usually, for want of a better word, modular. They did not mix them together. ABDACOM was not to be like that at all. It could not be like that; the resources available were just too slim. Instead, everything available was thrown into one pot. American pilots would fly alongside Dutch pilots taking orders from a British commander. Rather than having separate squadrons for Americans, British, Dutch, and Australians, each of which would report to their own commanders, who would in turn report to the force commander, instead a single seagoing force would have all the ships regardless of nationality answer to the same force commander. As a concept of military organization, this was highly unusual.

ABDACOM may have been slapped together from everything that was lying around Southeast Asia, but it did not just appear out of the blue. It was the culmination of

THE ABDA AREA OF OPERATIONS AND THE PHILIPPINES

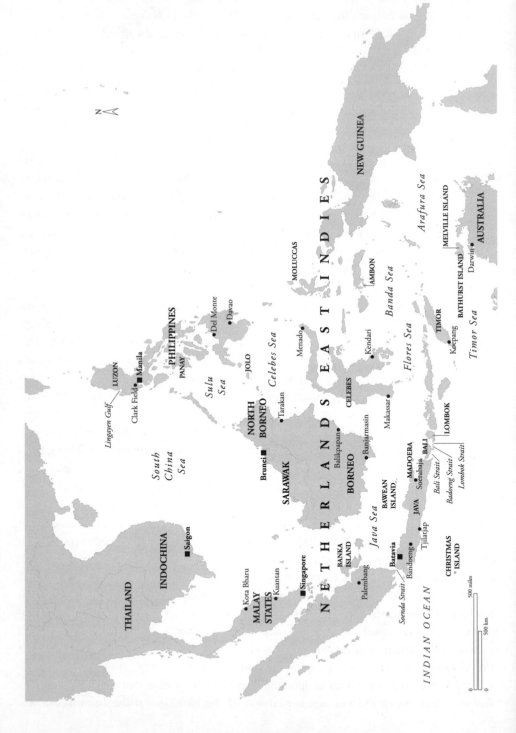

organizational work from those prewar conferences between the ABCD powers (American–British–Chinese–Dutch) and their confusing alphabet soup of acronyms – ADA, ABC-1, ABC-2, ADB – that had formally broken down before war started. Still, there was informal coordination, including such instances as the four US destroyers ordered to Singapore to join Force Z. But the real single proximate catalyst for the formation of ABDACOM was the Arcadia Conference at the end of December 1941 between President Roosevelt and Prime Minister Churchill at which they reaffirmed that their number one priority was the defeat of Nazi Germany and set up a combined British–American command in Washington called the Combined Chiefs of Staff. The inability to reconcile their differences on Singapore notwithstanding, America's entry into the war helped bridge those differences. But no one had bothered to consult with the Australians or the Dutch.

Since the Australians had been serving under British command for some time during the war in Europe, the new element in the war here was the Dutch whose territory was the primary objective of the Japanese war effort. The "East Indies" consists of thousands of islands in which the Dutch had had a presence for four centuries, with a few ports, mostly centered on Java, which they leveraged in the late 19th and early 20th centuries into control of what is today known as Indonesia.

Except that even that "control" was in name only. Most of the development in the Indies was in the coastal regions and ports of the four "big islands" of (most of) Borneo, Sumatra, the Celebes, and Java, along with some more important smaller ones like Bali, Timor, and Ambon in the eastern part of the Indies the interior of whose islands consisted of almost impenetrable jungle, containing numerous different ethnic groups who were often not on good terms with each other except for a unified dislike of their Dutch colonial "masters."

Since the middle of the 19th century, the Netherlands had maintained a policy of "aloofness" in foreign affairs, a central feature of which was strict neutrality. Although this had successfully kept it out of the carnage of World War I, it also caused the Netherlands, a country with a very strong naval tradition, to allow its military to atrophy. As the inexorable movement toward war continued in the late 1930s, the Netherlands would move much closer to Britain in defense matters, but defense spending and preparations always lagged. Although the Dutch Army was considered less an adversary than an annoyance by the Wehrmacht, the real decline was in the Royal Netherlands Navy. The famous Dutch Admiral De Ruyter would not have recognized the withered force of World War II. The Dutch had skipped the *Dreadnought* era altogether and had no battleships or even heavy cruisers. In its defense of the Netherlands East Indies, the Royal Netherlands Navy could deploy a surface fleet that consisted of only three light cruisers (actually two light cruisers *De Ruyter* and *Java*, one light cruiser-destroyer type ship called the *Tromp)* and seven destroyers of the *Admiralen* class (named after famous Dutch admirals – *Evertsen*, *Piet Hein*, *Van Ghent*, *Kortenaer*, *Witte de With*, *Banckert*, and *Van Nes*; an eighth, the *Van Galen*, had been sunk by the Germans in 1940). They also had the usual assortment of minor combatants such as minelayers and minesweepers. For the job it was asked to do in defending the Netherlands East Indies, this force was pitifully inadequate. The Dutch depended on Royal Navy patrols in the area to supplement its own patrols within its own territory.

Many of the Dutch Navy ships were of questionable quality. The light cruiser *Java* is a case in point. When her keel was laid down in 1916, the *Java* was intended to be a namesake for a class of three light cruisers specially designed for operations in the East Indies. It was intended for her to have ten 5.9in guns scattered across the main deck in single-gun mounts behind large gun shields, making the *Java* more than a match for the cruisers of her day. But labor problems and funding issues delayed her completion until 1925, by which time her day was done.[27] Cruisers now had enclosed multigun turrets with dedicated, reinforced ammunition magazines, not open single-gun mounts. Yet it was on this class of ship that the defense of the Indies depended for the next decade. Her sister ship, *Sumatra,* was chronically beset by engine trouble; a third sister, to be called the *Celebes*, was never completed.

But inadequate did not mean incompetent, and in many ways the Royal Netherlands Navy was both shrewd and insightful. Its crews were well-trained in submarine and antisubmarine tactics; they had a small but very high-quality submarine force that had already made its presence felt during the war, and even the old *Java*, though without torpedoes, had depth charges. The Dutch also placed a high priority on mine warfare. In a joint effort with the Royal Netherlands Indies Army Air Force a large number of airfields were also built across the Indies. An organization whose backbone was long-range flying boats, the Royal Netherlands Naval Air Service was among the best of its kind in the world, having trained extensively for operations in the Indies, working closely with the navy on such issues as communications and reconnaissance. And they were among the first to recognize that the most dangerous ships in the Imperial Japanese Navy were not the aircraft carriers or the big battleships, but the heavy cruisers. The Dutch had designed a version of the battlecruiser known as a "cruiser killer" to deal with just this threat. Three of them, called "Project 1047," were under construction when the Wehrmacht overran the Dutch homeland.[28] Perhaps knowing that the cruiser killers would not be ready in time for the war, in April 1939 the Dutch asked to buy three British battleships immediately, offering to pay with hard cash. In the midst of their own war preparations and taken aback by this bizarre request, the British had no battleships to sell.[29] It was a mark of Dutch desperation, too little and much too late.

The Dutch operated from three principal ports in the Indies, all of which were on Java, the political, commercial, and industrial center of the Indies. Their principal naval facilities were at Soerabaja on the northeast corner of Java. Soerabaja had a sheltered harbor because it was separated from the Java Sea by the island of Madoera (Madura) to the northeast, which created two entrances to the port, which is sometimes called Perak. The western entrance, the Westervaarwater, gave access to the Java Sea; because it ran north to south, it was also called the northern entrance. The eastern entrance, the Oostervaarwater, gave access to Madoera Strait and went east to join the Bali Strait. Unfortunately, both were too shallow for heavy ships. The eastern entrance could handle nothing bigger than a destroyer, while the northern entrance was dredged in 1940 to allow the battlecruisers that would never be built. Most of the Dutch naval facilities were centered on Soerabaja; perhaps too many: the seaplane base at Morokrembangan (perhaps the best seaplane base in the far east), the well-equipped submarine base, a standard airfield at Perak, along with Marine barracks and two floating drydocks.[30] It was not Pearl Harbor, Seletar, or even Cavite, but it could have been worse, as was the case elsewhere on Java.

On the northwest part of the island was Tandjoeng Priok (now Tandjung Priok or Tandjong Priok), the port for the capital Batavia. While modern Jakarta has now enveloped the port, Tandjoeng Priok, some 8 miles from the capital, was originally to Batavia what Long Beach is to Los Angeles. It was (and is) a very large civilian port, but had almost no naval facilities, with only a seaplane base.[31] The area around Batavia had two airfields, both south of the city.

The third port, and the only port of consequence on the south coast of Java was Tjilatjap. The town is now called Cilacap, and is pronounced "CHIL-a-chap," with the English "ch" approximating the Dutch "tj," though US Navy sailors typically pronounced it "Slapjack" or "that lousy dump."[32] With almost no natural harbors on the south coast of Java, Tjilatjap, located at a wide spot in a river near the inappropriately named Schildpadden (Turtle) Bay, was the best available, but even it wasn't very good: the entrance was twisting and very narrow, with tricky currents and dangerous shallows and rocks. With war approaching, the Dutch government tried to improve Tjilatjap so it could handle 250,000 tons of cargo each month, with mixed results. Critically, Tjilatjap also lacked an airfield of any kind.

In what would prove to be a Godsend, in mid-December the Dutch managed to place an 8,000-ton floating drydock in Tjilatjap, adding the Royal Netherlands Navy repair ship *Barentsz* in early January 1942.[33] It wasn't much for repair work, but it was something.[34]

The loss of the Netherlands had been a catastrophe for the Dutch in the Indies. Their government-in-exile, headed by Queen Wilhelmina, at this time in London, was almost totally dependent on the British. The Indies' military readiness had been effectively frozen. There would be no reinforcements and no spare parts, which now had to be cannibalized. They could no longer build their own ships and aircraft; they had to purchase them from Britain and the United States. With those countries using much of their industrial capacity to support their own war efforts, the Dutch were left with items the Americans and British no longer wanted, like obsolete aircraft such as the Martin B-10 bomber, called the Glenn Martin in the Indies, and more of the ubiquitous but largely ineffectual Brewster Buffalos. Even worse was a factor that has been perhaps underrated: with access to the mother country cut off, the Dutch seem to have been suffering from a critical manpower shortage. Several warships of the Royal Netherlands Navy were manned, if at all, with skeleton crews that impaired battle effectiveness. After the sinking of the *Prince of Wales* and *Repulse*, Admiral Helfrich had requested their survivors be sent to the Indies to crew the *Sumatra*, two submarines, and a few torpedo boats but for reasons that remain disputed, the obviously complicated details could not be worked out.[35] The destroyer *Evertsen* had been commissioned only since December 1, 1941, and her crew was not ready for combat.[36] The destroyer *Witte de With* was only fully crewed by transferring the entire crew of her sister ship *Van Ghent*, upon the latter's destruction.[37]

This military weakness, much but by no means all of which was self-inflicted, would play a role not just in the conduct of ABDACOM but in its organization. The Dutch military and civilian leaders were furious that they had been shut out of the senior positions in the command, with a particular anger over Admiral Helfrich not having been named ABDAFLOAT. On paper, there was a certain validity to their anger inasmuch as only one of the top nine posts within ABDACOM was occupied by a Dutchman, General Hein ter Poorten, the commander of Dutch Army Forces in the Indies, who was serving as ABDARM (sometimes called ABDARMY or ABDA-army), army commander. The Dutch wanted more of a presence on the naval staff, they said, because the Indies were their islands and they knew these difficult waters better than anyone.

But these arguments were more than a little self-serving. While the Dutch had only one of the top nine spots in ABDACOM, their one spot was among the top four (overall command, army command, navy command, and air force command), and the army command was the one in which the Dutch had by far the most to contribute. On a superficial scale at least, the Dutch seemed to want all the military forces from the ABDA countries but to keep all the commands to themselves. Their position was neither reasonable nor realistic.

In terms of the navy command that was such a sore spot for the Dutch, the US Navy was making equally as large a contribution as the Royal Netherlands Navy. The post of ABDAFLOAT chief of staff had been offered to Admiral Helfrich's chief of staff, Captain Johan Jasper Abraham van Staveren, which would have given the Dutch one more member of the top nine posts in ABDACOM, but it was turned down because Helfrich said he "could not spare him."[38] It is easy to wonder if Helfrich blocked the move in a fit of pique.

In fact, quite a number of the political problems that infected ABDACOM could be traced to Admiral Helfrich. Helfrich was not simply commander of the Dutch naval forces in the Indies, but was part of the civilian government as minister of the navy. General ter Poorten, as commander of the East Indies Army, held no such civilian appointment – and, moreover, was a "territorial" officer rather than a "royal" officer like Helfrich – and Helfrich resented being further down in the ABDACOM chain of command to someone who was lower in status in the Netherlands East Indies civilian government.[39] In Admiral Hart's view:

> In his [Helfrich's] relations as a subordinate commander under ABDAFLOAT, Admiral Helfrich
> at times seemed to be motivated somewhat from the political angle and at other times altogether

from the standpoint of a Naval commander in war. At times he would be entirely frank and open in any matters which were under discussion, while at other times he acted more as in a civil capacity.[40]

With all these issues of politics and status evidently occupying his thoughts, one may wonder where Helfrich found the time and effort to actually fight the war that was threatening them all.

But based on combat results, Admiral Helfrich could actually make a better case publicly for being ABDFLOAT than could Admiral Hart, for Helfrich's Dutch forces had so far shown themselves to be far more aggressive and successful than the US Navy. Well before the Japanese declared war on the Netherlands, the Dutch knew that their East Indies territories would be the main Japanese target. Thus they declared war on Japan and with their limited, largely obsolete forces moved in support of their British allies to try to take the offensive to the Japanese aggressors.

And they did, starting at the Pacific War's first battlefield off Malaya. On December 8, 1941, Admiral Helfrich signaled all the Dutch ships WAR WITH JAPAN HAS BROKEN OUT. The Dutch submarines were placed under the operational control of the British in Singapore, who concentrated the boats against the incoming Japanese invasion convoys. The Japanese submarine *I-56* launched an unsuccessful attack on the Dutch submarine *K-XVII*. On December 12, the Dutch submarine *K-XII* torpedoed and sank a Japanese Army cargo ship, possibly the luckless *Awagisan Maru*, off Kota Bharu. Not to be outdone, the submarine *O-16*, under the command of Dutch submarine ace Lieutenant Commander Anton Jacobus Bussemaker, delivered an incredible performance by sinking Japanese Army cargo ships *Tozan Maru*, *Kinka Maru*, and *Asosan Maru* off Singora.[41] Unfortunately, the water was shallow enough for the Japanese to eventually recover both. Even worse, both the *O-16* and *K-XVII* struck mines and were sunk while returning to Singapore. Of their crews, all but one were lost.

It was off Borneo that the Dutch made a serious nuisance of themselves to the Japanese, if not to overall Japanese plans. On December 15, the Japanese occupied Brunei, on the northwestern coast of Borneo. The next day, a Japanese invasion convoy, part of Admiral Ozawa's Western Force, left Cam Ranh Bay bound for Miri in Sarawak, a British-ruled area in north Borneo. The close escort consisted of the light cruiser *Yura;* the destroyers *Shinonome, Shirakumo,* and *Murakumo*; the seaplane tender *Kamikawa Maru*, a few subchasers, and two minesweepers. Also present was a covering force of half of the Japanese 7th Cruiser Division, with the heavy cruisers *Kumano* and *Suzuya*, the light cruiser *Kinu,* and the destroyers *Sagiri* and *Fubuki*. It was not a long trip and the invasion fleet reached Miri around midnight on December 16, where their 2,500 troops, landing almost unopposed, quickly captured it.[42]

Even though Miri was British territory, the Dutch launched a counterattack. First on the morning of December 17 was a flight of Glenn Martin bombers, but these B-10s were unsuccessful. Then came an attack from three Dutch Dornier Do-24 flying boats of the

Royal Netherlands Naval Air Service operating out of Tarakan in northeast Borneo. One was apparently shot down by a floatplane from the *Kamikawa Maru*, but two pressed home their attacks. Because of heavy cloud cover, one managed to sneak in completely unnoticed. The first the Japanese knew of the attack was an explosion near the stern of the destroyer *Shinonome*. The result of what were two 200kg (440lb) bomb hits, the explosion seemingly detonated the magazine for the aft gun mount, sending up a massive smoke column. A near miss also ruptured her hull plating. The destroyer immediately stopped, her stern breaking off. Within minutes she was gone. A second Dornier dropped its bombs on a freighter, with no hits. The Japanese never saw either Dutch flying boat.

Next came the Japanese landing at Kuching, in Sarawak on Borneo's northwest coast. On December 22, a convoy of transports left Miri for Kuching. They were escorted again by the seaplane tender *Kamikawa Maru*, the light cruiser *Yura*, and the destroyers *Shirakumo* and *Murakumo*, with the *Usugumo* replacing the sunken *Shinonome*. Once again, they had a covering force of *Kumano* and *Suzuya*, the light cruiser *Kinu,* and the destroyers *Sagiri* and *Fubuki*. Dutch Dornier flying boat X-35 of the Royal Netherlands Naval Air Service spotted the convoy and immediately signaled the Dutch submarine *K-XIV.* At 8:40 pm on December 23, *K-XIV,* under the skillful direction of Lieutenant Commander Carel A. J. van Well Groeneveld, managed to sneak inside these defenders and wreak absolute havoc. He first torpedoed and sank the transport *Hiyoshi Maru*. Next he torpedoed and sank the transport *Katori Maru.* Hundreds of Japanese troops drowned. The *K-XIV* then turned her torpedoes on the *Hokkai Maru*, which was heavily damaged and beached to prevent her sinking. Finally, one more ship, either *Nichiran Maru* or *Tonan Maru No. 3*, was scarred by van Well Groeneveld's torpedoes, although the ship did not sink.[43] This was a perfect example of the close and efficient cooperation between the Royal Netherlands Naval Air Service and the navy.[44]

As December 23 turned into December 24, Dutch submarine *K-XVI,* under Lieutenant Commander L. J. Jarman, got into the act by sending a torpedo into the Japanese destroyer *Sagiri*. The *Sagiri's* torpedo stowage caught fire and detonated, blowing off her stern. She sank within minutes.[45] The *K-XVI's* victory was short-lived, as later that morning the Japanese submarine *I-66* caught her on the surface, and launched one torpedo that blew the Dutch submarine in two, sinking it with all hands.[46] The Dutch topped off this merry mischief on December 26 when a flight of the obsolete Glenn Martin bombers operating out of the Samarinda airfield on Borneo swooped in to sink the minesweeper *W-6* and collier *No. 2 Unyo Maru*.[47]

While the Dutch successes sound impressive – and they were – the Japanese conquest of northwest Borneo was not delayed by even a day. Nevertheless, the Royal Netherlands Navy was left feeling "particularly cocky," as Admiral Hart would later describe it, bolstering Admiral Helfrich's credibility as a military leader. At one point the American press called him "Ship-A-Day" Helfrich because of the success of his submarines, whose success he publicly held over Hart against the relative lack of success of the US Navy to that point.[48] And it certainly fed the Dutch sense of entitlement to the ABDAFLOAT position. During these early days, with the Japanese advancing ever closer to Java, Helfrich spent a major effort using the Dutch successes and his own bureaucratic skills to create political problems, especially for Hart.

Those political problems would quickly become military problems.

MORE US TORPEDO PROBLEMS

Admiral Hart was a former submarine man who placed high hopes on the ability of the Asiatic Fleet's submarines to at least make the Imperial Japanese Navy pay a high price for its advance. He had even had a hand in developing the Mark 6's magnetic exploder for the submarine torpedoes, which, ultimately, would prove to be an achievement better left off his resume. Nevertheless, painful as it was for Hart to admit, Admiral Helfrich and General MacArthur's criticism were entirely justified regarding the lack of success.

And if it was dispiriting for Admiral Hart, his submarine skippers had to feel absolutely crushed. Some mentally cracked, others asked to be relieved of duty, still others were the subject of suspicions, justified and otherwise, from their own crews.

But a tough few decided to do something about the poor performance of the boats and their suspicions, now shared by Admiral Hart, that something was seriously wrong with their torpedoes.

Commander Tyrell Jacobs brought his command *Sargo* into Soerabaja at the end of her patrol for a chat with Captain Wilkes that was not entirely friendly. Wilkes had received Jacobs' unfavorable reports about the Mark 14 torpedo and the Mark 6 exploder. Wilkes agreed that the torpedo might be running too deep, but he criticized Jacobs for deactivating the Mark 6 magnetic exploder. Jacobs pleaded for the *Sargo* to be allowed to fire a test shot through a fishing net. He was denied, on account of the shortage of torpedoes.[49]

The US Navy Bureau of Ordnance flew a torpedo expert named Lieutenant Commander Walker out to Soerabaja to investigate the *Sargo*'s torpedo issues. The submarine was put through maintenance, handling, and firing drills with no problems surfacing. During one regimen in which they prepared a torpedo for firing, Walker, after going over the torpedo, directed the *Sargo*'s torpedo officer, Doug Rhymes, to lock the gyros, which set the torpedo's course once it is launched, into place. Unfortunately the torpedo expert flown in by the Bureau of Ordnance had put the torpedo gyro in backwards. Such a mistake would cause the torpedo to run erratically or even make a circular run, which could result in the destruction of the submarine. As Rhymes later told it, "I turned the gyro to the correct alignment, locked it in place and told Walker that we preferred to attack the enemy ships instead of our own. His face fell half a foot."

But this long-lasting moral victory was a short-lived bureaucratic victory. Even though Lieutenant Commander Walker found nothing wrong with the *Sargo* or her procedures, Walker's report, backed up by the Bureau of Ordnance, reasserted that the Mark 14 torpedo ran at its proper depth. Why were the Mark 14 and its Mark 6 exploder not hitting anything? To summarize Lieutenant Commander Walker's report in two words: User error.

THE STORMCLOUDS OPEN – JANUARY 10–20

The ominous concentration of Japanese forces at Davao and Jolo had not gone unnoticed by the Allies, but their response had been relatively ineffectual. There was the disastrous raid on Jolo by Patrol Wing 10 and the subsequent raid by that single Dutch Dornier flying boat. On January 4, B-17 Flying Fortresses based in Java bombed the former US Navy anchorage at Malalag Bay, where the *William B. Preston* had hidden and where now the Japanese 5th Cruiser Division – three heavy cruisers of the *Myoko* class – was holed up. The attack resulted in one hit on the *Myoko* herself, which had to return to Japan for repairs. On January 10, the submarine USS *Pickerel* torpedoed and actually sank the gunboat *Kanko Maru* off Cape San Augustin at the mouth of the Davao Gulf. That same day, the USS *Stingray* sank the Japanese cargo ship *Harbin Maru* with torpedoes off the south coast of Hainan Island, while the Dutch submarine *O-19* sank the cargo ship *Akita Maru* and damaged the freighter *Tairyu Maru* in the Gulf of Siam. But none of these successful actions delayed the approaching Japanese storm.

That storm hit on January 11, 1942. The Japanese officially declared war on the Netherlands, more than a month after the Dutch had declared war on Tokyo. Their first target was Tarakan in northeastern Borneo, which was to be occupied by the Imperial Japanese Army's 56th Regimental Combat Group and the Navy's 2nd Kure Special Naval Landing Force. The Dutch were struggling to adequately defend the oil-rich port. Even by the current hopeless standards of ABDACOM, the defense of Tarakan was bizarre.

Trying to scrape up enough combatants to throw in the path of the Japanese advance, the Dutch pressed back into service the submarine *K-X*, a 19-year-old submarine that had not been modernized and seems to have been in pretty bad shape.[50] Under the command of Lieutenant Commander P. G. de Back, the *K-X* huffed and puffed her way around the Indies, eventually being sent to Tarakan, where it was hoped she would help defend against the Japanese landings. But by the time she got to Tarakan on January 8, she was having trouble with her diving controls and her engines. She made some temporary repairs, took on supplies, and set about resuming her war patrol, only to have a compressor on one of the engines go out. It could not be repaired at sea, so *K-X* had to return to Tarakan the next day, where she moored alongside the Dutch minelayer *Prins van Oranje* while the compressor was taken ashore for repairs. The two Dutch naval craft took to hiding from expected Japanese air raids. Sure enough, early on January 10 the air raid alarm sounded, and the *K-X* dove to the bottom. Lieutenant Commander de Back took a look through the periscope and saw what looked like an aircraft carrier but, oddly enough, no aircraft. There was a good reason for this: the "carrier" was the USS *Langley*.

In the meantime, the Japanese had arrived offshore. To counter them, the minelayer *Prins van Oranje* had augmented the existing minefield protecting Tarakan's harbor. With the engine still not repaired, the *K-X* seemed to be trapped inside the harbor. Nevertheless, she was ordered by Admiral Helfrich to do all she could to stop the invasion. The *Prins van Oranje* gave Lieutenant Commander de Back a map through the minefield. It was not a very good map, but it would have to do.

At 4:30 pm on January 10, the *K-X*, required to stay on the surface by the shallow depth of the harbor, set out to navigate her way through the minefield to the north of Tarakan. On approaching the minefield she was attacked by a Japanese seaplane. From low altitude, the aircraft dropped one bomb that exploded some 25yd off the bow. The *K-X* retaliated with her antiaircraft machine gun, which promptly jammed. The aircraft made a second bombing run, resulting in a miss 20yd astern. The Japanese aircraft then made a strafing run, raking the crew members on deck with machine gun fire. There were no injuries as a result of this attack, but the map through the minefield was lost. Fortunately, *K-X* was able to safely navigate through the rest of the minefield and quickly submerged as soon as the water was deep enough only to spot attacking aircraft and antiaircraft fire to the east: Dutch Glenn Martin bombers operating out of Samarinda were attacking the Japanese invasion convoy.

After dark Lieutenant Commander de Back had his boat surface to try to attack the invasion convoy. But the engine was still not repaired; a problem that frustrated his attempts to get into attack position. Beset by continued mechanical issues, he returned to Soerabaja.

Meanwhile the Dutch defense of Tarakan was largely ineffectual. The *Prins van Oranje*, trying to escape on the night of January 11, was discovered and sunk by the Japanese destroyer *Yamakaze* and patrol boat *PB-38*.[51] Dutch army shore batteries would take out two Japanese minesweepers, *W-13* and *W-14*, and the Japanese destroyer *Asagumo* suffered damage when she ran aground, but the Japanese would make that trade anytime.[52]

It would have been helpful if the Dutch military had managed to destroy their airfield at Tarakan before it fell to the Japanese, but they did not. The Japanese captured it intact, and thus set the pattern for the entire Netherlands East Indies campaign. With amazing foresight, the Dutch had peppered the Indies with these airfields for use in case of war. With equally amazing lack of foresight, they did not follow through on those preparations, so these airfields usually had few if any aircraft and were poorly defended. The Japanese would capture these airfields intact and then use them against the Dutch.

That same day, naval paratroopers of the 1st Yokosuka Special Naval Landing Force occupied Menado in northern Celebes. Other elements of 1st Special Naval Landing Force followed up by landing at Menado and Kema, Celebes. The Japanese now controlled the northern entrance to the Makassar Strait, between Borneo and the Celebes, the driveway to Java.

This was the situation that greeted ABDACOM on its first official day of existence on January 15, 1942. Meanwhile General Wavell had flown into Java, establishing his headquarters in the mountains of central Java at Lembang, 10 miles from the Netherlands East Indies military headquarters in Bandoeng, and held a meeting with all the major ABDA commanders.[53] Then, however, he had flown back to Singapore.

This was yet another example of the lack of coordination between the ABDA countries. Throughout the campaign General Wavell's overriding concern was predictably Singapore, as the British, not unreasonably, considered Singapore to be critical to the defense of the "Malay Barrier." The phrase "Malay Barrier" – that stretch of islands running from Sumatra eastward through Java, Bali, Lombok, and the Lesser Soenda Islands to Timor in the east – would be important from now on. The barrier had to be held so that the Japanese could not pour through its cracks – the Strait of Malacca, Soenda Strait, Bali Strait, Lombok Strait, and others to the east – into the Indian Ocean to threaten Australia or India.

The British saw Singapore as the left flank of the Malay Barrier. Without it, the islands could simply be rolled up from the west. As such, General Wavell immediately returned to Singapore to see if he could shore up the defenses of the British commander in Malaya, General Arthur Percival. Certainly the British and the overall war effort might have been better served if Wavell had simply stepped in to take over from the overmatched Percival.

Ultimately ABDACOM ended up being a primarily British-led operation. And the British imprinted their military doctrines on ABDACOM, which were not always to the benefit of the Allied cause, as in the allocation of air power. The ABDA air force (ABDAIR) was under the command of Air Chief Marshal Sir Richard E. C. Peirse of the Royal Air Force and all the ABDA air assets were grouped under ABDAIR. Peirse enforced the British doctrine that the air force should not coordinate with the army or navy service branches, and that philosophy was imposed on ABDAIR. Thus, for instance, all the prewar training the Royal Netherlands Navy had with the Royal Netherlands Naval Air Service, the training that had enabled the submarine *K-XIV* to wreak such havoc off Kuching, went out the window. Eventually, a special reconnaissance section was set up including Patrol Wing 10 and the Royal Netherlands Naval Air Service and placed under the command of the Dutch. But Peirse often usurped elements of it to defend Singapore.

Another issue was the British naval policy, which emphasized convoying above all else. It was an understandable belief on their part; Britain was an island nation dependent on transoceanic shipping, and it was fighting a war in which that shipping was the target of submarines, namely German U-boats. What the British did not grasp – understandably so for this early period in the war – was that the Imperial Japanese Navy was not the Kriegsmarine, and the Japanese did not use their submarines in the same way as Germans. While U-boats were used as strategic weapons in striking supply convoys to strangle Britain, the Japanese generally used their submarines tactically to attack warships. More importantly, however, the British seemingly did not understand that ABDA countries simply did not have enough ships in theater both to protect convoys and to defend.

For all of the later charges of being defeatist and not aggressive enough, Admiral Hart constantly tried to create a naval striking force to counterattack against the Japanese. But his efforts were always undermined by the insistence of the British in using their own ships and the Dutch ships to escort convoys to Singapore over other, more urgent needs. A frustrated Hart could never pull enough ships from convoy duty to put together a force of overwhelming firepower.

Frustration was the status of nearly everyone involved in ABDACOM, from the senior officers to the lowliest enlisted men. The British were ecstatic to have the United States now allied with them in the war, and the relationship between the two was quite good, but it was not all rosy. The British were not always able to hide their belief that their American comrades were not-quite-ready-for-prime-time, a belief that was not entirely incorrect. General Sir Henry Pownall, Wavell's chief of staff, was described by one American sailor as "a snotty bastard who thought the Americans needed to be put in their place."[54] The Americans sometimes took the British to be stubborn and not given to listening to suggestions and concerns from others, with the elitist attitude of "you furnish the iron and we will furnish the brass."[55] In fact, so did the Dutch and Australians, who also felt they had been taken for granted by London. The Australians and Americans generally got along well at all levels, as both were former British colonies and, again, the Australians were elated to have the United States standing behind them.

Relations between the Americans and the Dutch were complicated. The staff officers generally got along fairly well, but among the lower ranks it was hit-and-miss. The language barrier was obviously significant, but it was much more than that. When the Asiatic Fleet first began arriving in the Indies, the Dutch were often surly and suspicious. One of the few who welcomed the Americans was Lieutenant Commander Antonie Kroese, captain of the Dutch destroyer *Kortenaer*. He actually invited his US Navy counterparts to his house on a number of occasions.[56] So appreciative were the Americans of Kroese's hospitality that they nicknamed him "Cruiser" – a play on the pronunciation of his surname.[57]

Aside from Lieutenant Commander Kroese, however, the Americans accused the Dutch of being completely unappreciative of American efforts to help them defend their colony, especially since the United States as a society was deeply suspicious of colonialism. One officer of Patrol Wing 10 called the Dutch "damn krauts," while another was of the opinion that "[The Dutch] had the attitude that it was your duty to do these things for them, and you were honored to do it."[58] For their part, the Dutch were often disrespectful of the US Navy's fighting ability after the retreat from the Philippines, and were resentful that the Americans had so easily given up what the Dutch had considered to be a shield against Japanese invasion of the Indies.[59] The anger was understandable if misplaced; it was an example of how many of the Dutch commanders and civilians felt entitled to have others protect them when they for so long had been unwilling to protect themselves. Chief among those who felt entitled to American help (as well as help from the British and Australians) was the Dutch Admiral Helfrich. Paradoxically, however, he was deeply appreciative of that same help.

As an aside, within these pages it may seem at times as if Conrad Helfrich was a villain second only to the Japanese. It must be emphasized that this was not the case. Helfrich may have been arrogant, conniving, bullying, unreasonable, and aggressive to the point of recklessness, often seeming to care little for the lives under his command, but he was no villain. He was not to blame for the desperate straits that the Netherlands East Indies or any of the other ABDA countries found themselves. He was by no means an incompetent commander, having effectively deployed his naval air assets and his submarines where they could do maximum damage to the enemy (though unfortunately suffering maximum damage to themselves). And while he felt entitled to the position of ABDAFLOAT, he did so in part because he felt he could do the best job of anyone at protecting the Indies. He was also a team player, inasmuch as he often turned over operational control of his ships to the British in support of Singapore. Helfrich on multiple occasions expressed his gratitude for the help given him by the other ABDA countries. As later events would show, he even backed up his feeling with a gesture that, while small, was nevertheless quite meaningful. For now, however, Helfrich was as much a hindrance as he was a help.

And so it went for ABDACOM. It may have been mostly unified in structure and purpose, but it was not in strategy or tactics. The British were doing everything possible to protect Singapore. The Dutch were far more worried about protecting the Netherlands East Indies. The Americans were more interested in counterattacking to regain the Philippines. The Australians were most focused on protecting Australia, which was starting to become a major concern for everyone.

The port of Darwin, in Australia's Northern Territory, had been designated the main logistics base and staging area for ABDACOM. Supplies would be accumulated here and forces would be grouped here before being shipped off to the front – most likely Singapore. The Japanese were aware of Darwin's potential as a port and were taking steps to neutralize it. On January 11, the US Army transport *Liberty Glo* was torpedoed by the Japanese submarine *I-166* about 10 miles southwest of the Lombok Strait. The US destroyer *Paul Jones* and the Dutch destroyer *Van Ghent* took the damaged ship in tow, but were unable to bring her back to port. They beached her on the shores of Bali in sinking condition.[60] Then mines started to appear in the main approaches to Darwin, starting in the Clarence Strait, connecting Van Diemen Gulf and the Timor Sea. These mines came courtesy of some Japanese submarines, namely the *I-121* and the *I-122*. Mines appeared next in the Bundas Strait, presents left by the *I-123* under the command of Lieutenant Commander Ueno Toshitake. She followed it up with an unsuccessful attack on the Asiatic Fleet oiler *Trinity* in the Beagle Gulf, some 60 miles west of Darwin, at 6:24 am on January 20; prompt reaction by the *Edsall* and *Alden* kept the submarine submerged and enabled the *Trinity* to make Darwin.[61] Then the *I-124*, under the command of Lieutenant Commander Kishigami Koichi, mined the waters off Darwin itself.[62] But Kishigami had signed his own death warrant; a January 19 report that he had made to Tokyo about a small convoy entering Darwin, quickly decoded by Allied codebreakers and used to warn of her presence off Darwin, turned out to be his last.[63]

With mounting evidence of Japanese submarines lying in ambush off Darwin, Darwin's Naval Officer in Charge, Captain Ernest P. Thomas, ordered three Australian corvettes *Deloraine, Katoomba*, and *Lithgow* to hunt down and kill the underwater predators. Kishigami greeted them at 1:35 pm with a torpedo aimed at the *Deloraine*, evaded by the corvette with a starboard turn.[64] This only served to anger the Australians, who, with help from two Catalinas and a Vought-Sikorsky OS2U Kingfisher floatplane from Patrol Wing 10, performed a series of relentless and devastating attacks on the submarine. Quickly picking up the *I-124* on asdic, the *Deloraine* launched her first depth charge attack at 1:43 pm, which produced oil and bubbles to the surface. A second attack five minutes later caused the submarine's bow and periscope to broach the surface and left her down by the stern with a 20-degree list to port. Before the *I-124* could submerge again (willingly or otherwise), she was simply thrashed by a depth charge from the *Deloraine* that detonated 10ft from the submarine's periscope and by a bomb from a Kingfisher from the *Langley*.[65] This attack apparently drove the submarine to the bottom where she gouged a trench in the sea floor, but she was not dead yet.[66] The Australians and Americans were determined to put the *I-124* under for good.

An attack by the *Deloraine* a little before 3:00 pm brought large amounts of air bubbles, oil, and debris to the surface. Her depth charges now expended, the *Deloraine* gave way to the *Lithgow*, who was soon joined by the *Katoomba* and later the *Edsall* and *Alden*. The attacks continued for the rest of the day and night and into the next morning, the *Katoomba* even attempting unsuccessfully to use a grapnel on the *I-124*.[67] Air bubbles, debris, and oil – apparently from tanks the submarine carried on her deck for refueling aircraft – continued to reach the surface.[68] The attacks were called off at about noon on January 21 due to inclement weather. The Australians believed that three submarines had been destroyed – two by *Deloraine* and one by *Katoomba* – but it was only one, the *I-124*, whose hatches had apparently been blown open by the attacks.[69] It was the first Imperial Japanese Navy unit to fall to the Royal Australian Navy.

But yet another problem surfaced, one that would plague ABDAFLOAT throughout its existence: operational accidents and mechanical breakdowns. On January 20, US submarine *S-36* ran aground on Taka Bakang Reef in the Makassar Strait some 30 miles southwest of Makassar City and had to be scuttled by her crew the next day. On January 23, the *Edsall* was attempting to sink another Japanese submarine in the Clarence Strait with depth charges, but the concussions were magnified in the shallow Howard Channel and backfired on the *Edsall*, apparently rupturing her stern plating and damaging her propellers and shafts, leaving her unfit for combat; she could only perform convoy duty.[70]

The Royal Navy also joined in the hunt for Japanese submarines. While escorting transports through the Banka Strait on January 17, British destroyer *Jupiter*, under the command of Lieutenant Commander Norman V. J. T. Thew, heard a distress call from a transport that had been torpedoed in the Soenda Strait. *Jupiter* engaged in a two-hour asdic hunt before dropping two depth charges on the Japanese submarine *I-60* some 25 miles north northwest of Anak Krakatau, the remnant of the famous volcano Krakatoa. For reasons known only to the submarine's skipper, Lieutenant Commander Hasegawa Shun, the heavily damaged *I-60* surfaced. She was just astern of the *Jupiter*, so close that the destroyer's main guns could not depress sufficiently to hit her, so it may have been a desperate bid to board the destroyer. Or she may have been just too badly damaged. In any event, she was ready for a fight. The submarine's crew manned her 4.7in deck gun and sent a flurry of shells at the *Jupiter*, one knocking out her "A" twin 4.7in gun mount, killing three and wounding nine. The destroyer responded with a withering fire from her 20mm Oerlikon antiaircraft guns and, after launching two torpedoes that missed, moved off so that she could bring her main 4.7in guns to bear on the submarine. The 4.7in shells hammered the already badly hurt *I-60* and set it afire before the *Jupiter* sent a shallow depth charge to explode near the boat's conning tower, shattering it and finally finishing off the submarine.[71] *Jupiter* had to return to Soerabaja for repairs.[72]

But these actions only highlighted the overemphasis on convoying. Sinking submarines had no potential to stop or even slow down the Japanese advance. Ships that could be used to stop the Japanese were wasted on convoys when there was no real danger – Admiral Hart would later say that if all of the convoys had been unescorted, they might have lost one ship.[73] That was why he had resisted sending Asiatic Fleet ships to western Java and Singapore for useless convoy duty. He kept them in the east, where he could at least maintain the potential for combat operations to blunt the enemy spear. That potential became a reality on January 20 when a Japanese invasion force was spotted in Makassar Strait.

No more convoying. Now it was time to attack.

CHAPTER 7
LUCK – THE BATTLE OF BALIKPAPAN

FORTUNE FAVORS THE BOLD – JANUARY 16–24

The Japanese had moved on the Minahassa Peninsula, the northernmost appendage of the oddly shaped island of Celebes.[1] In the predawn hours of January 11, the Japanese 1st Sasebo Special Naval Landing Force had landed at the ports of Menado and Kema. They were supplemented by a pair of parachute drops, also by 1st Sasebo Special Naval Landing Force.[2]

Admiral Hart suspected that this landing would be a jumping off point for further attacks against southern Celebes, particularly the port of Kendari, the real strategic gem of the island. This meant that the Japanese transports – unarmored and vulnerable – would be an inviting target.

Hart moved to assemble a striking force. The cruisers *Boise* and *Marblehead* and the destroyers *John D. Ford*, *Pope*, *Parrott*, *Paul Jones*, *Pillsbury*, and *Bulmer* set up a rendezvous at Koepang on Timor, where the natives promptly made clear that the Americans were not wanted.[3] The striking force was organized as Task Force 5 under the command of Admiral Glassford. Five of the destroyers would sail at night in column formation and launch all their torpedoes from their tubes on one side, then reverse course and launch all their torpedoes from the other side, filling the water with their deadly fish. Then the destroyers would leave, and the *Marblehead*, with Admiral Glassford on board, would fill the water with yet more torpedoes. Then she would use her 6in guns to enable everyone to withdraw. If they could not, the *Boise*, screened by the *Pillsbury*, could give cover with her 15 rapid-fire 6in guns.[4]

In theory this was a good plan; a high-speed torpedo attack at night, without the use of guns whose flashes would reveal the destroyers' presence, could cause chaos and heavy damage among the enemy ships. Of course, night torpedo attacks were already standard in the Imperial Japanese Navy. In many respects, the US Navy (and, indeed, the Dutch) was playing catch up to the Japanese. But the logic behind leaving his single most powerful warship – the *Boise* – out of the action seems rather elusive.

On January 16 Task Force 5 began speeding up the hazardous Makassar Strait for Kema and their massed Japanese prey. And they were almost there when, on January 17, they received a report from the US submarines *Pike* and *Permit*, who had been sent in to scout the Kema area – the Japanese ships were gone. The attack was cancelled.[5] Too soon, as it turned out: on January 21 the submarine *Swordfish* returned to Kema and found the harbor full of Japanese shipping. Her skipper Lieutenant Commander Chester Smith could not get into attack position, but he bided his time and was rewarded on January 24 when, just after noon, he managed to plunk two torpedoes into the gunboat *Myoken Maru* that sent her to the bottom.[6]

And so ended the first ABDAFLOAT attempt at a counterattack.

Admiral Glassford ordered his ships to retire to Koepang (Kupang) on Dutch Timor to refuel, which was much too far behind the front line for Admiral Hart's liking.[7] What Hart did not know was that the *Marblehead* suffered a turbine casualty while heading for Koepang, necessitating the shutdown of one of her propellers and limiting her speed to 28 knots.[8] The refueling rendezvous was moved to Kebola Bay, on Alor Island just to the north of Timor.[9]

Also arriving for this refueling party were reinforcements: the *John D. Edwards* and *Whipple*; and, on January 17, the *Houston*, *Alden*, and *Edsall*.[10] Now *this* was a striking force of some serious power. Admiral Hart had received a report from the Dutch that the Japanese were massing at the northern end of the Makassar Strait headed for Balikpapan with an estimated 16 transports, 12 destroyers, one light cruiser, and an unknown number of armed auxiliaries such as patrol boats and minesweepers.[11] Hart ordered an attack. With his reinforcements in hand, Admiral Glassford adjusted his plan. Now all eight destroyers would accompany the *Marblehead*, while the *Houston* and *Boise* would remain 50 miles astern to use their guns to cover their withdrawal. The historian and US Navy commander Walter Winslow thought the plan was a "one-way ticket to oblivion" for the old *Marblehead* and the even-older destroyers.[12]

But oblivion would have to wait. The meeting in which Admiral Glassford presented his plan had not even concluded before they were told that the Dutch intelligence information was, as Admiral Hart would later call it, "wholly false" and the mission was scrubbed.[13]

And so ended the second ABDAFLOAT – rapidly earning the nickname "ABDAFLOP" – attempt at a counterattack.[14]

The assembled ships of Task Force 5 scattered to attend to other matters. The *Houston* was sent off with the *John D. Edwards* and *Whipple* for convoy duty.[15] Late in the afternoon on January 18, the *Trinity*, with the *Alden* and *Edsall* as escorts, left Kebola Bay headed for Darwin and their encounter with *I-123*.[16]

On January 20, Dutch intelligence reported a Japanese advance down the Makassar Strait.[17] US submarines were deployed in the Strait to try to peck at it as best they could. But the effort started off badly with the fatal grounding of *S-36* off Makassar City. That night the submarines *Porpoise, Pickerel,* and *Sturgeon* moved to intercept the convoy in Makassar Strait, while the US submarines *Spearfish, Saury,* and *S-40* and the Dutch submarines *K-XIV* and *K-XVIII* maneuvered into position off Balikpapan.[18]

Admiral Hart attempted to get Task Force 5 reassembled as best he could. With the *Houston* and her consorts gone on convoy duty, Task Force 5 was back to its original formidable configuration: light cruisers *Boise* and *Marblehead* and destroyers *John D. Ford, Pope, Parrott, Paul Jones, Pillsbury,* and *Bulmer*. Again, they rendezvoused at Koepang. Admiral Glassford's battle plan was largely the same – *Marblehead* and five destroyers would go in for a night torpedo attack while *Boise*, screened by *Bulmer*, covered their withdrawal.

But the ABDA naval forces would continue to be plagued by operational accidents and mechanical breakdowns that would badly hamper their efforts against the Japanese. That plague would be no better exemplified than by this operation.

Back on January 18 the *Marblehead* had suffered a turbine casualty, reducing her speed to 28 knots. This was not good, but workable. Not so workable, however, was what had happened to the *Boise*, to which Admiral Glassford had been forced by the *Marblehead*'s issues to transfer his flag.[19] While traversing the Sape Strait into the Flores Sea on January 21, the *Boise* struck an uncharted reef off Kelapa Island, an unfortunate incident that was the result of a lack of accurate navigational charts of the Indies as opposed to any negligence on the part of her skipper, Captain Stephen B. Robinson.[20] The English language charts were often hundreds of years old, and with coral sometimes growing at a rate of 6in per year, the difference could be crucial. The Dutch had accurate charts, but they were in Dutch and the Americans could not read them. ABDAFLOAT could have used some of the Dutch navigational pilots, but the Dutch had none available, or so they said; Admiral Hart seemed less than completely convinced of the validity of that claim.[21] Given Admiral Helfrich's behavior, Hart had good reason to be suspicious.

But the upshot of the accident was disastrous. *Boise* suffered a 120ft gash in the port side of the keel. Her machinery was damaged by the subsequent flooding, water tanks were punctured, one of her condensers was filled with coral, and she would ultimately have to head to a British drydock in Bombay for repairs.[22] So now arguably the most powerful ship in the already overmatched ABDAFLOAT, owing to her 15 rapid-fire 6in guns, and the only Allied warship in the Far East to have surface search radar was now out of this particular fight, never to return.

Admiral Glassford ordered the two cruisers, with the *Pillsbury* and *Bulmer* as escorts, to head for Waworado Bay on Soembawa, much to the disgust of Admiral Hart, who again thought they were too far out of position.[23] There, on January 22, the *Marblehead* refueled from the damaged *Boise*, and Glassford transferred his flag back to the old cruiser.[24] But in the interim, the *Marblehead*'s engine problems had proven to be far worse than initially thought – she had to limit her speed to 15 knots and shut down one shaft or the engine would be ruined.[25] Now, Glassford's two most powerful ships were maimed.

"Oh, for a little LUCK!" wrote Admiral Hart in his diary.[26]

Once the refueling was done, *Boise* and *Pillsbury* were ordered to Tjilatjap to determine the extent of the cruiser's damage; the remaining four destroyers stayed in attack position near the Postillion Islands, while *Marblehead* and *Bulmer* were ordered to make for Soerabaja.[27]

So the initial formidable task force of three cruisers and eight destroyers had been pared down to all of four destroyers – *John D. Ford, Pope, Parrott,* and *Paul Jones* – of Destroyer Division 59 under the command of Commander Paul H. Talbot. Minimal though they were, they were all that was available, and Admiral Hart was determined to use them. For on January 22, the Japanese advance was confirmed. The Catalinas of Patrol Wing 10 had reported nine transports, four cruisers and 14 destroyers moving toward Balikpapan in small groups.[28] The US submarine *Pike* reported 26 enemy transports, escorted by 14 destroyers, headed for Balikpapan.[29] The submarine *Sturgeon* picked up the contact report and moved into attack position. After dark, her sonarman detected destroyers and a "heavy-screw ship" they thought was an aircraft carrier. Skipper Lieutenant Commander William Leslie "Bull" Wright launched four torpedoes. They heard hits and explosions. After hiding from the resulting Japanese antisubmarine counterattack for a while, Wright sent back a message: *STURGEON* NO LONGER VIRGIN, thinking he had sunk the carrier. In reality, there had been no carrier and the torpedoes had registered no hits – again.[30]

The withdrawal of the *Marblehead* and *Bulmer* was stopped and they were moved to a supporting position off the southeastern tip of Borneo. At 12:05 pm Admiral Hart gave the eagerly awaited order:

GOOD LUCK GOING IN ... ATTACK ENEMY OFF BALIKPAPAN ... IF NO CONTACTS BY 0400 ZONE TIME RETIRE AT BEST SPEED ... GODSPEED COMING OUT.[31]

The key word was "attack." The men of Destroyer Division 59 were elated to get the chance to strike back at the Japanese aggressors. But when the normally cool, capable Commander Talbot read the latest intelligence about the enemy numbers he was facing – "two cruisers, eight destroyers and possibly more plus transports" – he uttered two words: "My God."[32]

The Japanese were not the only enemies Commander Talbot was facing. Talbot was suffering from severe pain and blood loss as a result of a particularly nasty case of hemorrhoids.[33] Yet the choice between protecting one's health and commanding the first US Navy surface battle since the Spanish–American War in 1898 was obvious. While the skipper and bridge crew of Talbot's flagship *John D. Ford* were aware of the situation, Talbot kept his agony to himself and stayed in his command chair, however painful that may have been, to carry out his orders and protect his crews as best as his considerable ability would allow.

Talbot's little group made a feint to the east, hoping to fool enemy scout planes into thinking the destroyers were headed for Menado Bay, Celebes. In this effort he was aided by a storm that was building as his ships continued onward. For one of the few times in the campaign, however, the Japanese scouts were nowhere to be seen.

At 7:30 pm, as the column approached Cape Mandar on Celebes, Talbot ordered a sharp column turn to port, course 310 degrees True.[34] Destination: Balikpapan, keying on the position of the harbor's lightship. By some miracle, these old flush-deckers managed to increase speed to 27 knots on a diagonal run across the Makassar Strait to the target. By blinker light, Talbot reiterated orders that he had issued that afternoon:

PRIMARY WEAPON TORPEDOES. PRIMARY OBJECTIVE TRANSPORTS. CRUISERS AS NECESSARY TO ACCOMPLISH MISSION. *ENDEAVOR* LAUNCH TORPEDOES AT CLOSE RANGE BEFORE BEING DISCOVERED … SET TORPEDOES EACH TUBE FOR NORMAL SPREAD. BE PREPARED TO FIRE SINGLE SHOTS IF SIZE OF TARGET WARRANTS. WILL TRY TO AVOID ACTION EN ROUTE … USE OWN DISCRETION IN ATTACKING INDEPENDENTLY WHEN TARGETS LOCATED. WHEN TORPS ARE FIRED CLOSE WITH ALL GUNS. USE INITIATIVE AND DETERMINATION.[35]

"Use initiative and determination" – music to a destroyerman's ears.

The column was now heading into the teeth of a gale, battered by heavy winds and enveloped by rain, giant waves crashing over bows, tossing the little ships about, forcing the exposed gun crews under cover and splashing salt water on bridge windows.[36] But slowly, almost imperceptibly, the water in the air was joined by something else: fog. Except that this was no normal fog; it was greasy, somewhat irritating, and had a burnt, chemical odor.[37]

After midnight, the lookouts reported seeing strange, surreal lights, some just a flash, others in the clouds. Off the starboard bow a large fire was observed on the water.[38] Beyond it they could see an orange-red glow in the clouds with more fire on the horizon.

It was an environment worthy of Dante's *Inferno*, but all too real. The fire on the water was the transport *Nana Maru*, set alight earlier that evening by a Dutch air attack of nine B-10 bombers from the Samarinda airfield, subsequently abandoned, and now serving as a midnight beacon guiding the four-pipers in to their target.[39] The fog wasn't just oily – it was oil. From the fire they could see ashore and, reflected in the clouds, Balikpapan's burning oil fields, oil tanks, and oil refineries, with the storm winds blowing the smoke some 20 miles out over the Makassar Strait.[40]

The commander of the Japanese 56th Infantry Regiment and 2nd Kure Special Naval Landing Force Division had sent a message to the commander of the Dutch garrison at Balikpapan warning them not to damage the oil installations or they would "be killed without exception."[41] He may have hoped the record of the Imperial Japanese Army in China would be more effective in terrorizing the Dutch into acquiescence than it had been for the Chinese, but as had been the case in China, the threats backfired – literally. The Dutch may have been lacking in numbers and modern equipment, but they were not lacking in courage. They would rather die on their feet than live on their knees.[42] There would indeed be reprisals for destruction of the oil facilities – severe reprisals – but the damage to the oil fields and refinery would delay the Japanese, a delay that would help the Allied war effort.[43]

Right now, the damage was both helping to cover the approach of the US destroyers with an effective if irritating smokescreen and providing another beacon to their target.

At 2:35 am, a lookout in the crow's nest of the *John D. Ford* reported a column of four Japanese destroyers about 3,000yd ahead – a short distance, indicating that the rain and smoke were definitely hampering visibility on this already-moonless night – crossing from starboard to port.[44] These destroyers had been the source of the strange lights, their searchlights reflecting off the clouds and flashing in the darkness.

Had the Americans been spotted? Is this why these big Japanese destroyers were now speeding by?

The gunners and torpedo crews on the old flush-deckers tensed, training their weapons on the Japanese and waiting for the order to fire. But the crews' extensive training was paying off. These were professionals who would not panic. Talbot ordered a slight column turn to starboard (325 degrees True) to clear the enemy tin cans.

Three of the four Japanese destroyers passed by. The fourth passed and then flashed a challenge to the Americans. Using a blue light, the Japanese destroyer was essentially asking, "Who are you?"

Now surely the Americans had been found out. The US Navy sailors tensed, ready to fire. But Talbot coolly ignored the challenge and the American column disappeared into the glowing murk, while their Japanese rivals continued heading out to sea.[45]

Now where were the Japanese going?

The American column had sailed straight into the arms of the transports' escorts, the Japanese 4th Destroyer Flotilla, under the command of Rear Admiral Nishimura Shōji. The flotilla comprised ten destroyers led by a light cruiser, as Japanese destroyer squadrons usually were, in this case the *Naka*.[46] Nishimura was a competent, professional and steady if unspectacular commander.[47] As the war progressed, however, he would reveal himself to be unable to adapt to changing circumstances or even to acknowledge them.[48]

But on this night, Admiral Nishimura had his 11 ships alert and ready for battle – with a submarine.

ABDAFLOAT's dispatch of submarines to attack the invasion force was paying off. Unbeknownst to Talbot, on this night (and for once and arguably the only time in this naval campaign), the ABDA force was operating with something of a guardian angel. Lurking out to sea was the Dutch submarine *K-XVIII*, under the redoubtable and very talented Commander Carel Adrianus Johannes van Well Groeneveld, who was always

THE BATTLE OF BALIKPAPAN, JANUARY 24, 1942

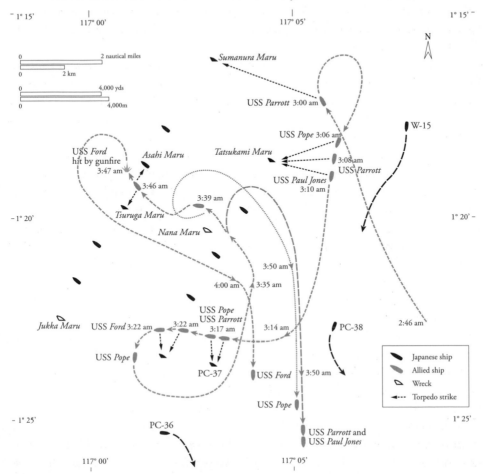

willing to cause trouble. The boiling sea caused by the storm prevented use of her periscope, so *K-XVIII* had to run on the surface, where that same storm also prevented the normally excellent Japanese lookouts from seeing her. She managed to creep through the Japanese escorts to get a clean view of the best target available, the light cruiser *Naka*. *K-XVIII* fired four torpedoes from her bow tubes at Admiral Nishimura's flagship. There were no successful hits. But the Japanese transport *Tsuruga Maru* was hit by one of van Well Groeneveld's torpedoes at about 12:45 am.[49] It is not clear, but the torpedo that hit the *Tsuruga Maru* may have come from the same round that had sped past the Naka.[50]

The plucky submarine was rapidly becoming a menace to the Japanese ships. Admiral Nishimura ordered the 4th Flotilla eastward out into the strait to hunt down the bothersome K-boat, which was exactly what the naval textbooks said he should do, *unless* he also had a column of enemy destroyers bearing down on the flock he was supposed to protect. So these ten destroyers and one light cruiser went off into the strait to make life difficult for Commander van Well Groeneveld and easy for Commander Talbot. After sailing straight into the arms of the Japanese 4th Destroyer Flotilla, the Americans sailed straight out again. The door was unguarded and wide open. And through it sailed the US destroyers with their eager crews, who could not believe their luck.

"In battle, victory goes to the brave," said the *John D. Ford*'s gunnery officer Lieutenant William P. Mack.[51] Then Mack added, "the fool-hardy."[52] The *K-XVIII* went to ground. Commander van Well Groeneveld had been warned of a pending attack by US destroyers and did not want to become involved in any friendly fire incidents. The Dutch submarine submerged, sitting down to watch the show and report on the results.

It was around 2:45 am that the sneaking American destroyers sighted their targets: the Japanese transports, sitting in two parallel lines roughly southwest to northeast, some 5 miles outside the harbor of Balikpapan: motionless and silhouetted by the massive fires ashore.[53] Guarding them were only three patrol boats converted from World War I-vintage destroyers, four minesweepers, and four subchasers.[54] As if on cue, the angry seas calmed down; the four-pipers had entered the lee of Balikpapan. It was time for Paul Talbot and company to go to work. The American column turned to the north to make a high-speed pass at the outer line of five transports. Their torpedo tubes had been trained outward for some time; now the destroyers selected their targets and let their torpedoes loose.

The *Parrott* fired three torpedoes from her portside tubes at a Japanese transport. It was motionless, backlit, a perfect setup. The Americans counted down the time to when their deadly fish should strike but there was no resulting explosion. About two minutes later, the *Parrott* thought she had spotted a destroyer or maybe a cruiser heading away some 1,000yd to starboard; that is, seaward of the American column. She let loose with five torpedoes from her starboard batteries. Yet again there was no explosion.

This was a frustrating experience by itself, made even more so by the fact that two of the torpedoes had been fired unintentionally. Even worse, her target had been neither a destroyer nor a cruiser, but the 700-ton minesweeper *W-15*. It was not a valuable target, to be sure, but no one should hold it against the *Parrott*'s crew; target identification was always difficult even on a sunny day, let alone on a stormy, smoky night. The *W-15* herself made the not-uncommon mistake of believing the American destroyer to be the flagship *Naka*, until she spotted a second Naka and then a third and a fourth. She radioed the actual *Naka*, but before *W-15* could take any other action, the ships seemingly disappeared.[55]

The *Ford* launched one torpedo from her port tubes at an anchored transport astern. The transport was immobile and unsuspecting – but yet again there was no explosion.

The *Paul Jones* fired one torpedo at a target to starboard, which turned out to be the *W-15*, who was attracting a lot of attention for a minesweeper. The US sailors counted down to … nothing.

Ten torpedoes launched at short range but with no hits. The destroyermen had heard stories that the submarine's torpedoes were defective. Were their own torpedoes defective as well?

It was now about 3:00 am. The US column had now passed the Japanese transports to the north, and Talbot, frustrated but not discouraged, ordered a column turn to starboard to make another pass. Just before she turned, the aggressive *Parrott* sighted a target to starboard and launched three torpedoes. Once again, the countdown began.

Finally. One large explosion, maybe more, right on target – the 3,519-ton transport *Sumanoura Maru*, at the north end of the inner line of transports. The minesweeper *W-16*, at the northern end of the transports, saw the explosion and, nearby, a shadow moving south. She raced to help, but before she arrived the transport had sunk, with only nine survivors.[56]

The hit also alerted the Japanese that they were under attack. The transports and their close escorts started signaling each other and getting under way. In their confusion they even signaled the US destroyers, thus unwittingly giving away their positions.[57] The *W-15* tried to alert Admiral Nishimura that surface forces were attacking, but the admiral refused to believe that enemy ships could penetrate the anchorage. He believed the attack must be coming from the same submarine he was hunting.[58]

Talbot was in good position to take advantage of the Japanese confusion. The American destroyer column was compact and unified, making anyone not in the column a target. The column was also between groups of enemy ships in conditions of low visibility. The normal Japanese excellence in night spotting was hampered not only by the smoke, clouds, and lack of a moon, but also by the oil fires on the coast that crippled night vision. With the American ships now threading their way among the Japanese ships, the defending escorts would have severe problems identifying the Americans without risking friendly fire incidents. The bigger question for the Americans was how long could they keep their formation compact and unified in the low visibility?

The *Ford* led the column southward again at around 3:00 am. Talbot ordered a cut in speed; maybe they would have better luck if they proceeded more slowly.

Once again, the elderly tin cans of the US Navy slashed at the outer Japanese transport column. One unfortunate target silhouetted to starboard attracted five torpedoes from *Pope* at 3:06 am, then *Parrott* fired one more at 3:08 am, and *Paul Jones* fired yet another at 3:10 am.[59] The destroyers were not coordinating their targets so, instead of spreading their torpedoes out on multiple targets, they were wasting torpedoes by inadvertently targeting the same ships. In this case, however, all seven torpedoes may have been needed. They resulted in exactly one hit; but that hit created a spectacular explosion as the 7,064-ton ammunition ship *Tatsukami Maru*, already damaged by that Dutch air raid earlier in the day, sank.[60]

At 3:14 am the *John D. Ford* stopped slashing at the outer Japanese line and led a column turn to starboard to stab at the inner transport line. Five minutes later, the *Pope* fired two torpedoes from her port tubes at what appeared to be a destroyer less than 2,000yd away; *Parrott* fired three torpedoes at the same target. In the dark and smoke, the target had the appearance of a destroyer, and indeed she had been once long ago, but due to obsolescence she had lost her name *Hishi* and was converted to a patrol boat – *PB-37*.

Allegedly damaged earlier by the *K-XVIII*, the unfortunate little patrol boat was now overwhelmed with three torpedo hits, two near the bow and one near the stern, which sent her to the shallow bottom of Balikpapan harbor.[61]

At this point the 5,175-ton freighter *Kuretake Maru* got under way. At 3:22 am *Ford* and *Paul Jones* each fired one torpedo at the freighter from their port tubes at a range of about 1,000yd. Because she was under way, *Kuretake Maru* had power to maneuver and managed to evade the torpedoes. No matter. Talbot led the column on a loop around the freighter and back outside the outer column of transports. *Paul Jones* took one more shot, a single torpedo that found its mark and put the *Kuretake Maru* under. *Ford* finished her loop around the stricken freighter and led the column back north.

Pope, *Parrott*, and *Paul Jones* now signaled: ALL TORPEDOES EXPENDED.[62] *Pursuant* to his previous orders, Talbot ordered them to commence firing with their 4in guns. All three engaged multiple targets to port. The low visibility, which even a starshell fired by the *Parrott* could not overcome, prevented any confirmation of damage claims.[63]

Keeping ships together during night combat operation is extremely difficult and after having stayed together for almost an hour, the American column now disintegrated. At 3:35 am the flagship *Ford* turned northwest, around the still burning hulk of the *Nana Maru*, now standing on end, and went back through the outer line of transports.[64] Then, at 3:40 am, the *Ford* swung sharply to port and slowed down for reasons that remain disputed; the ONI Narrative says that she believed that she was entering a minefield (although it gives no reason why), but her gunnery officer later indicated that it was to avoid colliding with a sinking transport.[65] *Pope* had to swerve to port to avoid the flagship, *Parrott* and *Paul Jones* swung to starboard to avoid the *Ford* and whatever wreck was in the way. *Parrott* and *Paul Jones* then looped around, settling on a course to the south and breaking off the action. The *Pope* passed the stopped *Ford*, then circled to starboard around the flagship and followed her two sister ships out of the action.

Talbot was not quite finished. The *John D. Ford* started moving once again and at 3:46 am fired her last two torpedoes at a group of three transports. When her gunnery officer Lieutenant Mack got the order to "Commence firing," he began unloading on the Japanese at ranges of 500–1,500yd, so close that no complicated targeting mechanics were needed. At the same time, the *Tsuruga Maru*, earlier damaged by the *K-XVIII*, now went to a watery grave in a ball of fire, sunk by the last torpedoes of the *Ford*.

But that particular victory was short-lived. The *Ford*'s next target transport, *Asahi Maru*, was armed. For a few minutes the *Ford*'s topside crew watched uneasily as shells from the freighter fell like a textbook creeping barrage, getting closer and closer with each strike.[66] When the *Ford* was straddled the crew knew what was coming; at 3:47 am, a shell hit the destroyer's aft deckhouse, setting fire to gasoline and starshell ammunition nearby and wounding four men, none seriously.[67] The hit caused the *Ford* to leave a trail of fire like a rocket, but within 30 seconds the burning materials were jettisoned.[68] They continued to burn on the water and even attracted Japanese fire. The *Ford* then turned the tables on her assailant and riddled the *Asahi Maru* with gunfire as she passed, wounding 50 men. Next target for her guns was the *Tamagawa Maru*, which received ten 4in shell hits.

Now the *Ford* was getting close to shoal water. Concerned about running aground, the destroyer made a port turn and doubled back. Her lookout reported no visible targets. With torpedoes expended and her destroyer consorts gone, the *Ford*'s captain asked for permission to withdraw. Talbot was reluctant. "If we had the other ships we could go back in. I'm not sure the torpedoes did too much good. The 4-inchers were much more impressive, but then *Ford* has pressed it's [sic] luck too long, permission granted."[69]

The *Ford*'s skipper, Lieutenant Commander Jacob E. Cooper, now ordered the destroyer to make a hard turn to starboard, course 180 degrees True, and wanted all the speed the engine room could provide.[70] At one point, the *John D. Ford* was reported to have been going almost 32 knots, the fastest she had gone since her sea trials.[71] By 4:00 am, she was heading south along the Borneo coast looking to rejoin her sister four-pipers. They were certain that the Japanese would chase them, with their light cruiser and the *Fubuki*-class destroyers.

The Americans needn't have worried. Admiral Nishimura believed that the voluminous gunfire and starshells had come from that same annoying submarine. At 4:08 am he radioed the *P-36* asking if she was mistaking his destroyers for the enemy. As late as 4:20 am the *Naka* and her destroyers were still some 7,000yd east of the transports.[72]

The Japanese already faced long odds in catching the American destroyers. Though the sky was beginning to lighten in the east, to the west it was still dark; between that darkness, the smoke, and the night vision crippled by the fires, they would have had difficulty spotting the four-pipers against the backdrop of the coast of Borneo. Eventually, the *Naka* and destroyers *Minegumo* and *Natsugumo* arrived on the scene but found no enemy ships. Nishimura remained convinced that this was all the work of that meddling *K-XVIII*; *Naka*'s after-action report discusses only the action with the Dutch submarine and nothing about the American destroyers.[73]

The *K-XVIII* had not wrought havoc inside Balikpapan Harbor, but she did have a role to play. Commander van Well Groeneveld had taken his submersible to periscope depth to watch, with considerable amusement, the chaos caused by the American Destroyer Division 59; he left only when, in his words, "I saw that my friends were doing very well."[74] Admiral Hart was very pleased. Now all that remained of this operation was to get Destroyer Division 59 back to port. He radioed Admiral Glassford in the *Marblehead* to look for their return.[75]

Talbot continued speeding south as fast as the ancient engines on the *John D. Ford* would go. But that did not diminish the magnitude of their accomplishment. At 6:42 am the *Ford* caught up with her consorts, and the *Parrott*, *Paul Jones*, and *Pope* now fell in behind the flagship. Talbot ordered a signal flag hoisted on the *Ford*: WELL DONE.[76]

The lookouts remained on constant scan for the Japanese pursuit – the ships that were bigger, faster, and better armed than the American four-pipers with the floatplanes that would herald the ships' approach. Their fears seemed realized when, at 7:10 am, a floatplane was sighted,[77] except that it came from the south and flashed a message: its mother ship *Marblehead* was 50 miles to the south and coming to meet them.

By 8:00 am the relieved destroyers were under the limping light cruiser's protection. Admiral Glassford greeted them with a flag signal: WELL DONE.[78] A rather happy Admiral Hart sent a wireless message of his own: WELL DONE.[79] Repetitive these messages may have been, but after a combat operation, especially one in a war going as badly as this one, there can never be too many such messages. The kudos was badly needed and very much welcomed.

Commander Talbot would not make it to Soerabaja, at least not sitting in his command chair. Weakened by stress, lack of sleep, pain and blood loss, he collapsed while climbing the ladder down from the bridge to the well deck. But a victory can salve many wounds and ease many stresses. On Task Force 5's return to Soerabaja, the Royal Netherlands naval officers and men, who had been suspicious and slightly contemptuous of their American counterparts after their flight from the Philippines, were now friendly, enthusiastic, and helpful.

Now the critiquing began, however, and there was a lot of it, doing little to improve the frosty relationship between Admiral Hart and Admiral Glassford. Hart wondered what Glassford had been doing by keeping his ships in Koepang and Waworado. If he had kept them closer to the front line, maybe he would not have lost the use of the *Boise*. Glassford wanted more credit for the victory, even though he had been more than 100 miles away from the action, because he had developed the battle plan. He was also angry that Hart had sent the attack order to Commander Talbot himself rather than through Glassford as was proper for the chain of command. So furious was Glassford that in his private diary he declared either he or Hart would have to go.[80]

But by far the most painful criticism was implied: the four destroyers had actually sunk only four of 12 relatively unguarded transports.

And there really was no answer for that. Commander Talbot took some heat because the high speed of his initial run was thought to have impaired the accuracy of the torpedoes. Talbot made no excuses whatsoever, only saying that the high speed is what allowed his destroyers to escape. This was a hit *and run* operation, after all.

But Admiral Hart knew something else was at work, something that was not the fault of Commander Talbot or even Admiral Glassford, something far more serious than slightly imperfect tactics. They had heard stories from the submarine crews about the lack of success against the enemy, their complete frustration and loss of confidence. The submarines, the destroyers, possibly the aircraft carrier pilots as well, they all had a traitor in their midst … their torpedoes. Simply put, their torpedoes did not work.

Still, for now, the Allies had achieved their badly needed victory. It may have only delayed the Japanese advance by at most a single day, but it was still a victory. The US Navy, in its antiquated, outnumbered, and isolated ships in the Far East, could still hold its own against the Imperial Japanese Navy.

CHAPTER 8
BLOODY SHAMBLES

Air Chief Marshal Robert Brooke-Popham was gone, having been replaced as British Commander-in-Chief, Far East by Lieutenant General Henry Pownall at the beginning of 1942 shortly before Far East Command itself was folded into ABDACOM. But his statements about how the Brewster Buffalo was "quite good enough for Malaya" and Malaya was "the easiest country in the world to defend," had lived on, at least inasmuch as the Japanese performance had made a mockery of them.

After the disastrous aircraft losses in the first days of the Japanese invasion of Malaya, London was belatedly realizing that the Buffalo was not, in fact, good enough for Malaya and was now rushing aerial reinforcements in the form of the Hawker Hurricane to the region in order to secure the western flank of the Malay Barrier.

Although outclassed by both its Japanese and German counterparts, it would generally give a good accounting of itself in combat. The Hurricane was simple, durable, reliable, and versatile.

On January 3, 51 crated Hurricanes, along with 24 pilots, had arrived in Singapore. So simple was the Hurricane's construction (and so effective was the work of the 151st Maintenance Unit) that within 72 hours the fighters were assembled. It was a major morale boost to the defenders of Malaya.[1] "Our troops are elated at the appearance of the newly-arrived Hurricanes" wrote Australian General Gordon Bennett.[2] And the Hurricanes lived up to those hopes – until the next Japanese air raid.

In midmorning on January 20, three flights totaling some 80 Japanese army and navy bombers made the largest air attack yet on Singapore. The Hurricanes operating out of Seletar officially entered combat as part of No. 232 Squadron (Provisional), newly formed around the 24 newly arrived pilots, during which they were sent to defend their airfield against one group of 27 army Mitsubishi Ki-21 "Sally" bombers. It was claimed the Hurricanes shot down eight Sallys with no losses to themselves; however, Japanese records indicated no bomber losses.[3] The Hurricanes tangled with the bombers' escort of Nakajima Ki-43 fighters. The Hurricanes shot down three of these Zeros against a loss of three of their own.[4] Although it was a respectable performance for the Hurricanes, the Japanese had replacements for the lost Zeros close by, while replacements for the lost Hurricanes had to be shipped from the United Kingdom. As the pilots of the Buffalos and the Warhawks had had to learn the hard way, so the pilots of the Hurricanes had to learn the hard lesson that they simply could not dogfight the Zero.[5] And they did, suffering painful losses in the process. By January 26, the No. 232 Squadron (Provisional) was down to nine serviceable Hurricanes.

The British commander of Malaya's land defense, called Malaya Command, and on whom the defense of this western flank of the Malay Barrier depended was Lieutenant General Arthur Percival, a highly intelligent and successful staff officer who had served with distinction on the front line during World War I. However, quite simply he was completely in over his head as a commanding officer in the defense of Malaya, especially going against the Japanese General Yamashita Tomoyuki, widely considered the best of a very mediocre and thuggish Imperial Japanese Army officer corps.[6]

Repeatedly, British, Australian, and Indian troops would set up defensive roadblocks along the one main road cited by Brooke-Popham, and Yamashita's troops would go around them, either through the supposedly impenetrable jungle using – of all things – bicycles, or through small amphibious landings on the east coast of Malaya using boats the Japanese had captured from the British (much to Winston Churchill's disgust) in Panang.[7] Though Percival's troops outnumbered the Japanese, through a combination of these Japanese tactics and a level of ineptitude totally uncharacteristic of the British Army, they were driven down Malaya, usually in a panic. As the Japanese advanced, they captured more airfields, until Singapore Island became untenable for the Royal Air Force, forcing it to begin staging many of its assets to an air complex at Palembang on Dutch Sumatra. Percival was left to try to withdraw his army to Singapore in some semblance of good order before the Japanese could cut them off.

That withdrawal may have seemed in danger when, at 7:45 am on January 26, two Royal Australian Air Force Hudsons of No. 1 Squadron spotted two Japanese transports escorted by two cruisers, 12 destroyers, and three barges 10 miles north of Endau, on the east coast of Malaya some 80 miles north of Singapore, heading south. The Hudsons were prevented from reporting the sighting immediately by the jamming of their radios by the Japanese, and then were jumped by three Japanese Army Air Force Nakajima Ki-27 "Nate" fighters of the 11th Air Group. The Hudsons escaped, however, and landed safely at Sembawang at 9:20 am to report the contact.[8]

Endau and the nearby beach town of Mersing were at one end of a major east–west road across Malaya that intersected the main road down Malaya; if the Japanese captured them, they could conceivably move along that road and cut off the retreating British Army troops.[9] Malaya Command had anticipated a Japanese invasion at Endau–Mersing, and so had filled potential landing beaches with defensive fortifications. But with the British retreat in western Malaya, Endau had become superfluous, so the Australian troops manning the defenses withdrew down the lateral road to hold a blocking position.

Furthermore, the Japanese were not really invading Endau. Certainly the Japanese had originally intended to land infantry units at Endau, but the campaign was proceeding so well that General Yamashita cancelled the infantry invasion, not wanting to expose his troops to unnecessary air attack at sea.[10] The landing operation was revived, however, but only to land air units to bring airfields at nearby Kahang and Kluang online.[11] The Japanese landing force consisted of two transports, the *Canberra Maru* and the *Kansai Maru*, carrying the 96th Airfield Battalion and their supplies, with a strong escorting force consisting of the 3rd Destroyer Flotilla, last seen invading Kota Bharu – light cruiser *Sendai*; destroyers *Fubuki*, *Hatsuyuki*, *Shirayuki*, *Amagiri*, *Asagiri*, and *Yugiri*; auxiliaries *Otawa Maru* and *Rumoi Maru*; five minesweepers (creatively named *W-1*, *W-2*, *W-3*, *W-4*, and *W-5*); and three subchasers, all under the command of Admiral Hashimoto Shizuo, with the usual Japanese assortment of warships in the Gulf of Siam designated as "distant support" for the invasion but in reality so far away as to be completely useless.[12]

For reasons known only to the British, upon receiving the Hudsons' report, Malaya Command, working with elements of the Eastern Fleet, decided to throw most of their slender remaining air and naval resources into a counterattack – over a position the British did not need against an invasion that was not taking place.[13] They proceeded with what was planned to be a three-pronged strike – by air, surface ship, and submarine – at the landing zone.

This was to be, in short, a second Balikpapan. But while at Balikpapan the battle plan came together well so that the Allies could give the Japanese a bloody nose, the high-risk, low-reward operation at Endau fell apart early and often.

COUNTERATTACK AT ENDAU: FIRST PHASE – JANUARY 26

The first phase in the counterattack was the air phase. The Royal Air Force in Malaya used every strike aircraft it had available in multiple bombing attacks. The first attack group would comprise 12 British Vickers Vildebeest torpedo bombers – nine from No. 36 and three from No. 100 Squadrons – escorted by six of the ubiquitous Brewster Buffalos, remnants of the No. 243 and No. 488 Squadrons so shredded by losses that they had combined into a single unit. Assigned to join this attack en route were nine Australian Hudsons from No. 1 and No. 8 Squadrons operating out of Sembawang. Their escort would consist of six Buffalos of the remnants of the Royal Air Force No. 21 and No. 453 Squadrons, also combined into a single unit due to losses, and nine Hawker Hurricanes of No. 232 Squadron (Provisional), operating out of Seletar. A second wave of nine Vildebeests from No. 100 Squadron and three modern Fairey Albacores of No. 36 Squadron, along with all torpedo bombers operating out of Seletar, would be escorted by fighters remaining from the initial raid. The third wave was to consist of six Lockheed Hudson bombers of No. 62 Squadron based at Palembang on Dutch Sumatra while five Bristol Blenheim bombers, also from Palembang, would attack separately later in the day.

With heavy Japanese aerial opposition expected, coordination of the air groups was essential to their survival, in particular that of the Vildebeests. The Vildebeest was a biplane torpedo bomber like the Swordfish, but it struggled to top 100mph – so slow that in the eyes of one reporter it "gave the impression of being suspended motionless in mid-air."[14] With gallows humor, the Vildebeest's aircrews called themselves "The Suicide Boys."[15] For this reason, the Vildebeest had been relegated almost exclusively to making night attacks. The orders to commit this daylight attack off Endau left the aircrews shocked and horrified.[16] Unfortunately, coordinating fast (or at least faster) fighters with lumbering biplanes would be difficult under the best of circumstances, and was made even more difficult when Malaya Command's orders to the escorting Buffalos of No. 243 and No. 488 Squadrons left off such details as the destination and the target, saying only to "escort them to where they are going and bring them back."[17] The result was a very tangled and confused melee.

The first counterattack started at 3:05 pm.[18] In the face of unusually intense antiaircraft fire from the Japanese warships, the Vildebeests pressed home their bombing attacks, mostly on the *Canberra Maru*, and found themselves shredded by 19 Nate fighters of the Japanese Army Air Force's 1st and 19th Air Groups providing air cover to the invasion. The escorting Buffalos, who had been forced to zigzag to bleed their excess speed over their biplane charges, were overwhelmed, and four Vildebeests were shot down.[19]

Racing back to Singapore, the remaining eight Vildebeests led the Nates on a merry chase – straight into the incoming Australian Hudsons and their escorting Buffalos and Hurricanes. The Hudson bombers were pounced on by the Nates about a mile short of the anchorage. Once again, the escorts were simply overwhelmed by the Japanese fighters. The Hudsons scattered to make individual low-level bombing runs in the face of unusually intense antiaircraft fire. The attack ended around 3:43 pm.[20]

At around 5:30 pm – almost two hours after the last attack ended – the second wave of nine Vildebeests and three Albacores arrived at an altitude of 10,000ft. Due to a mixup in scheduling, they took off 40 minutes before their planned escort of nine Hurricanes and four Buffalos, all of which had survived the first strike, could be turned around. Knowing that their slow, lumbering biplanes would enter the combat zone without any fighter protection and would be slaughtered, the pilots were furious.[21] And slaughter is exactly what happened. Gunfire from the cruiser *Sendai* directed ten Nates of the 1st Air Group and two Nakajima Ki-44 fighters, codenamed "Tojo," of the 47th Independent Squadron toward the incoming biplanes. As they started their bombing approach, the leading three Vildebeests were immediately shot down in flames. The following aircraft had much the same reception – two of the three Albacores were shot down, followed by two of the next three Vildebeests. The final three Vildebeests, under the command of Flight Lieutenant R. J. Allanson, made their attacks and returned to Seletar riddled with bullet holes, each with a wounded gunner.[22]

Too late to be of any use, their escorts finally arrived off Endau – four Buffalos and seven of the planned nine Hurricanes. Nevertheless, the angry fighter pilots tried to extract some measure of revenge, losing one of the precious Hurricanes to a Tojo in the process, but doing little damage.[23] By Allied estimates, only four of the biplanes were able to complete their bombing runs.[24]

Next up in this parade of pitifulness was a 6:10 pm strafing run on the landing beaches by two Buffalos of No. 243/488 Squadrons, with cover provided by another two Buffalos, all of whom returned to Sembawang without any losses. Finally came the last attack, the six Hudsons from Palembang, making low-level bombing attacks. After completing their runs they made for Singapore, but were chased by six Nates of the 1st Air Group. Two of the Hudsons were so badly damaged by the Nates that they crashed in the Johore Strait short of Sembawang.[25]

The British and Australian pilots – what few of them returned – made fantastic claims of bombing successes against the Japanese, but the Japanese landing was unhindered and neither of the transports suffered anything more than a near miss, which caused splinter holes. These splinter holes cost the British ten Vildebeests, two Albacores, two Hudsons, and a Hurricane. Two more Vildebeests had to be written off as total losses upon their return to base, and a further ten aircraft were damaged.[26] The Royal Air Force's strike capability in Malaya was effectively destroyed.

Of the 72 aircrew manning the biplanes, 27 were killed, seven wounded, and two captured. Air Vice Marshal Paul Maltby, second in command of the Royal Air Force in Malaya, visited the survivors of the Vildebeests and Albacores to congratulate them on their gallantry and to promise that further daylight operations would not be necessary.[27] Whether his audience was receptive to his words of comfort is another matter. Upon his return to Seletar from the second attack, one of those survivors, Flight Lieutenant Allanson, stormed in to report to the air operations officer the results of the second attack. The furious Allanson's words would become famous:

> Our Ops Officer started to question me but I was so damned angry that I told him it was nothing less than a "bloody shambles." I added that I would tell Command AHQ myself. And I did. For I was just about certain who it was who had ordered those two suicidal sorties.[28]

"Bloody shambles" became an apt description for the British defense of Malaya.

SECOND PHASE – JANUARY 26/27

The second phase of this all-out counterattack was a nighttime naval raid that made just as much (or as little) sense as the air phase. Admiral Layton had taken over the Royal Navy Eastern Fleet and moved it to Ceylon, where he was trying to build up his forces for a counterattack. The few old and outclassed ships he left behind to help with the defense of Malaya were divided into two groups. One group, whose mission was to escort convoys into Singapore, was based at Tanjoeng Priok. This force of ships based in Indonesia for the defense of Malaya was called, somewhat surprisingly, the "China Force" and was commanded by Captain John Collins, who had been promoted to commodore for this assignment. The second, based at the Singapore Naval Base and commanded by Rear Admiral Ernest Spooner, was dedicated to the defense of Singapore itself and antisubmarine protection of convoys.

It was on Admiral Spooner's command that the responsibility for this counterattack would fall. This would have been a perfect assignment for the *Prince of Wales* and *Repulse*, but with both ships now on the bottom of the South China Sea, Spooner had extremely limited options – nominally his force consisted only of the World War I-era destroyers *Scout*, *Tenedos*, and *Thanet*, one minelayer *Abdiel*, some minesweepers, and small auxiliary patrol craft.[29] On this day, all Spooner had available were two destroyers that had arrived with a convoy of reinforcements two days earlier on January 24: the *Tenedos* of his own command and the *Vampire*, an Australian destroyer of Commodore Collins' "China Force" and already a grizzled veteran of this war. They were a poor substitute for the *Prince of Wales* and *Repulse*, to put it mildly. The *Vampire* had been commissioned in 1917; the *Thanet* in 1919. Both destroyers, armed only with 4in guns in addition to their torpedoes, had been considered unfit for front-line duty long before World War II, particularly the *Thanet*, a tiny ship that despite being two years newer than the *Vampire* was the product of an older design. As one Australian sailor described them, "In *Thanet* and *Vampire* one would have been hard pressed to find two older, more obsolete destroyers still in the front line role for which they had been designed, in any of His Majesty's navies."

Admiral Spooner called both skippers, Commander William Moran of the *Vampire* who would command this operation, and Commander Bernard Davies of the *Thanet*, to the Singapore Naval base. The plan was for the two destroyers to sail at 4:30 pm and head up the east coast of Malaya to strike after dark. The returning pilots indicated that the Japanese force had two transports escorted by a cruiser and 12 destroyers. The destroyers' mission was to sink the two transports and, if they could manage it, the cruiser, before returning to Singapore before dawn.

It was a tall order, made even taller by the apparent inability of Admiral Spooner to give the captains anything more than the vaguest idea of where their targets were and the fact that the two aged destroyers were not fully armed, carrying only seven torpedoes between them. But Spooner, who does not seem to have been totally sold on this mission, had some idea of the long odds. He told the skippers that if they were sighted they should immediately bail on the mission and try to lead the Japanese over British minefields in the area.

And so at 4:30 pm, right on schedule, Commander Moran had his *Vampire* lead the *Thanet* out of the Singapore Naval Base and up the coast, delaying somewhat so they would strike after the moon had set, giving them the cover of maximum darkness but also complicating their ability to find the transports. While en route, at 10:55 pm Moran received a report from Admiral Spooner stating that the two transports, damaged in the airstrikes, were still disembarking troops and unloading equipment. Their escort was now erroneously reported as one cruiser, also allegedly damaged, and two destroyers. Maybe the odds weren't so bad after all.

But before the two destroyers had even sailed, Admiral Hashimoto had been given a report of two approaching British cruisers. The erroneous report should have put his force on guard for surface action that night, but for some reason he kept his ships deployed in a semicircle, each end anchored on the Malayan coast, around the two transports. This was a logical deployment to protect the transports, except that the most likely direction for a surface attack was from the south and east, towards Singapore and the British naval base, so now most of the Japanese ships would not be between the transports and the Royal Navy's most likely approach vector.

At 2:37 am the *Vampire,* approaching the Japanese semicircle from the east, sighted a vessel that she believed was a destroyer off the starboard bow. The destroyer, apparently the *Amagiri*, made no reaction, and as Commander Moran needed to strike at the transports, his little force pushed onward.[30] Three minutes later, the *Vampire* sighted another vessel that she believed was a destroyer and this time decided to fire two of her three torpedoes. It was a bad bet. The torpedoes missed, and the "destroyer," which was actually minesweeper *W-4*, gave the alarm – or tried to. For reasons that remain vague, it would be some 20 minutes before a message of the attack got through to Admiral Hashimoto's flagship *Sendai.* Observing no reaction from the *W-4* or a "cruiser" (apparently the *Sendai*) that the *Thanet* had seen in the distance indicating the British ships had been spotted, Moran turned to the southwest and towards Endau, where the very transports he was supposed to sink were sitting with only minimal defense.

The vaunted Japanese night fighting capability, a capability that the Royal Navy believed it matched, apparently did not include a night guarding capability. For the second time in the Java Sea Campaign – indeed for the second time in 24 hours – the Japanese had allowed a small raiding force to penetrate their defensive screen to get at their virtually unprotected transports. But this would not be a repeat of Balikpapan. The luck that had temporarily abandoned the Japanese had returned. In the now moonless night against the dark mass of Malaya, the British lookouts, so close to their prey, could not see the transports. At 3:13 am, having seen nothing, Commander Moran turned his tiny force back toward Singapore.

In the meantime, at 3:05 am, Admiral Hashimoto finally received, through the destroyer *Fubuki*, *W-4*'s report of possible intruders. The minesweeper was not having a good night, and had compounded her error in not sending the vital sighting report directly to her admiral by getting the position of the sighting wrong, sending the Japanese defenders looking in the wrong direction.

But the Japanese were soon to get a better idea of the location of their enemy. At 3:18 am, the Royal Navy lookouts spotted one Japanese destroyer off the port bow and a second destroyer tailing the *Thanet.* Commander Moran ordered all remaining torpedoes – four from the *Thanet* and one from the *Vampire*, fired at the first destroyer, apparently the *Shirayuki*. There was extreme consternation on the bridges of both ships when the torpedoes missed. *Shirayuki* reported to Admiral Hashimoto that she had been attacked by torpedoes.[31]

That report finally spurred a reaction from the Japanese, though not quite up to their usual standards. The result was yet another confused melee. After challenging the now fleeing intruders without a response, one Japanese destroyer, apparently the *Yugiri*, flipped on her searchlight and caught the *Thanet* in its beam.[32] Soon the little destroyer was caught in three other searchlight beams, while *Vampire* was illuminated by the *Shirayuki's* searchlight. At 3:31 am, *Shirayuki* opened fire on the *Vampire*, only to have her guns silenced by a tripped circuit breaker two minutes later, but she was just the start. At 3:38 am the *Yugiri* opened fire on the *Thanet*. Having also spotted the *Vampire*, at 3:45 am she signaled Admiral Hashimoto: THE ENEMY IS TWO DESTROYERS. The admiral responded by ordering ADVANCE TOWARDS THE ENEMY, followed by FIRE WITH SEARCHLIGHT ILLUMINATION AT THE ENEMY DESTROYERS. The Japanese ships responded with a very irresolute pursuit of the action, *Amagiri* proceeding slowly at 18 knots, and the flagship *Sendai* herself never even leaving her patrol zone. But they would be damaging enough for the Allies. Destroyers *Shirayuki*, having gotten her guns back online, *Hatsuyuki, Fubuki*, and *Asagiri*, minesweeper *W-1*, and the *Sendai* herself joined in the rain of 5in and 5.5in shells on the two Allied destroyers.

Both the *Vampire* and the *Thanet* returned fire while zigzagging and making smokescreens in a desperate effort to evade the Japanese gunfire. Commander Moran had the *Vampire* in the lead, effectively making smoke with her funnels, smoke generators, and even smoke pots launched from the ship; the smoke reflected the Japanese searchlights, effectively blinding the Japanese gunners. That left the *Thanet*, as the trailing ship, on the unfortunate receiving end of most of the Japanese attention. *Thanet* laid a smokescreen and tried to move behind its cover, but before she could do so, at around 4:00 am, after her main guns had fired only three salvoes, *Thanet* took a 5in round, apparently from the *Yuguri*, through the port side in the engine room that severed both her main and auxiliary steam lines and sent up a shower of sparks and smoke pouring from her hull. The *Thanet*, like many ships of her generation, did not have redundant systems that could be isolated in case of battle damage, so with both steam lines down she lost propulsive power. Unable to move, the old destroyer was quickly surrounded by her Japanese tormentors and blasted to pieces. Commander Davies realized that the situation was hopeless and ordered the destroyer abandoned.

Outnumbered, outgunned, and desperately trying to elude the broadsides of the *Sendai*, Commander Moran with his *Vampire* could not help the *Thanet* and had to leave her to her fate. *Vampire* lost her Japanese pursuers in her smokescreens, *Sendai* apparently switching her target to a Japanese destroyer in the confusion caused by the darkness and smoke. Moran last saw the *Thanet* listing to starboard, settling by the stern, and pouring forth smoke as the *Vampire* sped away. The *Thanet* sank at about 4:18 am in the morning.

Admiral Spooner was anxious as to the fate of his destroyers. At 5:10 am, *Vampire* signaled the fate of the *Thanet*, as well as the damage they believed they had caused off Endau. With the area still too hot for a rescue, there was little Spooner could do. Five officers, including Commander Davies, and 61 men from the *Thanet* made it back to shore and eventually Singapore. One officer and 11 men were killed in the action. The *Shirayuki* picked up 31 survivors, turning 30 of them over to Imperial Japanese Army units at Endau on January 28. The prisoners were never heard from again; postwar investigation revealed no information as to their fate.

THIRD PHASE, AND EVACUATION OF SINGAPORE – JANUARY 27–30

The third and final phase of this high-risk, low-reward British counterattack was anti-climactic: the newly arrived submarine HMS *Trusty* made her own sortie to the landing zone. She found nothing and returned to Singapore.

The Endau counterattack was unnecessary, poorly planned, poorly executed, and disastrous to the already dwindling British chances in Malaya. As one naval analyst described it: "[B]oth air and sea components of the … raid were grossly inadequate and heavily outgunned … There was no compulsion to throw these forces away in an ill-conceived gesture; they could have been employed elsewhere in the fighting yet to come."[33]

The British realized that their grip was slipping away and continued to desperately feed reinforcements, particularly of Hurricanes. But they could not get to Malaya quickly enough. On January 27, the freshly repaired British aircraft carrier *Indomitable* arrived at a position just south of Christmas Island in the Indian Ocean where she was to catapult off 48 Hawker Hurricane fighters of No. 232 and No. 258 Squadrons to Batavia. The Hurricanes were flown by Royal Air Force pilots inexperienced in – and in many cases horrified by – navigation over water, so the plan was to guide them in with a pair of Blenheim bombers operating out of Batavia.[34] But the first pair of Blenheims sent out could not find the carrier, nor could the second. The third did so easily by looking for a rather obvious feature ignored by the first two: Christmas Island itself.[35] The Hurricanes eventually got to Batavia and were parceled out to airfields on Sumatra and Singapore.

But it was not enough. By the end of January, with Britain still desperately trying to send reinforcements, the people of Singapore had lost confidence in Britain's ability to protect them. Admiral Spooner was preparing the demolition of the Singapore Naval Base. Civilians flocked to grab whatever transportation they could to get out of what they believed was a doomed island and get to someplace safe – like Java. As the refugees flocked, so did the ships to carry them, and those unarmed ships attracted increasingly frequent Japanese air attacks. On January 30, bombers from the Genzan Air Group, the same aircraft that had sent the *Prince of Wales* and the *Repulse* under, pounded Allied shipping in the Straits Settlements and at Keppel Harbor, Singapore's main harbor.

A US transport, two British transports, and a freighter were hit by bombs. As a result, two US transports embarked passengers that included dockyard workers from the Singapore Naval Base, their families, and Royal Navy and Air Force personnel. They headed for Tandjoeng Priok.

The evacuation of Singapore had begun.

CHAPTER 9

CAN'T CATCH A BREAK – THE BATTLE OF THE FLORES SEA

Japan's advance into the "Southern Resources Area" has, on more than one occasion, been likened to an octopus – grabbing so many targets at once. But octopi are rarely so vicious, so malevolent, so willful. For Japan was not just grabbing Malaya piece by piece with ruthless efficiency, her forces were also simultaneously seizing Hong Kong, Guam, Philippines, Wake, New Georgia, New Guinea, prior to securing its main target: the Netherlands East Indies. Japan, it seemed, could be everywhere at once, while the Allies were seemingly nowhere.

And the Allies were certainly nowhere on Japan's next piece of the Indies: Kendari, on the island of Celebes. The Japanese had already seized Kema and Menado, on the island's Minahassa Peninsula, on January 11. But Kema was not what the Japanese really wanted on Celebes; nor, for that matter, was Makassar City, the island's capital.

The real gem of Celebes, at least in military terms, was on the east coast of the island's Southeast Peninsula: Kendari. Kendari was considered by many to have the finest port and airdrome in the Indies. The city itself had a port and small harbor, but just to the south was Staring Bay – large, sheltered, and a perfect anchorage for, say, a fleet of aircraft carriers. Even better was Kendari's airdrome system, consisting of several airfields. One airfield, known as Kendari II, not in Kendari but in the town of Amoito about 12 miles to the southwest of Kendari, was believed by many to be the finest airbase in Southeast Asia – large, with paved runways, plenty of hangars and room to park and disperse aircraft, storage facilities for fuel and munitions, and comfortable barracks.[1] But as with most of their other airfields in the Indies, the Dutch had been unable to put many actual aircraft at this very nice airbase. A few B-17s had used it as a forward staging area, but the only aircraft present now was one disabled B-17.[2] Kendari II was also poorly defended with 400 Indonesian troops of suspect loyalty and commanded by just two Dutch officers.[3]

The US seaplane tender *Childs*, under Lieutenant Commander J. H. "Doc" Pratt, had been sent to Kendari to deliver 30,000 gallons of aviation fuel for the airbase. Like the *Peary* before her, in an effort to hide from air attack, the *Childs* had been painted green and was kept hidden in small coves among trees in the daytime, traveling only at night. Steaming up the south channel into Kendari's small harbor, the *Childs* arrived on the evening of January 22. The crew spent all night unloading the fuel. Unable to get under way by dawn, they moved to a hiding place chosen by the Dutch, where they tied the *Childs* to some coconut trees. However the Dutch had failed to mention that the hiding place went dry at low tide. The *Childs* was left in the mud and very nearly tipped over, the ropes tying her to the trees going taut. It was at this time that a Japanese reconnaissance aircraft flew over. Apparently thinking the green, "listing" ship in the mud was a derelict, the scout plane ignored it. Pratt and the crew were quite happy when the tide came back in and the *Childs* returned to the upright position.[4]

An encounter with a schooner whose owner seemed suspicious and too interested in the affairs of the *Childs* – and who also happened to have a transmitter capable of reaching Japan – convinced Pratt that his ship was being watched by the Japanese and that the *Childs* should leave as soon as possible. The tender got under way just before dawn on January 24. On her way out, she spotted four Japanese destroyers. One challenged her with the repeated recognition signal A8Y. Rodney Nordfelt, the quick-thinking signalman on the bridge of the *Childs*, flashed the same signal in return, confusing the Japanese long enough for the *Childs* to speed away under cover of a rain squall. The destroyers later gave a half-hearted chase, but the *Childs* made good her escape, enduring one bombing attack from a lone Japanese cruiser floatplane and earning a reputation as "one of the luckiest ships of the Asiatic Fleet during the Java campaign" before getting back to Soerabaja safely.[5]

The four Japanese destroyers had been from what had been designated the 1st Base Force, with eight destroyers led by Admiral Kubo on the light cruiser *Nagara*, and air cover provided by the seaplanes of the tenders *Chitose* and *Mizuho*.[6] They were escorts for the 1st Kure Special Naval Landing Force – essentially Japanese "Marines" with a reputation for extreme toughness and just as extreme brutality – who had been scheduled to land at Kendari on January 22. That landing was delayed because the route to the landing point was at first believed to be blocked by Allied submarines; the submarines turned out to be a dozen or so suspicious-looking whales.[7] But the Japanese luck returned as a storm front covered the Japanese advance. The invasion transports anchored off Kendari Bay around 2:00 am on January 24 and landed some two and a half hours later.[8] They easily overcame the resistance of the Dutch and native troops that, in the words of one prominent historian, "did not merit the description 'token.'"[9] Within 12 hours, Kendari II was in Japanese hands. The 400 troops fled. The Dutch officers, in a panic, had been unable to complete the demolition of the airbase.

Once again, the Japanese had controlled the skies before making their landing, but it did not seem to matter. The aircraft carriers *Hiryu* and *Soryu*, two of the six monsters that had attacked Pearl Harbor, sent 54 aircraft to attack Ambon, but they had to bomb ground installations because they found no Allied aircraft or even ships.[10] The Kendari operation had cost the Japanese two wounded and a very unpleasant day for the destroyer *Hatsuharu*. Acting as reinforcements with the *Nenohi*, *Hatsushimo*, and *Wakaba* of Destroyer Division 21, the *Hatsuharu* had arrived off Kendari where she collided with Admiral Kubo's flagship *Nagara*.[11] She also was damaged by a too little, too late attack by US bombers.[12] Both *Hatsuharu* and *Nagara* were compelled to go to Davao for very minor repairs.[13]

But for the Japanese those did not even rise to the level of irritants. "[T]he best air base in [sic] Dutch East Indies was secured for our forces," said a Japanese summation of the campaign: an airbase from which the principal Dutch naval base at Soerabaja was within easy reach.[14] Japan had captured its fine runways and even its stores of aviation gasoline, much of which had been just dropped off by the *Childs*. Kendari II now simply needed some aircraft. The next day 30 Japanese fighters and reconnaissance aircraft from the Toko Air Group staged into Kendari II, followed in short order by more fighters and the Nell and Betty bombers that had been so devastating to Force Z, these from the Kanoya and 1st Air Groups of the 21st Air Flotilla.[15]

For ABDACOM, things were about to go from bad to worse.

ESTABLISHMENT OF THE ABDA STRIKING FORCE

After more than a month of disaster after disaster, the American victory at Balikpapan had done much to bolster Allied confidence and shore up morale. Unfortunately, its effect on the strategic situation was negligible. The Japanese moved their 23rd Air Flotilla into the Balikpapan airfield, only to discover that it was "unfit" for their bombers. It quickly became a fighter base from where they would provide air cover to continue the advance.[16]

On January 31, the Japanese landed on Ambon, chasing off Patrol Wing 10, the Royal Australian Air Force's No. 2 Squadron, and the Dutch ground crew who had stayed behind to service them. The Dutch and Australian troops defending the island were not so fortunate; most of them were killed or captured after fierce resistance. The Japanese then set to work removing the Dutch mines that had nearly crippled the *Peary*. But the Imperial Japanese Navy did not have the Royal Netherlands Navy's affinity for mines and it showed: the Dutch mines sank the minesweeper *W-9* and damaged *W-11* and *W-12*. The Japanese were not happy about these losses and took it out on the captured Dutch and Australian troops: more than 300 of them were murdered in an orgy of bayoneting and beheading at the Laha airfield by the vicious Special Naval Landing Force troops.[17] It was among the worst of a very long list of Japanese war crimes.

With the airfields at Balikpapan, Kendari II and now Ambon in enemy hands, ABDACOM desperately needed aircraft. But simply getting aircraft to the Indies was a difficult and dangerous undertaking. The United States was churning out B-17s, LB-30s, and P-40s aplenty, but getting them to the front line was a major problem. Even the long-range Flying Fortress was having severe issues getting across the Pacific, and it could actually fly from island to island; the Warhawk fighter, with its limited range, was finding it almost impossible. Nevertheless, by late January, 112 P-40s had arrived in Australia, with 160 more on the way. Once in Australia, as part of General Brereton's reconstruction of the Far East Air Force they were hastily organized into "provisional" units. The first such unit for deployment was formed with new trainees around a cadre of fighter pilots withdrawn from the Philippines and designated the 17th Pursuit Squadron (Provisional) under Major Charles E. Sprague.[18] Once the P-40 arrived at Sydney, Australia, it had to fly across southern Australia to Perth, then to Darwin on the northwest coast before island hopping to Timor (now threatened by the Japanese occupation of Ambon) and then to Bali's Denpesar airfield before landing at Soerabaja. It was a grueling journey, taxing in the extreme for both pilots and aircraft; only 13 of Sprague's 17 Warhawks reached Soerabaja, while a later reinforcement attempt of 16 pursuits left Darwin but only eight arrived at Soerabaja due to crashes, mechanical issues, and problems for the army pilots navigating across water.[19] To secure more reliable reinforcement, General George Brett, General Wavell's deputy in ABDACOM, was working with Admiral Hart to use the seaplane tender *Langley* (currently based in Darwin) to ferry aircraft to Java.

Admiral Hart was struggling to get ABDAFLOAT in a position to be able to offer consistent resistance to the Japanese. Little seemed to be going right, and what did go right always came with a caveat. He tried to repeat the success of Balikpapan by sending the freshly repaired *Marblehead* and four destroyers into Makassar Strait on January 29, but the *Marblehead*'s Captain Robinson called off the mission two days later after being shadowed by a Japanese aircraft.[20] ABDAFLOAT needed a main base, but Hart was not happy with the designated base at Darwin – it had very strong tides and, if a ship was sunk there, the harbor was too deep for salvage efforts such as those being done at Pearl Harbor. For that reason, he ordered the destroyer tender *Black Hawk,* the submarine tenders *Holland* and *Otus*, and the oiler *Trinity,* escorted by the destroyers *Alden* and *Edsall*, to sail from Darwin (which they did on February 3) back to Tjilatjap to set up supply and maintenance functions there. And he continued to look for opportunities to counterattack. He believed that Balikpapan was a success on which the Allies could build if they could only avoid doing things like running aground and blowing turbines. Their chances of success would be bolstered further if they could augment the slender US naval forces available (even more slender with the *Boise* under repair) with some from the ABDA allies.

So on February 1 Admiral Hart, with the approval of General Wavell, formed the ABDA Striking Force using American and Dutch warships. The Striking Force was to consist of the heavy cruiser USS *Houston*, the light cruisers Hr. Ms. *De Ruyter*, Hr. Ms. *Tromp*, and USS *Marblehead*, and the US destroyers *Stewart*, *Edwards*, *Barker*, *Bulmer*, *Paul Jones*, *Whipple*, and *Pillsbury.* In terms of combat power, this was a very respectable unit.

Admiral Hart called a meeting between himself, Admiral Helfrich, Admiral Glassford, and Commodore Collins in Lembang on February 2 to discuss his next order of business: selecting the commander of the ABDA Striking Force, in which he had some political issues to finesse.[21] He neither trusted nor liked Admiral Glassford. Nor did the American crews, who, after the incident off Panay and the issues of the *Marblehead*, referred to him as "15-Knot Glassford."[22] So Hart wanted to keep him out of operational command and preferably out of any command.[23] He also had to deal with the Dutch, still angry over not getting command of the ABDA naval forces operating in what they believed were their waters. Complicating that problem further was Admiral Helfrich, still angry about not being named ABDAFLOAT, still conniving to replace Hart, and, in the process, somewhat undermining the naval defense of the Indies. Hart understood Helfrich's feelings, later writing, "I did not like to be commanding Admiral Helfrich on his home ground."[24] So, bowing to political realities and practicalities, Hart selected the man whose name would become symbolic of the Java Sea Campaign – Real Admiral Karel W. F. M. Doorman of the Royal Netherlands Navy.

Karel Willem Frederik Marie Doorman was born in Utrecht, Holland, on April 23, 1889. After graduating from the Royal Netherlands Naval College in Den Helder in 1910, he served on various ships before getting his wings and becoming a naval air force pilot in 1915. With flight still in its infancy, the young Karel Doorman would be on the cutting edge of aviation for the Royal Netherlands Navy – so much so that he would survive 33 emergency landings (in part a reflection of his duties as a flight instructor, one of the first in the Royal Netherlands Navy), before going to the Naval Staff College in 1921.[25] Doorman's wartime decisions, for which his courage has often been questioned, should be read in this context. A person who became a pilot at the dawn of aviation has shown courage in abundance. A person who managed to land an aircraft in emergency conditions even once, let alone 33 times, has demonstrated a cool head in crisis.

After completing the Naval Staff College, Karel Doorman held several staff positions and served as skipper on a variety of destroyers and cruisers, moving up through the ranks until August 17, 1938, when he was placed in command of the Royal Netherlands Naval Air Service in the East Indies. Doorman very much understood the importance of naval aviation, so he focused on rigorous training of the Naval Air Service pilots, coordination between aircraft and ships, and making certain his men had the best possible equipment and supplies then available to the Dutch military. Under Doorman's leadership, the Royal Netherlands Naval Air Service attained a very high level of quality.[26]

On May 16, 1940, Karel Doorman was promoted to *schout-bij-nacht*, the Dutch equivalent of rear admiral, and subsequently given command of the Navy's East Indies Squadron, which normally included the bulk of the navy's warships.[27] He held this command serving under Admiral Helfrich as the clouds of war darkened in the Far East, doing his best to keep his little force trained and ready for action. In Admiral Hart's eyes, Doorman's command of the East Indies Squadron more than qualified him for command of the ABDA Striking Force.

Karel Doorman's service record is easy enough to find and highlight, but discussion of him as a person, at least in English-language media, is scant. He was fluent in English and had a reputation for "exceptional charm."[28] One historian described him as "a very special and very difficult man, not only to others, but also to himself."[29] Despite driving his men hard, he was well respected in the Royal Netherlands Navy, both by fellow officers and by those under his command. He was considered "a clever man and an experienced sailor and his views on strategic and tactical problems had always been logical and sound."[30]

Yet assessing the few fragments available of Karel Doorman the person suggests that while he may have been charming and at ease in his element, he was not entirely comfortable socially. He was stoic and soft-spoken. The few pictures of him hint at an unease in being photographed. Doorman was nicknamed "The Tank" for his ability to drink vast quantities of alcoholic beverages.[31] This was not seen as a character flaw; he could definitely hold his liquor: nowhere in the mountain of abuse that has been heaped on Doorman since World War II have there been any charges of his being drunk while on duty or of alcohol influencing his judgment in any way.

Admiral Doorman also had a second nickname, "The Knot," arising out of his posture that usually featured hunched shoulders. Some attributed this bowed posture to the incredible pressure on his shoulders from commanding a polyglot task force under an unappreciative superior in a losing campaign, but most attributed it to neglected dysentery, which had flared up shortly before Pearl Harbor and was known to have caused him considerable discomfort. While his crews respected him, considered him kind, and may have even liked him for the concern he always showed for their well-being, Doorman was not one to mingle with them aboard ship. When off duty on his flagship *De Ruyter*, he would simply retire alone to his cabin, where, through a window, some sailors were able to surreptitiously watch him play a solitary card game known as Patience – and cheat.

This quiet, solitary nature would not help Doorman's postwar reputation. While playing some sort of politics is inherent in achieving flag rank, he seems to have had few close friends or allies and thus no one to defend him when he could no longer defend himself. He appears to have been a very private person as well; at the very least, he kept his tactical analyses to himself, making it difficult for those around him or those assessing his performance to determine what he had been thinking. Thus it has been easy for those who find fault with his performance – and there was at least some fault, to be sure – to define him, and many found fault with him at the outset.

By selecting Admiral Doorman, Admiral Hart had his ABDA Combined Striking Force of American and Dutch ships organized and ready, except for one detail: the Dutch ships and their admiral were missing. Admiral Helfrich had ordered them to Karimata, between Borneo and Sumatra, based on a report of Japanese activity there. If Helfrich had told Hart about the report, Hart could have told him it had already been determined false. But Helfrich had not.[32] As Hart later explained it, at the February 2 meeting Helfrich "was still found not disposed to be entirely frank as regards the state and readiness of his forces. At this conference he did not disclose that he could get a considerable force of his own Cruisers and Destroyers to sea – which would have strengthened our current weakness to the eastward of Java."[33]

Admiral Hart was furious with Admiral Helfrich, believing that Helfrich had misled him about the availability of the Dutch ships. Hart could only hope that the two-day delay caused by Helfrich's actions would not prove significant.

SOERABAJA ATTACKED – FEBRUARY 3

Sunrise in Soerabaja on February 3, 1942, brought a new day and a new nightmare.

For most of the people of Soerabaja, the first inkling that something was different about this day came at midmorning with the eerie, mournful wail of air raid sirens.

The previous day had contained an ominous portent – 17 Japanese Zeros and a single Babs scout plane of the Tainan Air Group operating out of Balikpapan performed a ighter sweep over Maospati airfield near Soerabaja. The material damage was not much, but they did shoot down an airborne B-18, killing its entire crew, several badly needed radar experts, and the new commander of the US Army Air Force's 7th Bomb Group, Major Austin A. Straubel, who died the following day from burns he suffered while trying to rescue the crew.[34]

But the situation would rapidly worsen. The losses of Balikpapan and Kendari II were about to make themselves felt: in response to an order from Vice Admiral Tsukahara Nishizo, commander of the 11th Air Fleet which had been the bane of Allied existence since the very first day of the Pacific War, for an "air annihilation operation" against eastern Java, an aerial armada of Japanese bombers and fighters was descending like a plague of locusts on the Soerabaja area.[35] From Kendari II came 72 Nell bombers – 26 of the Takao, 27 of the Kanoya, and 19 of the 1st Air Groups – to bomb the ABDA airfields at Soerabaja, Madioen, and Malang, respectively, "probably with our gas," as *Childs* skipper Doc Pratt would point out.[36] War is filled with such irony.

Supporting the bombers were 44 Zeros – 17 of the Tainan and 27 of the 3rd Air Groups – providing air cover, while three C5M Babs reconnaissance craft – one of the Tainan and two of the 3rd Air Groups – were on hand to provide navigational guidance and battle damage assessment.[37] Clearly Japanese intelligence gathering had been very good.

The air defenses of Soerabaja, manned by the Royal Netherlands East Indies Army, were better than those of Cavite. There were eight 80mm antiaircraft guns throughout the city and port. The airbase at Perak had four 105mm and four 40mm Bofors antiaircraft guns, while the seaplane base at Morokrembangan could contribute two 20mm guns. These were modern, effective weapons – the Bofors was generally acknowledged to be the best medium antiaircraft platform in the world – but there were far too few of them to make a difference. Perak and Morokrembangan were supplemented with 7.7mm and 12.7mm machine guns, but these were useful only against strafing aircraft.[38]

But Soerabaja did have some interceptors to protect it – or to try to. The Dutch courageously scrambled seven obsolete Curtiss Hawks and 12 equally obsolete Curtiss Wright CW-21B Demon fighters from their own army air force at Perak airfield, and seven P-40 Warhawks of the US Army Air Force's recently arrived 17th Pursuit Squadron (Provisional) with P-40 Warhawks, who were based at a very well camouflaged airfield at Ngoro. Dutch spotters had warned the squadron at Ngoro of the approaching attack some 20 to 25 minutes beforehand, so the P-40s scrambled and climbed to an interception altitude of 21,000ft, which as always with a P-40 took a painfully long time.[39] Too long; the Dutch had not given them enough warning, and the Nells of the Takao Air Group, unescorted because of a logistical mixup, had bombed Soerabaja before the Warhawks even came into range.[40]

The Japanese attack was large and coordinated. The Dutch fighters were held off by Zeros; three Zeros were shot down at a staggering cost of five Hawks and seven Demons.[41] In Soerabaja, the Nells damaged the naval base and the Perak airbase. Strafing by Zeros destroyed three Catalina flying boats on the water. Madioen was heavily damaged, and at the Singosari airfield at Malang, the American bombers of the 19th Bomb Group were caught standing on the runway loaded for take-off – targets of strafing Japanese aircraft. Four B-17s were destroyed on the ground, and the fifth was damaged and spontaneously combusted the next day.[42] Yet another B-17 was shot down 10 miles south of Malang, while a damaged B-17 crash landed on Arends Island, off Borneo.[43]

Back at Soerabaja, the Nells damaged the naval base and the Perak airbase. Strafing by Zeros destroyed three Catalina flying boats on the water. At around this time, the P-40s of the 17th Pursuit finally showed up over Soerabaja, their climb to interception altitude complete. Frustrated that their slow rate of climb had denied them the chance to prevent this carnage, the vengeful American pilots took out their anger on the Japanese bombers headed back to Kendari II, shooting down one Nell; in a separate engagement they shot down one Zero at a cost of one of their own.[44] But the little damage that the Americans caused could not make up for the massive damage inflicted by the Japanese Naval Air Force. Again. On this day, ABDAIR had had 16 fighters, three flying boats, and two B-17s shot down or crash from battle damage while five B-17s and 10 to 13 seaplanes had been destroyed on the ground or at anchor.[45]

The frustrated pilots of the 17th returned to Ngoro, sometimes called Blimbing, which was the closest town. They were joined by three of the surviving Dutch fighters.[46] Ngoro was a curious little airfield that the Dutch had gone to extreme lengths to hide. They would need it in the weeks ahead.

The Combined Striking Force assembles – February 3

While their base at Soerabaja was being blasted, the ships of the ABDA Combined Striking Force, including the Dutch contingent led by Admiral Doorman, had finally managed to rendezvous at Boenda Roads, east of Soerabaja in the Madoera Strait, to try to counterattack.

The assembled ships were a visual spectacle, the largest force ABDACOM had ever put to sea: the *Houston*, the most powerful ship on hand, with a confidence and strength that came from more than just her guns and armor; the newly repaired *Marblehead*, eager to get her guns into action after her star-crossed sortie at Balikpapan; the four-pipers *Pillsbury*, *Stewart*, *Bulmer*, *Edwards*, *Paul Jones*, *Barker*, and *Whipple*, all old but feisty and full of fight; and the *Pecos*, a tanker.

New to the group were two Dutch ships, the *De Ruyter* and *Tromp*. The *De Ruyter*, designed to be the flagship of the Dutch East Indies Squadron and currently the flagship of Admiral Doorman, was a beautiful, graceful light cruiser. Her most striking feature was her foremast, a "conning tower" design that gave her more than a passing resemblance to the late German battleship *Bismarck*.

Unfortunately for the Dutch, *De Ruyter*'s similarities to the German monster ended there. Born at a time when the Dutch politics was governed by pacifists who did not want to fund construction of weapons of any kind, the light cruiser was built on the cheap and it showed. She was initially designed to have six 6in guns in three dual turrets, one forward and two aft. Not surprisingly, the Royal Netherlands Navy protested this appalling lack of gunpower and through supreme effort was able to get one more 6in gun, in a single mount forward. Even after this minor improvement, the fact remained that some of the best and brightest minds in the Dutch government had thought it a good idea to have most of the guns of their East Indies flagship facing *behind* her.[47]

Nor was this all. Unlike most of her European counterparts, the *De Ruyter* had no torpedo tubes, mirroring the US Navy's decision. Between the relative lack of gunpower and the total lack of torpedo tubes, the *De Ruyter*'s surface armament, by cruiser standards, was nothing short of pitiful. She did have the state-of-the-art Hazemeyer fire control system, giving her excellent targeting, but it was the equivalent of putting a laser sight on an air gun.

The bizarre design decisions for the *De Ruyter* did not end there. She was badly underarmored. This flagship of the East Indies Squadron lacked a flagship-quality bridge. She did have a very good medium antiaircraft package, however – five twin-barreled Bofors 40mm antiaircraft guns; but unfortunately, they were all placed on a single platform behind the smokestack, where they could all be destroyed by a single bomb or shell hit. Even worse, they were unable to fire forward as they would have hit the bridge; therefore, virtually the entire front of the cruiser was without any aircraft defenses. And, although most cruisers were driven through the water by four propellers, or "screws," the *De Ruyter* had only two. If rudder control was lost, the only way to steer a ship was by varying the speed of its screws; this was one reason to have redundant screws, as if one was lost the ship could still be steered. The *De Ruyter*, if she lost a screw, would be unable to steer. This beautiful, intimidating ship when examined closely was nothing more than a hollow shell.

Also warped by Dutch pacifism was the *Tromp*, but in a completely different, much more positive way. When the Dutch Navy requested the *Tromp*, she was to be bigger than a destroyer, similar to a light cruiser, and armed with 6in guns, also like a light cruiser. However, the navy insisted she was not a light cruiser but was instead a "destroyer flotilla leader." She was to lead destroyer flotillas in the same way the Japanese used their light cruisers.

This nice bit of necessary bureaucratic subterfuge, necessitated by a pacifist government, was matched by an equally nice bit of ship design. Although the *Tromp* was little bigger than a destroyer, she had six 6in guns – only one less than the much larger *De Ruyter* – in two dual turrets forward and one aft. Even better, the *Tromp* carried six torpedo tubes.[48] Between her guns and torpedoes, the *Tromp* was arguably the most powerful ship in the Royal Netherlands Navy.

The underachieving *De Ruyter* and the far better *Tromp* were now added to the ABDA Combined Striking Force. Still to be added en route to the target were three Dutch destroyers – *Piet Hein*, *Banckert*, and *Van Ghent*. Like all of the Dutch destroyers, these were of the *Admiralen* class, which was technically an amalgamation of two almost identical classes of destroyers, both of which were named after famous Dutch admirals. Though not much younger than the American four-pipers, they were at least a generation ahead of their counterparts from the Asiatic Fleet and so were of a typically modern design, with enclosed 4.7in gun mounts, torpedo tubes, and depth charges. Probably their most interesting feature was their ability to carry aircraft. The *Admiralen* destroyers were designed to carry one floatplane aft. Not the way most cruisers and battleships did; the *Admiralen* had no cranes or catapults, and the aircraft covered the aft 5in mount and thus prevented its use.[49] This feature disappeared in the late 1930s, the experiment apparently deemed a failure, but it was a very creative concept that exemplifies the high priority the Dutch placed on naval aviation.

So Admiral Hart finally had his Striking Force ready to attack the Japanese who continued to mass in the southern end of the Makassar Strait. Hart had discussed the plan with Admiral Doorman and both agreed that the Striking Force should go out immediately to attack the Japanese convoy headed for Makassar City. They would leave the roadstead at midnight February 4, head east, and then make the dash northward towards Celebes. This plan would require transiting the Flores Sea in broad daylight, well within range of Japanese air power, but that could not be helped. Admiral Purnell, Hart's chief of staff, visited the *De Ruyter* to go over last minute details of the plan with Doorman.

At around this time, the air attack on Soerabaja had ended and the Japanese raiders were heading back to base. The four SOC Seagull floatplanes of the *Houston* had been launched and were flying overhead to avoid becoming fire hazards in the event of air attack, while the PBY Catalina that had brought Admiral Purnell was told to take off and hide. Upon the Catalina's return to pick up the admiral, it was jumped by one of the Babs reconnaissance planes, this one from the 3rd Air Group, who thought the fat, slow flying boat would be an easy target. The gunners of this Catalina, P-27, piloted by Ensign

Leroy Deede, promptly showed the Japanese pilot the error of his ways, sending the Babs crashing into the sea in a sheet of flame. Deede landed and recovered the Japanese pilot's chart.[50]

But this surprising aerial victory could not make up for the fact that the returning Japanese aircraft had spotted the ships of the Striking Force.[51] The sailors knew their upcoming mission had just lost the element of surprise.

This would be no Balikpapan.

THE STRIKING FORCE AT SEA – FEBRUARY 4

Shortly after midnight on February 4, 1942, Admiral Doorman and his *De Ruyter* led the Combined Striking Force out of Boenda Roadstead, heading east through the Madoera Strait at 15 knots. The tanker *Pecos* and a few escorting destroyers were left behind. Doorman was well aware that the Striking Force had been spotted on the afternoon of February 3, but he hoped that, with a head start and an after-dark departure, he could disappear again. The Striking Force made for a 5:00 am rendezvous off Meyndertsdroogte Light with the three Dutch destroyers, which it successfully accomplished. It then arranged itself into cruising formation. The cruisers were in column, with the *De Ruyter* in the lead, followed by the *Houston*, *Marblehead*, and *Tromp*, at 700yd intervals. The US destroyers *Barker*, *Bulmer*, *John D. Edwards*, and *Stewart* formed screens off the port and starboard beams, while the three Dutch destroyers *Piet Hein*, *Van Ghent*, and *Banckert* followed astern.

Admiral Doorman's original plan seems to have been to make the rendezvous and then dash north between Madoera and the Kangean island group across the Java Sea toward Makassar City. The log and track charts of the *Marblehead*, however, make clear that the Striking Force continued on a course 087 degrees True – almost due east – between Kangean and Bali.[52] The reason for the change has never been explained; the planned course itself would later be the subject of controversy.[53] One possible explanation could be that it was trying to avoid new Japanese air searches. If that was indeed the idea, it failed.

At 9:35 am, while still heading east, Admiral Doorman relayed a report of 37 twin-engine bombers having taken off from Kendari. It was believed they were headed for another raid on Soerabaja.[54] More accurately, it was *hoped* they were headed for another raid on Soerabaja. The loss of Kendari II was making itself felt once again.

With brilliant sunshine, visibility was only as limited as the horizon, with the masses of Sapandjang, the easternmost of the Kangean group, some 20 miles to port, and Bali and Lombok more than 40 miles to starboard. The day was bright and the sky was clear – except for a few Japanese floatplanes of the Toko Air Group that suddenly appeared to the east at an altitude of 5,500ft. The lookouts on the *Houston* first raised the alarm at 9:49 am: STRANGE AIRCRAFT SIGHTED.[55]

Twenty-seven Betty bombers of the Kanoya Air Group were spotted to port, bearing 30 degrees True – northeast.[56] Behind them were nine more Bettys of the Takao Air Group, followed by 24 Nells from the 1st Air Group. All were based at Kendari II.[57]

Admiral Doorman had spent most of his life immersed in naval aviation. More than anyone else in the Striking Force, probably more than anyone else in ABDACOM, he understood the power of aircraft against ships. He understood what these Nells and Bettys could do. So Doorman must have been horrified when he realized that these Japanese bombers were not coming to bomb his base – they were coming to bomb *him*.

All ships went to battle stations, lighting boilers to give maximum speed and maneuverability and preparing for air defense. This early in the war, however, naval air defense was hampered by two factors. The first was a general overestimation of the effectiveness of antiaircraft artillery against attacking aircraft. The *Prince of Wales* and the *Repulse* were part of the rapidly growing body of evidence that, against massed bodies of aircraft, antiaircraft guns were nowhere near as effective as airborne interceptors.

The second factor was faulty air defense tactics. Later in the war, Allied air defense doctrine would call on ships under air attack to bunch together so that they could mass their combined antiaircraft fire against the attackers. But early in the war, the prevailing doctrine was called "fighting room" with the ships spreading out. The idea was two-fold. First, each ship would gain maneuvering room to turn and avoid bombs and torpedoes without hitting other ships. Second and more importantly, it would force the attacking aircraft to split up into smaller groups. While each ship would effectively be on its own for antiaircraft protection, the attacking aircraft would be more vulnerable in isolation.[58] However, what was never considered was what would happen if the aircraft did not split up but instead focused all their efforts on one ship. So Admiral Doorman ordered his ships to scatter, as he was supposed to do, but they would suffer for the Allied theorists' lack of vision.

At 9:53 am, the attacking bombers were seen splitting into attack groups, headed for the cruisers.[59] Captain Arthur G. Robinson of the *Marblehead* had his executive officer Commander William B. Goggins head to the wardroom, his General Quarters station, so the skipper and his second-in-command would not both be caught on the bridge together.[60] Arthur Maher, the gunnery officer of the *Houston*, was high up in the fire control station atop the *Houston*'s tripod foremast, in charge of bringing the Houston's guns online: .50cal machine guns, 1.1in pom poms, 5in antiaircraft guns, and even the main 8in battery. While the main guns could not be elevated enough to strike aerial targets, it was thought that a salvo in front of approaching torpedo aircraft would cause such a massive shell splash that the attackers would be swamped.[61] A creative idea, it would end up being an understandable but disastrous mistake.

The *Houston* tried to launch her four floatplanes and get these fire hazards away from the cruiser. Only one would be blasted down the catapult and into the air in time. The antiquated 3in guns of the *Marblehead*, which had to fire independently, were ready. Commander Maher had the four 5in guns on the *Houston*'s port side target the incoming

Nells and Bettys. The main antiaircraft fire director was rendered useless by the smoke from the cruiser's funnels, so the secondary director had to be used.[62] They were ready. But now Admiral Doorman would learn about a third factor hampering his air defense, one that was completely inexcusable.

At 9:58 am, Maher's four 5in guns all fired at the approaching bombers, sending what were in essence four grenades into the air to explode among the Nells and Bettys, ripping them with shrapnel. Sitting on the catapult waiting for launch, a *Houston* Seagull floatplane had its tail fabric blown off by the concussion of the guns. The aircraft's skeletal remains were dumped over the side. The other two SOCs were returned to the hangars.[63] That floatplane would be the only aircraft damaged by the *Houston*'s first antiaircraft salvo. The gunners had shot four 5in shells into the air, but had seen only one explosion among the Japanese aircraft. A second salvo got a similar result. The 5in rounds had been set properly; they were rechecked and found to be in apparent working order.[64]

Although the *Houston*'s gunners were shocked and furious at their obviously defective ammunition, it was no surprise to the commander Captain Rooks and his staff, or to Maher.

Several months earlier, the assistant gunnery officer Jack Galbraith had seen a notice that, during some recent antiaircraft gunnery exercises at one of the US Navy's West Coast bases, some 75 percent of the 5in antiaircraft rounds were found defective. The *Houston* carried the same model of 5in shell. Captain Rooks had requested permission to conduct live-fire tests of the ammunition, but the navy denied the request. Out of cost concerns, the navy bureaucracy had for years been extremely resistant to live-fire exercises of any kind, which could have revealed such problems. Now, the magazines of its ships were full of ammunition as the navy had intended; but while aging might improve a fine wine, it erodes ammunition, and so was thought to be a factor in the 5in failures. Rooks had requested new 5in ammunition, but it had not arrived. Concerned for the morale of the crew, Rooks, Maher, and Galbraith had agreed to keep this depressing news to themselves.[65]

But now the word was out: once again, the US government had sent its men to war with defective ammunition. First, torpedoes on submarines and destroyers, now ammunition on ships. As a result, the *Houston* was effectively in a gunfight firing blanks. True to the reported percentage, three out of every four shells fired by the cruiser's 5in guns failed to explode. The gunners were as "mad as scalded dogs."[66]

Nine Japanese aircraft made their approach to the *Marblehead*, followed by another eight. They were watched closely. At the moment when he thought they were about to release their bombs, Captain Robinson turned the wheel of the *Marblehead* hard over – left full rudder. But the Japanese passed overhead without bombing. Another psychological maneuver, perhaps, but they were also trying to get their timing right. The 3in guns of the light cruiser stopped firing and Robinson had her again on an easterly course.[67]

That pattern would be repeated. At 10:05 am, having circled around, eight of the Mitsubishis were again approaching, this time from the port bow. They were trying to line the cruiser up to provide the maximum target for bombers, which was the opposite of the maximum target for torpedo aircraft. The *Marblehead* opened fire again with her 3-inchers, and Captain Robinson ordered emergency full speed and another hard turn to port. Again the bombers passed overhead without bombing. Now the cruiser was on a course of 345 degrees True – north northwest.[68]

The Japanese aircraft came around for a third pass. Again, the 3-inchers barked, even though at an altitude of 14,000ft the bombers were out of reach. This time, Captain Robinson ordered right full rudder, and the cruiser swerved to a course of 10 degrees True – north northeast.[69] This time, the Mitsubishis released their bombs; luckily, Robinson had guessed correctly, and although the old cruiser was straddled, all the bombs missed, landing some 100yd off the port bow.[70] One of the Bettys of the Takao Air Group was seen slowly losing altitude, hit by either the 40mm Bofors of the *De Ruyter* or one of the few 5in shells from the *Houston* that actually exploded.[71] The aircraft turned to make a suicide run on the *Marblehead*. The .50cal machine guns of the *Marblehead* poured fire into the dying bomber, apparently killing the pilot, and the aircraft slowly spun into the sea some 1,000yd off the cruiser's port bow.[72]

The other American cruiser, the *Houston*, was also receiving the attention of the Japanese. Nine Mitsubishis came after President Roosevelt's favorite ship. Captain Rooks was lying on deck, watching the bombers through his binoculars and trying to time their release point. Then he ordered hard to port – so hard that it jammed the antiaircraft fire director. The bombs came close to the cruiser. According to *Houston* pilot Walter Winslow, they landed 10ft on either side of the ship, to explode underwater. The explosions seemed to lift the heavy cruiser out of the water, sending up towering geysers of water as high as the foremast that deluged the main deck. But, as with the *Marblehead*, none hit.[73] Yet.

For there were plenty of other flights of Nells and Bettys, generally nine to a flight, arranged in a V-formation, as they had been for the attacks on the *Repulse* and the *Prince of Wales*. Only a few minutes later another flight of seven Nells from the 1st Air Group approached the *Marblehead* from the starboard bow. Again, Captain Robinson ordered left full rudder. This time, his guess as to their release point could not overcome their skill. It was 10:27 am.[74]

Some of the Japanese bombs again straddled the *Marblehead*, but two of the bombs struck the old light cruiser. One hit in the forward section of the ship, about 10ft from the starboard side.[75] It sheared a motor launch and then exploded a mere 15ft aft of the wardroom, where the executive officer Commander Goggins was stationed.[76] The explosion demolished the wardroom and sickbay, bent the forward uptakes, and started a large fire. Goggins was flash-burned by the explosion of superheated gases and fire, but he remained on duty.[77]

The second bomb hit the quarterdeck about 4ft from port side. The deck's steel was bent upward, blocking the aft turret and rendering it useless. Even worse, the after steering room was wrecked.[78] Because the *Marblehead* had been in a hard-port turn when the bomb hit, the rudder was now jammed hard to port by the explosion. The cruiser could only steam in circles. Attempts to communicate with the after steering compartment were met with ominous silence.[79]

A third bomb did not hit, but it might as well have. The near miss exploded underwater near the port bow, lifting the ship upward and causing a heel to starboard.[80] The hull plating near the bow was ruptured, a dangerous injury because it meant mere movement would cause the ship to take in water.

The *Marblehead* had lost 15 killed and had 34 seriously wounded. She could only move in a tight circle, albeit at 25 knots. She was on fire, settling by the bow and listing 10 degrees to starboard, trailing an oil slick. She looked finished. The *Tromp*, under the command of Captain Jacob de Meester, approached to take off the crew before the cruiser sank.[81]

But Captain Robinson waved him off; he was determined to save his ship. The US Navy took pride in its skill at damage control – there would be no cases like the aircraft carrier HMS *Ark Royal*, sunk by one torpedo from a German U-boat and the carrier's inept damage control. Damage control on the *Marblehead* immediately went to work, and very efficiently, too, helped along by a fortuitous interlude in the air attacks. The damage control officer had the fire under control by 11:00 am.[82] In a daze, suffering from a neck wound and horribly burned, Commander Goggins went aft to see what he could do about the steering.[83] Captain Robinson tried to steer the ship with the engines, shutting down the starboard engine while setting the port engine to maximum. The *Marblehead* was still only able to move in circles, but at least the circles were larger.[84]

At 11:04 am, another attack appeared. Captain Robinson ordered full speed on both engines, but this just made the *Marblehead* steam in smaller circles.[85] Fortunately for the suffering cruiser, this next attack was setting up for a run at the *Houston*, which was made at 11:17 am. One crewman admired how Captain Rooks handled the heavy cruiser "like a motorboat" – turning, stopping, starting, reversing, speeding. Once again, the captain lay on his back, guessing at the bombers' release point. The *Houston* was straddled again, but no hits. Her luck had held, but how long could she keep this up?

Meanwhile, Captain Robinson was still trying to give the *Marblehead* some semblance of navigability. When it became obvious his ship was not the target, he cut the starboard engine again. Then Commander Goggins came to the bridge with bad news: the engines used for moving the rudder had been demolished. Hand steering was impossible. The crew in the aft steering compartment had all been killed. Goggins' team was trying to get the rudder centered so that they could steer using the engines. In shock, high on adrenalin and focused on saving the ship, he had hardly noticed any pain from his neck wound, or from his charred arms and legs, where the skin was now hanging from his flesh. But now the pain was kicking in. Robinson ordered Goggins, having performed his duty admirably and with dedication, to go to the conning tower to get his severe wounds treated. The gunnery officer was made the executive officer.[86]

But the attacks were not over. At 11:26 am another flight of bombers swooped in. This time it was not the staggering *Marblehead* that was their target, but the flagship *De*

Ruyter. Admiral Doorman had signaled Soerabaja SEND FIGHTERS, but he knew they would not be coming.[87] The *De Ruyter* just had to endure the bombing like her compatriots. Captain Eugène Edouard Bernard Lacomblé handled his ship well enough to avoid all the Japanese bombs, but the vaunted Hezemeyer fire control system was knocked offline.[88]

Yet another attack was developing, this one apparently from the 1st Air Group, also stationed at Kendari II. Concerned about the welfare of the *Marblehead*, Captain Rooks ordered the *Houston* to close on the staggering light cruiser to bring her under the protection of the *Houston*'s 5in guns.[89] It may have been a fateful decision. The target of the last attack, coming at 11:40 am from the *Houston*'s port side, can be disputed. Both Walter Winslow and Captain Robinson seemed to think it was directed at the *Marblehead*, noting that the bombs landed some 2,000yd away.[90] Level-bombing ships from 14,000ft is not always (or even usually) particularly accurate, as both the US Navy and the Imperial Japanese Navy were learning, but the Japanese bombs on this day had been unusually accurate and deadly. Winslow's and Robinson's belief notwithstanding, the bombs of the last attack may have been directed at the *Houston.* Captain Rooks had again lain on his back, guessing the bombers' release point. He had guessed correctly. The bombs missed the cruiser again – at least those bombs that had been dropped properly. One bomb, it has been speculated, hung a little too long in the rack; it dropped slightly after the rest.[91] As a result, Captain Rooks' brilliant work went for naught.

The bomb screamed downward and glanced off the mainmast, cutting through the searchlight platform, nicking the tripod support, and exploding about 3ft above the main deck between the mainmast and the No. 3 aft turret, trained to port as Commander Maher had directed.[92] If the No. 3 turret had been in train – that is, facing down the centerline aft – the bomb might have hit the heavily armored top of the turret. Instead, because the turret was trained to port, the detonation sent white-hot shrapnel into the turret's less-armored sides – and into the turret itself. The entire aft damage control party, directly under the bomb, was killed. A 12ft hole was blown in the deck. Fragments tore into the turret, killing its crew as well as those in the handling room below, gutting the turret, and setting fire to the powder bags in the hoists inside.

"Fire in Turret Number Three!" bellowed the loudspeakers on the *Houston.*[93] Everyone knew the alarming potential of a fire in a turret, with the magazine and its ammunition and powder bags directly underneath. If the fire reached the magazine and detonated it, the resulting explosion would be devastating – an explosion in the No. 3 turret would likely blow off the stern – and almost certainly doom the cruiser. Commander Maher came down from his perch high atop the *Houston*'s foremast to stand next to the blazing turret and direct damage control efforts, shouting orders to get hoses trained on the turret. Crewmen who had no set battle station, such as Winslow, a pilot, converged aft to try to put out the fire. Then came a sharp, loud BOOM! Everyone scattered – except for Commander Maher. He knew what had happened, as did everyone else when they stopped their momentary panic: the heat had cooked off one of the 8in rounds in the loaded guns of the turret, which fired. Sheepishly, everyone came back and went for the fire hoses again.[94]

Maher's heroism would be matched by Gunner's Mate Czeslaus J. Kunks, who was in charge of the aft main battery magazine. When he felt the jarring explosion of the bomb and realized that No. 3 turret and its attendant handling room were on fire above him, Kunks immediately went to dog down the hatches to seal off the magazine from the fire. Then he activated the sprinkler system to douse the powder and ammunition with water. Kunks chased his men out of the magazine, checking to make sure everything possible had been done to prevent the fire from reaching these combustibles. Then, the last one in the magazine, he tried to climb out, only to have the metal door conk him on the head, knocking him unconscious as he fell back down the ladder. His men carried him out. Gunner's Mate Czeslaus J. Kunks had, quite literally, saved the ship.[95]

Meanwhile, the other crewmen were pouring water on the blazing turret, leaving some 6in of water sloshing on the deck. The task was made easier but grimmer when it was determined that no one was left alive in the turret. Altogether, the *Houston* had 48 men killed and 20 wounded. In the midst of this commotion came yet another air raid warning. But this time, there was just a single Japanese aircraft, with no intention of attacking. Circling for a while outside of gun range, he assessed his comrades' handiwork. Then he flew off.[96]

It was over. After this beating, with the element of surprise gone, Admiral Doorman cancelled the operation. At 12:25 pm, he ordered the Striking Force to head west toward the dubious safety of Soerabaja.

Trying her best to keep up was the *Marblehead*. By bleeding the hydraulic lines and yoking the rudder gears with chains, the damage control parties were able to lock the rudder at a 9-degree angle to port.[97] Close enough. With the rudder in more or less a center position, Captain Robinson could now steer with the engines, keeping the port engine running and varying the speed of the starboard. She moved with something of a sideways gain as her crew tried to counter the flooding by pumping and bailing as fast as they could, eventually reducing the list to a manageable 4 degrees to starboard. The destroyers *John D. Edwards* and *Stewart* came close by to lend support if needed.

Admiral Doorman checked on the status of the two damaged American cruisers. In response to their reports, at 2:15 pm he ordered them to head to Tjilatjap via Lombok Strait. They received some natural cover from rain squalls, which hid them from any more eagle-eyed Japanese aircraft. But Captain Robinson knew that, in trying to get his gravely wounded ship safely back to port, the *Marblehead's* main enemy was not the Japanese. It was the sea.

And, right now, the sea was winning.

CHAPTER 8

A THOUSAND CUTS

"War consists of long periods of boredom punctuated by moments of sheer terror." This unattributed quote, elegant in both its simplicity and its brevity, perhaps best describes the experience of war. Although it's the shooting, the bombing, the fighting, the killing, and the dying that are heralded in the newsreels, movies, and gripping tales of heroism and folly, the vast majority of war is the training, the guarding, the watching, the typing, the reporting, the filing, the signing, the requisitioning (if any word can capture the essence of military bureaucracy, it is "requisitioning"), the walking, the driving, the repairing – and the convoying. Putting supply trucks or ships in a convoy so they can be more easily protected. It is tedious grunt work, but it has to be done.

The way ABDACOM did convoying, however, leaves the logic open to question. Another old adage goes, "A good general thinks tactics, a great general thinks logistics." And there's definitely a lot of truth to that statement. But if it were completely true, then Julius Caesar was a terrible general and General Henry W. Halleck – "little more than a first-rate clerk," according to US President Abraham Lincoln during its Civil War – was a great one. A great commander must think of both.

Under General Wavell, ABDACOM was much more like Henry Halleck, but without the organizational skills. In keeping with British naval doctrine, Wavell placed a high priority on convoying. As previously discussed the Allies simply did not have enough ships both to guard every convoy and to mount an effective defense of the Indies. Given those options, Wavell made his choice clear – convoying.

On this day, February 5, the destroyer USS *Paul Jones* had the tedious task of convoying, if you can count one ship, the SS *Tidore*, as a convoy. But in war, tedious work is only tedious until it isn't, which would be on this day, February 5. The *Paul Jones* and the *Tidore* were south of Soembawa, headed for Tjilatjap, when at 11:00 am they spotted a large flight of Japanese bombers coming from the northeast. The loss of Kendari II was making itself felt once again.

The *Tidore* immediately ran herself aground to make certain the thin-skinned freighter would not sink, but *Paul Jones* skipper Lieutenant Commander John J. "Red" Hourihan had no intention of letting his ship suffer such an ignominious fate. He began a spate of wild evasive maneuvering as the Japanese Nells and Bettys made seven bombing runs against his ship. For two hours every US Navy voice radio in the vicinity was filled with his voice, giving both play-by-play and colorful commentary. Finally, Hourihan was able to report cheerfully: SEVEN RUNS, NO HITS, ALL ERRORS.[1]

At 3:55 pm, the *Paul Jones* returned to the stranded *Tidore* and rescued its officers and crew before destroying the ship and heading to Tjilatjap.[2]

The Japanese bombing attack had been intense, unusually so. They seemed to have sought out the *Paul Jones*. They knew where she was going to be and had sent a large airstrike to put her under. It seemed an unusual level of attention for just one destroyer.

Unless the Japanese had mistaken her for someone else, which, as it turned out, they had. They were hunting for another ship, and thought they had found her in the *Paul Jones*, because the *Paul Jones*, like all the *Clemson*-class destroyers, looked like a smaller twin to the light cruisers of the *Omaha* class.[3]

Like the *Marblehead*.

THE RETURN OF THE *MARBLEHEAD* – FEBRUARY 6

The men of the *Houston* marched up the road in the morning light in a long line, kicking up dust that covered their nice dress whites, especially those of Captain Rooks and his staff, who were marching in the back.

In the midst of this column were trucks carrying 48 wooden coffins, some still dripping the blood of their occupants.[4] All night the *Houston* had been full of noise and activity – the pounding of hammers, the sawing of wood, as, after scouring Tjilatjap for wood, crew members assembled coffins for their shipmates who had been taken by that one last Japanese bomb. Adding to the commotion was a fire alarm, again from the No. 3 turret. The dead had been removed and the gutted turret secured from the electrical system. But a guard nevertheless insisted he had seen sparks emanate from the blackened, tangled mess inside the turret.[5] His report had been in good faith but it had certainly not helped things.

Those fallen were the only ones sleeping on the *Houston* that night.

The *Houston* had safely arrived at Tjilatjap at around noon the day before, February 5, bloodied but by no means broken, determined to honor her war dead for their devotion to duty. Her colors had been lowered to half-mast. Now every officer and sailor not actively engaged in repairing and supplying the ship was in this funeral procession, marching its way through the town's dry, dusty streets. Lining those streets were Javanese residents, watching the spectacle with expressionless faces that betrayed at best a mild interest.

The procession would end at a Dutch cemetery where these brave souls would get full military honors, including the traditional 21-gun salute and the timeless, mournful tones of "Taps." Here, in a beach overlooking the Indian Ocean, on an island most of them had never heard of – Captain Rooks commented, "It's striking, isn't it? These boys are being buried in a town they'd never even heard the name of before." – they would be laid to rest until they could be returned to the United States.[6]

The skeleton crew left aboard the *Houston* had also wished to honor their fallen – the *Houston* had been an unusually happy ship – but they were stuck with making repairs: the large hole in the deck; the broken mainmast; the gutted, useless turret.

Their work stopped when they saw her making her way slowly, painfully up the channel with the help of tugs. She was large and vaguely sphinx-like, yet very familiar, coming in from the mysteries of the ocean, into the safe, welcoming harbor of what had once been christened "that lousy dump."[7] Tjilatjap's harbor, such as it was, was actually by itself neither safe nor welcoming, but the crewmen still on the *Houston* would take care of the latter. Normally when a friendly ship came by they would come to attention, but this time they came to the railing and cheered for the new arrival.

The *Marblehead* had made it to port.

Returning from the Flores Sea had been agonizing for the old girl and the men trying to keep her afloat. Most of the ship's fuel had to be dumped. They had managed to pump out the hand steering room and remove the bodies from it, but the rudder could not be made operable, so they had to steer by engine. Yet even by keeping the speed of the port screw steady while varying that of the starboard propeller to turn the ship in either direction, it was still a difficult job. It was slow, it was arduous, it was laborious.

But it was not nearly as laborious as trying to keep the still-flooding *Marblehead* from sinking. The pumps could not keep up with the inrush of water from the ruptured bow. Bucket brigades were set up. And they had to run a long, long time – some 48 hours, an eternity for such a physical, tedious, and boring but essential duty, with the flooding giving no breaks for dinner, sleep, or the restroom. But run they did. It was not expertise but effort.

The *Marblehead* had made it safely to port through the sheer will of Captain Arthur G. Robinson and his crew. This was an incredible work of seamanship – with assistance from the *Paul Jones*, who had unwittingly drawn off the Japanese bombers that had been looking to finish off the old cruiser.

After her crew returned the *Houston*'s cheers, with the help of the tugs the *Marblehead* crawled her way to the floating drydock. The Dutch, as with the *Houston* the day before, had made a hospital train available. Under the care of an Asiatic Fleet doctor, Lieutenant Commander Corydon McAlmont Wassell, the wounded, including Commander Goggins, were placed on board for a trip up the single railroad track to the Petronella Hospital in Djocja, outside Jogjakarta, where they could receive better medical care.

As bad as the debacle in the Flores Sea had been, two small but notable good developments came out of it. The first was on the cruiser *Houston*. Captain Rooks was a new skipper, having replaced Jesse B. Oldendorf the previous August. Oldendorf, who would go on to play an important part in the American recapture of the Philippines almost three years later, had been a popular and beloved captain. Living up to a high standard set by the previous skipper was a challenge for any new commander. The crew of the *Houston* had been willing to give Rooks a chance, but they had been wary.

Not any more. Captain Albert H. Rooks had more than earned their respect. They had been amazed and even awestruck at his handling of the *Houston* through the bombings. They had suffered the bomb hit, but the new, unknown skipper had remained calm, unflappable, and had kept the ship alive if not unharmed. "Everyone believed that the Good Lord had His hand on his shoulder for the things he brought us through," declared *Houston* sailor Paul Papish. More than respect, Rooks had earned their love. "I think they looked at him as just another god," said *Houston* seaman Melfred L. "Gus" Forsman, while some officers would later say, "Admiration for the Captain bordered on worship."[8] They now would go anywhere, do anything for Albert Rooks. It was the mark of an outstanding commanding officer. During the final two months of his life and that of his ship, Captain Rooks and the crew of the *Houston* fought as one.

The second development was much more subtle, but nevertheless important. The lack of respect shown the Americans by the Dutch rank-and-file had begun to subside. The first step had been the Battle of Balikpapan, an American victory that made many of the Dutch realize that the US Navy could and would indeed fight. It had not left the Philippines willingly, had not cut and run with its tail between its legs, but had been forced out violently.

Now, the action in the Flores Sea had seen the Americans fighting alongside the Dutch, fighting for the Dutch – and dying for the Dutch. It had been witnessed firsthand by the crews of the *De Ruyter* and *Tromp*, and the *Backert*, *Piet Hein*, and *Van Ghent* as well as by Captain de Meester, Captain Lacomblé, and Admiral Doorman. The action had been a defeat, and a costly defeat at that. But for the men of the Royal Netherlands Navy, it had been enlightening. War can divide people, but it can also bring them together, especially those fighting alongside each other. Whatever the political, strategic, and cultural differences that would erupt in the coming weeks, these men were now, in a sense, brothers-in-arms.

Furthermore Admiral Doorman had come to view the sailors of the US Navy operating under his command as just as important and deserving of just as much care and responsibility as those of his own navy.

That Doorman viewed the American sailors as his own is the most logical explanation for his behavior after the Flores Sea defeat, but it is also, admittedly, the most charitable. Admiral Doorman had kept the *De Ruyter* and the Dutch destroyers escorting the *Marblehead* until midnight on February 5. Then, satisfied that the crippled cruiser would make port and that any problems could be handled by the two escorting destroyers USS *Stewart* and *John D. Edwards*, he broke off and headed through the Soenda Strait to Batavia. It was a curious decision, one that would earn him some criticism.[9]

When he reached Tandjoeng Priok, Admiral Doorman went to speak with Admiral Helfrich, where they discussed the action in the Flores Sea. Helfrich would later tell Admiral Hart that the air attack "upset (Doorman) a little."[10] Hart did not learn for a full half a day that Doorman had cancelled the attack, due to communications issues and, some assert, a difference in Dutch reporting protocols.[11] And now the disharmony within ABDAFLOAT would turn into finger-pointing. Hart was furious with Doorman, for he felt that the attack could have still been carried out with the *De Ruyter* and *Tromp* and the remaining destroyers. Hart's anger, however, was mainly directed at Helfrich. He wrote in his diary, "If he had not misled me we could have had this joint force set up two days earlier."[12] That delay, caused by Helfrich's sending Doorman's ships on the useless Karimata mission, had indeed proven disastrous. Hart attempted to salvage the mission, ordering Doorman to reassemble the scattered ships after refueling. But when Doorman set a refueling point some 300 miles south of Java, way too far behind the front for Hart's taste, Hart wondered if Doorman had lost his nerve and seriously considered about relieving him of duty.[13]

Except that there was no one with whom to replace him. Hart would still not consider Glassford, and all the suitable British candidates had been drawn into the Singapore debacle. Admiral Hart simply called Doorman in for a meeting in Tjilatjap, where he found Doorman "visibly shaken" by the action in the Flores Sea, and "rather over apprehensive of enemy bombing attacks."[14] Hart later said that Doorman was "naturally a very cautious sea commander and not inclined to take commensurate risks."[15] Hart took great pains to explain to Doorman that while his withdrawal because of damage and lack of air cover may have been prudent in normal circumstances – which it indeed was – these were not normal circumstances. They had to take greater risks because their backs were against the wall. They either attacked without air cover or they did nothing.[16]

It is difficult to gauge what had happened to Admiral Doorman. The idea that he was lacking in courage does not seem entirely plausible considering his impressive pre-World War II service record. In light of his future actions, it is fair to say that Doorman was at the very least upset at losing so many men under his command while being helpless to protect them without withdrawing. The loss of the *Prince of Wales* and the *Repulse* to air attack was not an anomaly; the Flores Sea action was very nearly a repeat. Going to sea under enemy-controlled skies was risking destruction without a chance of appreciable gain. This was a fundamental disagreement between Doorman and Hart. Admiral Hart thought the circumstances justified the risk; Doorman was not convinced, which is ironic inasmuch as the Indies were governed not by the United States but by the Netherlands, and there is evidence that, from this point forward, Doorman believed that without air power the Indies were indefensible – a belief actually shared by Hart.

And so the Flores Sea action, like so much in this worsening Java Sea Campaign, became the basis for some controversy. Australia's official naval historian Herman Gill said that "given the known lack of air cover, [T]he timing of sailing, and route taken, would appear to have been ill-chosen."[17] Which begs the question of who developed the plan? Admiral

Hart had clearly discussed it with Admiral Doorman, but who came up with the details is disputed – a dispute further complicated by the visit that Admiral Purnell made to the *De Ruyter* in Boenda Roads to discuss the plan with Doorman the day before sailing. Samuel Eliot Morison said that Doorman "had plans for a try at Makassar Strait."[18] According to Admiral Helfrich, however, Doorman told him that "he didn't understand why he got orders to proceed for an attack on Balikpapan – a long way – without air protection and after being sighted the day before."[19] Helfrich certainly did not understand why Doorman took the route he did, nor did he know who had chosen the route. "In my opinion he should have gone through Sapudi Strait [along the east coast of Madoera] up north immediately."[20] Such a route would have taken the Striking Force out of the path of the Kendari-to-Soerabaja attack vector. If one reads the accounts to give both some credence, it would seem that the idea of the counterattack in the Makassar Strait was Doorman's but the operational details that proved so troubling were Hart's or, more likely, Purnell's.

If read in this light, while it is impossible to know what Admiral Doorman was thinking, it is easier to understand the reasons he may have had for being "upset." The operation, with which he at the very least agreed and may have even initiated, was threatened by the Japanese sighting of the Striking Force in Boenda Roads. The threat was compounded by a route that took his ships under the direct route from Kendari to Soerabaja for an extended period of time. The idea to head east for so long initially and then make the dash to Makassar City was likely intended to deceive Japanese scout aircraft. But that plan was developed before the Japanese raid on Soerabaja and their discovery of the force in Boenda Roads; that discovery had prompted the Japanese to plan the aerial ambush in the Flores Sea.[21] Nevertheless, while the circumstances had changed, the plan had not.

It is also easier to understand why Doorman aborted the mission and went directly to Batavia, even leaving the *Marblehead* to do so. If he was uncertain about Admiral Hart's leadership and his orders for the immediate mission, Admiral Helfrich was the best person to discuss his concern with. Helfrich, for once, understood his fellow countryman's concerns. Hart clearly did not, although interestingly enough, his report suggests that it was not Doorman's decision to abort the mission that had gotten Hart angry enough to consider relieving him, but rather Doorman's proposal to withdraw to the Indian Ocean some 300 miles south of Java to refuel. But even that proposal was understandable to Helfrich. "What could Doorman have done else?" he would ask. "He told me later it never was his intention to *stay* in the Indian Ocean. It was part of the 'hit and run' tactics, which I had ordered, before Hart arrived, as the only method to operate against a superior enemy, without air cover."[22] In this respect, at least, Helfrich was exactly right.

The issue of Admiral Doorman was neither the only nor even the biggest political problem faced by Admiral Hart. The sharks were circling the American admiral. In addition to Admiral Helfrich's campaign the Deputy Governor General Dr van Mook had been campaigning against Hart in Washington and London. In yet another example of the irony that was seeping into ABDACOM, they claimed that Hart was "not aggressive enough." Their words echoed the caustic insinuations of General MacArthur, who had far more political support in Washington than Hart could ever muster. Furthermore the British were starting to turn on Hart. Hart's efforts at finding out what his status was with General Wavell were met with claims of ignorance and noncommittal answers. On February 5, Fleet Admiral Ernest J. King, the commander-in-chief of the US Fleet and Chief of Naval Operations in Washington, informed Hart that "an awkward situation had arisen" and that as a result "it might be best if Hart were to ask for detachment on grounds of health."[23] His days as ABDAFLOAT were now numbered.

Below his rank, things were not much better. As a condition of accepting the appointment as ABDAFLOAT, the US Navy had ordered Admiral Hart to relinquish operational control of the Asiatic Fleet. This Hart had resisted, in part because he did not want to put Admiral Glassford in charge of the Asiatic Fleet as the navy had wanted. But Admiral King issued a direct order to Hart to relinquish command to Glassford. When Glassford found out about the order on January 25, he threw a party for his staff at the Simpang Club in Soerabaja.[24] Barely containing his fury, Hart, as ordered, put Glassford in charge of the Asiatic Fleet, which was now renamed "US Naval Forces, Southwest Pacific," an awkward name that Asiatic Fleet sailors resented and refused to use.[25] The new title meant a promotion for Glassford from rear admiral to vice admiral, so, with the Japanese menace coming closer and closer with no apparent way to stop them, Glassford celebrated by throwing another party.[26] Admiral Purnell, who as Asiatic Fleet chief of staff had been Glassford's superior, was now answerable to him as chief of staff of the "US Naval Forces, Southwest Pacific." It was all very confusing.

Far worse was the state of the American ships. Admiral Glassford had sent the fleet's materiel specialist to check out the ships. It was not a pretty picture. The *Boise* had already left Tjilatjap, returning to the United States because of the gash in her hull caused by her grounding. The most modern American ship in the Far East and the only one with radar was gone. At least she had left her good 5in ammunition behind for the *Houston*.

The *Marblehead* was another matter. She had come into port with 30 of her compartments flooded. The floating drydock at Tjilatjap was too small to accommodate her. Through the ingenuity of a Dutch naval architect, the *Marblehead* was moved into the drydock so that when it rose (as floating drydocks usually do to lift the ships they are servicing out of the water), it lifted up her bow. It was exceedingly dangerous but it enabled the drydock workers to place a temporary patch on her bow.[27] Unfortunately, they could not, dared not, attempt this trick with the stern. If the cruiser fell, the propellers, shafts, and rudder would all be smashed and probably driven into the hull, so the rudder could not be made operable. There were also still the ruptured hull plates that could not be repaired, so the *Marblehead* could not be made entirely watertight. There was no choice but to send her back to the United States as well. Admiral Hart ordered her to head back through Ceylon, where the British base at Trincomalee could make temporary repairs. With no guarantee that the *Marblehead* would make it, Hart ordered the submarine tender *Otus* to escort her.[28] It was an unusual order for a submarine tender, but Hart could spare no other ships. If the worst happened and the *Marblehead* sank, at least the *Otus* could take off the crew.

While not the most dangerous problem, one of the most taxing was that of the *Houston*. Her No. 3 turret was completely useless, the insides burnt, the circuits and controls melted. It could not be repaired outside a shipyard. But there was no shipyard nearby. Normally such damage would necessitate a trip back to the United States. But there was no ship available to replace the *Houston*; the cruiser *Phoenix*, a sister ship of the *Boise*, was due to come in March, but until then, even with her aft turret out, the *Houston* was still the most powerful ship Admiral Hart had.

After inspecting the *Houston* in Tjilatjap, the admiral had an extended discussion with Captain Rooks on the dock. Not hearing the substance of the conversation, *Houston* crewman Otto Schwartz watched the two officers talking and looking back at the ship. He later said, "It was quite evident from the events that followed that some kind of decision had been made at that time."[29] Admiral Hart had determined that even in her damaged condition the *Houston* was "capable of escort duty, at least," but would not make a decision as to whether to send her home because of her battle damage without consulting with her skipper. Hart worried that ordering the *Houston* to stay in theater would amount to a death sentence for one of the best-trained and highest-morale crews in the fleet, and told Rooks that he "didn't want our folks to accuse him of manslaughter, and there was a battle coming that was already lost before it was fought."[30]

The captain, it is believed, personally would rather have gone home, but the officer in him did not want to leave the navy in the lurch in the Indies; and the warrior in him, like his crew, was furious and wanted another crack at the Japanese. In any event, Captain Rooks told Admiral Hart, "*Marblehead* has to go out and the [*Boise*] has already gone with a torn-out bottom. We are the only one left. *Houston* has one good strike on her, but she has two good strikes left there and we can shoot all the ammunition that is left from [the *Boise*]. We don't think we should go out."[31] Hart would later say of this exchange, "Of course, I was the one who had to decide it. But it would have been very hard to send you home when the ship's people feel that way."[32] Based on this discussion, Hart ordered the *Houston* to stay until the *Phoenix* arrived. Reportedly, he also told Rooks that because of the loss of the aft turret, he would never order the *Houston* north of the Malay Barrier again.[33] Then again, Hart had told Rooks and crewmen on the *Houston* of his pending replacement, so it would not be his call for much longer. Of the decision to keep the *Houston* in theater, Hart would later say, "I had to make a decision which I now wish that I had reversed. It was largely her captain's decision."[34]

A dockside crane was used to move the turret to train it aft, and canvas was placed over its riddled side, so that at least it looked operable. A steel plate was acquired from a nearby farmer to patch the hole in the deck, and railroad rails were welded in to patch damaged interior longitudinal girders. The *Houston* was thus made ready for combat again.

So the *Houston* was sent to escort a convoy of troops leaving Darwin to reinforce the defenses at Koepang on Timor, the farthest east of the major islands in the Malay Barrier, which was now threatened by the Japanese capture of Ambon.

And so began the death by a thousand cuts. ABDAFLOAT would be constantly losing ships. Not a lot – at first, anyway. Just one here, another there. Little by little. Those that were sunk could not be replaced. Those that were damaged, by combat, accident, or mechanical breakdown, could not be fixed locally and so had either to be sent home – such as *Boise* and *Marblehead* – with no replacement available, or kept in their damaged condition – such as *Houston*, *Peary*, and *Edsall* – with no replacements from home.

It only reinforced the disheartening feeling that they were all alone. So far from God, so close to Japan.

Makassar City invaded – February 8–10

Sunset on February 8, 1942, was the end of another horrible day for ABDACOM. The British destroyer *Express*, survivor of the debacle of Force Z, was on her way to Ceylon and eventually South Africa and out of the fight as a result of a major fire in a boiler room. When the destroyer was lifted out of the water as the *Prince of Wales* capsized, the bump had damaged a boiler room bulkhead next to a fuel tank. The Eastern Fleet engineering officer had complained that the repairs made on the *Express* at the Singapore Naval Base were incomplete, leaving cracks in places that could lead to a fire, but the base said the repairs were adequate and refused to perform any more work. Sure enough, the *Express* was on convoy duty when, on February 6, that fire occurred.[35] Yet another loss to Allied resources in the Indies.

The Japanese air attacks on Soerabaja were continuing, every day at around 9:00 or 10:00 am, from high altitude. The 17th Pursuit Squadron (Provisional) would try its absolute best to intercept the attackers, but the Dutch air defense command could never get the word to them in time. The pilots of the 17th would take off from their base at Ngoro, but after the excruciatingly long time it took to get the P-40 Warhawk to altitude, the enemy bombers had already finished their work. The Warhawks would give chase, but the P-40 was not turbocharged; its performance suffered markedly at high altitude, so the Nells and Bettys could usually outrun the US fighters.

Further to the north, the debacle that had hit the ABDA Striking Force on February 4 meant there was now no surface force capable of stopping a Japanese move to Makassar. Doorman had reassembled his force at Tjilatjap but it was a case of being too weak and too late. The enemy was going to win this battle.

But it was possible to win every battle and still lose the war. Just because there was no surface force capable of stopping a Japanese move to Makassar City did not mean that there was nothing there with which to resist them, strike back, and start turning this into a war of attrition. The solution lay with US submarines.

The US submarine *S-37* was, like the other S boats, the submarine version of the "four-pipers," constructed shortly after World War I and now outclassed by newer models.

Those newer models were the "fleet" submarines, usually named after fish or other sea creatures. The fleet submarines had more torpedo tubes, better fire control and navigation gear, better endurance and range, and even air conditioning (always important in a completely enclosed submarine) than the S-boats. As with the four-pipers, the Asiatic Fleet had had an unhealthy proportion of these aged models, which were in the process of being phased out.

But a sword that is old is still a sword, and throughout the war these old "sugar" boats would repeatedly prove themselves. They did also have one unintended advantage over their newer brethren: they were too old to use the Mark 14 torpedo and the Mark 6 magnetic exploder, so they used the earlier Mark 10 torpedo with its simple contact exploder.[36]

The *S-37* maintained a solitary position off Makassar City, keeping a watch on the harbor by periscope. The Japanese Eastern Force had sent out an invasion convoy from Staring Bay on February 6 – four transports and a replenishing vessel, carrying the Sasebo Combined Special Naval Landing Force and the 5th and 6th Naval Construction Units. The convoy was escorted by the light cruiser *Nagara* and 11 destroyers, two minesweepers, and three subchasers.[37] Based on heavy air raids on Ambon, ABDACOM had presumed Ambon would be their target and had accordingly pulled a submarine cordon out of the Makassar Strait to intercept it.

But just before midnight on February 6, the convoy was spotted in a rainstorm by the submarine USS *Sculpin* under the command of Lieutenant Commander Lucius H. Chappell. The convoy was heading south, which meant it was clearly not going to Ambon. Chappell reported in and fired two torpedoes at *Nagara*, but once again without any success. In another quality performance for the US Mark 14 torpedo, one exploded prematurely and the other missed.[38]

This convoy, the Makassar Occupation Force, another renamed element of the much larger Eastern Force under Admiral Takahashi, continued down the east side of Celebes, around the South Peninsula, and north into the Makassar Strait. Now there were no Allied ships to face the invasion convoy and no submarines – except for the *S-37* in her lonely vigil off Makassar City.[39]

At dusk on February 8, the *S-37*'s periscope, manned by executive officer Lieutenant W. H. Hazzard, spotted a thin shadow on the barely discernible horizon. The shadow quickly became a mast, which soon brought with it over the horizon a Japanese destroyer, charging toward the submarine fast – too fast to make much use of her sound gear. She sped by, not toward the submarine, but toward Makassar City.[40]

Lieutenant Hazzard discussed it with his skipper, Lieutenant James Charles Dempsey, and they agreed: the destroyer was a high-speed scout. But for what?

The answer soon revealed itself. Coming out of the gloom were four more vague forms in a slow-moving column – more destroyers. Behind them were even more shadows, too dark and too far away for periscope identification, but Lieutenant Dempsey ascertained that this was an invasion convoy headed for Makassar City. More importantly, it was also headed straight for his boat. Dempsey moved off to the east and sat down to await an opportunity to attack.

As the convoy got closer, Lieutenant Dempsey could see the flashing of Aldis lamps signaling between ships and, from somewhere back in the darkness, a searchlight sweeping the sky. Surfacing so that it could achieve greater speed, the *S-37* began stalking the convoy.

At this stage of the war and especially in this campaign, Dempsey's targets were to be the ships of the convoy itself – the troopships, freighters carrying supplies, and tankers. Not the escorts, and especially not the escorting destroyers. Submarines had two major enemies: destroyers and aircraft. Aircraft could spot even a submerged submarine, especially at periscope depth or in shallow water. Aircraft could also drop depth charges on a submarine, while a submarine could generally not strike back against aircraft. However, aircraft could carry only a very limited number of depth charges, and since aircraft had no sound detection equipment, a submarine could dive deep and usually escape.

A destroyer was a much more serious problem. Small and fast, destroyers were hard to hit with a torpedo, and usually of limited value – at least in the eyes of US Navy theorists – so they weren't usually worth a torpedo strike. They could also overtake a submarine on the surface and easily riddle its unarmored hull with gunfire. They had sonar (asdic) sound detection gear and plenty of depth charges. A destroyer was a submarine's nightmare, especially for an old submarine like the *S-37*.

But after stalking the convoy for some time, Lieutenant Dempsey found he could not get around the escorting destroyers. Under US Navy doctrine, if he could not get at the convoy, it was permissible to attack the destroyers. This is exactly what he did: at 8:30 pm he launched one torpedo at each of the four destroyers in the column at a range of 800yd.[41]

One torpedo at a small target at night was a tough shot, but Lieutenant Dempsey was rewarded with one flash in the dark on the third ship in the column, the 1,900-ton *Natsushio*, flagship of Destroyer Division 15 under Captain Sato Torajiro. The torpedo hit between the smokestacks, flooding the boiler rooms and causing the stacks to belch flaming soot. The explosion left eight dead and two wounded, and buckled the destroyer midships some 20ft over the bow and stern, indicating that the *Natsushio*'s back had been broken. With the rest of Destroyer Division 15 headed his way, Lieutenant Dempsey decided that, having stung the enemy, it was time for the sugar boat to submerge and retire from battle. *S-37* evaded depth charge attacks and made her escape.

Antisubmarine tactics were never a strength of the Imperial Japanese Navy. Destroyer Division 15's counterattack was likely further crippled by the incapacitation of its flagship. Captain Sato transferred his flag to the *Oyashio*. The *Kuroshio* tried to take the stricken destroyer in tow, but the *Natsushio* was breaking in two; a broken keel meant that there was little that was structurally holding the ship together. The crew was removed, and on February 9 the *Natsushio* foundered 22 miles south of Makassar City.[42]

The Japanese troop landing was carried off successfully on February 9. Some 8,000 troops landed in two detachments, one of which got into a skirmish with native troops of the Royal Netherlands Indies Army defending a bridge. After the native troops surrendered, the Japanese marines, resentful that these Asian natives had actually shot back at them, tied the captured troops in groups of three and threw them from the bridge into the water below.[43] Japanese propaganda attempts to get the Asian peoples to side with them against the Europeans curiously failed to mention this incident.

Makassar City was now Japanese. Although three US LB-30 Liberators that claimed a bombing attack on February 10 resulted in direct hits on a "converted aircraft carrier" which then "exploded and was left burning" – it was actually the seaplane tender *Chitose* which was damaged by a single bomb hit but was able to remain in service – the only Japanese naval loss had been the *Natsushio*, a pittance for such an important conquest.[44] But it was a harbinger of things to come. *Natsushio* was the first of 39 Japanese destroyers to be sunk by US submarines during the war. The US Navy would change its doctrine to make destroyers higher priority targets. An early practitioner was Lieutenant Dempsey; the *S-37*'s patrol featured five attacks on destroyers, though only the one on the *Natsushio* was successful. The S-boat's patrol ended when it ran aground in the Lombok Strait and had to return to Soerabaja for repairs.[45]

Nevertheless, two years later, the Combined Fleet would be critically short of destroyers, unable to protect supply convoys, and barely able to even protect its larger surface forces.

But that was two years into the future. Right now, it was ABDACOM that was short of destroyers and, for that matter, just about everything. And what it did have was dwindling fast.

DISAPPEARANCE OF THE USS *SHARK*

It was during this time period that those Japanese destroyers got some revenge for the sinking of the *Natsushio*, in the form of the US submarine *Shark*.

After her chauffeur duty for Admiral Hart was done, the *Shark* had supplied up at Soerabaja and on January 5 went out on her second war patrol. The next day a Japanese submarine welcomed the *Shark* back to the war by firing a torpedo at her. It missed. Barely. On February 2 *Shark* reported to Soerabaja that she had been in a battle of her own some 10 miles off Tifore Island with a destroyer later identified as the *Amatsukaze*, being depth-charged and launching an unsuccessful torpedo attack. On February 7, Commander Shane reported chasing an empty cargo ship heading northeast, a message that drew a rebuke from Captain Wilkes for breaking radio silence for this rather trivial information. The *Shark* was never heard from again.

Post-war examination of Japanese records, which the US Navy described as "notoriously inaccurate and incomplete, especially during the early part of the war," indicated several possible incidents that could have been the end of the *Shark*. The most likely took place at 1:37 am on February 11, when the destroyer *Yamakaze* sighted a surfaced submarine in the darkness some 120 miles east of Menado, an area consistent with the last orders issued to the *Shark*. The destroyer opened fire with her main guns, expending a total of 42 5-inch shells and 60 rounds of machine gun ammunition. Surprise was complete, and the submarine was quickly sunk, the *Yamakaze* abandoning any survivors to their fate in the dark off Celebes.

ADMIRAL HART DEPARTS – FEBRUARY 14–15

The sharks that had long been circling Admiral Hart now finally got their prey. After the admiral had, as ordered, requested relief from his duties as ABDAFLOAT for reasons of health, General Wavell was ordered "to let Hart maintain the nominal title of ABDAFLOAT but delegate his operational duties to Admiral Helfrich," while Helfrich himself was instructed to relieve Hart on February 14.[46]

It was a very confusing and ultimately dishonest change of power. While Admiral Hart had friends in the US Navy who well understood that Douglas MacArthur and the Dutch were trying to make him a scapegoat – and succeeding – he had very few friends in the Washington establishment, with one of his bitterest critics being President Roosevelt himself. Dutch complaints had also turned General Wavell and Prime Minister Churchill against him. But the reasons for his relief extended far beyond him. There was the belief in Washington that the Java Sea Campaign was not going to end well, and for that reason the Dutch should assume responsibility for it.

The treatment of Admiral Hart sparked considerable resentment among the men of the Asiatic Fleet, directed at Washington and, especially Douglas MacArthur.[47] Hart was not necessarily a popular character – many detested him personally – but he was very well respected professionally. Admiral Hart does not seem to have cared too much about being relieved of duty, but he hated the idea of leaving his men in desperate straits under someone else's command. Hart would later write in his diary, "Oh, it was hard … leaving them out here in the face of a dangerous enemy and commanded by God knows whom or how."[48]

That "whom" was Dutch Admiral Conrad Helfrich, which did not please the men of the Asiatic Fleet. The pending change in ABDAFLOAT quickly made its way through the rumor mill of the fleet. The men knew that in Hart they had a commander who would look out for them. Lieutenant Commander David A. Harris, who had taken over command of the destroyer *Bulmer* on January 28, summed up the fleet's feelings: "We've been thrown to the wolves by the God Damned politicians. With Hart gone, we have no chance. We're dead."[49] As *Stewart* sailor Lodwick Alford described it, "There was a feeling of we are in for it now, God help us!"[50] There was widespread mistrust of Admiral Helfrich. "All of us on the *Stewart* had unbounded admiration and confidence in Admiral Hart but none for Helfrich," Alford added. The *Houston*'s Commander Maher later said, "There was some reaction against the Dutch command. We didn't figure the Dutch were qualified to take over command at sea."[51]

After one last reception was thrown in his honor, Thomas C. Hart was last seen standing on a dock in Batavia, in civilian clothes, waiting for the old British cruiser *Durban* to take him to Ceylon for the first leg of his trip back to the United States and Washington, where yet more knives awaited him.[52]

The decision to remove Hart may have been a political judgment from Washington and London, but it was a disaster for the US sailors trapped in the East Indies. Now ABDAFLOAT was the Dutch Admiral Helfrich, while his chief of staff was the Royal Navy's Admiral Palliser. There was no American officer with a formal post in the leadership of ABDAFLOAT, even though the US was providing a significant part of the ships. Admiral Glassford remained the US Navy's representative as Commander US Naval Forces, Southwest Pacific, but he had no title within ABDACOM and no authority.

When told he was finally ABDAFLOAT, Helfrich had four words for his secretary: "In charge at last."[53]

FALL OF SINGAPORE – FEBRUARY 15, 1942

For the men of the Asiatic Fleet, February 15 was "Black Sunday" – the day Admiral Hart departed the scene. But even the men of ABDACOM would acknowledge that the departure of Hart was not the only, or even the worst, of the disasters of Black Sunday. For this was the day that General Percival surrendered Singapore, "the Gibraltar of the East," to the Japanese.[54]

The troops of Japanese General Yamashita's 25th Army had marched – or, more accurately, pedaled – all the way to the Johore Strait in an advance that would be christened the "Bicycle Blitzkrieg." Bicycles were hardly novel in warfare – the Germans had used them in their 1940 invasion of France, for instance – but to General Percival these bicycles might as well have been Guderian's panzers.

When the Japanese reached the Johore Strait, Singapore Island still had ample supplies, more than enough troops, and a natural defense in the Johore Strait itself that should have enabled it to hold out for some time. But the incompetence that Malaya Command had displayed throughout the campaign now reached new heights. Singapore Island was linked to the mainland by an 1,100ft man-made causeway across the Johore Strait. After the British had retreated to the island, their engineers dynamited the causeway. But they were only able to blow a 70ft breach. Even worse, the breach could be (and was) forded at low tide.

The British Malaya Command would have been far better served if the experienced and capable General Wavell had just taken over from General Percival. General Wavell had warned General Percival that British intelligence expected the Japanese to attempt a landing on the northwestern part of Singapore Island, where the Johore Strait was at its narrowest. Percival expected the Japanese to land on the northeastern part of the island, where the Johore Strait was at its widest, and so stationed his best troops there.[55] When on February 8, the Japanese landed – on the northwestern part of the island, just as Wavell had predicted – they faced Percival's weakest troops. Moreover, Percival had muddled the deployment of his troops so that they could not be moved quickly, had scattered them across the island, including in many places where combat was unlikely, and had failed to set up a reserve.[56] If this was not enough, almost no fortifications had been constructed in the projected landing areas. Requests made to Percival the previous December to build the defenses had been rejected on the grounds that they were bad for civilian morale. When presented with the resulting nakedness of the northern shores of the island on a January 9 visit, an infuriated Wavell had ordered Percival to build the fortifications, but by then it was too late.[57]

Unable to react quickly to the invading Japanese, the British were driven back towards Singapore City. The airfields at Sembawang, Seletar, and Tengah had become untenable due to Japanese shelling, and the last eight Hawker Hurricanes had been withdrawn by February 10. When Yamashita's troops captured the island's reservoir, resistance was doomed. And so on February 15 came General Percival's surrender and the icing on this multilayer cake of ineptitude. As General Yamashita later admitted:

> My attack on Singapore was a bluff – a bluff that worked. I had 30,000 men and was outnumbered more than three to one. I knew if I had to fight long for Singapore I would be beaten. That is why the surrender had to be at once. I was very frightened the British would discover our numerical weakness and lack of supplies and force me into disastrous street fighting.[58]

But General Percival, a courageous and highly intelligent officer out of his depth as a battlefield commander, never did, and, bluffed by General Yamashita into believing he was massively outnumbered, surrendered Singapore. For the Japanese, it was "one of the most brilliant feats of arms in the war, perhaps in modern military history."[59]

Some 90,000 British, Australian, and Indian troops passed into the hell of Japanese prisoner-of-war camps. The Kempeitai carried out a plan that became known as *Sook Ching* – "purification by elimination" – a name earned by the murder of 30,000–50,000 Chinese.[60] The Malaysian population, quickly disavowed of any idea of Japanese benevolence towards the conquered islanders, began three years of Japanese occupation that Malaysians would universally describe as cruel and brutal.[61]

The Japanese were determined that there would not be another Dunkirk at Singapore in which a British army could escape. Fleeing ships, transports and boats, whether civilian or military, were hunted down and attacked with utter ruthlessness. Exact numbers will never be known, but it is estimated that more than 70 vessels were sunk or otherwise permanently disabled, killing between 2,000 and 5,000 servicemen and civilians.[62]

Among those deaths were Air Vice Marshal Pulford and Admiral Spooner, whose boat *ML310* was driven aground on Tjebia (Chebia or Cebia) Island by Japanese destroyers. The Japanese never found these two high-ranking British officers or the other 42 refugees, but they found the boat and smashed the engines, marooning them on an island with no communications and little food but plenty of malaria. Accounts differ, but somehow, the castaways got a message to ABDACOM of their plight.[63] Captain Wilkes ordered the submarine *S-39*, under the command of Lieutenant James W. (Red) Coe, to attempt a rescue. On February 27 she arrived at an island it was thought was Tjebia but the blinkered messages she sent that night received no response. The next night brought no better luck, so the following night Coe led a search party ashore, but found no one.[64] It is now speculated that Coe landed on the wrong island, which given the thousands of little islands in the Indies, is easy to do. Most of the marooned survivors, including Pulford and Spooner, ultimately died of malaria, with the remainder eventually taken into Japanese custody.[65]

The defeat was a national embarrassment. Churchill himself described it as "the worst disaster and largest capitulation in British history."[66] It was a hammer blow for the British Empire from which it never recovered.

And it was the shatterpoint for ABDACOM. The next day General Wavell told Churchill, "Landings on Java in near future can only be prevented by local naval and air superiority. Facts given show that it is most unlikely that this superiority can be obtained."[67]

INVASION OF SUMATRA – FEBRUARY 10–16

So well had the operation in Malaya and Singapore been going for the Japanese (and so badly for the British) that they were able to use troops not needed in Malaya to accelerate the timetable for the next phase of their operations in the East Indies: the occupation of Sumatra.

Sumatra was one of the major gems of the East Indies. The island is just over 1,000 miles long, and some 230 miles wide, lying roughly northwest to southeast parallel to the Malay Peninsula, from which it is separated by the Strait of Malacca, which at its narrowest point is only some 30 miles wide. The reason Sumatra was so valuable was Palembang, which lay inland on the southern part of the island. Palembang was home to major oil fields and two major oil refineries near Palembang at Pladjoe (Pladju), owned by Royal Dutch Shell, and Soengai (Sungei) Gerong, owned by Standard Oil. It was also home to an airbase complex of two major fields: Palembang I, about 10 miles to the north, and Palembang II, about 35 miles to the southwest. The Royal Air Force, who called the airfields P1 and P2, respectively, had been given permission by Dutch General Hein ter Poorten, ABDARM, to operate from the airfields and defend them with antiaircraft batteries. The Dutch were to provide ground troops for defense. Unusually for an inland city, Palembang was extremely vulnerable from the sea, being connected to the Banka Strait some 50 miles away by the Moesi (Musi) River, which was navigable to ocean-going vessels.[68]

Once again, Japanese intelligence had done its job extremely well. Japanese commanders were aware that the Moesi River was navigable and they were prepared to take advantage of it. Once again, the job fell to Admiral Ozawa and his Western Striking Force. On the morning of February 10, Ozawa departed from Cam Ranh Bay, Indochina, in the luxurious heavy cruiser *Chokai*. With him was the 7th Cruiser Division and its four heavy cruisers of the *Mogami* class (those ships that the failed Washington and London treaties were supposed to prevent), light cruiser *Sendai*, and destroyers *Fubuki*, *Hatsuyuki*, and *Shirayuki*, escorting 25 transports whose objective was to head up the Moesi River to Palembang. Some 50 miles behind them was the light carrier *Ryujo*, rapidly becoming an Allied nemesis, and the destroyer *Shikinami*. The carrier now had an air group of 12 Mitsubishi A5M4 "Claude" fighters and 15 Nakajima B5N1 "Kate" attack aircraft.[69]

This time ABDACOM knew about the invasion and would try everything humanly possible to stop it. US intelligence had long been able to decipher Japanese naval codes to varying degrees of success and they picked up the departure of the convoy. Captain Wilkes of the Asiatic submarine command sent a message to Lieutenant Commander Theodore Aylward and his submarine *Searaven* vectoring them to an intercept position. Upon arriving, the *Searaven* submerged and waited in ambush.

The next day, February 11, the seas were heavy but the convoy appeared on cue. In heavy seas, *Searaven* moved in on two of the *Mogami*s. Lieutenant Commander Aylward fired two Mark 14 torpedoes at each of the cruisers from close range. This entire operation had been well planned and well executed, a credit to US intelligence, the US submarine command, and ABDACOM. Except for one thing: of the four Mark 14 torpedoes fired not a single one scored a hit.[70]

ABDACOM had other irons in the fire, if only they could pull them out. ABDAIR had been watching the movements of the Japanese convoy.[71] Two attempted attacks by Royal Air Force Blenheim bombers failed.[72] General Wavell ordered General ter Poorten to reinforce Palembang; ter Poorten responded by sending a battalion of Dutch East Indies troops to Palembang and a second, curiously, to Banka and Billiton islands. Wavell further ordered the Striking Force to assemble in western Java for an attack on the convoy. Admiral Doorman had the cruisers *De Ruyter* and *Tromp*, and the destroyers *Van Ghent*, *Banckert*, and *Piet Hein* (remnants of the force that had attempted to stop the Makassar City invasion) south of Soembawa in the Lesser Soenda Islands, where Admiral Hart had ordered him to wait in an attempt to resume that operation. Doorman was ordered to move 800 miles west to a rendezvous point near Oosthaven (now Bandar Lampung), on the extreme southeast tip of Sumatra, where the Dutch maintained a small fueling base.[73] And Doorman dutifully headed there as fast as he could, so fast that, in foggy, stormy conditions on the night of February 12, the *De Ruyter* plowed into the forward starboard side of the destroyer USS *Whipple* off Prigi Bay in eastern Java, where the Dutch flagship had stopped to refuel.[74] Damage to the Dutch cruiser seems to have been negligible, but the collision bent the *Whipple*'s bow 45 degrees to port, requiring a stay in Tjilatjap's floating drydock and leaving her no longer fit for combat duty.[75]

ABDAFLOAT was rounding up all the ships it could. The USS *Houston* had been shipped to Darwin to assist in the defense of Timor, now threatened by the Japanese Eastern Force, and was not immediately available. But the Dutch light cruiser *Java*, that old, little ship with the heart of a warrior, and the destroyer *Kortenaer* were finally pulled off convoy duty in the Soenda Strait and ordered to Oosthaven. So was the Australian light cruiser *Hobart*. Some heavier support showed up at Oosthaven in the form of the British heavy cruiser *Exeter*, who had been on convoy duty since the war began and who had just finished escorting a convoy to Batavia. Under the command of Captain Oliver Louden Gordon, the *Exeter* was a veteran cruiser with an impressive pedigree, having had a hand in the sinking of the German pocket battleship *Admiral Graf* Spee off Montevideo, Uruguay. She was immediately the strongest ship in ABDAFLOAT. She may have carried only six 8in guns to the nine the *Houston* normally carried, but unlike the US Navy, the Royal Navy had not been foolish enough to remove the torpedo tubes from its cruisers. Rounding out the force were six US destroyers: *Bulmer*, *Barker*, *Stewart*, *Parrott*, *Edwards*, and *Pillsbury*, who arrived on February 14. With the Americans, the British, the Dutch, and the Australians all contributing ships to save Palembang, this was truly an ABDA Striking Force.

Admiral Helfrich, now in charge of ABDAFLOAT, had ordered Admiral Doorman to "consider the advisability of an attack by day as well as by night in view of the considerably increased firepower of his force."[76] Doorman flew from Oosthaven to meet with Helfrich in Batavia. The shortest route to intercept the convoy went through the Banka Strait, but there was concern that the Japanese had already mined it. So the Striking Force was to take the longer, more difficult route north through the Gaspar Strait, a hazardous area lacking navigational aids, and head north of Banka Island "destroying any enemy force seen."[77]

But the Japanese struck first. Smoke from massive fires in Singapore drifted southward and covered the route to Palembang. The smoke provided cover for bombers and transports carrying 360 Japanese Special Naval Landing Force paratroopers to strike Palembang. P1 was heavily bombed, but the Royal Air Force aircraft were not caught on the ground – they were out over Banka bombing the invasion convoy. Bristol Blenheim bombers from No. 211 Squadron managed to sink the transport *Inabasan Maru* with bombs.[78] Upon return, the British aircraft were rerouted to P2. That afternoon, 11 Blenheims from the No. 84 and No. 211 Squadrons, escorted by 15 Hawker Hurricanes, went after the *Ryujo*, but were bounced by defending Claudes that shot down two bombers and damaged six others for no losses in return.[79] Of the 360 Japanese paratroopers, 260 captured P1 – the other 100 had been redirected to seize nearby oil refineries – but suffered severe losses in the process. The Dutch Army troops were confident the airfield could be recaptured. The British, dispirited by the Singapore disaster, were not.

At 4:00 pm on this chaotic Valentine's Day, the Combined Striking Force left Oosthaven. They formed two columns, with the Dutch cruisers *De Ruyter*, *Java*, and *Tromp* to starboard and the *Hobart* and *Exeter* to port, in that order. The six US destroyers screened ahead and three Dutch astern. The fourth, veteran *Banckert*, had been sent ahead as a navigational beacon and rejoined the force later on.[80]

But things went badly almost from the start. The Combined Striking Force took the ordered route, the Dutch destroyers leading in a line-abreast formation, but the night of February 14/15 was dark and stormy, with low visibility. Sailing into an area notorious for navigational hazards this was a recipe for disaster. And sure enough, at approximately 5:20 am, the destroyer *Van Ghent*, the most starboard of the leading destroyers, ran fast aground on the Bamidjo Reef in the Stolze Strait between Banka and Billiton islands, starting a fire in her forward boiler room.[81] And so yet another cut was added. Admiral Doorman would be criticized for having his destroyers steam abreast in this narrow and dangerous strait.[82] In fairness, he may have been trying to use the destroyers as a submarine screen; certainly during this campaign the Dutch seemed concerned about Japanese submarines out of all proportion to the threat those submarines actually presented, a concern that would cost ABDACOM dearly. The *Banckert* was left behind to take off the *Van Ghent*'s crew, salvage as much equipment and supplies as she could, and scuttle the ship with explosives and gunfire.[83] Dutch claims that they knew these waters better than anyone seemed rather hollow after this.

At 6:00 am, the *De Ruyter* sent off her floatplane to scout out the enemy. It reported back at 8:37 am, having sighted seven cruisers and three destroyers 10 miles northeast of Pulau Laut (some 45 miles north of Banka Island) heading northwest at high speed.[84] Admiral Doorman kept on his course, clearing Gaspar Strait and heading east of Banka Island. But if the Japanese were headed northwest, he would never catch them. They must know he was coming. Any lingering doubts about whether the Japanese knew about the Allied task force were dispelled when a Japanese cruiser floatplane was sighted at 9:23 am.[85]

The floatplane was from the *Chokai*, Admiral Ozawa's flagship.[86] His surface forces could easily outgun and out-torpedo Admiral Doorman's but Ozawa was an astute naval commander. A surface fight could be dangerous – his ships could be damaged or even sunk, his men killed, his ammunition expended. This was an unnecessary risk when he had air superiority. He could keep his ships and his men safe by ordering the transports to hold back and simply sending his attack aircraft to bomb the Allied force into oblivion.

And so it began. Shadowed throughout the day by floatplanes, Admiral Doorman and his Combined Striking Force would never get the opportunity to defend Palembang. What he and his sailors had to endure was not only terrifying but also completely ridiculous.

At 10:20 am, four Kates from the *Ryujo*, each armed with one 250kg (550lb) bomb and four 60kg (130lb) bombs, attacked, focusing on the *Exeter*. Admiral Doorman had the ships spread out but maintain their course, and implemented new antiaircraft protocols learned in the Flores Sea action.[87] The ABDA ships maneuvered to air defense positions, twisting and turning to avoid the bombs, while their heavy antiaircraft fire forced the Japanese attackers to stay at high altitude. The Kates registered no hits, but they would get many, many more chances.[88]

Next came 23 Mitsubishi G3M2 "Nell" bombers from the Genzan Air Group, the killers of the *Prince of Wales* and *Repulse*, who had relocated to airfields at Kuching on Borneo. They scored near misses on the destroyers *Barker* and *Bulmer*, rupturing the hull plating on both.[89]

Around 11:30 am, it was seven Kates from the *Ryujo*, each armed with one 250kg (550lb) bomb and four 60kg (130lb) bombs. They got no hits, but a near miss on the *Exeter* damaged her Supermarine Walrus floatplane sitting on its catapult and rendered it inoperable.[90]

By this time, after three Japanese air attacks, the Combined Striking Force was some 40 miles east of Banka Island and some 80 miles from Admiral Ozawa's ships.[91] Admiral Doorman realized that the Japanese were not going to let him get anywhere near their warships, let alone their transports. At 12:42 pm, he cancelled the operation and ordered a retreat to Tanjoeng Priok.[92] But the Japanese were not through with him or his sailors yet.

Next came 27 Nells of the Mihoro Air Group, operating out of Kuantan.[93] To the defiant shouts of "Missed again" from the ABDA crews that would be heard most of this day, all of the Nells' bombs fell harmlessly into the sea.[94] About half the bombers were damaged by antiaircraft fire.[95]

At 3:29 pm it was six Kates from the *Ryujo*. Again, they went after the *Exeter*, but registered no hits.[96] At 4:30 pm it was seven Kates from the *Ryujo* – again scoring no hits.[97] At 7:00 pm, it was six Kates, concentrating on the *De Ruyter*, which with her *Bismarck*-like tower mast the Japanese had mistaken for a battleship. But she too escaped unscathed.[98]

Then came one more attack from 17 Bettys of the Kanoya Air Group – after a five-hour flight from Thú Dâu Môt.[99] One last time, they registered no hits.

It may sound as if the ABDA Combined Striking Force had had a good day, surviving so many relentless air attacks, but in reality it had been a miserable day. With no air cover whatsoever, the Allied ships had to run and pirouette like ballerinas for the entire day until sunset offered them some respite. Only skillful handling of the ships – and the learning of some key lessons from the Flores Sea action – prevented any major losses. Captain Harry Leslie Howland of the *Hobart* would comment:

> [T]he bombs fell close enough for me to see the ugly red flash of their burst and to feel the heat of their explosions across my face – but the ship steamed clear … There have been occasions when I have had to call for the most violent manoeuvring of the main engines, and the instant answer has resulted in swinging the ship in a manner I hardly thought possible. On one occasion I found it necessary to go from 24 knots ahead to 24 knots astern on one engine, while going full ahead on the other.[100]

They had shot down no enemy aircraft. The crews were exhausted. The ships were scattered, and it would take time to reform the force. Fuel was becoming an issue, especially with the fuel-hungry destroyers. The Japanese clearly knew where the Combined Striking Force was; they were prepared to pound it until it either withdrew or was destroyed. The only option for Admiral Doorman was to retreat.

And so Palembang would fall. The Combined Striking Force withdrew from what *Kortenaer* skipper "Cruiser" Kroese called "bomb alley" and through the Stolze Strait, where they saw the wreck of the *Van Ghent*, now burning as a result of her demolition by the *Banckert* and still more Japanese air attacks.[101] The destroyer's grounding may have drawn off yet more air attacks that would have otherwise targeted the exhausted ABDA ships.

Admiral Doorman attempted to go into Tandjoeng Priok on February 16, but every berth in the port was crowded and at least 30 ships were anchored in the harbor, so the *De Ruyter* led the *Hobart, Exeter, Tromp, Barker,* and *Bulmer* into the harbor where they anchored at 9:52 am.[102]

Because of the crowding at Tanjoeng Priok, the *Java*, Dutch destroyers *Kortenaer* and *Piet Hein*, and the American destroyers *John D. Edwards, Parrott, Pillsbury,* and *Stewart* were sent to Oosthaven to refuel – before the retreating Dutch could destroy the refueling facilities there.[103] Oosthaven was the point of evacuation for Sumatra. The island with its oil fields and refineries was now lost. And the Japanese were not going to let the Dutch evacuate unscathed.

As part of the reinforcement of Sumatra, General ter Poorten had ordered a battalion of Dutch East Indies troops to reinforce Banka and Billiton islands. It was a nonsensical idea, and Admiral Helfrich said so; the war in the East Indies had clearly shown it was impossible for a small garrison to defend an island from an enemy who controlled the sea. But ter Poorten was insistent, and General Wavell supported him. An angry Helfrich had acquiesced, using the *Java* to guard the transport carrying these troops on February 5.[104] He would soon have even more reason to be angry.

With the retreat from Sumatra came, on February 17, the retreat from Billiton. Admiral Helfrich, after having been forced against his will to use some of the few ships under his command to place these troops to their worthless defensive position, now had to use some of the same few ships under his command to evacuate these troops. The transport *Sloet van de Beele*, escorted by the destroyer *Van Nes*, was sent to Billiton, where the crews quickly embarked the troops and numerous civilians from the island. Then they headed home, but not before attracting the attention of a floatplane from the cruiser *Mogami*.[105]

Once again, a seaplane was the harbinger of doom. Fifteen Mitsubishi Nells of the Genzan Air Group and ten Kates from the *Ryujo* armed with bombs headed to cut them off. They arrived around 4:40 pm. With no air cover and no ships to help them, the transport and the destroyer were truly alone.

The cruiser *Tromp* and PBY Catalina Y-45 of the Royal Netherlands Naval Air Service would be the only Allied witnesses, via radio, to the plight of these two lonely ships on a nightmarish afternoon of February 17. *Van Nes* skipper Charles Albertus Lagaay signaled CONVOY HIT BY BOMBERS.[106] There was nothing anyone could do. Shortly thereafter the PBY picked up another signal from Lagaay that the destroyer had been SLIGHTLY

DAMAGED. Then a third signal that the Sloet van de Beele had been sunk – victim of a direct hit from the Nells. She had lasted barely five minutes and the *Van Nes* herself was now under heavy air attack.[107] Then silence. Corkscrewing like a rollercoaster, the *Van Nes* had initially managed to evade several bombs from the Kates, but was soon hit by three in rapid succession. At around 5:00 pm, she broke in half near her second stack, sinking immediately.[108] Of her crew, 68 were lost; 86 were rescued, 52 of whom were picked up by the Dutch Dornier Do-24 flying boat X-18 and taken to Batavia, after spending 92 hours in the sea without food or drinking water. No one knows how many were on the transport, though some have quoted figures in excess of 1,000, but only 272 were ever recovered, 38 by a Dutch minesweeper, the remainder by the Royal Netherlands Naval Air Service.

As a victim of the redoubtable Kate bomber from the *Ryujo*, the Hr. Ms. *Van Nes* was the first allied warship sunk by Japanese carrier aircraft since Pearl Harbor. But Japanese carrier aircraft would send more to join her soon.

Preparing to defend Timor – *Houston* saves a convoy, February 15–16

The Combined Striking Force was not the only ABDA force suffering from the affliction of Japanese air attacks on February 15.

Admiral Hart had not been able to send the *Houston* home because the cruiser was still considered useful for convoy duties. So on the evening of February 8, on orders from Hart shortly before his own departure, Captain Rooks had sailed the *Houston* out of Tjilatjap for Darwin, arriving at 11:00 pm on February 11.[109]

At Darwin a reinforcement convoy for Koepang was forming at the orders of General Wavell. While the western tentacles of the Japanese Kraken were finishing up at Singapore and grabbing Sumatra, the eastern tentacle – the Eastern Force under Admiral Takahashi – was now aiming for Dutch Timor, at the far eastern end of the Lesser Soenda Islands. This was yet another disaster in the making for ABDACOM. One of the few ways to get aircraft to Java, especially badly needed P-40 Warhawk fighters, was to have them fly in stages, from Darwin to the Koepang (Kupang) airfield on Dutch Timor (the other, eastern half of the island was under the rule of neutral Portugal) then to the Denpesar airfield on Bali and then to Soerabaja. If the Japanese captured Timor, that supply route would be cut off.

So it was essential to increase the defense of Koepang. Four transports – the army transport *Meigs*, the SS *Mauna Loa*, the SS *Port Mar*, and the British transport *Tulagi* – would carry US Army troops of the 147th and 148th Field Artillery and Australian troops of the 2/4th Pioneer Battalion. Escorting the transports would be the *Houston*, the US destroyer *Peary*, and the Australian sloops *Swan* and *Warrego*.[110]

Steps were taken to conceal the reinforcement. The convoy left Darwin under cover of darkness a little before 2:00 am on February 15 and headed west southwest. It was not the most direct route to Timor, but it was hoped that it would fool the Japanese. It did not even fool Tokyo Rose, who taunted the convoy, naming each ship and the destination in the process.[111] At around noon on February 15, the *Houston* went to battle stations for air defense. One of the ubiquitous Japanese seaplanes – a four-engine Mavis of the Toko Air Group – had been sighted circling outside of gun range.[112] It was a shock to the crew; they had presumed that being south of the Malay Barrier meant they were safe from air attack. Well within aircraft range of Darwin's airfield, Captain Rooks immediately radioed for fighter cover. It would come – to a degree – but for now they were on their own.[113]

The main concern of Captain Rooks was for the troops on the thin-skinned transports. So it was very fortunate that the Mavis chose as the target for its bombs the *Houston*. Even more fortunate was that the *Houston* now had the 5in antiaircraft rounds from the *Boise* on board. The gunners eyeballed their Japanese stalker. At around 2:00 pm, the Mavis came in on a bombing run, only to be forced to cut it short by the shell bursts of the *Houston*'s 5-inchers.[114] The bombs fell harmlessly into the sea.

Captain Rooks' request for fighter cover was answered at this time – in the form of a single P-40 Warhawk, one of only two fighters available, piloted by Lieutenant Robert J. Buel, a survivor of the 21st Pursuit Squadron.[115] Buel could not find the Mavis, and the *Houston* could not communicate with him or tell him where the Mavis was. Even gunfire from the cruiser's 5-inchers in the direction of the Mavis apparently went unnoticed by the pilot. The Mavis went on its second bombing run, which was again cut off by accurate gunfire from the *Houston*'s newly effective 5in guns. Again, the bombs fell into the sea. The Mavis then fled, the Warhawk finally on its heels. The gunners and lookouts on the *Houston* lost sight of the two aircraft, only to see a flash on the horizon shortly thereafter. Neither the Mavis nor Buel's Warhawk was ever seen again.[116]

As usual, the Japanese seaplane was the harbinger of doom. Nothing happened during the night, other than the disheartening news of the surrender of Singapore, but the crews knew that dawn on February 16 would be dangerous.

And so it was. The day was sunny and bright. They were 300 miles from Darwin, well outside the protection, such as it was, of its fighters. Visibility was excellent, especially for the Mavis flying boat that spotted the convoy at 9:15 am.[117] She was keeping contact for the airstrike that followed at 11:00 am: 35 Betty bombers of the 1st Air Group and ten Mavis flying-boats of the Toko Air Group, all from Kendari II.[118]

This would not be an all-day marathon, like the Banka Strait action. Instead, it would be an hour of terror. The 45 aircraft attacked in four waves of nine, one wave of five, and one wave of four.[119] This time, for one of the very few times in the Java Sea Campaign, convoy duty would save ships and lives.

For instead of going after the helpless transports, the attackers went after the *Houston*, which was just fine with Captain Rooks. This was not the Flores Sea. The cruiser's antiaircraft gunners were now armed.

On this day the *Houston* would spend 903 rounds of 5in ammunition. The fire of the *Houston* was both heavy and accurate, forcing the bombers to stay at high altitude. After the disaster in the Flores Sea Captain Rooks was now an old hand at avoiding bombs.

And *Houston* floatplane pilot Thomas Payne had used his aerial skills, his observations from the Flores Sea action, and his common sense to develop a table – a cheat sheet, if you will – to tell Rooks when to throw the rudder hard over to avoid the bombs. Rooks drove the cruiser hard through the convoy, trying to protect the helpless transports by drawing the attention of the bombers. And succeeding – almost all the bombers targeted the cruiser and not the transports. "The skipper nearly turned the *Houston* over protecting those ships. In fact, he dipped the quarterdeck at one point; the water came up to my knees," remembered crewman Griff Douglas. The *Houston* was not hit once.

The last wave, of five flying boats, went after the transport *Mauna Loa*. Captain Rooks had the *Houston* race over. Her 5in antiaircraft guns delivered a barrage which made her guns look "like a continuous sheet of flame." The captain of the transport *Meigs* was heard to shout, "Look at those bastards go!" One *Houston* survivor said the cruiser was "twisting in and out of that convoy like a mother hen protecting her chicks." The *Mauna Loa* received a near miss that injured three, one mortally, but no direct hits. After the attackers withdrew around noon, the *Houston* steamed by to check on the transports. Hundreds of men – army troops and crewmen – went to the rails of the transports and gave a thunderous ovation for the work of the cruiser. The captain of the *Meigs* signaled EXCEEDINGLY WELL DONE.

But ABDACOM recalled the convoy at 3:15 pm and they headed back to Darwin. Captain Rooks turned south rather than southeast – the most direct route to Darwin – hoping to avoid prying Japanese eyes. He requested fighter protection from Darwin for February 17, and at midmorning it came – in the form of a single Lockheed Hudson bomber. The crews were aghast; the Hudson was worse than useless in an air defense role.

Nonetheless, in the early morning hours of February 18, the convoy was back in Port Darwin and found it heavily congested: more than 20 merchant ships, an Australian hospital ship, the seaplane tender *William B. Preston* with three Catalinas, several smaller ships, two Australian corvettes, the *Houston*, and the *Peary*.

It was while in Darwin that the crew of the *Houston* found out that Admiral Hart had officially been relieved by Admiral Helfrich. Hart's promise to never send the *Houston* north of the Malay Barrier again was now moot, and Helfrich immediately ordered the *Houston* and *Peary* to return to Java.[120] Captain Rooks quickly had the cruiser's fuel bunkers filled to the brim; he did not want to stay any longer than he absolutely had to. At 10:00 pm, the *Houston* and *Peary* left Darwin for Tjilatjap. Just outside the harbor and its protective boom, the *Peary* made a sonar contact. As the *Houston* cleared the area, the *Peary* stayed behind to pin down whatever submarine was lurking, dropping some depth charges in the process. She returned to Darwin to top off with fuel.[121] It seemed like an easy enough task, but for the *Peary* nothing was ever easy.

The *Houston* did not go directly to Tjilatjap, but instead southwest to recover a floatplane she had launched before the air attacks. Communications issues prevented the rendezvous and she made her way towards south Java, relatively relaxed, as there were no reports of Japanese ships or aircraft south of the Malay Barrier. However, Rooks and his crew did not know the full reasons why the convoy had been called off.

General Wavell had received intelligence information that indicated that an invasion of Timor was imminent. The air attack on the *Houston*'s convoy was one major piece of that evidence, but by no means the most disturbing.

At 9:00 am on February 18, enemy fighter aircraft had been reported over Dili in Portuguese Timor. Just after noon the next day, an American bomber aircraft en route from the Malang airfield on Java to Darwin reported being attacked by three enemy fighter aircraft some 200 miles west northwest of Darwin.[122]

There were no Japanese air fields in the area that could have flown off such short-range fighters. They could only have come from an aircraft carrier. But there was only one Japanese aircraft carrier in the theater, at least as far as they knew. The light carrier *Ryujo* was operating off Sumatra so it could not be her. That could mean only one thing.

Air battle over Soerabaja – February 19

The morning of February 19 began as it usually did in wartime Soerabaja: with the ominous wail of air raid sirens. The Japanese were coming for another attack – 18 Betty bombers out of Kendari II escorted by 23 Zero fighters of the Tainan Air Group, operating out of Balikpapan.[123]

The Japanese had been getting sloppy of late. The previous day a flight of nine Bettys of the Takao Air Group operating out of Kendari II missed their rendezvous with their escorting Zeros of the Tainan Air Group coming in from Borneo, and flew into an ambush by Captain Grant Mahoney and 12 P-40 Warhawks of the 17th Pursuit Squadron (Provisional) operating out of Ngoro. The P-40s quickly shot down two Bettys and damaged several more before being driven off by the late-arriving Zeros, who shot down only one of the Warhawks, its pilot parachuting to safety.[124] But the terrible luck of the Dutch continued. The Bettys got their revenge with a bomb hit on the *Banckert* in Soerabaja's Perak Harbor and a second bomb that splashed into the water – right on top of the Dutch submarine *K-VII*, hiding underwater to avoid the bombs. All 13 on board, including skipper Lieutenant Commander P. J. Mulder, were killed, either by the explosion or by suffocation when desperate efforts to reach the stranded submarine failed.[125] The Zeros took out their vengeance on a fighter sweep of the Malang airfield, where fighter ace Sakai Saburo found a patrolling Fokker floatplane – W-12 from the *De Ruyter* – and shot it down.[126]

On this day, however, the Zeros and Bettys had managed to rendezvous successfully, and much of the 17th Pursuit Squadron (Provisional) was on a more pressing mission. Soerabaja braced for another pounding.

But the worsening weather conditions forced the Bettys to abort their attack, so the Zeros left their charges for a fighter sweep. Although the Japanese pilots had been warned that ABDAIR was massing airpower near Soerabaja, when they arrived over the city around 11:30 am, they were startled by the sight that greeted them: 30 to 50 fighters, mostly Dutch P-36 Mohawks and Brewster Buffalos but also 16 P-40 Warhawks of the 17th Pursuit Squadron (Provisional), again led by Captain Mahoney. The defenders were stacked at three levels at least 10,000ft above the city, patrolling counterclockwise.[127]

Through superhuman effort, the Dutch had assembled every fighter they could. This time, the Dutch had warning of the Japanese approach. This time, they were ready. This time, they were going to give everything they had – determination, courage, heart – to defend their city from the Japanese menace. "[P]repared and eager for a fight," was how Sakai described them.[128] And they outnumbered the Japanese Zeros, possibly by more than two to one.[129]

The Allies didn't last even ten minutes.

It was the biggest air battle of the Pacific War so far, a giant dogfight in the skies over Soerabaja. But many of the Dutch aircraft were the hopelessly obsolete Mohawks and the detested Buffalos, which seemed to be everywhere they shouldn't. And the first rule of aerial combat in the Pacific was: *Never, ever dogfight a Zero.*

Sakai, the Zero pilot who would become Japan's top ace, feasted on the Dutch Mohawks in this attack. The Zeros simply mauled the Mohawks and Buffalos. The Warhawks too never stood a chance. Upon returning to Ngoro, 17th Pursuit pilot Lieutenant Butch Hague would lament "the bastards are a thousand percent more maneuverable than us."[130] Determination, courage, and heart are no substitute for superior experience and superior equipment.

When the biggest air battle of the Pacific War so far was over, the Japanese had shot down some 40 Dutch and American fighters, three of which were the modern Warhawks, at a cost of one of their own.[131] ABDAIR had been driven from the skies over Java and would never again be a factor in the campaign. According to Sakai, "It was this fighter-versus-fighter air victory – and not raids by our bombers against enemy airfields – which denied the Allied warships their air cover, and contributed so completely to their destruction."[132]

Soerabaja could take some comfort, albeit of the cold variety, in that now the Japanese were also bombing the other end of Java as well. For on this day five Ki-48 Lilly bombers of the Japanese Army Air Force's 84th Air Group, escorted by 19 Oscars of the 59th and 64th Air Groups, struck the Semplak airfield near Batavia, destroying nine ABDAIR aircraft on the ground and shooting down five Buffalos.[133] Soon, Batavia and Tanjoeng Priok would be getting the same treatment as Soerabaja.

Yet as bad as the battle over Soerabaja had been, a far, far more devastating battle was taking place some 1,200 miles to the east.

Destruction of Darwin, February 19

Darwin, in Australia's Northern Territory, was made ABDACOM's main logistics base simply for lack of alternatives. It was hardly ideal as a logistical hub. It was too far from the front line. Its harbor, though providing a relatively spacious anchorage, had huge tides

JAPANESE ATTACK ON DARWIN

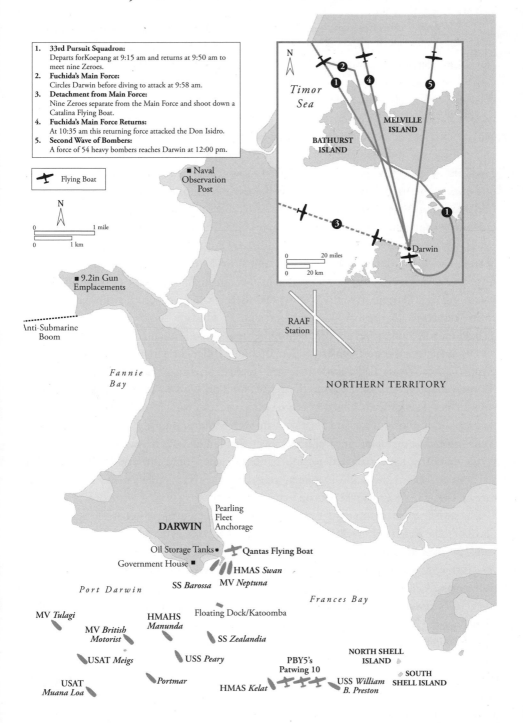

1. **33rd Pursuit Squadron:**
   Departs forKoepang at 9:15 am and returns at 9:50 am to meet nine Zeroes.
2. **Fuchida's Main Force:**
   Circles Darwin before diving to attack at 9:58 am.
3. **Detachment from Main Force:**
   Nine Zeroes separate from the Main Force and shoot down a Catalina Flying Boat.
4. **Fuchida's Main Force Returns:**
   At 10:35 am this returning force attacked the Don Isidro.
5. **Second Wave of Bombers:**
   A force of 54 heavy bombers reaches Darwin at 12:00 pm.

Flying Boat

N

0   1 mile
0   1 km

N

Timor Sea

MELVILLE ISLAND

BATHURST ISLAND

0   20 miles
0   20 km

Darwin

■ Naval Observation Post

■ 9.2in Gun Emplacements

Anti-Submarine Boom

Fannie Bay

RAAF Station

NORTHERN TERRITORY

Pearling Fleet Anchorage

DARWIN

Oil Storage Tanks ● | Qantas Flying Boat
Government House ■ | HMAS *Swan*
Port Darwin   SS *Barossa*   MV *Neptuna*

Frances Bay

MV *Tulagi*

HMAHS *Manunda*   Floating Dock/Katoomba

MV *British Motorist*   SS *Zealandia*

NORTH SHELL ISLAND

USAT *Meigs*   USS *Peary*

PBY5's Patwing 10   **SOUTH SHELL ISLAND**

USAT *Muana Loa*   *Portmar*   HMAS *Kelat*   USS *William B. Preston* (in excess of 20ft) and was so deep that a ship sunk there could not be salvaged.[134] And that was just the harbor.

In an Australian continent and an Australian nation known for independence and ruggedness, the small town of Darwin epitomized both. While located on mainland Australia, from a transportation standpoint Darwin was essentially an island. The easiest way to get there was by sea, though that was not the easiest way to get in: Darwin's port consisted of a single L-shaped wharf that could handle only two ships at a time, with two mobile hand-operated cranes.[135] As Darwin historian Peter Groese would comment, "If anyone had set out to design the worst possible port facility imaginable they might have easily come up with the Darwin Harbour of the first half of the 20th century."[136] The town itself, generally considered a hellhole, was small and consisted almost entirely of wooden buildings.[137] If one hadn't known any better, one might think this was in the Old American West, Wyatt Earp, Doc Holliday, and Billy the Kid drinking up at the bars, except for an insidious red dust that seemed to get into everything.

The Allies had done what they could to make Darwin serviceable as a logistical center. Warehouses and storage tanks were built. An airfield on the northwest side of town was improved. At this time the US 33rd Pursuit Squadron (Provisional) was stationed there, patrolling over Darwin, but it was scheduled to fly off to Java. A new airfield northeast of town was home to the No. 13 Squadron and its Hudson bombers, while at the civil airfield closer to town were five Wirraway fighters of No. 12 Squadron.[138]

Nevertheless, the port's position as an obvious choice for a logistics base and a staging area to protect Timor had already attracted Japanese attention. January had seen Japanese submarines detected near Darwin; the *I-124*, sunk on January 20, had been one of these submarines. Part of their job had been to mine the approaches to the port, mines which had started breaking loose and floating ashore.[139] More ominously, Japanese flying boats were spotted with increasing frequency over the Timor Sea. It was one of these flying boats that may have attracted Japanese interest when on February 10 it reported an aircraft carrier at Darwin. The crewmen were close; they had actually seen a former aircraft carrier, the USS *Langley*, who left on February 11.[140]

As morning on February 19 came around, it seemed like a relatively quiet day in Darwin. The freighter *Neptuna*, carrying material for the extension of the harbor boom and 200 tons of depth charges, was at the wharf's outer berth; the Australian freighter *Barossa*, with wood to extend the wharf, was also present. There were three American transports, *Meigs, Mauna Loa,* and *Port Mar* of the returned Timor convoy; and the *Admiral Halstead* loaded with drums of aviation fuel originally intended for the Philippines. There was the British ship *Tulagi*, also from the returned Timor convoy. The British tanker *British Motorist* was there to replenish Darwin's stocks of fuel. The hospital ship *Manunda*, originally bound for Singapore, was in the anchorage; as was the Australian freighter *Zealandia*, carrying ammunition.[141] Destroyer USS *Peary* was trying to get topped off with fuel to head to Java. The *William B. Preston* was servicing its Catalinas, its skipper Etheridge Grant having gone ashore for a meeting.[142] There were some 47 vessels in all.[143]

Air operations were very limited – and not encouraging. At the civil airfield, No. 12 Squadron's five Wirraway fighters, usually fairly ineffectual, were more so than usual today because all of the aircraft were down for repairs.[144] Six Hudsons from No. 2 Squadron, bringing evacuees from Timor, appeared over Darwin outside of their designated flight path, drawing a warning shot from the town's 16 3.7in high-angle heavy antiaircraft guns and sparking a fight between the air force pilots and the army gunners after the Hudsons landed at the main airfield.[145] Five PBY Catalinas of Patrol Wing 10 had gone out on a routine patrol over the Timor Sea; curiously one of those Catalinas – P-9, under the command of Lieutenant Thomas Moorer, assigned to patrol the area around Bathurst Island – had not reported in.[146]

Ten P-40 Warhawks of the US 33rd Pursuit Squadron (Provisional) under Major Floyd Pell took off at 9:15 am, heading west for Koepang on the first leg of their journey to Java, but were recalled 20 minutes later because of bad weather.[147] While they were returning to base, at around 9:37 am, Father John McGrath, a coastwatcher on Bathurst Island some 50 miles north of Darwin, reported "Big flight of planes passed over going south. Very high."[148] Even though the returning Warhawks would have been coming from the west, Darwin assumed the report was actually referring to the returning Warhawks.[149]

Aircraft were constantly coming and going through Darwin and reinforcements were always urgently required. So when Tom Anderson, a mechanic for Patrol Wing 10 saw a large flight of incoming aircraft, he was excited. "Oh, boy. Look at those reinforcements. We're finally getting a carrier out here."[150] That last part was true, albeit in not quite the way Anderson was considering. He started counting the aircraft – until he noticed the insignia on their wings. "Those aren't reinforcements. Those are Japs!"[151]

Admiral Nagumo's carrier force, consisting of four (*Akagi, Kaga, Hiryu, Soryu*) of the six carriers that had attacked Pearl Harbor, had sailed from the Palaus on February 15. The *Kaga* was limited to 18 knots because she had struck an uncharted reef while shifting mooring positions, but, typical of the Allied luck, she merely shrugged it off.[152] Their destination was the newly acquired anchorage at Staring Bay, Celebes. The loss of Kendari was being felt by the Allies once again.

After supplying at Staring Bay, *Kido Butai* headed off to kick the already-shaky legs out from under the ABDA table in the Indies. It had reached a position east of Timor and northwest of Darwin, where, according to Japanese records, it launched 36 Zero fighters, 71 Aichi D3A carrier bombers, codenamed "Val"; and 81 Nakajima B5N carrier attack planes, the now-dreaded Kate torpedo bombers functioning as high-level bombers. The attack was led by Fuchida Mitsuo, who had led the attack on Pearl Harbor.[153] In an effort at some deception, Fuchida had the flight loop around Darwin and come from the southeast.

The first Japanese aircraft to arrive were nine Zeros that had broken off from the main group to shoot down Thomas Moorer's Catalina. They quickly engaged five P-40 Warhawks of the 33rd still in the air as they attempted to protect the other five who were already landing. Four were quickly shot down.[154] The five Warhawks which had landed were shocked to discover that they were under attack by Japanese Zeros that should not have had the range to reach Darwin.[155] They tried to take off again. Squadron leader Major Charles "Slugger" Pell was able to get airborne. He was chased northeast of Darwin, where, with his aircraft riddled with bullets, he was forced to bail out at an altitude of only 70ft. Miraculously, he survived, only to be machine gunned as he tried to crawl to safety.[156] Lieutenant Robert McMahon's Warhawk was badly shot up, but he stayed airborne and in the fight until he ran out of ammunition and parachuted to safety.[157] The other Warhawks on the ground were destroyed as they tried to take off.

The air raid sirens of Darwin sounded at 9:58 am.[158] The 16 3.7in heavy antiaircraft guns opened fire. The ships in the harbor that could do so got under way to try to achieve some evasive capability. The US Navy ships Peary and *William B. Preston* were among the first, *using* their antiaircraft guns to defend their unarmed brethren.

The situation deteriorated rapidly. Both *Barossa* and *Neptuna*, at the dock, took early bomb hits and were set afire. The three PBYs of Patrol Wing 10 on the water were destroyed by gunfire. *William B. Preston*, being conned by her executive officer Lieutenant Lester O. Wood with skipper Grant ashore, took a bomb hit astern and was set afire.[159]

But it was the destroyer *Peary* that was the largest warship in the harbor, and she took more than her share of *Kido Butai*'s attack. She circled and twisted to avoid the Japanese bombs, but she was essentially a fish in a barrel facing the best carrier pilots in the world. After evading the first few bombs, the *Peary* took five bomb hits in rapid succession. Getting five hits on a destroyer shows an incredible level of skill by the bomber pilots, but the crew of the destroyer were in no condition to appreciate it. The first hit was on the fantail, flooding the steering engine room and slicing off one of the propellers. The second, an incendiary, landed between the smokestacks and set the four-piper afire. The third went through the fire room without exploding – not that it mattered. The fourth detonated the forward ammunition magazines, the cataclysmic explosion blowing the heart out of the destroyer and killing Commander Bermingham. The fifth, another incendiary, exploded in the after engine room.[160]

Nothing had come easy for the destroyer *Peary*, who had done everything asked of her, and in return had endured far more suffering than she deserved: a collision, bombed in its dock in Cavite, bombed by friendly aircraft, nearly running into a friendly minefield, her own fleet seemingly oblivious to her troubles. In yet another of the ironies of war, she had, as ordered, run from the Philippines, all alone, all the way to what was supposed to be a safe haven in Australia, only to be cut to pieces in Darwin's harbor. Even now, nothing went right for the *Peary* and her battered crew; abandoning ship was virtual suicide because the destroyer was surrounded by blazing oil.[161] Her heartbreaking story came to an end around 1:00 pm, when she sank stern first, two of her machine guns firing. Of her crew, 80 officers and men were lost; 52 of her crewmen and only one officer, Lieutenant W. J. Catlett, survived.[162]

The tragedy of the *Peary* was but one of many in Darwin this day. The port and harbor were racked by an almost volcanic explosion as the 200 tons of depth charges on the blazing *Neptuna* detonated and sent shock waves through the harbor. The port administrator described the explosion: "[T]he vast cloud of black smoke shot with flames into the sky. The explosion shook the whole town and blew the ship to pieces. The stern and engines went down near the wharf and the bow floated for a few minutes, turned on its side, and then sank."[163] The nearby *Barossa*, being towed clear when *Neptuna* exploded, had to be beached, her timber cargo completely lost.

Commander Grant, trying to return to the *William B. Preston* in a boat, was dumped in the harbor by the shockwaves from the blast and had to cling to a buoy for life.[164] The fuel lines to the destroyed wharf ruptured and blazing oil poured into the harbor. US transport *Meigs* was ablaze aft and sinking. *Mauna Loa* had a broken back and was going down by the stern, although her entire crew was rescued. *British Motorist* was sinking by the bow. *Portmar* was beached. *Zealandia* would not last much longer. *Manunda*, a marked hospital ship, was the victim of two Japanese bombs, a clear violation of international law.[165]

But today the Japanese would not make the same mistake they had made at Pearl Harbor by attacking only the ships. They wanted to destroy Darwin as a base, so the real focus was on its shore installations. The warehouses, docks, cranes, oil tanks, both airfields, even the town itself. They were smashed and left in smoldering ruins. The Japanese pilots flew on strafing runs so low that the defenders on the ground could see their faces; reportedly they were smiling.[166]

At 10:10 am, less than 15 minutes after it had started, *Kido Butai*'s attack was all over and the Japanese headed back towards their carriers. Admiral Nagumo's biographer described the operation as "using a sledgehammer to break an egg," while Fuchida would later say that "the job to be done seemed hardly worthy of the Nagumo Force."[167] As they headed back, however, they passed over two Philippine cargo schooners, the *Don Isidro* and the *Florence D.* For the sake of completeness, they attacked both. *Don Isidro* had to be beached in sinking condition. *Florence D.* was sunk, marking a very rough day for US Navy pilot Thomas Moorer and his crew. He had been the pilot of the Catalina that had disappeared shortly before the Darwin raid, shot down by the attack force's escorting Zeros, which had shot out his radio before he could make a report. They had been fished out by the *Florence D.* only for her to be bombed and sunk. One member of Moorer's crew and three of the 37-man ship's complement were killed in action; the survivors, after some uncomfortable days in the bush on Bathurst and Melville islands, were picked up by Australian minesweeper HMAS *Warrnambool* and mission boat *St. Francis*.[168]

Darwin's agony was not over yet, however. At around noon came 54 Mitsubishi bombers of the Kanoya and 1st Air Groups, operating out of Kendari II.[169] The bombers concentrated on both airfields. With no aircraft left to oppose them, both airfields were destroyed. Runways were cratered and more aircraft were destroyed on the ground before the bombers departed.

At the end of this horrific day in Darwin, nine ships had been sunk, 11 P-40s destroyed in the air; two more P-40s, six Hudsons, and one LB-30 on the ground. Some 250 people had been killed, mostly on the *Peary* and *Neptuna*.[170] Darwin was destroyed as a serviceable base. Fearful of an invasion, the town was completely evacuated.

That fear had little basis. The Japanese had no intention of invading Australia and could not have done so. But the evacuation shows the psychological effect on the Australians. For them, the air raid on Darwin was every bit as traumatic as Pearl Harbor had been for the Americans.

However, Japan's only immediate plans were for Timor, the next target for Admiral Takahashi's Eastern Force. On February 17, nine transports carrying the 228th Infantry Regiment had left Ambon for Timor in preparation for a February 20 invasion. The convoy was escorted by Rear Admiral Tanaka flying his flag in the light cruiser *Jintsu* leading the 2nd Destroyer Flotilla. The *Nachi* and *Haguro* of the 5th Cruiser Division were also on hand with three destroyers, and air cover was provided by the seaplane tender *Mizuho*.[171]

The Dutch and Australian troops defending Timor put up a stiff fight, but in three days they were defeated, the remnants melting back into the countryside to conduct a guerilla campaign for the next year. Koepang airfield was gone. There was now no way to ferry fighter aircraft to the front line.

Java and the American, British, Dutch, and Australians trying to defend it were hanging by a thread. And the scissor blades of the Japanese Western Force and the Eastern Force were about to start cutting.

CHAPTER 11

TOO CLEVER BY HALF – THE BATTLE OF BADOENG STRAIT

The ancient maxim divide and conquer holds that the best way to defeat an enemy that is larger, more numerous, or more powerful is to divide it and defeat the individual pieces in detail. Confederate General Thomas "Stonewall" Jackson used it during the American Civil War to flummox Union armies in the Shenandoah Valley. Napoleon also used it to good effect, though his last, most famous attempt at Waterloo was a disastrous failure.

The Japanese, however, would turn "divide and conquer" on its head. While most commanders like Stonewall Jackson sought to divide the enemy forces, the Japanese much preferred to divide their own. Samuel Eliot Morison described the Japanese concept in this way: "division, deception and odd forces popping out at unexpected places."[1] Sometimes division of force cannot be avoided – the Japanese advance into the Southern Resources Area virtually required separate eastern and western prongs – but more often than not, the emperor's admirals would divide a force seemingly for the sole purpose of dividing it.

It is very difficult to find instances during the Pacific War where this doctrine actually contributed to a Japanese victory. Much easier to find are instances where it contributed to a Japanese defeat: including amongst others Coral Sea, Midway and Leyte Gulf. The Japanese actually seemed to have more success *not* using this doctrine; two of their most spectacular naval victories – at Savo Island and Tassafaronga, both off Guadalcanal – involved simply assembling a single force of ships and sending them off. But that was in the future.

In the present came something of a weird interlude in the inexorable advance of the Rising Sun. While the Japanese were consolidating their hold on newly acquired Sumatra and Timor, they moved on another target: Bali.

Bali and the Battle of Badoeng Strait – February 17–20

Located just east of Java across the Bali Strait, Bali, an island shaped somewhat like an inverted triangle, is famous for its superb weather. Even Admiral Ugaki Matome, Admiral Yamamoto's chief of staff, would call it "the paradise of the world."[2]

What attracted the Japanese military, however, was its airfield, located at the island's capital of Denpesar, near the southeastern coast. Their capture of Kendari II may have become the bane of ABDACOM's existence, but the Japanese Naval Air Force had a few minor issues with the base. The distance from Kendari to Soerabaja was a little long, and the weather over the big airbase was not ideal, though it was far better than that over a newly- captured airfield at Bandjermasin, on the south coast of Borneo, where incessant rain turned the runways into quagmires. As a result, almost a week of combat missions in early February had been prevented by bad weather.[3] Primitive Denpesar did not have the luxurious facilities of Kendari II – the runway was dirt, for example – but it was much closer to Java and would allow Japanese aircraft to range out into the Indian Ocean to cut off reinforcement of Java from the south and even bomb the last remaining Allied naval base at Tjilatjap.

So, in a rather impromptu action, Imperial General Headquarters added Bali to its list of targets in late January, and an invasion force was quickly formed at Makassar City under the command of Admiral Kubo Kyuji.[4] The convoy would consist of the transports *Sasago Maru* and *Sagami Maru,* carrying one infantry battalion of 48th Japanese Infantry Division under command of Major Kanemura Matabei (and thus called the Kanemura Detachment).[5] Their objective was Sanoer (Sanur) Roads, on the southeast coast of Bali on the Badoeng Strait, the closest landing point to Denpesar. Destroyers *Asashio, Oshio, Arashio,* and *Michishio* would provide close escort for the transports. The light cruiser *Nagara,* flagship of Admiral Kubo, and the destroyers *Hatsushimo, Nenohi,* and *Wakaba* would follow behind but hold back, providing a distant covering force from a position in the Banda Sea to the north.

The invasion force was divided like this because, in the Japanese view, Bali was so close to the major ABDA bases on Java that there was considerable risk of air and sea attack. While there was to be fighter protection courtesy of Zeros of the Tainan and 3rd Air Groups operating out of Makassar City, Admiral Kubo wanted to achieve a successful landing with minimum exposure for his ships – deploying only four destroyers for the landing itself and keeping his cruiser and three other destroyers far removed from the action. The force left Makassar City on the night of February 17, 1942.[6]

ABDACOM had noticed the Japanese ships massing in Makassar City, but could not determine where they were going. It was not until late in the afternoon of February 18 that it became obvious and by then General Wavell was at pains to counter them.[7]

Admiral Kubo's force landed at Sanoer Roads at around 2:00 am on February 19.[8] Ground resistance to the Japanese landing was typically light for the East Indies. The

600 native Indonesian troops of the Dutch *Korps Prajoda*, under command of Dutch Lieutenant Colonel W. P. Roodenburg, whose main mission was either to defend or to destroy Denpesar airfield, managed to accomplish neither. Surprised in their barracks, the troops quickly surrendered. With a display of the same level of competence that had been shown at Kendari, Dutch plans to demolish the airfield were botched, and it was captured completely intact.[9] Nevertheless, according to one Japanese source, "just about when we thought this landing would culminate in success, all of a sudden B-17s flew over and bombed our convoy. Repeated bombings by enemy airplanes delayed our landing operation."[10]

With daybreak on February 19, ABDAIR attempted those repeated bombings with its pitifully small force of bombers. First three B-17s operating out of Malang, flying without the fighter escort that would be tied up in the air battle over Soerabaja, managed to evade the pair of Tainan Air Group Zeros providing air cover, but didn't achieve any hits. Shortly after 6:00 am four more bombers were bounced by the two covering Zeros. Those same two Zeros also intercepted three LB-30s at 6:45 am, who once again failed to score any hits, all suffering damage in the process. Then at 8:00 am came two more B-17 attacks, which were just as ineffective. Finally came two A-24 Banshee dive bombers of the 91st Bomb Squadron. They managed to put a bomb into the engine room of the transport Sagami Maru. The transport did not sink; even American bombs seemed to be ineffective.[11] Admiral Kubo had her head back to Makassar City, escorted by the *Arashio* and the *Michishio*. The bomber pilots returned with reports that the Japanese had four transports, two cruisers, and five to six destroyers in Sanoer Roads, and claimed three direct hits with heavy bombs on one or more cruisers; two direct hits on a transport; and eight near misses on destroyers; and hits with lighter bombs on one cruiser and one transport.[12] Sighting reports with overestimations of enemy forces are not unusual, but in this case they may have warped planning for a naval counterattack by ABDAFLOAT.

The Japanese landing on Bali came at a particularly bad time for ABDAFLOAT. The only Allied forces near Sanoer Roads were the American submarine *Seawolf*, already positioned in the Badoeng Strait as a contingency against the invasion, and the British submarine *Truant*. Their experience, particularly that of the *Seawolf*, could be seen as a microcosm of the entire Java Sea Campaign.

Seawolf, under Lieutenant Commander Fred B. Warder, first encountered the Japanese at 2:00 am on February 18, right in the heart of the invasion. Somehow, *Seawolf* managed to sneak through the Japanese destroyers while surfaced. Though subsequently forced to submerge, Warder was within the destroyer screen and in good position for an attack. But the lack of adequate charts of the area would trip up the *Seawolf* as it had the *Boise* earlier. Attempting to navigate the difficult currents of the Badoeng Strait in the dark through a periscope without adequate charts, Warder became thoroughly lost.[13]

Even so, at dawn, sighting several enemy ships through the periscope, Warder moved in to attack – and ran aground on a sandbar. The *Seawolf* backed off and tried again, only to run aground again. Unable to back off this time, Warder ordered the submarine to blow the main ballast tanks, which is done only in emergencies to quickly get to the surface. Unfortunately, in this case *Seawolf* would be surfacing in full view of the Japanese. And surface she did, bursting from the water in the midst of a fortuitous rain squall. Thanking their luck, Warder used the storm as cover while he approached the convoy on the surface for the next half hour, submerging when the squall dissipated. Finally in torpedo range, the *Seawolf* turned around, fired two torpedoes from her stern tubes, and tried to escape. Two explosions were heard, but the *Seawolf* had no chance to confirm damage as Japanese destroyers located the submarine and pounded her with 43 depth charges in the shallow strait, normally a death warrant. Somehow Warder managed to get his boat through it all without serious damage, either from the Japanese or from the grounding.[14]

Yet it was all for naught. *Seawolf*'s torpedoes had not touched any Japanese ships. They had either missed and detonated against the shore of Bali, or once again exploded prematurely.

The British submarine *Truant* had been ordered to sortie from Soerabaja. In yet another commentary on the organization of ABDAFLOAT, the *Truant* was sent with no briefing and no idea that another Allied submarine was in the area. Fortunately, left as she was to wing it, as submarines often must, the British boat would end up *not* entering the Badoeng Strait, avoiding the potential for a friendly fire incident with the *Seawolf*, who had similarly been uninformed of the *Truant*'s presence. But while not making it to Bali per se, the *Truant* nevertheless showed up to the battle. While transiting to Sanoer Roads, the British boat came across Admiral Kubo's covering force in the Banda Sea. Easily penetrating the destroyer screen the submarine fired six torpedoes at Kubo's flagship *Nagara* without securing any hits. The *Truant* was then chased off by Kubo's destroyers and returned safely to Soerabaja.[15]

Meanwhile Admiral Helfrich was struggling to put together a counterlanding force. The ABDA ships were scattered across the Indies, many being engaged in the seemingly endless, fruitless rounds of convoying. The *Houston* was returning from Darwin after her aborted convoy run (and was very fortunate to be doing so). The cruisers HMS *Exeter* and HMAS *Hobart*, and destroyers Hr. Ms. *Evertsen*, HMS *Tenedos*, and HMS *Scout* were escorting transports in the Soenda Strait. The Dutch destroyer *Van Ghent* had been lost in the Banka operation, her crew rescued by the *Banckert*, who had taken them to Soerabaja. The Dutch handling of the loss of the *Van Ghent* was unique, inasmuch as the Dutch manpower shortage had left her sister destroyer *Witte de With* laid up for overhaul without a crew. Now the *Van Ghent*'s entire crew, including skipper Lieutenant Commander Pieter Schotel, was simply transferred to the *Witte de With* as she was brought online, but she would not be ready until February 22.[16] The *Banckert*, in drydock at Soerabaja from her bomb hit on February 18 was also not ready.[17] USS *Barker* and *Bulmer* had been damaged by near misses in the Banka Strait bombing and were laid up at Tjilatjap, about to be sent to Australia for repairs. Four other US destroyers, *Stewart, Parrott, John D. Edwards,* and *Pillsbury,* returning from the aborted action in the Banka Strait, were refueling for the last time in southern Sumatra at Ratai Bay, near Oosthaven, before those installations were destroyed so as to deny them to the advancing Japanese.

Nevertheless, the Allies were able to assemble a formidable force to attack the Japanese landing site at Denpesar, but they faced two very serious issues. The first was a question of time, of which ABDAFLOAT was unaware. Admiral Kubo was determined to get the transports in and out as fast as possible. In fact, the Allied counterattack, even had it been successful, would have started out too late to have any impact on the outcome on Bali. The Japanese landing had been completed. The second major problem was that the available ships were divided among Soerabaja, Tjilatjap, and Ratai Bay. Admiral Helfrich met with Admiral Doorman on February 17 to consider the Japanese ships then only massing at Makassar City.[18] What eventually emerged was a plan for a counterattack for the night of February 19/20. Precisely who came up with this plan is unclear, but Helfrich ordered Doorman not to wait until the forces had been concentrated completely, but to make a series of raids in successive "waves."[19]

The counterattack would take place in three waves. The first would be under the direct command of Admiral Doorman, using the serviceable ships on hand at Tjilatjap. The Dutch light cruisers *De Ruyter* and *Java* would lead the modern Dutch destroyers *Kortenaer* and *Piet Hein* and the less-modern American destroyers *Pope* and *John D. Ford* up through the Badoeng Strait, the 15-mile wide channel between Bali and the tiny island of Noesa Besar, to attack the Japanese at Sanoer Roads and then leave, heading north through the Lombok Strait, which separates Bali and Noesa Besar on one side from Lombok on the other, to rendezvous at Soerabaja.

The second wave would consist of the serviceable ships at Soerabaja: Dutch light cruiser *Tromp*, whose skipper Captain Jacob de Meester would command the wave, and American Destroyer Squadron 58, with the *Stewart, Parrott, John D. Edwards,* and *Pillsbury*, who had to do the maritime equivalent of burning rubber to make it back in time to take part. They would leave Soerabaja through the east channel, sail down the Bali Strait, loop around the southern coast of Bali and, like the first wave, enter the Badoeng Strait through its southern entrance before retiring to the north through the Lombok Strait and returning to Soerabaja.[20]

The third wave, on the suggestion of the Soerabaja Naval District Commander, Admiral Pieter Koenraad, consisted of the Dutch motor torpedo boats *TM-4, TM-5, TM-6, TM-7, TM-9, TM-10, TM-11, TM-12,* and *TM-13*.[21] Also coming from Soerabaja, they too would go through the Bali Strait and, after a stop at Pangpang Bay to refuel from the Dutch minelayer *Krakatau*, sweep through the south entrance to the Badoeng Strait and torpedo any cripples before following the first two waves to the north through Lombok Strait.[22]

This operational plan has been heavily criticized by historians. At the very least, it was slapped together due to the severe time considerations. "Unavoidably, it was a bad plan, dictated by grim necessity," declared Java Sea historian Tom Womack, while fellow historian David Thomas would opine, "Doorman's plan for attacking the Bali occupation force was not a good one, but it might be argued cogently that it was the best plan available."[23] *Houston* survivor Walter Winslow, in his respected history of the Asiatic Fleet, put it bluntly: "Based upon intelligence that failed to perceive that the Japanese were already ashore and all but four of their destroyers and one transport had withdrawn from the area, this hastily conceived, poorly orchestrated operation should never have taken place."[24]

It was not a naval tactics textbook plan, to be sure, with the primary defect being economy of force. The Allies' overwhelming force was diluted by dividing that force and attacking at different times. In theory, the warships from Tjilatjap and Soerabaja should have combined to form one overwhelming attack group.

In fairness to Admiral Helfrich, there were several mitigating factors. First, as a practical matter, the awkward positioning of ABDAFLOAT's naval assets made concentration problematic, as some historians have been willing to acknowledge. Trying to amalgamate the available forces was almost impossible. For the ships of the first wave to rendezvous with the ships of the second wave the former would have had to wait for several hours that Helfrich believed they did not have. After traveling a significant distance separately along different routes, the first and second waves would have had to rendezvous after dark, probably at the southern end of the Bali Strait, with enemy ships in the vicinity. The Allied ships would have risked not only ambush but also friendly fire, which would prove to be the norm in night actions in World War II. Additionally, the motor torpedo boats, because of their fuel requirements among other things, could not operate with the heavier warships. Finally, and this point is frequently forgotten, while there was some belief that the air and submarine attacks had inflicted significant damage on the Japanese invasion force, ABDACOM believed its naval forces were outnumbered and outgunned.[25]

As a result of these considerations, the plan had a different objective, one that seems to have been misunderstood by many historians. This was not to be the all-out attack that many believed it was supposed to have been, or, for that matter, should have been. As Admiral Glassford would later explain, the groups "were to strike at the enemy as in a raid. A 'battle' was not contemplated. The work was to be done while simply passing the enemy."[26]

Nevertheless, it is difficult to understand precisely what Admiral Helfrich hoped to accomplish with this operation. The plan fits his profile – aggressive to the point of recklessness, throwing anything and everything at the enemy with scant thought given to such details as organization, methodology, or even objectives. Helfrich later admitted that he simply felt they had to do something.[27] Even so, however flawed the operational plan was, given the circumstances it was at least defensible and understandable.

Less understandable was the tactical plan, or at least that plan used by the first wave, which was most likely developed on the fly by Admiral Doorman, since he was in tactical command of the first wave and had radioed the plan to his ships en route. The cruisers *De Ruyter* and *Java* were to lead the charge, opening with gunfire on what would essentially be a drive-by shooting before heading out to the north, clearing the area so that the destroyers who were following at a significant distance could use their torpedoes on the Japanese ships.

To be blunt, this was not a good plan; indeed "poorly orchestrated" may well be the most charitable way of describing it. Given their pride in night fighting and the amount of training the Royal Netherlands Navy had put into it, the tactical plan may have been in line with their doctrine, but it certainly was not consistent with their shrewd understanding of the Imperial Japanese Navy and the importance it placed on cruisers and air power. It does bear some similarity to how the Battle of Balikpapan played out, and the Dutch admiral may have been hoping for a repeat performance. At Balikpapan, the Japanese escorts were drawn away, however unintentionally, by a submarine, leaving the transports open for attack by destroyers; here the escorts would be drawn away by the *De Ruyter* and *Java*, leaving the transports open for attack by the destroyers, who would be following at such a distance that they would be hidden by the darkness.[28]

The lesson from Balikpapan was not in luring the Japanese escorts away to leave their charges undefended; it was in realizing that it is much easier to hit enemy ships with torpedoes when those ships have no idea the torpedoes are coming; therefore, opening a night battle with torpedoes while withholding gunfire could maximize the chances of success. In other words, torpedoes before guns. Doorman's plan had guns before torpedoes. It was exactly backwards.

The Japanese had learned this lesson a long time ago and made it part of their night fighting doctrine. Whatever his other faults, Admiral Glassford was among the few in the gunnery-dominated US Navy who understood this principle as well, which is in part why he developed the Balikpapan plan of attack as he did. Lieutenant Commander Edward N. Parker, who had taken over command of Destroyer Division 59 from the sidelined commander Talbot and thus would be leading the US destroyers in this operation, was unhappy with the plan, as were most of those under his command, and he let Glassford know about it. Glassford acknowledged the inherent flaw but said that, since Admiral Doorman was in charge, he had no say in the matter.[29]

The Dutch admiral may have had other considerations as well, primarily dealing with the issue of communications. Admiral Doorman, like most admirals before radar was commonplace, tended to lead from the front. It would have enabled him to get a feel for the enemy firsthand, rather than through someone else's opinion as communicated over a basic communications system – once again, there had been no time to develop a common code system or communications protocols – so he could make better decisions more quickly. If he wanted to stick with this philosophy and stay in front, Doorman might have been forced into this less-than-ideal formation by the lack of torpedoes on the *De Ruyter* and *Java*.[30]

Another concern may have been the ships' lack of experience working together. While ABDACOM was intended to be fully integrated, and was indeed at times fully integrated on a tactical level, it often was not (especially at the strategic level); and this was one of those times. Like multinational forces from millennia past, Admiral Doorman's force was modular, with a Dutch contingent in the two cruisers leading another Dutch contingent in the *Piet Hein*, and *Kortenaer* leading an American contingent in the *John D. Ford* and *Pope*. The two American destroyers, replacements in the Striking Force for the damaged *Barker* and *Bulmer*, had never worked with Doorman or the Dutch before, and, once again, there had been no time to train together. These considerations notwithstanding, while most of the voluminous criticism Karel Doorman has received over the years has been unfair, the negative assessment of his plan here is largely justified.

First wave – cruisers attack, February 18–19

It was a bad situation with a bad plan that started out badly, as the plague of operational accidents and mechanical breakdowns continued. While the torpedo boats were leaving Soerabaja on the evening of February 18, *TM-6* ran into a light buoy in the harbor and was so badly damaged that she could not continue. Worse happened at Tjilatjap. A sense of teamwork and appreciation was buoyed by the crew of the *De Ruyter* all coming topside and cheering for the *John D. Ford* and the *Pope* for their work at Balikpapan.[31] But as Admiral Doorman's force started out at 10:00 pm, the *Kortenaer* lost rudder control in the port's channel to the sea and ran aground.[32] Fortunately, the other ships were able to get around her. If Admiral Doorman could not afford to wait a few hours to rendezvous with the ships of the second wave, he certainly could not wait for morning when the tide would allow the *Kortenaer* to be removed. He was forced to leave her behind. The destroyer would sail to Soerabaja to join the increasing line of damaged ships waiting for repair.[33]

And it would only get worse. As February 18 turned into February 19, Admiral Doorman's force moved into its night cruising formation, with the *Piet Hein* in front and the US destroyers on the flanks of the Dutch cruisers, moving at 22 knots. The *John D. Ford* slowed temporarily to deal with a torpedo running hot in one of her tubes. At 2:25 am on February 19, Doorman signaled his tactical plan for the first wave. At sunset, the destroyers were to drop back behind the cruisers "at [the] end of visibility."[34] Operating in column, the *Piet Hein* was to follow behind the cruisers by some 3 miles, leading the US destroyers *John D. Ford* and *Pope*, to attack "shortly after" the cruisers stopped firing and then "retire immediately."[35]

Being outside the range of Japanese aircraft – for now – Admiral Doorman's force went undetected through the day on February 19. At 6:31 pm, he switched to battle formation; the *De Ruyter* and *Java* were now in the lead at 1,000yd intervals, the *Piet Hein* was some 5,000yd behind the cruisers, the *John D. Ford* and *Pope* some 2,000yd behind the Dutch destroyer, dropping back to about 5,000yd shortly thereafter.[36] That may not have been quite as dictated by Doorman's plan; there is some suggestion that the US destroyers were supposed to be closer to the *Piet Hein*. As it was, the distance may have contributed to some tragic results.

At 10:25 pm, Tafelhoek, the southern tip of Bali, was reached, and Admiral Doorman turned to course 25 degrees True to enter Badoeng Strait about 3 miles offshore, raising speed to 27 knots.[37] The sea was calm. The night was cloudy and very dark, with almost no natural illumination.[38] Still uncertain of just what they would be facing, the lookouts would have to be on the hunt not for ships, but for shadows, ill-defined shapes just slightly more black than the black around them, and would have to try to determine if each shadow was a deadly enemy warship or merely a trick of tired eyes.

Not long after entering the strait began the very confusing series of engagements known variously as the Battle of the Badoeng Strait, the Battle of the Lombok Strait, or the Battle of Bali. At 11:20 pm the *De Ruyter* spotted a shadow to starboard. She tried to train her guns on the target, but it disappeared behind Noesa Besar. Postwar examination of Japanese records revealed no Combined Fleet ships in that location; her sighting was either a mirage or a local craft.[39]

Five minutes later, lookouts on the *Java* were able to make out three vague forms against the dark shore of Bali, which were identified as a destroyer, a transport, and a landing craft. Some confusion reigned on the Dutch ships, with the skippers apparently waiting too long for Admiral Doorman to give the order to fire. *Java* opened her searchlights to pin the targets and fired starshells to backlight them, following up with her first salvo at a range of 2,200yd – point-blank range – against the destroyer.[40]

Her target turned out to be the *Asashio*. She and her sister ship *Oshio*, misidentified as a landing craft, had been standing by the 9,258-ton transport *Sasago Maru,* which had already disembarked her troops and was preparing to return to Makassar City. The Allied presence had caught the Japanese by surprise, but Destroyer Division 8 commander Captain Abe Toshio, sailing in the *Oshio*, recovered quickly, making a contact report to Admiral Kubo, and implementing a very aggressive defense. *Asashio* quickly snapped on her searchlight, but it did not stay on for long in the face of withering fire from the *Java's* 40mm Bofors antiaircraft guns. Nevertheless, neither side scored any hits, though some sources claim the *Asashio's* searchlight was knocked out.[41]

Abe's command consisted of two state-of-the-art destroyers, *Asashio* and *Oshio*, ships with working torpedoes that were the best in the world. As soon as the ships got up enough steam to make speed, with a confidence born of years of training in night fighting, Abe had them turn east and charge the two Dutch cruisers.

The destroyers' course enabled them to attempt to perform an old maneuver known as "crossing the T," by which they would cross the path of the Dutch cruisers and in so doing could use both their forward and aft guns while restricting the cruisers to their forward guns. Admiral Doorman, like most flag officers of his generation, was trained to avoid this maneuver and turned to the northeast. *Asashio* returned the *Java's* fire, whose searchlight provided a fine point of aim in the darkness. Asashio was rewarded with a hit on the *Java's* port side near the stern, but effective damage control prevented a fire and left only negligible damage. The *Java* may have drawn blood with a 5.9in hit on the *Sasago Maru*, but apparently also with negligible damage.[42]

Oshio, the more northern of the destroyers, went after *De Ruyter*, who was struggling to train her guns to port after having been pointed to starboard at the earlier sighting. Sources disagree on whether the *De Ruyter* even got off a shot, but no hits were scored either way.[43]

The Japanese destroyers did end up crossing the T in a way, from behind. But it did not matter. The extreme darkness and high speed made targeting extremely difficult, resulting in little damage to either side.

The *De Ruyter* and *Java* raced off to the northeast, out of the Badoeng Strait and into the Lombok Strait. The entire exchange had lasted less than ten minutes. The Dutch cruisers believed they had inflicted major damage; in reality, they had achieved nothing.

If Karel Doorman had hoped the Japanese escorts would follow his cruisers, he was to be sorely disappointed. The *Asashio* tried to follow but could not build up enough speed in time, so she continued east for several minutes and then turned southeast. *Oshio* went a little further east before turning to the southeast, on a course parallel to that of her sister.[44]

They had found new game.

First wave – the loss of the *Piet Hein*, February 19

The Hr. Ms. *Piet Hein*, although technically not in this operation alone, or even in this attack wave, might as well have been. Being in the middle of a 6-mile gap between the two Dutch cruisers and the two American four-pipers, this lonely destroyer had no one in supporting distance, another result of the faulty tactical plan put together on the way to battle. In hindsight, one wonders if, once the *Kortenaer* was disabled, the *Piet Hein* should have simply been grouped with the American destroyers. But now, when February 19 was about to turn into February 20, it was too late.

As the *Piet Hein* headed north, her lookouts observed gunfire and tracers in the dark ahead. Sighting a dark object off the port bow, her captain, Lieutenant Commander J. M. L. I. Chömpf, ordered three torpedoes launched at this target, which turned out to be the *Sasago Maru*.[45] She then trained her guns on the transport, only to be greeted with the *Asashio* and the *Oshio*, having freed themselves of the Dutch cruisers, now bearing down on her. The *Piet Hein* launched two torpedoes and opened gunfire at the *Asashio*. She then made a smokescreen with both black and white smoke and, at about 11:30 pm, swerved to starboard and the southeast, either to duck behind her own smokescreen or to engage a target that just appeared out of the dark.[46] Her torpedoes would miss, and the smokescreen would prove ineffective – in more ways than one.

The *John D. Ford* and the *Pope*, 5,000yd behind the *Piet Hein*, were closing rapidly on this fracas. At 11:37 pm, the *Ford* launched three torpedoes from her portside tubes against the *Sasago Maru*, which were followed shortly thereafter by two from the *Pope*. Though they claimed to have seen "two dull explosions on the waterline of the transport," the torpedoes registered no hits.[47] They followed up with gunfire and claimed several hits on the transport. When they came upon the destroyer melee, as is often the case in night battles, they were not quite sure what they were seeing. What had looked like three destroyers now appeared to be two destroyers hidden by a smokescreen made by the third. The four-pipers opened fire.

Her smokescreen having screened Captain Abe's destroyers from the Americans without screening herself, the *Piet Hein* was engaged in a running gun battle with the

Asashio about 1,000yd to port. The Dutch destroyer made a sharp turn to port, then took two hits from gunfire, one demolishing the searchlight platform and starting a major fire that served as a point of aim in the darkness, the other severing the steam pipe to the aft boiler room and knocking out power. As the *Piet Hein* drifted to a stop, she was riddled by the *Asashio's* 25mm antiaircraft guns. By some miraculous work, Commander Chömpf's damage control teams managed to restore some power and get the ship moving again – but not fast enough. *Oshio* had joined her sister in beating up the *Piet Hein*, and *Asashio* loosed a spread of torpedoes against the helpless ship. At 11:37 pm one of her Long Lances blew a hole in the *Piet Hein's* port side and started her on a trip to the bottom.[48] As the *Asashio* and *Oshio* passed the sinking destroyer, they raked it with machine-gun fire. Most of the crew was killed, including Commander Chömpf, who was posthumously awarded a medal for gallantry in action.[49]

The *John D. Ford* and the *Pope* drove through the *Piet Hein's* smokescreen, swerving to avoid the sinking destroyer and coming face to face with the oversized Japanese destroyers of Captain Abe's command who blocked their way northward.[50] They were at a severe disadvantage – "these two little 1,190-ton destroyers were no match for the giants who had just eaten up the 3,500-ton *Piet Hein*," wrote one survivor – but Commander Parker was determined to give as good as he was getting.[51] *Ford* made a smokescreen and swerved to port; the *Pope* followed, trying to unmask her starboard torpedo tubes. Still uncertain about what he was facing, Abe had his destroyers reverse course, keeping themselves between the four-pipers and their planned route of escape.

Now approaching the coast of Bali, Commander Parker tried another tack. He began a long counterclockwise circle to port, likely hoping that the Japanese destroyers would pursue. If they chased him around the circle, the route to the north out of the Badoeng Strait would be free and he could put the Japanese behind him. It was a nice idea, but Captain Abe quickly caught on. The *Asashio* and *Oshio* did not pursue. Instead, they reversed course again, heading back to the southeast. The Japanese destroyers still blocked the Americans' route of exit, but now the Americans were facing them with empty port torpedo tubes, unable to bring their loaded starboard torpedo tubes to bear.

Another running gun battle began, with the *John D. Ford* and the *Pope* heading southeast on a course about 120 degrees True, parallel with the *Asashio* and the *Oshio* roughly on their port quarter.[52] Commander Abe's ships were pouring a murderous fire into the old US destroyers, rapid and very accurate, constantly straddling the old four-pipers, though not connecting. Commander Parker decided that this was not working and had the *Ford* and the *Pope* veer to port, heading toward Noesa Besar and cutting in front of the Japanese destroyers.[53] Parker's hope was that the dark mass of Noesa Besar behind him would help obscure his ships while enabling him to unmask his starboard torpedo batteries for an attack. In the latter, at least, he would be successful, to a degree: *Pope* launched five torpedoes from her starboard tubes (a sixth jammed in the tube). But it was another dismal performance as not a single torpedo secured a hit.

But in trying to camouflage himself Parker was cursed to be foiled again, this time by a searchlight. *Ford* was caught in a bright beam of light from so far up in the air that the Americans thought it was coming from a cruiser. Momentarily convinced he had just stumbled across the *De Ruyter*, Commander Parker flicked on the *Ford*'s recognition lights for 15 seconds.[54] In response, he received an avalanche of 5in gunfire, with shell splashes so thick that crewmen on the *Pope* thought the *Ford* was finished.[55] But all the shells missed the *Ford*, and, coincidentally, disavowed Parker of any idea that he was facing friends. The searchlight was likely up on the mast of the *Oshio*. Being caught by the searchlight of an enemy ship in a night battle can be terrifying. Even amongst his shipmates, a sailor could feel all alone in that glare, not so much like being alone in a spotlight on a stage, but in the glare of a guard tower's searchlight during a prison break.

Of course, that searchlight also makes a fine point of aim in the darkness – except that in this case it was so close that it blinded the *Ford*'s gunners, who could not get an accurate aim.[56] Even if they could, the 4in guns were good for tearing up transports, freighters, and tankers as at Balikpapan and the upper works of modern warships, but were ineffectual against such warships' hull armor.

Commander Parker had one more trick up his sleeve, which he used to rid himself of his persistent hunters and their rapid-fire 5in guns. He dropped the *John D. Ford* back behind *Pope* and ordered a smokescreen, which served to blind Captain Abe and his gunners just long enough for the Americans to pull away to the southeast. Parker decided they had had enough. It was clear they were not going to break through to their assigned route of egress to the north. By 12:10 pm, the *Pope* and *Ford* were retreating to the southeast, course 135 degrees True, and preparing to set course for Tjilatjap.[57]

Having lost contact with the American destroyers, the *Oshio* and the *Asashio* turned to the north. As they were doing so, the *Asashio* encountered a destroyer seemingly out of nowhere, and opened fire. So did the *Oshio*, at about the same time. Both claimed to have sunk these new targets by gunfire – but, as it turned out, the *Asashio* and *Oshio* had been firing at each other, which goes to show the difficulty of identification and battle damage assessment in night battles. Although both claimed a sinking in their after-action reports, this incident did not appear in either of their log books.[58]

Seeing the flashes of gunfire behind them as they retreated, the crews of the *John D. Ford* and *Pope* found some humor in the thought of their tormentors now tormenting each other. To the very limited amusement available this night was added the tale of the *Ford*'s whaleboat. During the first exchange of gunfire with the Japanese destroyers, a 5in shell cut the afterfalls of the *Ford*'s whaleboat. The sailors cut the dangling motorized boat loose and it fell overboard.[59] It landed right side up, and 13 survivors of the *Piet Hein* claimed it. They tried to start the engine but failed – it had been drained of gasoline to minimize the possibility of fire. No matter. Just before dawn they were amazed to find a large gasoline drum floating close by. The drum, for the boats on the destroyer *Pope*, had been jettisoned during the battle, again to minimize the possibility of fire. Thanking their luck, these *Piet Hein* survivors started the engine, recovered 20 more survivors, and managed to get the boat back to Java.[60]

But these would be the only humorous aspects of this disastrous night for the first wave. The numeric superiority of the first wave had been totally dissipated by the strung-out formation that essentially created three different engagements. First it was two light cruisers – indeed two underarmed light cruisers – versus two overstrength destroyers. Then it was one destroyer versus the same two overstrength destroyers, a fatally lopsided matchup for the single *Piet Hein*. Then it was two old destroyers versus these same two overstrength destroyers. Only in the first did the Allies have anything resembling superiority, and then only barely. Admiral Doorman's tactical plan had pulled apart his ships and left his force unable to bring its full power to bear on the enemy.

The Allies were very fortunate that the only ship to pay a price for this faulty plan was the *Piet Hein*, forced into that one-on-two fast break. Even so, the sinking of the *Piet Hein* has caused some controversy and remains a bit of a mystery. While it appears undisputed that the destroyer was sunk by the *Asashio*'s torpedo, it is still unclear whose gunfire hit the *Piet Hein* and caused her to lose power, leaving her vulnerable to that torpedo. Most official histories attribute the hits to the 5in guns of the *Asashio*, but there has been some belief, especially among Dutch sources, that the hits were actually friendly fire from the US destroyers *John D. Ford* and *Pope*.[61] The thinking seems to be that the American destroyers lost track of the *Piet Hein* in the darkness (and vice versa), a consequence of being too far behind her. They later saw a destroyer laying smoke that screened the Japanese destroyers, assumed that destroyer was Japanese and attacked accordingly, not immediately realizing the ship was friendly – an understandable assumption, which the Dutch are careful to admit.[62] Once the Americans realized their error, it was too late. The *Piet Hein*'s late swerve to port away from the American destroyers and towards the Japanese fits in with this theory. However, against this suggestion is the fact that, unless they poured on such an avalanche of fire that they overwhelmed the target, the four-pipers' 4in guns were usually ineffectual against more modern warships. Furthermore, some American eyewitness accounts indicate that they never lost sight of the *Piet Hein*.[63] For those reasons, although the possibility that US gunfire disabled the *Piet Hein* cannot be totally ruled out, it seems very remote.

Inextricably linked to this controversy is a second mystery concerning the *Piet Hein*'s smokescreen. The smokescreen laid by the Dutch destroyer in turning away from the attacking Japanese may surely qualify as the worst smokescreen of all time. It not only failed to screen the *Piet Hein* from the Japanese but it actually screened the *Asashio* and *Oshio* from the US destroyers, thus at the very least confusing the Americans and possibly helping convince them that the *Piet Hein* was enemy.

A prominent story about the incident has been that the smokescreen was actually an accident. This theory holds that a button marked MAKE SMOKE was on a wall at the back of the bridge. When the *Piet Hein* swung to starboard, the story goes, a member of the bridge crew was thrown against the button.[64] Precisely how this generated the smoke has never been made clear. Dutch sources simply say that the cause of the smoke was unknown.[65] A warship can make smoke using two methods. In one, the engineering crew alters the fuel mixture in the boilers, releasing what is usually black smoke through the ship's stacks. In the other, a dedicated smoke generator, if the ship has one – and the *Piet Hein* did – releases what is usually white smoke. The alleged button at the back of the bridge would have either activated the smoke generator, or signaled the boiler room crew and the generator crew to make smoke.

The theory has never been proven, however, and is likely apocryphal on several grounds. The first is that, on its face, having smoke available at the simple press of a button, when practically everything else on a ship involves orders and acknowledgments through various means of communications, seems preposterous. While gunnery can be delegated to the gun director or the individual gun mounts, most major tactical decisions, such as speed and course, are controlled directly by the bridge. It is unlikely that a major decision like making smoke would be delegated to engineering or the generators. It would have to be controlled from the bridge. Making smoke would thus involve an order, and it is unclear how a single button could communicate that order.

Moreover, eyewitness accounts of the *Piet Hein*'s actions indicate that the destroyer made both black and white smoke, suggesting that smoke was coming from both her funnels and her generators. How such an order, if mistaken, could get past both the engineering crew and the generator, not to mention the bridge crew who would see the smoke as it was being made, is unknown.

Finally, the entire theory is insulting to the efficiency of the Dutch in both operations and ship design. Having something like a "MAKE SMOKE" button on the wall can lead to accidents, exactly like the one claimed in this case. And the inability of the Dutch crewmen either to prevent the accident or to limit it unnecessarily calls into question their competence. Particularly when there was a very valid tactical reason for making smoke – Commander Chömpf wanted to launch an attack and retire under cover of smoke. As the *Piet Hein* swung to starboard, Chömpf ordered the smokescreen, and the crews in the boiler rooms and the smoke generators executed it perfectly. While it ended up being a bad call, it was hardly unreasonable or illogical.

For the *John D. Ford* and the *Pope*, the smokescreen had fouled their attack, but the real culprits were the unusually aggressive tactics of the *Asashio* and the *Oshio*. Heading back to Tjilatjap, the four-pipers crossed the southern entrance to Badoeng Strait. Lookouts reported gunfire and flares to the north.[66] The second wave had arrived.

Second and third waves – February 19–20

Captain de Meester's group was in a more traditional combat formation than Admiral Doorman's group, with US destroyers *Stewart*, *Parrott*, *John D. Edwards*, and *Pillsbury* under the command of Commander Thomas H. Binford leading the light cruiser-destroyer leader *Tromp*. At around midnight the *Tromp* dropped back some 5 miles behind the destroyers.[67] The plan was to use her 5.9in guns to finish off any ships the destroyers had crippled. Again, this was a hit-and-run tactical plan, much better than Doorman's. But the idea of the single strongest ship dropping back so far astern in a night battle was questionable and would come with consequences.

They passed through Bali Strait and saw searchlight beams and gun flashes on the far side of Tafelhoek in the Sanoer roadstead. Picking up snippets of radio conversation between the *John D. Ford* and the *Pope*, Commander Binford tried to reach Commander Parker in the *Ford* to get information on what they were facing, but he could not make contact and as he continued to head south away from the gunfire it seemed to die out around 11:00 pm.[68] The second group had gone out expecting to face "a large number of transports and … a group of three or four cruisers and seven or eight destroyers," but now they were, again, sailing in with no more information than they had when they left Soerabaja.[69] The destroyers went to battle stations at 12:15 am and passed the Dutch torpedo boats of the third wave, who were waiting for their cue to enter the Sanoer Roads stage. At about 12:45 am the destroyers turned toward the east to pass Tafelhoek some 3 miles offshore, and at 1:10 am they set course 20 degrees True, speed 25 knots, entering the Badoeng Strait.[70]

The Japanese ships were the same that had faced the first wave: destroyers *Asashio* and *Oshio* and the transport *Sasago Maru*. They had not yet been able to leave the Sanoer roadstead, and may have been tending to the damaged transport. Admiral Kubo had been told that the Denpesar beachhead was under attack. He was in his flagship *Nagara* with destroyers *Wakaba*, *Hatsushimo,* and *Nenohi*, designated as "distant support" for the invasion, but could not help because the Japanese had chosen to emphasize the "distant" part of that equation. So Kubo ordered the destroyers *Arashio* and *Michishio* to stop escorting the limping transport *Sagami Maru* back to Makassar City and instead rush to help Captain Abe's embattled destroyers. Until these reinforcements could arrive, however, *Asashio* and *Oshio* were on their own.

As was, for all intents and purposes, the *Tromp*, simply because she had dropped back so far behind the US four-pipers. At 1:30 am, Captain de Meester's ship was on the receiving end of a signal of flashing green lights: a recognition signal, but from whom he could not say. The strike force had not had a chance to work out night signals, and ABDAFLOAT, with representatives of four different countries and three different navies speaking two different languages, was bad with communications in any case.

The immediate effect was negligible. The *Stewart* led the *Parrott, John D. Edwards*, and *Pillsbury* toward the anchorage. At 1:34 am, the *Stewart* sighted two shadows to port at a range of 2,000–2,500yd; Commander Binford ordered a course change to 30 degrees True, slightly to starboard, to clear them. One of the Japanese destroyers, either the *Oshio* or the *Asashio*, flashed a challenge to the *Stewart*. Commander Binford responded by ordering an immediate torpedo attack. At 1:36 am, the *Stewart* and *Parrott* each fired a salvo of six torpedoes and *Pillsbury* three, all from their port tubes, into the Sanoer roadstead. Their runs ended only in "loud oaths and groans of disappointment."[71] Fifteen torpedoes had all failed to secure a hit.

Captain Abe once again adopted an aggressive defense and the *Oshio* and the *Asashio* charged out. At 1:43 am the *Stewart* snapped on her searchlight and opened fire with her three 4in guns. Her crew was aghast at the massive ship – actually the *Oshio* – caught in the light's beam; they immediately assumed that it was a cruiser.[72] Behind the *Stewart*, John D. Edwards set up to fire four torpedoes to port. Two stuck in the tubes. The other two launched successfully but without any hits.[73]

At 1:45 am, the *Oshio* and *Asashio* launched torpedoes at the US destroyers, then opened up on the *Stewart* with "rapid and accurate fire" from their rapid-fire dual 5in mounts.[74] With her searchlight making a nice point of aim and then caught in the beam of the *Asashio*'s searchlight, the *Stewart* was hit by a flurry of 5in shells. One passed clean through without exploding. Another at 1:46 am ricocheted off the water, killing one seaman and wounding her executive officer.[75] Shrapnel tore into her No. 3 stack. A third at 1:47 am blew a 4ft hole that flooded the after steering engine room and damaged the steam line that powered the steering engines, but the *Stewart* remained navigable and she continued on, ceasing fire at 1:48 am after 12 salvoes. She then changed course to 65 degrees True to put the *Asashio* and the *Oshio* behind her. The crew saw the annoying searchlight disappear in a shower of sparks.[76]

The *Stewart*'s sudden course change caused the naval equivalent of a train derailment. The *Parrott*, following behind the *Stewart*, nearly plowed into her. The third destroyer in the column, the *John D. Edwards*, had to veer off to starboard to avoid the *Parrott*, passing the *Stewart* in the process. The *Pillsbury* swerved even further to starboard to avoid the mess of ships in front of her, nearly colliding with the *Parrott*, and adopted a parallel course.[77] At 1:57 am the *Stewart* turned to starboard – 75 degrees True – and reunited with the *John D. Edwards* around 2:00 am, retaking the lead sometime before 2:11 am.[78] With *Pillsbury* now to starboard of the *Stewart* and *Edwards*, the *Parrott* adopted a parallel course to port close to the Bali coast.

The charge of the *Oshio* and *Asashio* had kept the US destroyers out of the anchorage. For the second time this night, fortune had favored the bold Abe Toshio. He had his destroyers cut behind the *Stewart*, *Parrott*, and *John D. Edwards* to concentrate on the *Pillsbury*, but they could not isolate her and moved back toward the anchorage.[79]

Now, having closed to some 3,000yd behind the *Pillsbury*, came the *Tromp*. Captain de Meester had his light cruiser-destroyer leader raise its speed to 31 knots. To starboard she sighted the *Oshio* and *Asashio*. Expecting reinforcements and not sure of the identity of this new ship, the Japanese destroyers again flashed a challenge. At 2:05 am, De Meester responded snapping on one of the cruiser's searchlights.[80] This was a bad idea.

At 2:07 am, a flurry of 12 5in shells from *Asashio* riddled the Dutch cruiser. One damaged the fire control of the portside torpedo tubes; another destroyed the fire director, forcing all her guns to go to local control for the rest of this nine-minute gun duel. A full nine shells smashed the bridge. The last hit pierced the *Tromp*'s hull below the waterline, briefly causing some flooding.[81] Without the fire director, coordinated and accurate gunfire was problematic, and Captain de Meester's ship was unable to return fire until 2:10 am, her 5.9in guns targeting the *Oshio* and the 40mm Bofors antiaircraft guns operating against the *Asashio*.[82] At 2:16 am, *Oshio* fired three Long Lance torpedoes, but the *Tromp* managed to avoid them. At 2:11 am Captain Abe's *Oshio* took one hit on the bridge and a second into the portside torpedo magazine; such was the Dutch luck that the 5.9in shell did not cause the torpedoes to explode, which would have finished off the destroyer. As it was, the *Oshio* lost seven dead.[83] The *Tromp*'s 40mm shells took their toll on the *Asashio*, killing four, wounding 11, and destroying that annoying searchlight.[84] For having fired 71 5.9in shells and several hundred rounds of 40mm ammunition, however, it was not a good hit ratio.

Nevertheless, this heat was a bit too high for Captain Abe and he broke off, moving back to protect the transport. Captain de Meester also pulled away to the northeast. The *Tromp* had been badly damaged – there was flooding, the bridge was smashed, and her fire control was gone – with ten dead and 30 wounded. But now Admiral Kubo's reinforcements, destroyer *Michishio* and *Arashio*, arrived on the scene, surprising the badly scattered ABDA ships. *Parrott* was hugging the Bali coast, *Stewart* and *John D. Edwards* in column in the center; *Tromp* 8,000yd behind the *Edwards* off her starboard quarter, and the *Pillsbury* 3,000yd off the *Tromp*'s starboard beam. They were in no semblance of formation to take on the newcomers.[85]

But as scattered as the Allied ships were, the *Michishio* and *Arashio*, heading southwest, blundered right into the middle of them, with the *Stewart* and *John D. Edwards* to starboard and *Pillsbury* and *Tromp* to port.[86] For once, the Japanese were surprised and at a severe disadvantage, with one Japanese survivor admitting, "Their [the Americans'] rapid attack surprised us because we did not expect it so soon. We lost our minds momentarily."[87]

At 2:19 am, the Japanese destroyers opened fire – very inaccurately – on the *Stewart* and were rewarded by being caught in an unintentional crossfire. The *Stewart* immediately changed course to 85 degrees True. The *Pillsbury* snapped on her searchlight and directed it on the *Michishio*, pinning the Japanese destroyer and allowing the *Stewart* to open fire with her 4in guns and launch six torpedoes from her starboard tubes at 2:19 am.[88] But once again without any success. The *John D. Edwards* also fired her 4in guns and launched six torpedoes from her starboard tubes at the *Michishio* – with no torpedo hits. *Pillsbury* also fired her remaining three portside torpedoes, again without any success. The *Parrott* was unable to join the unplanned ambush; at 2:19 am while hugging the Bali coast, her rudder had jammed full left and, despite ordering emergency full speed astern, a sudden maneuver that threw overboard a chief petty officer, she had run aground on Bali.[89] She was not able to free herself until 2:26 am and continued onward steering by engine.[90]

The *Michishio* and *Arashio* now saw their predicament and turned to flee. *Arashio* made good her escape but the *Michishio* was hit with an avalanche of fire. A 4in shell from the *John D. Edwards* hit the Japanese destroyer in the engine room and left it disabled. The *Pillsbury* and *Tromp* hit the midships antiaircraft platform amidships and smashed the bridge. The *Michishio* was burning, "drifting, submerged to sea level from the middle to aft deck," with 13 dead and 83 injured.[91]

Now, the Allies had a Japanese ship dead to rights, dead in the water and alone. But the Allied ships were in no mood to finish her off. They had taken their own beating this night. They still believed they were badly outnumbered and seemed satisfied with the damage they had inflicted – or thought they had inflicted. Captain de Meester's second wave thus sped off to the north out of the Badoeng Strait into the Lombok Strait, showing no interest in finishing off the *Michishio*. Thus spared, the next day she would be towed to Makassar City by her sister ship *Arashio* for emergency repairs; ultimately, she would be out of action until late October.[92]

Some three hours after the attack on the *Michishio* came the third act of Admiral Helfrich's drama when the seven Dutch motor torpedo boats entered Badoeng Strait. They split into one group of three boats, which came in close to shore, and a second group of four, which stayed some 4 miles out. Sitting low in the water, they could not see much, and saw no ships in the strait. One of the boats reported a shadow to the south, but was unable to close as it retired at high speed; they may have seen the *John D. Ford* and *Pope* leaving.[93] The motor torpedo boats returned to Pangpang Bay and refueled again from the *Krakatau* before returning to Soerabaja.[94]

Daylight on February 20 saw the *Tromp* reunited with the US four-pipers. It also saw nine Mitsubishi bombers operating out of Makassar City. The ABDA ships managed to avoid all the Japanese bombs. Although the ships repeatedly called for fighters, the air battle over Soerabaja the previous day had destroyed what little pursuit capability the Dutch had in Java.[95]

There was some celebration in Soerabaja, in the mistaken belief that they had given the enemy a bloody nose. But even so, they knew that nothing they had done had made any difference. Bali was gone. The Denpesar airfield was now Japanese. Enemy aircraft could now attack reinforcements and supplies in the Indian Ocean. The last safe Allied port in Tjilatjap was now in range of the dreaded Nells and Bettys.

With Sumatra in the west and Bali in the east now in Japanese hands, for all practical purposes, Java was cut off. General Wavell believed ABDACOM now had a lifespan of two weeks.[96] He would be overly optimistic.

CHAPTER 12

NO BREATH TO CATCH – PRELIMINARIES TO THE BATTLE OF THE JAVA SEA

With the string of Japanese victories the world was closing in for the Allies in the Far East, and was about to be turned upside down – in the case of one group of American sailors, quite literally.

The destroyer *Stewart* led the US destroyers into Soerabaja around noon on February 20.[1] Discussions between Commander Binford, *Stewart*'s skipper Lieutenant Commander Harold P. Smith and the Dutch naval authorities determined that the destroyer should immediately go into the 15,000-ton floating drydock, the larger of Soerabaja's two floating drydocks, to repair her damage. As she was being tied up alongside, the *Tromp*, with her blackened, twisted bridge, came into the harbor and passed the *Stewart* to port. Commander Smith called the crew to attention on the port side for an official salute to the Dutch cruiser. The crewmen had their own ideas, however. At attention they loudly shouted cheers for their Dutch comrades-in-arms. The crewmen of the *Tromp* returned the favor.[2] They had seen each other fight the enemy, both taking and giving blows. The ships had the scars to prove it and the respect was genuine.

But the hope was to get rid of those scars as quickly as possible and make the ships battle worthy again. For the *Tromp*, that hope could not be fulfilled in Soerabaja, or even in Java. Her damage was too extensive to be repaired locally. She would have to go to Australia. The *Stewart* fortunately only required quick repairs in the floating drydock.

The destroyer was maneuvered inside the drydock. Blocks were placed under her keel and wooden braces to her sides. At 4:05 pm, the floating drydock started to rise. Like a giant hand, palm underwater but fingers out of it, the dock would lift the destroyer *Stewart* out of the water, to rest on those keel blocks that had been placed beneath her, so that workmen could perform repairs and maintenance on her hull.[3]

While the dock was rising, Commander Smith was in a meeting with the officers in the wardroom, discussing the urgent repairs needed for the destroyer. Being immobilized in a drydock within range of enemy air attacks was not a pleasant prospect, especially for destroyers. Already during the Pacific War, three US Navy destroyers – the *Shaw*, *Cassin*, and *Downes* – had come to grief as a result of bombing in drydock, all during the Pearl Harbor attack.

So, air attack was everyone's first thought when, at 4:15 pm, there was a loud crash. Commander Smith and everyone in the wardroom were thrown against the wall. The room now seemed at an almost 45-degree angle. They scrambled to get off the ship.[4] What happened? Was it indeed an air attack? Had they been hit by a bomb?

No, but they almost wished they had. As Signalman William Kale described it, "One of the strangest and toughest accidents that could have befallen a ship happened to us."[5]

The *Stewart* had simply tipped over in the drydock. As the dock rose out of the water, the destroyer was supposed to rest on the keel blocks, but the blocks were not set properly, the timber supports could not support her weight, and, with the drydock not even fully raised, the destroyer had rolled over to port. She was now lying at a 37-degree angle.[6]

Commander Smith was heartbroken. The damage the Japanese had caused off Bali was nothing compared to this. In collapsing, the *Stewart*'s port propeller shaft – a most unlucky ship component for the Allies during this campaign – had been bent into the hull, cutting into the engine room. A fire room and both oil tanks were leaking into the drydock as well.

While the skipper may have been devastated, the crew were livid. Loud curses flew through the air at Dutch incompetence. One crewman of the *Stewart*, sleeping in his bunk when the accident dumped him on the floor, vented at "The God damned Dutchmen, they lead us up to the enemy, then they turn and run allowing the bombers to pick us off. Now their God damned drydock crew, have really fixed us. With Allies like them, who needs enemies?"[7] They repurposed a popular jingle: "Oh, there's the Veendam Dutch and the Amsterdam Dutch, there's the Rotterdam Dutch and the goddam Dutch. …"[8] For the moment, the bravery, toughness, and camaraderie of the *Tromp* were forgotten. But only for the moment.

What precisely happened to the *Stewart* has never been fully explained. All that is known is that the blocks were not properly set beneath her bilge keel, or properly attached, as the Dutch would later explain, but why is not known. The drydock was a commercial operation, used to dealing with flat-bottomed merchant vessels, not warships with rounded keels. But the "ownership manual" for the *Stewart* had been given to the Dutch naval authorities for just such a purpose. And those plans had supposedly been given to the management of the drydock. So either the management or their workmen had made a major mistake. This brought up another, unpleasant possibility: while the management was Dutch, the workmen were native Javanese. Had the Japanese gotten to members of the work crew for the *Stewart*? The question seems to have been considered and dismissed rather quickly.[9]

Whatever the cause, the resulting damage to *Stewart* was severe. It was estimated that it would take three weeks to three months to repair her, and this was assuming they could get spare parts. Part of the problem was the damage to the drydock itself. It was a total mess, and could not be raised without further engineering work on the *Stewart* lest the destroyer slip further and cause even more damage. With the Japanese believed to be headed for Java, time was not on the *Stewart*'s side.[10]

The question of what to do with the wrecked destroyer was considered for about a day. The crew actively campaigned to simply patch up the hull; they were determined to take the *Stewart* to Australia on one propeller if necessary. These four-pipers may have been old and of limited effectiveness, but they were loved by their crews. "[G]ive the ship a chance," they demanded.[11]

But love would not be enough. At 1:30 pm on February 22, the word came through that the *Stewart* would be abandoned. There was simply no time to repair her. The crew's outrage and resentment at losing their ship, not in battle, was rekindled.[12] The crew were dispersed among the destroyers *Parrott*, *Pillsbury*, and *John D. Edwards*. Commander Binford shifted his command ship to the *Edwards*, who still had torpedoes. She would remain in Soerabaja for the last-ditch naval defense of Java. The *Parrott* and *Pillsbury* had no torpedoes and little ammunition left, so they were sent to Tjilatjap as the first leg of their withdrawal to Australia.[13]

The *Stewart* was just the latest in a bizarre series of what might be called "unforced losses" – operational accidents and mechanical breakdowns – suffered by ABDAFLOAT. The list was already a long one. The *Boise* had run aground; she was unavailable for the counterattack off Balikpapan, had to be sent home and was lost for the duration of the campaign. The *Marblehead* had blown out a turbine; she, too, had been lost for the Balikpapan operation. The *Peary* had been damaged by a friendly air attack in a case of mistaken identity. The *Edsall* had been damaged by her own depth charges and was unfit for combat. The *Whipple* had collided with the *De Ruyter*; consequently, the destroyer had to be fitted with a soft bow that left her, too, unfit for combat. The *Van Ghent* had run aground, a total loss. The *Kortenaer* had run aground and was lost to the Bali counterattack. Now the *Stewart* had rolled over in drydock.

And there were even more unforced losses to come.

PLAYING FOR TIME

The fall of Singapore was the single biggest development in the Java Sea Campaign. Not only had it broken the western flank of the Malay Barrier and freed up Japanese military assets to be used in the conquest of Java, it had been the political shatterpoint for ABDACOM.

Up until that event, the Americans, British, Dutch and Australians had been united in purpose if not in strategy or tactics. As has already been seen, the British had been focused, to the exclusion of virtually everything else, on holding Singapore. The Dutch had been intent on keeping the East Indies in general and Java in particular, the Australians wanted to protect Australia and the Americans wished to re-take the Philippines, though even they admitted that was extremely unlikely, leaving their strategy as mostly a delaying action to buy time until the United States could fully bring its manufacturing superiority to bear. Yet they all were in agreement on one thing: the Japanese had to be kept out of the East Indies.

But after Singapore fell to the Japanese, the British seemed to lose interest in trying to achieve this aim. London had maintained all along that holding Singapore was key to defending the Indies. Singapore was the west flank. If it was lost, the Japanese could just roll up Sumatra and take Java from the west. There was most definitely a military logic to that position. London used that logic to convince the Dutch to use their ships and aircrafts in support of the British efforts in Malaya, especially in convoying. In so acting in support of the British, the Dutch sacrificed actions they could have taken to protect the East Indies, such as counterattacking against the Japanese advance units as Admiral Hart had advocated.

To be sure, Prime Minister Churchill was still intent on fighting for Java, cabling General Wavell: ANY QUESTION OF ABANDONING JAVA IS UNTHINKABLE. ALL FORCES IN THE ISLAND OF WHATEVER NATIONALITY SHOULD RESIST TO THE END. Churchill went on to request diversionary airstrikes by American carrier aircraft.[14] On February 20, the Combined Chiefs of Staff in Washington cabled Wavell echoing the prime minister's sentiments: EVERY DAY IS OF IMPORTANCE. THERE SHOULD BE NO WITHDRAWAL OF TROOPS OR AIR FORCES OF ANY NATIONALITY, AND NO SURRENDER.[15]

That statement, in a nutshell, was why the Americans, the British, and the Australians continued fighting for the Indies – "playing for time," as *Stewart* survivor Lodwick Alford would call it. Conspicuously, however, there was no mention of reinforcements, due partly to an assessment by the First Sea Lord Sir Dudley Pound and the chiefs of staff that reinforcement of the ABDA forces in Java was both pointless and next to impossible, in large part because, with Singapore gone, it was impossible to hold the East Indies. The day after receiving the Combined Chiefs' cable, Wavell responded:

I AM AFRAID THAT THE DEFENCE OF ABDA AREA HAS BROKEN DOWN AND THAT DEFENCE OF JAVA CANNOT NOW LAST LONG. IT ALWAYS HINGED ON THE AIR BATTLE ... ANYTHING PUT INTO JAVA NOW CAN DO LITTLE TO PROLONG THE STRUGGLE: IT IS MORE QUESTION FOR WHAT YOU WILL CHOOSE TO SAVE ... I SEE LITTLE FURTHER USEFULNESS FOR THIS HQ ... I HATE THE IDEA OF LEAVING THESE STOUT-HEARTED DUTCHMEN AND WILL REMAIN HERE AND FIGHT IT OUT WITH THEM AS LONG AS POSSIBLE IF YOU WOULD CONSIDER THIS WOULD HELP AT ALL.[16]

The underlying message of retreat was thinly veiled within what was an accurate evaluation of the situation in the East Indies. The best thing to do, in the view of the field marshal and the other British commanders, was to pull all the remaining forces – British, American, Australian, and Dutch – out of the Indies to save them for better use elsewhere. Again, there was definite military logic to it.

But, as eminent Pacific War historian H. P. Willmott puts it, "Of all the unpalatable aspects of the campaign in the Indies the most distasteful surely must be the rapidity and totality with which Wavell, London, and Washington recognized Java's indefensibility after so long and stubborn a refusal to abandon Singapore."[17] Indeed. It was easy for London to advocate abandoning the East Indies; the East Indies were Dutch, not British. It seemed somewhat convenient that while London had enjoyed Dutch support for the British defense of Singapore, now that it was time to return the favor, the British wanted to back out. The Dutch were indignant at this view; to say they felt used is an understatement. They immediately pushed for General Wavell's removal.[18]

Both the United States and Great Britain had badly underestimated the emotion that the Dutch attached to the East Indies. With their homeland under Nazi occupation, the East Indies in general and Java in particular were the closest thing the Dutch had to a homeland at this point. An air of unreality hung over the Dutch in Java. The parties continued in Batavia, Bandoeng, and Soerabaja even as the Japanese made their final approach. Many civilians were blissfully unaware, willfully or otherwise, of just how badly the war was going. Others did everything they could to avoid recognizing or considering the horror that was about to befall them. The East Indies government had done little to prepare the European population for the possibility of evacuation or Japanese occupation. Even the Dutch military, who knew how badly the war was going, could not accept that the Dutch presence in the Indies was near an end.

Nevertheless, the fall of Bali drove home the truth that, however callous the British position on the East Indies, the accuracy of their assessment was undeniable. Now there was no place on Java safe from air attack. Batavia and its port Tanjoeng Priok were vulnerable to the Japanese airfields at Palembang. Soerabaja was vulnerable to Kendari, Makassar, Balikpapan, Banjermasin, and now Bali. The fall of Bali had drawn Tjilatjap and the sea approaches thereto into bombing range.

Admiral Helfrich vehemently disagreed with General Wavell's assessment. In Helfrich's view, because, he claimed, the Soenda and Bali straits were still open, Java could be held if London and Washington could send reinforcements – ships, aircraft, guns, men – and if they would act "with extreme speed, grim resolution, and take all risks."[19] Wavell was unmoved.

The issue of air power was especially sensitive. With the Japanese having air superiority over the main naval base at Soerabaja, ABDAFLOAT was crippled. The only interceptors in eastern Java were the US Army Air Force's 17th Pursuit Squadron (Provisional) at Ngoro, which was being depleted by attrition, and the few Dutch aircraft that had survived the disastrous February 19 battle over Soerabaja. Between February 21 and 26, the pilots of the 17th claimed ten enemy aircraft shot down, having lost three of their own. As of February 26 it had only 13 serviceable P-40s to fight an enemy that had hundreds of aircraft.[20] Warhawk pilot Robert S. "Spence" Johnson lamented in his diary, "Every day a nightmare! More raids, more Japs, never ceasing air raids and the native tom-toms which forecast their arrival. Half our outfit left or killed and no aircrafts coming. We are encircled and terribly outnumbered!"[21]

Very minimal offensive power was present with a handful of heavy B-17 and LB-30 bombers and a few Douglas Banshee dive bombers of the V Bomber Command of the Far East Air Force – not enough to do much of anything to support naval operations. Only the British had significant air resources in Java, all in the western part around Batavia after having been withdrawn from Palembang. In keeping with British doctrine, however, the Royal Air Force refused to use its aircraft to support naval operations. So the Dutch began pressuring American forces on Java. It would become commonplace for Dutch officers to accost their American counterparts. "Our honor requires that we go down fighting," they would say. "Are you with us?" The Americans would almost always say they were with them to the end, but took great pains to point out that what they viewed as "the end" was not necessarily the same as the Dutch view. To the Americans, "the end" was when continued commitment of military resources would serve no purpose. The Americans had no intention of dying or going to the hell that was a Japanese prisoner of war camp for a lost cause.[22]

Similarly, Admiral Helfrich pressed Admiral Glassford, asking if the US Navy would stay. Adroitly, Glassford responded that his orders were to give full support to the Dutch. Even so, he began preparations for pulling out of Java.

The Americans understood the logic of the British position. On February 18, General Wavell's Deputy, US Army General Brett, had told the War Department obliquely that Java was lost, advocating the view that the one chance of overcoming the odds against the Allies was to launch an offensive through Burma and China, while building up strength in Australia. Again, it was completely logical. But logic and the right thing were not necessarily the same. Washington tried to navigate this thorny issue of military and morality by fully supporting the Dutch to the best of its ability while trying to convince them that the British were right. The Dutch disagreed. Nothing anyone said – not Wavell or Glassford or Roosevelt or Churchill – could move the Dutch.

Back and forth discussions took place between Bandoeng and the Combined Chiefs of Staff. General Wavell and General Brett had "dignified, frank, and painful" discussions with Governor General van Starkenborgh Stachouwer.[23] No one wanted to stay to fight for Java and no one wanted to abandon the Dutch. So a compromise of sorts was reached. General Wavell would relinquish control over ABDACOM, which would be transferred to Dutch command. The remaining British and American forces would remain under the Dutch as long as resistance was practical, but, aside from aircraft, no reinforcements would be sent. The multinational force was still there but the command had become national.

While Admiral Glassford was supportive of Admiral Helfrich he sent Admiral Purnell to Exmouth Gulf in Australia, to begin setting up a new submarine base. Captain Wilkes pulled out the tenders of the US submarines.

Curiously, though, the Americans were still sending reinforcements of aircraft. Admiral Glassford had informed his superiors that there were no more than 15 fighters left in Java. So the Americans had been arranging some of that desperately needed air power. Heading for Java were 36 ready-to-fly P-40 Warhawks, complete with pilots, on the seaplane tender USS *Langley*, and 26 crated P-40s, together with pilots and 250,000 rounds of .50cal ammunition in the hold of the freighter *Sea Witch*. But would they arrive in time? Would they arrive at all?

Planning the defense of Java – February 23–24

On February 23, ABDACOM was still in existence, though no one seems quite sure what it was called – ABDACOM, ABDA-Area, Combined Headquarters, Unified Command, or somesuch – but was now commanded, nominally at least, by the Dutch Governor General van Starkenborgh Stachouwer and Deputy Governor General van Mook. For all practical purposes, however, it was led by Lieutenant General Hein ter Poorten, formerly ABDARM and now "Commander-in-Chief, ABDA Area," who promptly moved ABDACOM from Lembang back to the more logical headquarters of Bandoeng.[24] An LB-30 Liberator was set aside for General Wavell's departure. He came aboard and, much to the disgust of the crew, promptly overloaded it with a very large set of luggage, two crates of bourbon and a set of golf clubs, forcing the pilot to leave his bombardier behind.[25] Wavell headed off to India to defend the "jewel in the crown of the British Empire" from Japanese invasion.

Back on Java, the Dutch were now in charge of all the defenses. ABDAIR was renamed "Java Air Command" – just as much of an aspiration as a title – under the command of Major General Ludolph H. van Oyen of the Royal Netherlands East Indies Army Air Force. He divided its operations into eastern and western groups.

Admiral Helfrich sent a message to the sailors of ABDAFLOAT that he "had assumed command of the Allied Naval Forces engaged in the defense of the NEI under the title CZM. "CZM" was a reference to *Commandant der Zeemacht* (Commander of Sea Forces), Helfrich's title in the days before ABDACOM.[26] ABDAFLOAT itself was not really renamed, though Helfrich had called it "Allied Naval Forces engaged in the defense of the NEI" and some others would call it "Allied Naval Forces in the Southwest Pacific."[27] Since neither title readily rolls off the tongue, most historians have continued calling both Helfrich and the naval forces under his command ABDAFLOAT, just as most have continued calling US Naval Forces in the Southwest Pacific the Asiatic Fleet. Helfrich continued his message by expressing his confidence that "all commanders of Forces and those under their command will give fullest support at this critical time."[28]

The Royal Navy's Admiral Palliser remained as Admiral Helfrich's chief of staff with orders to stay and support the Dutch until resistance served no useful purpose, then to withdraw the British ships to Ceylon. For his part, Glassford, as ordered by Washington, promptly reported to Helfrich for duty. Helfrich, to his credit, expressed his profound gratitude for the US Navy's "ever loyal" assistance.[29]

ABDAIR reconnaissance had detected the final Japanese invasion fleet destined for western Java. On February 18, 56 transports of Admiral Ozawa's Western Invasion Force had left Cam Ranh Bay in Indochina. The transports were carrying the headquarters of the Japanese 16th Army, the 2nd Division, and the 230th Infantry Regiment. They had a massive escort: Ozawa's flagship heavy cruiser *Chokai*; the four *Mogami*s of the 7th Cruiser Division; light cruisers *Natori*, *Sendai*, and *Yura*, each leading a flotilla of destroyers; light carrier *Ryujo*; and seaplane tender *Mizuho*.[30]

The next day, another invasion convoy had left Jolo. The Imperial Japanese Army's 48th Division was on board 41 transports of Admiral Takahashi's Eastern Invasion Force, with another large escort: Takahashi's flagship heavy cruiser *Ashigara* and her sister *Myoko*, freshly repaired from her bomb hit back in December; the two other *Myoko*s of Admiral Takagi's 5th Cruiser Division; and light cruisers *Jintsu* and *Naka*, each also leading a destroyer flotilla.[31] Their air cover was to be provided by Zeros operating out of Balikpapan. Their destination? Eastern Java.

Meanwhile Admiral Kondo, who was leading the entire Southern Expeditionary Force somewhere south of Java in the Indian Ocean, had now come out for battle on his own. He had his flagship, heavy cruiser *Atago*, plus her sister ships *Takao* and *Maya* (all sisters to the *Chokai*) and two battleships, *Kongo* and *Haruna*. Also south of Java was *Kido Butai*, the Japanese Carrier Striking Force under Admiral Nagumo, with the large carriers *Akagi*, *Kaga*, *Hiryu*, and *Soryu*; battleships *Hiei* and *Kirishima*; heavy cruisers *Tone* and *Chikuma*, and the light cruiser *Abukuma* leading a destroyer flotilla. Originally, *Kido Butai* had been set to cover the invasion of Java, but it was reassigned. After the Badoeng Strait action, Commander Abe had reported that his two destroyers had sunk two enemy cruisers and three destroyers, while damaging two further destroyers. It was preposterous, but Admiral Yamamoto accepted it as true, further drawing from it that Allied naval forces were no longer a threat. So instead of covering the invasion forces, *Kido Butai*'s mission now was to cut off Java from retreat or reinforcement.[32]

The number of ships available to Admiral Helfrich to oppose these forces was pitifully small. Operating out of Tanjoeng Priok were the remaining Royal Navy ships under Commodore Collins: heavy cruiser *Exeter*; light cruisers *Hobart*, *Dragon*, *Danae*, and the very recently arrived *Perth*; and destroyers *Electra*, *Encounter*, *Jupiter*, *Tenedos*, and *Scout*, plus a single Dutch destroyer, the *Evertsen*, most of which were on convoy duty. At Soerabaja he had most of the remaining Dutch and American ships under Admiral Doorman: light cruisers *De Ruyter* and *Java*, and destroyers USS *John D. Edwards*, and Hr. Ms. *Kortenaer*, *Witte de With*, and *Banckert*. Operating out of Tjilatjap was the heavy cruiser USS *Houston* and US destroyers *John D. Edwards*, *Alden*, *John D. Ford*, *Paul Jones*, *Pope*, *Whipple*, and *Edsall*.

It was not a pretty picture. Light cruisers *Boise* and *Marblehead* were long gone, and the light-cruiser-destroyer-leader *Tromp* had left on February 23 for Australia and major repairs after the action off Bali. Dutch destroyers *Van Nes* and *Piet Hein* had been sunk; the *Van Ghent* was a total loss after her grounding, her crew now manning her sister ship *Witte de With*; and the *Evertsen*, newly crewed just the previous December, had no combat experience. US destroyers *John D. Ford* and *Pope* had to be dispatched from Tjilatjap to meet the destroyer tender *Black Hawk* near Christmas Island and take off her last 17 torpedoes. The tender would then go to Australia, escorted by the US destroyers *Barker* and *Bulmer*, who were out of torpedoes and suffering from leaky condensers that limited their speed as a result of the Banka bombing. Destroyers *Pillsbury* and *Parrott*, without torpedoes and in need of refitting, had been detached and ordered to Tjilatjap. Destroyer *Peary* had been sunk, while the *Stewart* was completely inoperable as a result of the drydock accident and likely could not be made seaworthy before the invasion of Java. Considering the Royal Navy assets, destroyer *Thanet* had been sunk off Endau, while destroyer *Express* had been sent off for more repairs after the shoddy repair job done by the Singapore Naval Base.

Of the remaining Allied ships, almost all had major issues. The *Exeter* was in serious need of a refit, had lost her floatplane, and was having train problems with her aft turret, though not nearly as bad as those of the *Houston*, who had lost her aft turret. The *Perth* had just arrived with a case of whiplash, having been ordered to the East Indies twice only to be recalled twice before this charmed third time.[33] Destroyer *Edsall* was damaged from the shallow depth charging, and the *Whipple* had a soft bow from her collision with the *De Ruyter*. The other US four-pipers were suffering from leaky condensers, old and worn machinery, and bottoms biofouled with barnacles and other marine life. The *Kortenaer* was dealing with a leaky boiler after her grounding and the *Witte de With* had been hurriedly brought online from overhaul and given the *Van Ghent*'s crew, and though the two destroyers were sister ships, sister ships are rarely identical. The *Dragon*, *Danae*, *Scout*, and *Tenedos* were just as ancient as the four-pipers and the *Thanet*, while the *Jupiter* and *Encounter* still had their engine issues.

Overshadowing these problems was one that potentially could immobilize the entire fleet – oil. While the East Indies was a major oil producer, Japanese forces had overrun most of the oil production centers. There was oil in Java, both oil fields and stored oil, but the oil fields were inland and most of the maintenance crews had fled. Some 50,000 tons of oil remained at Soerabaja, but the Dutch, still believing they could hold the Indies, refused to move it until it was too late. On February 19, all ABDAFLOAT ships had received a message that the fuel situation was very serious.[34] The oil situation had an impact on the disposition of the Allied ships; although both Soerabaja and Tanjoeng Priok had oil, neither had enough to supply the entire fleet, so the fleet had to be divided between the two ports.

Admiral Helfrich poured his heart into defending Java. His first order of business was reorganization. On February 21, even before the final nail was placed in ABDACOM's coffin, he had pulled the ships at Tanjoeng Priok off convoy duty and formed them into the Western Striking Force, forming the ships at Soerabaja into the Eastern Striking Force. At Tjilatjap, the *Whipple* and *Edsall* were not combat-ready due to their damage, but the *Alden* and *Paul Jones* were available to replace the *John D. Ford* and *Pope* while they were off being refitted with torpedoes. There was also the *Houston*, who, even with her aft turret out, was still almost the most powerful ship he had. That same day, he ordered the *John D. Ford* and *Pope* to finish replenishing their stores and return to Soerabaja as soon as possible. That same day, the crew of the *Houston* got the order they had been dreading: escorted by the *Alden* and *Paul Jones*, they were to head for Soerabaja, back to the north side of the Malay Barrier, into the potential trap that was the Java Sea.

Falling back on a traditional area of expertise for the Royal Netherlands Navy, Admiral Helfrich had minesweepers work off the Java coast in the Soenda Strait. While not a bad idea, this seemed rather pointless in that the Japanese would soon be using the strait. He ordered minefields laid in likely landing areas on the north coast of Java near Rembang and off the island of Madoera. This was a good idea, to be sure, but the Dutch would claim that they had mined *all* the waters off Madoera. The Americans in particular found this laughable and similarly pointless.[35]

As the fall of Java approached, Admiral Helfrich's orders would increasingly strain the limits of rationality. The first to feel his whip were the submarines. Helfrich had had considerable success driving Dutch submarines relentlessly – and ruthlessly. Commodore Collins related a story about a Dutch submarine skipper returning from a patrol in which he attacked a Japanese cruiser without success. Helfrich promptly sacked him, saying, "I do not want unlucky Captains in command of my submarines." The skipper may have been unlucky, but he was luckier than his boat; on its first patrol without him it was sunk.[36]

Now Helfrich was extending that ruthlessness to all ABDAFLOAT submarines. He recalled them all to be near the Java coast in position to intercept the invaders, and the Dutch submarines *O-19*, *K-VIII* and *K-X*, the British *Truant* and the American *S-37* and *S-38* moved into a concentration near Madoera, where he expected the landing to take place. The US Navy had never agreed with Helfrich's submarine tactics, and they did not now. US Navy doctrine would have the submarines attack the convoy en route and cause disruption, delays, and, hopefully, losses while reporting on the convoy's progress. Helfrich preferred to use the submarines for close-in defense. But his authority was nevertheless respected – until Captain Wilkes pointed out to him that there was no way the US submarines could meet Helfrich's timetable. The Dutch admiral said they could meet the timetable if they traveled on the surface. Captain Wilkes angrily countered that traveling on the surface under enemy-controlled skies was suicide. Helfrich shouted back that if US submarines took greater risks, they might be more effective.[37] The exchange was Conrad Helfrich at his absolute worst: emotional, unreasonable, unconcerned for the welfare of those under his command.

There was one interesting and underreported move. The *Java* was ordered to perform a night bombardment of the Denpesar airfield, with the *Banckert* providing illumination with starshells, and a bomber spotting the fall of shot. The effort was an attempt to silence what had now become the major source of air attacks over eastern Java.[38] It was a good concept that could have yielded some immediate albeit temporary results. But it had to be scrubbed when on February 24 the Japanese bombed Soerabaja again, leaving the *Banckert* with a hole in her stern from near misses and requiring repairs in the drydock.[39] This was yet another cut; one less ship with which to stop the Japanese. But this was a bigger loss than a single destroyer: the *Banckert* was a veteran of this new war, with a veteran crew, and had been with the Striking Force for most of the campaign. Now she could not help when she was needed most.

And that was the only way the invasion convoys could be stopped: by ships at sea. The few remaining bombers and fighters were focused on neutralizing the Denpesar airfield on Bali and the Palembang airfields on Sumatra, with little success. The remaining Catalina flying boats of Patrol Wing 10 – all three of them – were still on the job, however, and had been monitoring the progress of the convoys, determining that the Eastern Force was closer. Admiral Helfrich decided to assemble a countering force in Soerabaja with the hope that they could stop the Eastern Invasion Force with enough time to move west and destroy the Western Invasion Force. It was not really a plan with a major chance of success, but it was indeed the best one available. Helfrich ordered the Royal Navy heavy cruiser *Exeter*, light cruisers *Hobart* and HMAS *Perth*, and destroyers *Electra*, *Encounter*, and *Jupiter* to detach from the Western Striking Force to join the Eastern Striking Force to re-form the Combined Striking Force. His order contained the explanation, SACRIFICE IS NECESSARY FOR THE DEFENSE OF JAVA.[40]

But not every sacrifice. While in Batavia, the *Exeter*'s Captain Oliver Louden Gordon had taken the liberty of collecting all the merchant ships still in Tanjoeng Priok that could still move into a convoy. Then he escorted them some 50 miles outside Soenda Strait, where he told them to make for Ceylon. This move quietly saved tens of thousands of tons in Allied shipping and hundreds of lives.[41]

It would take the British warships a few days to arrive in Soerabaja. So when the *Houston*, along with destroyers *Alden*, *Paul Jones*, *John D. Ford*, and *Pope* came in as scheduled on February 24, Admiral Helfrich was as happy as he could be under the circumstances.[42] The crew of the *Houston* were less so: when Walter Winslow had asked the navigator where they were going, he responded, "Son, we're going to hell, we're going to hell."[43] Meanwhile, as the cruiser was going through the Soenda Strait on February 23, one sailor was heard to remark, "Say, didn't I just hear a gate clang shut behind us?"[44]

Captain Rooks had his cruiser berth right next to the *De Ruyter*, after which they were treated to Japanese air attacks. The attack on February 24 was particularly punishing. In addition to heavily damaging the *Banckert* and *Stewart*, the Japanese set fire to a freighter filled with rubber, the *Kota Radja*.[45] The crew of the *Houston* watched with some amusement as Dutch patrol craft tried unsuccessfully to scuttle the burning ship.[46]

It was the same theme over and over again. With the rising sun life was at the mercy of a Japanese bomb falling from the sky. No one could fix or fuel a ship because of Japanese air attacks.

But for Admiral Helfrich the issue of a commander for the Combined Striking Force was a more pressing concern than even the unremitting Japanese air attacks. Admiral Doorman had been commanding it ever since its formation, but he had not gotten results. Except for the men on his Dutch ships, no one was happy with Doorman – not the ABDA governments, not the skippers, not the officers, not the crews – and his courage and competence were openly questioned. The American seamen in particular had lost confidence in Doorman, saying that he lacked "the bayonet spirit" and viewing their combat activities so far as "sighted enemy, ran like hell."[47] That such views were unfair – they would have been slaughtered by the Japanese for no gain if not for Doorman – was irrelevant. Admiral Helfrich, Chief of Staff Admiral Palliser, and Admiral Glassford discussed the matter, and the name of Commodore John Collins, the British naval commander in Batavia, came up as a possible replacement. Glassford in particular liked Collins, who would ultimately serve with distinction.[48] But there were political considerations, and, more importantly, replacing a commander on the eve of battle is always a dangerous proposition. They would stick with Karel Doorman.

THE WESTERN STRIKING FORCE DEPARTS – FEBRUARY 26–28

With Admiral Helfrich's orders to bolster the Eastern Striking Force with the best ships from the Western Striking Force, all that was left in Tanjoeng Priok was a skeleton defense: the *Dragon* and the *Danae*, old light cruisers whose namesakes seemed no more mythical than the chances of successfully defending Java, and two equally old destroyers, *Scout* and *Tenedos*, the latter a survivor of Force Z.

Also on hand was the modern light cruiser *Hobart*. Though she had been ordered to Soerabaja, the *Hobart* could not leave with her Royal Navy consorts; she was delayed when the tanker from which she was fueling was hit by a bomb in a Japanese air attack. She was now assigned to the Western Striking Force. She was supported by the inexperienced Dutch destroyer *Evertsen*. Even on paper, this force was not impressive, with all but the *Hobart* considered so useless that even a Combined Striking Force desperate for ships did not want them. But they were all that was left. Commodore Collins would later call the Western Striking Force "a misnomer, as they had little force with which to strike."[49]

On February 26 a Royal Air Force aircraft on reconnaissance reported a fleet of 20 transports protected by cruisers and destroyers near the east coast of Sumatra, about 100 miles north of Batavia. In another example of the declining rationality of his orders, Admiral Helfrich directed this small collection of ships to leave that night to sweep the western side of Java, searching for and attacking the Japanese Western Invasion Force. This little group was ordered to do battle with Admiral Ozawa's eight cruisers, three flotillas of destroyers, an aircraft carrier, and a seaplane tender. There was no way the Western Invasion Force could even make a dent in Admiral Ozawa's armada. They would likely be slaughtered.

But under the command of Captain Harry Leslie Howden of the *Hobart*, they dutifully left Tanjoeng Priok and made their night sweep. They found nothing and, after a bombing by eight Japanese aircraft that left the *Hobart* slightly damaged, returned to Batavia at 2:20 pm on February 27 short of fuel.[50] That day, Allied aircraft reported a convoy of 30 transports escorted by four cruisers and three destroyers 55 miles south of Banka Island, but steering away from Java, towards Banka Strait. The Japanese were trying to avoid the Western Striking Force, largely because they had mistaken the *Hobart* for a battleship.[51]

The feeling was mutual, as the savvy Commodore Collins, not wanting his ships used in a suicidal gesture, was playing a very careful game. After some campaigning from Commodore Collins and Admiral Palliser, Admiral Helfrich reluctantly consented to let these ships withdraw if they did not find the Japanese. As Helfrich later explained it, the decision to withdraw these ships "was against [his] better judgment."[52] With this in hand, Collins sent a very carefully worded set of orders to Captain Howden under which his force was to make another northward sweep, but if he failed to meet the enemy by 4:30 am on February 28, he was to retire through Soenda Strait to Ceylon.[53] In fact, Collins had designed his orders to make it impossible for his ships to meet the Japanese.

In due course, the Western Striking Force did not meet the Japanese, and, except for the Dutch destroyer *Evertsen*, which became separated in a storm and returned to Tanjoeng Priok, the ships successfully transited the debris-clogged Soenda Strait and headed to Ceylon.[54] Historian David Thomas said it best in his respected book on the Battle of the Java Sea: "It is unnecessary to observe that failure to meet the enemy was a deliverance from suicide."[55] But would Admiral Doorman and his ABDA ships receive a similar deliverance?

The defense of the Bawean Islands – Doorman in conference, February 26

The man at the head of the conference table – tall, distinguished, charming, dressed in his tropical white short-sleeved naval uniform – gave the appearance of confidence. Just behind him in a corner was his chief of staff, Commander J. A. de Gelder and the skipper of his flagship, Eugène Edouard Bernard Lacomblé. There was little evidence of how draining the previous 24 hours had been for Karel Doorman.

The day before, February 25, had been eventful. Scouting reports indicated that the Japanese were coming. On February 24, PBY Catalina P-42 of Patrol Wing 10, piloted by Lieutenant John Robertson, was performing a nighttime reconnaissance flight when just before dawn he found three transports and a submarine at anchor in Makassar harbor. Robertson started his return. There was a reason why the Catalina flights were now limited only to the night: experience in this campaign had shown definitively that daytime flights for the Catalinas were too dangerous in the face of Japanese air superiority, but Captain Wagner ordered Robertson to turn around and attack the freighters, now in the morning sunlight, all the same. Dutifully, Robertson turned around, only to be met by two Zeros from the Tainan Air Group before he even reached his target.[56] AM BEING ATTACKED BY FIGHTERS, he signaled.[57] Ducking in and out of clouds, he made his attack and headed for home. At 7:16 am, while he was over the Makassar Strait, Robertson sent a plain language message, AM BEING ATTACKED BY AIRCRAFT. NORTH MANY PLANES AND FLEET.[58] Neither he nor his crew was ever heard from again. The fact that the message was not in code indicated his desperation to get this information out. It was indeed a heroic last act. The PBY had been shot down by Zeros from the Tainan Air Group operating out of Balikpapan after Robertson had stumbled across the Eastern Invasion Convoy.[59]

That same day, it was learned that an enemy advance team had landed on Batan Island, one of the Bawean Islands, some 80 miles north of the Westervarwaater to Soerabaja. They were setting up a radio station to act as a beacon. Upon orders from Admiral Helfrich, submarine *S-38* bombarded the island with her 4in deck gun, using up her entire stock of 4in ammunition.[60]

It was the occupation of Bawean that was the most immediately troubling, but it had also been calculated that the enemy convoy could, at a speed of 12 knots, reach the north coast of Madoera Island by the morning of February 26. That night, Admiral Doorman took the ships he had available, cruisers Hr. Ms. *De Ruyter* and *Java*, and USS *Houston*; and destroyers Hr. Ms. *Kortenaer* and *Witte de With* and USS *John D. Edwards*, *Alden*, *John D. Ford*, *Paul Jones*, and *Pope*. They made a sweep around Madoera Island and found nothing. By daybreak, they were back in Soerabaja's Perak Harbor, the crews exhausted after a full night at battle stations. At around 11:00 am, the Japanese welcomed them back with yet another air attack. This time, though, the Nells and Bettys got a surprise from the *Houston*'s 5in antiaircraft guns. The ammunition left over by the *Boise*, though starting to run low, had a major impact. The Japanese bombers were driven to a higher altitude and their bombing was not nearly as effective. Another bombing run that afternoon had similar lackluster results, but the crew of the *Houston* were grimly aware that they were the only ones shooting back at the Japanese. Its antiaircraft guns knocked out, the once playful, elegant, and energetic city of Soerabaja was silent. Walter Winslow said, "it was like a city of death, defended only by the *Houston*'s guns."[61]

Upon his force's return to Soerabaja, Admiral Doorman apparently flew off to see Admiral Helfrich. According to Helfrich, Doorman's surprise visit was to explain that his men were exhausted and he himself was barely coping with the situation. Helfrich's staff said Doorman looked pale and dead tired, and walked with a stoop, while Helfrich told his staff, "Doorman looked incredibly tired, too." Exhausted though he may have been, Doorman nevertheless greeted the staff on his way out. The meeting lasted less than an hour.[62]

That day the main Japanese convoy was located. A report came in that as of 11:55 am an enemy force consisting of 30 transports protected by two cruisers and four destroyers was at position lat. 04°50' S., long. 114°20' E. (near the Arends Islands off the southeast coast of Borneo) on a course 240 degrees True, speed 10 knots.[63] That is, they were not headed for Madoera, but more towards Toeban Bay west of Soerabaja. Admiral Helfrich had guessed wrong; now both his mines and his submarines were out of position. A few of the submarines were shifted west, but they would struggle to catch the convoy, which is one reason the US Navy typically does not use its submarines for close-in defense. Helfrich ordered three Dutch motor torpedo boats to be stationed off Toeban and three off Madoera.

Admiral Helfrich, now back in Bandoeng, transmitted this report to Admiral Doorman at 12:50 pm, along with orders to PROCEED TO SEA, ATTACK AFTER DARK, THEN RETIRE TOWARD TANDJOENG PRIOK. The idea was to stop the eastern convoy then head west to stop the western convoy. Subsequent to these instructions at 8:55 pm, Helfrich added a rather unfortunate order: YOU MUST CONTINUE ATTACKS UNTIL THE ENEMY IS DESTROYED.[64]

While it may seem counterintuitive, the fact is that this supplemental order was not a good one. As Admiral Frederick Sherman in his history of the Pacific War later stated, "It was utterly beyond the capabilities of the ships employed."[65] It is tempting to conclude that, once again, Admiral Helfrich was showing a lack of concern for the men under his command, and that may well have played a part here, but a more likely, albeit more charitable, explanation is Helfrich's lack of experience. An experienced officer would have realized that the major need was not to *destroy* the Japanese invasion force, though that was certainly preferable, so much as to *stop* it.

One major example from World War II relevant in showing the difference would occur just a few months later at the Battle of the Coral Sea, when a Japanese invasion convoy was forced to turn back when the aircraft carrier providing its air cover was destroyed. Using this example, a possible battle plan for the Combined Striking Force begins to emerge: attack whatever Japanese ships are encountered, either the convoy or the escorts. Without the escorts, the convoy would be forced to retire. Driving the convoy back would have at least bought the Dutch some time to assemble more air reinforcements, and might have even convinced Britain and the United States that the defense of Java was not so hopeless after all.

Unfortunately, Admiral Helfrich's orders to attack "until the enemy is destroyed" precluded such a strategy. Admiral Doorman would have to go and find the transports, spending as little effort on their escorts as possible, while those same escorts could focus their efforts on him. It amounted to a virtual death sentence for him and his ships.

They had to fight. After receiving the sighting report and his orders – and, it would seem, news of other ABDA officers leaving – Doorman telephoned Helfrich, asking, "Are we going on with the war, or are you leaving, too?" Helfrich answered, "No, there has to be a fight." Doorman responded, "Then I'm leaving tonight."[66] He seems to have spent the afternoon making preparations for this second sortie. The result was the battle plan presented at this conference to his skippers.

Merely putting this conference together took some doing. They had to use a conference room at the large private office of the ANIEM, the Netherlands East Indies Electricity

Company, because the Soerabaja naval base was untenable due to the air attacks.[67] Admiral Doorman did not want the captains to have to dive under the table at the air raid alarm. As it was, the air raid sirens went off during the meeting, but as this building was not believed to be a target, the disruption was minimal. The admiral was driven to the conference in his limousine, which he graciously shared with one of his sailors; that day was the sailor's wedding anniversary, and Doorman was having his limousine drive the sailor to see his wife.[68]

Around the conference table, on which sat a large map of the Java Sea and several smaller maps, sat most of the skippers of the Combined Striking Force: Captain Philippus Bernardus Maria van Straelen of the light cruiser *Java*, Lieutenant Commander Antonie Kroese of the destroyer *Kortenaer*, Lieutenant Commander Pieter Schotel, formerly of the destroyer *Van Ghent*, now of the destroyer *Witte de With*; Captain Albert Rooks of the heavy cruiser *Houston*, Commander Thomas Binford of US Destroyer Division 59, Lieutenant Commander Edward N. Parker of US Destroyer Division 58 and Lieutenant Commander Henry Effingham Eccles of the destroyer *John D. Edwards*. Binford's destroyers were having trouble getting fuel because the fuel lines at the Holland Pier had been ruptured by Japanese bombing, so he had Eccles represent his destroyer skippers while Lieutenant Commanders *Lewis Elliott* Coley of the *Alden*, Jacob Elliott Cooper of the *John D. Ford*, and John Joseph Hourihan of the *Paul Jones* worked on the fueling issues. Ultimately the destroyers would have to refuel from a Dutch tanker, and would not even be able to get full loads because of time constraints.

Newly arrived were the Royal Navy skippers – Captain *Oliver Loudon* Gordon of the heavy cruiser *Exeter*, Captain Hector Macdonald Laws Waller of the light cruiser HMAS *Perth*, and Lieutenant Commanders Cecil Wakeford May of the *Electra*, Eric Vernon st. John Morgan of the *Encounter*, and Norman Vivian Joseph Thompson Thew of the *Jupiter*, whose ships had just come in and made a great impression on the American sailors who had witnessed their entrance.[69] Admiral Doorman had asked them to get him their fuel requirements. He had then sent a driver to pick them up to bring them to the conference. As Gordon later told it, they "only arrived at the risk of our lives in the fastest and most dangerous motor car ride through traffic we had ever experienced."[70] Doorman greeted each of the newcomers with a cordial handshake.

Speaking English fluently, Admiral Doorman opened the conference by describing how serious the situation was and that everyone had to do their best to hold Java. The Japanese invasion they had long expected was on its way. The ships available to the Combined Striking Force were the *De Ruyter*, *Java*, *Exeter*, *Houston*, *Perth*, *Witte de With*, *Kortenaer*, *Electra*, *Encounter*, *Jupiter*, *John D. Edwards*, *Alden*, *John D. Ford*, and *Paul Jones*. He reminded them that the *Houston* had no aft turret, which made using her as the rear ship in the formation a bad idea, bringing a sheepish grin from Captain Rooks. He also advised that the boilers of the *Kortenaer*, damaged when she ran aground off Tjilatjap before the Bali operation, were still not repaired, so the speed of the force would be limited to 26 knots. Finally, *Pope* would not be able to sail with the Combined Striking

British battleship *Prince of Wales* leaves Singapore Naval Base and heads out to sea, December 8, 1941. (Australian War Memorial)

British battlecruiser *Repulse* leaves Singapore Naval Base, December 8, 1941. (Australian War Memorial)

Prince of Wales (top) and *Repulse* (bottom) maneuver under the first Japanese attack following Pearl Harbor on December 10, 1941. *Repulse* is smoking as a result of a bomb hit. (US Naval History and Heritage Command)

Repulse (top), *Prince of Wales* (middle), and destroyer *Express* (foreground) take evasive action under Japanese air attack, December 10, 1941. This picture was most likely taken during the first torpedo attack. (US Naval History and Heritage Command)

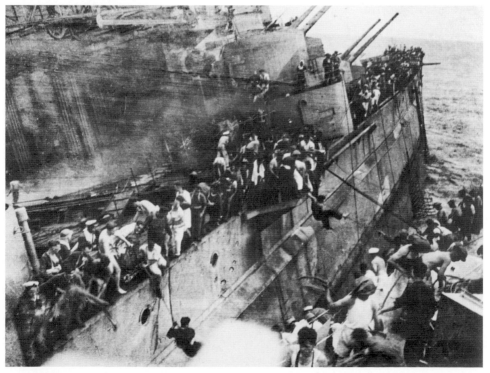

The destroyer *Express* (right) evacuates survivors from the badly listing *Prince of Wales*, who had initially waved off the destroyer, December 10, 1941. (Australian War Memorial)

Allied commanders in the Far East (right to left): US Admiral Thomas C. Hart: Hart's Chief of Staff US Admiral William Purnell, Dutch Admiral Conrad E.L. Helfrich, and British Admiral Sir Geoffrey Layton. (Koninklijk Instituut voor de Marine)

Cavite Navy Base burns after a Japanese bombing attack, December 10, 1941. Partially visible at the far right is submarine USS *Sealion*, settling by the stern. (US Naval History and Heritage Command)

Acres of charred wood and molten slag: the ruins of Cavite Navy Base following the Japanese attack. This photo was taken on December 17, 1941. The wreck of USS *Sealion* can be seen in center. (US Naval History and Heritage Command)

The scourge of Allied servicemen in the Far East: Japanese Mitsubishi G4M bomber, Allied reporting name "Betty." (Australian War Memorial)

Cruiser USS *Houston*'s aft turret (visible in the center) was disabled on February 4, 1942 by a Japanese air attack in the Flores Sea. Taken from cruiser USS *Marblehead*, which was disabled in the same air attack, *Houston* is photographed as she was towed into port, two days after the attack. The crew of the *Houston* is cheering for their shipmates on the *Marblehead*. (US Naval History and Heritage Command)

Stern of USS *Marblehead* showing the bomb damage caused by the Japanese attack of February 4, 1942. (US Naval History and Heritage Command)

Her striking appearance could not make up for her flawed design: Admiral Doorman's flagship Dutch light cruiser *De Ruyter* photographed shortly before her loss at the battle of the Java Sea. (Australian War Memorial)

The commander of the ABDA Combined Striking Force, Dutch Admiral Karel W.F.M. Doorman. Asked to do the impossible, he made saving his men a high priority. (Collection Dutch Navy Museum, The Netherlands)

Dutch light cruiser *Java*. Her aged design had her main guns scattered in single-gun mounts. (Australian War Memorial)

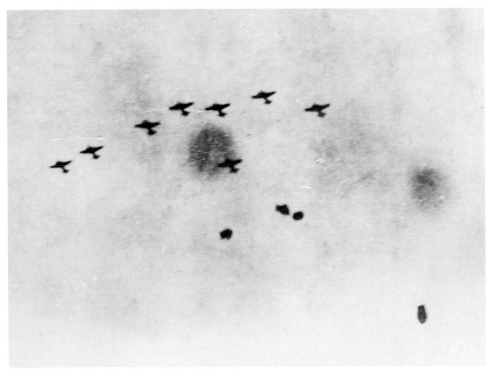

A dreaded, daily, and all-too-common occurrence for the Allies: Japanese bombers in attack formation. This photograph was taken from cruiser HMAS *Hobart*, near Banka Island, on February 15, 1942. (Australian War Memorial)

British cruiser HMS *Exeter* fires her antiaircraft guns at attacking Japanese bombers near Banka Island, February 15, 1942. (Australian War Memorial)

Japanese bomb explodes near Dutch cruiser *Java* off Banka Island, February 15, 1942. (Australian War Memorial)

Cruiser HMAS *Perth* transits the Indian Ocean on her way to the East Indies, February 15, 1942. This photograph was taken from HMAS *Adelaide*. (Australian War Memorial)

Cruiser USS *Houston* (right) and destroyer USS *Peary* (left) in Darwin Harbor, February 1942. (US Naval History and Heritage Command)

"Australia's Pearl Harbor": merchant ships *Barossa* and *Neptuna* burn in Darwin Harbor after coming under attack from Japanese Carrier Striking Force *Kido Butai* on February 19, 1942. (Australian War Memorial)

Tanker *British Motorist* (left) and hard-luck destroyer USS *Peary* (right) sinking in Darwin Harbor, February 19, 1942. (Australian War Memorial)

The Allied nemesis: Japanese heavy cruiser *Haguro*. Along with her sister ships *Nachi*, *Ashigara*, and *Myoko*, she helped destroy the Combined Striking Force. (Australian War Memorial)

America's first aircraft carrier, USS *Langley*, photographed after her conversion to seaplane tender. (US Naval History and Heritage Command)

HMS *Exeter* sinking in the Java Sea, March 1, 1942. Taken from a Japanese float plane. (Corbis)

Destroyer USS *Edsall* takes survivors off the disabled *Langley* on February 27, 1942. The photograph was taken from destroyer *USS Whipple*. (US Naval History and Heritage Command)

Modified still from Japanese film of destroyer USS *Edsall* sinking under gunfire and air attack from *Kido Butai*, March 1, 1942. The Japanese intentionally misidentified the ship in the picture as the *Pope* and murdered the *Edsall*'s survivors to help cover up their poor performance against the destroyer. The sinking was originally filmed by the Japanese cruiser *Tone*. (US Naval History and Heritage Command)

Drawing by J.H. Hoowij showing the *De Ruyter* leading the Combined Striking Force past the survivors of sunken Dutch destroyer *Kortenaer* during the night of February 27, 1942. Note the ship immediately behind the *De Ruyter*, which appears to be the USS *Houston*, reflecting the confusion still prevalent as to the events of that night. (Koninklijk Instituut voor de Marine)

Force. A weld had split in her "hot well" – a large pipe that provided fresh water to her boilers.[71] If the fresh water all leaked out she would have no engine power. While her consorts were fighting it out in the Java Sea, she would be forced to stay behind in Soerabaja – a target immobilized under Japanese air attacks because of an extended welding job.

Admiral Doorman continued. "But fortunately I have more cheerful news than these tales of damaged ships and losses. There is a possibility," he deadpanned, "that in this action we may have some fighter protection." That brought howls of bitter, derisive laughter from the men around the table. They had all heard the same thing time and again, usually only to get the stuffing blown out of them by Japanese bombers. At least they now had a ship with radar – the *Exeter* had air warning radar – so while they might not be able to do anything about the air attacks, they might at least have more warning. Doorman also told them about incoming aircraft reinforcements: P-40 Warhawks coming in on the *Langley*, to which one American skipper shook his head and muttered, "Too little, too late."[72]

The Dutch admiral went on to detail his plan. The enemy was projected to land either at the already-mined Madoera or near Toeban Bay, where a minefield was scheduled to be deployed. He did not want to make a sortie to the northward into the Java Sea because he might miss the convoy and not be able to catch up before it reached the Java shore, so they were to make another sweep to the eastward, north of Madoera Island, and then proceed toward Rembang. The British and Dutch destroyers were to form the advance screen, while the US four-pipers, much more vulnerable with their thin armor and light gun armament, would bring up the rear. "In case of contact British and Dutch destroyers were to attack at once and retire, then cruisers attack and retire, then United States destroyers come in and deliver a torpedo attack." Retirement was to be towards Tanjoeng Priok.[73]

Specifically, the British and Dutch destroyers would do their utmost to get in amongst the Japanese transports and secure as many victims as possible by gun and torpedo. The cruisers were to remain aloof from the closely engaged destroyers and transports and would endeavor to pick off enemy vessels from a distance by concentrated gunfire. Finally, the light US destroyers would employ the superior advantage of their heavy torpedo armament to sink as many transports as possible during the confusion of battle.[74] After this retirement they would go out again to deal with the western convoy.

Admiral Doorman went over the order of leaving harbor, cruising order, night recognition signals, and battle disposition, in which the cruisers would be in a column formation. At some point, either at this meeting or just before sailing, Doorman gave the verbal order that disabled ships and survivors of sunken ships were to be "left to the mercy of the enemy."[75] Because the Combined Striking Force simply had no ships to spare to help them, Doorman would have to be as ruthless as Admiral Helfrich. Or so it seemed.

Two particular features of his plan are notable and would generate critical comments. The first concerned the floatplanes from the cruisers. Because a night combat action was expected, the floatplanes would be left behind. The biggest impact would be on the SOC Seagull floatplane of the *Houston*.

Temporary disposal of floatplanes in preparation for a night battle was standard operating procedure in Allied navies. Unless a cruiser had a hangar in which to stow its floatplane – neither the *De Ruyter* nor the *Java* had hangars and the *Java* did not even have a catapult – its floatplane would be left ashore. The rationale was that a floatplane on deck was a fire hazard.[76] Any fire on deck – even a small one like burning paint – could reveal a ship's position and serve as a point of aim in the darkness for enemy guns. Accordingly, because of the expectation of combat the previous night, pilot Tom Payne had been told to hide his SOC in a swamp. After this conference he was ordered to move it to the Dutch seaplane base at Morokrembangan, where he was to remain on call to perform scouting or spotting duties.[77]

Admiral Doorman's use of the Seagull floatplane, or lack of use to be more accurate, is well known. It has been the subject of very heavy criticism since almost immediately after the end of the battle, by historians, naval analysts, and even the crews of the British and American warships. Less well known, at least in English-language media, is the fact that Doorman had attempted to arrange for a flight of US LB-30 Liberators with naval liaisons aboard to serve the Combined Striking Force. The US air commander had even agreed to the plan but was overruled by Java Air Command.[78]

Admiral Doorman's reasoning for trying to use the Liberators instead of his own floatplane will never be known, but his efforts here place the refusal to use the SOC floatplane in a new light and merit some digression.

The Consolidated LB-30 Liberator was an early model of what would become the famous B-24 Liberator heavy bomber. Bombers were frequently used for armed reconnaissance in places where the skies were contested or controlled by the enemy and thus too dangerous for thin-skinned, lightly armed seaplanes. What is unusual here was the presence of naval liaisons aboard the Liberators. This suggests that the bombers were not to be used just for armed reconnaissance, but to be under the direct control of the Combined Striking Force, as the SOC would have been. Moreover, the naval observers would have allowed the LB-30 to spot for gunnery, which the LB-30 normally could *not* do because, unlike the SOC Seagull crew, the Liberator's crews were not trained for this.

If indeed this is what Admiral Doorman was thinking – and this is only a theory – then it was a very inspired, creative idea. It would show that despite his lack of success, the Dutch admiral was nevertheless a resourceful, practical commander with a very sophisticated understanding of aviation. It is unfortunate that he could not get the LB-30s and the liaison officers. All that would be available was the SOC Seagull.

It would also suggest that, far from forgetting about the Seagull ashore, Admiral Doorman made a conscious decision not to use it. Again, the question would be why. Here it might help to recall that, unlike Japan, the United States had not placed a very high priority on floatplanes. Even before World War II the SOC Seagull biplane was considered badly obsolete (the more modern Kingfisher monoplane was also obsolete), but because no replacement had yet materialized it was still in use. Doorman had already shown that if there was no reasonable chance of success, he would not risk his men. It also helps to recall that on February 18, the *De Ruyter's* own Fokker floatplane, W-12, had been shot down during a Japanese air raid, which may have given the impression that floatplanes were helpless in the face of Japanese air superiority. Given that record, he may have thought it more likely that use of the SOC under these conditions would just result in the death of the pilot, Tom Payne, for no gain.

In addition to the disposal of the floatplane, a second issue from a historical standpoint was Admiral Doorman's battle formation, of which two elements have received close scrutiny and criticism. One was the positioning of the heavy cruisers *Exeter* and *Houston*. Typically they would have been in the rear of the column, with the light cruisers in front, so that everyone could bring their guns to bear on the enemy at the same time. Obviously, however, the *Houston* with her disabled aft turret could not be in the rear. Admiral Doorman's column led with his flagship light cruiser *De Ruyter*, which was then followed by the *Exeter*, *Houston*, *Perth*, and *Java*, in that order. Why he used this order is not clear. A possible reason is communications. Because communications were so bad, he may have wanted to keep a tighter control on his most powerful ships. It should be noted that Doorman used a similar formation in the Flores Sea and Banka Strait actions. A hint that communications were an issue in the formation was the positioning of the *Java*, with the shortest gun range of any of the cruisers, in the rear. She was the only other Dutch cruiser in the column, and would be in a position to herd the US and Royal Navy ships in the event of a breakdown in communications.

The second issue in Admiral Doorman's battle formation was insistence on keeping the American destroyers in the back of the force. He made clear that their 4in guns were ineffectual and their armor thin, but they still had very good striking power because they had the most torpedo tubes of any ship in the force. So he verbally stated that once their torpedoes were expended they were to withdraw.

Commander Eccles of the *John D. Edwards* was, to say the least, unimpressed with the substance of the conference. In an after-action report he pointed out that, "There were no common flag signals nor signal books available nor were there any tactical plans save of a most rudimentary nature." Later in that same report he would state:

It was evident that the Dutch had little tactical experience, their knowledge of communications was rudimentary and they went on the assumption that a hastily organized, uncoordinated force of ships from three navies could be assembled and taken into a major action after a one-hour conference. It is impossible for anyone who did not go to sea in the Striking Force to comprehend the utter lack, in the Dutch, of any knowledge of tactical organization and employment of a force as a unit. They were individual ship men and went to their deaths with grim foreknowledge. The Allied Force was little more than a column of strange task groups which entered the battle with a vague general directive and no specific missions."[79]

Military reports generally make for dry reading. The report of Commander Eccles, however, ranks as one of the most interesting simply because it is both well-written and colorful, tinged with sarcasm and more than a hint of understandable bitterness over the defeat in the Java Sea. His specific criticisms are not uncommon for the Java Sea Campaign, but while some of those criticisms are valid, some are misdirected and at least a few are more than slightly unfair.

The ONI Narrative effectively lists the problems and their causes:

> [The Combined Striking Force] was composed of ships of four nations which had had little opportunity of joint training or of working out common tactical doctrines. There was no opportunity to promulgate a well-considered plan of battle. Communication was inadequate and broke down completely during the battle. It was carried on by flashing light in plain English or by Dutch high-frequency radio to the *Houston*, which relayed to our destroyers. Lieut. Otto Kolb, communication officer for Commander Destroyer Squadron 29, was on board the *De Ruyter* and his work made this system possible.[80]

Indeed it did, as did the work of Signalman Marvin Edward Sholar.

Communications had always been a problem for ABDACOM in general and ABDAFLOAT in particular. Remember that ABDACOM had been put together from parts that were on-hand. This was all being done on the fly, simply because the Japanese advance offered no time. As it was, all three navies had different communications systems, which were never fully bridged. The Combined Striking Force had been at sea constantly, with its ships rotated in and out because of damage, maintenance, or convoy duty. There was simply not time to work out the communications issues. In fact, this conference was the first time Admiral Doorman had had the *Perth*, *Electra*, *Encounter*, and *Jupiter* under his command. And, by order of Admiral Helfrich, they were leaving for battle in a matter of hours. Captain Gordon of the *Exeter* admitted that the time constraints left Doorman's instructions "necessarily brief."[81] Precisely when was he supposed to fix the communications issues?

The "most rudimentary nature" of Admiral Doorman's battle plan was caused by multiple factors. One was the aforementioned lack of time training and working together. Admiral Hart, when he formed the Striking Force at the beginning of February, admitted that there would be little, if any, time for training and communications, which would necessitate keeping the tactics "simple."[82] Of this occasion Admiral Glassford would report, "The striking force was assembled hurriedly – the British units especially were engaged before proper indoctrination could possibly have been effected. It is doubtful that Doorman had opportunity to promulgate a well considered plan of action."[83] The second was the most rudimentary nature of their intelligence information. No amount of intelligence on enemy dispositions is ever enough, but ABDAFLOAT had only an idea of where the convoy was and only a very limited knowledge of its composition, especially its escorting warships. James Hornfischer, in his respected book on the *Houston*, would comment, "Karel Doorman's force would enter that fight one-eyed if not blind, and with only the dimmest sense of the forces marshaled against it."[84] It is extremely difficult to develop a detailed battle plan when you have little idea of what you will be facing. And what they did know had only been told to them a few hours before they were to go to sea. A battle plan is only there to give structure to what a force will be doing, because every battle requires deviation from that plan and even improvisation. There was always going to be more than the usual element of improvisation in this battle.

And so the conference broke up and the skippers returned to their ships. Admiral Doorman's presentation had been business-like, well-intentioned, and optimistic.[85] But the admiral returning to his flagship *De Ruyter* bore little resemblance to the confident, charming commander of just a few minutes before. The meeting may have simply been an acting job, as every good commander must do to boost morale. As he approached the gangplank to come aboard, Admiral Doorman was hunched over and looked "broken."[86] It may have been pain from the neglected dysentery that had tormented him for so long. Or it may have been that he knew this was a one-way mission. Before the *Tromp* left for Australia on February 23, Doorman had told Commander de Meester, "Jan, You still have a chance, but we will not see each other again."[87]

But an officer who has demonstrated care and consideration for the men under his command – by, for example, driving a sailor to see his wife on their anniversary – will often find that care and consideration returned, as Admiral Doorman did now. As he stepped on the gangplank, the crew of the *De Ruyter* applauded their admiral.[88]

RUN-UP TO BATTLE: THE COMBINED STRIKING FORCE SETS SAIL – FEBRUARY 26–27

The departure of the Combined Striking Force from Soerabaja took place at 6:00 pm, as sunset approached. It was a solemn event, like the departure of the *Prince of Wales* and *Repulse* from Singapore not even three months before. A throng of civilians, mostly Dutch, watched from shore as the ships sailed off, the apprehension and fear obvious on their faces.[89] These people at the docks knew what was at stake. Everything had come down to this.

And so the Combined Striking Force's sortie to defend Java in this last big climactic battle got off to a typical ABDAFLOAT start: the *De Ruyter* collided with a tug and water barge on the way out of Perak Harbor. Both the tug and barge were sunk. The force was delayed slightly. The crew of the tug was taken on board.[90]

Admiral Doorman had requested to be informed promptly of any reconnaissance reports which might come into Bandoeng. His request would be only sporadically met. At 2:45 pm, before the Combined Striking Force had even left port, he had received a report from Admiral Helfrich of two *Isuzu-* class light cruisers, two destroyers. POSITION: LAT. 06°25' S., LONG. 117°13' E., COURSE 315 DEGREES, SPEED 10–20 KNOTS. The report had come in at 2:40 pm; the delay in Helfrich getting the report and forwarding it to Doorman had been five minutes, very quick in World War II terms. It was a good start.[91]

Some time after 7:00 pm, Admiral Doorman received another report that at around 5:00 pm, a Dutch reconnaissance aircraft had been attacked by two Japanese cruiser catapult aircraft at lat. 06°05' S., long. 113°15' E., and lat. 05°40' S., long. 113°05' E. (near the Bawean Islands). The pilots had made the report upon their return to Soerabaja; the report was immediately forwarded to Doorman.

But next came a significant failure. At 6:30 pm US Army Air Force bombers attacked the Japanese convoy. They reported its course unknown, position: lat. 05°30' S., long. 113°00' E. (northeast of Bawean). At the time of the attack, the Combined Striking Force would have been emerging from the Westervaarwater. Unfortunately, the report of this attack at 6:30 pm did not reach Soerabaja until 10:20 pm, when the Combined Striking Force was approaching Sapoedi Strait, which he had set as the eastern limit to his sweep. Interception now would be difficult. Their report was immediately forwarded to Admiral Doorman, who was understandably not happy with the delay.

Upon reaching the Sapoedi Strait at around 1:30 am on February 27, Admiral Doorman turned westward. He received a clarification of the report from 2:20 pm the previous day: CONVOY LAT. 05°30' S., 113°00' E., 18 OR MORE SHIPS, 1 POSSIBLE AIRCRAFT CARRIER OR BATTLESHIP. SIX FIGHTER AIRCRAFT PROTECTING CONVOY REPORTED BY DUTCH NAVY AIRCRAFT AT 1440/26. The six fighter aircraft were likely Zeros of the Tainan Air Group operating out of Balikpapan, who had been assigned to provide air cover to the eastern convoy in the absence of aircraft carriers of *Kido Butai*.

By dawn of February 27, the Combined Striking Force, its crews having been up all night at battle stations – once again – was now west of Soerabaja near Rembang. Just before 9:00 am came the inevitable attack, not a massed one but single aircraft acting independently flying at high speed and high altitude. For reasons unknown the aircraft focused on the British destroyer *Jupiter*, dropping three bombs that missed badly. The *Houston* drove the aircraft off with her 5in guns.

It has been commonly thought that this air attack caused Admiral Doorman to end the sweep and return to Soerabaja, but upon closer examination that does not seem to be the case. Rembang had been the western limit of his planned sweep. At 9:30 am, he turned the force around to return to Soerabaja. The reversal of course coincided with the air attack, but does not appear to have prompted it. Nevertheless, by this time, Doorman had searched all night for the Japanese force and found nothing. Without surface radar, his force was restricted in its search of the big Java Sea to what they could see visually. Their reconnaissance reports had obviously been wrong and were unreliable. Worse, he was beginning to suspect that another Banka scenario was taking place, where the Japanese would keep the convoy away from him until their air power had disposed of his force. Now it was daylight, and since he had no air cover their opportunity to destroy his force was here. No doubt the normally stoic Dutch admiral was frustrated. So he would go to

Soerabaja to rest (as much as possible under repeated air attacks) and wait until he received good information on which to act. There is no telling what his reaction would have been had he known the aircraft that had bombed the *Jupiter* was a US Army Air Force B-17.[92]

The crews of the Combined Striking Force, tired as they were from being at battle stations all night, understandably attributed the withdrawal to the air attack and were disgusted. "We just turned east. Doorman just saw a plane and I guess we are headed for the barn," complained one of the bridge crew of the *John D. Ford*.[93]

Admiral Helfrich, having received Doorman's report on the air attack and his reversal of course, had drawn the same conclusion and was himself disgusted, prompting a rather remarkable exchange. He signaled: NOTWITHSTANDING THE AIR ATTACK YOU ARE TO PROCEED EASTWARD TO SEARCH FOR AND ATTACK THE ENEMY.[94] Admiral Doorman attempted to set the record straight: WAS PROCEEDING EASTWARDS AFTER SEARCH FROM SAPOEDI TO REMBANG. SUCCESS OF ACTION DEPENDS ABSOLUTELY ON GETTING GOOD RECONNAISSANCE INFORMATION IN TIME, WHICH LAST NIGHT FAILED ME. DESTROYERS WILL HAVE TO REFUEL TOMORROW.[95]

It has been suggested that during this time period of cruising fruitlessly, Admiral Doorman should have been exercising the Combined Striking Force in, at the very least, common signaling procedures, but also some common maneuvers.[96] It is a fair point, but it seems to have been made with the benefit of hindsight. The Combined Striking Force had spent the entire night and morning at battle stations in the belief that an attack, either from the air or from the sea, was imminent. Troops generally do not train on the battlefield itself in full view of the enemy. If the enemy attacked while training in signaling or in maneuvers, the result could have been disastrous.

At 12:40 pm Admiral Doorman signaled Bandoeng: PERSONNEL HAVE THIS FORENOON REACHED POINT OF EXHAUSTION. This was just a reinforcement of the decision to withdraw. Shortly after this message came yet another air attack, this not by B-17s but by eight actual Japanese bombers from the Kanoya Air Group. Once again the focus of the attack was on the British destroyer *Jupiter*, but there were no hits.[97]

About an hour later a flurry of reconnaissance reports started coming in:

1:40 pm: 20 SHIPS, UNKNOWN NUMBER OF DESTROYERS. POSITION: LAT. 04°45' S., LONG. 112°15' E., COURSE 180 DEGREES.

1:45 pm: ONE CRUISER. POSITION: LAT. 04°04' 5., LONG. 111°07' E., COURSE 220 DEGREES.

1:50 pm: GREAT FLEET WITH 2 CRUISERS, 6 DESTROYERS, 25 TRANSPORTS. POSITION: 20 MILES WEST OF BAWEAN, COURSE SOUTH.[98]

Admiral Doorman received these reports at 2:45 pm, just as the Combined Striking Force was, in two columns, entering the swept channel through the minefield in the Westervaarwater to Soerabaja.

The others ships watched with surprise as the *De Ruyter* turned around in the channel, a turn that took her into the minefield itself. The cruisers followed as Commander Binford on the *John D. Ford* who had never been confident in the alleged Dutch skill at minelaying, watched with horror, telling skipper Eccles, "Well, we are committed, there goes the *Houston* around in *Exeter*'s wake. Captain, just be sure to follow in the cruiser's wakes, being on the end of the column gives us the privilege of having the others sweep for us."[99] Fortunately, despite some anxious moments for the navigators, none of the ships hit any mines.

A message was flashed from the *De Ruyter* explaining the move: AM PROCEEDING TO INTERCEPT ENEMY UNIT. FOLLOW ME. DETAILS LATER.[100] Admiral Doorman never provided the details, but with action imminent the tired crews were filled with adrenalin.[101]

A Japanese floatplane from the cruiser *Nachi* saw the Combined Striking Force turning around. It dropped a few bombs ineffectually, but did its real damage when it reported the reversal of course.[102] Admiral Doorman asked for fighter protection and was told that none was available.[103]

And so, Karel Doorman and the American, British, Dutch, and Australian ships of the Combined Striking Force headed to sea and their fate. The crews thought they were going to lose, but they were ready for the fight, eager to dish out what they had been taking, fueled by the pent up anger from all the abuse the Japanese aggressors had dumped upon them.

The crews of the American ships were stunned to see the British unfurl the flag that they traditionally only flew in battle, the giant White Ensign, the same type of flag that had flown on the *Prince of Wales* and *Repulse* in the Gulf of Malaya. It was universally described as awe-inspiring, a point of pride for everyone.

Several of the ships also played music. Standing out in particular so that everyone could hear it was the song blaring from the loudspeakers of the *Exeter*: "A Hunting We Will Go."[104]

CHAPTER 13

NERK NERK NERK – THE SINKING OF THE *LANGLEY*

On August 24, 1912, a large hull slid down the ways at the Mare Island Navy Yard in Vallejo, California, on San Francisco Bay. After fitting out, this new ship was commissioned April 7, 1913, as the USS *Jupiter*. She was not intended or designed to be "glamorous," to earn the "glory" of fighting in war. Rather, she was intended to support other ships that were. The *Jupiter* was a collier.

She was one of a class of four colliers, the *Proteus* class, all of which were named after figures from Greek and Roman mythology: *Proteus*, *Nereus*, *Cyclops*, and *Jupiter*. These were big ships, 19,000 tons, with a forest of derricks and cranes up top to provide coal to warships. Like most supply ships, they were slow, ugly, mostly defenseless and generally disliked by their crews, but important. The fleet could not function without them.

But this *Proteus* class left a rather curious record in that three of its four ships simply disappeared without a trace, the most famous instance being that of the *Cyclops*.[1] Not the *Jupiter*, however. Far from disappearing, the *Jupiter* would leave her mark on history, though not as a humble collier.

On March 24, 1920, the *Jupiter* was officially decommissioned, not to be put in mothballs like her sisters, but to be converted into the first US aircraft carrier. She would emerge almost exactly two years later, with a new flight deck, a new designation as CV-1, and a new name, the *Langley*.

Like her namesake, Samuel Pierpont Langley, the *Langley* would blaze a trail in flight, this time with experiments in aviation at sea. For the next 14 years, hers would be a career of testing, training, and firsts – first aircraft launched from the deck of a ship in US Navy history, first carrier landing, first aircraft catapulted from a carrier. She would become a beloved ship, earning the affectionate nickname "Covered Wagon."

By 1936, the *Langley* had helped create a sound enough foundation for US naval aviation that she was no longer needed in the carrier role – in fact, naval aviation had advanced beyond what the *Langley* could offer – so she was returned to Mare Island Navy Yard for her second conversion, this time to a seaplane tender. She emerged on February 26, 1937, with a truncated flight deck and a new classification, AV-3, but the same old name, *Langley*, and the same old standard of excellence for she was immediately the best seaplane tender in the world.

The Imperial Japanese Navy had purpose-built seaplane tenders, but even they were not nearly as good as the *Langley*. Thanks to her size the former first aircraft carrier had plenty of room to stow supplies like aviation fuel, spare parts, munitions, and provisions. She had kept about two-thirds of her old flight deck, so she had space for seaplanes either on her flight deck or in the hangar beneath. She had only one major drawback: she was very, very slow. Her top speed was 13 knots, much slower than her modern or even converted counterparts.

It was the *Langley*'s slow speed which had effectively kept her out of the war, up to this point. When the war began, the tender had been immediately moved out of the Manila area towards the Indies. But unlike the other seaplane tenders of the Asiatic Fleet, the *Childs*, *William B. Preston*, and *Heron*, the *Langley* was not deployed for reconnaissance operations in the Indies. She was instead sent to Darwin.

So now the question became: what do we do with the *Langley*?

A ROLE FOR THE *LANGLEY* – FEBRUARY 10–22

Even if all the ABDA nations had pooled their aircraft at the start of the war, they still would not have had parity with the number of aircraft the Japanese had, let alone superiority. But they could have at least remained in the field, so to speak, taking losses but causing losses as well, tying up Japanese air assets and making them work for their gains.

Any chance for that disappeared when Douglas MacArthur allowed the Far East Air Force to be destroyed on the ground in the opening hours of the war on December 8. The loss of so many aircraft without causing commensurate loss or any real damage to the Japanese permanently crippled Allied air efforts in the Far East. The Japanese were now able to use the aircraft they had *not* lost in the Philippines to gain massive local air superiority at any point they chose, wiping out local air opposition and easily gaining control of the skies for ground and sea operations.

MacArthur's incompetence had left the Allied nations constantly playing catch up in the aircraft department, especially in the area of pursuit aircraft to counter the Japanese fighters. It was a tall order, because the Far East was a long way from the United States and Great Britain. The Combined Chiefs of Staff adopted the policy of sending every plane as soon as they could – right off the assembly line – and every pilot they could – immediately out of flight training.

It was extremely difficult, however. The range of an American B-17 Flying Fortress or an LB-30 Liberator allowed it to be flown from island to island. But the Curtiss P-40 Warhawk fighters had too short a range to allow for such island hopping. They had to be shipped across the ocean, usually disassembled in crates, to Australia, where they would be assembled, which could be an adventure. There might be problems locating necessary parts and tools (not to mention coolant, which was in very short supply). Reassembly also required an experienced aircraft mechanic, but such were few and far between in Australia. The ground crews of the 7th Bomb Group assembled 138 P-40s between December 23, 1941, and February 4, 1942.[2] Not all of these crewmen were experienced or even trained in aircraft assembly, but they were the best available.

As the aircraft were sent to Australia as fast as possible, so were the pilots, most of whom were fresh out of flight training. Veteran pilots of the Far East Air Force withdrawn from the Philippines took to putting the newcomers through an improvised training program in flying pursuits. The pilots were organized on the spot into provisional pursuit squadrons: the 17th, 20th, 3rd, 33rd and 13th.[3] And therein resurfaced the same problem: how do we get these squadrons to Java and the front line?

The obvious solution was to fly these aircraft to Java. The 17th Pursuit Squadron (Provisional), formed around a cadre of Far East Air Force veterans, had managed to do so, to a degree. By January 25, 13 of the original 17 aircraft had arrived in Soerabaja, where their pilots underwent more training before occupying the Ngoro base on February 1.[4] It was not perfect, but it could have been worse, as it was on the next ferry attempts to Java. Between January 29 and February 11, the Warhawks of the 3rd and 20th Pursuit Squadrons (Provisional) and A-24 Banshee dive bombers of the 91st Bomb Squadron tried to make the trip from Brisbane to Soerabaja through Darwin and the Lesser Soendas.

Flying from Darwin to Soerabaja may seem inconsequential in today's interconnected world, but for a World War II pursuit like the P-40 Warhawk, especially flown by a pilot not experienced with the Warhawk (or with fighters in general, for that matter), it could be harrowing. The pilots had to cope with weather, lack of fuel, and lack of navigational aids (as an army fighter, the Warhawk was not designed to be flown over water, so its navigational aids were simple), combined with lack of familiarity with the aircraft as many of these newly- trained pilots were flying a pursuit for the very first time with this ferry flight. The process here was just impractical, as became clear. The squadrons ended up losing 60 percent of their aircraft simply trying to reach Java. The 3rd and 20th were so beaten up that they were no longer viable as independent squadrons and were folded into the 17th. After these losses, for all practical purposes, there would be no more American fighters island-hopping to Java.[5]

But the aircraft, especially the P-40 Warhawk fighters, were desperately needed to try to counter Japanese air superiority. If the pursuits could not be flown to Java, how on earth could they get there?

The obvious solution was to ship the aircraft to Java on freighters. That came with two problems. The first was that merchant ships were slow. The second was that shipping on freighters meant the aircraft would have to be disassembled and shipped in crates, to be reassembled in Java. But constructing the aircraft could take days or even weeks, and that was with a qualified aircraft mechanic, of which there were few in Java, while the crated pursuits might even be destroyed on the ground before they could be built.

So, what to do? The British had had the aircraft carrier *Indomitable* shoot off 48 Hawker Hurricanes in January. She was supposed to make a second trip with more Hurricanes. The US Navy, however, did not have an aircraft carrier available to do that. Or did they?

Enter the old *Langley*. The *Langley* was sitting at Darwin, and she certainly looked the role of an aircraft carrier. Indeed, the Dutch submarine *K-X* had a moment of panic after mistaking her for an aircraft carrier when the *Langley* stopped in Tarakan in January. Japanese reconnaissance aircraft flying over Darwin on February 10 had identified the *Langley* as a carrier, which caused some excitement at their headquarters and probably played no small part in Japanese planning for the attack on Darwin.[6] The "Covered Wagon" still had two-thirds of her flight deck, plus her hangar – perfect for carrying fully assembled aircraft, aircraft that could be used as soon as they were offloaded. The solution was seemingly obvious: have the *Langley* bring fighters to Java.

Not so obvious was how to get the fighters to the *Langley*. Ideally, the P-40s would fly to Darwin, where the *Langley* would load them. But it was found that there was no way to get the aircraft from the airfield to the docks.[7] So, on February 10, ABDACOM ordered the *Langley* to go to Fremantle, the port of Perth, on Australia's western coast. The seaplane tender left on February 11, thereby missing the Japanese attack on Darwin.[8]

In the meantime, several pursuit squadrons were available in Australia. The 13th and the other part of the 33rd were in Brisbane, flying fully assembled fighters. On February 11, General George Brett at ABDACOM sent orders for the remainder to fly alongside the 13th – a total of 36 P-40 Warhawks – across Australia to Perth. The aircraft would be moved to Fremantle and loaded on the *Langley*.

Two other pursuit squadrons were available in Australia: the 35th, which was training at Sydney, and the 51st, which was due to arrive in Melbourne on February 1 with 33 crated P-40s. And so another piece of this improvised plan began to form. The 35th, which apparently did not have any P-40s, the 51st, and the 51st's crated P-40s would be loaded on freighters in Melbourne.

So on February 12, at 4:30 pm, the convoy designated MS-5 left Melbourne for Fremantle and then, accompanied by the *Langley*, Java. The convoy consisted of five ships. The American freighter *Holbrook* had six Warhawks from the 51st and part of its personnel complement, with the remainder of the personnel aboard the Australian freighter *Katoomba*. The Australian freighter carried the personnel of the aircraft – less 35th Pursuit. The remainder of the aircraft – 27 crated P-40s – all of the 51st's jeeps and trucks, and some 750,000 rounds of .50cal ammunition, were on the American freighter *Sea Witch*.

Escorting the convoy was the light cruiser USS *Phoenix*. A sister to the *Boise*, the *Phoenix* was ultimately supposed to relieve the battered *Houston* in the East Indies when this convoy was completed. The *Phoenix* may have had only 6in guns to the *Houston*'s 8in, but she had 15 of them; with their rapid-fire capability they could lay an avalanche of ordnance on a target very quickly.

All of these disparate elements were supposed to come together in Fremantle. On February 17, after a 2,400-mile, six-day journey across the Australian countryside – a journey made all the more exciting by getting lost, mechanical breakdowns, and landing accidents – the 13th and 33rd Pursuit Squadrons landed in Perth. The next day the *Langley* arrived, followed shortly thereafter by Convoy MS-5. Getting the aircraft from Perth to Fremantle proved to be no simple endeavor. The tail of each plane had to be tied to the bed of a truck. With little in the way of help, the pilots had to drive the trucks towing the fighters from Perth to the docks at Fremantle, with members of the 51st Pursuit's ground crew sitting in the back of the trucks to make sure that the trucks and the aircraft stayed connected. After what must have been a bizarre sight to the people of Perth, the Warhawks of the 13th and 33rd Pursuits made it to the docks on February 22, at which point they were hoisted aboard and tied down – 27 on the truncated flight deck and five on the main deck beneath.

More bizarre were the discussions taking place surrounding what was supposed to happen with the *Langley*; MS-5; and the 13th, 33rd, 35th, and 51st Pursuit Squadrons and their aircraft. An integral part of this reinforcement effort seemed to be confusion and miscommunications. Even before everyone had arrived in Fremantle, Deputy ABDACOM General Brett had changed his mind and decided that reinforcing Java following the loss of Singapore was pointless. On February 17, Brett re-routed Convoy MS-5 from Java to India.

This decision left the Dutch outraged. They desperately needed the P-40 Warhawks. But some of their anger may have been misplaced, inasmuch as the *Langley*, while she would travel with MS-5, was, in theory, not actually part of MS-5. No one seemed particularly sure, however. The seaplane tender got her orders from Admiral Glassford. Whether the Dutch government understood that is not clear. What they did understand was that the *Sea Witch* had 27 crated P-40s. After vehement protests by the Dutch, General Brett agreed to detach the *Sea Witch* with the *Langley* to go to the last remaining safe port in Java, Tjilatjap.

General Brett's order meant the inexperienced 13th and 33rd Pursuit Squadrons would go to Java, along with their 32 ready-to-fly Warhawks, in the *Langley*, with an additional 27 crated aircraft in the *Sea Witch*. This fulfilled the US commitment to the Dutch, giving them the most aircraft and the ones that could be put into action the most quickly. Meanwhile, the more experienced 35th and 51st Pursuit Squadrons and the remaining six crated Warhawks in the hold of the *Holbrook* would go to India, where they would be reequipped.

And so, at noon on February 22, the *Langley* sailed with the *Phoenix*, the *Sea Witch*, and the other ships of Convoy MS-5.[9] At the docks, an Australian army band gave the ships a sendoff with a song that, for the *Langley*, would prove all too appropriate: "Farewell to Thee."[10]

THE *LANGLEY* HEADS FOR JAVA, FEBRUARY 22–27

The skipper of the *Langley*, Commander Robert P. McConnell, was a veteran. McConnell had dropped out of the University of California at Berkeley to fly in World War I. Having earned his commission, he had worked his way up through the ranks until, only recently, he had taken command of the Covered Wagon. He had maintained the *Langley*'s reputation as a happy ship. Nevertheless many would later report a sense of foreboding concerning this mission.[11]

Commander McConnell knew the plan. The *Langley* and the *Sea Witch* were to stay with the Convoy MS-5 until February 25, when they were off the Cocos Islands. Then the seaplane tender and the freighter would break away from the convoy and make the dash to Tjilatjap.[12] Complicating matters was Japanese air superiority over Java, especially their control of the Denpesar airfield on Bali, which enabled them to attack targets south of Java in the Indian Ocean. So, the timetable for the *Langley*'s journey was very carefully set. The transit to Tjilatjap was timed so that the last 120 miles would be covered at night with the two ships due to arrive on the morning of February 28.[13] But the plan was changed almost immediately.

On the evening of February 22, Admiral Helfrich issued orders directly to the USS *Phoenix* to have *Langley* leave the convoy that night and head for Tjilatjap alone.[14] The *Sea Witch* stuck to the original schedule and left the convoy a few hours later. The decision was one of desperation. As Admiral Glassford told it, there were no more than 15 fighters left in all of Java.[15] They actually had more than that, but not many more.

Admiral Helfrich's order here would cause considerable controversy. One problem was that he had no direct authority over the seaplane tender, which fell under the command of Admiral Glassford. Theoretically, Helfrich should have ordered Glassford to order the *Langley* to break from the convoy and come in. It may seem academic but the chain of command can be very important, especially in a multinational organization like ABDACOM. An order comes from authority. With authority comes responsibility. Admiral Glassford had the authority to ask for instructions from Washington or even turn down Helfrich that Commander McConnell did not. Helfrich was essentially ordering American units without American authority.

Why would he do this? In a word, as Admiral Helfrich later explained it to Admiral Glassford: time. Glassford had simply not been immediately available to issue the order. Helfrich's order to the *Langley* moved its arrival timetable up by a day, so that the seaplane tender was still traveling the last 120 miles to Tjilatjap and arriving in the morning, but at 9:30 am on the morning of February 27 rather than February 28.[16] His story is true as far as it goes.

But, not for the first time in this campaign, Admiral Helfrich's honesty in this matter has been questioned.[17] He may well have been concerned that if he had tried to run the order through Admiral Glassford, the latter might have refused. In any event, Admiral Glassford would prove Helfrich's concerns unfounded. After Helfrich explained what he had done and expressed regret for how he had done it, Glassford agreed with the order and affirmed it.[18] And, indeed, it is hard to argue with it: the fighters carried by the *Langley* were desperately needed in Java, so it made sense to move the timetable up – if it could be done safely. So the change in orders to the *Langley* was, at worst, defensible. What followed was not.

With the *Langley* making its stately progress toward Tjilatjap at 13 knots, confusion reigned as ABDACOM disintegrated. The tender's orders would change daily. They did not yet impact the final arrival time, but they showed the first sign of the Japanese airfield at Denpesar – the big Sword of Damocles hanging over this entire operation – slipping out of Admiral Helfrich's focus. One of these changes involved meeting the US destroyers *Whipple* and *Edsall*, who would provide an antisubmarine escort into Tjilatjap, just before dawn on February 27.[19]

Protection from submarines was important, to be sure, but they were not the threat that Japanese air power was. The *Langley*'s clock was ticking. She simply *had* to arrive at Tjilatjap at 9:30 am on February 27. Any later that day and she risked air attack from Denpesar.

Tjilatjap was readying herself for the arrival of the *Langley* and her P-40 Warhawks, which was no small matter as Tjilatjap had no airfield. The plan seems to have been to use the quay, which was long and flat and ran parallel to the docks, as an improvised runway. The East Indies Army moved in to clear obstacles, such as trees, light posts, signs, shacks, crates, and parts of buildings.[20] The commotion it created in Tjilatjap was considerable, and soon the arrival of the *Langley* and her fighters was known to everyone in town – including, according to Admiral Glassford, Japanese agents.[21] But short of working only at night it is hard to see how it could have been avoided.

Meanwhile the repeated changes in orders became downright dangerous. At 1:00 pm on February 26, the tender's lookouts sighted two unidentified aircraft. Hearts stopped until it was shown they were not Japanese but Dutch Catalinas.[22] One flashed a message to the *Langley*; her antisubmarine escort, some 16 hours too early, was 20 miles to the west. Commander McConnell dutifully changed course to the west.[23]

After losing valuable time, the *Langley* came upon her antisubmarine escort: not the USS *Whipple* and USS *Edsall* as planned, but a Dutch minelayer, the Hr. Ms. *Willem van der Zaan*.[24] She and the Catalinas would provide an antisubmarine screen for the *Langley* on the stretch run to Tjilatjap. This latest change originated from Admiral Helfrich. At first glance, it does not seem like a bad idea. While designed as a minelayer and occasional training ship, the *Willem van der Zaan* was a decent antisubmarine platform, carrying both asdic and depth charges. In addition, the *Willem van der Zaan* actually had better antiaircraft armament than the US four-pipers.[25] However the *Willem van der Zaan* was having difficulties with leaking boiler tubes that limited her to 10 knots, even slower than the *Langley*.[26] If the seaplane tender stuck with this escort, her timetable for arrival at Tjilatjap would be wrecked and she would be vulnerable to air attack.

Commander McConnell decided he could not risk it. He was already dangerously behind the timetable. He informed Admiral Glassford of the issue, bailed on the minesweeper, and made for Tjilatjap.

But several hours later Admiral Glassford sent another message. He had checked with Admiral Helfrich and the *Langley's* orders were confirmed: she was to proceed to Tjilatjap with the *Willem van der Zaan* and the two Catalinas. Helfrich seemed obsessed with submarines and had completely forgotten that Japanese air power could reach south of Tjilatjap. Utterly exasperated, Commander McConnell turned his ship around, to the south, away from his destination, and toward his panting escort.[27]

The *Langley* was now a true pawn of war, being jerked back and forth as the Japanese lurked, ready to pounce. Things went from bad to worse for just as the *Willem van der Zaan* came into view, Commander McConnell received new orders: the *Langley* was to meet the *Whipple* and *Edsall* some 200 miles south of Java, as originally planned, for antisubmarine escort into Tjilatjap. By now, McConnell had to be pulling his hair out. He turned around – again.[28] Admiral Helfrich's meddling by entangling the *Langley* with the *Willem van der Zaan* had completely destroyed the timetable that had been so carefully set to avoid disaster.

Commander McConnell signaled Admiral Glassford. The original timetable was now out the window. He estimated the *Langley's* time of arrival in Tjilatjap for 5:00 pm on February 27. Because his ship would be making the most dangerous part of this trip in broad daylight, vulnerable to Japanese air attack from the Denpesar airfield, McConnell requested air cover.[29] Admiral Glassford discussed the issue with Admiral Helfrich, wondering if the *Langley's* arrival should be delayed until the morning of February 28, her original arrival date, to allow her to come in with the *Sea Witch* under cover of darkness. Helfrich said that time was of the essence; every minute counted, because the Japanese convoys were known to be approaching Java and could be landing within a day. There had not been any air attacks south of Java – yet – and 5:00 pm was too late to bomb Tjilatjap itself. He decided against any delay. Glassford concurred. Commander McConnell was ordered to press on.[30]

Admiral Helfrich, to his credit, repeatedly told Admiral Glassford the responsibility was his alone. He even ordered Glassford to tell Washington that. But Glassford, to his credit, refused to allow Helfrich to take that responsibility alone.[31] The clock was ticking down to disaster – just not the disaster they were considering.

Commander McConnell believed his ship was reasonably safe after dark. However, at around midnight the lookouts on the seaplane tender saw two series of brilliant flashes far off in the darkness off the port bow. Commander McConnell thought they looked like flashes of gunfire. He ordered general quarters and a 90-degree turn to starboard. This course took the *Langley* into a series of rain squalls that helped cover her tracks and hide her from whatever was causing the flashes. When he was reasonably certain it was safe, McConnell turned back towards Tjilatjap.[32] Though two Japanese forces, *Kido Butai* and Admiral Kondo's battleships, were operating south of Java, precisely who or what the *Langley* saw that night remains a mystery.

The sun that rose on February 27 had a decidedly less friendly appearance than it had the previous day. The morning saw a brilliantly blue sky with only a few high, scattered clouds, a light northeast wind and high visibility. A very pleasant day, in the minds of most, but not to Commander McConnell or those on board the *Langley*. Commander Lawrence Divoll, the *Langley*'s popular executive officer, would later say she "had no business being there."[33]

At about 7:20 am, the two destroyers that were supposed to be the *Langley*'s escorts, *Whipple* and *Edsall*, finally came into sight, with two Dutch Catalinas circling over them. They immediately took positions as an antisubmarine screen. And it was a good thing they did, for it turned out that there was indeed a submarine threat. The *Whipple* signaled that the *Edsall* had made a sonar contact and was holding down what she believed was a Japanese submarine. Commander McConnell ordered a course change to keep them 12 miles from the contact as they passed by. The *Whipple* moved into position between the tender and the submarine. When the contact was lost and the *Langley* had passed, the *Edsall* raced back to join her sister ship at 8:44 am and the two Catalinas to form a protective screen around the seaplane tender.[34] Now Japanese submarines would have a difficult time even approaching the *Langley*.

But Admiral Helfrich's determination that the *Langley* be protected from Japanese submarines, to the exclusion of everything else, would come with a price. At around 9:00 am, a time when the *Langley* was originally supposed to be entering Tjilatjap, lookouts sighted an unidentified aircraft at high altitude, coming from the east.[35]

Commander McConnell sent an emergency message to Admiral Glassford stating that the *Langley* had been sighted by the Japanese, expressing his belief that an air attack could be expected in two hours from land-based aircraft, or sooner from carrier-based aircraft. He also requested that fighters be sent to protect the tender.[36] But he knew that few if any fighters were available; that was the very reason why the *Langley* was making this run in the first place.

Tjilatjap was only about 100 miles away on Java, but it might as well have been a million miles away on Jupiter. Commander McConnell stood on the bridge, seething with rage at the incompetence that had just doomed his ship and his crew.[37] A pawn of war was needlessly about to be sacrificed. The skipper told Commander Divoll that it might be a good time to say something to the crew about the imminent air attack. The popular executive officer picked up the microphone: "Boys, I'm just a little bit scared. We're going to catch hell and I want everybody to concentrate and do his job. I wish you all the best of luck."[38]

LAST HOURS OF THE *LANGLEY*, FEBRUARY 27

Admiral Glassford, in his report on the Java Sea Campaign, expressed a belief that the journey and mission of the *Langley* had been betrayed to the Japanese:

> It has generally been assumed that the enemy was informed of the LANGLEY, and her mission. Her loading of assembled planes at FREEMANTLE [sic] it appeared could hardly be disguised. On my arrival later at FREEMANTLE I was made aware by the Lieutenant Governor and other

military and naval officials of other leaks of information to the enemy. It is quite possible the enemy was fully informed. That the LANGLEY alone was attacked, and the SEAWITCH [sic] unmolested may be of significance with respect to a leak.[39]

The narrative of the Java Sea Campaign published by the US Navy's Office of Naval Intelligence in 1943 is much more circumspect: "Large numbers of people knew that the work had to be completed by a certain time. The voyage of the *Langley* and the date of her expected arrival were no secrets."[40]

Under this theory, the *Langley* was subject to an aerial ambush, similar to what the US military arranged for the Japanese seaplane tender *Nisshin* the following year off Bougainville.[41] But though the theory happens to fit the facts, there is little in the way of evidence to support it.[42]

What is known is that a Japanese submarine had spotted the *Langley* the previous day en route to Tjilatjap. Her contact report generated considerable excitement among the Japanese, understandable since the submarine had identified the *Langley* as an aircraft carrier.[43] With her flight deck filled with aircraft, the *Langley* certainly looked like one. The unidentified aircraft following up on that contact report had been a Kawanishi flying boat of the Takao Air Group operating from Denpesar on Bali.[44] Sixteen Mitsubishi G4M bombers, the Bettys that had been murderous so far, took to the air, escorted by 15 Zeros of the 3rd and Tainan Air Groups.[45]

The timing worked just as Commander McConnell had anticipated. At 11:40 am the *Edsall* signaled AIRCRAFT SIGHTED.[46] Due to antisubmarine measures the *Langley* was zigzagging on a base course of 357 degrees True, almost due north.[47] He ordered battle stations. Within moments the skipper was told, "All guns report manned and ready."[48] For whatever that was worth. The *Langley*'s armament was almost prehistoric. She had four 5in guns, two on the forecastle and two on the stern under the flight deck, but they were only for surface gunnery and were useless in an antiaircraft role. She had four World War I-vintage 3in antiaircraft guns on the flight deck, but they were similar to the ones that had proven so useless at Cavite – they could only reach targets of 12,000ft or less and they had a slow rate of fire of four rounds per minute. The *Langley* also had four .50cal machine guns, which were similarly useless against aircraft at high altitude. Finally, and bizarrely, she had men stationed on the flight deck prepared to use the Browning Automatic Rifle (BAR) as an antiaircraft weapon. The fire control system for the *Langley*'s guns consisted of a group of sailors inside a circle of sandbags on the flight deck with a jury-rigged device.[49] In short, the *Langley* was virtually defenseless. All she could do was maneuver wildly and hope the bombers were inaccurate.

NERK NERK V 1MCZ 1MCZ BT AIR AIR RAID RAID, signaled the wireless telegraph in the Langley's radio room.[50] "Nerk" would be interpreted as "air raid."[51]

There would be a lot of "nerks" over the next few hours and, for that matter, the next few days. The radio room of the *Langley* would give play-by-play and color commentary for the disaster that followed.

Standing on the signal bridge, which was an open area on top of the actual bridge structure, Commander McConnell saw the Bettys swing around the starboard quarter to approach from directly astern at an altitude of 15,000ft. It was a standard bombing tactic. He ordered his guns to open fire.

Through his binoculars, Commander McConnell watched the approach of the first flight of seven Mitsubishis, divided into two Vs of three aircraft each with the seventh tucked in behind the second V. The flight was under the command of Lieutenant Tanabata Yoshinobu of the Japanese Naval Air Force.[52] Tanabata and his pilots ignored the antiaircraft fire from the *Langley* and her escorts – it was too low to hit them in any case – and concentrated on their bombing run. So did McConnell.

As the aircraft approached, the skipper of the *Langley* tried to gauge when the bombs would be coming by the angle of the bombers' elevation, at which point he would throw the rudder. But when they had reached 80 degrees elevation over the flight deck, Commander McConnell could wait no longer. "Hard right rudder!" he barked. The Covered Wagon veered to starboard, and the seven 250kg (550lb) bombs dropped by Lieutenant Tanabata's flight fell some 100ft off the port bow sending up towering columns of water. McConnell had guessed correctly.[53]

NERK NERK V 1MCZ 1MCZ BT AIR AIR RAID RAID/WE OK.

Two of the bombs were so close that the *Langley* shook "like a dishrag" and was sprayed with splinters and shrapnel.[54] Shock waves ruptured hull plates and sent tons of water flooding into the *Langley*'s engine rooms. There, a potentially catastrophic problem developed. The concussion from the bombs had ruptured the lines for the fire and bilge pumps. As seawater poured in, the pumps could no longer keep pace with the flooding. It might not be that significant a problem on another ship, but the *Langley* was both blessed and cursed by design. She was the first US Navy ship to have electric drive propulsion, but those motors were located in the lowest part of the ship, in open box-like structures called motor pits. If the flooding continued, eventually it would reach the top of the motor pits and force the shut down of or even flood the motors themselves. And the *Langley* would be immobilized and completely helpless. To compound the problem, damage control could not locate the source of the leak in the hull.[55] The damage report added to Commander McConnell's feeling of dread.

But the skipper had other, more pressing matters to deal with, such as the approaching second flight of nine Bettys. These were under the command of Lieutenant Adachi Jiro. Adachi had watched Lieutenant Tanabata's attack and made some observations. First, the antiaircraft fire of the *Langley* and her escorts seemed to be topping out well below his altitude of 15,000ft, so they had reached their maximum altitude and therefore need not concern him. Second, there was no evidence of enemy fighters in the vicinity. Third, this American captain was good. Very good. His late twist had thwarted Tanabata's attack. Adachi had better be at his best.[56]

The Japanese Naval Air Force pilot organized his flight of Bettys into three Vs of three aircraft each, one following another. It was a repeat of the first attack, lining up on the *Langley*'s stern. When they had reached 80 degrees elevation over the flight deck, Commander McConnell barked, "Hard left rudder!" The Covered Wagon swung to port.[57]

But no bombs fell. At the last minute, Lieutenant Adachi had realized his approach was too fast and he overshot his bomb release point.[58] Adachi led his flight around to make another pass at the *Langley*.

Again they came from astern, this time at the slowest speed Lieutenant Adachi could manage. The slow speed apparently convinced Commander McConnell that he needed to try something different. As the Bettys got close to their release point, McConnell had the *Langley* veer to port. Adachi's aircraft adjusted. Then, McConnell ordered the rudder thrown to starboard.[59] It was too early by just a fraction of a second.

Lieutenant Adachi's flight dropped its nine 250kg (550lb) bombs. Five hit the *Langley* and three just barely missed. It would prove to be "the most accurate or the luckiest" high-level attack by Japanese bombers against ships at sea during the Pacific War.[60] The ONI Narrative was even more blunt: "Seldom has a ship been hit more severely by one salvo."[61]

NERK NERK NQO NQO V NERK NERK BT *LANGLEY LANGLEY* BEING BEING ATTACKED BY SIXTEEN AIRCRAFT 0435 K.

One hit was forward and severed power lines. The second and third hits were on the port side of the flight deck near the elevator, setting afire the P-40s parked under the flight deck and engulfing the port side beneath the flight deck in a fire that caused more P-40s to explode. A fourth was on the port stack sponson, its detonation sending up shrapnel and debris that tore through even more P-40s. The fifth bomb penetrated the flight deck aft, jamming the rudder 35 degrees to starboard and setting another large fire that cooked off the ready 3in antiaircraft ammunition, causing yet another large explosion that blew crewmen clear off the ship.[62]

In response the ONI Narrative described the devastating results of Lieutenant Adachi's bombing run:

Aircraft on deck were burning, there were fires below deck, fire mains were broken, the ship was taking water forward and was listing 10 degrees to port. But she could still be steered and her engines were still running in spite of the water rising in the engine room.

"The ship was maneuvered to obtain a zero wind" and the fires were somehow put out. The shattered planes on the port side were pushed overboard and counterflooding was carried out in an attempt to correct the list. It was useless; water continued to rise in the engine room and the list was increasing.

NERK NERK NERK ... GOT A HIT ON THE FOCL [FORECASTLE THAT PUT US

OUT FOR] A FEW MINUTES … LOST LOCAL CONTROL … TRANSMITTER WENT
OUT BUT I PLUGGED IN RAK RAL BATTERIES AND AM BACK NOW.

The radio room had lost power with the first bomb and had switched to batteries, but
within a few minutes their power was restored.[63]

The *Langley* was in bad shape, but she still had what appeared to be undamaged P-40s
on what remained of her flight deck. That was enough for Lieutenant Yokoyama Tamotsu.
His flight of six Zeros from the 3rd Air Group made two strafing runs on the battered
wagon, ripping up the remaining aircraft on the flight deck with 20mm cannon fire.[64]

The Japanese fighters then turned their attention to the *Langley*'s escorting Dutch
flying boats, or at least what they thought were the *Langley*'s escorting flying boats. In a
midair tussle that even Commander McConnell observed, the Zeros shot down an
unarmed four-engine civilian flying boat that had been chartered by the US Army Air
Force to make runs between Java and Broome, Australia. They also shot up the Dutch
PBY Y-65, which managed to stagger back to Tjilatjap with such severe damage that she
was written off as a total loss. But it would be fair to say that the slow, lumbering Dutch
Catalina got the better of that exchange, managing to shoot down one Zero flown by
Sakai Toyo-o.[65] After this exchange, the Japanese withdrew.

The radio room got philosophical:

NERK NERK NERK WE ARE ALL OK SO FAR … MAMA SAID THERE WOULD BE DAYS
LIKE THIS … SHE MUST HAVE KNOWN … HIT ON FLIGHT DECK ON PLANES AND
ONE ON WELL DECK ONE ON FOCL … GAS FUMES ON THE WELL DECK.

Damage control had managed to contain the fires, but the portside list was threatening to
literally upend everything. The *Langley* had been constructed not as a warship but as an
auxiliary and thus did not have the interior compartmentalization common to most
warships that could limit flooding. Moreover, the addition of the flight deck made her top
heavy. That the flight deck was currently holding hundreds of tons of aircraft – now
wrecked – made her even more top heavy.[66] She was in serious danger of capsizing.

As a precautionary measure, Commander McConnell had given orders to prepare to
abandon ship. The operative word here was "prepare," but in the chaos the operative word
was not heard and men began to jump overboard. Others had been blown overboard by
explosions or forced to jump by the fires. The destroyer *Edsall* saw what was happening
and carefully moved in to fish men out of the water.[67]

Commander McConnell on the bridge now realized the *Langley* was slowing down.
Sure enough, word came from the engine room: the motor pits had flooded. The engines
were now offline.[68]

NERK NERK NERK JAP PLANES WERE … TOO HIGH FOR OUR GUNS … WE
HAVE A DECIDED LIST … POWER OFF ON SHIP AC TO BATTERIES.

Commander McConnell considered his situation. His mission was obviously a failure, though, it should be emphasized, through absolutely no fault of his own. Most, probably all, of the P-40 Warhawks were destroyed. The *Langley* was still some 75 miles south of Tjilatjap, the only port within a reasonable distance. The seaplane tender had no propulsive power and was immobilized. McConnell wanted to head for Java and beach the ship, but her rudder was jammed hard over so even if she could move, it would be only in circles.[69] Even if there were seagoing tugs in Tjilatjap, it would take them some ten hours to reach the stricken ship. His destroyers might be able to tow the *Langley* to port, but the flooding had left her too deep in the water for the shallow channel to Tjilatjap's harbor.[70] Damage control could not stop, indeed could not even locate the source of, the flooding. In fact, the flooding was coming from multiple small breaches of the ship's hull on the port side.[71] The *Langley*'s list and progressive flooding suggested a capsize was imminent. The Japanese could return at any moment to kill the crew and sink or even capture the ship. It was heart breaking, but the necessary course of action was clear.

NERK NERK NERK THE JAPS ARE JAMMING US AS MUCH AS POSSIBLE … WE ARE SECURING SOON … THE SHIP IS LISTING … SHOT TO HELL.[72]

At 1:32 pm, Commander McConnell gave the order to abandon ship.[73] This time, there was no misunderstanding. The crewmen rushed over the sides but were by no stretch of the imagination panicked or disorderly. The destroyers were ready for rescue operations, standing by with nets deployed and knotted ropes over the sides for the swimming men to grab, *Edsall* on the *Langley*'s port side and *Whipple* to starboard.[74]

NERK NERK NERK SIGNING OFF PER LEL CRM.[75]

A few officers and chiefs made their way around the ship making sure it was now empty. Commander McConnell himself oversaw the destruction of the *Langley*'s top secret documents – code books, charts, logs, maps – which were burned or weighed down and dumped overboard. Her radios and decoding machines were also dumped overboard.[76] After that was completed, McConnell then ordered his own senior staff to evacuate. They noticed he was making no move to join them. In fact, Richard McConnell, heartbroken over the fate of his ship, was determined to go down with her. The officers refused to leave until he did. Moved by their concern for his well-being, McConnell relented and joined them in abandoning ship.[77]

Aboard the *Langley* had been 484 officers and men, including 33 pilots and 12 crew chiefs of the Army Air Force. The Takao Air Group's attack had left a grand total of seven killed, five missing and 11, including two pilots, wounded.[78] Though the casualties were all individual tragedies whose significance merits recognition, the total count was miraculously low. The major reason so many lives were saved was the skillful rescue work done by the destroyer *Whipple*, under the command of Lieutenant Commander Eugene

S. Karpe, and the destroyer *Edsall*, commanded by Lieutenant Joshua J. Nix. It was their amazing performance of this delicate and painful task that gave so many men hope to be returned to the front and eventually to their families.

With their rescue work completed, the destroyers' final task was to ensure that the sinking *Langley* did actually sink. However the Covered Wagon was presenting the paradoxical spectacle of a sinking ship that refused to sink. In fact, she was going down very, very slowly. Too slowly. At 2:28 pm, the destroyer *Whipple* fired nine 4in shells at the tender's waterline to no effect. On a suggestion from Commander McConnell, at 2:32 pm she fired a torpedo into the *Langley*'s starboard side near the stern, hoping the aft magazine would detonate. It didn't; in fact, the seaplane tender now seemed to right its portside list and came to an almost even keel. The *Whipple* moved around to the port side and fired one more torpedo. This one started a massive fire aft and the *Langley* began to settle lower into the water. But she still did not sink.[79]

It was feared that the Japanese could reappear at any time. With the destroyers, inadequately armed for air defense, now packed with *Langley* survivors to the point where they were practically bursting, the situation was increasingly dangerous. Commander E. C. Crouch, commander of Destroyer Division 57, decided that they could not wait for the stubborn tender to take its final plunge. At 2:46 pm, the *Whipple* and *Edsall* with the survivors cleared the area at high speed, going off to the west. Commander McConnell signaled Admiral Glassford to this effect.[80]

Left behind was the USS *Langley*, America's first aircraft carrier, an amazing ship that had done everything asked of her, forlorn and alone in her dying moments.

At the request of Commander McConnell, Admiral Glassford sent the gunboat *Tulsa* and the minelayer *Whippoorwill* out from Tjilatjap to search the area for survivors and confirm the *Langley*'s sinking.[81] They found nothing. Later that evening a Dutch PBY reported that the *Langley* had indeed finally sunk.[82]

Unknown to the suffering men of the *Langley* and her escorts, while the Japanese had been ruining the seaplane tender's desperate mission with her precious cargo, back on Java, there had been a massive argument over giving the *Langley* some semblance of aerial protection. In Bandoeng, Major General van Oyen, the head of the optimistically titled Java Air Command, had been told that the *Langley*'s arrival had been delayed to the point where she would arrive in the daytime. Worried about her vulnerability to air attacks, he asked General ter Poorten about getting the *Langley* some air cover. His request was denied. Furious, van Oyen protested to no avail.[83]

The last remaining operational fighters on Java had been combined and organized at the Ngoro airfield. The 14 remaining serviceable P-40 Warhawks of the 17th Pursuit Squadron (Provisional) had been reinforced by seven Dutch Brewster Buffalos and six Dutch Hawker Hurricanes.[84] But they could not be and were not used to protect the *Langley*.

They had another, even more critical mission.

CHAPTER 14

ONE SHELL – DAY ACTION OF THE BATTLE OF THE JAVA SEA

THE SCENE IS SET – FEBRUARY 27

The campaign to conquer the Southern Resources Area had not been perfect, but it had so far exceeded the Imperial Japanese Navy's most optimistic hopes. The campaign was ahead of schedule and losses had been minimal. It would be unfair to say that the Combined Fleet had crushed enemy resistance, but only because the enemy had so rarely been able to even offer resistance.

Four times ABDA naval forces had sortied to contest Japanese landings. Twice they had been turned back by air attack – in the Flores Sea and in the Banka Strait – before coming anywhere near the landing forces or their escorts. Once – off Bali – they had arrived too late and been too scattered to stop the landings or even cause much damage. Only once – off Balikpapan – had ABDA forces been able to effectively strike back against the Japanese. Balikpapan was the only significant blemish on a performance that had, so far, been nothing short of spectacular. And even that blemish was minor; Japanese operations at Balikpapan had been delayed by only a single day at the most.

But Commander Hara Tameichi and his superior, Rear Admiral Tanaka Raizo, were not ones to take anything for granted. Scout aircraft had reported that ABDA naval forces were coming, in their strongest numbers yet, to try to stop the Japanese landings on Java. Hara and his ship, the destroyer *Amatsukaze*, were ready; Hara was certain Tanaka was also ready, but he knew they were in the minority.

For the relatively unimpeded string of victories had allowed arrogance, overconfidence, and sloppiness to begin slowly seeping into the Japanese naval war effort. This had started back in Japan on Admiral Yamamoto's current flagship *Nagato*, sitting rather uselessly in Hashirajima anchorage. Yamamoto had reached the conclusion that the ABDA ships that had been massing in Soerabaja were "no potential threat" to the Japanese advance. He would go on to declare that the landings on Java "[did] not require the support of a major task force," which was why he had pulled the Carrier Striking Force away from covering the landings. Yamamoto later said the ABDA fleet was "completely demoralized" and "no longer in shape to attempt any major action."[1]

This attitude had rapidly permeated the Combined Fleet. The object of the Imperial Navy's protection – and the Combined Striking Force's sortie – was the Imperial Japanese Army's 48th Division crammed into a convoy of 41 troop transports in two columns, with 600m (650yd) between ships and 2,000m (2,200yd) between columns, zigzagging at 10 knots to avoid the ABDA submarines that Admiral Helfrich had already moved out of their path. Actually, calling these ships "troop transports" is perhaps a little misleading. Most of these ships were civilian, with civilian captains who were neither used to nor particularly happy about being under military authority.[2] The Japanese could spare only two destroyers to directly shepherd the convoy, making sure all the ships got their orders and executed those orders properly, preferably without colliding with each other.

Moreover, the transports were not taking this operation seriously, at least in the eyes of Commander Hara:

> The 20 mile long convoy was quite a spectacle. An obvious laxity prevailed in the transports with their ill-trained crews. Many transports emitted huge clouds of black smoke from their funnels. Many used their radios in violation of "no transmission" orders, or failed to observe blackout rules at night.[3]

The Combined Fleet had put together an escorting force to protect the Eastern convoy from ABDA interference, but it was not nearly as strong as it could or perhaps should have been. The Japanese convoy of 56 transports assigned to land in western Java, for instance, had an escort centered on the four oversize heavy cruisers of the *Mogami* class, and air cover in the form of the carrier *Ryujo*. The eastern convoy, by contrast, had no aircraft carriers and minimal air cover; in theory it was supposed to have fighter protection from Balikpapan, but no one ever saw any fighters – ultimately, the weather over Balikpapan was too bad for the Tainan Air Group to provide the requested air cover – and Balikpapan was too far away to provide effective fighter cover in any instance. The convoy did have 18 warships as escorts, centered on only two older heavy cruisers. The disparity was odd, since the eastern convoy was nearer to the main ABDA naval base at Soerabaja and thus more likely to face resistance.

It was not the Imperial Japanese Navy's style to have these 18 ships merely guard the convoy and sweep aside resistance. In typical Japanese fashion, these 18 ships were divided three ways, this time along unit lines. Admiral Tanaka was commander of the Japanese 2nd Destroyer Flotilla, consisting of his flagship, the light cruiser *Jintsu*, and, for now, only four destroyers.[4] Also present was the veteran Admiral Nishimura, the possessor of the lone Japanese defeat during this campaign, and his 4th Destroyer Flotilla, with the light cruiser *Naka* and six destroyers.[5] Forming the backbone of the escorting force were the heavy cruisers of Rear Admiral Takagi Takeo's 5th Cruiser Division.

Part of the problem for the Japanese here was organizational, the result of prior operational decisions that made little sense. The 5th Cruiser Division normally consisted of three of the four heavy cruisers of the *Myoko* class: the *Myoko*, *Nachi*, and *Haguro*. The *Myoko*s were somewhat older ships but each was still the typical Japanese heavy cruiser – with the characteristic raked funnel and low profile, giving it a sleek appearance, backed up by a high top speed of 34 knots. Their armament consisted of ten 8in guns and 16 fixed torpedo tubes (eight on each side) capable of firing the devastating Type 93 "Long Lance" torpedo, the armament that made the Japanese heavy cruiser, pound-for-pound, the most dangerous warship in the Pacific.

And here was where the Combined Fleet's decision-making showed signs of carelessness. The fourth member of the class, the *Ashigara*, had been designed and designated as a fleet flagship, which was precisely how she was employed in this operation as flagship for Admiral Takahashi Ibo, commander of the 3rd Fleet or, as designated in this campaign, the "Eastern Striking Force." In December, the *Myoko* had, as usual, been the flagship of the 5th Cruiser Division, but she took a bomb hit off Mindanao and returned to Japan for repairs. When these were completed, however, the *Myoko*, now designated the "Second Section of the 5th Cruiser Division," was assigned to pair with the *Ashigara*. Together these two cruisers were to serve as "distant support" for the invasion. The *Ashigara* and *Myoko* would play no role in the battle this day.

The arrogance and overconfidence typified by the Japanese use of the *Ashigara* and *Myoko* was personified by the commander of the 5th Cruiser Division (less Second Section), Rear Admiral Takagi Takeo, the Officer in Tactical Command of these three forces escorting the convoy. Though Takagi had commanded surface ships for several years, he was trained and had spent most of his career as a submariner. Perhaps that training and service history explain some of Takagi's rather curious actions.

Nicknamed "King Kong," Takagi Takeo was, as described by historian Arthur Marder, "A stout, broad-shouldered, round-faced officer, friendly, down to earth, easy to work with, and morally courageous. He was a brilliant torpedo specialist and submariner, but not a naval tactician. Neither was he a leader – a commanding officer prepared to take the initiative."[6]

However by his description of Takagi's actions in his book *Japanese Destroyer Captain*, Commander Hara would paint a very different picture of the admiral's personality – arrogant, overconfident, sloppy.

It began with Admiral Takagi's method of escorting the extremely important and vulnerable convoy, whose destination was Java, the final major objective for which Japan had started the war. He had left Kendari with the *Nachi*, *Haguro* and their four escorting destroyers on February 24. He was supposed to rendezvous with the convoy, but he was, to use Commander Hara's description, "haughtily" following the convoy some 200 miles away, seemingly in no particular hurry to catch up and, in a rather unique tactical choice, content to guard the convoy from this position.[7] "[E]xhibiting the supercilious leisure of a triumphant fleet," was how *Houston* historian James Hornfischer would describe it.[8] Nor was that all.

Like Admiral Yamamoto and many others, Admiral Takagi seems to have completely dismissed the possibility that the ABDA forces might actively resist his invasion force. He had been informed of the Combined Striking Force's sortie that morning, but was rather sanguine about it, only launching the *Nachi*'s floatplane to keep an eye on the enemy ships and ordering the convoy to temporarily turn around to the north (more work for the harried destroyers with the convoy) to keep clear of them.[9] When on February 27 at 3:10 pm the *Nachi*'s aircraft reported that the ABDA ships were returning to Soerabaja, well after the daily Japanese air attacks on the city, Takagi laughed. "The enemy ships were merely staying clear of our air raids on [Soerabaja]. The enemy is in no shape to fight us. We will stick to our original plan and schedule. The [convoy] will turn and head south again."[10]

However, at 4:30 pm, the *Nachi*'s scout aircraft radioed, THE ENEMY FLEET HAS TURNED AROUND AGAIN. THE DOUBLE COLUMN FORMATION IS NOW SHIFTING TO SINGLE COLUMN. THE ENEMY IS GAINING SPEED AND IS HEADED ON A COURSE OF 20 DEGREES. At 4:40 pm came another: "THE ENEMY SPEED IS 22 KNOTS. IT IS HEADED DIRECTLY FOR OUR CONVOY."[11]

At this point Admiral Takagi ordered the convoy temporarily to turn around – again – which left Hara disgusted as he noted, "Many [in the convoy] were baffled at the repeatedly changing orders and they were unable to respond quickly."[12] Takagi then had the *Nachi* and *Haguro* launch their floatplanes to keep watch over the incoming ships, ordered his own warships into, as Commander Hara called it, "fighting formation," and – finally – had the *Nachi* and *Haguro* increase their speed to catch up.

Commander Hara was concerned – Takagi's absence meant that Hara's unit was effectively on point, about to be forced to face the ABDA force of five cruisers and nine destroyers with only *Amatsukaze*, three other destroyers, and one light cruiser.

That one light cruiser was the *Jintsu*, Admiral Tanaka's flagship. In contrast to the sleek, graceful, almost artistic Japanese heavy cruisers, Tanaka's flagship, like her sister ship *Naka* and most other Japanese light cruisers at this point in the war, was blocky, tall, and ugly, with straight funnels and an awkward-looking bridge tower. Also like most other Japanese light cruisers, she had been designed as a "destroyer leader," flagship for a flotilla of destroyers. Her gun power was somewhat lacking with only seven 5.5in guns – she was outgunned by the *De Ruyter* – but she also had eight torpedo tubes in two rotating quadruple mounts, making her a dangerous foe, particularly when leading her destroyers – but not so dangerous that she could take on a force of five cruisers and nine destroyers and expect to survive victorious.

Later in the war Tanaka would make it a habit of overcoming such long odds, becoming one of the most brilliant naval commanders of the war and, with his flagship *Jintsu*, a nemesis to the US Navy, but he was a careful and capable commander who did not seek such odds.[13]

Commander Hara had spent the last few hours nervously looking out the bridge windows ahead of him, watching for the arrival of the enemy, and turning around to see if Takagi's cruisers had finally arrived behind him. "Without [the *Nachi* and *Haguro*] I did not see how we could fight the powerful enemy fleet," he later wrote.[14]

Nevertheless, like any good knight of Bushido, he had prepared himself to face those odds. He would fight to the best of his ability, would fight to the end – an end that seemed much closer when the bridge spotter shouted "Enemy ship," pointing to a weird, dark shape that had appeared over the southern horizon. Some of the Japanese thought it looked like a creature from Mars – which it was, of a sort – or the head and long neck of some prehistoric monster of the sea, a dinosaur slowly emerging from the depths to wreak havoc on the surface. The head kept rising out of the water, eventually revealing itself to be not some ancient menace, but a modern one – the ominous tower mast of the *De Ruyter* – some 20 miles to the south.[15] Japan's enemy had arrived.

This was it. Commander Hara looked behind him. Nothing. He shouted, "Gunners and torpedomen, get ready. Our target is the lead cruiser in the enemy column!" But shortly thereafter, at 5:30 pm, the bridge spotter shouted again. "Commander, look! *Nachi* and *Haguro* there!" Over his destroyers he could see a pair of masts and funnel smoke plumes just starting to peak above the eastern horizon.[16] The good luck of the Japanese – and the bad luck of the Dutch – had held. The *Nachi* and *Haguro* had arrived.

Hara Tameichi could now breathe a little more easily.

ATTACK AND COUNTERATTACK

It started with the seaplanes – as it always did – the harbingers of doom.

The destroyer *Electra* and her cohorts in the van of the Combined Striking Force, heading on a course 315 degrees True, saw the seaplanes – the floatplanes from the *Nachi* and *Haguro* – at 4:00 pm, flying in from the northern horizon to hover over the Allied ships out of antiaircraft range.

These two opposing forces looked relatively equal on paper, the Combined Striking Force with two heavy cruisers, three light cruisers, and nine destroyers; the Japanese eastern convoy's escort with two heavy cruisers, two light cruisers, 14 destroyers – and a few floatplanes.

But the two sides were in fact far from equal for a variety of reasons:

8in guns – the *Nachi* and *Haguro* each carried ten 8in guns in five dual turrets. The *Houston* nominally had nine 8in guns in three triple turrets, but with her aft turret out she had only six. The *Exeter* had six 8in guns in three dual turrets. So in terms of the most powerful rifle on this battlefield, the Japanese outnumbered the Allies 20 to 12.

Torpedoes – the cruisers and destroyers of the Japanese escort force carried a combined 144 torpedo tubes, 138 of which fired the legendary Type 93 "Long Lance." The Combined Striking Force only had 100 tubes, 48 of which were on the ancient US destroyers.

Speed – the slowest of the Japanese ships was rated for 33.8 knots. In contrast, because the *Kortenaer*'s speed was limited as a result of her grounding and the consequent boiler damage, the Combined Striking Force was limited to 26 knots – and the elderly US destroyers could barely keep up with that. The situation was highly unusual; as Hornfischer would note, "Destroyers were called many things ... but never albatrosses."[17] Except today.

Age – the oldest of the Japanese ships was the destroyer *Harukaze*, completed in 1922. All the remaining Japanese destroyers had been completed in the 1930s and were top-of-the-line, *Fubuki*-class or later. All the Japanese cruisers had been completed in the mid- to late 1920s, but they had been extensively modernized. For the ABDA navies, the *Java*, with her poor compartmentalization and single unenclosed gun mounts, had been obsolete before she had even finished fitting out in 1925. The US destroyers, completed in 1919–20, had thin armor, three unenclosed 4in gun mounts each, and extremely poor antiaircraft armament. Although the *Exeter* had radar, it was air search radar, useless for tracking surface ships.

Maintenance – the Japanese had been able to maintain their ships properly from secure bases. The ABDA ships had been desperately trying to stop the Japanese advance and had little time to perform repairs or essential maintenance. Worse, their primary base and repair facility at Soerabaja had been under daily air attack from Japanese bombers based in Kendari and Bali. So like a football team going into a playoff game with most of its players having nagging injuries, the ships with which the Combined Striking Force went into battle were a battered lot. The *Houston*'s aft turret could not be repaired. The *Exeter* was having fire control problems generally and train issues with her own aft turret. The *Kortenaer* was slowed by her damaged boiler. The American destroyers all suffered from leaky condensers, old boilers, and bottoms biofouled with such annoyances as barnacles that could slow them down.

Crew conditions – the Japanese sailors, riding high on a wave of victories, had been able to rest and recuperate from action in safe ports under Japanese-controlled skies. In contrast, the Allied crews, like their ships, were exhausted – constantly moving to stop the Japanese advance, frequently called to battle stations to fend off Japanese air attacks, and their home base under daily Japanese bombing. Nevertheless, their mood was high. Marine Private First Class Marvin Robinson of the *Houston* would say, "We realized help would come, but not today. The feeling was – and I think the skipper [Captain Rooks] had a large part to do with this feeling – 'Looky fellows, let's give them hell. Let's give them all we've got. They'll be here.'"[18] They had been at battle stations for the last 24 hours; now they were running on adrenalin.

Training – the Japanese crews were all part of the same navy and thus had the same training and operated under the same tactical doctrine. Lack of time meant that the sailors of the Combined Striking Force had never trained together. Lieutenant Harold S. Hamlin, Jr, commanding the *Houston*'s No. 1 turret, compared it to 11 all-stars playing the Notre Dame American football team without a single practice together.[19]

Communications – the ABDA forces came from four different countries in three different navies and spoke two different languages. They all had different communications codes, techniques, and protocols. Aside from the Dutch quickly learning how to use semaphore, little had been done to adopt a common communications or coding system. Admiral Doorman issued orders in Dutch, which were then translated by Allied signalmen on the *De Ruyter* and transmitted to the other ships.

Air power – the Japanese had cruiser floatplanes, which could monitor the movements of the Allied forces and spot for cruisers' guns. Despite Admiral Doorman's best efforts, the Combined Striking Force had no reliable air support for spotting shellfire or reconnaissance.

The Combined Striking Force had considerable combat power, to be sure, and a very definite chance of accomplishing its mission, but it was a brittle force. Admiral Doorman needed everything to go right to have a chance of turning back the invasion of Java. And already, even before contact with enemy ships had been made, things had gone wrong.

Steaming to the northwest under the watchful eye of the Japanese floatplane, Admiral Doorman adopted a column formation, which is very common. Lighter ships with relatively short gunnery ranges would usually be in the front of the column, with the heaviest ships at the back. If the destroyers were not part of the column itself, they would usually screen it to the front or the sides in order to be positioned to launch a quick torpedo attack.

The usual formation was not adopted here, however. Admiral Doorman did lead in his flagship light cruiser *De Ruyter*, with seven 6in guns, but the second ship in the column was the Allies' heaviest ship, the 8in armed heavy cruiser HMS *Exeter*. Immediately behind her was the Allies' second-heaviest ship, the heavy cruiser USS *Houston*, followed by the 6in armed light cruiser HMAS *Perth*. Bringing up the rear was arguably the lightest ship, the light cruiser Hr. Ms. *Java* with her ten old 5.9in guns. This formation was likely adopted because of the aforementioned communications issues and the *Houston*'s disabled aft turret. It may explain his thinking; but it does not necessarily justify it.

Admiral Doorman's positioning of the ABDA destroyers, even more curious, seems to have been brought about by the aborted attempt to enter Soerabaja as well as by the air attack that greeted them when they turned around. In order to conduct mass attacks with destroyer torpedoes, he had divided the destroyers into two groups, with the Dutch and British destroyers (*Kortenaer*, *Witte de With*, *Electra*, *Encounter*, *Jupiter*) in one group, and the US destroyers (*John D. Edwards*, *Alden*, *John D. Ford*, *Paul Jones*), almost useless in a gun fight, in the other.

The American accounts of the battle are very clear that the formation used by the destroyers was different than the cruising formation used earlier. The Combined Striking

Force had to move into a double column, cruisers in one, destroyers in the other, to navigate the cleared channel into Soerabaja. When Doorman had them turn around, not all of the destroyers could get back into formation; the subsequent air attack that forced the ships to scatter before the attackers were driven off by the *Houston* did not help. The British destroyers took their lead positions, as before, but the *Kortenaer*, hampered by the boiler trouble, could not get back into position. The US destroyers tried to adjust to their position in the battle formation in the van on the disengaged side of the cruisers behind the Dutch destroyers. However, the *Kortenaer*'s boiler problems and consequent lack of speed again held her back, dragging her sister *Witte de With* along until they were still on the port beam but closer to the back of the formation. In terms of speed, the US destroyers were not much better off than the *Kortenaer*, but they had a separate problem – at some point, Doorman had given them the specific order, "Do not pass Dutch destroyers."[20] This made their orders contradictory inasmuch as when the *Kortenaer* dropped back, they were forced to drop back as well. Ultimately, the US destroyers fell back to their original position behind the *Java* in the very back of the cruiser column.[21]

Why the Dutch admiral did not slow down the column to allow the Dutch and American destroyers to take their proper positions is unknown. It may well have been difficult communications issues once again. It may have simply been determination to engage the Japanese as quickly as possible to preclude being turned away by another air attack, as had happened in the Flores Sea and the Banka Strait; certainly he had no way of knowing that the extent of the Japanese air support was only their floatplanes.

Nevertheless, Admiral Doorman did have a few advantages, albeit advantages he may not have been aware of due to his lack of airborne reconnaissance. The first is that he had more 6in guns than the Japanese – 25:14.[22] However, this was only an advantage if he could get in range.

Secondly, while Admiral Doorman has been criticized for using the column formation, it did keep his ships centralized and together, massing their firepower for maximum effect. The Japanese, as mentioned earlier, were divided into three separate groups, each of which was by itself inferior in firepower to the Combined Striking Force; Admiral Takagi even reinforced that division by ordering them into separate columns.[23] That those columns were in supporting distance of each other did not necessarily negate that division. If the Combined Striking Force could isolate each group from the others, it could destroy each in turn.

At 4:10 pm, shortly after spotting the floatplanes, the destroyer *Electra*, in the starboard van, spotted masts poking over the horizon. Soon enough these masts would reveal themselves as the light cruiser *Jintsu* with her flock of destroyers following her on a southwesterly course, crossing the Allies' course from starboard to port. At 4:12 pm *Electra* signaled: ONE CRUISER, UNKNOWN NUMBER LARGE DESTROYERS BEARING 330, SPEED 18, COURSE 220.[24] Racing up to support the 2nd was Admiral Nishimura's 4th Destroyer Flotilla, still out of sight of the Allied column. Three minutes later, *Electra* reported: TWO BATTLESHIPS TO STARBOARD. There was one minute

The Initial Phase of the Battle of the Java Sea, February 27, 1942, c.3:55 pm–5:15 pm

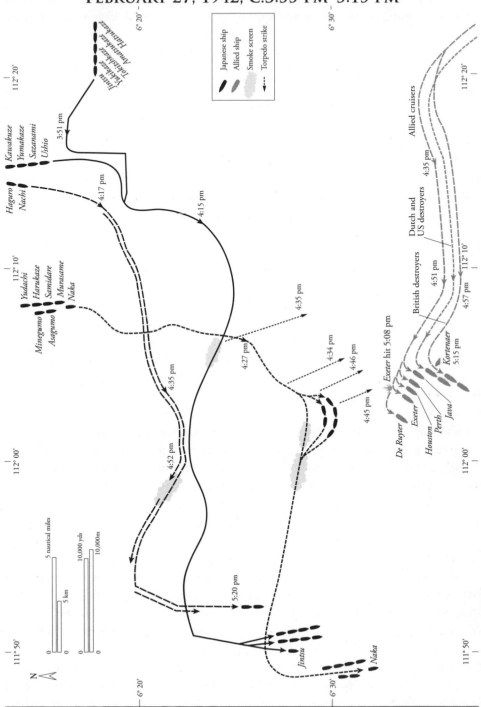

of pure horror for the crews of the ABDA ships before *Electra* sheepishly corrected her report: TWO HEAVY CRUISERS. She had spotted Admiral Takagi's 5th Cruiser Division speeding in from the northeast and angling to keep the destroyer flotillas on his flanks.[25]

The quiet, soft-spoken Karel Doorman had an unfortunate habit of keeping his thoughts and plans to himself, so that while it is known for certain that he intended to engage both the escorts and destroy the transports, pursuant to his orders, it is not possible to know for certain what he was thinking. But if the information and considerations Doorman had and the actions he later took are examined, the broad outline of his battle plan starts to form.

A primary consideration for Admiral Doorman seems to have been keeping the Combined Striking Force between the Japanese and the coast of Java. He evidently wanted to avoid making blind thrusts into the middle of the Java Sea. By holding a blocking position, he could make the transports come to him.

A secondary consideration appears to have been to keep a line of retreat open to his base at Soerabaja. This is not entirely consistent with his orders from Admiral Helfrich who seemingly intended for him to use the Combined Striking Force as a kind of "ABDA Kamikaze Corps," or even with his own orders that sunk or disabled ships were to be "left to the mercy of the enemy." This disconnect would become more apparent as the battle wore on.

A third consideration that seems to have hung like an amorphous dark cloud over everything else, shackling Admiral Doorman's movements, was that seemingly small thing often overlooked by the histories – the reduced speed of the *Kortenaer*. Although that speed issue would be of little consequence when facing slow transports, the Japanese escorts, whose top speed exceeded 33 knots, could literally run circles around a Combined Striking Force limited by the *Kortenaer* to 26 knots. If the Japanese escorts got around the Allied force, their superior speed could enable them to maintain a blocking position of their own and prevent any attack on their transports. This third consideration would manifest itself again and again and again, always to the detriment of the Allies.

By 4:05 pm, the 5th Cruiser Division's *Nachi* and *Haguro* had closed to within 13,000yd of the worried 2nd Destroyer Flotilla. The 5th's screening destroyers broke off and joined the 2nd.[26] Precisely who opened gunfire first is disputed, with both sides saying they responded to the other's fire. Admiral Takagi gave the order and at 4:15 pm, Admiral Tanaka's *Jintsu* opened fire with her 6in guns on the *Electra*, on the Combined Striking Force's starboard wing, at an extreme range of 18,000yd, straddling her and sending her and *Jupiter* scurrying to the disengaged side of the Allied cruisers. One minute later *Nachi*, having finally sighted the Combined Striking Force at a range of 28,000yd, let loose a salvo of 8in shells – which fell 2,000yd short of their target, either the *Exeter* or the *Houston*.[27] This would be emblematic of Takagi's gunnery throughout the day.

Admiral Doorman had not given the order to return fire, but the *Exeter*'s Captain Gordon, finding it "undesirable from many points of view to act as a target without replying," realizing the *De Ruyter* was not yet in gunnery range, and understanding "the limitations of inter-ship communication," took the liberty of opening fire with his 8in guns at 4:17 pm.[28] Following at 4:18 pm were those of the *Houston*, firing in anger for the first time in the Pacific War, returning fire on their tormentors.[29] The *Houston's* shells contained red dye to make identification of the fall of her shots easier; her shell splashes sent up towering columns of water colored blood red.[30] The splashes surprised the gunners on the *Houston* and even Captain Rooks – the red dye had been a Navy Department secret kept from everyone on the ship except for Chief Gunnery Officer Maher – and terrified many of the officers on the *Nachi*.[31] Admiral Takagi and his chief of staff, Nagasawa Ko, both fighting their first surface combat action, were less than amused.[32] The bridge crew of the *Nachi* noted how Nagasawa held the bridge railing with white knuckles.[33] Takagi and his staff seemed mentally unprepared for the possibility that the enemy might actually shoot back.[34]

The Combined Striking Force now made its planned adjustment from approach to combat formation, moving into three columns. The column closest to the Japanese held the cruisers, flagship *De Ruyter* in the lead, followed by the *Exeter*, *Houston*, *Perth*, and *Java*. With no quick torpedo attack in the offing, the Dutch destroyers *Witte de With* and *Kortenaer* and the four ships of US Destroyer Division 58 redeployed to the disengaged side of the cruisers in a second column. Moving to yet a third column, this on the disengaged side of the US and Dutch destroyers, were the British destroyers led by *Electra*, followed by *Jupiter* and *Encounter*. The two columns of destroyers now had to deal with "overs" – Japanese shells overshooting the Allied cruisers and landing near the destroyers.

From this point forward, the accounts of the Battle of the Java Sea begin to diverge, that divergence growing as the battle goes on. This is completely understandable; in battle, individual sailors and officers are normally focused on their assigned task, gathering only glimpses of the overall action. With the Battle of the Java Sea, those glimpses are often the only pictures of the engagement available. Over the next 36 hours all of the ships that took part, except for the four US destroyers, were sunk and their records lost. Most of the senior officers were killed; those who were not were captured and had to report their recollections of the battle years later after being liberated from hellish Japanese prisoner-of-war camps. Therefore, it should be no surprise that no two accounts of the Battle of the Java Sea are alike. What is presented here is an effort to amalgamate the various accounts and glimpses of the battle into a coherent story.

The albatross of the *Kortenaer* made itself felt at 4:21 pm when Admiral Doorman turned his column 20 degrees to port, course 295 degrees True, keeping a speed of 25 knots. He was apparently concerned that the Japanese cruisers were about to "cross his 'T'" and thus bring their full broadsides to bear.[35] But he need not have worried: the Japanese were turning to a westerly course to parallel his. Admiral Takagi literally jumped for joy when informed of this course change, shouting, "Now I can catch up with our fleet."[36] Takagi seems to have been determined to fight this out at extreme range, using the superior range of his torpedoes and 8in guns to win the battle without coming in range of the Allies' 6in armed cruisers. This was not an unreasonable strategy by any means, and Doorman was certainly playing into it by not closing more quickly. Unfortunately for Takagi, his strategy required a large amount of ammunition, for as the range went up, the accuracy went down.

The long-range gunnery duel continued for approximately half an hour. The 5th Cruiser Division's gunfire followed a pattern: each salvo was tightly spaced (a diameter of 150yd), with every third or fourth one a straddle, in which shells of the salvo would land on both sides of the target without hitting it; "first 25 yards short, then 25 yards over" was how one officer on the *Perth* described them.[37] Pumping out 8in salvoes at a rate of five or six every minute, the *Houston* on her tenth salvo claimed a hit on the *Haguro*'s aft turret – Lieutenant Hamlin in the *Houston*'s No. 1 turret cheered, "We've just kicked the Hell out of a ten-gun Jap cruiser!" drawing a cheer from the crew – but the Japanese recorded no such hit.[38]

Perth claimed a hit with her second salvo on a destroyer, after which the flotilla turned away behind smoke. But the *Nachi* and *Haguro* remained out of range of the Allied 6in guns. The *Perth*'s Captain Waller said in his report, "I found a long period of being 'Aunt Sally' very trying without being able to return the fire."[39] In return, the *Perth* endured eight straight straddles, which Waller, a veteran of two surface actions in the Mediterranean, likely found even more trying, having once commented, "I'd rather 1000 bombing attacks than to stand one enemy shelling."[40] The Japanese finally started finding the range when they landed an 8in shell on *De Ruyter* at 4:31 pm (this one in the auxiliary engine room) and another at 4:53 pm.[41] Both shells were duds. *Houston* was also hit by a dud 8in shell in the engine room at about 5:06 pm.[42] A second dud a few minutes later ruptured an oil tank.[43] A Marine on one of the *Houston*'s aft 5in mounts quipped, "Those little bastards. If they're not careful they're going to hurt somebody."[44]

The *Houston* was now having trouble with her main guns. The electric rammer for the starboard 8in rile in the No. 1 turret had stopped functioning when a fuse box damaged in the February 4 bombing had fallen off the bulkhead wall. Crewmen were now ramming the 250lb shells into the gun by hand – a feat considered impossible in peacetime.[45] The Japanese ships and the Combined Striking Force continued exchanging gunfire on their slowly converging courses.

Admiral Doorman was facing a tactical dilemma. The long-range gun duel was not to his advantage; he needed to close the range both to make the gunfire of his 8in cruisers more effective and to bring in his 6in guns, which were currently outranged. But as the range between the Japanese cruisers and their ABDA counterparts continued to close, Doorman could see that the Japanese were, once again, about to "cross his T" and place his Combined Striking Force at a severe disadvantage, albeit only a temporary one. At this point came what many consider to be the critical decision in the Battle of the Java Sea by Admiral Doorman, a decision which has been heavily criticized and merits some examination.

"Crossing the T" is a maneuver dating back to the Age of Sail in which one or more ships cross in front of and perpendicular to one or more opposing ships, allowing the crossing ship to fire all of its guns, located only on the ships' sides in the Age of Sail, at the target while the target would be unable to fire back. With the advent of battleship and cruiser turrets, the tactic was modified so that the crossing ships could fire all of their main guns, trained to the side of the enemy, while the targets would only be able to fire back with their forward guns. This would confer a significant and, in the case of the Battle of Tsushima, for example, perhaps a decisive advantage in gun power.

Applied to the Battle of the Java Sea, if Admiral Doorman had continued on his course, the *Nachi* and *Haguro* would have crossed the "T," trained their main gun turrets to port, and fired their combined 12 forward and eight aft 8in guns, for a total of 20 guns. The Combined Striking Force could theoretically respond with the four 8in forward guns of the *Exeter* and the six 8in forward guns of the *Houston*, her only remaining operational 8in guns. With the range continuing to close, Admiral Doorman could also, theoretically, bring in the three forward 6in guns of the *De Ruyter*, four forward 6in guns of the *Perth*, and four 6in guns of the *Java*. In short, Admiral Takagi could cross Doorman's T and the Dutch admiral would still have the advantage: 21 guns to Takagi's 20. Using this calculus, Doorman would in theory have been justified in holding course.

But it was not quite that simple. As the *Nachi* and *Haguro* crossed in front of the Allied column, the only Allied cruiser with a clear field of fire would have been the *De Ruyter* with her three forward 6in guns. The *Exeter*, right behind her, would have had her guns obstructed for a period of time by the *De Ruyter*, during which she would have been unable to fire for fear of hitting the flagship. The *Houston*, behind the *Exeter*, would have also had her range fouled both by the *De Ruyter* and by the *Exeter*. It would have continued all down the column. In short, crossing the T here would mean that the Japanese could bring the 20 8in guns of the *Nachi* and *Haguro* against the three 6in guns of the *De Ruyter*. This would be a massive firepower advantage for the Japanese, albeit for a short period of time.[46]

Moreover, those 20 8in guns would also have a targeting advantage. While the ABDA column would present a narrow target, especially for direct gunfire, ballistic (or indirect) gunfire is much more likely to over- or undershoot the target than miss side-to-side, known as "deflection." The ABDA column was narrow but long, where even one shot with inaccurate range could cause damage. Worse, the main target for the Japanese would be the lead ship in the column: Admiral Doorman's flagship *De Ruyter*. Twenty 8in guns at short range would make short work of the under-armored light cruiser. With communications in the Combined Striking Force at this point little better than tin cans connected with string, the loss of the *De Ruyter* would have the potential for effectively ending the battle with the Allied column disintegrating in confusion.

A microcosm of the dilemma Admiral Doorman was facing could be seen in the difference of opinion on the *John D. Ford* as to Doorman's tactics. Gunnery officer Lieutenant William P. Mack complained, "Damn, Doorman is letting them cross our 'T.'" But when a lookout in the crow's nest spotted, "Many masts on the horizon, but they seem to be headed north. They are definitely getting smaller," Commander Parker responded, "They must be the transports. With their damn floatplanes spotting our position we will never get at them, not with their bully boys holding us off. Doorman has got to go in … So we get hurt, but some of us will overtake the transports."[47]

One more factor apparently entered Admiral Doorman's consideration, this one a familiar one: the speed of the *Kortenaer*. If the 5th Cruiser Division crossed the T and continued on its present course, the Combined Striking Force would have no way to catch up once the Japanese got past, at least not in any coherent combat formation.

With these considerations in mind, Admiral Doorman apparently decided to split the difference. At 4:29 pm he turned further to the west to a heading of 248 degrees True, changing course to 267 degrees True – almost due west – six minutes later.[48] The range would continue to close, but not as quickly, and the Japanese would not cross his T. Doorman's decision here has been very heavily criticized by his colleagues (most notably Admirals Helfrich and Palliser), by historians and by his own crews (most notably Captain Waller and Commander Parker) because it did not allow him to immediately close the range to bring in his considerable 6in firepower.[49] Waller fumed, "What possible bloody good can we do here? We should be in there having a whack at them – not sitting here waiting to be sunk!"[50] While the criticism is valid, in actuality the dilemma Doorman faced had no obvious solution. His course change at this time represented a judgment call. That it ultimately did not work out in favor of the Allies should not obscure the fact that, under the circumstances, the decision was logical and tactically sound.

But Admiral Doorman was not acting in a vacuum; Admiral Takagi was making tactical decisions of his own. Happy to keep the range long – for now – Takagi ordered a torpedo attack a little after 4:30 pm.[51] Admiral Nishimura, in his flagship *Naka*, led the 4th Destroyer Flotilla south, southwest across the bows of the other two Japanese columns; by 4:30 pm, he was closest to the Allied column.

At 4:34 pm Nishimura launched what would be the first massed torpedo attack of the war. *Naka* launched four Type 93 torpedoes at a range of 15,000yd. The six destroyers of his division followed suit between 4:40 pm and 4:45 pm sending another 27 torpedoes toward the Combined Striking Force at ranges between 13,000 and 15,000yd. *Jintsu* added four at 4:35 pm. *Haguro* launched eight from her port tubes at 4:52 pm at a range of 22,000yd; *Nachi* was unable to launch because a valve left accidentally open had bled all the air pressure from her tubes.[52] The massed torpedo attack would become a Japanese specialty, but this was not one of their better ones; when the Japanese launched their torpedoes, the Allied column was heading toward them, giving themselves a narrow bow profile that would allow the Allies to comb the torpedoes without making much of a move. To make matters worse, today they were not quite performing up to the normally high standards of the Long Lance; a dozen or more of the torpedoes detonated before reaching the targets, either in premature explosions or as a result of colliding with other torpedoes.[53]

As something of an interlude, at about this time (5:00 pm) a pitifully small Allied airstrike, three A-24 Banshees, led by Captain Harry Galusha of the 91st Bombardment Group (Light), flew over the battlefield. They had taken off from Malang at 3:00 pm on a mission to attack the Japanese transports. Near Soerabaja they joined up with their bodyguards of ten P-40s of the US 17th Pursuit Squadron (Provisional), broken into two flights led by Lieutenants George E. Kiser and Jack D. Dale, and five Dutch Brewster Buffalos led by Lieutenant G. J. De Haas.[54] It was this mission that resulted in Admiral Doorman being told he could not have air cover. Or so it seemed.

Captain Galusha flew over the battlefield and saw the ABDA and Japanese ships already shooting at each other. But his mission was to hit the convoy, or, preferably, an aircraft carrier or tender that had been reported. Finding no carrier he went after the transports. The attack produced little in the way of results; they claimed one hit on a transport of an estimated 14,000 tons, but the hit caused no apparent damage and the transport steamed on. Galusha reported his attack and the location of the Japanese transports by radio at 5:00 pm. Commander Hara would later say that Zeros flying out of Balikpapan shot down the Banshees, but Galusha's bombers all returned to Malang unescorted.[55]

Because his fighter escort had broken off, Lieutenant Kiser's Warhawks and Lieutenant De Haas' Buffalos had a second mission: to provide air support for the Combined Striking Force. It was through supreme effort, Admiral Helfrich's pestering, and the sacrifice of fighter cover for the *Langley* that Java Air Command had assembled these 15 P-40s and Buffalos (the Hurricanes were still unavailable). Admiral Doorman was finally getting his wish fulfilled – fighter protection against Japanese aircraft. Unfortunately the communications at Soerabaja were so bad that no one told him, so he and his crews understandably assumed that any aircraft they saw was enemy. The fighters ended up taking antiaircraft fire from both sides.[56] The fighters had no way to communicate directly with the Allied ships and vice versa, so they could not be vectored in to shoot down the ubiquitous Japanese floatplanes that continued to keep watch over the Combined Striking Force; the fighter pilots would have to find them on their own. Flying a rectangular circuit around the two forces at about 25,000ft, with grim fascination the American and Dutch pilots watched the battle below.[57] Lieutenant Spence Johnson called the scene "chilling to my blood," while Lieutenant Lester J. Johnsen said it was "a sight that made my stomach sink."[58]

Allied stomachs were about to sink some more. Walter Winslow said, "Throughout this madness, everyone was painfully aware that torpedoes were knifing through the sea toward us, yet Admiral Doorman took no evasive action."[59] In fact, there was no real need to because the Combined Striking Force was already decently positioned to comb the torpedoes. For now.

Impatient at the ineffective long-range duel and concerned that the battle was moving too close to the precious transports, Admiral Takagi signaled his ships TO CLOSE AND CHARGE THE ENEMY.[60] The 5th Cruiser Division had concentrated its fire on the *De Ruyter* and the *Exeter*. Eventually the *Exeter* was straddled and even sustained a near miss underwater well aft. The explosion lifted the entire ship and flooded several underwater compartments, but fortunately the *Prince of Wales*' aft hit was not repeated.[61]

At 5:08 pm, the *Exeter* took one direct hit believed to have come from the *Haguro*.[62] An 8in shell passed through a 4in gun shield on the starboard side aft and entered Boiler Room "B," where the shell did not actually detonate as it was intended to do, but landed inside a boiler where the extreme heat caused it to explode, severing one of the main steam pipes. Although only two of the cruiser's eight boilers were put out of action, another four were knocked offline by the severed pipe. Superheated steam burst from the pipe with a deafening roar and poured out from the new hole in the *Exeter*'s side. With the six boilers offline, the cruiser's speed was immediately cut to 11 knots. The damage also caused a temporary failure of the High Power electrical system, which put the main armament out of action.[63]

It was at this point that the ramshackle nature of the Combined Striking Force and especially its communications would come home to roost.

Captain Gordon of the *Exeter* realized that his abrupt decline in speed meant his ship was in danger of being rammed by the *Houston* from behind. Trying to get out of the *Houston*'s way, he swung the *Exeter* on a 90-degree turn to port. However, the steam now billowing from the *Exeter* acted as a smokescreen to all of the ships behind her, blocking the view of the flagship *De Ruyter* in front of her. *Houston*'s Captain Rooks saw the *Exeter* turn and thought he had missed a signal from Admiral Doorman for an immediate simultaneous turn. He set the *Houston* on a 90-degree turn to port as well, which now put him on the *Exeter*'s port side. Captain Waller of the *Perth* also guessed that he had missed a signal TO TURN AWAY TO LET TORPEDOES COMB THE LINE and turned the *Perth* 90 degrees to port, as did Captain van Straelen of the *Java*.[64] The cruisers were now essentially stampeding in a line directly toward their destroyers, which threw the destroyers into chaos as well.

Admiral Doorman had just about brought the *De Ruyter*'s 6in guns into range of the *Nachi* and *Haguro* when he noticed to his horror that no one was following him; he was attacking the two Japanese vessels alone. He saw that, instead of the somewhat orderly column they had started out in, the other ships of the Combined Striking Force were now milling around in confusion like cows on a pasture. Possessed with a gift for understatement, he said to Captain Lacomblé, "That's not right." Doorman scribbled a note for the radio room to signal FOLLOW ME and ordered the *De Ruyter* to immediately turn around.[65]

With the British and Australian ships having their own communications to which the Americans and Dutch were not privy, the *Exeter* reported to Captain Waller that she had taken a bad hit.[66] Waller quickly had *Perth* make a smokescreen to protect the wounded *Exeter*. Destroyers *Electra*, *Jupiter*, and *Encounter* soon joined in. As the *Perth* sped by, the *Houston*'s gunnery officer Commander Maher calmly ordered, "Check fire. *Exeter* has been hit."[67] In Turret One, Lieutenant Hamlin was awestruck by the sight of the *Perth* protecting her wounded consort:

I'll never forget the *Perth* as she came by there. She was a magnificent sight. Absolutely at top speed, streaming smoke and with battle flags flying at both yardarms and a great big white ensign aft, all guns firing, she looked like a warship really should. One of the finest sights I have ever seen.[68]

On Japanese destroyer *Amatsukaze* Captain Hara was amazed at the Allied tactics. He assumed the turn was a method for avoiding the torpedoes.[69] In reality the line turn was the last thing Admiral Doorman wanted to do. Hitting a target with a torpedo is very different than hitting a target with gunfire. Because of the accidental port turn, instead of facing the Japanese with a narrow bow profile that almost guaranteed no damage, the Combined Striking Force was now showing a large beam profile that virtually guaranteed a hit.

And now the torpedoes began appearing in the midst of the confused ABDA ships. *Jupiter* turned sharply to starboard across the bow of *John D. Edwards*, signaling TORPEDO, and a few minutes later a torpedo passed between the *Edwards'* stern and the *John D. Ford*.[70] *Ford* had to avoid a second torpedo spotted on her port quarter. At about the same time *Edwards* put her rudder hard left to avoid yet another torpedo ahead.[71] One Long Lance actually hit the *Houston*, but only a glancing blow as it drifted along after the end of its run, not enough to detonate.[72] Upon seeing a few of the Long Lances explode prematurely, someone on one of the destroyers reportedly quipped, "Even Japanese torpedoes commit suicide if their attack is a failure."[73]

Unfortunately, one of the torpedo attacks was not a failure. Destroyer *Kortenaer*, under the command of "Cruiser" Kroese, was crossing in front of the *Perth* and some 700yd to starboard of the *John D. Edwards* when at 5:13 pm a torpedo that came from behind exploded on her starboard side in her engine room.[74] A horrified Commander Binford on the *John D. Edwards* cried out, "Oh my God, there's my friend 'Cruiser!'"[75] The explosion broke the destroyer's back. She immediately capsized to starboard, her now-upturned bow and stern folding upward like a jackknife and momentarily standing in the water. Dutch sailors were seen scrambling over the sides – and tossing over Indonesian members of the crew who were too scared to jump.[76] One survivor, apparently the ship's doctor, was seen clinging to one of the *Kortenaer's* still-turning propellers – no one could figure out how he got there – while another was seen clinging to the destroyer's mast waving the Allied cruisers by to avenge his ship – "Go get 'em!"[77] Kroese, as it turned out, had been thrown off the bridge by the explosion.[78] The *Kortenaer* sank in one minute 50 seconds according to the *John D. Edwards*.[79] "No ship stopped to take on survivors," noted Walter Winslow – not yet, anyway – "for any that did could easily have shared the same fate."[80] The *Houston* did manage to toss over life preservers.[81]

There has been some thought that the *Kortenaer* intentionally took a torpedo meant for the *Perth* or the *Houston*, but while she may have indeed taken a torpedo that would have otherwise hit the cruisers, there is no indication it was intentional; Kroese certainly did not mention it in his well-respected history of the Java Sea Campaign.[82] Neither the ship nor even the group of ships that launched the torpedo that struck the *Kortenaer* has ever been conclusively determined. This uncertainty stems from the fact that the

Japanese launched three torpedo attacks in relatively short order. The location, vector, and timing of the torpedo hit have led to a limited consensus that the torpedo, possibly aimed at the *Houston*, came from the *Haguro*, but the nature of mass torpedo attacks and the passing of time means the truth will likely never be known with certainty.[83]

The appearance of the torpedoes left the Allied crews mystified and more than a little worried. According to the *Exeter*'s gunnery officer Lieutenant Commander Frank Twiss, "[T]hey came as a complete surprise. The Japanese destroyers were 15,000 yards away, and well out of torpedo range – *our* torpedo range. So what the hell ...?"[84] That they had come from the Japanese ships, still little more than specks on the horizon, seems to have never entered their minds. Captain Waller believed they had run into a submarine ambush; his lookouts reported sighting a periscope, at which his pom-poms opened fire.[85] At about 4:58 pm, torpedo wakes and a periscope had been reported on the *John D. Edwards'* port quarter. Two minutes later lookouts saw a "huge geyser of water resembling a torpedo explosion" with debris and "two large pieces of metal observed falling end over end" in the same area. The Americans thought the Japanese had accidentally torpedoed one of their own submarines; in actuality it was one of their torpedoes either prematurely detonating or colliding with another torpedo.[86] The Dutch destroyer *Witte De With*, under the command of *Van Ghent*'s former skipper Commander Schotel, started dropping depth charges on top of their alleged new tormentors.[87]

Other Allied ships had joined the *Perth* in blanketing the *Exeter* in a protective smokescreen, so much so that, according to Walter Winslow, "The entire area became so heavily curtailed with smoke that it was impossible to determine accurately who was where, or what Admiral Doorman had in mind for his next maneuver."[88] The smokescreen protecting the *Exeter* was of only limited value; Admiral Takagi still had the floatplanes of the *Nachi* and *Haguro* aloft; they could simply fly over the smoke and continue reporting to him by radio. Incredibly, the floatplanes seem to have been missed completely by the Allied fighters above the Combined Striking Force, the fighters that had been assembled at such a devastating cost. It seems likely that the Allied pilots were so fascinated by the naval action taking place below them – one, Lieutenant Johnsen, even took photographs with a small camera, believed to be the only pictures of the Battle of the Java Sea – that they failed to notice the Japanese floatplanes.[89]

Takagi had been informed of the air attack on the convoy, and the reports he was getting from his floatplanes indicated that the *Exeter* was in trouble and the ABDA column in confusion. In this first hour of action, the Japanese had fired 1,271 8in rounds, 171 5.5in rounds, and 39 torpedoes; they hit with exactly five 8in shells, of which four were duds, and one torpedo.[90] But here was an opportunity to finish off the crippled British cruiser and get rid of these Allied nuisances. He ordered an immediate attack. The 5th Cruiser Division and both destroyer flotillas formed up and charged eastward at the disorganized Allied column.

Meanwhile, Admiral Doorman was speeding back to his reeling ships. He needed to protect the staggering *Exeter*, as well as buy time to get the column reorganized before it completely disintegrated. He had one move immediately available, probably his only one. At 5:25 pm, the *De Ruyter* flashed an order to the British destroyers: COUNTERATTACK.[91]

Too scattered to mount a coordinated torpedo attack, the *Electra*, *Encounter*, and *Jupiter* nevertheless all charged, supported by the *Witte de With*. The skipper of the *Electra*, Commander C. W. May, announced to his crew, "The Japanese are mounting a strong torpedo attack against the *Exeter*. So we are going through the smoke to counterattack."[92] Commander May was the epitome of calm, but her veteran crew knew the *Electra*'s hour had come. The destroyer now charged into the smokescreen she had just laid and came out on the other side to find the light cruiser, the *Jintsu*, and eight overstrength destroyers, operating in two parallel columns of four following their light cruiser. They were alone. "All our friends had vanished," noted senior *Electra* survivor Lieutenant Commander T. J. Cain. "We were naked to our enemy. We were beyond the smoke."[93] The minds of many of the destroyer's crew were filled with chilling thoughts of dying alone, so far from home. But only for a moment. "[W]e cussed the Nip down to the most unmentionable depths, then jumped to our duties as the party opened, and the salvoes tossed the waters into storm." The *Electra* was now taking on the entire Japanese 2nd Destroyer Flotilla.

Admiral Tanaka's ships, about 6,000yd southwest of Admiral Takagi's cruisers, had been forming up to join Admirals Takagi and Nishimura in another mass torpedo attack. At 5:54 pm *Nachi* and *Haguro* each launched eight torpedoes at the limping *Exeter* at a range of 27,000yd. Admiral Nishimura's 4th Destroyer Flotilla had circled back behind the 5th Cruiser Division and the 2nd Destroyer Flotilla while reloading his torpedo tubes – another rude surprise for the Allies was that the Japanese carried one set of reloads for their torpedo tubes – before settling some 6,000yd east southeast of the 2nd on its port beam. At 5:50 pm *Naka* launched her spread from about 18,500yd; four minutes later *Jintsu* launched hers at the *Exeter* from 20,000yd. Tanaka ordered his eight destroyers to launch torpedoes; one destroyer cockily answered back: IT'S SIMPLE. EXACTLY LIKE A MANEUVER.[94] The destroyers closed range to 15,000yd before launching and then immediately reversed course. All but two of Nishimura's destroyers closed to 10,000yd before launching at 6:04 pm. The other two, the *Asagumo* and the *Minegumo* comprising the Japanese Destroyer Division 9, closed to within 6,500yd before *Asagumo* launched. *Minegumo* was unable to launch; she had to first maneuver to avoid the friendly torpedoes being fired with such profligacy, and when she was clear, her firing solution had been ruined. In this attack the Japanese launched 92 torpedoes at the limping *Exeter* and achieved exactly zero hits.[95] In that respect, at least, the attack was, indeed, exactly like a maneuver.

It was in the midst of Admiral Tanaka's effort to join the Japanese torpedo attack that Commander May's *Electra* found herself cut off from her allies by the smokescreen. She began slashing away at the Japanese destroyers. "It was a fierce encounter, tooth and claw," wrote T. J. Cain.[96] *Electra* had had an amazing wartime career, serving with the *Hood* and *Prince of Wales* in their ill-fated duel with the *Bismarck*, and rescuing the only three survivors from the *Hood*. She had also rescued the survivors of the *Repulse* off Malaya. Now, the proud *Electra* was in the fight of her life. Facing ten Japanese destroyers as well as the ubiquitous light cruiser *Jintsu*, neither May nor his crew cared about the odds. The British destroyer was magnificent, "[standing] up to the punishment in the best traditional manner," to quote Cain.[97] "Time after time had [May] brought *Electra*, twisting like a hare, into the spot where the last salvo had dropped, thus causing confusion among the Nips as they adjusted their ranges in accordance with the previous fall of shot."[98] Meanwhile she was dishing out all the fire her 5in guns could manage. She got herself in a gun duel with the destroyer *Asagumo* at a range of 5,000yd, ripping her with 5in shellfire and scoring a direct hit on her engine room that left the Japanese destroyer dead in the water.

But *Electra*'s charmed life could not last forever; it ended with three hits in rapid succession from the destroyer *Minegumo*. The first cut off all communications from the bridge to the rest of the ship, and severed the communications link between the main gun director and the guns. The second hit the main switchboard and wrecked the electrical system in the forward part of the ship. But the third was the most damaging, detonating in the engine room, shattering a boiler and the pipes to the steering gear. The destroyer staggered to a stop with a slight list to port.[99]

No longer able to avoid the avalanche of shells, the *Electra* fought on as long as she could. She continued landing shells on the *Asagumo*. She scored hits on the destroyer *Tokitsukaze*, and *Minegumo*. She even hit the *Jintsu* with one 5in shell, killing one and wounding four. But unable to move, the destroyer was in real trouble. The engineer reported that he could have propulsion restored in a half hour.[100] He wouldn't get half a minute.

The Japanese surrounded the *Electra* and smothered her in gunfire, her principal tormentors being the *Asagumo*, the *Minegumo*, and the *Jintsu*. First, the *Electra*'s A gun was knocked out by a direct hit, then a fire began under B gun and took her offline. The searchlight platform was smashed and a fire started aft. One of the aft turrets (X or Y) exploded, and the other ran out of ammunition. In desperation, the *Electra* launched her torpedoes at the *Minegumo*, but since she was stopped, she could not get them to spread and all of them missed.[101] Pounded into a wreck, the *Electra* slowly foundered as the Japanese passed her by, deeming her finished. Commander May gave the order to abandon ship, but ignored the exhortations of his crew to abandon it with them. He was last seen waving from the bridge as the destroyer rolled over to port and sank at around 6:00 pm, the White Ensign still flying defiantly from her mast.[102]

In the gathering darkness, the *Electra*'s cohorts were doing their best to give some support to the destroyer that had entered the smoke and never came back. At 6:00 pm, the *Minegumo* drew the ire of Lieutenant Commander Eric Vernon St. John Morgan's destroyer *Encounter*, and the two destroyers settled into a ten-minute gun duel on parallel courses at ranges of 3,000yd or so without inflicting damage. *Witte de With* was racing up in support when she suffered an underwater explosion aft. Two of the depth charges she had readied to attack the suspected submarine had been swept overboard port side, one detonating under her stern. The concussion damaged her propellers and knocked out two

300

of her dynamos; one was restarted in short order.[103] The *Witte de With* had been brought online in a hurried manner not even a week earlier and given the crew of the *Van Ghent*; it is fair to wonder if this set of circumstances contributed to this mishap.

The *De Ruyter* had looped around on the other side of the Allied ships from the Japanese, flying the signal flag FOLLOW ME from her mast and repeating the signal by voice radio to get the ABDA ships to fall in behind the flagship and reform the column. As he passed the *Exeter* at 5:36 pm, Admiral Doorman signaled: WHAT IS YOUR DAMAGE?[104] Captain Gordon responded: HIT IN ONE BOILER ROOM. MAXIMUM SPEED FIFTEEN KNOTS, a signal he repeated for the benefit of Captain Waller in the *Perth*.[105] Although the *Exeter's* engineers had been able to get her speed back up to 15 knots and restore power to her turrets, there was a limit as to what they could do until the engine rooms had cleared of the superheated steam and the temperature was reduced to levels that would not melt human skin. Doorman ordered her to return to Soerabaja.[106]

It had taken some 20 minutes but by 5:29 pm Admiral Doorman had managed to reconstitute the Allied column, with the *De Ruyter* in the lead, followed by the *Perth*, *Houston*, and *Java*. They headed east southeast, parallel to the *Exeter* on the British cruiser's starboard beam before crossing the bow of *Exeter* and positioning themselves between the British cruiser and the Japanese who were still determined to finish her off. The destroyer *Encounter* now joined by the *Jupiter* and *Witte de With*, continued screening Captain Gordon's limping command, but while *Exeter* may have been maimed, she was, as always, still full of fight. Admiral Nishimura's light cruiser *Naka* and her destroyers were moving in to finish off the heavy cruiser when they got a rude surprise: the *Exeter's* 8in guns were back online. The *Houston*, with her aft turret out, also trained her forward guns on the *Naka*, maneuvering back and forth to do so.[107] A few straddles, a shower of shrapnel, and a severed antenna later, *Naka* and her destroyers were scurrying away under a smokescreen, having treated the staggering *Exeter* to 24 torpedoes, all of which somehow missed.[108] Now, on orders from Doorman, *Witte de With* flashed a signal to *Exeter* to follow her back to Soerabaja.[109]

In spite of the gathering darkness and the smoke that hung over the battlefield, all of these movements were being witnessed by the Japanese floatplanes. Gunnery Officer Maher of the *Houston* banged on the door of the gun director for the forward 5in guns, shouting "Shoot down that goddamn airplane!"[110] But the aircraft remained out of range, circling, almost taunting them.

The continuing combat with the escorting Japanese warships was accomplishing nothing. To Admiral Doorman's increasing frustration, the Combined Striking Force was getting nowhere nearer the convoy. Doorman told US Signalman Marvin Sholar, "We can't get to the transports this way. Their floatplanes keep the Japanese advised as to our every move, our every trouble, the beginning of every course change."[111]

That seems to have been the motivation behind Admiral Doorman's next set of orders. At 6:06 pm, the *De Ruyter* flashed a one-word signal to the four-pipers of US Destroyer Division 58: COUNTERATTACK.

The officers and crews of the *John D. Edwards, Alden, John D. Ford*, and *Paul Jones* had been getting increasingly frustrated and angry at their lack of orders to attack. Commander Eccles of the *John D. Edwards* was especially brutal, "The crystal ball was our only method of anticipating the intention of Commander Combined Striking Force."[112] Now they were running low on fuel and would have to head back to port soon. But at last they would get their chance to attack.

Then the next order flashed from the *De Ruyter*: CANCEL COUNTERATTACK. Then another order: MAKE SMOKE. Finally, one last order from the flagship: COVER MY RETIREMENT.

With sunset rapidly approaching at 6:20 pm, Admiral Doorman's idea appears to have been to break free of the Japanese escorts so he could sneak up on the convoy under cover of darkness – night fighting being a specialty of the Royal Netherlands Navy.[113]

Although Doorman's idea was sound in theory, its execution with a confusing series of orders did not resound to the Dutch admiral's credit. The crews of the US destroyers were thoroughly confused. Commander Thomas Binford of US Destroyer Division 58 discussed what to do with Commander Eccles; with fuel running desperately low, they decided on a torpedo attack.[114]

So, like the *Electra*, the four destroyers of Destroyer Division 58 charged through a smokescreen at the enemy who significantly outgunned them: Admiral Takagi's *Nachi* and *Haguro*, still some 22,000yd distant off the starboard bow.[115] As they countercharged at 28 knots, a member of the bridge crew of the *Alden* was heard to remark, "I always knew these old four-pipers would have to go in and save the day!" Everyone on the bridge laughed.[116] Lodwick Alford, formerly of the *Stewart*, called this type of attack "a destroyerman's dream."[117]

And, indeed, Commander Binford was doing exactly what Admiral Doorman had intended.[118] "Good! He needs no orders," the Dutch admiral told Signalman Sholar. "He'll die if [the *Nachi* and *Haguro*] don't turn. He is so low on fuel, he doubts that he will make Soerabaja, but he is not going to get sunk with a full division of destroyers, lying dead in the water with no fuel."[119] While he probably overstated the *kamikaze* desire of Binford and US Destroyer Division 58, he was generally correct.

Admiral Takagi guessed what was happening and turned the big guns of the *Nachi* and the *Haguro* on these new interlopers. Their salvoes fell 800yd short of the four-pipers.[120] But Commander Binford was well aware that the 5th Cruiser Division would correct its aim eventually and blast his destroyers to bits if he got too close. His torpedoes were set for broadside fire, which would force the destroyers to present the biggest possible target – their sides – to the cruisers, so he set the sluggish US torpedoes for long-range fire.[121] At 6:17 pm, the destroyers launched 20 torpedoes from their starboard tubes at their maximum ranges of 10,000–13,000yd; *John D. Edwards* had only three torpedoes for her starboard tubes and one of *Paul Jones'* torpedoes misfired.[122] As these torpedoes hit the water, there was a large explosion on "the right hand" enemy ship, the *Haguro*, apparently the result of the *Perth*'s gunfire. Then the destroyers reversed course in a column turn and, at 6:27 pm, launched 21 torpedoes from their port tubes; once again, the *John D. Edwards* had only three torpedoes for her portside tubes.[123] Lieutenant Commander Lewis Elliot Coley of the *Alden* observed that at this time, "the rear ship of the enemy column appeared to be on fire aft, and to have a fire in her high forward turret or superstructure."[124] At this point there may have been a shell hit on the *Haguro* that set fire to the aviation fuel for her floatplanes, near her catapults, but it was quickly extinguished.[125]

Knowing that the American torpedoes were inbound – and not knowing that their chances of detonating were slim – Admiral Takagi easily avoided the attack by turning the 5th Cruiser Division toward the north. Indeed the US four-pipers lived to fight another day and, chased by shell splashes, sped to the south to find the protection of their cruiser cousins. But all their torpedoes had missed. It was an expensive way to "cover his retirement," but under the circumstances Admiral Doorman's use of his torpedoes made sense.

Admiral Takagi was also taking stock of the situation and reassessing his strategy. The Soerabaja lighthouse was now in sight, and he had earlier observed explosions among the Allied ships, which made him worry he was about to enter a minefield.[126] As it happened, the explosions he had observed were his own torpedoes malfunctioning. Nevertheless, things had been going rather well for the Japanese. The Combined Striking Force was retreating. Takagi ordered his forces to retreat and reform, and for the convoy to change course – again – to the south. The fight was over.

But the fight wasn't over. At 6:31 pm the *De Ruyter* signaled to the Combined Striking Force: FOLLOW ME.[127]

Far from retiring, Admiral Doorman wanted to renew the fight and to renew the hunt for that ever-elusive invasion convoy. Instead of heading into the Soerabaja roadstead, the Combined Striking Force turned northeast. Walter Winslow was uneasy: "Admiral Doorman, we knew, was doggedly determined to intercept the transports and, if necessary, die in the attempt. In all probability, he would take the rest of us with him."[128] He did not know, could not have known, that the truth was far more complicated.

Admiral Doorman had no information as to where the convoy was. He had deduced that it was to the north or northwest, but that was at best a guess. The Combined Striking Force now had the *De Ruyter* leading the *Perth*, *Houston*, and *Java*, with the *Jupiter* screening to port and the four American destroyers to starboard rear. Doorman was now reduced to blind probes headed northeast then northwest. Commander Eccles was appalled:

> Darkness set in and we followed the Main Body endeavoring to regain station, and having not the slightest idea as to his plans and still only a vague idea as to what the enemy was doing, we reported the expenditure of torpedoes. Airplane flares indicated the enemy was following our movements closely … During this whole movement we received no instructions nor signals.[129]

But he still could not escape the notice of the ubiquitous Japanese floatplanes. His fighter cover – for all the good it did – had been forced to retire due to darkness and lack of fuel.

Admiral Takagi had presumed that the Allies might try again for the transports. He now had to gather his scattered forces and put them into some semblance of order for night combat. The *Asagumo* had managed to restart her engines and, with the *Minegumo*, headed back to the convoy, depriving Admiral Nishimura's 4th Destroyer Flotilla of their services. Though it had suffered negligible damage, Admiral Tanaka's 2nd Destroyer Flotilla had completely disintegrated. The destroyers *Sazanami* and *Ushio* had not been able to rejoin *Jintsu* until 6:45 pm. All of Tanaka's other destroyers, scattered by their torpedo attacks, were unable rejoin him until 7:07 pm.[130]

But the abominable luck of the Dutch continued, and the Combined Striking Force was not able to take advantage. At 7:20 pm the *Jintsu*, now with her eight destroyers back, sighted the *De Ruyter*, leading the Combined Striking Force on a northwesterly course. The two forces were on a parallel course heading north at a distance of 17,500yd. The *Nachi* and *Haguro* were also in the area, some 16,000yd to port of the Allied column. Their sighting of the *De Ruyter* put Admiral Takagi into a panic; he bit his lip so hard it drew blood.[131] Both his cruisers were completely stopped to recover their floatplanes, but no one in the Combined Striking Force spotted the 5th Cruiser Division stopped and dead to rights on the other side of the *Jintsu*.[132] Once the two cruisers recovered their aircraft, they went full speed almost immediately, and prompted a change to Imperial Japanese Navy policy: floatplanes would no longer be recovered at sea.[133]

Although the Combined Striking Force had missed the heavy cruisers it had sighted the *Jintsu. De Ruyter* signaled: TARGET TO PORT. *Perth* and *Houston* launched starshells and, joined by the *Perth,* opened fire on the Japanese light cruiser at 7:33 pm. They then observed a string of flashes on the *Jintsu*. Guessing – correctly – that the flashes were firing primers for torpedoes, indicating a torpedo launch, the Allied ships made an immediate line turn to starboard 60 degrees True at 7:36 pm.[134] The Japanese increased speed, made smoke, and withdrew. No damage was reported to either side.

Frustrated by his lack of success, Doorman commanded the Combined Striking Force to turn around and head south again.

Admiral Doorman could not have known that his deductions had been correct, that the convoy for which he had been desperately searching for the last 24 hours was in fact only 20 miles away to the northwest.[135] It was just over the horizon, and they had been headed straight for it before they turned to proceed to the south.

"The next six hours will, I am sure, remain a bitter memory to those of us who have survived," Lieutenant Hamlin would later write. "On the plotting board were 55 enemy surface warships in the east end of the Java Sea … Opposing them were now four cruisers and a half a dozen destroyers, low on fuel, ammunition, and torpedoes."[136]

The Combined Striking Force now headed south. Admiral Doorman took the opportunity to try to determine the fate of the *Electra* and the *Encounter*, signaling

REPORT YOUR POSITION, COURSE AND SPEED at around 8:00 pm.[137] He would never hear from *Electra*. *Encounter* was still some ways back trying to help the *Exeter*. The lookouts reported a sighting to starboard. The *Perth* fired off starshells, but they could not see anything.[138]

But the Japanese could. Out of nowhere appeared eight green parachute flares to illuminate the Allied squadron as it moved. A floatplane from the *Jintsu* passed along word to Admiral Takagi that the Allied column was apparently heading toward the south.[139]

Finally, at 9:00 pm, the Allied column reached the coast of Java near Kodok Point, west of Soerabaja.[140] The *De Ruyter* led the Combined Striking Force on a column turn to the west as Admiral Doorman attempted to find the elusive invasion transports.

Destroyer Division 58 did not follow. Commander Binford had a decision to make about his thirsty four-pipers. Knowing that Admiral Doorman planned to go eventually to Batavia, Binford spoke with Commander Parker of Destroyer Division 59 on the *John D. Ford* about what to do.

"I'm not going in there after Doorman," he told Lieutenant William J. Giles, Jr, conning officer for the *John D. Edwards*. "That Dutchman has more guts than brains."[141] Commander Binford later explained it a little more tactfully: "Realizing that I had no more torpedoes and that further contact with the enemy would be useless, since my speed and gunpower were less than anything I would encounter … I retired to Soerabaja, which was about 50 miles away."[142]

As the *John D. Edwards* led the *Alden*, *John D. Ford*, and *Paul Jones* through the cleared channel of the minefield into Soerabaja, the aircraft from the *Jintsu* dropped a flare above them.

Behind them, Admiral Doorman and the remnants of the Combined Striking Force – *De Ruyter*, *Perth*, *Houston*, *Java*, and *Jupiter* – disappeared into the darkness.

CHAPTER 15

A TURN TOO FAR – THE SECOND PART OF THE BATTLE OF THE JAVA SEA

ENEMY RETREATING WEST. CONTACT BROKEN. WHERE IS CONVOY?[1]

So had transmitted the wireless telegraph of the *De Ruyter* to Admiral Helfrich in Bandoeng at 6:30 pm. Helfrich had no new information for him, and replied that Doorman would have to guess.[2]

In fact 25 minutes previously, at 6:05 pm, Admiral Helfrich had transmitted to Admiral Doorman a report that, at 5:57 pm, 35 ships, including one cruiser and four destroyers, were on course 170 degrees True at lat. 05°10' S., long. 111°35' E. That is, northwest of the Bawean Islands. Moreover, at 4:30 pm, five large ships and several small ones were at lat. 06°20' S., long. 115°30' E., on course 315 degrees True. It was this second group that had been attacked by Captain Galusha's bombers. Helfrich had done his job in sending this information almost immediately, but Doorman apparently never received it.[3] Helfrich, assuming Doorman already had this information, did not repeat it when Doorman asked him for the convoy's location. Similar incorrect assumptions had contributed to the misunderstanding between Admiral Phillips and his chief of staff Admiral Palliser, now coincidentally Helfrich's chief of staff, that had contributed to Force Z's catastrophe off Malaya.

So now Admiral Doorman and the rapidly dwindling number of ships under his command were searching the Java Sea blindly in the dark for a convoy guarded by superior enemy forces of whose location they had no idea.

Admiral Doorman's turn to the south when, unbeknownst to him, his objective was only 20 miles away, had been the result of this complete lack of information about

Japanese movements and dispositions. In turning to the south, Doorman had likely despaired of finding the convoy by poking blindly, randomly in the dark in the middle of the Java Sea. He appears to have developed a better idea: to go to the convoy's landing site and work back along their projected course track.

Allied intelligence had a prediction of the convoy's landing site: Toeban Bay, on Java's northern coast about 50 miles west of the northern channel to Soerabaja. To prepare for the predicted landing, a Dutch infantry contingent had been stationed at Toeban, and Admiral Helfrich had ordered the minelayer *Gouden Leeuw* to lay a minefield at the southern end of the bay. Doorman was informed of the minefield and had passed the information along to his commanders.[4] In fact, the Combined Striking Force had made a point of specifically searching Toeban as part of its earlier unsuccessful sweep.

That the prediction of the Japanese convoy landing at Toeban was little more than an educated guess mattered little. It was not necessarily good information, but it was the best Doorman had, and so his best remaining option was to act on it. The placement of the infantry would prove to be fortuitous, though not for reasons the Dutch had been considering; the minefield, surprisingly, would not.

The Combined Striking Force steamed westward about 4 miles off the coast of Java in a slight zigzag to throw off enemy submarines.[5] The ships were in a column of five – *De Ruyter*, *Perth*, *Houston*, *Java*, and *Jupiter*. The *Encounter* was still operational and was trying to catch up to the column after being separated while screening the *Exeter*, but she was well out of sight and so far behind that she was of little tactical use.[6]

Any hopes Admiral Doorman may have had of evading Japanese notice against the coast were dashed soon enough. A magnesium parachute flare appeared to port, then another. Worse, mysterious yellow lights seemed to float up to the surface of the water – all along the Allied column's course as they passed, as if they were dragging "a long string of Christmas lights," in the words of *Houston* Marine Private Jim Gee.[7] "As fast as we passed one group of lights astern, another popped up about a hundred yards to port," said Walter Winslow.[8]

One of the ubiquitous Japanese floatplanes, this one from Admiral Nishimura's *Naka*, who had taken over from the *Jintsu*'s floatplane at 9:20 pm, was shadowing the Allied column in the moonlight.[9] It reported the Combined Striking Force's position and every move, dropping magnesium flares attached to little parachutes to backlight the cruisers themselves, and calcium floatlights that burned on water – the yellow "Christmas lights" the *Houston*'s crew had seen – to mark their course.

The Allied sailors had never seen or even heard of floatplanes being used like this. "We felt fairly safe after the sun went down," *Houston* sailor Bill Wessinger would later say, "until we heard those planes. We just couldn't believe they were flying over water at night. Then they started dropping flares."[10]

Far from being an equalizer as the Dutch had hoped, the night was tipping the scales more and more against them. "[I]t was soon obvious that our every move in the moonlight was being reported, not only by [wireless telegraphy] but also by this excellent visual

Second and Third Phases of the Battle of the Java Sea, February 27, 1942, 5:20 pm–6:00 pm

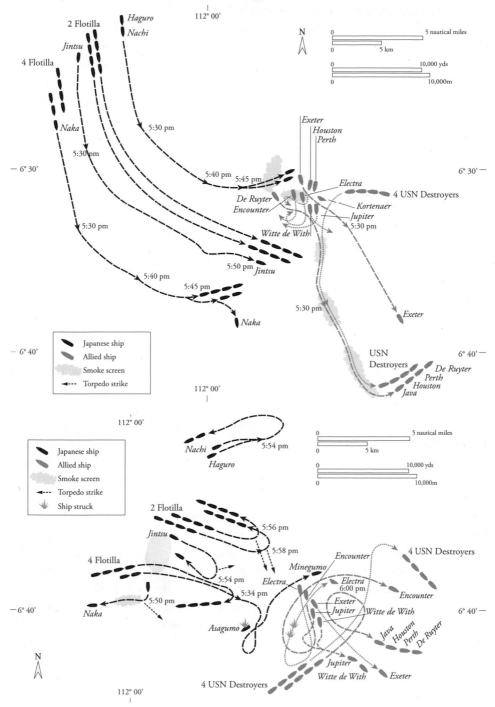

means. The enemy's disposition of his forces must have been ridiculously easy,"[11] declared *Perth*'s Captain Waller. Beyond frustrated, the normally calm, stoic Karel Doorman cursed the floatplane softly under his breath.[12]

So often during the day, indeed during the entire campaign, the Japanese floatplanes had been modern-day harpies – screaming the Allies' movements, position, and actions; snatching away any and all hope for an Allied victory and fouling the battlefield with unwanted enemy ships. At least by heading to the Japanese landing site, the Allies had partially nullified the advantage given by the floatplanes; if the convoy was headed to Toeban it had only a limited number of maneuvers it could make. But the floatplanes did mean that any chance of working his way around Admiral Takagi's escorts was gone; he would have to fight his way through them.

The ever-present floatplanes and his ever-diminishing number of ships were hardly the only problems Admiral Doorman had to deal with. The ships were wearing out. The life of an 8in gun is approximately 300 salvoes. The No. 1 turret on the *Houston* had fired 97 that afternoon, 261 since its installation. The No. 2 turret had fired 100 that afternoon, 264 overall. Liners ran on the insides of the big gun barrels both to rifle the shots and to prevent the barrels themselves from being damaged. The strain had been so much that afternoon that the linings had crept out of the muzzles by an inch or more. This may not sound like a lot, but if the lining had pulled out much more, the *Houston* would have been unable to fire. The gun casings were so hot they could not be touched.[13] With inadequate ventilation below decks, men worked in heat that often reached 140 degrees. Lubricating grease on the gun slides melted, and men were forced to work in pools of grease, sweat, and urine 3in deep.[14] The Combined Striking Force's biggest remaining guns and their crews were rapidly reaching the breaking point. Nor was that all.

Ammunition was fast becoming a serious problem. The *Perth* had only 160 6in shells remaining.[15] The *Houston* had fired 303 rounds of ammunition for each of her forward turrets. Now she was reduced to having her crew haul up 8in shells (each weighing around 150lb) and the necessary powder bags (each weighing 63lb) from disabled No. 3 turret to the forward magazines.[16] She had fewer than 300 8in rounds left – 50 per operational gun.[17] The *Houston* informed the *Perth* that she was running low on ammunition. *Perth* passed on the information to Admiral Doorman on the *De Ruyter*,[18] highlighting yet another ongoing problem with the Combined Striking Force: communications. The already ramshackle arrangements for communication were close to complete collapse. At some point during the evening, the voice radio used on the *De Ruyter* for communication with the other ships in the task force went out. An identical Dutch voice radio installed on the *Houston* to streamline communications went offline as well.[19] The cause of both these radio malfunctions was common in this early part of the Pacific War – the concussion caused by the firing of the main guns. The Battle of the Java Sea was the first action in which the *De Ruyter* and the *Houston* had fired their main armaments for extended periods, and the vibrations they caused threw off the delicate settings of the radios.[20]

There has been considerable confusion on this point because while the *De Ruyter*'s voice radio went out, other parts of the Dutch cruiser's radio suite, specifically her wireless telegraph, remained operational. During the night she was able to send at least two messages to Dutch shore installations.[21] But the wireless telegraph was ill-suited to the fast pace of battlefield communications and could even be dangerous. For all practical purposes, the flagship of the Combined Striking Force was now without a radio.

And that was not the end of the *De Ruyter*'s communications problems. During the afternoon action, Doorman had frequently given orders by flags run up the cruiser's mast – his famous command "Follow Me" had been in the form of a flag. But it was almost impossible to see flags at night. Signal by semaphore was similarly useless. A favorite method of communications at night involved the use of mounted lights called Aldis lamps that blinked or flashed messages. Unfortunately, the same gun concussions that had knocked out the *De Ruyter*'s voice radio had also shattered her mounted blinker lights.[22] The *De Ruyter*'s massive searchlights, which could have been similarly used, were similarly shattered by the concussions.[23] The only method left to Doorman for communicating with his force was by use of a small, hand-held blinker lamp, also known as an "Aldis lamp," flashing signals in plain English.[24]

At this time, the communications situation had to be endured; the crews were too busy with more immediate priorities. The tired, battered little column continued steaming along close to the Java coast, rapidly coming upon the Toeban lighthouse. Their course soon became a concern for the *Houston*. Being the heaviest remaining ship and the only heavy cruiser left, the *Houston* had a deeper draught than the other ships. Pharmacist's Mate Griff Douglas, leaning on a rail and looking over the side, remarked to a chief petty officer that the water looked funny. The response he got was alarming: "We're in shallow water." Antiaircraft officer Jack Galbraith saw "this great big wave behind us. It must have been six or eight feet high. The ship began to vibrate and I reported to the bridge that I thought we were running into shoal water."[25]

Fearing that his ship was in imminent danger of running aground, Captain Rooks swung the heavy cruiser out of column onto an offset course – parallel to that of the other four squadron mates.[26] It may have saved his ship.

At around 9:30 pm, as the Allied column passed north of Toeban Bay, the *Jupiter*, last in the column, suffered an underwater explosion on her starboard side that wrecked her No. 2 engine room and caused her to lose all power. She blinkered a signal to the *Java* ahead of her, I AM TORPEDOED, presumably by a Japanese submarine.[27] Doorman apparently checked on the big British destroyer, but with no power to pump out the water pouring into her hull or even to move, her wound was mortal.[28] As one survivor described it, "We had not blown up. We had not sunk. We had, in fact, just stopped, and the same oppressive silence of a ship in dock during the night watches descended on us."[29] In a remarkable display of seamanship, the *Jupiter*'s skipper, Lieutenant Commander Norman Thew, managed to keep her afloat for another four hours, long enough to get the crew off. Fortunately, the destroyer was disabled so close to the Java coast that much of her crew was rescued, helped by the presence of the Dutch Army contingent.[30] Either seeing or otherwise being convinced that the destroyer was close enough to shore to save most of the crew, Doorman continued onward to the west.[31] The *Jupiter* sank at 1:30 the next morning.

The cause of the *Jupiter*'s loss has never been conclusively determined. That night the Allied crews were not convinced the culprit was a submarine torpedo; postwar research would reveal no Japanese submarine in the area that could have been responsible for the explosion. While the Dutch, who long took pride in their expertise with mines, at first indignantly denied responsibility, Allied suspicions focused on the recently laid Dutch minefield nearby in Toeban Bay.[32] The explanation that has been accepted is that one of the mines had broken loose and struck the *Jupiter*. A "drifting Dutch mine" appears to be the most popular description. This has led to even more abuse heaped on Admiral Doorman for having blundered into his own minefield, costing the Combined Striking Force and the British Royal Navy a precious ship in the process. The most recent scholarship suggests, however, that none of these descriptions do this bizarre incident justice.

Even the eminent Dutch historian F. C. van Oosten would later admit "the minefield was not laid with the necessary accuracy."[33] But that is an understatement – the minefield, it seems, was not laid at all. En route to the location, the *Gouden Leeuw* was spotted by one of the ubiquitous Japanese seaplanes. Convinced an air attack was imminent, the minelayer apparently just dumped the mines, only a few of which were active, well north of their assigned position, and left the area.[34] After earlier encountering no mines in what was supposed to be a minefield, now the Combined Striking Force found mines where there were supposed to be none.

Having passed Toeban Bay and not found the Japanese convoy, Admiral Doorman proceeded to work his way back along the convoy's projected route. The *De Ruyter* led the column on a starboard turn to the north on a base course 0 degrees True.[35] Doorman had the column run at very high speed and, without orders, zigzag slightly. This was a tactic normally used to throw off submarine firing solutions, though at the expense of staying in the vicinity of the submarine. In this case, Doorman probably wanted to confuse the trailing Japanese floatplanes as well. In this, once again, he failed. As *Houston* Ensign C. D. Smith explained:

> They picked us up from the phosphorus wakes made by our speed … began dropping flares right alongside us, disclosing our identity to any Japanese ships in the area, telling them where we were, what course we were on, and almost how fast we were going. We maneuvered radically, but as long as we remained at high speed, it was impossible to shake these planes off.[36]

At around 10:15 pm, the crews began hearing voices coming from the water.[37] This northward thrust had them cross the area of the afternoon action, and pass the survivors of the sunken destroyer *Kortenaer*, still trying to survive on the sea. The *Kortenaer*'s skipper Commander Antonie "Cruiser" Kroese, in his book *The Dutch Navy at War*, relates the experience of one of these survivors:

About midnight we heard the sound of movement on the water. We looked up and suddenly we saw, clearly outlined in the moonlight, the shape of ships making straight for us. Would we be picked up? The ships loomed nearer, obviously going at top speed. Soon we saw the rising water foaming at the bows. Still they continued on their course directly towards us. But this was getting dangerous! These were not rescuers, but monsters which threatened to destroy us. They were going to run us down in their mad career and crush us in their furiously churning propellers.

We yelled like madmen, not to be picked up but to warn them off. And then suddenly we saw that they were our own cruisers racing along in the moonlit tropical night. Probably they saw us, too, for the leading *De Ruyter* changed course slightly. As they charged past us, almost touching us, the rafts were turned over and over in the wash. But we cheered and shouted, for there high on the gun turrets we could clearly see our comrades. In the noise and turmoil they raced past – the Dutchman, the Australian, the American, and last another Dutchman, four cruisers going at top speed under a tropical moon. I did not know that it could be such an impressive spectacle. While they were speeding past, some Americans on the *Houston*'s stern dropped a flare. It floated on the water, a dancing flame on the sea. We followed the ships with our eyes until they were out of sight. They had no destroyer protection any longer and their course was north towards the enemy. Had Rear Admiral Doorman from his bridge on the flagship looked down on us with his quiet smile and given us a sympathetic thought? "This is the last time we have seen them," said one of the officers of the *Kortenaer* as the ships faded from sight. "I hope they smash the ribs of the Japs before they go down themselves," said a sergeant vindictively, and from the bottom of his heart, added "The bastards!"

All was quiet again around us. Near us danced the flare. We couldn't take our eyes off it, for it was like a flame of hope. Slowly the hours passed. Then another ship appeared above [sic] the horizon. First we saw it from the beam. Suddenly the vessel changed course and came straight for us. It was some lonely destroyer or small cruiser, seeming a straggler in this sea full of action. Perhaps it was a Jap that had been damaged and was now withdrawing from the scene of battle. We had not been in the water long enough to appreciate being rescued by the enemy to be made prisoners of war. Intently and suspiciously, we watched the approaching ship. "An English destroyer," shouted one of the officers. "It's the *Encounter*," shouted another. We all stared silently, then a shout of relief and joy broke out. It was the *Encounter*! It almost seemed as if the flare from the *Houston* shared our joy and danced with pleasure, too. Cleverly, the Commander of the *Encounter* manoeuvred his ship alongside the rafts. Nets were dropped, and all who could climb swarmed monkey-like up the ropes. The wounded and those who were too weak had to be hauled aboard. When we all had the firm deck of the destroyer under us, our hearts overflowed with gratitude. We could have hugged the British sailors, but even if that's what you are feeling, you can't just show it. You give your rescuers a firm hand-shake, and let them see that you appreciate very much the glass of grog they give you and the warm, dry clothes they provide from their own scanty wardrobes.

"Bad luck!" said the British sailors, shaking their heads because we had lost our ship.[38]

This would be the last time anyone would see the Combined Striking Force before its final battle.[39] The *Encounter* picked up 113 survivors and was supposed to return them to

Batavia, but upon hearing of a "strong enemy force" to the west – from whom is unclear – dropped them off in Soerabaja instead.[40]

Lieutenant Commander Eric St John Morgan's *Encounter* was most certainly a Godsend to the survivors of the *Kortenaer*. Precisely who ordered him to pick them up – Admiral Doorman or the *Perth*'s Captain Waller – is disputed.[41] What seems to have happened is that Doorman, because he had no voice radio, signaled the *Perth* to use her radio to have the *Kortenaer*'s survivors picked up. Doorman had the authority to order the survivors picked up, but not the means. Waller had the means to order the survivors picked up, but not the authority. Doorman's signal seems to have gone straight to the *Perth*'s radio room, without Waller (a former signalman and a known stickler for signals) being made aware of it.[42] What is known for certain is a voice message to that effect was sent out by the *Perth* shortly thereafter, oddly enough to the *Electra* and the *Jupiter*.[43] The *Encounter* picked up the message and acted on it. The *Houston* had apparently also been informed that the survivors were to be picked up and tossed out a "flare" or, as other translations call it, a "light." It was likely a small buoy with a battery and light bulb, used to mark the position and make it easier to find in the darkness.[44]

By around 10:00 pm, the Japanese floatplanes from the *Jintsu* and the *Naka* had been forced to retire for lack of fuel, so now Takagi's advantage of knowing Doorman's movements was gone.[45] The Combined Striking Force and the Japanese were now equally blind as to each other's movements. The Allies could even have had an advantage here. At 7:00 pm Patrol Wing 10's Captain Wagner had ordered Catalina P-5, piloted by veteran Duke Campbell, to search for the Japanese convoy. At 10:22 pm, Campbell spotted the convoy in the moonlight and immediately sent a contact report. Then for the next 70 minutes he continued shadowing the convoy, aghast at its size as "running time from the head of the convoy to the tail … took exactly eight minutes."[46] Even as the number of its flying boats dwindled to almost nothing, ABDACOM had continued to rely on Patrol Wing 10 because of its superior communications performance.[47] But could Admiral Koenraad get that information to Doorman in time?[48]

Indeed, even with both forces "equally" blind, Doorman had a small advantage, if only he had realized it. Takagi knew the Allies' last course, courtesy of his floatplanes. A radical change of course after the withdrawal of the floatplanes might have left the cocky Takagi fumbling to find the Allied cruisers once again. But without knowledge of the convoy's location, such a move would have been a risky proposition.

And so, in desperation, having passed Toeban Bay, Doorman made his last dash north to find the convoy, hoping against hope that he had outflanked them to the west.[49] "He had no idea how close he came in this last magnificent attempt." So says the ONI Narrative, adding a small bit of hyperbole to an otherwise dry missive.[50] But it is not out of place. With only four ships, dead tired crews, low ammunition, and outnumbered by the enemy, Doorman's attempt to strike the convoy was the naval version of Thermopylae, if ultimately less successful.

The final chapter began at 11:15 pm, when the *De Ruyter* signaled to the *Perth* behind it: TARGET AT PORT. FOUR POINTS.[51] The Dutch cruiser's lookouts had sighted

NIGHT-TIME ENGAGEMENT DURING THE BATTLE OF THE JAVA SEA, FEBRUARY 27, 1942

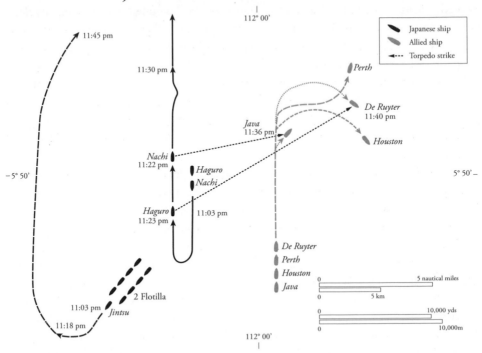

the *Nachi* and *Haguro* in the moonlight, 45 degrees off the port bow at a distance of about 9,000yd.[52]

It must be emphasized that, although reports and other evidence from earlier in the battle could be confusing, ambiguous, or even contradictory, at this point they become much more so. No one agrees on when events took place in relation to other events, or in some cases whether those events occurred at all. This is understandable, for most of the evidence for this last phase of the battle consists of eyewitness testimony, normally the least reliable form of evidence in the best of times, and notoriously unreliable in times of extreme stress.

For much of the war, the specially trained and equipped Japanese lookouts, using oversized and polarized binoculars, would outperform even American radar. Here, where neither the Americans nor their allies had radar, the Japanese had already spotted the cruiser column at 11:03 pm at 16,000yd.[53] The 5th Cruiser Division was in column on a course 180 degrees True – due south. Some sources indicate that the Japanese had taken the Combined Striking Force under fire even before the *De Ruyter* spotted the cruisers, but if so the fire was completely ineffective, as the Allied reports do not even mention it.

The situation for the Japanese appears to have been more difficult than is generally recognized. Admiral Tanaka, whose 2nd Destroyer Flotilla had been screening the convoy to the west northwest, ordered a course reversal to the northeast, keeping his squadron between the Allies and the convoy. According to Commander Hara, Admiral Takagi, still headed due south, ordered the *Nachi* and *Haguro* to slow down so he could develop a good firing angle for his torpedoes.[54] The 5in secondary battery of the *Houston* fired starshells at a range of 10,000yd but these fell short. The American cruiser fired two more salvoes of starshells, this time at a range of 14,000yd. These, too, fell short.[55] The Japanese fired illumination rounds of their own. These fell short as well, but the Allies' terrible luck continued: the glare of the Japanese rounds concealed the *Nachi* and *Haguro* behind them, essentially blinding the Allied gunners.[56] With the starshells ineffective, according to Lieutenant Hamlin, "We stopped shooting starshells and settled down to just shooting at each other by starlight."[57]

Admiral Takagi was getting a second chance to finish off the ABDA Combined Striking Force. His crews were both mystified and furious at Takagi's earlier order to withdraw, and Takagi himself later admitted that it was a bad call.[58] At this point, Takagi may have intended to launch torpedoes, because he would have had a good firing solution for his Long Lances, but he did not, for reasons that remain vague. He may have underestimated the Allied column's speed or, more likely, he may have been concerned that a torpedo launch might move his cruisers out of position in blocking the convoy and allow Doorman to get behind him. As it was, Doorman was able to get slightly north of Takagi's cruisers by perhaps a little more than 1 mile – not enough to make a difference.[59] The *Nachi* turned to starboard and poured on speed. *Haguro* followed, but apparently was slow to get her speed up and fell significantly behind the *Nachi*.[60] The 5th Cruiser Division now spent the next 20 minutes trying to close the range with the Combined Striking Force.[61]

What followed next was the naval equivalent of two exhausted football teams fighting it out in a sudden death overtime of the most literal kind – a slow exchange of fire as the Japanese labored to close the range. The *Java* kept her guns trained on the Japanese, but since she was outranged – again – she did not fire.[62] Because of the *Houston*'s desperate ammunition situation, Doorman ordered her not to fire unless she could be certain of a hit. In this action she fired exactly once.[63]

So this last confrontation was between the 8in Japanese heavy cruisers *Nachi* and *Haguro* and the 6in Allied light cruisers *De Ruyter* and *Java*. It was not an even match. As it had been throughout the day, Japanese gunfire was tightly spaced and accurate. The *Houston* was dangerously straddled near her stern. One shell came so close to the *De Ruyter* that the other ships thought she had been hit on her quarterdeck, but Dutch accounts make no mention of such a hit.[64]

The exchange of gunfire, a violent contrast to the peaceful backdrop of the bright moon and stars, was slow and sporadic, as a result of the dwindling supply of ammunition and the crews' exhaustion. By this time, the battle had taken seven hours and both sides were extremely tired, the Allies much more so for having been at battle stations 24 hours beforehand. So slow was the exchange that it took a moment to register when the Japanese actually stopped firing.[65] This was an ominous silence – Admiral Doorman realized that the cease fire could mean only that the Japanese had launched torpedoes.[66]

Japanese tactical doctrine called for an ambush of enemy forces in a night attack using torpedoes before opening gunfire. The Imperial Japanese Navy would use this doctrine very effectively during the war in places such as Savo Island and Tassafaronga. But the doctrine depends on the element of surprise, meaning that it is important not to tip off the enemy that torpedoes are being launched – which is precisely what Takagi did at this point by ceasing fire.[67]

Thus informed, Admiral Doorman ordered an immediate 90-degree turn to starboard in an attempt to comb the torpedoes.[68] Because each ship was to turn as fast as possible, this would break the column and would result instead in a line of ships four abreast headed east – what is sometimes called a "line turn," a "simultaneous turn," or, if the turn is delayed as it is passed behind, an "echelon turn."[69] Captain Waller does not record whether such an order was flashed back to the *Perth*, but he did not need the order: the wily veteran was well aware of the danger and ordered the *Perth* into an immediate 90-degree turn to starboard, conforming to the *De Ruyter's* turn and leaving the *Perth* behind and somewhat to starboard of the flagship.

One way or another, word was passed back to the *Houston*, who began her own 90-degree turn to starboard. Word also reached the *Java*, 900yd astern of the *Houston*.[70] The *Java* began her turn but she was too late.[71]

At 11:36 pm, while early in her turn, the *Java* suffered an underwater explosion port side aft, the end result of one of eight torpedoes fired 14 minutes earlier by the *Nachi*.[72] Now the *Java's* aged design, with her poor internal compartmentalization and obsolete gun layout, would be her death knell.

Very quickly after the first explosion came a second.[73] This blast was not so much larger than the first as it was cataclysmic, sending a huge fireball into the night sky. Horrified lookouts on the *Houston* saw "bodies flying through the air, silhouetted by flames, the water burning."[74] The blast was actually felt by crewmen aboard the *Perth*.[75] And in a mass of smoke and fire, the stern of the *Java* disappeared.

When the smoke cleared enough to see, the *Java's* stern had been replaced by a blazing, "jagged," "tangled mess."[76] The *Nachi's* torpedo had caused the *Java's* aft magazine, not nearly as well protected as those of her more modern brethren, to explode, blowing off some 100ft of the cruiser's stern, including the No. 7 gun.[77] There was no hope for the ship; the truncated stern section could not be sealed off and the engine room was flooding.[78] After some very brief discussions, Captain van Straelen gave the order to abandon ship. Initially there was no panic in the veteran crew of the *Java*, but that changed because of a very questionable policy; the cruiser's life vests had been locked in a room.[79] The room had one door, and the rush to get in and out through that one door became a panicked mob. With little time to launch the lifeboats, crewmen tossed anything overboard that might float and then jumped after them. Less than 15 minutes after the devastating torpedo hit, the bow of the *Java* reared up and the shattered stern led the rest of the ship to the depths. One of her crewmen in the water shouted, "There goes the old tub."[80] Out of a crew of 528, only 19 survived.[81]

For the mortified crewmen of the *Houston*, their horror was mixed with a sense of bewilderment. Captain Rooks had to maneuver the ship to avoid torpedoes "that zipped past us 10 feet on either side."[82] But where had they come from? They were still unaware of the range and capabilities of the Japanese Type 93 torpedo, and the *Nachi* and *Haguro* had disappeared into a rain squall. A number of the crew believed that they had run into a submarine ambush.[83] So the men of the *Houston* could be forgiven for being transfixed on the catastrophe behind them, so much so that they were in danger of missing the catastrophe unfolding in front of them.

While the loss of the *Java* was devastating, it could have been significantly worse. Admiral Doorman, guessing what the cessation of Japanese gunfire meant and acting quickly on that presumption with the 90-degree starboard turn, had likely saved his other three ships. It was time to reform the column. As he had done twice earlier in the day, Doorman would reform the column by having his flagship circle his remaining ships so they could fall in behind him. To that end, he ordered the *De Ruyter* to make a further turn to starboard, either in a continuation of the original turn or as the start of a new turn.[84]

Because this turn would take the *De Ruyter* across the track the Japanese torpedoes had followed, Doorman must have been convinced that the threat of the Japanese torpedoes had passed. Possibly his staff had made calculations based on the estimated firing time and torpedo track.[85] More likely, the *De Ruyter's* lookouts had seen torpedoes pass by; as it was, the *Houston* had watched torpedoes bracket the US cruiser. And, indeed, those remaining from the *Nachi* had actually passed the column and were churning away from the action.

So the *De Ruyter* turned to the southeast, her forward guns swinging around to starboard to remain trained on the Japanese cruisers, apparently convinced that the immediate danger had ended.[86] So there was surprise and extreme consternation on the bridge of the *De Ruyter* when a telegrapher spotted wakes approaching from relative bearing 135 degrees.[87] "What is that?" The response from Admiral Doorman was calm and matter-of-fact. "Oh, that? That's a torpedo."[88]

The flagship was still turning to starboard when a Type 93 lanced into the starboard side aft, near her reduction gearing.[89] A Dutch Marine remembered, "It was like the ship was lifted from the water; all lights went out, we were listing heavily and fire broke out on the AA-deck …"[90]

The *De Ruyter* had turned too far, turning into the path of one of four torpedoes fired by the *Haguro*. The *Haguro* had fired her spread at 11:23 pm, one minute after the *Nachi*.[91] Significantly behind her flagship, *Haguro* had had to use a different firing solution to that of the *Nachi*. The track of her torpedoes had actually crossed those of the Nachi, and the southernmost of the Japanese cruisers was thus able to hit the northernmost of the Allied ships. Whatever calculations the Dutch had made had been based on the *Nachi's* tracks, which were very different from the *Haguro's*.

The *Haguro*'s torpedo does not seem to have been immediately fatal to the positive buoyancy of the *De Ruyter*, but it might as well have been. The hit knocked out the dynamos, causing the loss of power. The explosion started a fire that spread with extraordinary speed, and within minutes everything aft of the catapult was an inferno. Why the fire spread so quickly is unclear. What is known is that one of the ship's oil tanks had ruptured and probably leaked flammable bunker fuel both inside and outside the ship. The antiaircraft deck was also rapidly succumbing to the spread of the fire.[92] There the fire was especially dangerous, as it contained the five twin-barreled 40mm Bofors antiaircraft mounts – and ready lockers full of 40mm ammunition, which presently began to explode with devastating effect.[93] Walter Winslow remembered, "[A]mmunition, detonated by the intense heat, sent white-hot fragments flying into the night sky like demonic fireworks."[94]

The cruiser's damage control teams went to work and may have kept it from immediately sinking, but the damage to the dynamos, now engulfed in flames, meant no power for water pumps for firefighting or reversing the flooding. The *De Ruyter* was in a fatal conundrum – the fire could not be put out without restoring power, yet power could not be restored without putting out the fire. The ship was doomed.

As if to emphasize the point, the fire on the antiaircraft deck reached the cruiser's pyrotechnics locker, and flares, signal rockets and starshells shot into the sky "like the Fourth of July on the Chicago waterfront."[95]

Admiral Doorman ordered, "Everyone down below,"[96] while Captain Lacomblé lamented, "Now it's all over …"[97]

But it was not over, not yet, for the *Perth* and the *Houston*. How long it remained that way this night remained to be seen, for the *De Ruyter* had been crossing in front of the two cruisers in an attempt to reform the column. When the flagship lost power she staggered to a halt – right in the path of the speeding *Perth* and *Houston*.

For Captain Rooks of the *Houston*, aft of and starboard of the *Perth*, the decision was easy. The *Houston* turned to starboard and came within 100yd of the stricken flagship's starboard side and bow before heading off to the southeast.[98]

With the Dutch flagship's bow pointed to the southeast, away from both cruisers, a starboard turn would have been the preferred choice for the *Perth*'s Captain Waller but for the presence of the *Houston*. A starboard turn by the *Perth* would have sharpened the *Houston*'s starboard turn, and given both cruisers' high rate of speed would have almost guaranteed a very damaging collision for the only remaining operational Allied ships in the Java Sea.

The only other option available to avoid shearing off the *De Ruyter*'s blazing stern, which was pointed northwest toward the *Perth*, was a very sharp port turn. Waller had to shut down one of his port engines to enable his starboard engines' torsion to swing the ship's bow over further to port.[99] The *Perth* came so close to the *De Ruyter* as to feel the heat of the flames and "smell burning paint and a horrible stink like burning bodies."[100] But she managed to clear the Dutch cruiser's stern and head northeast. This desperate swerve may have had an interesting consequence.

On the cruisers of the 5th Cruiser Division, now northwest of the remnants of the Combined Striking Force, the crews could see the explosions of the *De Ruyter* and the *Java* through the rain, and they filled the drizzly air with dancing and shouts of "*Banzai!*"[101] Admiral Takagi crept towards the pyres of the Dutch cruisers and coolly noted, "Ah, they're finished." Hoping to finish off the remaining Allied ships, Takagi had the *Nachi* and *Haguro* dash in what he thought was pursuit – to the northeast. Hara called it Takagi's last mistake of the battle.[102] Why he chose northeast has never been determined; it seems the *Nachi* may have seen the *Perth*, backlit by the burning *De Ruyter*, in her port swerve to the northeast and may have followed.[103]

But Captain Waller had no intention of continuing to the northeast. He had the *Perth* reverse course, likely to port to keep from being silhouetted again, and head toward the stricken flagship, slowing down slightly.[104] One may speculate here that the *Houston*, already headed southeast, also slowed down and probably turned to port. Both Waller and Rooks wanted to check on the status of the obviously troubled *De Ruyter* and find out what Doorman wanted to do. Doorman had given orders that disabled ships and surviving crews were to be left "to the mercy of the enemy." But now that it was he who would be left behind, would he change his orders?

An Aldis lamp on the *De Ruyter* flashed their answer: DO NOT STAND BY FOR SURVIVORS. PROCEED TO BATAVIA.[105]

While the use of the Aldis lamp requires brevity, neither the format nor his innate stoicism could take away from the meaning of this last order of Rear Admiral Karel Doorman, and it has not gotten the attention it deserves.[106]

A commanding officer whose courage had been questioned and ridiculed, telling the remaining ships under his command to leave him behind and save themselves. Not only did he tell them to save themselves, he *ordered* them to do so, giving them legal cover for doing so and hopefully sparing Captain Waller of any feelings of guilt for seemingly having abandoned the cruiser's survivors. Whatever the faults of Karel Doorman, he deserves recognition for this one selfless act.

But this act was also the culmination of a pattern of behavior that strongly suggests that Admiral Doorman did not entirely share the desire of Admiral Helfrich, safely ensconced behind his desk in Bandoeng, for his Combined Striking Force to act as ABDA *kamikazes* hurling themselves at the Japanese. Though Doorman had given those orders that disabled ships and surviving crews were to be left "to the mercy of the enemy," he had repeatedly deviated from those orders in efforts to save those ships and their crews. Far from being suicidal, it was almost as if Admiral Doorman, knowing he was likely to go down to defeat, was trying to preserve the remaining ABDA ships, if not his own, to fight another day.

Certainly Captain Waller was doing his very best to make sure that the depleted force would survive to fight another day. Waller says that at this point as senior surviving officer he "took *Houston* under [his] orders." [107] He most likely signaled the *Houston* to continue heading southeast and the *Perth* would catch up. At around midnight, the *Perth* caught up to her American brethren, but in a fashion much more dramatic than anyone would have liked.[108]

The *Houston* was speeding to the southeast towards Soerabaja when her lookouts thought they spotted torpedoes – it bears remembering here that all day the crews, not knowing the capabilities of the Japanese Type 93 torpedo, had thought they were being stalked by submarines, who in their minds had claimed the *Kortenaer*, *Jupiter*, and now *Java* and *De Ruyter*. Now here were more, or so it seemed.

Captain Rooks ordered a hard turn to starboard to avoid the torpedoes – except there were no torpedoes and the *Perth* was trying to pass the American cruiser to starboard to take the lead position in this now two-ship column. Captain Waller's difficult turn to avoid the *De Ruyter* and the *Houston* would have been for naught but for a member of the *Houston*'s bridge crew, Ensign Herb Levitt, who literally pushed the helmsman aside, seized the wheel and swung it to port. Collision was avoided by a mere 25yd.[109]

Captains Waller and Rooks took the opportunity of this meeting to discuss their options. Waller recommended they head to Batavia at 20 knots; Rooks countered that they should head there at 30 knots.[110] In his report, Waller would explain his decision:

> I now had under my orders one undamaged 6in cruiser, one 8in cruiser with very little ammunition and no guns aft. I had no destroyers. The force was subjected throughout the day and night operations to the most superbly organized air reconnaissance. I was opposed by six cruisers, one of them possibly sunk, and twelve destroyers. By means of their air reconnaissance they had already played cat and mouse with the main striking force and I saw no prospect of getting at the enemy (their movements had not reached me since dark, and even then the several reports at the same time all gave different courses). It was fairly certain that the enemy had at least one submarine operating directly with him, and he had ample destroyers to interpose between the convoy and my approach – well advertised as I knew it would be. I had therefore no hesitation in withdrawing what remained of the Striking Force and ordering them to the pre-arranged rendezvous after night action – Tanjong Priok.[111]

That may sound perfectly logical, but it did not to Admiral Helfrich, who was furious over Captain Waller's refusal to continue his pursuit of the enemy:

> Strictly speaking the return of *Perth* and *Houston* was against my order 2055/26 – "You must continue attacks till enemy is destroyed." This signal was intended to make it quite clear that I wanted the Combined Striking Force to continue action whatever the cost, and till the bitter end. *Perth* did receive this signal. Both cruisers were undamaged [*Houston*'s after triple turret was out of action] and it was not right to say in anticipation "It is no use to continue action", considering the damage inflicted upon the enemy cruisers, which in my opinion must have been severe. However, it is possible that other facts had to be considered, such as shortage of fuel or ammunition.[112]

To this the official Australian naval historian G. Herman Gill, after correcting Admiral Helfrich's factual efforts, offered the following retort:

> In his desire for "the Combined Striking Force to continue action whatever the cost, and till the bitter end", Helfrich disregarded a major point in warfare: "When is it the right time to disengage?" On numerous occasions in the history of battles, he who found the right answer to that question has been rewarded with victory – a prize that has seldom been given in recognition of military suicide. Here were no conditions warranting a Thermopylae, with commensurate rewards for the sacrifice. Had none but military considerations governed the use of the Allied naval forces in the Java campaign, the time for their disengagement and withdrawal was reached long before Waller took his absolutely correct action in disengaging and withdrawing the remnant under his command. In that action he did his duty to the Allied cause, which would have been much better served by his saving the two ships and their trained crews for future use.[113]

As the fall of Java became more and more certain, Helfrich's actions bordered increasingly on the irrational.

While not avoiding Conrad Helfrich's sizable ire, somehow Captain Waller's fugitives managed to elude Admiral Takagi's hunters. Admiral Nishimura reported seeing them in the darkness and demanded that the Japanese go after the Allied fugitives, but Takagi, more concerned about the convoy and his own fuel and ammunition situation, turned back to tend to his main mission.[114] According to Commander Hara, Takagi would be heavily criticized for "his series of blunders," which included opening gunfire at extreme range and wasting ammunition.[115] One disgusted gunnery officer said of Takagi, "He's a submariner, and doesn't know how to use guns."[116] During the afternoon action the Japanese fired 1,271 8in shells, of which only five hit, and four of those were duds. Of 153 Type 93 torpedoes fired by the Japanese during the Battle of the Java Sea, only three hit – but each of those three hits was fatal.[117]

And so, to quote Walter Winslow, "The *Houston* and *Perth* raced on into the night."[118] And to their own date with destiny and legend. "Behind us blazed the funeral pyres of our comrades-in-arms, whom we deeply mourned."[119] Before the *Houston* lost sight of the Dutch flagship over the horizon, her lookouts had counted nine separate explosions.[120]

At about this time, to add insult to grievous injury, Admiral Koenraad sent out the following signal:

CONVOY CONCENTRATED TO 39 TRANSPORTS IN TWO COLUMN, 1500 YARDS BETWEEN COLUMNS, COURSE NORTH, SPEED TEN. 3 DESTROYERS IN COLUMN RIGHT FLANK, 1000 YARDS. 1 CRUISER, 2 DESTROYERS IN COLUMN LEFT FLANK 1000 YARDS. 2 CRUISERS AND SIX DESTROYERS CONCENTRATING ON CONVOY AT HIGH SPEED POSITIONS PROBABLY, LAT 05-36S, LONG 112-46E/0227 1842.

The information the Combined Striking Force had been waiting for all day and night, in the form of this contact report from Duke Campbell, was finally available – 20 minutes too late. A furious Admiral Helfrich would call the inability to get these reports to Admiral Doorman in a timely manner a "scandalous lack of coordination."[121] Now the Combined Striking Force was in no shape to act on it. What would have been precious news was now useless to the beleaguered Admiral Doorman.

The Dutch admiral could only oversee the evacuation of the glowing blast furnace that his flagship had become. Amidst the continuing explosions and with the power out, lowering lifeboats and other life preserving equipment was next to impossible. Nevertheless, Doorman personally made certain that the only whaleboat that could be lowered without power was filled with wounded and a few sailors who could row, and then saw it pushed away from the ship.[122] Captain Lacomblé had the nets and rafts tossed overboard and gave the order to abandon ship, "Jump, lads, she's had it. God speed."[123] Not all of the wounded were able to leave, however, and the ship's surgeon chose to stay with them and share their fate.

His work done, Admiral Doorman turned away to his own fate. Survivors described him at this time as being calm as usual but obviously distraught, and apparently, like Admiral Phillips on the *Prince of Wales*, determined to follow that old, sad ritual of a captain going down with his ship. Precisely what happened to him is disputed. Some say that he and Captain Lacomblé were seen in the water or in lifeboats, already dead.[124] Others say he returned to the bridge and disappeared.[125] The most recent scholarship has identified a survivor who saw Admiral Doorman and Captain Lacomblé talking in a burning passageway before they retired to a cabin, where, it is believed, they shot themselves.[126]

Still aloft was P-5, Duke Campbell's US PBY Catalina flying boat that had found the convoy, and Campbell had done his best to get the information to those who needed it most. As Campbell was returning home, he spotted several sharp flashes in the distance, followed by several heavy explosions. Then he spotted two ships in the moonlight, leaving the area at high speed. Campbell dutifully reported the sighting, and wondered what it meant, not hopeful that it was anything good.[127]

On the north coast of Java, people were wondering what was behind the ominous sounds they had been hearing throughout the night from far out to sea. Many thought it was a storm; indeed it was, though not of the meteorological variety. Others, like one American B-17 pilot, knew better: "I could hear a dull rumble in the midnight air coming from far over the water. The people in the blacked-out streets assumed it was distant thunder. I knew it was the little Dutch Navy in its final agony out there in the dark."[128] Said another pilot, "Java died that night in the gunfire which came rolling in over the water."[129]

The sounds of gunfire and explosions would end that night when the *De Ruyter*, the repeated blasts having ruptured her hull, the raging inferno having heated it to near-incandescence, rolled over and slipped beneath the dark waters of the Java Sea with an unpleasant steaming hiss. The time was 2:30 am.[130]

CHAPTER 16

A HOPELESS PLAN – THE ESCAPE FROM JAVA

The four octogenarian American destroyers of Destroyer Division 58, the *John D. Edwards*, *Alden*, *John D. Ford*, and *Paul Jones* finished their trek through the minefield of the Westervaarwater to Soerabaja just before February 27 turned into February 28. As they arrived in Perak harbor, the entire city was darkened, the docks silent, the native dockworkers having fled the air raids. The naval base was a shambles. At the Holland Pier, the *Exeter* was doing what she could to get propulsive power restored. Her engineers cleared the debris from the boiler that had been the victim of the *Haguro*'s 8in shell. They even found the baseplate for the shell itself. It was stamped "Made in Britain" – they did not find the irony amusing.[1]

With the battered *Exeter* was the battered Dutch destroyer *Witte de With*, paying a hefty price for a dislodged depth charge, now figuring what to do with propeller damage and a dynamo out.

Commander Binford had decided not to follow Admiral Doorman in his westward trek along the coast of Java. There has always been some ambiguity in Binford's action here. Many histories, including the US Navy's official narrative and Samuel Eliot Morison's authoritative history, state that Binford had orders to retire once his torpedoes were expended, but no one seems to know exactly when that order was made and, in any event, Binford did not retire, but instead followed Doorman until the Combined Striking Force started its westward sortie, at which point he and his destroyers returned to Soerabaja. None of which suggests that any such order was in place.

That being said, Commander Binford's action was a reasonable and, as it turns out, accurate interpretation of what the Dutch admiral wanted him to do. The US destroyers were in the force for their powerful torpedo batteries, nothing more. With their torpedoes expended and, worse, their fuel reserves dangerously low, he decided that his destroyers had served their purpose and decided to break off and return to port, at the very least, for some fuel. He tried to inform Admiral Doorman, but could not raise the *De Ruyter* on the radio; not surprisingly, since the *De Ruyter*'s voice radio was out. Ultimately, he had the information relayed to Doorman by wireless from the Soerabaja Naval District. As the destroyers were entering the swept channel, at 9:52 pm the district relayed a message back from the Dutch admiral affirming Binford's actions and ordering him to Batavia to refuel and get additional orders for fresh torpedoes.[2] Binford immediately had his destroyers turn around to head out the channel and make for Batavia, but then stopped. He conferred with his skippers by voice radio who agreed that the danger was too great as they would run into enemy cruisers and destroyers.

Instead Binford sent Soerabaja a message for relay to Doorman stating that he would refuel at Soerabaja then proceed as ordered.[3] He would never hear from Karel Doorman again. The Allied sailors spent most of the night wondering what was happening in the Java Sea.

But the American destroyermen had much more pressing issues. Exhausted as they were, there would be no rest for the weary sailors of Destroyer Division 58. They were out of fuel and, with the native dockworkers having long fled to the hills, Holland Pier was now a self-service facility. Being out of torpedoes – their main weapon, and, in the case of these four-pipers, practically their only weapon – the crew searched in the darkness through the battered naval establishment and its warehouses, weapons caches, and dockyards, but their hopes were quickly dashed. The destroyers were now virtually unarmed.

However, the fifth remaining member of Destroyer Division 58 – the *Pope* – was not. She had missed the Battle of the Java Sea due to a bad leak in her hot well, but Javanese dock workers had welded it shut, doing a much better job than the destroyer's engineer had ever seen out of the Cavite Navy Yard. Like a dog waiting for its owner to come home, the *Pope* had waited outside the cleared channel for a chance to rejoin the Combined Striking Force.[4] She returned with her four squadron mates. So she had torpedoes and her crew was fresh, albeit wary after enduring air raids while immobilized in port. Theoretically, she was ready for a fight. Unfortunately for her, she would get one.

For the classically educated, the aged American destroyers this night, trying desperately to get fuel and weapons as the Japanese were storming ashore in Java, could elicit images of the aged Trojan King Priam, struggling to put on his armor in the last night of Troy to face Pyrrhus, the brutal, vengeful surviving son of Achilles, leading heavily armed Greeks into the palace. But the flush-deckers were not alone. All these ships – *Exeter*, *Witte de With*, *John D. Edwards*, *Alden*, *John D. Ford*, *Paul Jones*, and *Pope* – these magnificent ships, with their amazing crews, had spirits willing and able but bodies weakened and exhausted, having been pushed beyond the limits of physical, mental, and now material endurance.

The last night of Java was at hand. The Java Sea, where they had operated all this time, was now a trap, and the Japanese were rapidly moving to close the few exits through the Malay Barrier: the Bali Strait, Lombok Strait, and Soenda Strait. They had to move quickly but rumors swirled around the cruiser *Exeter*. With her boiler damage, her maximum speed of 16 knots left little hope for escape. There was talk that the cruiser was to be abandoned and scuttled, possibly to block the entrance to Soerabaja.

The US destroyers, once they managed to fuel up, moved out to the anchorage, their crews all on board and their boilers up so they could leave as soon as they got the word. Commander Binford went ashore to use the secret "Green Line" telephone to Admiral Glassford's headquarters in Bandoeng to request instructions. He sent the following frank message: urgent and to the point: "I've got four ships and 700 men. The bottom's dropped out. I want to get out of here and go to Australia. If we stay twenty-four hours, it will probably be too late to escape."

The operations officer replied, "I'll tell the boss and let you know."[5]

PERTH AND *HOUSTON* IN TANJOENG PRIOK – FEBRUARY 28

At 1:30 pm, the *Perth* and the *Houston* were led by a Dutch harbor boat through the minefields into Tanjoeng Priok.[6] At the other end of Java from Soerabaja, Tanjoeng Priok looked little different from its eastern counterpart. A bombed freighter lay on her side near the breakwater. At various places across the harbor lay the blackened skeletons of what had been ships, now twisted into grotesque forms. Many of the harbor installations were now burnt out or broken open. Burning oil tanks darkened the sky with massive black plumes of oily smoke. There was no noise and little action in this normally bustling port. The native workmen had fled. A few Dutch troops were wiring the dock facilities for demolition. The only active ship there was the Dutch destroyer *Evertsen*, having just returned from the Western Striking Force. Otherwise, Tanjoeng Priok, like Soerabaja, was as silent as the grave. As one survivor described it, "Defeat was everywhere. It was something you could almost reach out and touch. It covered everything like the smoke from the splintered tanks a half mile away."[7]

Nevertheless, for the crews of the *Perth* and *Houston*, eerie Tanjoeng Priok looked like a veritable paradise, if only a temporary one. Between two full days at battle stations and a naval battle that had lasted some eight hours, the crews were beyond exhausted. They had not slept in the last 30 hours, and none had changed clothes in three days.[8] In his report, Commander Maher wrote, "The physical condition of both officers and men was poor and in some cases treatment for exhaustion was necessary. More than four days had elapsed since most of the crew had received adequate rest. Battle stations had been manned more than half of this time and freedom from surface contacts or air alarms never exceeded four hours at a time."[9] The condition of the ships was not much better. The concussions of both ships' main guns had wrought havoc with their own interiors. Walter Winslow noticed that on the *Houston*:

Every unlocked dresser and desk drawer had been torn out and the contents spewed all over. In lockers, clothes were wrenched from hangars and dumped in muddled heaps. Pictures, radios, books, and anything else not bolted down had been jolted from normal places and dashed to the deck … Broken clocks, overturned furniture, cracked mirrors, charts ripped from the bulkhead, and large chunks of soundproofing jarred loose from the overhead added to the thick rubble underfoot. The glass windows on the bridge were shattered … Fire hoses, strung along passageways with pressure on for emergency use, were leaking so that the deck had become slippery. The *Houston* was battle-scarred and battle-weary, but there was still plenty of fight left in her.[10]

Conditions on the *Perth* were little different. Captain Waller had been so strained that his crew said, "He had been off color for days," jaundiced, ill from gall bladder trouble. After the battle he had gone back to his cabin and collapsed into his bed – after sweeping it clean of a mess of broken glass.[11]

As bad as their night had been, the *Perth* and *Houston* well knew it could have been worse. And it had been worse, much worse, for a good many of their friends. En route *Perth* signaled Admiral Pieter Koenraad in Soerabaja: RETURNING TO BATAVIA. *DE RUYTER* AND *JAVA* DISABLED BY HEAVY EXPLOSIONS IN POSITION 6°S 112°E.[12] Admiral Helfrich immediately sent the hospital ship *Op ten Noort* to the location to pick up survivors. He was in radio contact with the ship when it was suddenly cut off. A PBY later reported seeing the ship being escorted by two Japanese destroyers, one of which, Commander Hara later admitted, was his *Amatsukaze*.[13] Seizing a hospital ship was a violation of international law, but the Japanese had always considered the conventions of war more "guidelines" than actual rules.

About 60 miles outside Batavia, the cruisers sighted yet another Japanese floatplane and requested air support to drive it off.[14] For once, they got it: five Royal Air Force Hawker Hurricanes were scrambled from the Tjililitan airfield near Batavia to give them air cover.[15] The floatplane had disappeared. But it would be back.

As the *Houston* came into harbor, it was keeping watch for its floatplane, piloted by Lieutenant Payne, flying to rejoin the cruiser from where his aircraft had been hidden at Soerabaja before the battle. In short order, a floatplane did appear, a Japanese one, out to sea, where it was dueling with a Dutch patrol boat. Two Hawker Hurricanes were still covering the *Perth* and *Houston*, but they were not in radio communication with each other, and the Hurricanes were completely oblivious to the whole exchange, which may go a long way to explaining how that flight of Warhawks and Buffalos sent to protect the Combined Striking Force had managed to miss the Japanese floatplanes that would prove to be the decisive edge. The floatplane eventually lost interest and left, the Dutch patrol boat apparently little the worse for wear.[16] The thought of that aircraft reporting back to its parent cruiser, which could be waiting just over the horizon, filled the sailors with dread.[17]

Meanwhile, another floatplane appeared, a single-engine biplane, flying straight into the middle of the harbor. *Houston* would be happy to be reunited with its floatplane.

Except that this floatplane did an abrupt turnaround and opened fire with its aft machine guns on the *Perth*, the red "meatball" on its wings and fuselage now apparent. The *Houston* shot back, but the aircraft was too far away and moving too fast for the return fire to have any effect before it flew away.

Determined not to get burned like that again, when another floatplane appeared, the Dutch antiaircraft gunners opened fire. Naturally, as the crew of the *Houston* immediately recognized, this was Lieutenant Payne's SOC Seagull, having survived a blown oil line to make the trek from Soerabaja to Batavia.

"You dumb bastards," Payne yelled over the radio. "Don't you know I'm one of you?" The aircraft pulled back out to sea, and then, to the amazement of the Dutch, landed near the entrance to the bay. A Dutch motor torpedo boat went to check it out, and proceeded to lead it and its angry pilot through the minefield into the harbor, where it was hoisted aboard the *Houston*.[18]

During the Java Sea battle, Lieutenant Payne had been waiting at the Dutch naval air station, hoping he would be called for his services. That hope was in vain, leaving the *Houston* pilot furious. It could not have been improved when rumors apparently began circulating that the *Houston* herself had been sunk. A member of the US ground crew had handed a poem that had begun circulating to Payne.

THE BATTLE OF THE JAVA SEA
The Admiral was in charge of us
And I swear upon the cross
He put the airplane on the beach,
And that is why we lost.
He took the beautiful Houston
And said, "Just follow me."
And off he took our other ships
Out into the Java Sea.
He looked around to find the Japs
A lesson them to teach,
But he didn't have the eyes to sea –
His plane was on the beach.
The Japs they had their airplanes
Flying around in the sky.
But the Admiral didn't use such things
It really makes me cry.
Had he realized the value
Of a single spotting plane,
The Battle that he tried to fight
Might not have been in vain.
His ship was lost and lots of others

Because of this mistake.

The beautiful, brave Houston later followed

In De Ruyter's wake.

For lack of a plane, the battle was lost,

Just like the shoe and the nail.

The loss of Houston and most of her crew

Was all to no avail.

Had the Admiral not left his eyes behind

Those brave men might not have been slain,

Why, in the name of God, I ask

Didn't he use his spotting plane?[19]

Lieutenant Payne must have been happy to reunite with his *Houston* safe and sound – for now – but his anger, like that of the British pilots at Singapore who were never called in to save Force Z, was undiminished. Like most of the survivors, he did not know that Doorman had tried to get the LB-30 Liberators to serve as his reconnaissance aircraft. Like most of the survivors, he did not view the surprising use of floatplanes at night by the Japanese as indicative that the issue with the Allied floatplanes was not with Doorman, but with doctrine.

The mistakes of the day before were on the minds of the crews of the *Perth* and *Houston*, but eventually those minds switched to more immediate concerns. The sailors went everywhere left on shore trying to restock their supplies, but the Dutch were less than cooperative, more interested in rendering everything useless to the Japanese than in helping the few remaining Allied ships. The sailors managed to divvy up life rafts they had found. They also raided a canteen filled with goods like whiskey and cigarettes that had been designated for the "Victualling Officer, Singapore."[20] The crews figured that the aforementioned Victualling Officer wouldn't be receiving it in any case.

But cigarettes could not be fired from the main guns and whiskey could not be sprayed into the boilers to power the ships, yet that was about as close as the crews of the *Perth* and *Houston* could come to meeting these two most critical of needs. There was simply no 8in ammunition available for the *Houston*'s main guns or 6in ammunition for the *Perth*'s main guns. They found some 4in ammunition lying around, but that was of little comfort.[21] *Houston* still had fewer than 50 rounds left for each of her functioning guns, and Perth still had fewer than 20 for each of hers.

Just as desperate and even more infuriating was the situation with fuel. With the oil from Sumatra and Borneo now cut off, Java was now limited to what she could produce herself, some 22,000 tons per month. Unfortunately, that oil was in the mountains; with the native workmen gone, there was no way to transport it to the naval bases. As it was, the Dutch facilities in Tanjoeng Priok had only some 750 tons of fuel left.[22]

Both the *Houston* and *Perth* tried to get fuel, but the Dutch authorities were miserly. Pursuant to Admiral Helfrich's orders, they were saving the little remaining fuel for the

Dutch warships. When informed that almost all of the Dutch warships were now at the bottom of the sea, most having been sunk in the last 24 hours, the Dutch position did not change. Admiral Glassford had issued orders for US Navy ships to fuel only from the tanker *Pecos*, except the *Pecos* was, rather obviously, not here.[23] The reaction from the *Houston* and the *Perth* was exasperation: Tanjoeng Priok had been the designated rendezvous point for the Combined Striking Force even before the Battle of the Java Sea yet it had no fuel for the ships?[24] Eventually, the *Perth* was able to find some 300 tons, which brought her up to about half capacity. The *Houston*, by contrast, was able to get only "a dribble."[25] Nevertheless, both cruisers were told that they had enough fuel to make it to Australia if they husbanded it properly.[26]

Meanwhile, Captains Waller and Rooks had gone ashore to the British Naval Liaison's Office. There they managed to find Commodore Collins. They knew, as did Collins, that there was no saving Java now, no way to stop the Japanese invasion or to even resist it. All they could do was try to escape and fight another day. Waller and Rooks wanted to know what their new orders were, hoping, praying they would be to make for Australia and safety.

They would be disappointed.

DEPARTURE FROM SOERABAJA – FEBRUARY 28

Throughout the day, amidst the continuing air raids by the Japanese, little by little, survivors of the Battle of the Java Sea made their way into the naval base at Soerabaja. With them came news of the magnitude of the catastrophe that had taken place the previous evening.

Sometime around noon the destroyer *Encounter* came in, having hauled in as many survivors of the *Kortenaer* as she possibly could. Much to the delight of the US sailors, one of those survivors was the *Kortenaer*'s skipper Commander "Cruiser" Kroese. Back in the early days of the American presence in Java, Kroese, almost alone among the Dutch naval officers, had been welcoming to the Americans. They remembered it even now, and did everything in their power to repay his hospitality.

Also creeping in was a Dutch patrol boat. She had just rendezvoused with the US submarine *S-38* to transfer 54 British survivors of the destroyer *Electra* that the submarine had fished out of the water.[27] Then came another, bringing in US Navy Signalman Marvin Edward Sholar, who had survived the sinking of the *De Ruyter*; his communications mate, Otto Kolb, had not. US submarine *S-37*, badly damaged by depth charging, had come across a boatload of the Dutch cruiser's survivors. Unable to take them all on board, she just took the American survivors, causing some consternation among the Dutch. *S-37* did leave them with five days' provisions and towed them to within sight of the Java coast.[28]

At the other end of the spectrum was the grim task of burial of the war dead. During the afternoon, with the full cooperation of the Dutch, Captain Gordon led a detail to bury the *Exeter*'s dead at the European cemetery of Kembang Koening.[29] Commander Kroese, leading a Dutch detail to pay honors to a wounded *Kortenaer* sailor who had died on board the *Encounter*, thought it sadly symbolic: "It was all very tragic, the impressive ceremony, the beautiful uniforms, the immobile faces, and as background the lost cause of the Allies in the Indies."[30]

As if to emphasize the lost cause, a little after 2:00 pm came 12 Betty bombers out of Makassar City to bomb the port area, escorted by 12 Zeros of the Tainan Air Group, including the Japanese ace Sakai Saburo. Java Air Command scrambled four Dutch Buffalos and a dozen P-40s of the 17th Pursuit Squadron (Provisional) out of Ngoro. But the worn out Warhawks could not reach the bombers and the dejected Americans turned back. The Dutch Brewsters aggressively tried to defend Soerabaja but it was no contest. Mystified by the "lack of caution" of the Dutch pilots, Sakai shot down one Buffalo; a squadron mate shot down one more.[31] The Bettys went about their task unmolested, although the *Exeter*'s 4in high angle antiaircraft guns managed to keep them somewhat at bay, but not enough to protect the hard-luck Dutch destroyer *Banckert*. Sitting in drydock to repair the damage to her stern from the near miss on February 24, *Banckert* now took another near miss that added more damage to her stern.[32] There was no way the destroyer could be repaired before the Japanese came. The Allied ships obviously could not stay in Soerabaja much longer.

Java Air Command tried to strike back as best they could. In the morning they sent three B-17s against the eastern convoy. That evening they sent eight Vildebeests and one Albacore, then a second attack by those same Albacores, followed by six B-17s and one LB-30. These pitifully small attacks did little if any damage and achieved nothing. The bombers' airbase at Madioen would be evacuated that night.[33]

As the afternoon dragged on, the frustration of the British and American sailors grew as they waited for instructions from Bandoeng. Here they were, enduring yet more Japanese bombs, while their superiors Admiral Glassford, Admiral Palliser and, especially, Admiral Helfrich, safely ensconced in the mountains, dithered in deciding their fate. Finally, the tension got too much for Commander Binford. He telephoned Glassford's office.

"We sent you a signal," said the voice on the other end of the line. "We told you to go to Australia. But the *Pope* has to wait and help escort the *Exeter*." "If she does, she's a goner," warned Binford, knowing that the crippled cruiser had little chance of escaping. The response contained no hint of sympathy. "That's too bad. *Pope* wasn't in the battle and still has her torpedoes. She has to escort *Exeter*."[34]

During this time Admiral Helfrich, Admiral Palliser, and Admiral Glassford had been in discussions about what to do with the remaining ABDA ships. But for the most part Helfrich did not listen to his British and American subordinates. Palliser and Glassford believed that Java could not be saved; Helfrich insisted on continuing the fight. The resulting orders left absolutely no one happy, except perhaps Helfrich.

Commander Binford had received permission to take his destroyers *John D. Edwards*, *Alden*, *John D. Ford*, and *Paul Jones* to Australia for "rearming."[35] At least they could now leave. They were told to leave Soerabaja through the Oostervaarwater and go into the Madoera Strait; from there to take the Bali Strait between Java and Bali to the Indian Ocean and Australia. At 5:00 pm, the *John D. Edwards* and *Alden* got underway, heading for the Oostervaarwater. Shortly thereafter the *John D. Ford* headed for the Westervaarwater, and the *Paul Jones* headed for the Oostervaarwater. As they passed the *Exeter*, the crews on deck gave the British cruiser a loud cheer, for her courage and heroism the previous day and for encouragement in the extreme trial that awaited her.[36] The trials of war can bind anyone together, even people from different countries, from different navies, and from different traditions, and the US Navy appreciated the work done under extreme duress by their British counterparts. The *Ford* then turned around and joined her cohorts heading out through Soerabaja's east exit into the Madoera Strait.[37] This unusual method of leaving had been done knowing they were being watched by Japanese floatplanes, in the hopes of convincing them that the US destroyers were merely sounding the route for the *Exeter* to leave.

At 5:00 pm, as the destroyers of US Destroyer Division 58 were getting underway, additional orders came in from Admiral Helfrich: the destroyers *Encounter*, *Pope*, and *Witte de With* were to report to the *Exeter* for duty. Captain Gordon flashed a message to the destroyer captains to board the *Exeter* for a conference.[38]

At 5:20 pm, the skippers of the destroyers who would be escorting his crippled command arrived: Commander St John Morgan of the *Encounter*, Lieutenant Commander Welford C. Blinn of the *Pope*, and Commander Schotel of the *Witte de With*. Now Captain Gordon would give them the appalling plan from Bandoeng, as it was relayed to him by Commodore Collins.

The *Exeter* was too badly damaged to continue with combat operations, so Admiral Helfrich had authorized her to go to Colombo, Ceylon for repairs.[39] There was nothing unreasonable in that, until Captain Gordon relayed to the destroyer skippers just how they were to get from Soerabaja to Colombo:

> Rear Admiral A.F.E. Palliser, RN, of Staff has determined that the *Exeter*'s best chance of escape, considering intelligence reports, *Exeter*'s material casualties, and her deep draft, [is] to pass to the east of Bawean Island, head northwest then west for a daylight run to Soenda Strait, where an after dark transit could be made into the Indian Ocean. The Japanese have landed to the west of us and we must skirt their supporting naval units."[40]

To give a short background, the *Exeter* had a severe problem getting out of the rapidly closing trap in the Java Sea. There were three routes she could use to get into the Indian Ocean. To the immediate east of Soerabaja between Java and Bali was the Bali Strait. On the other side of Bali was the Lombok Strait. Far to the west at the other end of Java was the Soenda Strait. The Bali Strait had been ruled out because it was believed to be too shallow for the *Exeter*. The Lombok Strait was considered and was advocated by Admiral Glassford. It was the shortest and fastest route out of the Java Sea for the *Exeter* and her cohorts and would give them much more room to maneuver, but the route did have the disadvantage of passing through the strait in broad daylight within visual range of the Japanese-held Denpesar airfield and lying within the range of the ever-menacing airbase at Kendari II.

Admiral Palliser pushed the option of the Soenda Strait. It required the *Exeter* and her escorting destroyers to loiter for an entire day just off the southern coast of Borneo in the Java Sea, an area now infested with enemy ships and under skies continually patrolled by the enemy, until they could make a night dash through the strait, hopefully evading the Japanese units that would control the strait by that time, and into the Indian Ocean.

It is very difficult to understand why the Soenda Strait route was chosen over the Lombok Strait route. To be sure, the Soenda Strait had two, maybe three potential advantages. The first was that the Japanese might be so busy with their advance that they would not look behind them, which is where the *Exeter* group would be "hiding," if one considers sailing in broad daylight in enemy-controlled seas under enemy-controlled skies "hiding." That was a slim reed, at best. The other, apparently, was the Japanese fuel situation. By Admiral Palliser's calculations, the Japanese warships in the Java Sea would be running out of fuel, and with the landing operations completed by that time should be on their way to get their fuel bunkers refilled, or be so restricted in their movement by low fuel as to be willing to let the ABDA fugitives go. A third possible advantage was this: the Japanese would not expect a senior officer to be so stupid as to try this route.

"The problem of [the *Exeter*'s] route was carefully considered."[41] So states the narrative of the Java Sea Campaign produced by the US Navy's Office of Naval Intelligence. If it sounds defensive, that is because it is and it should be. This route may have been carefully considered, but apparently it was carelessly decided, and would prove to be controversial postwar. The *Exeter* was believed to have a slim chance of escape in any case, but with this route that chance became none. Trying to force the Lombok Strait and get into the Indian Ocean where she would have far more maneuvering room was the obvious and logical choice, one that, while hardly guaranteed, gave the *Exeter*, *Encounter*, *Pope*, and *Witte de With* the best chance of escape. This was more a prayer than a plan. For all of Admiral Palliser's alleged mistakes in handling the air cover of Force Z, this route for the *Exeter* was a far greater error and hard to explain inasmuch as it seems to violate common sense.

The reaction to this plan from the crews was not entirely supportive. Lieutenant John Michel described how these orders were received on the *Pope*:

> The immediate effect of this information on the officers of the *Pope* was to curse the Dutchman responsible for that order. The next things to be cursed were the torpedoes (without them we would have been ordered to proceed with our own destroyers out past Bali). The *Black Hawk* received her share of vituperation for having given us the torpedoes in the first place – and on general principles.[42]

That the order came from an Englishman and not a Dutchman did not gain it any better a reception on the *Exeter*. "Our preference was for a run to the East and so down into the ocean south of Java and the islands with a dash for Darwin or an Australian port, risking the mines and seeking more room to manoeuvre," the *Exeter*'s gunnery officer Lieutenant Commander Frank Twiss would say.[43] Captain Gordon thought, "It looked to me that we hadn't a hope in Hades of getting through."[44]

Captain Gordon was bound to obey his orders. He went over the specifics of their route and their formation. He also announced at least some encouraging news from his engineers; they would probably be able to get two more boilers online by about 11:00 pm, giving the *Exeter* a total of four operating boilers, though just how much they could give would depend on power trial at sea. She had a potential to reach 24 knots. They would be leaving at 7:00 pm.[45]

At this point, Captain Schotel of the *Witte de With* interrupted. "Not knowing of this assignment sooner, I granted shore leave to my crew. It will be impossible to round them up in the time allowed," he said, adding, "The drydock was to be made available tomorrow."[46] With the Japanese landing on Java mere hours away, with the trap of the Java Sea rapidly closing as the emperor's ships moved to seal the exits, with time remaining to escape that trap now down to mere hours, and being docked in a bombed-out city, Captain Schotel had given his crew shore leave.

Captain Gordon replied, "My orders are to leave tonight. Do the best you can in rounding up your crew, then follow at your best speed to catch up."[47] Ultimately, the *Witte de With* was scheduled to leave at 9:00 pm. She was given projected courses and speeds to allow her to catch up and meet the *Exeter* around midnight.[48]

At 7:00 pm, under the cover of "a beautiful tropical night," the *Exeter* led out the *Pope* and the *Encounter* through the winding Westervaarwater out of Soerabaja for the final time.[49]

PERTH AND *HOUSTON* MOVE OUT – FEBRUARY 28

At Tanjoeng Priok, talk of what had gone wrong the day before had become rumors of what was to come for the cruisers *Perth* and *Houston*. These were happy rumors, in some cases. "Our spirits were high. We thought we were going home," *Houston* Marine Private Lloyd Willey would later say. Antiaircraft officer Lieutenant Leon Rogers thought, "Thank God, we're going to get out of this Java Sea." Lieutenant Commander Richard Gingras, the *Houston*'s chief engineer, was upbeat: "You know, I had no hope that we would ever get away from all this, but now I think we've got it made."[50]

Java was gone, as any sane person could see. Rumors abounded on the *Houston* that they were going back to the United States. Similar happy rumors were amok on the *Perth*.

But amidst the happy rumors came some ominous portents. Sailors, whether military or merchant, can be a superstitious lot. On the *Perth*, the portrait of the Duchess of Kent, who had renamed the cruiser upon its entry into Australian service in 1939, had fallen from the wardroom bulkhead and crashed to the floor.[51] Someone remembered they had two chaplains on board. As *Perth* historian Ronald McKie would write, "One chaplain was bad enough, but two – that was lethal."[52] Someone on the *Houston* remembered their trip northward through the Soenda Strait into the Java Sea on February 23, when he had heard the sound of a gate clanging shut. The most worrying signs of all were from the cats. Red Lead, the *Perth's* feline mascot for over a year, tried three times to jump ship. Eventually, to keep her onboard, she was clamped in "irons" – a kerosene can with holes cut out for her paws.[53] The *Houston's* cat tried desperately hard to escape as well.[54] Cats seemed to be a theme on the *Houston*, where many of the crew worried that the *Houston* "like a cat, had lost eight of her nine lives, and that this last joust with fate would be too much."[55] Did the cats know something?

Whatever terror the cats felt were matched by the exasperation and disgust felt when Admiral Helfrich's orders for the *Houston* and *Perth* came down. Captain Waller and Captain Rooks were at the British Naval Liaison Office. They were told they would not be going to the United States, or even Australia. Helfrich, "stubborn and obtuse to the last," had ordered the two cruisers and the destroyer *Evertsen* to leave Tanjoeng Priok as soon as they were ready, sail through the Soenda Strait and make for Tjilatjap.[56] Rooks responded that Tjilatjap "did not appear to be a very desirable destination."[57] In breaking the news to Waller, Commodore Collins was almost apologetic, saying he had no choice.[58] Admiral Glassford made it clear to Rooks that he disagreed with the orders and hoped they would be changed to send the cruisers to Fremantle, Australia or Colombo, Ceylon.[59] The two captains spent part of the afternoon talking aboard the *Perth*.

The one piece of good news they got at the British Naval Liaison Office was that the Soenda Strait, the cruisers' only route of escape, was still open. The only information the *Houston* and *Perth* were given as to Japanese dispositions was that a group of cruisers and destroyers was escorting a large enemy convoy headed east about 50 miles northeast of Batavia. Otherwise, they were told, a Dutch reconnaissance aircraft had reported that as of 3:00 pm there was no Japanese force within ten hours of the strait.

"Perhaps it was best that none of us knew the awful truth," as Walter Winslow wrote.[60]

But some did know. Captain Rooks had briefed his senior officers about Admiral Helfrich's new orders. They were less than supportive, with their common sense expressed by senior aviator Lieutenant Payne: "My God, the war was over! There wasn't anything left to fight with. That was like going to your own funeral."[61]

Captain Rooks tried to lift everyone's spirits. "We're getting out of the bottleneck." He informed them of the latest ABDA intelligence showing no Japanese force within ten hours of the strait.[62]

Lieutenant Payne was unconvinced. "I told Captain Rooks it was wrong. I had seen a Jap cruiser seventy miles northeast of Batavia that afternoon. Also, the plane that came in just before I did had to come from somewhere, and it was a ship based plane."[63]

The *Perth* and *Houston* were set to leave at 6:30 pm, just after sunset. Just before they left, Australian Sub Lieutenant Gavin Campbell, Captain Waller's secretary, handed the report on the Battle of the Java Sea that he had written in Waller's name to Commodore Collins. For him:

> [T]hat Battle Report [was] utter trauma. I had only a few hours to get it together from all heads
> of departments and then DO it. I held back the Commodore's driver so that he could take the
> finished report before the ship sailed, otherwise, as it happened, no one would have known what
> had occurred.[64]

Indeed, his was the only report by a senior officer of the Combined Striking Force written contemporaneously with the Battle of the Java Sea.

With that administrative detail completed, all they needed was a pilot to take them through the minefield. An hour later, when that pilot had not shown up, Captain Waller decided that trusting his navigators and charts to risk the minefield was preferable to waiting in this veritable trap for a pilot who might or might not arrive. The two cruisers got under way.[65]

As they were slowly moving towards the harbor entrance, Captain Waller noticed that the Dutch destroyer *Evertsen* did not seem to be getting ready to move. He hailed her and asked why she was not getting under way. *Evertsen*'s skipper, Lieutenant Commander Walburg Marius de Vries, replied that he had no orders to do so. Waller "strongly recommended" that he get those orders and get the *Evertsen* underway. De Vries responded that his boilers were not up, so he did not have engine power, and could not do so for another hour.[66] And so the *Evertsen*, like the *Witte de With*, was left behind to catch up as best she could, another example of the strange lack of urgency on the part of the Dutch.

Cautiously the *Perth* led the *Houston* through the minefield, trusting her charts, her navigators, and her navigators' memories to make up for the missing pilot. Eventually, they cleared the mines and raised speed to 22 knots – a speed dictated by considerations of their less-than-optimal fuel situation.

As they left Tanjoeng Priok, Captain Waller received a report that at 4:00 pm air reconnaissance had spotted an enemy convoy of ten transports escorted by two cruisers and three destroyers about 50 miles northeast of Batavia heading east. Waller remarked to his navigator Lieutenant Commander J. A. Harper that it looked as though the Japanese would land east of Batavia that night. Harper replied that it was unlikely, with a convoy to look after, that the Japanese escort would trouble *Perth* or *Houston*. Waller agreed.[67]

Once clear of the minefields, the hopes of the crews were dashed. On the bridge of the *Perth*, Captain Waller made the announcement over the cruiser's loudspeakers:

> This is the Captain speaking. We are sailing the Soenda Strait for Tjilatjap on the south coast of
> Java. Shortly, we will close up to the second degree of readiness. Air reconnaissance reports that
> the strait is free of enemy shipping, but I have a report that a large enemy convoy is about
> 50 miles northeast of Batavia, moving east. I do not expect, however, to meet enemy forces.[68]

The disappointment was palpable. On the *Perth*, the captain's words left members of the crew "restless and full of foreboding – full of unspoken, unpronounceable fears like whispers in the dark."[69] Engineer Lieutenant Frank Gillan of the *Perth* had a sense that at sundown was a dividing line between the past and the future and that somewhere a decision had been made affecting his life and the lives of them all.[70] The crew of the *Perth* had never been to Tjilatjap, had never even heard of it, but the *Houston*'s sailors had had quite enough of "that lousy dump."

With that unpleasant duty done, Captain Waller simply lay on the deck. "Kick me if anything happens," he told the Officer of the Watch, and was soon fast asleep.[71] Eccentric, utterly unpretentious, this Hector Waller – "Hec" as he was known to everybody – was a well-known, well-respected character, and dearly beloved by his men, who "would follow him to hell if that was absolutely necessary." *Perth* historian Ronald McKie said of Waller, "He was, among other things, perhaps the greatest fighting captain the Royal Australian Navy has produced."[72]

On the *Houston*, Walter Winslow, a pilot without a plane, had no duty station at this time, so he was allowed to go back to his cabin to get some sleep. The cruiser was dark; the only lighting Winslow had to guide him to his cabin were beams of blue lights along the floor. On his desk sat a wooden head, a beautiful ornament from Bali that he had purchased on the cruiser's first visit to Soerabaja and had named "Gus." He asked Gus, his "silent friend," "We'll get through this OK, won't we, Gus?" Though he could see nothing in the dark, Winslow was certain that Gus had nodded.[73]

And soon he, like Captain Waller, was fast asleep, sleeping the sleep of one who had been stressed for so long, denied rest and relaxation for so long, that the fatigue had seeped into his skin and bones.

Everyone on the *Perth* and *Houston* was in that very same predicament: simply saturated with exhaustion. But for those of the crew on duty, even mere sleep was a luxury they could not afford. They had a ship to watch and protect, but it is not a good thing to have helmsmen with tired eyes, gunners with tired eyes, lookouts with tired eyes. Especially during the hours of darkness. It was why none of those tired eyes noticed in the night the small, dark, silent shape that had started following them.

CHAPTER 17

DANCING IN THE DARK – THE BATTLE OF SOENDA STRAIT

ABDACOM had always been very good at gathering information. This is due in large part to the incredible work of Patrol Wing 10 and the Royal Netherlands Naval Air Service under extremely dangerous conditions, as well as the signals analysis that was becoming a staple of Allied intelligence work. But communications was another matter entirely.

Whether it was not getting Admiral Doorman the critical information regarding the location of the Japanese convoy for four hours or not telling Commander Binford, the *Evertsen*, or the *Witte de With* that they could leave, ABDACOM had more than its share of instances where the left hand did not know what the right hand was doing. The consequences could be, and often were, fatal.

On the morning of February 28, Sergeant Geoff Dewey, an Australian pilot in the Royal Air Force's No. 84 Squadron, took off in his Bristol Blenheim bomber from the Kalijati airfield in western Java, and headed west northwest over the Java Sea. Dewey was a veteran pilot, having flown numerous antisubmarine patrols over the Atlantic earlier in the war. His target that day was Palembang, whose airfields had become just as much of a bane to Batavia as Kendari's had for Soerabaja.[1] The Royal Air Force based in the Batavia area had been trading blows with the Japanese Army Air Force's Palembang airfields, doing considerable damage and hindering Japanese aerial efforts to a degree. But the British were running out of aircraft and the Japanese were not.

At around noon, he and his observer spotted a massive convoy of transports stretching as far as they could see. In front of the convoy were two light cruisers and no fewer than six destroyers in an arrowhead formation headed directly towards Java.

Sergeant Dewey immediately recognized the importance of what he had just found. Breaking radio silence, he radioed a report of the ships, their position, and course to Kalijati and received an acknowledgment. He then went on to complete his bombing mission over Palembang. On the way back to base, he sighted the same convoy again. He radioed his sighting once again. After landing at Kalijati, he also verbally reported what he had seen.

Dewey's report was the most recent information available. It showed that the Japanese Western Invasion Force was far closer to the Java coast than previously believed. They were not ten hours away; they were only four.

Kalijati forwarded at least two of Dewey's reports to Bandoeng. Combining Dewey's report with analysis of the Japanese radio signals, they assembled a picture of what was approaching the western coast of Java: 50 to 60 transports and support ships, the carrier *Ryujo*, four heavy cruisers of the 7th Cruiser Division, three light cruisers, one of which was the *Natori*; and numerous destroyers.[2] Their course would put them off St Nicholaas Point at about 11:00 pm.[3]

However, as one well-respected air force history put it, "On reporting the sighting, very little notice was apparently taken amid the confusion prevailing."[4] Bandoeng did send out a warning of what was coming – to the Netherlands East Indies Army. For some indiscernible reason, no one thought to tell the Dutch Admiral Helfrich or the remaining Allied naval units such as the *Houston* and *Perth* that the Japanese ships were coming close to Java and the landing was imminent.[5]

The warning took the form of a piece of paper on the desk of Major General Wijbrandus Schilling of the Netherlands East Indies Army's 1st Infantry Division in Batavia. Although Schilling's office was in the same building as that of Commodore Collins and the British Naval Liaison Office, he did not tell Collins about the report. The general did not know that the *Perth* and the *Houston* were in Batavia; nor did he know that they would be leaving for the Soenda Strait and Tjilatjap that night. Nor did Collins think to ask him.[6] After all, why would the report not have been forwarded to Collins at the naval command in the first place?

Captain Waller and the *Perth*, Captain Rooks and the *Houston*, and hundreds of Australian and American sailors were heading straight into the middle of the massive Japanese Western Invasion Force.

Two cruisers, one already damaged, both almost out of ammunition, against half of the Imperial Japanese Navy. And they had no idea.

BATTLE OF SOENDA STRAIT, FEBRUARY 28–MARCH 1

After a short nap, Captain Waller roused himself from the floor of *Perth*'s bridge. It wasn't the Waldorf Astoria or even his stateroom, but it had served well enough for a power nap and a quick if incomplete recharge of his batteries. He went to the back of the bridge to help himself to a cup of coffee.[7] Faithfully following some 900yd behind the *Perth* was the *Houston*, Captain Rooks on steady watch. Still further behind, and as yet unnoticed, was a shadow low on the water.

As they had seen signs that they were closing in on the entrance to the Soenda Strait, the sailors on watch had allowed their hopes to build. First, off to starboard came the lighthouse at Babi Island, off the northeastern side of Bantam Bay on the extreme northwest corner of Java. Their plan was to cross the mouth of Bantam Bay and make for St Nicholaas Point, marking the northern entrance to the Soenda Strait, on the far western side of the bay. It wasn't quite the course they had been ordered to follow – Admiral Helfrich had wanted them to loop around further to the north and enter the strait nearer its western side near the coast of Sumatra – but this course was faster, with any increased risk of meeting the Japanese mitigated by the report that no Japanese were within ten hours of the strait.[8]

Nevertheless, as they got closer to the exit, the danger increased as well. Bantam Bay gave a dark backdrop where enemy ships could hide at night undetected. So did Babi Island to starboard and Pandjang Island at the mouth of the bay. "They could hide a battleship out there and we'd never see it until attacked," said *Houston* Marine Walter Standish.[9] Captain Waller ordered speed increased to 28 knots. As the hopes of the crews increased, their vigilance increased as well in this dangerous corner of Java.

Their hopes rose a little higher when they saw the light of St Nicholaas Point in the distance, now only some 5 miles away. Their escape, their salvation, had just come into view.

But something else came into view as well. A dark, vague form near St Nicholaas Point.

"Ship, sir, bearing green oh-five," came the call from one of the *Perth*'s lookouts. Captain Waller and the bridge crew took a look. They could barely make out the low silhouette off the starboard bow.

It was probably one of the Allied patrol boats still on station. They had been warned to be on the lookout for these boats, still on duty, so as to avoid friendly fire casualties.

"Very good. Make the challenge," came the order from Captain Waller. The *Perth* flashed the challenge on an Aldis lamp.[10] Behind her, Captain Rooks and the bridge crew of the *Houston* watched the exchange with concern. This unidentified ship seemed to be moving very fast for a patrol boat.[11]

The unknown ship flashed back two green lights. The signalmen understood them to be Morse code for "UB." This was not the Allied Night Recognition Signal. Captain Waller could not have been pleased. A former signalman, he was famous for being a stickler for proper signaling and could get very testy if proper protocols were not followed. "Challenge again," Waller snapped, the turrets of the *Houston* astern training in on the unknown ship, as that unknown ship turned away, making smoke, showing its full silhouette, its full long silhouette, that unmistakable low silhouette with the raked funnels of a Japanese destroyer.[12]

"Jap destroyer. Action stations! Sound the rattles!"[13]

The destroyer, *Harukaze*, sped into Bantam Bay, making smoke the entire way and launching a red flare.[14]

"For'ard turrets open fire!"

Behind the *Perth*, on the *Houston*, the clangs of General Quarters brought the sleepy Lieutenant Walter Winslow out of bed. He staggered to the bridge, not fully awake, to be greeted with the blinding flash of the No. 2 turret firing. "We were desperately short of those 8in bricks," wrote Winslow, "and I knew they were not being wasted on mirages."[15]

Captain Rooks ordered starshells fired to see what they were dealing with. But the first salvo at 7,000yd fell short. So did the second at 10,000yd and the third at 14,000yd.[16] Once again, American starshells were not nearly the equal of the Japanese illumination rounds.

As the fugitive Allied cruisers passed Babi Island, they saw the precise reason why the *Harukaze* had been so quick to make smoke. The spectacle left them aghast. Flying Officer Allen McDonough caught the shock and awe of it: "There are four to starboard … There are five on our port side … By God, they're all round us!"[17]

At the far western end of Bantam Bay were dozens of masts – transports.

Captain Waller and Captain Rooks had unwittingly stumbled into Admiral Ozawa's Western Invasion Convoy.

The convoy, consisting of 56 transports carrying the 16th Army, plus escorts, had left Cam Ranh Bay, Indochina, on February 18. It had later split up. One group of transports had split off with *Yura* and the destroyers *Satsuki*, *Minatsuki*, *Fumitsuki*, and *Nagatsuki* to land at Merak in the Soenda Strait. Another, escorted by the light cruiser *Sendai* and the destroyers *Amagiri*, *Asagiri*, and *Yugiri*, had split off and headed east, away from Soenda Strait, to land at Eretan Wetan on the north coast of Java. It was the latter force that had been spotted by the Dutch PBY and reported to Captain Waller.

But the rest, 27 transports, were here, in Bantam Bay, with their escorts.

Bandoeng's analysis had been surprisingly accurate. There was the aircraft carrier *Ryujo*, fast becoming an American nemesis. With her was the seaplane tender *Chiyoda*. There was the 7th Cruiser Division, under the command of Rear Admiral Kurita Takeo, with the four heavy cruisers of the *Mogami* class, even bigger than the large cruisers the *Perth* and the *Houston* had faced two days ago. There was the 5th Destroyer Flotilla: seven destroyers (*Shiratsuytu*, *Shirakumo*, *Murakumo*, *Shirayuki*, *Hatsuyuki*, *Asakaze*, and *Ahikinami*) with the light cruiser *Natori*, flagship of Rear Admiral Hara Kenzaburo, who was in overall command of the convoy.[18] Seemingly, the Combined Fleet was taking the protection of this landing very, very seriously.

The *Ryujo* and *Chiyoda* were well to the northwest in the Java Sea, with Admiral Kurita's flagship *Kumano* and sister ship *Suzuya*, and the destroyers *Isonami*, *Shikinamni*, and *Uranami*. The other half of the 7th Cruiser Division, the *Mogami* and *Mikuma*, were north of Pandjang Island in the Java Sea. Admiral Hara was with the *Natori* and her destroyers north of St Nicholaas Point. With the convoy in Bantam Bay were two

The Battle of Soenda Strait, March 1, 1942

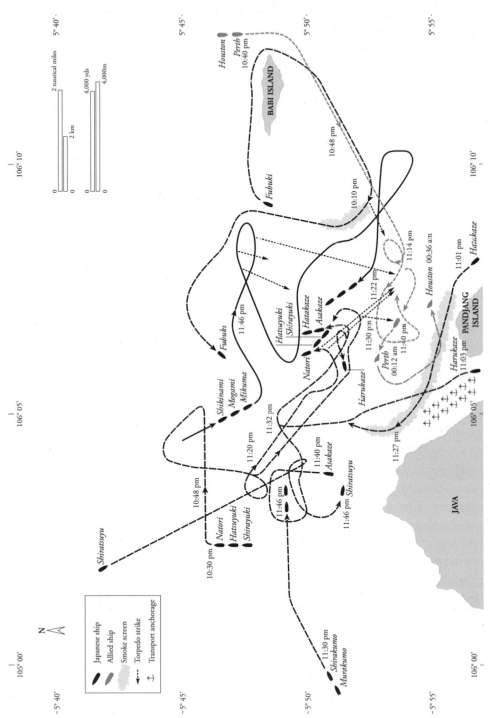

destroyers, the *Harukaze* and the *Hatakaze*, and four minesweepers, creatively named *W-1*, *W-2*, *W-3*, and *W-4*, while one more destroyer, the *Fubuki*, was north and east of Bantam Bay near Babi Island.[19]

It was an overwhelming collection of warships when compared to the *Perth* and *Houston*. Although Japanese intelligence had lost track of the two cruisers after the Java Sea battle, floatplanes had sighted the two cruisers in Tandjoeng Priok, just east of Bantam Bay, throughout the day on February 28. Yet any reports of the *Perth* and *Houston* in Batavia seem to have vanished before reaching anyone in the Japanese fleet who could use them. Communications problems were not limited to ABDACOM.[20]

Admiral Hara would later say that he was trying to lure the *Perth* and *Houston* to their destruction, using his flagship *Natori* as bait, and then spring the trap with the *Mikuma* and *Mogami*.[21] But, aside from the admission that he had abdicated his responsibility for guarding the transports, his story smacks of a cover up for what was one of the Imperial Japanese Navy's most inept performances of the war. For nothing about Admiral Hara's force this night suggests any sort of a plan, more like a sense of panic.

A panic for which there was good reason. Despite the last known presence of the enemy cruisers *Perth* and *Houston* in Batavia or, at least, the eastern Java Sea, the only Japanese warship between Batavia and Bantam Bay was the lone destroyer *Fubuki*. The only Japanese warships between Batavia and the convoy were three destroyers, the aforementioned *Fubuki*, *Harukaze*, and *Hatakaze*. And the *Perth* and *Houston* had managed to get by the *Fubuki*, that low shadow that had been following the two cruisers, and were now between the majority of the Japanese warships and the transports those warships were supposed to be guarding.

Admiral Hara's ships were not deployed to protect the convoy. They were deployed to catch Allied ships trying to escape into the Soenda Strait.

Arrogance, overconfidence, sloppiness: all were manifesting themselves with increasing frequency in the Imperial Japanese Navy. This time, it would cost them.

The *Perth* and *Houston* had slipped by the *Fubuki* by hugging the coast while the destroyer was at the northern end of her patrolling course, but they had not done so unnoticed. The only Japanese warship between Bantam Bay and the ABDA base at Batavia had sent out a warning: TWO MYSTERIOUS SHIPS ENTERING THE BAY.[22]

And yet the Japanese were still not ready for them. They had wanted to catch escaping Allied ships such as unarmed civilian craft or small patrol boats, but apparently not warships, especially not heavily armed cruisers or "battleships," as the *Fubuki* had assumed them to be.[23] Making smoke, the *Harukaze* had run away toward the transports, while her sister *Hatakaze* had run to the north seeking help from Admiral Hara's *Natori* group and from the 7th Cruiser Division.[24] Even worse, the 7th's commander Admiral Kurita, showing that same instinct that would make him so famous in action in the Philippines some 30 months later, chose to hang his own flagship back and let the *Mogami* and *Mikuma* handle the intruders.

It was into this careless, panicked mess that the *Perth* and *Houston* entered. If Admiral Doorman and the *De Ruyter*, the *Exeter*, and the rest of the Combined Striking Force had been with them, they might have been able to strike a major if ultimately meaningless victory against these helpless transports. But they were not; there was just the *Perth* and the *Houston*, battered, exhausted, and almost out of ammunition. As historian Samuel Eliot Morison would state, "Although *Houston* and *Perth* were only trying to escape, they had accidentally fulfilled the long-felt desire of Hart and Helfrich" and an object that Doorman had given his life in seeking: "They had run into an enemy amphibious force at its most vulnerable moment. But alas, they were so few and the time was so late."[25]

Captain Waller and Captain Rooks likely never knew the composition of the forces against them, and only gradually realized that they were badly outnumbered and outgunned. The reconstructed log of the *Houston* would state, "No number of enemy ever accurately known but estimated about 2 heavy cruisers, 3 light cruisers, 11 destroyers and about 35 transports."[26] "It looks like a bit of a trap," Waller was heard to say.[27] But they would still try to escape. *Fubuki*, still trailing the cruisers, decided she needed to do something to stop the intruders and decided to follow the apparent maxim of Japanese surface ships: when in doubt, launch torpedoes. At 11:14 pm she let loose with at least nine Type 93 torpedoes before running away to the north under cover of a smokescreen.[28] It was a bad bet; the cruisers were moving away from the destroyer, presenting a decreasing stern profile. The slim chance of a hit became none when Captain Waller on the *Perth* led the *Houston* on a long loop to starboard to unmask her forward turrets against the targets that were rapidly revealing themselves to the west. *Houston* had finally sighted the stalking destroyer, but with her aft turret out she could do little except feel self-conscious.

The *Fubuki*'s torpedoes sped by their intended targets and headed for the mass of Japanese transports anchored at the other end of Bantam Bay.

The Japanese had been poorly deployed to protect the transports, but Admiral Hara tried to recover by ordering all his warships to converge on the *Perth* and *Houston*.[29] It made sense, but the execution was chaotic, destroyers arriving in ones and twos. The *Houston*'s log would say, "Fight developed into a melee – *Houston* guns engaged on all sides, range never greater than 5000 yards."[30] The unrelated Commander Hara Tameichi of the destroyer *Amatsukaze*, not a participant in this battle, would describe Admiral Hara's ships as "scrambled in confusion and chaos."[31] The chaotic nature of the engagement off Bantam Bay continues to confound historians trying to piece together what happened. With so many Americans and Australians killed, so many US and Australian records lost, so frenzied a Japanese response, and so many Japanese who wanted to cover up the ineptitude of their performance, the Battle of Soenda Strait remains a puzzle missing several pieces. The precise sequence of events in this engagement will probably never be known.

Destroyer *Hatakaze* opened gunfire on the two cruisers and was shortly thereafter joined by the *Asakaze* and the *Harukaze*, the latter turning back to the battle, some 2.5 miles east of St Nicholaas Point.[32] The *Houston* and *Perth* were now deluged with

5in shells from the destroyers, their searchlights sweeping across the water trying to pin down their elusive targets with a spiderweb of unwanted light, but the targets were doing some deluging of their own. The *Harukaze*, hit by both *Houston* and *Perth*, suffered minor damage to her bridge, engine room, and rudder, with three crew dead and 15 wounded. At 11:26 pm, *Perth* took a 5in shell in her forward funnel, rupturing a steam pipe.[33] Six minutes later another shell hit the flag deck.[34] But the damage was only superficial.[35]

Destroyer *Shiratsuyu* was charging in from the west; behind her were the destroyers *Shikinami* and *Murakumo*, but the last two were still about 3.5 miles west of any action. Moving to hold the blocking position were the *Natori, Hatsuyuki, Shirayuki, Hatakaze, Asakaze,* and *Harukaze*. The *Perth* responded with her 6in main battery and 4in secondary guns, while the *Houston* roared with her six functioning 8in main guns and her 5in secondary.

At 11:30 pm Captain Waller turned the *Perth* to the south. Upon nearing Pandjang Island eight minutes later, he looped back to the northeast in a dance to avoid the shells coming her way. The *Houston* followed, as she would throughout the battle. Surrounded by so many targets, Captain Waller decided to allow his turrets to go to local control and fire at any available targets they chose. He also ordered the *Perth*'s torpedoes launched. The *Houston*'s Captain Rooks tried going to local control as well, only to find that the cruiser's dance to avoid incoming fire made it impossible to target, so targeting was switched back to the main battery director.[36] A rain of shells fell around the cruisers. Nothing was hitting – yet – but they soon would be facing far deadlier munitions than the small 5in shells of the destroyers.

For, like the *Fubuki*, Admiral Hara, too, was following the maxim of when in doubt, fire torpedoes. At 11:40 pm, two of his destroyers, *Hatsuyuki* and *Shirayuki*, launched nine torpedoes each at a range of 4,000yd.[37] They missed. At 11:43, *Asakaze* launched six torpedoes, also from about 4,000yd.[38] They, too, missed. One minute later, Hara's flagship *Natori* made her dramatic entrance with 29 rounds of gunfire and four torpedoes launched at the *Perth*.[39] They, too, missed. Walter Winslow would later swear that he saw two torpedoes – exactly whose is unclear – coming directly at the *Houston*, but instead of hitting they passed underneath.[40] If this is true, the torpedoes were set to run too deep, perhaps a reflection of the *Fubuki*'s initial belief that the Allied ships were battleships instead of cruisers. The *Natori* turned away to the north under a smokescreen. Hara ordered the destroyers to form up on his flagship and to reload their torpedo tubes.[41]

But Admiral Hara's trump card in this particular game was about to arrive: the Japanese heavy cruisers *Mogami* and *Mikuma*, of the Second Section of the 7th Cruiser Division, two overstrength treaty violations now with ten 8in guns each, a dozen torpedo tubes, and magazines stocked full of ammunition. Screened by the lone destroyer *Shikinami*, they made their fashionably late entrance from the north at around 11:46 pm and promptly launched floatplanes. *Mikuma*'s skipper Captain Sakiyama Shakao, who was commanding this half of the 7th Cruiser Division, decided that their first move would be to a course parallel to that of the Allied fugitives, heading northeast, while firing full broadsides with their 8in guns. One shell penetrated the *Perth*'s hull near the waterline and started flooding.[42] At 11:49 pm they launched six torpedoes aimed at the *Perth* from their starboard tubes. They missed. Before the two speeding Japanese cruisers could do much else, they found that Babi Island was in their immediate path and they had to do a hard port turn to avoid grounding on the tiny island.[43]

Once that near embarrassment was avoided, the 7th Cruiser Division, using searchlights to pin their targets, opened fire on the *Houston*. The "Galloping Ghost of the Java Coast" took a hit on the forecastle that set the forward paint locker on fire, giving the Japanese a point of aim until it was extinguished seemingly an eternity later.[44] Somehow continuing to find 8in ammunition in the darkest reaches of her nearly- empty magazines, the *Houston* gamely returned fire. She was rewarded with a near miss on the *Mikuma* that at 11:55 pm tripped the Japanese cruiser's circuit breakers, knocking her searchlights and main battery offline for about five minutes.[45]

With their bigger cruiser brethren now at hand, the Japanese destroyers became bolder and bolder, although not necessarily smarter. The Allied crews got some entertainment value from the Japanese ships, unable to pin the *Perth* or *Houston* with their searchlights, firing at each other.[46] In one instance, the Japanese actually turned their searchlights on each other, illuminating their own ships for the Allied gunners.[47] Destroyer *Shikinami*, screening the 7th Cruiser Division, took a battering on the port side from Allied guns and damage to her propeller from a near miss that reduced her speed to 24 knots.[48] Destroyer *Harukaze* suffered damage to her rudder, while *Shirayuki* took a 6in hit from the *Perth* on her bridge, killing one and wounding 11.[49]

The waters just outside Bantam Bay were a scene of pandemonium. But within that chaos, the *Perth* and the *Houston* were now surrounded. There would be no escape. The lack of ammunition on the Allied cruisers was now becoming desperate. At around midnight Captain Waller was informed that the *Perth*'s 6in ammunition was almost gone and they were reduced to using practice rounds. He responded with, "Very good."[50] Hector Waller, a veteran officer who had served with distinction in the Mediterranean as skipper of the destroyer HMAs *Stuart*, spent the night calmly and quietly issuing orders in the mist of this maelstrom. The secondary guns were also out of ammunition, now firing starshells and practice rounds. When those rounds were almost gone, one of the sailors asked what to do next. An older man suggested they raid the potato locker.[51]

Waller decided to make one last attempt to force their way past St Nicholaas Point into Soenda Strait. He began a looping port turn back to the southwest at full speed.[52] His objective would be Toppers Island, in view just beyond St Nicholaas Point at the northern end of the strait. Captain Rooks and the *Houston*, as always, followed. But there were too many ships arrayed against them.

Too many ships even for the Japanese, perhaps, who were acting more like a circular firing squad than a noose to be squeezed tight to win a battle that by rights should not have been even this close. More Japanese torpedoes were launched, heedless of the fact that they were *surrounding* the Allied fugitives. At 11:57 pm the *Mogami*, now north northwest of Pandjang Island, launched six torpedoes from her portside tubes at the *Houston* to the south at a range of about 10,000yd.[53] They missed – and went on bubbling towards the mass of Japanese transports anchored to the south in Bantam Bay.

Off in Bantam Bay, the commander of the Japanese 16th Army, General Inamura Hitoshi was in the 8,160-ton modified transport *Ryujo Maru*.[54] Earlier, one of his aides had "heaved a sigh of disappointment to think that this landing operation was to be made without firing a single rifle or gun or without bloodshed."[55]

The arrogant aide's wishes probably changed when, as he was working to unload the second wave of Imperial Japanese Army troops, gunfire erupted offshore. On the *Ryujo Maru*, "[T]he facial expression of the soldiers changed to anxiety," and General Inamura watched the naval battle drift closer and closer to his transports with increasing annoyance. That annoyance turned to something worse when, at 12:05 am, the *Ryujo Maru* suffered an underwater explosion that tossed the general off the ship and into the warm waters of Bantam Bay.[56]

The thin-skinned *Ryujo Maru* had been hit by a torpedo. Explosions from torpedoes also rocked the transports *Sakura Maru*, *Horai Maru*, and *Tatsuno Maru*.[57] They all sank in the shallow waters of Bantam Bay. General Inamura's aide remembered "tanks and automobiles and freight which had been loaded on the deck fell into the water beside us with a dreadful sound."[58] Tons of army equipment was destroyed and hundreds of troops drowned.

Precisely whose torpedoes struck the transports has never been conclusively determined. The only thing on which naval historians agree is that the torpedoes did not come from the *Perth* or, obviously, the *Houston*. The Japanese themselves seemed to think the torpedoes had come from the *Fubuki*, fired at the beginning of this engagement from the other, eastern end of Bantam Bay.[59] But a Japanese investigation could not determine who fired the torpedoes.[60] Over the years others have claimed that the cruiser *Mikuma* was responsible with a launch whose exact time is unclear.[61] Given the timing of the explosions on the transports, the spread launched from the *Mogami* was most likely responsible.[62] General Inamura believed the *Houston* was responsible, which in a manner of speaking she was; the Imperial Japanese Navy was all too happy to accept that version of events to cover up their own incompetence.[63]

The *Mogami* was not alone in launching torpedoes at will. At 11:56 pm the *Harukaze* fired five torpedoes, followed a minute later by six from her squadron mate *Hatakaze*. *Shirakumo* and *Murakumo*, coming from the west, each launched nine torpedoes at midnight. Admiral Hara would later say that his ships experienced more than a few near misses from the 7th Cruiser Division's torpedoes, saying, "We felt very much in danger."[64] The unrelated Commander Hara would relate the story of how the Japanese spent almost as much time avoiding their own torpedoes as they did firing at the Allied ships.[65]

The *Perth*, now reduced to firing starshells, and the *Houston* did not take this new harassment lying down. The destroyer *Shirakumo* was hit and damaged by the *Houston*, and more shells ripped into the *Harukaze*, killing three and wounding five men. At

12:07 am, the minesweeper *W-2* was hit, capsized, and sank, possibly struck by one of the *Mogami*'s torpedoes.[66]

The destroyers' searchlights were now finding the Allied cruisers. On the decks of the *Perth* and the *Houston*, it now felt like they were performing on a stage, stars of a show in which they wanted no part, but were giving virtuoso performances nonetheless. Now began a somewhat bizarre game. Waller gave orders to shoot out the searchlights – "For God's sake shoot that bloody light out!" was one of Waller's few heated exclamations during this entire engagement – and the Australian and American sailors working their machine guns proved fairly proficient at it.[67] The Japanese responded with one destroyer having the cruisers in her searchlight, then snapping it off before she could be targeted, only to have another searchlight from someone else pin the fugitives. The destroyers' searchlights served to illuminate the *Houston* and *Perth* for the guns of the *Mikuma* and *Mogami*, hiding in the darkness somewhere behind the glare of the lights.[68] Everywhere across the sky Japanese flares and illumination rounds floated down like slow-falling meteors. As the destroyers came closer and closer, the *Houston* opened up with her 1.1in pom-poms and .50cal machine guns.

There is no adjective superlative enough to describe the performance of the *Perth* and the *Houston* in this, the last hour of their lives and the lives of Hector Waller, Albert Rooks and a good portion of their crews. In their last stand, dead tired, surrounded, almost out of ammunition, chances of escape gone, they roared in defiance at the Japanese aggressors, firing every gun they had with every piece of ammunition they had, holding on for as long as they could. Somewhere, Leonidas and his 300 Spartans from Thermopylae must have looked on with approval. But there were just too many torpedoes.

The *Perth* had just settled on her new course, still trying to make Toppers Island, when at 12:05 am she was hit by a torpedo, probably from *Harukaze* or perhaps the *Hatakaze*, on the starboard side between the forward engine room and Boiler Room "A."[69] The *Perth* suddenly lost speed and became sluggish to the helm. With the flooding caused by the earlier shell hit near the waterline, the torpedo hit seems to have been particularly bad. And Captain Waller knew it.

"Christ, that's torn it. Prepare to abandon ship."

"Abandon ship, sir?" responded the gunnery officer.

Waller shook his head. "No. Just prepare for it."[70]

The skipper was getting very discouraging reports of damage, to which he always responded "Very good" to these pieces of news that were anything but. A few minutes later, two more torpedoes hit, probably from *Shirakumo* and *Murakumo*.[71] One hit the starboard side near the forward magazine for A-turret. Seawater and oil were splashed over the bridge, knocking down a number of men, including Captain Waller. Picking himself up off the deck, he ordered the crew to abandon ship.[72]

As the crew was evacuating, the third torpedo hit, again on the starboard side, this time aft under the "X" turret. The senior officers on the bridge tried to get Captain Waller to leave, but the skipper refused. He remained with his hands clamped to the bridge railing looking over the forward 6in turrets, now silent forever.[73] He ordered the crew off the bridge and was never seen again. It was a grave loss to the Royal Australian Navy, to lose such a fine commanding officer. Commodore Collins would later write, "[Waller] was a fine fighting sailor, a tower of strength, and beloved by all. The loss of *Perth*, her fine Captain, and her tried and true company was a sad blow to the RAN."[74] But those who survived to be treated to the hell of a Japanese prisoner-of-war camp might have wondered if Waller had the right idea.

The Japanese now closed in on the helpless *Perth*, still staggering her way forward as she settled lower and lower in the water, and, with the cruiser pinned by multiple searchlights, blasted her with gunfire of pitiless efficiency. A fourth torpedo, from whom is unknown, stuck the cruiser on her port side, but it was superfluous. With her Australian ensign illuminated by the searchlights, the *Perth* was still moving, being driven by her only remaining functioning propeller. As her survivors would say she "did not sink" but instead "she *steamed* out" into the deep, some 9.5 miles north northeast of St Nicholaas Point at 12:25 am on March 1, 1942.[75] Of the 686 souls aboard the *Perth* that night, 351 were lost, including Captain Hector MacDonald Laws Waller. Another 106 died in the hospitality of Japanese prisoner-of-war camps.[76]

The crew of the *Houston* watched the death of their cohort with sadness and anger. They were next and they were alone. Captain Rooks gave up the idea of forcing his way to Toppers Island and turned around to make the Japanese pay. "When Captain Rooks realized that the *Perth* was finished and escape was impossible, he turned the *Houston* back toward the transports, determined to sell his ship dearly," wrote Lieutenant Winslow.[77] She fought on with even more ferocity. She was now caught in the glare of three searchlights, with the *Houston* using her 8in, 5in, pom poms and .50cal machine guns against the Japanese searchlights. One of her Marines somehow managed to shoot out a Japanese searchlight with a rifle.[78]

At 12:20 am Captain Sakiyama had the *Mikuma* and *Mogami* maneuver to again adopt a parallel course to the *Houston* and began another exchange of gunfire, in which the *Houston* was severely punished. She received a serious hit, believed to be from an 8in shell, though some believe it was a torpedo, in the aft engine room. A second full salvo went through the wardroom. The hit ruptured steam lines and killed everyone inside. The cruiser's speed was cut to 23 knots.[79] Another shell hit the No. 2 turret in the face plate just as powder was exposed for loading what would have been the *Houston*'s 28th salvo from her main battery. The hit was a dud, but the sparks ignited the powder, causing a fire which forced the flooding of the forward magazines.[80] Now both forward turrets were silent forever. The *Houston* gamely returned fire, hitting the *Mikuma* on the bridge, killing six and wounding 11 Japanese. The *Houston*'s 5in guns were now reduced to firing off their starshells, though the range was now so close that even the starshells were deadly to the Japanese crewmen, immolating them on deck.[81] But it was an unequal fight.

So many torpedoes appeared that there was almost no way of tracking them all. Precisely how many torpedoes hit the *Houston* is still unknown. Based on her reconstructed log, the general belief is at least four. Commander Maher, the cruiser's gunnery officer, would later say, "Because of the overwhelming volume of fire and the sheer rapidity with which hits were being scored on the *Houston*, it is impossible to determine in many instances whether a shell, torpedo or bomb hit had occurred."[82]

Her first hit by a torpedo, apparently from either *Shirakumo* or *Murakumo*, was on the starboard side beneath the bridge.[83] Two more came in quick succession, all on the starboard side. The *Houston* was now disemboweled, quickly taking on a 10-degree list to starboard.[84]

That was it. It has been claimed that Captain Rooks considered beaching the cruiser on the beaches of Bantam Bay, where the crew would disembark and fight on shore back to civilization, such as it was, but in any event he did not do so.[85] Having been forced from the bridge by the fire in the No. 2 Turret, Rooks summoned the Marine bugler, Jack Lee, and said to him, "Bugler, sound abandon ship." Lee played it into the ship's PA system. One survivor marveled at Lee's composure: "He never missed one beat on that bugle. It would have been absolutely beautiful if it had been anywhere else but that time."[86] On this night, everyone on the *Houston*, even the bugler, was at his absolute best.

The crew began abandoning ship. Motor torpedo boats were joining the Japanese destroyers in raking the *Houston*'s decks with machine-gun fire. Some of the *Houston*'s gunners refused to leave their posts until their ammunition was exhausted and dealt punishing blows to the boats with their .50cal machine guns. It was a last gesture of defiance. Officers and crewmen streamed over the sides.

Walter Winslow shook hands one last time with Captain Rooks, then climbed down a ladder to the deck below – just in time to see a hit where he had been standing with the skipper. Rooks was hit by shrapnel in the head and upper torso. The captain staggered and fell, covered in blood, some 10ft away from Ensign Charles D. Smith. The ensign injected Albert Rooks with two tubes of morphine. "He died within a minute," Smith would later write. The ensign covered him with a blanket and went to report the skipper's death to the *Houston*'s executive officer, Commander David W. Roberts, who was now in command, and navigator Commander John A. Hollowell, Jr. Sometime later, Captain Rooks' cook, Ah Fong, who had come with the *Houston* from Shanghai, was seen cradling the skipper's lifeless form in his arms. His voice trembling with emotion, the cook, known to the crew as "Buda," repeated over and over again, "Captain die, *Houston* die, Buda die, too."[87]

The *Houston* was caught in the glare of the Japanese searchlights, burning, blackened, twisted, slowly heeling over to starboard, sinking. But a sinking American ship was not good enough for the Japanese; they wanted her sunk. So they fired one last torpedo at the already-sinking *Houston* at point blank range, hitting her high on the port side. Who fired it is disputed. The *Houston*'s log indicates that it was fired by a motor torpedo boat, but a postwar examination of Japanese records suggests the torpedo was fired at 12:29 am by the destroyer *Shikinami*.[88] It was pointless and academic.

In response to this latest insult added to her grievous injury, the *Houston* merely continued her roll to starboard, her bow dipping beneath the waves. Every single primary source, from her log to Walter Winslow, mentions the state of her flag, caught in the Japanese searchlights, catching a breeze and flying defiantly from her mainmast just above the water: " … a sudden breeze picked up the Stars and Stripes still firmly two blocked on the mainmast, and waved them in one last defiant gesture. Then with a tired shudder she vanished beneath the Java Sea."[89] Sources do not agree on the time she disappeared forever. Some place it at 12:36 am but other, mainly American, sources estimate it to have been 12:42–12:45 am, March 1, 1942.

Only 368 of the *Houston*'s 1,061 officers and men survived the sinking.[90] They were now floating, swimming, in the Java Sea, some trying to make it to shore, others just trying to avoid the Japanese troops searching for them, shooting some of the survivors in the water, knocking others out with hits from rowboat paddles. A total of 102 of the *Houston*'s survivors died in POW camps.

One more individual was in the water: General Inamura. After being thrown from his flagship when it was sunk by friendly fire, he spent 20 minutes on a piece of wood before being picked up by a boat, then three hours making his way to the beaches of Bantam Bay.[91] Once back on terra firma, he sat down on a pile of bamboo, wet, black with oil and exhausted.

His arrogant aide, also a dripping wet, oil-covered survivor from the *Ryujo Maru* and perhaps a bit chastened now, came up to him with a touch of the humor that is always needed in a war.[92]

"Congratulations," he said, "on the successful landing."[93]

CHAPTER 18

NOWHERE TO RUN – THE SECOND BATTLE OF THE JAVA SEA

For years afterwards, until after the end of the war when Japanese records could be examined and prisoners of war recovered, the official position of the US Navy and the Royal Australian Navy was that they did not know what had happened to the *Houston* and *Perth* other than that they had vanished somewhere off western Java on the night of February 28/March 1, 1942.

This official position was due to their inability to get precise details to confirm their suspicions. Sometime after 11:00 pm on February 28, various Allied units in the East Indies theater had begun intercepting cryptic signals on the wireless telegraph. At least two came from the *Perth*, one a report of ONE UNKNOWN, the second clarifying the first as ONE DESTROYER.[1] These were picked up by the Allied station at Darwin and by *Perth*'s sister ship *Hobart*, now off the southern coast of Sumatra and making for Ceylon.[2] But they could only get bits and pieces of information.

Around 11:30 pm came another cryptic signal, this one from the *Houston*. Intended for Admiral Glassford, the US naval forces in the Philippines, and Admiral King in Washington, it read: ENEMY FORCES ENGAGED. Ominously – and, for those monitoring the situation, frustratingly – that was the last anyone heard from the *Houston*.[3]

But there was one visual witness, of a kind, to the bedlam off Bantam Bay: the Dutch destroyer *Evertsen*.

The *Evertsen*, under the command of Lieutenant Commander Walburg Marius de Vries, had been playing an odd role in the Java Sea Campaign. Though the Dutch had been desperately short of ships, she had been kept on convoy duty until February 26, when she was pulled to join the *Dragon*, *Danae*, *Tenedos*, and *Scout* as part of the Western

Striking Force. It is very revealing that though Admiral Helfrich had felt compelled to transfer the *Exeter*, *Perth*, *Hobart* (who ultimately could not go), *Electra*, *Encounter*, and *Jupiter* from the Western Striking Force to the Eastern Striking Force, on the grounds that they were the best and most modern ships available, he did not transfer the *Evertsen*, which was in physically better shape than, say, the *Kortenaer*. It suggests a lack of confidence in the destroyer's ability. The fact that the crew of the *Evertsen* was not fully trained may explain Helfrich's handling of the destroyer, as well as her actions during the last few days of the campaign, actions that have left historians mystified.[4]

The sweep of the Western Striking Force ended with the *Evertsen* in company with the force heading towards the Soenda Strait. But the destroyer got separated from the other ships in a storm.[5] All alone, she returned to Tanjoeng Priok on February 28.[6]

On the evening of February 28, the *Evertsen* was supposed to leave in tandem with the *Houston* and *Perth* for Tjilatjap. But, for whatever reason, with the Japanese landing on Java mere hours away, Commander de Vries does not seem to have been in any particular hurry to get out of Batavia. Unlike the US destroyers in Soerabaja, he had not kept his boilers boiling and thus had no engine power to be able to leave with Captain Waller. She was left behind.[7]

The *Evertsen* did not leave Tanjoeng Priok until two hours after the *Perth* and *Houston*. Commander de Vries had only two of his three boilers up, because, it would seem, he did not want the added smoke the third boiler would emit, which could tip off the Japanese to the destroyer's movements in the darkness. She cleared the minefield protecting Tanjoeng Priok at 9:15 pm.[8] The skipper seems to have planned to take a route to Soenda Strait closer to that originally conceived by Admiral Helfrich; that is, not hugging the Java coast but looping around and instead hugging the Sumatra coast down the Soenda Strait.

While so doing, at around midnight, when the *Evertsen* was near the Agenieten Islands, her lookouts spotted flashes of gunfire, tracers, searchlights, and flares to the south. Commander de Vries dutifully reported that they could see a sea battle in progress off St Nicholaas Point. Admiral Helfrich seems to have been surprised by the message – like the *Perth*'s Captain Waller and the *Houston*'s Captain Rooks, he had not been given the latest intelligence showing just how close the Japanese convoy was to the Java coast. Nevertheless, Helfrich reacted to the report by sending the following orders to *Houston*, *Perth*, and *Evertsen*: EVERTSEN REPORTS SEA BATTLE OFF ST. NICHOLAS POINT … IF ANY OF ADDRESSEES ARE ENGAGED WITH ENEMY, OTHERS RENDER ASSISTANCE AS POSSIBLE.[9]

After receiving this order, Commander de Vries seems to have tried everything he could to avoid engaging the enemy in the sea battle he was witnessing. It was perhaps not the most valorous of decisions, but it is certainly defensible. With the *Perth* and *Houston* facing two heavy cruisers, a light cruiser, about a dozen destroyers and numerous smaller craft like minesweepers and motor torpedo boats, the *Evertsen* was not likely to make a difference. With an untrained crew, more likely than not, she would have gotten herself sunk for no appreciable gain.

De Vries instead headed for Poelau Moendoe (Pulu Mundu), Sumatra. There he turned south into the Soenda Strait, hugging the Sumatra coast, hoping that the *Evertsen* would not be spotted in the moonlight against the dark shore.[10] But that hope proved to be mere wishful thinking. At around 2:00 am, while near the island of Dwars in de Weg, the *Evertsen* was pinned by the searchlights of the Japanese destroyers *Murakumo* and *Shirakumo*. Fresh off their drubbing of the *Perth* and *Houston*, the two destroyers were speeding on a southerly course looking for fugitives, of which the *Evertsen* was one. The *Murakumo* and *Shirakumo* promptly opened fire.[11]

With one of her three boilers not boiling, the *Evertsen* could not outrun the Japanese destroyers; de Vries had gambled and lost on that count. He turned to starboard to hug the Sumatra coast, again hoping that the *Evertsen* could disappear against the dark shore. It was no use. The gunfire from the *Murakumo* and *Shirakumo* was scoring hits. One knocked out the *Evertsen*'s fire control. The Dutch destroyer's feeble efforts at returning fire were completely ineffective. A series of hits pounded the *Evertsen*'s after section, starting a large fire. Damage control could not put out or control the fire, nor could the aft magazine be flooded.[12]

Seeing that this was going to end badly, de Vries did what he could to save his crew. He drove the *Evertsen* towards Seboekoe Besar (Sebuku Besar), another island in the Soenda Strait. With the *Murakumo* and *Shirakumo* in hot pursuit, the *Evertsen* let loose with her torpedoes, again ineffectually. Then the Dutch destroyer intentionally ran aground on Seboekoe Besar, driving ashore till her bow was high out of the water. The fire on the stern cooked off the aft magazine, which exploded with such force that, as with the light cruiser *Java*, the stern was blown off.[13] The crew abandoned ship and headed as far inland on Seboekoe as they could; their skipper signaled Bandoeng that the *Evertsen* "had been intercepted by two cruisers and had beached herself in a sinking condition" on Seboekoe.[14]

All of the survivors were eventually captured by the Japanese and given the treatment that was typical for the Imperial Japanese Army and the Kempeitai. Of the *Evertsen*'s crew, 57, including Lieutenant Commander de Vries, died during the sinking and subsequent imprisonment; 111 survivors were returned to the Netherlands after the war.[15]

With the loss of the *Evertsen* alongside the *Perth* and *Houston*, the Soenda Strait was now closed to Allied ships. No one was going to get through.

That gate had clanged shut and been locked up tight.

Through the Malay barrier – February 28–March 1

Not closed to the Allies – yet – was the Bali Strait. Thanking Heaven they were able to head through it were the skippers and crews of the four destroyers of US Destroyer Division 58: the *John D. Edwards*, *Alden*, *John D. Ford*, and *Paul Jones*. Of all the ABDA ships, they had the best chance of escape.

But just because the Bali Strait was not closed did not necessarily mean it was without serious danger. The Dutch had informed Commander Binford that a Dutch ammunition ship had been sunk on February 27, and that on February 28 a Dutch merchant ship had been sunk by a Japanese cruiser and a destroyer (actually, as it turned out, two Japanese destroyers, the *Wakaba* and the *Hatsuharu*), both in the Bali Strait.[16]

Trying to leave as little to chance as possible, Commander Binford made what preparations he could for his division. At around 8:30 pm the destroyers went to battle stations. With a full moon out that night, the crews paid particular attention to covering all reflective surfaces. Binford would later say that, "My idea was to fight off the enemy and to retire to the south as quickly as possible, because I expected other enemy forces in the immediate vicinity."[17]

At 12:07 am on March 1, US Destroyer Division 58 finally cleared the mined channel of the Oostervaarwater and entered the narrowest part of the Bali Strait, where it is only about a mile wide.[18] The waters in this area are hazardous, and the navigators were glued to their fathometers, which in places registered depths of only 25 or 30ft.[19] Lieutenant Commander Cooper of the *John D. Ford* was desperately hoping the Dutch had not mined the area, especially not with the quality of mining they had shown in the Gulf of Toeban.[20] Dangerous as it was, the destroyers had to hug the Java coast as much as possible and, like the *Evertsen*, hope their silhouettes would be lost against the dark backdrop of the land.[21]

But Commander Binford was more prepared than his counterpart on the *Evertsen*; he had kept all his boilers going, knowing that his best chance at escape was speed. The American destroyers cleared the narrows at about 1:15 am and increased speed to 26 knots on a course of 130 degrees True – southeast, still hugging the Java coast.[22]

And, unlike the *Evertsen*'s, this gambit seemed to be working when, at 2:05 am, an enemy destroyer was seen some 8,000yd on the port bow.[23] The Japanese destroyer came about and adopted a parallel course five minutes later. Dim flashing lights were seen to the southeast, from where came two more Japanese destroyers, who promptly joined the first destroyer to form a column.[24] The three destroyers were part of Destroyer Division 21, which actually consisted of four destroyers: *Wakaba*, *Nenohi*, *Hatsuharu*, and *Hastushimo*, commanded by Captain Shimizu Toshio.[25] Either they did not see the Americans against the land or they were waiting for an opportunity to fire.

That opportunity arrived at about 2:30 am. The four US destroyers, still hugging the Java coast, turned east to avoid the reef off the eastern tip of Blambangan Peninsula, where the troops of a Dutch garrison were watching the proceedings. With the Americans now silhouetted in the brilliant moonlight, the Japanese destroyers opened fire on relative bearing 225 degrees at an initial range of 5,000–6,000yd.[26]

For some reason, the Japanese destroyers focused on the *John D. Ford*, the third destroyer in the now strung-out American column. The first salvo straddled her, and subsequent ones were so close that her skipper, Lieutenant Commander Cooper, was convinced they were using radar.[27] Nothing came anywhere near the other US destroyers.

Lieutenant Commander Coley, skipper of the *Alden*, said that the 5in shell splashes were about 1,000yd short. Commander Binford would report that, "Enemy fire was well over and splashes nowhere near the formation."[28]

The US destroyers increased speed to 27 knots and began returning gunfire. The 4in guns of the four-pipers were ineffectual against Japanese destroyers, but their objective now was not so much to injure the enemy as to keep them away. Commander Cooper described the tactic: "An attempt was made to keep up a rapid volume of fire rather than an effective fire... Our aim was to keep the enemy outside effective torpedo range."[29] Then again, the US Navy had no idea of the effective range of the incomparable Japanese Type 93 torpedo.

But Commander Binford had one ace up his sleeve. The US destroyers had no torpedoes, but they did have firing primers, which were used to blast the torpedoes from their tubes. The firing primers flashed when a torpedo was launched. During the Battle of the Java Sea, the US destroyers had witnessed such flashes when the Japanese light cruiser *Jintsu* launched a torpedo attack, and it is fair to wonder if this is where Commander Binford got the idea. Firing just the primers was the torpedo equivalent of firing blanks. Where they did not have firing primers, they used dummy charges. The torpedo tubes were trained directly at the Japanese destroyers and "fired."

After this the Japanese destroyers seemed less than full-throated in their pursuit of the Americans. The Japanese dropped directly astern, from where the US destroyers were not so visible in the moonlight. By 2:36 am, the Japanese had stopped firing, but remained in pursuit. Oddly, however, the old four-pipers were actually opening the range on the normally much faster Japanese destroyers.[30]

Having rounded the reef, the American destroyers turned southwest along the Java coast on a course of 205 degrees True.[31] The Japanese did not follow. At 3:21 am, the US destroyers observed flashes from over the horizon astern – gunfire, "sometimes in timed salvo fire, sometimes in irratic [sic] bursts," matched by a corresponding dull rumble that came shortly afterwards. The firing stopped after seven minutes or so. At 3:50 am the lookout on the *John D. Ford* reported hearing a continuous low rumble from astern. Perhaps a ship sinking? The bridge could not confirm the low rumble.[32] There is no record of a combat action at this time and precisely what the gunfire was about remains a mystery. The US destroyer skippers suspected that the Japanese were firing blindly, hoping to provoke the Americans into responding with gunfire that would reveal their position.[33]

The four destroyers of Destroyer Division 58 seemed to lead a charmed existence. They had escaped the Java Sea and had gotten through the Malay Barrier, encountering Japanese vessels who seemed rather uninterested in stopping them. The Americans assumed that the Japanese destroyers had reported their position, and they braced themselves for the daylight that would bring the inevitable air attacks. But on this day, March 1, the air attacks did not appear. Even though they were well within range of the Denpesar airfield on Bali and Kendari II on Celebes, and *Kido Butai* was known to be lurking in the Indian Ocean south of Java, the Japanese aircraft never showed up for reasons that remain unclear. The *John D. Edwards*, *Alden*, *John D. Ford*, and *Paul Jones* went at their best speed, gas-guzzling for Australia.

They had escaped, but now they wondered about the fate of the last of their kind, still trapped north of the Malay Barrier in the Java Sea: the USS *Pope*.

NOT SO LUCKY: THE *EXETER, ENCOUNTER,* AND *POPE* – FEBRUARY 28–MARCH 1

Just off the southern coast of Borneo in the Java Sea, the officers and men of the *Pope*, like those of Destroyer Division 58, were wondering about her fate as well.

Captain Gordon's little group of ships spent the late evening of February 28 still working their way out the Westervaarwater, the northern entrance to Soerabaja. They then assumed cruising formation, with the *Encounter* and *Pope* taking positions off the port and starboard bows, respectively, of the *Exeter*.[34] On board the cruiser, the Royal Navy engineers were still trying to work miracles with their damaged machinery. And they had some success. At around 11:00 pm, they were able to bring two more boilers online, giving them four boilers total – all on the starboard side.[35] The *Exeter*'s speed went back up to 23 knots, but they could not get any more than that.[36]

On the bridge, Captain Gordon was happy he did not have to worry much about Japanese aircraft at this hour, but he kept a wary eye out for Japanese ships. He also had his radio room keep a watch for signals from the *Perth* and the *Houston*. They were going through the Soenda Strait, as his little "force" was supposed to do, much to the disgust of his crew. Like him, they thought that their proposed escape route had little chance of success. They might have a fighting chance – literally – if they headed east. Gordon, ever the consummate professional, would never let on that he shared the crew's unhappiness about it.[37]

In fact, no one was happy about it, not on the *Exeter* nor on the *Encounter* nor on the *Pope*. Some of the officers tried to keep spirits up in the face of Admiral Palliser's insane plan. When a boatswain's mates asked the *Pope*'s Lieutenant Michel about their chances, he replied, "It's a cinch. Our orders are to avoid action because *Exeter* is damaged. Besides, the Japs will be so busy with their landing that they'll never notice us." The answer seemed to satisfy the mate, if not Michel himself.[38]

It was Commander Blinn's *Pope* that first realized there was another, far worse problem than simply surviving the day tomorrow. That problem became apparent in the ominous bits and pieces of information coming out of the Soenda Strait. Coming as it did from their planned route of escape, the information did not go unnoticed by the *Exeter*, *Encounter*, and *Pope*. At around 11:30 pm, the radio room on the *Pope* intercepted a message indicating that "a severe sea battle was in progress off entrance to Sunda Strait."[39] They had apparently gotten hold of the *Houston*'s signal of ENEMY FORCES ENGAGED.

At that point, Captain Gordon's ships were 20 miles east of Bawean Island, heading north.[40] All the ships monitored the message traffic coming out of the Soenda Strait. Gordon would later state with some frustration that he could not get any information as to the numbers of enemy ships involved.[41]

By 2:00 am, the messages coming from the Soenda Strait had ceased, and no one could raise the *Houston* or the *Perth*. An unknown ship was sighted off the port bow and Captain Gordon promptly ordered a change of course to the east, hoping to remain unseen.[42]

On board the *Pope*, Commander Blinn and his staff had deduced that the *Perth* and *Houston* had been sunk by superior enemy forces in the Soenda Strait. Blinn asked that this information be kept from the crew. There was some hope on the bridge of the *Pope* that the news from Soenda Strait might convince Captain Gordon to abandon the hopeless course set out for them by Admiral Palliser and to instead head east. Blinn ordered his navigator to prepare analyses of what their best speed would be for Australia based on their current fuel.[43] But any hopes for a more sensible course to the east were dashed at 2:05 am when Captain Gordon ordered a course change to 345 degrees True – north northwest.[44] All they could do now was hope Admiral Palliser knew more than his orders suggested.

The plan had been to turn westward at 4:00 am, but before that could happen, in the light of the setting moon, the lookouts sighted three ships – two large and one smaller – to the west approximately 10 miles away, heading south southwest. They believed them to be two merchant ships escorted by a cruiser or destroyer, on a course to pass west of Bawean Island. Attempting to evade them, Gordon turned the *Exeter* and her cohorts away to the east, looping around back to the north and returning to the original course of 345 degrees True at around 4:30 am. Subsequently, they began curling their course more towards the west, as at 6:00 am they turned to course 290 degrees True and at 7:00 am course 280 degrees True.[45] They were still desperately hoping to somehow remain unseen.

In short, it was not even dawn yet and Captain Gordon's force had already had at least one and probably two encounters with Japanese ships. It was a miracle they had not been seen. The idea that loitering off Borneo for an entire day trying to avoid such incidents gave the *Exeter*, *Encounter*, and *Pope* the best chance of escape was nothing short of ludicrous. When dawn did come on March 1, 1942, they were some 60 miles south of Tanjoeng Poeding on the south coast of Borneo.[46] The day was warm, clear and bright, the seas calm – the worst possible weather for hiding from the Japanese.

At 7:50 am, a lookout on the *Exeter* reported the masts of two ships, cruisers or larger, nearly dead ahead, steering to the north northeast. Captain Gordon decided to immediately reverse course back to the east and in the direction of the still-rising sun, in the hope that the Japanese would be sun-blinded and unable to see the *Exeter* and her cohorts.[47]

Those hopes seemed to be dashed when the masts turned, indicating that the ships, whose hulls were still below the horizon, were turning towards the Allied fugitives. But the masts turned back to their original course and soon disappeared. These ships were apparently the *Ashigara*, flagship of Admiral Takahashi, commander of the Eastern Invasion Force, and her sister ship *Myoko*.[48] Their job was to provide "distant support" to the invasion and its supporting naval forces. Gordon sent a contact report but received no acknowledgment. It seems the Japanese indeed did not see the *Exeter* hidden in the sun's glare. Their turn toward the east was supposedly to launch their floatplanes, although Gordon in his report later stated that the *Exeter*'s air warning radar did not show any aircraft nearby at this time.[49]

With the Java Sea swarming with Japanese ships, such near misses could not last. At 9:35 am, the *Exeter*'s lookout in the crow's nest reported the topmasts of "two large cruisers" bearing about 170 degrees True – almost due south – heading west. Once again, Captain Gordon tried to evade, turning to 320 degrees True – northwest, but the two Japanese cruisers turned toward the Allied ships.[50] These Japanese cruisers were Admiral Takagi's *Nachi* and *Haguro*, whom the *Exeter* had escaped less than 48 hours before.[51]

The Allied fugitives had been spotted. Admiral Palliser's plan had not even made it to lunch. With Palliser's absurd plan now out the window, Captain Gordon would have to improvise.

Gordon's turn to the north was met by two Japanese destroyers, the *Akebono* and *Inazuma*, charging right at them. At 10:20 am, the *Exeter*, *Encounter*, and *Pope* opened fire on these trespassers. The Japanese destroyers quickly made a smokescreen and scurried away – back to their bigger brethren who were coming up right behind them: the *Ashigara*, which Gordon identified, and *Myoko*. The two Japanese cruisers opened fire on Captain Gordon's group at a range of some 25,000yd.[52]

This was the worst case scenario that could have been imagined – a limping *Exeter* facing four enemy cruisers. The course set out by Admiral Palliser had unwittingly taken the Allied fugitives right into the midst of the Japanese 5th Cruiser Division. The destroyers *Akebono* and *Inazuma* looped around to the west and took up positions south of the Exeter near two other Japanese destroyers, the *Yamakaze* and *Kawakaze*, who had been screening the *Nachi* and *Haguro*.[53] Now the Japanese had four cruisers and four destroyers to face the Allies' one cruiser, which was limping, and two destroyers, one of which had no torpedoes. Captain Gordon assessed the situation as follows: "It was not encouraging."[54]

The *Exeter* immediately turned to the east, course 90 degrees True, and Captain Gordon ordered as much speed as his battered engines could give. They would try to make a run for it. Without orders, Lieutenant Commander St. John Morgan of the *Encounter* and Lieutenant Commander Blinn of the *Pope* bathed the *Exeter* in a smokescreen. The cruiser's chief engineer reported that he could get an additional boiler up and running in about an hour. Gordon told him to make it so, and in less time than had been anticipated, at around 11:00 am, the boiler was up and the *Exeter* was moving at 25 knots.[55]

Lieutenant Michel was chided about his previous, overly optimistic appraisal of the situation. "Say, Mr. Michel, didn't those guys get the word?" a torpedoman asked. "We're supposed to be avoiding them and they're supposed to be covering the landing on Java." And, truth be told, the torpedoman was right, but, as Michel replied, "Well, you can't expect these ... bastards to get the word."[56]

And so the chase, such as it was, was on. The *Exeter*, with the *Encounter* and *Pope* zigzagging around her, was running to the east. Following her on a parallel course to the northwest were the *Ashigara* and *Myoko*. On a parallel course to the south were the *Nachi* and *Haguro*. Between Gordon's ships and Admiral Takagi's two cruisers were the four Japanese destroyers *Akebono*, *Inazuma*, *Yamakaze*, and *Kawakaze*, also on a parallel course. Overhead were the ubiquitous Japanese cruiser floatplanes, doing spotting for the *Ashigara* and *Myoko*'s gunfire.

Though the odds of escape were indeed long, the crews of the Allied ships noticed something odd about the Japanese ships: they were riding high in the water.[57]

When a ship is fully loaded – a merchantman with cargo, a warship with munitions, both with fuel – its hull will sit low in the water. Its freeboard – the distance between the water and the main deck – will be relatively short. As it unloads cargo, delivers munitions or uses fuel, the freeboard will get longer and longer, as the ship rides higher and higher in the water. In short, a ship riding high in the water is relatively empty. That meant only one thing: the Japanese were low on fuel.

Admiral Palliser had been right.

In fact, the Japanese ships were desperately short on fuel. Admiral Tanaka, whose ships had worked with Admiral Takagi's during the Java Sea battle less than 48 hours previously, had to order Captain Hara in the *Amatsukaze* to make a run to Banjermasin to get a full load of fuel and return so that the remainder of Tanaka's 2nd Destroyer Flotilla could get just enough from the destroyer to make it back to port.[58] In short, Tanaka's group was essentially out of fuel in the middle of the Java Sea. They were in the worst shape of any of the Japanese ships, but neither Admiral Takahashi's nor Admiral Takagi's ships could have been in a much better situation.

Palliser's plan had been based on the hope that the Japanese would be returning to port to fuel. In fact they were not, but this does highlight another absurdity in the plan: the *Exeter* and her cohorts were directed to hide off Borneo, to which the Japanese ships would eventually be returning to refuel. Indeed, Palliser's planned course inadvertently took the *Exeter* and her cohorts right between two groups of Japanese cruisers of the 5th Cruiser Division.

Still, however deeply flawed Admiral Palliser's plan may have been, it did give Captain Gordon and the *Exeter*, *Encounter*, and *Pope* an opening to escape. They were now racing for their lives eastward across the Java Sea. But this was not a race of speed but rather of endurance. Captain Gordon was in better shape for fuel than the Japanese. If his ships could avoid taking damage, they could keep racing the Japanese until the Japanese were forced to break off for lack of fuel. It was not a great chance, but it was a chance.

From the start, the Japanese had been closely coordinating this operation. When the *Nachi* spotted the *Exeter*, Admiral Takagi believed that despite his numerical advantage he was in no position to take on the cruiser alone; in addition to being nearly out of fuel, he was also nearly out of 8in ammunition as a result of the Java Sea action.[59] So he maintained contact with the *Exeter* and called for assistance from Admiral Takahashi's *Ashigara* and *Myoko*, still with nearly full magazines. It would be Takahashi's cruisers who would take the lead in this particular action. And the Japanese kept coordinating their movements effectively. The *Ashigara* and *Myoko* adjusted their parallel course slightly to starboard, to close on the *Exeter*. To the south, the *Nachi* and *Haguro* mirrored the adjustment, turning slightly to port.

The two groups of cruisers were now on converging courses with the *Exeter*. On what would be a day to forget for Japanese gunnery, the *Ashigara* and *Myoko* would fire 1,171 8in shells, so far to little effect.[60] Their rounds seemed to get close to or even straddle the *Exeter*, but they could not manage a hit. They were being severely hampered by what was an extremely effective smokescreen created by the *Encounter* and *Pope*, which apparently not even spotting by the Japanese floatplanes could overcome. The *Exeter* even managed to shoot down one floatplane and damage another with her 4in guns.[61]

But the *Exeter* was having severe gunnery problems of her own. Very early in the action, the cruiser suffered a major failure in her gun director, the piece of equipment that takes entries of the target's course, speed, and distance to come up with an appropriate firing solution for the guns. The firing angle, which determines the range of the shot, seemed to be acceptable, but the deflection – where the shot lands left to right – was way off. The result was that all of the shots fired by the *Exeter*'s main guns were falling very wide of their targets. The *Exeter*'s fire control improvised with an old piece of targeting equipment known as a Dumaresq, but it was ineffective.[62]

Nevertheless, Captain Gordon found another reason for hope. At about 11:00 am he spotted on the eastern horizon two very slight rain squalls, which could provide a measure of cover. By this time, the *Exeter* had managed to reach 26 knots, zigzagging between 70 degrees True and 110 degrees True, or 20 degrees off her base course of 90 degrees True. The *Encounter* and *Pope* were working in and out, making smoke with their smokestacks and dropping smoke pots.[63] Gordon hoped they could reach the squall, which could allow his crew time to fix the gun director and permit him to focus on driving off one of the two cruiser groups instead of trying to hold them at bay all at once.[64] He could not have known that the *Nachi* and *Haguro* were low on ammunition.

But the *Ashigara* and *Myoko* had closed to 18,000yd on the port quarter. The *Nachi* and *Haguro* were also 18,000yd off the starboard beam. All four cruisers seemed reluctant to close the range further, apparently because they feared the *Exeter*'s torpedoes.[65]

The Japanese destroyers, however, were much more aggressive. They caught up to the *Exeter*, making pests of themselves off the starboard beam. The British cruiser engaged them with her 4in secondary guns.[66] The *Encounter* and *Pope* used their guns to try to drive off the *Akebono* and *Isazuma*, who were pressing especially hard.[67]

But everyone on the Allied ships knew their time was running out. Their only possible salvation – and that a temporary one at best – would be the two squalls. Seeing that the

Ashigara and *Myoko* had stopped closing the range, Captain Gordon played his last card by launching the *Exeter*'s torpedoes from her port tubes at the two Japanese cruisers from long range at 11:05 am. Five minutes later, the *Pope*, on the port side of the *Exeter*, launched four torpedoes from her port tubes at the *Ashigara* and *Myoko* at a range of 6,000yd.[68] The attacks forced the two Japanese cruisers to turn and make a complete 360-degree circle to avoid them, but avoid them they did.[69] Gordon's hope was that the attack would at least keep them at bay long enough to reach the squall.

Meanwhile, the *Pope* had crossed ahead of *Exeter* to her starboard side, where she launched her last five torpedoes from her starboard tubes at the *Nachi* and *Haguro*.[70] No hits were registered. Silent until now, Admiral Takagi's cruisers opened fire with their 8in guns at 11:15 am. They also launched torpedo attacks of their own, *Nachi* launching four Type 93 torpedoes at 11:20 am, followed two minutes later by four from the *Haguro*. The destroyer *Kawakaze* also fired two at 11:19 am. Two minutes later the *Yamakaze* launched four.[71]

The *Exeter*'s gun director was almost repaired. They had almost reached the squalls. But they were to remain forever almost there, as at 11:20 am all hope ended. An 8in shell (from whom is not clear) finally made a hit on the *Exeter*, and a devastating hit it was too. It landed in Boiler Room "A" on the starboard side, where four of the five still-functioning boilers on the cruiser were located.[72]

This single hit did irreparable damage to the jury-rigged propulsion system for the *Exeter*. The main steam pipe was cut. The main engines stopped. All power in the ship failed, except for one dynamo that remained functional for a short time. The main guns, now without power, were frozen in place; they could not train and could not fire. The fire control for the secondary 4in guns was out of action as well. Boiler Room "A" was on fire, which necessitated the flooding of the adjacent 4in magazine.[73]

The *Exeter* was finished. She was not sinking – in fact, her watertight integrity had not been impaired in the slightest – but she could not move and could not fight. She was surrounded by enemy ships and was in serious danger of being captured intact. Captain Gordon gave the only orders he could: scuttle the ship. At 11:35 am he followed that grave order with another equally grave: abandon ship.[74]

With the stoppage of the engines, the *Exeter*'s forward momentum began to slack off. The Japanese gunfire seemed more accurate now, against a hulk slowing to 4 knots. Aboard the *Exeter*, seacocks, condenser inlets, and flooding valves for magazines were opened to the sea. Explosive charges placed in the propeller shaft passages were detonated.[75] The crew evacuated calmly and without panic.[76] Joining the officers and men in abandoning ship was a small flock of ducks that had been kept to provide fresh eggs for Captain Gordon. With the *Exeter* being evacuated, someone had the presence of mind to release the ducks from captivity. They wouldn't get a spot on the lifeboats, but no matter. The ducks merely hopped over the side and were last seen "quacking merrily," swimming towards Borneo.[77]

The loss of power meant that the *Exeter*'s crew could not lower the large lifeboats, but anything else that could float was tossed over the side. The cruiser's continuing slow movement forward actually helped the crew by drawing Japanese fire away from the swimming Royal Navy men.[78] Ultimately 44 officers, including Captain Gordon, and 607 men survived to be rescued by the Japanese, mostly by the destroyer *Inazuma*.[79]

Before abandoning ship, Captain Gordon had given one last order by the still-functioning voice radio to the destroyers *Encounter* and *Pope*: "Make a run for it and do not pick up survivors."[80]

Lieutenant Commander Blinn of the *Pope* and Lieutenant Commander St. John Morgan of the *Encounter* could not leave their comrades on the *Exeter* in such extreme shape without giving them some assistance. Blinn had his destroyer turn around and laid one more smokescreen around the stricken cruiser to protect her crew during the evacuation before speeding off to the east.[81]

The *Exeter* was still pouring smoke from the fire in her boiler room and was showing a steadily increasing list to port.[82] She took a second hit from an 8in shell, this time in the vicinity of the "Y" (aft) turret.[83] The list was quickly ended at about 11:45 am, when the cruiser suffered an underwater explosion on the starboard side, the result of two torpedo hits from the *Inazuma*.[84] Captain Gordon would call this "the mortal wound."[85] The *Exeter* now quickly righted herself, then took a steadily increasing heel to starboard until she capsized and sank sometime around 11:50 am.[86]

Believing his work done, at 11:45 am Admiral Takagi had the *Nachi* and *Haguro* cease fire and headed southward again. They had fired only 170 and 118 rounds of 8in ammunition, respectively.[87] It is fair to ask precisely what Takagi's cruisers were doing so far in the Java Sea when they had been assigned to support the invasion still in progress at Kragan, Java. This divergence from their assignments almost ended in disaster, as they were the targets of a torpedo attack from the US submarine *Permit*. Skipper Lieutenant Commander Chapple crept up and launched three torpedoes from only 600yd. But he scored no hits – again.

The remaining Allied destroyers were indeed trying to make a run for it, as Captain Gordon had ordered. But while the *Pope* was already well to the east, the *Encounter* had been behind the *Exeter* when the cruiser took the decisive hit, and she could not disengage from the Japanese long enough to make a break for it. At 11:35 am, a very close miss from an 8in shell from either the *Ashigara* or the *Myoko* caused a catastrophic mechanical breakdown: a suction pipe was broken, disabling her lubrication system, knocking her engines offline and depriving her guns of power.[88] Commander St. John Morgan got the news from his chief engineer that the engines could be brought back online – in two hours.[89] But the *Encounter* didn't have two hours. She didn't even have two minutes.

With the *Encounter*, like the *Exeter*, now in serious danger of being captured intact, Commander Morgan, too, was forced to give the order to abandon ship and scuttle his destroyer. She sank at 12:05 pm.[90]

With that, the *Ashigara* and *Myoko* stopped firing. They had fired 1,171 8in rounds, for a grand total of two hits. The Japanese had also fired 35 torpedoes, for a grand total of two hits, both by the *Inazuma*. Six officers, including Commander St John Morgan, and 143 men of the *Encounter* were rescued by the Japanese, mostly, again, by the destroyer *Inazuma*.[91]

The only Allied ship left in the Java Sea, the only Allied ship north of the Malay Barrier, was now the single, old, four-piper destroyer USS *Pope*.

The *Pope* had been lucky. A little before noon, she had managed to reach the rain squall and was quite happy to hide in the "torrents" of rain that reduced visibility to 50ft.[92] She changed course to 60 degrees True – east northeast – to throw off potential pursuit.[93] But the *Pope* was having problems of her own. She had engaged the Japanese destroyers with her 4in guns, firing 345 4in rounds in some 150 salvoes in addition to the nine torpedoes she had launched.[94] Her forward magazines were empty, and her gunners spent much of this time transferring ammunition from her aft magazines to the depleted forward one. The concussion caused by her salvoes was taking a toll on the ship. The brickwork inside her No. 3 boiler had collapsed, forcing the shutdown of the boiler and permanently lowering her speed.[95]

Commander Blinn's ship cleared the squall, only to promptly run into a second squall. The crew's hopes began to rise. Maybe they would get out of this yet. And Blinn changed course to 40 degrees, again to throw off the Japanese, and optimistically began calculating a run through the Lombok Strait that night.[96]

The *Pope* emerged from the second squall at around 12:15 pm – too soon for the tastes of her crew – into a brilliant tropical day.[97] The sun was at its near-noon high, and there was nothing in the sky – except for a single Japanese floatplane.

The harbinger of doom for the entire Java Sea Campaign had been the Japanese seaplane. This one, a Type 0 "Pete" floatplane from the seaplane tender *Chitose*, was no different – sitting safely out of antiaircraft range while reporting the *Pope*'s position.[98]

And while the lookouts on the *Pope* could only watch helplessly in frustration, she was joined by another Pete. And another. And another. And another. Soon there were a total of ten Pete floatplanes, all from the *Chitose*, all following the *Pope*.[99]

The *Pope* sent a desperate message to Admiral Glassford: RETIRING TO THE NORTHEAST, REQUEST YOU DRIVE OFF TRAILING PLANES.[100]

At around 1:00 pm, the air attacks that everyone on the *Pope* had been dreading began. The floatplanes attacked independently, one at a time, with 132lb bombs using high level bombing tactics.[101] Commander Blinn adopted the now familiar tactic of having someone lie on his back on the deck with a pair of binoculars focused on the attacking aircraft, calling out when it dropped its bomb, at which point Blinn would turn the destroyer hard to port or starboard.[102] It worked – for a while.

Commander Blinn's handling of the *Pope* was masterful, but there are some things that even the best skipper cannot control. The destroyer's antiaircraft armament was limited to four .50cal machine guns and one 3in gun. Located on the fantail, the 3in gun was of limited use overall, but in this case was perfectly placed to drive off pursuing aircraft. Her gunners managed to keep the floatplanes at bay for a while. To be more precise, 75 rounds, at which point the gun jammed, or "failed to return to battery" to use naval terminology.[103] With the machine guns only able to reach low-level aircraft, the *Pope* was now practically defenseless.

The bombing attacks continued. The *Pope* continued to twist and turn to avoid the floatplanes' bombs and, while shrapnel from one near miss forward damaged the range finder and wounded two crew members, Commander Blinn mostly succeeded in avoiding those bombs.[104]

The 11th bombing attack resulted in another near miss off the port side near the stern. The concussion split several hull seams, but it did far worse to what was proving to be the Allied Achilles heel during this campaign: the port propeller shaft. The shaft was jarred out of line. Similar to what happened to the *Prince of Wales*, the offline shaft, spinning at high speed to propel the *Pope* as fast as possible, now sent a very heavy vibration through the ship. The shaft had to be shut down, reducing the destroyer's speed even more. But, similar to what happened on the *Prince of Wales*, the off-center spinning shaft had managed to shred the glands securing the shaft passage from the sea. Water now poured deep into the *Pope*'s innards through the shaft passage.[105]

Damage control was immediately directed to try to stem the flooding which, when combined with the loss of the propeller, had caused the *Pope* to become sluggish to the helm. Just in time for yet another air attack by six Type 97 "Kate" carrier attack planes from the Allied nemesis *Ryujo*.[106]

At 1:35 pm, the Kates began low-level bombing attacks on the *Pope*. Each Kate was carrying one 550lb bomb and four 132lb bombs.[107] With a sluggish, slowing ship settling by the stern, somehow Commander Blinn managed to avoid every single bomb.[108]

But that didn't matter now. The flooding through the shaft passage could not be controlled. The stern was nearly awash. More attacks could be expected. The *Pope* had not even been hit by a bomb, but she was finished and Commander Blinn knew it.

So the order was passed to abandon ship and scuttle the *Pope*. Everything was settled quickly and calmly. Two 10lb scuttling charges were set. Secret documents and equipment were destroyed. The depth charges were confirmed to be set on safe and then dumped. After all was done, the crew got into the destroyer's whaleboat and rafts. The demolition charges exploded and the crew began pulling away from the sinking destroyer – just as shell splashes began appearing in their midst.[109] The *Ashigara* and *Myoko* had arrived.

By now the *Pope*'s stern was under water and, though the damage had been to the port side, she was listing to starboard. Now, one 8in shell, apparently from the *Myoko*, exploded on the destroyer.[110] It only hastened her end. The USS *Pope*, the last Allied ship in the Java Sea, slid into that sea stern first at 2:20 pm.[111] Then, oddly, the Japanese ships simply left. All but one of the *Pope*'s 151 crew survived – that one had been killed not by the Japanese but by one of the scuttling charges – but they had to wait two days to be rescued by the Japanese destroyer *Inazuma* on March 3.[112]

To the credit of her skipper, Lieutenant Commander Takeuchi Hajime, the *Inazuma* seems to have made a special priority of rescuing these Allied survivors and even treating them with medical care and food. Unfortunately, such compassion would end as soon as the survivors were dropped off at Makassar City.[113]

And so, the Japanese naval combat operations north of the Malay Barrier came to a successful conclusion. Admiral Ozawa with his Western Invasion Force and Admiral Takahashi with his Eastern Invasion Force had done their jobs.

And in the minds of the Japanese, the *Ashigara* and *Myoko* had done their jobs by providing "distant support" for the invasion. That had not meant actually helping to protect the invasion by driving off Admiral Doorman's ships two days earlier at the Battle of the Java Sea, which they most definitely did not do. The emphasis in "distant support" had always been on "distant."

Instead, it had meant courageously chasing down and sinking three badly outnumbered, even more badly outgunned and crippled ships trying to flee.

CHAPTER 19

TO THE WINDS – ESCAPE ATTEMPTS FROM JAVA

Second Lieutenant James Moorehead was a fighter pilot, one of the few left in Java, with the US Army Air Force's 17th Pursuit Squadron (Provisional). On this day, February 27, he was not so much a fighter pilot as a guide. His job was to lead the pilots of the 13th and 33rd Pursuit Squadrons (Provisional) back to the 17th's base at Ngoro. These trained pilots, lacking in combat experience, along with their planes, were to arrive that afternoon in Tjilatjap on board the seaplane tender *Langley*.

Lieutenant Moorehead spent much of the 27th on an ancient train. When he stepped off in Tjilatjap, he found the town and its harbor area in a state of suspended chaos. The roads were clogged with military supply trucks and jeeps. The Dutch were setting up for demolition of the harbor installations and anything of military value to deny them to the Japanese. The town and its docks were clogged full of people – civilians and military, many in a panic – looking for a way to get out of a Java they knew was doomed.

But that was irrelevant to Lieutenant Moorehead. He pushed and shoved his way through the throngs to get to the long pier at which the *Langley* was supposed to dock but there was no sight of her.

When he saw the empty pier, Moorehead had a very good idea of what had happened.

His suspicions were confirmed by a reporter from the *Chicago Sun-Times*. "There'll be no *Langley*," he intimated in a solemn whisper. "The Japs got her."[1]

He could get no official confirmation but Lieutenant Moorehead would hear people discussing the sinking of the *Langley* on the streets of Tjilatjap. That was enough confirmation for him, or at least as much confirmation as he was going to get for now. He got back on board the train and returned to Ngoro.[2]

Communications had never been the strong suit of ABDACOM, but as the Japanese approached Java, whatever rudimentary system ABDACOM had managed to improvise fell apart completely. It had become a grab bag of missed messages, intelligence information unfathomably delayed or not provided at all, and conflicting orders as experienced by Admiral Doorman, Captain Waller, and Commander McConnell respectively.

This had been the case with the *Langley.* The seaplane tender had been sunk, but the Japanese would never have had the opportunity if the *Langley* had not received one order telling her to get to Tjilatjap as soon as possible and another to turn away from Tjilatjap to meet with her escort, a crippled minelayer. Orders pulling the *Langley* in opposite directions had pinned her in place for the Japanese air attack.

THE LAST DAYS OF THE *PECOS* – FEBRUARY 27–MARCH 1

The next victim of ill-thought out orders was the *Pecos*, the Asiatic Fleet's sole remaining tanker in the area. The role of the *Pecos* was to act as a mobile gas station, fueling the ships of the fleet, whether at sea or in port. This is exactly what she had been doing in Tjilatjap, fueling American, British, and Dutch ships in Tjilatjap from fuel that she received from bulk tankers.

Once the Japanese captured Bali and its Denpesar airfield, Commander Elmer Paul Abernethy did not like the idea of being cooped up in Tjilatjap's anchorage. He thought it would be safer if the *Pecos* was at sea, where he could still refuel ships but maintain some mobility. Admiral Glassford agreed, calling it "a procedure which appeared more desirable than to require our ships to fuel at Tjilatjap under constant threat of air attack while immobilized."[3] The Dutch, for reasons known only to them, did not. The *Pecos* was stuck.

In the meantime, Admiral Glassford continued his struggle to get fuel for his ships. It was a problem exacerbated by the Dutch unwillingness to acknowledge the dire straits they were in. The Japanese occupation of most of the East Indies had left the Dutch with only the oil production of Java to support themselves, and much of that oil was stuck in the mountains of central Java. There was no way to get the oil to the coasts because so many native Indonesian workers had gone into hiding with the start of the Japanese air attacks.

The problem was typified by Soerabaja. Soerabaja had largely been abandoned as a base due to Japanese air attacks – Admiral Glassford had described the naval base there as now "operating at 5% efficiency," but it still had 50,000 tons of oil in its storage tanks.[4] After cajoling and begging, Glassford managed to get the Dutch to agree to a plan to move some of its oil to Tjilatjap. Unwilling to risk the oiler *Pecos*, he sent the civilian bulk tanker *British Judge* to Soerabaja to recover some of the fuel. By some miracle, the *British Judge* made it there and back unhindered.[5] By the time it had returned to Tjilatjap, the *Pecos* had finally been cleared to leave, on February 27, but only because its dock was needed by the incoming *Langley.*[6]

Admiral Glassford's plan had been to have the *British Judge* offload its oil directly into the *Pecos*, after which the *Pecos* would take to sea. He had issued orders to this effect, but the Dutch ignored them and had the *British Judge* unload into their shore tanks.[7]

It was all taking too long, much too long for Commander Abernethy. In addition to the threat from the Denpesar airfield, aircraft carriers had been reported south of Java. Despairing over the fate of his ship, Abernethy ordered the crew to gather as many bamboo poles as possible. These improvised flotation devices were all tied down to the deck of the *Pecos*.[8]

Coming down by train from Jokjakarta on February 25 had been Dr Wassel and 40 patients from the February 4 attacks on the *Houston* and *Marblehead* in the Flores Sea. Of those 40, 30 were ambulatory and ten, including the badly burned Commander Goggins, were on stretchers. It was hoped that the *Pecos* could evacuate them all, but Commander Abernethy refused to take aboard the ten on stretchers or any non-ambulatory passengers – they would be helpless if the ship sank. Refusing to abandon his patients, Dr Wassel returned with them to Jokjakarta.[9]

So on the morning of February 27, escorted by the destroyer *Parrott*, the *Pecos* threaded her way out of Tjilatjap into the Indian Ocean, heading southwest towards Ceylon. Commander Abernethy doubled the lookouts, ordered all watertight hatches sealed, and had a steam blanket placed over the oil in the tanks to drive out volatile gas fumes and reduce the risk of fire and explosion.[10] A few hours later, the *Pecos* received the "nerks" of the *Langley*, which was under Japanese air attack and desperately calling for help. She was only 30 miles from the *Pecos*. Realizing that his oiler would be next-to-useless in this situation, Abernethy, a well-respected and practical skipper, prudently steered his ship well clear of the *Langley's* soon-to-be grave and sped westward.[11]

Even so, he could not escape the infection of the *Langley* disaster. Shortly thereafter, Commander Abernethy received orders to rendezvous with the destroyers *Whipple* and *Edsall*. The two destroyers were swamped with the survivors they had carefully picked up from the *Langley*. These badly needed ships could not be used for other duties until the survivors were offloaded. So the *Pecos* was directed to meet the *Whipple* and *Edsall* just off Christmas Island, where she would take on the *Langley* survivors and proceed to Australia. The rendezvous would occur on the north side of Christmas Island in a place called Flying Fish Cove, which would provide some protection from the winds blowing across the Indian Ocean.[12]

But the harbor could not provide protection from Japanese air attacks. By 8:20 am on February 28, the *Whipple* and *Edsall* had arrived off Flying Fish Cove and were waiting for the *Pecos*. Flying Fish Cove was home to the facilities of a phosphate mining company. An employee of the company, identified only as E. Craig, left the company dock in a small launch to offer to pilot the warships and warn them of navigational hazards. Instead, the boat was used to shuttle 32 combat airmen from the *Whipple* to the *Edsall*, which was to take the pilots to Tjilatjap. As the transfer was completed, the *Pecos* arrived, minus the *Parrott*, who had gone to escort the *Sea Witch* to Tjilatjap.[13]

A pilot boat from the *Edsall* came alongside the *Pecos* carrying Craig and Commander Thomas A. Donovan of the *Langley* to arrange the transfer, and promptly fouled its propeller in a line. In yet another example of the Allies' terrible luck during this campaign, just as the pilot boat was struggling to free itself, three Japanese twin-engine Mitsubishi bombers appeared from the direction of Sumatra.[14] Out of necessity the boat was cut loose. Craig lurched for the boarding ladder to the *Pecos* and made it, but Donovan could not. The boat was left adrift with Donovan aboard.[15]

As it turned out, the Japanese were there to bomb the phosphate mining facilities, not the ships. Not that this did Commander Donovan much good. Not wanting to be immobile in the face of an air attack, the *Pecos*, *Whipple*, and *Edsall* got under way. The Japanese pilots proceeded with their mission, dropping six bombs near the docks, making a low-level pass by the *Pecos*, and then flying back towards Sumatra. Donovan watched in horror as the three US Navy ships sped away toward a rainsquall to the south, leaving him behind. His horror was nothing compared to his feelings when the Japanese captured Christmas Island and took him prisoner.[16]

It seems like a heartless decision by Commander Edwin M. Crouch of Destroyer Division 57 aboard the *Whipple*, abandoning Commander Donovan, a popular officer, to a cruel fate. The survivors of the *Langley* certainly thought so. But the Japanese had undoubtedly reported the presence of the *Pecos*, *Whipple*, and *Edsall*. It was still very early in the day, and new air attacks could be expected. Additionally, during the attack a periscope had been sighted northeast of the cove. Under these dangerous circumstances, Crouch could not risk three ships, or even one ship, for one man.[17]

The squall covered the three ships for some 30 minutes, after which they found no more enemy planes. Commander Crouch kept the *Pecos*, *Whipple*, and *Edsall* running southward, trying to put as much distance as possible between them and the Japanese airfields on Sumatra and Bali. They still had to transfer the survivors, however, a task that was complicated by rough seas and winds as high as 26 knots.[18] The lee of Flying Fish Cove would have been helpful, but it was no longer an option.

So unfavorable were the conditions that the transfer had to wait until the next morning, March 1. At 4:25 am the transfer began in the heavy seas and windy conditions, using a whaleboat expertly handled by a boatswain named Robert J. Baumker; four hours later, 353 souls from the *Langley* had been transferred from the cramped destroyers to the much roomier *Pecos*. Then everyone went their separate ways. The *Whipple* headed westward, course 279 degrees True, toward a refueling rendezvous off the Cocos Islands with the British tanker *Bishopdale*.[19] The *Edsall* set about taking the pilots to Tjilatjap and into controversy and mystery of her own. The *Pecos* headed course 160 degrees True, south southeast, towards Fremantle, Australia.[20]

For the survivors of the *Langley*, the *Pecos* was a Godsend. After their home had been sunk, they had been packed aboard the *Whipple* and *Edsall* until the destroyers were practically bursting. The crewmen were literally piled in the hallways. They were ecstatic to be able to stretch their legs again. Except for those who were pulled for duty on the *Pecos*, few gave much thought to a repeat of their ordeal.[21]

But Commander Abernethy had been giving that matter quite a lot of thought. He would prove prescient. For at around 10:00 am, members of the crew reported hearing a humming sound, like an engine, coming from somewhere to port. Commander Abernethy ordered general quarters and, sure enough, an aircraft, shining in the sunlight, was spotted.[22]

The plane flashed recognition signals, which convinced some of the crew it was Australian. But the recognition signals did not match any known Allied code. Commander Abernethy ordered as much speed as the *Pecos'* engines could manage: 14.6 knots. The tanker's antiaircraft guns – two 3in guns located near the bow and ten water-cooled machine guns – opened fire. But the plane just circled twice and soon disappeared to the east.[23]

Commander Abernethy, along with the *Langley's* Commander McConnell and Executive Officer Lieutenant Commander Divoll, had been on the port wing of the bridge watching the scene unfold with a rising sense of dread. They knew what that single plane portended.

"We're in for it now," glumly observed Commander McConnell. Commander Abernethy would later say, "I felt we were in for serious trouble." The aircraft brought an unwanted sense of déjà vu all over again to many of the survivors of the *Langley*. One of them remarked, "It won't be long now."[24]

Indeed, it would not be. For the plane that had spotted them was not the usual telltale sign of imminent attack, death, and destruction: a seaplane, either a cruiser floatplane or a large Kawanishi flying boat. This was something far worse: a carrier plane. The reports of Japanese aircraft carriers south of Java had been correct. And those carriers now had knowledge of the *Pecos*.

Commander Abernethy held little hope for his ship, but though he held a lousy hand he still had a few cards to play. After conferring with Commander McConnell, at 10:40 am Abernethy ordered a change in course toward the west – 225 degrees True.[25] A half hour later they headed back south again closer to their original course. The navigator was keeping very careful, precise track of the *Pecos'* position, in the likely event that she needed to issue a call for help. The skipper kept reminding the lookouts to be sharp.[26]

"Here they come!"

The call had come not from one of the many, many lookouts, but a coxswain, identified only as J. Balitzki, who, at about 11:45 am, just happened to look up – and see a dive bomber, one of those Aichi D3As that would become known as the "Val," screaming right out of the sun, already late in its dive and ready to release its bomb.[27]

For most of the Java Sea Campaign, the Japanese relied on level bombing – an aircraft just flying along and dropping its bombs when over a target – usually from the twin-engine Nells and Bettys, or sometimes the Kate torpedo planes. The Japanese Naval Air Force had enjoyed unusual success with level bombing so far; normally, it was not very accurate against ships at sea, especially when tried from high altitude.

This attack was different. The Val's forte was dive-bombing: far more accurate and effective – but also much more difficult and dangerous. The plane's dive would serve to essentially guide the bomb on its way down to the target. At the end of the dive the plane would release the bomb and pull up, preferably in time to avoid crashing into the target, at least at this early point in the war. Momentum and gravity would direct the bomb the rest of the way.

There were two kinds of dive bombing. One was glide bombing, which usually involved diving from a shallow angle. Typically used by inexperienced pilots, it was not as effective as the other kind, sometimes called "hell-diving," in which the plane would dive from an angle approaching 90 degrees. It would scream straight down, adding its speed to the pull of gravity to direct the bomb to its target. It required the most skill and daring, but skill and daring were hallmarks of the Japanese Carrier Striking Force from which this Val dive bomber had come.

Despite all of Commander Abernethy's preparations and warnings to his lookouts, the Val's dive out of the sun, a common tactic for hiding approaching attackers, had caught the *Pecos* by surprise, allowing the aircraft to release its bomb before the tanker could open fire with its 3in antiaircraft and its machine guns. The bomb exploded in the water off the port side.[28]

Circling over the *Pecos* outside her antiaircraft range at an altitude of 16,000ft were five more Vals, their gull wings and spat-covered fixed landing gear conjuring images of the dreaded German *Stuka*. In short order, one of the dive bombers broke from the circle and dove on the tanker. A sharp turn to port enabled the tanker to avoid this second bomb, which detonated in the water to starboard.[29]

This seemed like a weird attack with the dive bombers attacking one at a time seemingly like target practice – which indeed, it was.

Just 80 miles away was *Kido Butai*, Admiral Nagumo's carrier force. It had not seen a lot of opposition since Pearl Harbor and was looking for some practice. When an Allied transport, the Dutch merchantman *Modjokerto*, was sighted at 9:55 am, Nagumo had his escorts engage in a little "firing exercise" with their main guns. With the carrier flight decks packed with spectators, the cruiser *Chikuma* moved in to pound the *Modjokerto* with gunfire. When that proved ineffective – the armor-piercing shells just passed through the thin-skinned transport's hull without exploding – the *Chikuma*'s furious skipper, Captain Komura Keizo, put her under with a torpedo, earning an immediate rebuke for wasting torpedoes on non-combatants.[30] Almost immediately thereafter, at about 10:30 am, came the report of an Allied "special service ship" nearby.[31]

There were no enemy fighters nearby. The sky was clear, with a few scattered clouds. Pilot Ensign Yamagawa Shinsaku would later say the "weather was ideal for bombing."[32] Now was a chance for more target practice, this time for Nagumo's dive bombers. First off was a flight of six Vals from the carrier *Kaga*, under the command of Lieutenant Watanabe Toshio.[33]

So far, they had shown they clearly needed the practice, as the first two Vals had attacked and missed.[34]

The third Val was piloted by Ensign Yamagawa. He was impressed by Commander Abernethy's handling of the *Pecos*, later saying, "[I]t really was something. The ship's captain certainly was skilled and superbly avoided our bombs." The *Pecos* was also putting up a level of antiaircraft fire that Yamagawa described as "fierce."[35]

No matter. At 12:03 pm, Ensign Yamagawa's 550lb bomb, released at approximately 1,500ft, found its target, exploding on the *Pecos'* main deck near the starboard 3in mount. Most of the gun's crew were killed. Four oil tanks were smashed, with the oil catching fire. Fire mains and oil lines were ruptured. Worse, the concussion knocked out the tanker's radios.[36]

Commander Abernethy now had his hands full. The *Pecos* was afire, her radios were out and, apparently as a result of the first bomb that had missed off the port side, she was developing a list of 8 degrees to port.[37] There were still three Vals of the *Kaga's* squadron left to make their attacks.

But the skipper was dealing with the situation admirably. The fat lady was not singing yet, but she sure was dancing, as adroit maneuvering by the large, slow, cumbersome *Pecos* managed to avoid the bombs of the three remaining bombers.[38] This display of Japanese bombing accuracy, or lack thereof, left the *Langley's* air officer Lieutenant Commander Harry Hale underwhelmed. A former dive bomber pilot, Hale kept up a running commentary on the apparent lack of skill of the Japanese pilots.[39]

Moreover, the fire was quickly brought under control. The list was stabilized and mostly corrected. The radios were quickly brought back online, or at least it was hoped they were. The 3in gun was quickly manned again. The *Pecos'* gunners were furious, throwing up everything they could at their Japanese tormentors – 3in rounds, .50cal rounds, .30cal rounds, bullets from Browning Automatic Rifles and Colt .45s, and, as they had on the *Perth*, potatoes.[40] The spud missiles may have been more a humorous morale booster than anything else and the small arms fire was nothing short of useless, but the plucky tanker was drawing blood; of Lieutenant Watanabe's six Vals, four were damaged, including Yamagawa's.

Upon his return to the *Kaga*, Watanabe proudly reported that the *Pecos* "was observed to sink after the attack."[41] This goes to show the unreliability of eyewitness accounts of damage, especially those of the Imperial Japanese Navy, which as the war went on would gain more and more of an inverse relationship to the damage actually inflicted. The *Pecos* had not sunk and was in no danger of sinking – for now, at least. The vaunted *Kido Butai* had been stymied by, of all things, a tanker. Commander Abernethy may have taken a bloody nose, but he left the *Kaga's* pilots with egg on their faces – or at least potato.

Nevertheless, the *Pecos'* supply of potatoes was limited, and her desperate predicament was not unappreciated by her crew and the survivors of the *Langley*. At 12:27 pm, as the *Langley* had done 48 hours earlier, her radio room began broadcasting her "nerks" and making her desperate call for help:

NERK V NIFQ ATTACKED BY BOMBERS SHIP HIT MAYBE SINKING LAT 15 LONG 106 K K ANYBODY K K.[42]

The immediate list had spooked the men in the radio room, though not nearly as much as the silence they received after they sent the message out.

What they did receive, at about 1:00 pm, was another attack: six Vals from the carrier *Soryu* under the command of Lieutenant Ikeda Masi.[43] This time the *Pecos* was ready, or at least as ready as she could be.

But though she had survived the first attack from the *Kaga*, the *Pecos* had still been hurt. The flooding caused by the near miss meant that she had hundreds of tons of water sloshing in her innards. It would be a serious drag on the already cumbersome tanker as she tried to defy the odds and avoid Lieutenant Ikeda's bombs.

NERK NERK NERK NERK NERK NERK ...[44]

Again, the *Pecos* put up an impressive barrage of antiaircraft fire, and some of the *Soryu*'s pilots were so put off by the barrage that they dropped their bombs early. But with the tanker's maneuverability hindered, the Japanese bombs hit home. The first one hit just forward of the bridge to starboard, blowing out the bridge's windows and some 20ft of hull on the starboard side, mostly above the waterline, and starting a fire. On the heels of the first hit came a second, which passed through the foremast, destroying the radio antenna before detonating in an oil storage tank amidships and collapsing the center line bulkhead. The list now increased, back up to 15 degrees, and the tanker temporarily lost steering.[45]

NERK NERK V NIFQ ATTACKED BY BOMBERS SHIP HIT MAYBE SINKING LAT 15 LONG 106 K K ANYBODY K K.[46]

For the survivors of the *Langley*, especially those not already actively involved in the defense of the *Pecos*, the repeat of their experience of just 48 hours earlier was rapidly becoming a crushing mental burden. Surviving the sinking of a ship, especially as a result of combat, is a traumatic experience. The survivors of the *Langley* had had only 48 hours before they were facing the same traumatic experience yet again. Without being able to focus their minds on their normal duties, many (but by no means all) of these men were in a daze, showing the famous "thousand yard stare." Attempts to get them to help with the *Pecos*' plight came to naught.[47]

As might be expected. These men, who had been strong enough and brave enough to join the military in the first place – not just the military, but the front-line Asiatic Fleet – were not weak or somehow lacking in necessary martial qualities. They had simply been thrust into the most inhuman of circumstances – twice – in 48 hours. Very, very few people could withstand that level of trauma. This was "combat fatigue" or, to use the more technical term, "combat stress reaction," a condition now acknowledged and treated by mental health professionals and the military. It can, and does, strike anyone. Even the crew of the *Pecos*: her antiaircraft plotter, Ensign E. J. Crotty, was driven temporarily mad by a bomb hit and had to be restrained.[48]

So it is no surprise that when someone near the stern shouted, "Abandon ship," many of these men snatched onto that supposed directive without thinking. No such directive had been given, but its rumor created a near panic at the stern of the *Pecos*. Before order could be restored, two boats, several life rafts, and numerous floatables were tossed over the side. People jumped overboard, only to watch helplessly as the tanker continued on its way. With the list, the *Pecos'* starboard propeller was now partially out of the water. One of the boats lowered over the side, filled with passengers, landed on the spinning propeller, with predictably gruesome results. None of the perhaps 100 unfortunate souls who abandoned ship during this time were ever seen again.[49]

While these unfortunates were literally diving headlong into oblivion, the attack continued. The next bomb missed, but the one after that, at 1:13 pm, landed on the forecastle between two 5in mounts, killing the crews of both. Immediately thereafter came another that went right through the hole created by the earlier hit near the 3in mount. It detonated deep inside the ship, crushing more bulkheads and frustrating the radio room's efforts to repair the antennas and get out the call for help on their assigned radio frequency. The tanker's repeated, desperate "nerks" continued to go unanswered.[50]

At 1:30 pm, yet another bomb just missed the *Pecos*, detonating off the port quarter. But she might as well have hit. The shock wave slammed into the tanker's side, rupturing hull seams, collapsing the brickwork in one of the boilers and freezing another, and knocking her speed down to 10 knots.[51]

Like the *Soryu's* dive bombers, now heavily perforated with evidence of the *Pecos'* defiance, the *Pecos* herself was now battered, bleeding, bruised. But she was not dead. The frozen boiler was restarted and her speed worked back up to 12 knots. By 2:12 pm, the list had been reduced to 10 degrees.[52] The vaunted *Kido Butai*, the same *Kido Butai* that had sunk practically all the battleships of the Pacific Fleet at Pearl Harbor, was now struggling to sink a tanker.

But the *Pecos'* wounds, though by no means mortal, had left her sorely hurt. Commander Abernethy ordered everything that could float to be brought up to the weather deck. And he ordered a radio electrician from the *Langley*, Charles A. Snay, to see if he could help with the apparent problems in the *Pecos'* radio room. Snay's extra set of eyes indeed helped. He assisted in making some temporary repairs, and between 2:14 and 2:28 pm, the *Pecos'* wireless, off frequency, cried out her nerks once again:

NERK NERK NERK NERK V [...] BOMBED MAY BE SINKING LAT 15 LONG 106 K K.[53]

To silence.

The *Pecos* was all alone. Except for the 18 Val bombers that appeared at 2:45 pm: nine from the *Akagi* under Lieutenant Chihaya Takehiko, and nine from the *Hiryu* under Lieutenant Shimoda Ichiro. Since the *Akagi* was the flagship of *Kido Butai*, her squadron had the honor of going last, so Shimoda's Vals attacked first at 2:50 pm. But instead of going one at a time, as they normally would for target practice, the *Hiryu*'s bombers all piled on the *Pecos* at once. Nine Val dive bombers, flown by the best pilots in the world, like an aerial execution squad, dropped their bombs on the staggering tanker, to send her finally to her grave – and they all missed.

The gunners of the *Pecos* had taken such casualties that her antiaircraft guns were now manned by a gaggle of untrained volunteers from the *Pecos* and *Langley*, with a few from the *Stewart*, *Marblehead*, and *Houston*. With a rage borne of their months of torment, they fired everything they had – 3in, .50cal, .30cal, potatoes – putting up a barrage far larger than a tanker had any right to. The storm of shrapnel was so vicious that Lieutenant Shimoda's pilots, not willing to risk their lives for target practice, were unnerved enough to drop their bombs early. All of them missed. Two exploded in the water just off the tanker's starboard side, the shock waves knocking out the *Pecos*' jury-rigged radios yet again.[54]

Finally, at 3:00 pm came Lieutenant Chihaya's nine Vals from the *Akagi*. Like Shimoda's Vals from the *Hiryu*, they dove all at once. For one last time, Commander Abernethy and his *Pecos* rose to the occasion. Once again, the maelstrom unnerved the plunging Vals. Some of them, apparently trying to get the perfect drop for their bombs, made multiple dives (earning scoldings from their air officer), but ultimately most still dropped their bombs too early. And, once again, all their bombs missed. Not that it did the *Pecos* much good.[55]

NERK NERK V 9VTW T L 9VTW YE82 O BT BOMBED MAY BE SINKING LAT 15 LONG 106 PLEASE COME.[56]

While seven of the bombs missed badly, two – the seventh and eighth bombs dropped – were near misses. The seventh detonated near the partially exposed starboard propeller, literally blowing people off the ship, wiping out the gun crews near the starboard quarter and hammering the engine room with its shockwaves.[57] But it was the eighth that was the last straw for the *Pecos*. It exploded off the port side forward, bashing in the hull below the waterline. The result was uncontrolled flooding forward and the *Pecos* started settling by the bow.[58]

That was it, and Commander Abernethy knew it. With the water rapidly approaching the forecastle, he ordered calls for help to be broadcast on the distress frequency and any other frequency they could find, and, at 3:30 pm he gave the order to abandon ship.[59]

CQ CQ DE NIFQ PLEASE COME LAT 1430 LONG 10630 AND PICK UP SURVIVORS OF *PECOS* AND *LANGLEY* CQ CQ DE NIFQ.[60]

So broadcast the wireless telegraph of the *Pecos* into the void to the sound of silence.

As the Japanese pilots circled overhead – except for four of Lieutenant Chihaya's planes who had been badly damaged by the *Pecos*' antiaircraft fire – the men of the *Pecos* and *Langley* (and *Stewart*, and *Marblehead*, and *Houston*) calmly evacuated the *Pecos* as her bow dipped further and further into the sea. But the tanker was not quite done yet.[61]

At 3:38 pm, the radio room of the *Pecos* broadcast one last message to anyone who would or could listen:

LONG 10630 PICK UP SURVIVORS CQ CQ DE NIFQ SENDING BLIND SENDING BLIND CASNAY RAD US NAVY SENDING CQ CQ DE NIFQ COM LAT 1430 LONG 10630 PICK SURVIVORS OF *LANGLEY* AND *PECOS* CQ CQ DE NIFQ … SINKING RAPIDLY AND THE JAPS ARE COMING BACK TO GIVE US ANOTHER DOSE OF WHAT THE US IS GOING TO GIVE BACK IN LARGE QUANTITIES.[62]

The pool of survivors in the water kept getting larger and larger, becoming an enticing target for Vals interested in machine-gun practice. A flight of three Vals started a low-level sweep over the helpless Americans, machine gunning the bobbing heads in the water. At the rear of the formation was a single plane that ominously had not yet dropped its bomb.

From the sinking *Pecos* erupted fire from two machine guns, a .50cal manned by the executive officer, Lieutenant Commander Lawrence McPeak, and a second manned by Ensign John W. Martin. The pilot of the Val with the bomb found his tail and the underside of his fuselage gashed by McPeak's fire. The bomb was dropped some 300ft from the rapidly sinking tanker, doing no harm, and the Vals withdrew.[63] So did the *Pecos*, in a way. Sinking by the bow, she corkscrewed to port, her stern lifting "until the ship was vertical," and slipped beneath the Indian Ocean at 3:48 pm.[64]

So now the survivors of the *Pecos* and the *Langley* – including Abernethy, McConnell, and Divoll – were left in the oil-covered water, some on boats or rafts, some holding on to bamboo or other floatables, still others hanging on by their life vests, a few just trying to tread water. They were in the middle of the Indian Ocean with no way to get to land and with no indication that any of their calls for help had been received; no indication that anyone knew where they were or what had happened to them. Some were wounded, others covered in oil, all were physically and mentally exhausted. With an enemy fleet nearby and with dark approaching.

The stress, the boredom, the bleak thoughts, the seeming hopelessness of their situation, became overwhelming for many of those in the water. Some suffered from combat fatigue. Others just gave up, shedding their life jackets to sink down into the watery depths, gone forever.[65]

Toward dusk the scattered survivors began hearing booming sounds from far over the horizon. Familiar booming sounds. They also felt spent shock waves in the water. Commander Abernethy would later report that at around 6:00 pm he "heard explosions towards the northeast as if some ship were being bombed." He certainly knew the feeling and feared it happening again. The mysterious sounds would continue for some two hours.[66]

As night fell, the sense of hopelessness and of isolation only increased. One could no longer see shipmates who were also in the water. Eyelids were heavy from exhaustion, and eyeballs burned from the oil in the water. Some survivors swore they saw the conning tower of a submarine.[67] Others thought they spotted a dark silhouette on the western horizon.

At 7:10 pm, it became clear that the dark silhouette was heading for them. Someone in one of the whaleboats used a flashlight to signal SOS SOS SOS. Commander Divoll looked carefully at the approaching ship. It had resolved itself into the very familiar shape of a four-piper US destroyer. At 7:16 pm, Ensign Michel Emmanuel, treading water, fired off a red flare. Others in the widely scattered pool of survivors began shooting off more flares, flashing lights, and shouting.[68]

At around 8:00 pm, sailing into their midst slowly, carefully, with boarding ladders, knotted ropes, cargo nets, fire hoses, and anything onto which anyone could grab hanging from the side, with crewmen lining the rails waiting to help, came the destroyer USS *Whipple*.

The *Pecos'* frantic calls for help had finally been successful. Her damaged radio suite had been knocked off her assigned frequency, and as a result her transmissions had gone largely unheard. Heading towards the Cocos Islands, the *Whipple* had just changed course from 279 degrees True to 225 degrees True to approach the islands from the south, trying to get in touch with Admiral Glassford, when she apparently picked up something. Commander Crouch and Lieutenant Commander Karpe seem to have put two and two together, for at 1:24 pm, when the *Whipple* was some 50 miles from the *Pecos*, the destroyer changed course to 180 degrees True – due south, parallel to the course of the tanker, moving at 16 knots.[69]

As the afternoon wore on, the *Whipple's* radio room struggled to lock on to the *Pecos'* off-frequency signal. The destroyer continued to receive occasional whole messages, but also just unintelligible fragments of Morse code. Nevertheless it was clear to Commander Crouch and Lieutenant Commander Karpe that the *Pecos* was under air attack and in deep trouble. Of course, if the *Whipple* went barreling in immediately, she would be, too. They decided to time their approach to arrive at the *Pecos'* location after dark. At 3:31 pm, the *Whipple* sped up to 19 knots and turned to a course to intercept her, 120 degrees True, which was adjusted to 102 degrees True a little before 6:00 pm.[70] Crouch and Karpe had timed their arrival perfectly, arriving after dark when the threat of air attack was negligible.

But air attack was not the only potential threat. Lieutenant Commander Karpe was repeating his maneuvers of two days earlier, carefully moving into the groups of survivors while his crew brought them on board and gave them food, clothes, and medical treatment. His destroyer was about to be swamped with cold, wet, and hungry men again, but it was better than the alternative.

The call from the sonarman on the *Whipple* came at 9:41 pm, after the destroyer had been moving through the widely scattered men in the water for almost two hours. "Submarine contact bearing 130 degrees True."

The rescue operations immediately stopped. The destroyer got up to speed and at 9:48 pm, dropped two depth charges in the water. Their detonations sent shock waves through the water, as they were supposed to do, but those shock waves slammed into the unfortunate souls still to be rescued.[71]

At 9:52 pm, the *Whipple* resumed fishing the survivors out of the water, only to be called away again four minutes later when the sonarman reported another submarine contact and, as if in confirmation, the sound of propellers less than 200yd ahead. The destroyer headed for the contact, again, and dropped four more depth charges (only one of which was heard to detonate) at 9:58 pm.[72]

The sonar contacts, the sound of the propellers, and the reports of some of the survivors that they had seen a submarine conning tower in the darkness came on top of a flurry of submarine contacts over the past 72 hours. When the *Langley* had first met up with the *Whipple* and *Edsall* on the morning of February 27, the *Edsall* was trying to hold down a submarine as the *Langley* passed. The attempt to transfer the *Langley* survivors at Christmas Island on February 28 was thwarted by not just the air attack, but the sighting of a submarine periscope. It was known that the Japanese had concentrated submarines in the waters south of Java. And indeed, though the Americans did not know it, it was a Japanese submarine that had reported the presence of the *Langley*. The repeated contacts by the same group of ships – *Whipple* and *Edsall* – in the same area suggest that a submarine had been stalking the *Langley* and her attendants.

This meant that Lieutenant Commander Karpe had to make a gut-wrenching, heart-breaking decision: the *Whipple* had to stop the rescue operations and clear the area immediately. Commanders Crouch, McConnell, and Abernethy concurred in the decision, a necessary decision to save the ship, but that did not make it any easier to leave hundreds of Americans to die, alone, in the cold, watery night.[73]

And so the *Whipple*, driven by necessity, left the scene, taking the 233 survivors she had picked up and heading for Fremantle. Commander Crouch had thought that most of the survivors had been rescued. But there had been more than 500 men in the water. Crouch later broadcast the news and position of the *Pecos* sinking, but a flight by a Consolidated PB2Y Coronado flying boat the following day found nothing. None of them was ever recovered.[74]

Cutting short the rescue had turned the sinking of the *Langley* and the *Pecos* from a military disaster into a humanitarian tragedy. When the *Pecos* had left Tjilatjap, her crew of 125 was swollen to 272 with additions from the *Stewart*, *Marblehead*, and *Houston*. Then she took on the survivors of the *Langley*, which consisted of all but 60 of the tender's crew and passengers, who had totaled about 430. There had not been enough time to record the names of everyone on board the tanker. The Navy would confirm 456 men as missing from the sinking of the *Pecos*, but most believe the death toll was closer to 500.[75]

Theoretically, it did not have to be this way. The *Whipple* had not been the only destroyer in the area. That morning the *Pecos* had met up with not just the *Whipple* but the *Edsall* as well. If both destroyers had been present, then more survivors could have been rescued, or one of the destroyers could have held down the submarine while the other fished the survivors out of the water.

But only the *Whipple* had responded to the *Pecos'* cry for help. What happened to the *Edsall*?

DISSOLUTION OF ALLIED NAVAL COMMAND – MARCH 1

The night of February 28 into March 1 had been a long one for Admiral Glassford and Admiral Palliser, though, to be sure, not nearly as long as it had been for those on the *Houston* and *Perth*. The US Navy commander and his Royal Navy counterpart, who also served as Admiral Helfrich's chief of staff, had talked deep into the night. They were planning what might today be called an "intervention" with Helfrich. The grim reports had come in continually through the night. The Japanese had landed troops at multiple points in western Java and at Kragan in eastern Java. *Kido Butai* was operating south of Java, and air attacks on Tjilatjap, the only remaining operating Allied base, were considered imminent. Japanese submarines were known to be lurking in the waters south of Tjilatjap. There was no way Java could now be saved. All that could be done was to withdraw all remaining forces so they could be used elsewhere at a later date before the Japanese could close the trap for good.

But, given his order for all remaining Allied warships to converge on Tjilatjap, Admiral Helfrich seemed hell-bent on defending Java to the last man. If by "last man" Helfrich meant the last Dutchman, that was tragic and foolish, but it was his right. Unfortunately, it was apparent that by "last man" Helfrich also meant the last American, last Englishman, and last Australian. Admiral Glassford and Admiral Palliser were both determined to convince Helfrich that their ships needed to withdraw. If Helfrich refused, however, Palliser had an ace up his sleeve that Glassford did not.

This meeting that promised considerable unpleasantness between the three admirals took place at 9:00 am on March 1, 1942, in Helfrich's office in Bandoeng. Admiral Glassford would "substantially" detail in his report the conversation that took place.[76]

Admiral Palliser, as Admiral Helfrich's chief of staff, detailed the current bleak military situation on Java using the latest intelligence reports. Based on this information and analysis, Palliser officially recommended that Helfrich cancel his order directing the surface ships to converge on Tjilatjap and instead order them to Australia or India. As they had feared, Admiral Helfrich refused: "I must decline to accept your recommendation. I must continue resistance as long as I have ships that can fight. I have already ordered a greater concentration of submarines against the enemy in the Java Sea. The enemy will make another attempt to land tonight near Rembang. He may succeed tonight but I shall attack the next wave of transports."

This plan to attack the next enemy landing was nonsensical when Japanese troops had already landed on Java.

Admiral Palliser would have none of it and was forced to play his trump card. "Then I must say to you as the senior British naval officer in this area that my instructions from the Admiralty are to withdraw [His Majesty's] ships from Java when resistance will serve no further useful purpose," Palliser said. "That time, in my judgment, has come. Therefore, I feel it my duty to order His Majesty's ships to India at once, and this I propose to do."

"You realize that you are under my orders?" Helfrich responded. "I do, of course. But in this vital matter I cannot do other than my duty as I see it," Palliser answered. Helfrich was indignant: "You know that I lent to the British when Malaya was threatened all of my fighting fleet – my cruisers, my destroyers, my submarines, my air – all of it was placed at your disposal for operation as you saw fit. In so doing we suffered grave losses. Furthermore you did not hold Malaya. Singapore is now in the hands of the enemy. You failed. I think the wisest course now is to let me continue to handle this situation and save Java."

There was more than a little air of unreality in the words of this burly, bullying naval officer. But in one major sense, Admiral Helfrich was exactly right. The British had indeed asked for Dutch help in defending Malaya, help which the Dutch dutifully provided. Malaya and the fortress of Singapore fell to the Japanese in any case. Now, when the Dutch needed the British to return the favor and help defend Java, the British were refusing. Helfrich and the Dutch had every right to feel they had been used and to a certain extent abused by the British.

But neither British callousness nor Dutch feelings were relevant to the cold, hard calculus of the situation in Java. With the truth on his side, Admiral Palliser held firm: "I cannot alter my decision."

"Will you delay one hour until I see the Governor General and inform him what you intend to do?" When all else fails, stall with bureaucracy. But this old trick of Helfrich's would not work in the rapidly deteriorating situation.

"I cannot delay any longer. Every minute counts now."

Helfrich turned to the American. "And you, Admiral Glassford, what do you intend to do?" Glassford used his considerable political skills to good effect:

> My instructions are to report to you for duty. Any order you give me will be obeyed at once. I wish to say to you, however, that I concur without reservation in the advice given you by your chief of staff. I am to retire on Australia by order of my commander in chief if necessary to abandon Java, but that is for you to decide.

Admiral Glassford does not mention it – he was writing a military report, not a play, after all – but it is easy to imagine Admiral Helfrich responding to Glassford's statement with a few seconds of grim, thoughtful silence. Helfrich was not a stupid man, by any means, and his operational and strategic abilities as a naval officer should not be underestimated, but he was emotional. And he had let emotion cloud his military judgment, as had much of the Dutch military and political establishment on Java in general. Yet he knew it was over, that he had lost, that the Dutch had lost. Glassford and Admiral Palliser were only forcing him to face that unpleasant reality.

"Very well, then. Admiral Palliser, you may give any orders you wish to [His Majesty's] ships. Admiral Glassford, you will <u>order</u> your ships to Australia."

In his report, Admiral Glassford underlined the word "order" to call attention to it. And it does deserve attention. Because, for all his bluster and intimidation, Admiral Helfrich had made a small but significant and thoughtful gesture. As when Admiral Doorman ordered the *Perth* and *Houston* to leave and save themselves, Helfrich was ordering Glassford and his forces to save themselves, thus relieving Glassford of both the mental burden of deciding when or if to leave and any guilt about abandoning the Dutch. It was one way of acknowledging the contribution made by Glassford and the US forces and expressing his appreciation for it.

Admiral Glassford immediately got to work. There were still ships aplenty in Tjilatjap: the destroyers HMS *Stronghold*, USS *Pillsbury*, and USS *Parrott*; the US Navy gunboats *Tulsa*, *Asheville*, *Lanakai*, and *Isabel*; the US Navy mine sweepers *Whippoorwill* and *Lark*; and a large number of civilian merchantmen. Glassford ordered all US Navy ships in the vicinity of Java to head for Exmouth Gulf, on the extreme west northwest tip of Australia; later he changed the destination to Fremantle. All vessels were to leave Tjilatjap immediately. These orders included a sort of rendezvous point. As Glassford described it in his report, "All vessels were to proceed by prescribed routing clear of enemy forces through a common rendezvous in Latitude 15 degrees South, Longitude 113 degrees East." He continued, "Vessels were not to remain at the above rendezvous. They were to pass through the rendezvous that there they might pick up vessels with which to proceed in company for mutual protection or escort." Admiral Palliser gave identical orders to his remaining ships. He also sent a signal to Commodore Collins to depart from Batavia.[77]

The US and British naval forces bow out – March 1

A little after 10:00 am, Admiral Helfrich told Admiral Palliser and Admiral Glassford that he had consulted with the Governor General and was now officially dissolving the Allied naval command in Java.[78]

At 10:30 am, Helfrich sent for Glassford and expressed "the gratitude felt by the Governor General and himself" for the "loyal support" of the US Navy in the defense of Java. He then cleared Glassford to leave Java and suggested he do so at once.[79]

So at approximately 11:00 am, Admiral Glassford sent his last message from Bandoeng, ordering Admiral Purnell, already in Fremantle, Australia, in the submarine tender *Holland*, to take charge until he arrived. He and his staff proceeded to destroy all their code books, communications equipment, and records. With these final acts completed, Glassford and his remaining staff piled into a car and headed for Tjilatjap. Admiral Palliser did the same.

The admirals shared a feeling of apprehension, not only for themselves but for their ships. Admiral Glassford's orders were specifically sent to the heavy cruiser *Houston*, light cruiser *Phoenix*, destroyers *Pope*, *Whipple*, *Edsall*, *Pillsbury*, and *Parrott*; submarine tender *Otus*; gunboats *Asheville*, *Tulsa*, *Lanikai*, and *Isabel*; and minesweepers *Whippoorwill* and *Lark*. The first to leave Tjilatjap was a small convoy, with the *Parrott* escorting the *Whipporwill*, *Lark*, *Isabel*, and *Lanikai*. A number of the ships were no longer in any condition to receive these new and desperately wanted orders. Already contact with the *Houston* and the *Perth* had been lost under circumstances that left little room for optimism. And the day had just begun.

The end of air resistance – February 28–March 8

With the Japanese landing on the north coast of Java during the night of February 28/March 1, the optimistically named Java Air Command threw every pursuit plane it could at the invasion beaches. The numbers were pitiful, the results negligible.

In western Java, at 5:30 am on March 1, nine Dutch Buffalos and three Glenn Martins set out from Andir to attack Eretan Wetan, to little effect. A dozen Hawker Hurricanes of the Royal Air Force's No. 242 Squadron operating out of Tjililitan went up and found the main Japanese landing "in a lovely bay 10–15 miles east of Batavia."[80] They made three attacks that achieved nothing. The pilots of No. 84 Squadron at the British bomber base at Kalidjati were told by Bandoeng "there was absolutely no danger" of ground attack from the Japanese beachhead only 30 miles away. But there was. With Japanese infantry attacking, the Royal Air Force commander, instead of ordering his men to escape, for reasons unknown decided to go into town.[81] After he was killed on the way, his men attempted to escape. Several Lockheed Hudsons managed to do so, but none of the Blenheim bombers escaped. About 20 of No. 84 Squadron's pilots and crewman were killed.[82]

In eastern Java, an attack on one beach was all their pitiful number of aircraft – nine P-40s of the 17th Pursuit Squadron (Provisional), six Hurricanes, and four Buffalos – would be able to handle. It would be the last major air mission from Java. The Japanese had prepared antiaircraft defenses at the beaches. The fighters braved the heavy antiaircraft fire to make low-level strafing runs on the beach, sinking several small boats, but it was spitting into the wind. Three P-40s were shot down, reducing the 17th to just six operational pursuits, all of which were damaged in the attack. They returned to Ngoro. But, with the Japanese having complete command of the air over Java, it was just a matter of time before the Ngoro airfield, though extremely well camouflaged, was located. That time had arrived. The Warhawks had been followed back to the airbase by Zeros of the Tainan Air Group operating out of Denpesar. Once the P-40s were on the ground, the Japanese aircraft made their first sweep over Ngoro, raking the airfield with machine-gun fire and destroying ten P-40s, two LB-30s, two Hurricanes, and five Glenn Martins.[83]

With this, the 17th Pursuit Squadron (Provisional), whose total number of serviceable aircraft had rarely been more than 20 at any one time, whose personnel had performed heroically against impossible odds to serve as much of a shield as they could for the Allied naval forces, was destroyed as a combat unit. Having done their best, the surviving personnel were moved to Jogjakarta, to be evacuated to Australia.[84]

Nevertheless, efforts at supplementing the rather nonexistent aircraft available continued. At around 10:00 am on February 28, the *Sea Witch* had dropped anchor safely in Tjilatjap, thanks to the good planning that had been so hastily abandoned in the case of the *Langley*, and to good luck in no small measure. In her hold she carried the precious 27 crated P-40s that had carried so high a cost.

The importance of the P-40s apparently could not overcome the chaos that was now Tjilatjap. The docks were so packed with refugees and ships trying to escape that the

Sea Witch had to wait for clearance to dock; the wait required her to maneuver constantly in tight circles to throw off submarines.[85] It was over a day before the *Sea Witch* was unloaded. When Admiral Glassford arrived in Tjilatjap on the evening of March 1, in the midst of his own flight from Java, he stopped to personally supervise the unloading of the *Sea Witch*. The crates had to be loaded onto lighters that would cart them ashore. The job was completed by midnight, and *Sea Witch* was personally ordered by Glassford to make for Exmouth Gulf, Australia (later changed to Fremantle), under the escort of the *Isabel*.[86]

Despite the presence of Admiral Glassford (or perhaps because of it), to this day no one is quite sure what happened to those P-40s on the *Sea Witch*. For the longest time, the official position of the US Navy was that, with too little time left to assemble the pursuits, the P-40s were destroyed in their crates on the docks in Tjilatjap.[87] This was based on what Admiral Glassford was told, or says he was told.[88] Some versions of the story get more specific, asserting that the Warhawks were dumped, still in their crates, off the lighters into the bay.[89] Or that they were burned on the docks. Some witnesses maintain that the crates were indeed dumped off the lighters into the bay, but that, in a sleight of hand, the crates actually contained ammunition and not the P-40s, which instead remained safely in the hold of the *Sea Witch* to be used elsewhere.[90]

None of this seems credible. Dumping the crated P-40s into the bay would have been pointless; the Japanese could just fish them out again. Dutch demolition teams were burning everything else of value in Tjilatjap, so the theory that they were destroyed on the docks is more plausible, except that the Dutch high command under General ter Poorten still had not given up hope of defending Java. And, indeed, the latest scholarship is at odds with the US Navy's story.

It seems that at least some of the crated P-40s were loaded onto trains in Tjilatjap to make the trek up to airfields at Bandoeng and Tasikmalaja for assembly by Dutch technicians. The Dutch pilots sent to Ngoro were recalled to Bandoeng, arriving on March 2, to man the new Warhawks. But when they arrived, their hearts sank – assembly of the pursuits was just beginning. There was no way they could be assembled before the Japanese overran the airfield.[91] With Japanese Army troops approaching the airfields at Bandoeng and Tasikmalaja on the night of March 7/8, the Dutch technicians had to destroy the half-assembled P-40s to deny the Japanese their use.[92] However, as with the airfields at Kendari II and Bali, the Dutch seem to have been less than successful in their efforts at destruction. Indeed, the latest scholarship has revealed photographs of several of the P-40s repainted with the Japanese "meatball" and in Japanese service.[93]

This, then, was adding insult to not just injury but also irony. Via air ferry, the *Langley*, and the *Sea Witch*, the US had tried to send 120 P-40 Warhawks to Java. Only 36 had arrived to see combat, and all of them had been subsequently destroyed in combat. The last, desperate efforts to ship the badly needed pursuits to Java had come with a horrendous cost – the *Langley*, the *Pecos* and hundreds of lives – and had not only failed in their mission, but had instead strengthened the enemy.

And the already horrendous bill was not yet completely paid.

THE FATE OF THE *EDSALL* – MARCH 1

South of Java, the men of *Kido Butai* were in something of a bored mood. "[W]e had more time on our hands than needed every day ..." Haraguchi Shizuhiko of the cruiser *Chikuma* would later write. They had faced almost no opposition so far in this war and, knowing their current mission was only "to cut off any escape of the Allied Forces," they knew they were not likely to meet significant opposition now.[94] This is not to say they were dispirited. Far from it; they were moving too much in the opposite direction. Their record was exemplary and they knew it.

It was during the late afternoon, while the carriers of *Kido Butai* were still recovering the Vals from the "target practice" against the *Pecos*, that the flagship *Akagi* got an astonishing signal: her escorting cruiser *Chikuma*: she had sighted an enemy "light cruiser" 15 miles away.[95]

Like her sister ship *Tone*, the namesake of this class of two ships, the *Chikuma* was designated a heavy cruiser, which, since she carried a main armament of eight 8in guns plus a battery of 12 torpedo tubes, was true as far as it went. And like most Japanese heavy cruisers, she was fast, overstrength, and exceedingly dangerous.

But she had her quirks. All of her 8in guns were in four dual turrets forward of her superstructure; she had no 8in guns near her stern. For her aft area was totally and bizarrely devoted to float planes. Japanese cruisers already carried three floatplanes, but the Imperial Japanese Navy wanted the *Tone* class cruisers to be scouting cruisers for *Kido Butai*. So they put all of their guns forward, which allowed the *Tone*s to carry five seaplanes. For that reason, while the *Tone* and *Chikuma* were officially "heavy cruisers," they have also been called "seaplane cruisers" or "scouting cruisers."

As the war dragged on, the *Chikuma* and *Tone* would prove that they weren't even particularly good at scouting. This sighting of the "light cruiser" was such an example. With all the great reconnaissance of *Kido Butai*, an enemy "light cruiser" had managed to get within visual range of the centerpiece of Japanese naval power, only spotted by the *Chikuma*, which was screening the battle group to port. Moreover, this enemy ship actually appeared to be chasing them, and, thanks to those two extra floatplanes, the *Chikuma* could not fire at targets behind her.

So, the carriers of *Kido Butai* – *Akagi*, *Kaga*, *Hiryu*, *Soryu* – stood off while their screening force – cruisers *Tone* and *Chikuma* of the 8th Cruiser Division, under the command of Rear Admiral Abe Hiroaki, and battleships *Hiei* and *Kirishima* of the 3rd Battleship Division, First Section, under the command of Rear Admiral Mikawa Gunichi – turned around and placed themselves between the precious carriers and the enemy light cruiser, which appeared to be a four-stacker much like the *Marblehead*.[96] Ever since the air attack in the Flores Sea on February 4, in which the *Marblehead* had been heavily damaged, the Japanese ships seem to have had a mild preoccupation with her. Although the *Marblehead* had long ago been withdrawn, the Japanese continued to regularly report sighting her.

But there was a logical reason for the constant sightings of the *Marblehead*, a reason that probably contributed to making this particular engagement one of the most bizarre in the Pacific War. For the ship sighted by the *Chikuma* was not the *Marblehead* or even a light cruiser, but a destroyer that bore a close resemblance to a miniaturized version of the *Marblehead*, a destroyer the Japanese would call "Edosooru" – the *Edsall*.[97]

The *Edsall* had last been meeting off Christmas Island with the *Pecos* and her sister ship *Whipple*. During the rendezvous, the *Edsall* had taken aboard pilots and ground crew, members of the 33rd Pursuit Squadron who had been on the *Langley*, from the *Whipple*. The *Edsall*'s skipper, Lieutenant Joshua J. Nix, was under orders to take these pilots to Tjilatjap although there were no planes in Tjilatjap for them to fly. In the words of *Pecos* historian Dwight Messimer:

> In what must rank as one of the monumentally stupid decisions of World War II, the airmen were to be put aboard the Edsall and taken to Java, where they would fight as infantry. This was to be done at a time when American, British, and Australian personnel were already leaving Java by whatever means available, and it was obvious the Japanese could not be prevented from taking the island.[98]

Precisely what happened on the *Edsall* between the time she left the rendezvous and the time she ran into *Kido Butai* has remained a mystery, for reasons that will soon become apparent. There is almost nothing in the way of hard evidence. What is known is that when she left the *Pecos* and *Whipple* she was on her way to Tjilatjap to deliver the pilots. After 9:00 am Admiral Glassford issued his order to clear Java and make for the rendezvous point. It has been reasonably assumed that the *Edsall* received this order, turned away from Java, and headed for the rendezvous point; as it was, when she stumbled across *Kido Butai* (or vice versa), she was headed away from Java.

But that may not have been all she was doing. The survivors of the *Pecos* initially expressed some anger that the *Edsall* had not responded to their distress call the way the *Whipple* had. But the latest scholarship, by historian Donald M. Kehn for his seminal work on the *Edsall*, *A Blue Sea of Blood*, offers a persuasive theory that the destroyer was indeed, like the *Whipple*, trying to respond to the distress calls sent by the *Pecos*. In support of the theory, Kehn points out that while the *Whipple* had extreme difficulty picking up the "nerks" of the *Pecos*, another ship much further away was able to pick them up with little difficulty. That may not be much in the way of evidence, but it does make sense, particularly since the *Edsall* was not much further away from the *Pecos* than the *Whipple* was. And the *Edsall* appears to have been headed in the direction of the *Pecos*.[99] Unfortunately, *Kido Butai*, only less some 80 miles from the *Pecos*, was blocking the way and, based on the sighting of the *Chikuma*, was also heading for the tanker.

The unexpected – and unwanted – sighting of the "light cruiser" changed *Kido Butai*'s priorities. Admiral Nagumo was not happy that enemy surface forces had come so close to his carriers. The 8th Cruiser Division took the lead in dealing with the intruder, and at

5:33 pm the *Chikuma* opened fire with her forward guns at an extreme range of 21,000yd.[100] At 5:37 pm, Admiral Abe on the *Tone* signaled ALL FORCES CHARGE, and both cruisers of the 8th Cruiser Division ganged up on the lonely destroyer.

The *Edsall* seems to have gotten off a contact report, but it was apparently jammed by the Japanese and no ally or person in authority received it.[101] Lieutenant Nix and his *Edsall* were caught in a classic fight-or-flight situation. Except that she could not flee. Even at her best speed she could not outrun the *Chikuma* and *Tone*, and her speed was reduced by the depth charge detonation under her stern, which likely left her with damage to her screws and propeller shafts. Having no real choice, Nix decided to fight.

One destroyer – one old, battered destroyer – was pitted against the force that had been rampaging across the Pacific: *Kido Butai*, with two heavily modernized battleships, two heavy cruiser-seaplane-tender types, one light cruiser, and eight destroyers, in addition to the headliners of four aircraft carriers. This was not going to end well for the *Edsall*. But it was also not going to end quickly. If it was to be her last stand, it would be a long one. Lieutenant Nix would see to that.

The *Edsall*'s first act was to make smoke. The Japanese recorded her "skillfully [laying] smokescreens from time to time."[102] Lieutenant Nix then began a series of evasive maneuvers that seemed more appropriate for a ballet than a battlefield. Nix also abruptly varied the destroyer's speed from 30 knots to full stop and back again. One of the *Chikuma*'s crew later wrote, "[T]his enemy ship was extremely maneuverable, and repeated changing speeds and courses, and ran away like a Japanese dancing mouse."[103] The officers of *Kido Butai*, still thinking the *Edsall* was a light cruiser, had never seen anything like this. The rain of 8in shells from the *Chikuma* did not register a single hit on the destroyer.

Meanwhile, Admiral Mikawa's battleships *Hiei* and *Kirishima* had maneuvered to a position east of the *Edsall* to cut off potential escape. At 5:47 pm, they joined in with their 14in main guns at a range of 29,500yd. The *Edsall*'s smoke and evasive maneuvers frustrated even these battlewagons. Though the *Hiei* managed to straddle the destroyer, she did not get a hit.[104] She launched all her floatplanes to aid in artillery spotting over the smoke, but it did little good.[105] The Japanese later reported, "[T]he enemy ship took evasive tactics, every other minute, and skillfully created a smokescreen so a strike could not be achieved."[106] The range was too great, so great that Lieutenant Nix was apparently able to avoid being hit by observing the flash of the Japanese guns and turning his ship before the incoming shell completed its trajectory.[107]

Frustrated beyond belief, Admiral Mikawa signaled from the *Hiei* FULL SPEED and, at 5:50 pm, ALL FORCES CHARGE.[108] Mikawa did not mean for the *Edsall* to charge, but she charged at her tormentors all the same. Lieutenant Nix ordered his 4in guns to open fire on the *Chikuma*, but their rounds fell short. Nevertheless, officers on board the *Chikuma* were shocked and unnerved when they saw torpedoes from the destroyer speed past their ship.[109]

Admiral Mikawa's order to charge managed to get his ships into position to identify the *Edsall* as a destroyer, not a light cruiser, but little else.[110] Twenty minutes later Mikawa ordered flank speed. He was rewarded with one hit on the *Edsall* from the *Tone* at

6:35 pm.[111] This was out of some 800 rounds fired by the 8th Cruiser Division and 1,400 rounds overall. However, this hit by the *Tone*, who had only been able to bring her guns to bear at 6:14 pm, seems to have accomplished nothing.[112] The *Chikuma* was forced to break off when she entered a squall, but soon emerged. The *Edsall* ducked behind a smokescreen once again.[113]

Kido Butai, the vaunted Japanese Carrier Striking Force that had sunk most of the US battleships at Pearl Harbor, was now struggling to sink a single destroyer.

Admiral Nagumo, "[s]eething with rage" according to Japanese accounts, now ordered his air crews to attack. The *Akagi*'s Vals were still being recovered from the target practice on the *Pecos*, but the dive bombers from the *Kaga*, *Hiryu*, and *Soryu* were available. A little after 6:00 pm, 26 Vals were launched from the three carriers.[114]

The *Edsall*'s smokescreen was of little good against attacking dive bombers. The Vals were all carrying 550lb bombs. It is not known exactly how many bombs hit the *Edsall*, but the destroyer was left completely ablaze and losing power.[115]

The *Edsall* was finished, but Lieutenant Nix still had one final act of defiance. It was small, but nevertheless worthy of Melville:

> *Towards thee I roll, thou all-destroying but unconquering whale*
> *To the last I grapple with thee*
> *From Hell's heart I stab at thee*
> *For hate's sake I spit my last breath at thee.*

Losing speed, Nix turned the *Edsall* to face the Japanese aggressors.[116] She had not run. She had made her last stand, like the *Houston*, in the best traditions of the US Navy.

And in the process she may have saved the destroyer *Whipple* and the survivors of the *Pecos*, who had been in the path of *Kido Butai*. They had been angry that the *Edsall* had not come to save them. It was only later that they realized that the booming they had heard in the distance marked the explosions and gunfire signaling the death of the little four-piper. Historian Kehn would rightfully say they "were the recipients of one of the Pacific war's great unsung acts of courage."[117]

For the Japanese now surrounded the helpless *Edsall*. The *Chikuma* used her secondary battery to pound away mercilessly at the destroyer.[118] His ship now down by the stern, Lieutenant Nix ordered the ship to be abandoned. Japanese lookouts on the *Chikuma* watched through their binoculars as someone who appeared to be the skipper oversaw the evacuation of the *Edsall*. After the crew had left the ship, calmly and without panic, many of them in boats and rafts, the man believed to be Joshua Nix was observed to return to the *Edsall*'s bridge. He was never seen again.[119] Still under gunfire, the *Edsall*'s stern settled lower and lower in the water before she capsized and sank at around 7:00 pm.[120]

The *Chikuma* closed on the *Edsall*'s sinking position to recover survivors, but was forced to cut off the attempt by an alleged submarine alert. The term "alleged" is appropriate here because little about the aftermath of the *Edsall*'s sinking was as it seemed.

The Japanese did pick up some survivors, at least eight, from the *Edsall*. Some were from the destroyer's crew, some were US Army Air Force pilots from the 33rd Pursuit Squadron (Provisional). No one else was picked up and no other survivors were ever recovered. The survivors picked up by the *Chikuma* were not treated badly, at least not by the crew of the *Chikuma*. Unfortunately for the US Navy, the survivors of the *Edsall* explained how the destroyer was able to evade the Japanese shellfire for so long.[121] These revelations, when reported to the Yokosuka Navy Yard in the home islands, resulted in major changes to Japanese surface tactics.

Upon the *Chikuma*'s arrival at Kendari, the few survivors of the *Edsall* were turned over to the Special Naval Landing Force and the *Tokkeitai*, the Imperial Japanese Navy's military police. After the war, their corpses were recovered in the hinterlands of Celebes off Kendari. They had all been decapitated.[122]

Loss upon loss – March 1–3

The order for immediate withdrawal did not include ABDAFLOAT's submarines, or at least those submarines on patrol, which was almost all of them. Those still in port were to leave, but those on patrol would just adjust their schedule to take into account having to return to a new base. In the case of the US submarines, this base was Fremantle in Australia, already established by Admiral Purnell and Captain Wilkes in anticipation of the evacuation.

Contrary to the doctrine of the US Navy, Admiral Helfrich had pursued a policy of concentrating the submarines near anticipated or actual Japanese landing sites. In the first month of the war, the policy had some success, including the spectacular work of Lieutenant Commander van Well Groeneveld off Borneo. The success of his submarines had buoyed Helfrich's reputation at the expense of Admiral Hart.

But while it most definitely would have its time and place, such a doctrine would come with risks. One major risk was that the Japanese would not land at the anticipated invasion site. Then the submarines would be out of position and unable to mount any significant resistance. Indeed, this is exactly what happened with the Japanese invasion of Java, when Admiral Helfrich guessed that the invasion point would be on Madoera and placed his submarines there, only to have the invasion convoy bypass Madoera and leave the submarines waiting in ambush in the dust.

And once the convoy had passed and established its landing site, it was extremely difficult for the submarines to get in and attack the transports. While antisubmarine warfare was by no means a strength of the Imperial Japanese Navy, it went into these invasion landings expecting undersea opposition and was prepared for it. It is not particularly difficult to seal off a small area near a coast from submarines, as the US Navy had found out in its belated attempt to contest what should have been an obvious Japanese landing site at the Lingayen Gulf in the Philippines. The Dutch paid a human price for their policy of concentration, as several submarines were lost early in the campaign trying to defend British Northwest Borneo and Dutch Borneo. And now the US Navy would pay a human price.

February 1942 had already been a disastrous month for the Asiatic Fleet submarines. Shark had dissapeared and they had managed to sink all of two ships: a troopship off Lingayen Gulf and the destroyer *Natsushio*.[123] And March was about to get off to an even worse start. The US submarine *Perch* had been one of the boats that Admiral Helfrich had sent to oppose what he thought would be the Japanese landing on Madoera. Under the command of Lieutenant Commander David A. Hurt, the *Perch* had departed Darwin on February 3 for her second war patrol and arrived in her patrol area of the Java Sea on February 8. ABDAFLOAT sent the submarine reports of Japanese ship concentrations, causing her to run hither and yon without accomplishing much.[124]

On February 25, as part of Admiral Helfrich's concentration of submarines to stop the Japanese invasion of Java, the *Perch* was directed to go through Salajar Strait and patrol northeast of the Kangean Islands. That same day, Lieutenant Commander Hurt reported that the submarine had made two attacks, but neither was successful. For her troubles the *Perch* had been rewarded with a shell hit on her conning tower, damaging her antenna trunk, so that while she could receive transmissions, sending them was extremely difficult.[125] It could have been a lot worse; a shell hit on a submarine is usually fatal.

Two days later, the *Perch* reported sighting two cruisers and three destroyers at lat. 6°08'S., long. 116°34'E. She was never heard from again.[126]

As usual with submarines, given their stealth, the silence that they must usually practice, and their combat that often takes place blind, the activities of the *Perch* on the final days of her life remain somewhat nebulous. What is known is that on February 28, she, like the other Allied submarines, received orders to abandon her patrol area and break for the Japanese landing point on the Java coast. But, as they had at Lingayen Gulf, the Japanese had effectively sealed off the area and were actively looking for submarines.

On the night of March 1, the *Perch* was about 35 miles north northwest of Soerabaja when she surfaced and promptly saw two destroyers, believed to be the *Amatsukaze* and *Hatsukaze*. After they tossed several shells in her direction, the submarine submerged again and allowed the destroyers to pass. They would later circle back – this was an obvious antisubmarine patrol – and Commander Hurt decided to attack the closer destroyer with his stern tubes. His wait for a clear kill shot was cut short when at a range of only 800–1000yd, the destroyer turned straight at the *Perch*. Hurt ordered a dive to 180ft. She was only halfway there when the destroyer passed over and dropped six depth charges.[127]

The *Perch*'s dive came to a crashing halt when she struck the bottom of the Java Sea at a depth of 147ft; Hurt's charts showing that the area was 200ft deep had been inaccurate. She was now stuck in the mud, unable to move, while the destroyer pounded her with depth charges. The *Perch* lost power to her port propeller.[128] The depth charging finally ended at around 4:00 am on March 2 when the *Amatsukaze* and *Hatsukaze* withdrew, thinking they had sunk the submarine based on the strong smell of oil in the area. The *Perch*, operating on one propeller, was able to free herself from the mud and surface.[129]

The *Perch*'s time on the surface, spent recharging her batteries and taking stock of the already heavy damage, was cut short when at 5:49 am, just before dawn, two Japanese destroyers were sighted. These were later identified as the *Ushio* and *Sazanami*. The *Ushio* now resumed the attack. The *Perch* dived again.[130]

And once again, her dive came to a crashing halt – literally – this time at a depth of 200ft. Now the *Perch* had so buried herself in the mud at the bottom of the Java Sea that she could not move. Commander Hurt and his crew could only sit there and take a vicious pounding. It is estimated that some 30 depth charges were dropped on the submarine, with the attack ending at around 8:30 am. Large air bubbles broke the surface, "emitting the characteristic stench of diesel oil," accompanied by an oil slick. Having lost sonar contact, the *Ushio* withdrew believing she had sunk the submarine.[131]

Not quite, but very, very close. Commander Hurt decided that discretion was the better part of valor and kept the *Perch* on the bottom the entire day. She had been very badly hurt. The concussions from the depth charges had caused two torpedoes to run hot in their tubes. The reduction gears were smashed. There were leaks everywhere, with the engine room hatch having a particularly bad one. The worst damage may have been to the electrical system, where battery jars were now broken, leaking deadly chlorine gas, and various circuits had shorted out.[132]

It took an hour of effort, but the *Perch* was somehow able to surface at sunset on March 2. She was in desperate shape. The deck gun was smashed. They could not restore power to the port propeller and the submarine could barely move with a top speed of just 5 knots. Commander Hurt prepared to scuttle the submarine.[133]

Before dawn on March 3, as submarines typically do with the sunrise, the *Perch* attempted to dive. But not only did the engine room hatch leak badly, but the conning tower hatch, once opened, could not be completely closed, letting in a 3in stream of water. The flooding could not be stopped while submerged. The submarine would sink if she continued the submergence, so Commander Hurt was forced to surface again. But she could only partially surface.[134]

A surfaced submarine in daylight is in grave danger. Submarines are small and have no armor, so they are very vulnerable to gunfire and bombs on the surface. Sure enough, while the *Perch* was surfaced, the *Ushio* and *Sazanami* came around again and opened fire.

The *Perch* could not fight and could not move. Commander Hurt ordered the submarine abandoned and scuttled. The entire crew got into the water safely and all were picked up by the *Ushio* and *Sazanami*. They were all taken to Japan where they were questioned then forced to work in the mines at Ashio. Both actions were in violation of international law, but the Japanese routinely ignored international law. Of the crew of the *Perch*, nine died and 53 were recovered at the end of the war.[135]

This was a Japanese antisubmarine success, no doubt, but the US Navy seems to consider it the equivalent of the sinking of the *Edsall*, less a victory and more a testimony to Japanese incompetence.

Still, even an enemy who lacks skill can succeed when given warning and when present in strength at the proper time and place. This was the problem with Admiral Helfrich's policy of concentration. The Japanese expected submarines to attack their landing points and were well prepared and well positioned. The *Perch* was an example of the weakness in this policy.

And so was the Dutch submarine *K-X*. The *K-X* as seen earlier, had been doing her best trying to defend Tarakan while suffering a series of setbacks. Her luck had not improved much since then. Commander de Back and his crew would gamely go out to try to take on the Japanese, only to have a mechanical breakdown of one form or another and have to return to port. On February 24, when the *K-X* was ordered to patrol the Soenda Strait, she ended up returning to Soerabaja the same day because of issues with the engines, pumps, and steering, many of which had been plaguing the submarine for the entire campaign. The repairs took two days.[136]

By 1:00 am on February 28, while the *De Ruyter* was still in her death throes and the Houston and Perth were trying to reach Tandjoeng Priok, K-X was back on the front lines, this time off Soerabaja. But she never got much further than that. Throughout the night and until the early afternoon on February 28, she was harassed by Japanese destroyers, apparently the *Minegumo* and *Natsugumo*, who subjected her to persistent if not entirely accurate depth charge attacks, forcing her to stay on the bottom. The sounds of the depth charges ceased around 4:00 pm, and she surfaced an hour later. Badly damaged, the *K-X* staggered back to Soerabaja.[137]

At the Royal Netherlands Naval Establishment, the *K-X* joined a long list of ships awaiting repair that were now trapped and could never leave, at least not under the colors of the Allies. The Hr. Ms. *Banckert* was almost completely immobilized, damaged in the bombing raid of February 24 and damaged further in one of the Japanese air raids on February 28. Now the Dutch tried to finish her off to deny her use to the Japanese. Her seacocks were opened and the deck gun of the submarine *K-XVIII* opened fire on the crippled destroyer as she sat docked. The *Banckert* caught fire and rolled over.[138] But the Dutch, who had established a pattern of allowing the Japanese to capture their military assets intact, continued to have issues with demolitions. While they considered the *Banckert* scuttled, the Japanese did not. After their occupation of Soerabaja, they would later raise the hulk and convert her to a patrol boat.

Similar ignominy would await the USS *Stewart*. Still in the floating drydock where she had tipped over, already half sunk, the destroyer took a bomb hit in the forward engine room from a Japanese air attack. A US Navy demolition team placed an 80lb demolition charge near the stern, believing its detonation would set off the depth charges stored there. It did not. The Dutch fired one torpedo into the drydock, sinking both. It was not enough. Like the *Banckert*, the Japanese raised the *Stewart* and converted her to a patrol boat.[139]

The Dutch destroyer *Witte de With* could not join the *Exeter*, *Encounter*, and *Pope* in their attempted flight because her skipper had, incredibly enough, given his crew shore leave pending the destroyer's admittance to the other floating drydock to have her propellers repaired. She was still in that drydock when she was heavily damaged by a bomb hit on her forecastle on March 1. Now she would never leave. Dutch attempts to scuttle the destroyer were at least successful this time.[140]

The queue of Dutch submarines was scuttled, but only some successfully. The *K-X* and *K-XIII* were successfully destroyed, but the *K-XVIII* was ultimately raised by the Japanese and used as an air defense platform.[141]

The Dutch struggle with demolitions would take a tragic turn. The skilled, successful submariner Lieutenant Commander van Well Groeneveld had been assigned to oversee the destruction of the stocks of Dutch submarine torpedoes at the naval base. On March 3, the demolition charges were set and detonated. The next day, van Well Groeneveld and a team went to inspect the damage to see if their work was complete. They found an unexploded demolition charge, which, unfortunately, took the opportunity of their visit to explode. Three members of the team, including van Well Groeneveld himself, were killed.[142]

The death of the 35-year old Carel Adrianus Johannes van Well Groeneveld was a major loss to a Royal Netherlands Navy submarine service, which had more than held its own in this losing campaign. But at least the young commander, who had been born in Batavia as a European native of the East Indies, was spared the indignity of watching the nightmare fully descend on his homeland.

THE END OF THE NETHERLANDS EAST INDIES – MARCH 1–8

It was pandemonium. Hundreds of people jammed the docks, panicked, desperately looking for a way to escape. The bedlam was punctuated by the booms of explosions. The harbor was jammed with ships in a barely manageable horde also trying to get away. Smoke and the occasional glowing ember filled the air, with huge fires lighting up the night sky.

Having abandoned their untenable base at Soerabaja, the last few PBY Catalinas of Patrol Wing 10 were in essence running an airlift between Tjilatjap and its forward base at Exmouth Gulf, Australia, where the tender *Childs* was operating. They were doing their best to get senior US officers and as many US servicemen and civilians as possible off the doomed island.[143] The 17th Pursuit Squadron (Provisional) had destroyed its last six serviceable P-40 fighters at Ngoro and taken the last B-17 flight out.

Catalina P-5, piloted by Ensigns C. C. Hoffman and B. C. Nolan, landed in the midst of the harbor at Tjilatjap. They were there to pick up Admiral Glassford and his staff. P-5 taxied to a service ramp near the explosions of the oil facilities. There they refuelled, where a Dutch officer, seemingly immune to the chaos, made them sign for the fuel.[144]

Not surprisingly, Admiral Glassford struggled to travel down the roads jammed with traffic to Tjilatjap and did not get to P-5 until around midnight. He found that Admiral Palliser had already arrived. Together, they boarded Catalina P-5, and Ensign Hoffman skillfully navigated the crowded harbor – actually just a wide area in the Shildpadden River – lit only by the fires ashore, and took off. As the rapidly dying island of Java receded behind them, Catalina P-5 made for Exmouth Gulf, arriving on the morning of March 2.[145] There, Admiral Glassford realized that Exmouth Gulf was not nearly as good a staging area and rendezvous point as he had been led to believe. The harbor was subject to weird tides, high winds, and storms. More serious was a logistical problem. Glassford had correctly guessed that many of the ships fleeing Java would be short of fuel, so he had ordered the tanker *George H. Henry* to sail up to the gulf to service them. However, the *Henry* had not gotten the order in time and was not there. Glassford quickly ordered everyone to make for Fremantle instead and headed there himself.[146]

Now the admiral could only watch the ships as they came in. The *Houston*, *Perth*, *Exeter*, *Encounter*, *Pope*, and *Edsall* would not. He hoped against hope the remaining Allied ships in Tjilatjap and off the southern Java coast could evade the Japanese aircraft carriers and battleships now hunting them in the Indian Ocean.

But yet more ships would disappear between Java and Australia.

First to enter the ether was the old British destroyer *Stronghold*. Under the command of Lieutenant Commander G. R. Pretor-Pinney, the *Stronghold* had been operating out of Tanjoeng Priok, but could not take part in the Battle of the Java Sea because she was off southern Java escorting the British merchantman *Ashridge*.

When her mission was done, the *Stronghold* went to Tjilatjap, where, like the other Allied ships, on the morning of March 1 she was ordered to clear the harbor and make for Australia. Low on fuel, she was forced to sail at a slow speed of 12–15 knots to maximize her limited supply. The old destroyer was some 300 miles south of Bali at about 9:00 am when she was spotted by a Japanese seaplane.[147]

Closest to the *Stronghold* was Admiral Kondo's "Main Body" force of the battleships *Kongo* and *Haruna*, the luxurious heavy cruisers *Atago*, *Takao*, and *Maya* of the 4th Cruiser Division; and the destroyers *Arashi*, *Hagikaze*, *Akatsuki*, *Hatakaze*, *Nowaki*, *Maikaze*, *Michishio*, and *Hibiki*. On March 1, already they had sunk the Dutch merchant ship *Parigi*, the Dutch motorship *Toradja*, and an auxiliary minesweeper, the HMS *Scott Harley*. They also captured the Dutch steamer *Bintoehan*. The sighting of the *Stronghold* promised greater rewards. The *Maya*, *Arashi*, and *Nowaki* were detached to chase down the destroyer. At 5:43 pm they gained a visual on the Royal Navy ship, hapless and alone. The *Maya* opened fire with her 8in guns at a range of 16,600yd. The *Arashi* and *Nowaki* joined in with gunfire of their own at 6:21 pm when the range was down to 11,300yd. The Japanese ships closed the range while maneuvering very carefully to surround the *Stronghold*. The *Maya* closed to 3,000yd off the *Stronghold*'s starboard bow and the destroyers 2,000yd off her port beam. By this time, the old British destroyer was afire and unnavigable. Lieutenant Commander Pretor-Pinney ordered the abandonment of the *Stronghold*, which blew up and sank around 7:00 pm. The next morning, 54 survivors were picked up by the *Bintoehan*, but the operation was cut short when the *Maya* came up and demanded that the survivors be turned over to her. They were, and, amazingly enough, were given medical treatment and even permitted on deck. None of the remaining 74 officers and crew of the *Stronghold*, including Pretor-Pinney, were ever recovered.[148]

Despite the victory, there was a source of some embarrassment for the Combined Fleet. Incredibly, given their well-deserved reputation for brutality, the Japanese seemed to have relied on the honor system in capturing the *Bintoehan*, declaring the steamship captured without leaving a prize crew on board. The *Maya* ordered the steamer to Bali, but, sensing opportunity, the Dutch crew sailed the ship to just off the coast of Java, where they scuttled it.[149] A small but meaningful act of defiance.

While the *Maya* and her friends were away, Admiral Kondo was informed of far bigger prey – the light cruiser *Marblehead* – just to the south. Once again, the Japanese seem to have had a serious preoccupation with the *Marblehead*, who had long since left for the United States. Kondo's luxurious flagship *Atago* and her sister *Takao* headed south to take on a ship who could lay almost as much claim to the title "Galloping Ghost of the Java Coast" as the *Houston* did. At 8:36 pm, in the midst of some nighttime squalls, the two Japanese cruisers found the "*Marblehead*," which was once again actually a four-piper US destroyer, this one the *Pillsbury*. Commanded by Lieutenant Commander H. C. Pound, the *Pillsbury* had been performing antisubmarine sweeps south of Tjilatjap when Admiral Glassford issued his evacuation order. She apparently took off for Exmouth Gulf as ordered. The squalls may have compromised her lookouts, for it seems the *Atago* and *Takao* took her by surprise. With help from their always-reliable illumination rounds, at 8:36 pm, the two Japanese cruisers opened fire with their 8in main guns at a range of 6,000yd. It took them only seven minutes to sink the *Pillsbury*. No survivors were ever recovered.[150]

With the Indian Ocean between Java and Australia now dotted with Allied ships, most of which were either unarmed civilian freighters or slow-moving military auxiliaries, Admiral Kondo's force had easy pickings. The gunboat *Asheville*, under the command of Lieutenant Commander Jacob W. Britt, had left Tjilatjap a little before 3:00 pm on March 1. She was last seen by the Australian corvette *Bendigo* late in the afternoon of March 2 heading for Australia as ordered. On the morning of March 3, the minesweeper *Whippoorwill* and the yacht *Isabel* from the convoy escorted by the destroyer *Parrott*, picked up a distress call indicating that the *Asheville* was under attack 300 miles south of Java and 160 miles southwest of Bali. Of course, they could do nothing. The *Asheville*, heading south, had had the misfortune to be sighted by the *Arashi* and *Nowaki*. The two Japanese destroyers turned from their westerly course to chase down the gunboat, opening fire at a range of 9,200yd. An early hit knocked out the *Asheville*'s engines, while other hits killed almost the entire crew. With the gunboat now sinking, Fireman Second Class Fred L. Brown and a few of the engine room personnel managed to abandon ship. The *Asheville* sank at 9:38 am. Brown was the only one rescued from the water by the Japanese destroyers. He was subsequently beaten to death while ill with dysentery at a Japanese prisoner-of-war camp in March 1945.[151]

Continuing their carnage just after sunrise on March 4, Admiral Kondo's ships found a feast – an Allied convoy: three ships escorted by the Australian sloop *Yarra* and the British motor minesweeper *MMS.51*.[152]

The *Yarra* was a sloop. She had some 4in guns on her as well as some antiaircraft guns, and she could drop a depth charge or two, but she was designed for patrolling and escorting, not surface warfare. Nevertheless, the *Yarra* had served with distinction in the Red Sea and Persian Gulf before being sent to the Far East with the outbreak of the Pacific War.

The previous week had been as confusing for the *Yarra* as it had been for anyone in the Allied service. Under orders for all British ships to clear Batavia, she had left Tanjoeng Priok around midnight on February 27 heading through the Soenda Strait for Tjilatjap. With the Indian corvette *Jumna*, she was escorting a convoy consisting of the depot ship HMS *Anking*; the tankers *War Sirdar*, *British Judge*, and *Francol*; and the minesweepers *Gemas* and *MMS.51*. Also in the vicinity was a convoy of Australian minesweepers. The weather was decent, with calm seas, light wind, and occasional showers, but the strait bore the evidence of war, filled with drifting debris and abandoned life rafts. And that evidence mounted, as at 4:20 am the *War Sirdar* went aground on Jong Reef, off Agentium Island, in the Thousand Island group just west of Tanjong Priok. The corvette *Wollongong* detached from the minesweeper convoy and tried to tow *War Sirdar* off, but Japanese air attacks cut the effort short, and *Wollongong* set out to rejoin the convoy after advising *War Sirdar* to abandon ship and land on Agentium Island. When *Wollongong* returned to the convoy, the tanker *British Judge* was torpedoed by a Japanese submarine just south of Soenda Strait. The *Wollongong* was now ordered to stand by the damaged tanker, which slowly limped her way toward Tjilatjap. Her own convoy of minesweeping corvettes was broken up by confusing orders and disparate fuel considerations.

The *Yarra*, *Jumna*, and their convoy arrived off Tjilatjap around 11:00 am on March 2, but they received an order from Commodore Collins, relayed through the corvette *Bendigo*, one of the corvettes that had arrived in Tjilatjap, forbidding them to enter the harbor unless fuel considerations dictated otherwise. With the Japanese prowling south of Java it was simply too dangerous to be in Tjilatjap. The convoy was followed by the Australian corvettes *Maryborough*, *Toowoomba*, *Ballarat*, and *Goulburn*, who did enter Tjilatjap as they were short of fuel. Like the corvettes *Bendigo* and *Burnie*, who had left before them, these four corvettes embarked refugees and made their way southward individually.

The scene outside Tjilatjap was chaotic. The *Jumna* was ordered to Colombo. The *British Judge* headed there as well. The *Gemas* was to be scuttled, which was accomplished by the *Ballarat* on the morning of March 3. Everyone else was ordered to Fremantle. The *Yarra*, now escorting the *Anking*, *Francol*, and *Tjisaroea* with the minesweeper *MMS.51*, headed for Exmouth Gulf, slowly at 8.5 knots to conserve fuel.

At some point, either on the evening of March 2 or on March 3, the convoy was sighted by a Japanese reconnaissance plane. This time the harbinger portended a delayed death; no attacks materialized on either day. The little convoy made decent progress and on the morning of March 3, the *Yarra* rescued survivors that she sighted in two lifeboats from the Dutch merchant ship *Parigi*, sunk on March 1. That night, a submarine contact was reported and the *Yarra* dropped two depth charges.

Dawn on March 4 brought "a glorious sunrise," not uncommon in that part of the tropics, but always appreciated. Not quite as appreciated were Japanese warships spotted, to the north northeast, by the lookouts on the *Yarra* at 6:30 am in the midst of that sunrise.

Once again, Admiral Kondo's force was about to score. His *Atago*, *Takao*, *Maya*, *Arashi*, and *Nowaki* had come across a full convoy whose only escort was a lightly armed sloop and a minesweeper. He launched two floatplanes to keep watch on the convoy and assist in spotting for gunfire.

Naval textbooks and training academies generally do not deal with such lopsided scenarios. But needing to improvise, Lieutenant Commander Robert William Rankin of the *Yarra* acted quickly. He sent out a contact report and ordered the convoy to scatter, a desperate tactic, but one that gave the best chance of at least some of the ships surviving. Rankin had the sloop lay down smoke in an effort to mask the ships' movements, unfortunately an effort that was nullified by Admiral Kondo's floatplanes. Lieutenant Commander Rankin then opened fire and ordered the *Yarra* to charge the enemy.

This warrants restating: Lieutenant Commander Robert William Rankin ordered his sloop *Yarra*, armed with only three 4in antiaircraft guns, to charge three heavy cruisers armed with a total of 30 8in guns, 24 5in guns, and 48 torpedo tubes, along with two destroyers armed with a total of 12 5in dual purpose guns and 16 torpedo tubes.[153]

It is extremely difficult, perhaps impossible, to come up with adequate words to describe the courage, the devotion to duty, and the selflessness it took to order the *Yarra* to charge into the enemy against these odds, knowing that the result was almost-certain death, in a desperate effort to protect the unarmed ships she was escorting. According to Australian War Memorial historian Daniel Oakman, it is "widely regarded as one of the bravest acts in Australian naval history."[154]

The *Yarra* paid an immediate price for her singular devotion to duty. She took a heavy pounding, especially from Admiral Kondo's flagship *Atago*, and was left burning with a serious list to port. Still, her guns kept firing.

The depot ship *Anking* was the next target. She was sunk in a matter of minutes. The *Francol* was shot up by one of the destroyers. The minesweeper *MMS.51* was set afire; the crew set scuttling charges and abandoned ship as one of the cruisers slashed at her with antiaircraft guns. The *Francol* then took her final plunge at around 7:30 am.

The *Yarra*, burning, listing, was now alone against three heavy cruisers and two destroyers. During all this time, she had kept shooting at tormentors she could barely scratch. Her fire had not saved her convoy, had not even saved herself, and had not hurt the Japanese. But still, she had accomplished a great deal.

The brave sloop with the big heart was now buried by a steamroller of 8in shells, 5in shells, and bombs from the cruiser floatplanes. Lieutenant Commander Rankin gave the order to abandon ship, only to be killed when an 8in shell exploded on the bridge. Sailor Ronald Taylor ignored the order and kept firing his gun until he was killed. Sometime after 8:00 am, the sloop finally succumbed and slipped beneath the waves. Of *Yarra*'s crew, 117 were killed in the action, 21 died on rafts, and 13 were rescued five days later by the Dutch submarine *K-XI*.

The next day *Kido Butai* staged a devastating air attack on Tjilatjap. Seventeen ships were sunk in the harbor, though the Dutch would claim that 16 of those ships were scuttled to prevent capture.[155]

The Japanese rampage was now largely over, as they headed back to Staring Bay. In all, the Japanese accounted for 20 ships – *Stronghold, Pillsbury, Edsall, Asheville, Pecos, Yarra*, and 11 others sunk; and three merchant ships captured. It had been open season on Allied ships, and Admiral Kondo's force in particular had feasted on the defenseless ships scattered between Java and Australia. But for the Allies it could have been worse – much worse. The performance of Admiral Nagumo's force in particular was curious. Aside from sinking the *Pecos* and the *Edsall* and bombing Tjilatjap, they seem to have done relatively little. The raid on Tjilatjap was relatively late, on March 5, after most of the more significant ships had already left.[156] Indeed, the Japanese let a lot of major targets slip through their fingers, in particular the light cruiser USS *Phoenix*, who had passed off her convoy to the British light cruiser HMS *Enterprise* and was returning to Fremantle during this period. Also escaping was the *Sea Witch*, who seemed to lead a semi-charmed kind of life throughout the disaster that had overcome the effort to reinforce Java. A final notable escapee was the tiny 300-ton steamer *Janssens* that, by the incredible, epic effort of Dr Wassell, was carrying both him and eight of the remaining ten wounded Americans, including the *Marblehead*'s badly burned Commander Goggins.[157]

Escape was all that was left. On orders from Governor General van Starkenborgh Stachouwer, Admiral Helfrich had flown out on March 3, heading to Ceylon to establish a new headquarters for the pitiful remnants of the Royal Netherlands Navy, their major surface forces now consisting of essentially just the *Tromp*. Following him was the Deputy Governor General, Hubertus van Mook. Admiral Doorman's widow and son were flown out.

Governor General van Starkenborgh Stachouwer chose to remain behind with his people, but he ended up trapped in Bandoeng. With him was the cream of the Dutch Army in the Indies, nicknamed Blackforce. But advancing Japanese troops, having already conquered Batavia and Soerabaja, surrounded the mountain town.[158] Resistance was futile.

On March 8, van Starkenborgh Stachouwer surrendered the Netherlands East Indies to the Japanese.

CHAPTER 20

AFTERMATH – NOT QUITE VANQUISHED

If ships had hands and knees, then the destroyer *Whipple* would have been crawling on them, pulling herself forward with her fingernails, when she pulled into Fremantle on March 4. Denied her opportunity to refuel by rescuing the survivors of the *Pecos* (as well as *Langley*, *Stewart*, *Marblehead*, and *Houston*), her skipper spent the time en route to Fremantle nervously watching his fuel supply, cutting speed more and more and more, until the *Whipple* was moving at the speed of continental drift. Even with all these precautions, according to some, she ran out of fuel just as she pulled up to the dock.[1]

The panting destroyer was packed with survivors. They and the *Whipple*'s crew were not so much happy to be relatively safe on dry land in Australia as relieved. Relieved, tired, despondent, confused. And angry. Very, very angry.

Angry at the Japanese for putting them through this hell for some four months. But also angry at the United States for seemingly abandoning them. They knew they were needed in the Far East to stall for time, but as far as they knew they were never supposed to be sacrificed. Not like this.

That anger needed an outlet. One way or another, it would come out.

And it did. Their anger at the Japanese could not be released. Not yet, anyway, though that day would come. But their anger at the Pacific Fleet for seemingly abandoning them bubbled to the surface. These sailors, staggering into Fremantle were astonished to see the USS *Phoenix* sitting at the dock.

The *Phoenix* had originally been sent with convoy MS-5 to go to Java. She had been intended to relieve the *Houston*, which was to be sent home to get badly needed repairs and badly needed rest. But she had come too late. Far too late for the schedule of the long-suffering servicemen in the East Indies, albeit on schedule as far as the US Navy was concerned.

With Java about to fall, General Brett had redirected convoy MS-5 to India. The *Phoenix* continued to accompany the convoy to a point in the Indian Ocean where it could rendezvous with the British light cruiser HMS *Enterprise*. The *Enterprise* would take the convoy the rest of the way. At that point, the *Phoenix* was still supposed to go to Java, but Admiral Glassford's order to avoid the doomed island came through and she instead made for Fremantle. En route, she passed the *Isabel* and the *Sea Witch*, completely uninterested in escorting the two to safety.[2]

Many survivors of the disastrous campaign to hold the East Indies had out of necessity congregated in Fremantle. They had started out with inadequate forces and had gotten almost nothing in the way of reinforcements or replacements. They had spent months looking up at the daytime sky with dread, wondering when the next Japanese air attack would show up. They had worked day and night keeping their ships and planes in some semblance of functioning order with duct tape, chewing gum, chicken wire, and rubber bands, because they knew there would be no replacements or spare parts coming from home. They had gotten no sleep because of continued Japanese air raids. They had been beaten and bombed by the Japanese on an almost constant basis. They had been worked and run to death, in some cases literally.

They had been alone.

Where was the Pacific Fleet? Well, here they were: the *Phoenix*. "[S]nugly sitting there in the harbor looking fat, dumb and happy."[3] "[D]amned, sleek [and] prissy."[4] Her crew in their *own* nice, clean uniforms, not something borrowed after they had been fished out of the water covered in oil and blood.

That the *Phoenix* had not known of the peril of the ships trying to escape Java – and would most certainly have helped if she had – did not matter. That she had survived the same danger in the Indian Ocean from *Kido Butai* that had put their own ships under did not matter. That, while she had not been in the Java Sea Campaign, she had survived sitting in the anchorage at Pearl Harbor on that fateful Sunday did not matter.

All they could see was that this modern monster of a ship, more powerful than anything in the Asiatic Fleet, had done nothing to help them.

When on liberty on Fremantle, the crews of the various Asiatic Fleet warships crossed paths with the crew of the *Phoenix*, who made some unjudicious remarks, to which the Asiatic Fleet sailors took exception. The result was chaos, a massive brawl on the streets of Fremantle on March 4. *Whipple*, *Pecos*, *Langley*, *Stewart*, *Marblehead*, *Houston*, and even the hated destroyer tender *Black Hawk* versus the *Phoenix*. Asiatic Fleet versus Pacific Fleet. The shore patrol had to intervene. Liberty for the *Phoenix* was cancelled for March 5.[5] When the *John D. Edwards*, *Alden*, *John D. Ford*, and *Paul Jones* arrived the same day, they were told that crews on liberty were to stay away from the *Phoenix*.[6] Ultimately, not everyone did, with cooler heads prevailing, visiting friends on the now-hated *Phoenix*. Her crew had been unaware of the disaster that had taken place in the Indies, the hell her fellow US American servicemen had gone through.[7]

Only then did the crew of the *Phoenix* learn the depth of their insult, the magnitude of the catastrophe that had overtaken the Allied cause in the Far East.

The fighting in the aftermath of the defeat in the Java Sea Campaign was not limited to the brawl on the dockside. As the officers arrived in Fremantle with their ships (or not), they wrote up their reports of what had happened as best as they could reconstruct. Reports are perhaps the quintessential symbol of military bureaucracy, but they both help the military in assessing what happened, what went wrong and what went right, and provide a record for posterity.

But there is a reason why eyewitness reports are considered the least reliable form of evidence. Concepts like time and sequence can get lost in the heat of battle. When writing up their reports after the battle, commanders have their secretaries check with the section chiefs and look over records to get details, but when those section chiefs, those records, or even the secretaries are unavailable it can be a problem.

Commander McConnell of the *Langley*, with his ship sunk, most of his records gone, and having to deal with two sinkings instead of one, wrote up his report dealing with the loss of his command and the events leading up to it after leaving Fremantle for Adelaide aboard the USS *Mount Vernon*. While it is certainly not a pleasant job, it may not seem like a difficult one, with the aforementioned factors taken into account. McConnell likely did not think so. Until he got Admiral Glassford's response to his report. Glassford had forwarded it to Admiral Ernest King, commander-in-chief of the United States Fleet, in Washington, with the following comments:

> 1. Forward. An examination of this report makes it doubtful that every effort was made to save the USS LANGLEY and that her abandonment and subsequent endeavors to assure her sinking failed to uphold the best traditions of the naval service.
>
> 2. This opinion was communicated to the Commander in Chief, United States Fleet, by despatch, with a recommendation that these matters be the subject of further investigation.[8]

The note was devastating. It had the potential to ruin Commander McConnell's career. McConnell responded, in an effort to defend himself and his actions in scuttling (or, more precisely, trying to scuttle) the *Langley*. But that was precisely what Admiral Glassford was questioning. Glassford thought that McConnell had tried too hard to sink his own ship and not hard enough to save it:

> If the *Langley* could have been kept afloat by the continued effort of any of her personnel who might have stood by her, it is possible that she could have been brought into a port by assistance sent out from Tjilatjap. This opinion is based on the fact that no further bombing attacks are

known by me to have been made on the *Langley* and it might be expected that the late hour would preclude further attacks that day and that the *Sea Witch* which followed about 12 hours behind the *Langley* entered Tjilatjap the … following morning without incident, and departed safely on the morning of 2 March. Operations in the general area off the south coast of Java were extremely hazardous but the fact remains that many ships were able to clear the area safely for Australia and elsewhere.[9]

In this matter, Admiral King sided with Commander McConnell, whose career seems to have been ultimately unaffected by this unfair accusation by Admiral Glassford.

And it was indeed unfair. Admiral Glassford himself gave a plausible reason for the loss of the *Langley*: "Operations in the general off the south coast of Java were extremely hazardous."

During World War II, it was not unheard of to scuttle a US Navy ship not in immediate danger of sinking out of tactical considerations or to prevent its falling into the hands of the enemy. Two incidents come to mind. After the Battle of Santa Cruz Islands during the Guadalcanal campaign in fall of 1942, the US aircraft carrier *Hornet* was disabled by Japanese air attacks, but was not in immediate danger of sinking. She could have been towed to a port, but a Japanese advance force was approaching and the decision was made to sink the ship to deny her to the Japanese. Ultimately, the attempt to scuttle the *Hornet* failed, thanks to the ineffectiveness of US torpedoes, though the carrier was so ruined by the attempt that the Japanese ultimately scuttled her themselves.

During the Battle of Leyte Gulf in 1944, the aircraft carrier *Princeton* was hit by a Japanese bomb and set afire. The fire ultimately detonated her torpedo stowage and blew off her stern. Still, oddly, she was not in immediate danger of sinking and even requested a tow. But it was decided to sink her instead, because the smoke from her fires could serve as a beacon for Japanese air attacks.

In the case of the *Langley*, it is hard to see what Commander McConnell could have done differently. The ship was immobilized, her rudder jammed. In the best scenario it would have taken some ten hours for a tug to arrive from Tjilatjap, and such a tug would possibly have arrived during the dark. But the *Langley*, even assuming she could be towed with the jammed rudder, would have been under tow during the next day, even more vulnerable to air attacks. Furthermore, simply towing her into Tjilatjap through its channel would have been a major problem. And once she got to Tjilatjap, then what? The Japanese were approaching quickly; if the seaplane tender had been in Tjilatjap under repair, she would have been vulnerable to capture.

It has been suggested that Glassford's opinion was influenced by an incident during World War I, in which the destroyer he was commanding suffered severe damage in a collision and was in grave danger of sinking. It was through "resolute persistence" that he was able to save the ship, for which he was awarded the Distinguished Service Medal. Since Glassford had done that himself, the theory goes, he may have believed that McConnell should have done so as well.[10]

Perhaps that is true, but his report on the Java Sea Campaign suggests another, darker possibility. William Glassford was a very political animal. He had some tactical skills, and without more evidence it would be unfair to say that he did not care about the best interests of his men, but his political skills and political senses were by far his greatest asset. Glassford was well aware of the controversy the *Langley's* doomed mission created. And his report on the Java Sea Campaign combined with his accusations against Commander McConnell can (though not necessarily should) be read as a masterful political sleight-of-hand.

His Java Sea Campaign report emphasizes his support of Admiral Helfrich's decision to have the *Langley* press onward in spite of the danger of air attack. However, in that same report he does not mention the reason the *Langley* was vulnerable to air attack – the delay imposed by Admiral Helfrich by insisting the tender be escorted by the crippled *Willem van der Zaan*. Without that delay, the *Langley* would have arrived in Tjilatjap on time. But Glassford either did not think it important enough to mention in his report – or thought it might lead to uncomfortable questions about his role in the entire affair.

In that context, the omission of the *Willem van der Zaan* seems rather convenient. So do the accusations against Commander McConnell. After the Japanese attacked the *Langley*, as Admiral Glassford presented it, her sinking was not the fault of Admiral Helfrich and his bizarre orders, orders in which Glassford had had a hand, but the lack of effort of McConnell in saving the ship.

Again, this is not necessarily what happened, not necessarily Admiral Glassford's motivation here. But because of how badly the operation turned out and the convenient omissions in Glassford's report, it is hard not to discount the possibility.

But none of that mattered now. Within a week, Admiral Glassford set up a new headquarters in Perth for the US Naval Forces Southwest Pacific. A short time later he was transferred to the Atlantic Theater for the remainder of the war.

Commander McConnell was not the only one being thrown to the wolves, though he was one of the few to be rescued.

On March 4, 1942, Commander Eccles, skipper of the *John D. Edwards*, submitted his report on "Battle of Bawean Islands – Report of Action; Events Prior and Subsequent Thereto" – the Battle of the Java Sea. In his description of the events of the Battle of the Java Sea, Eccles became one of the first to officially criticize the performance of Karel Doorman, with statements like the following: "There were no common flag signals nor signal books available nor were there any tactical plans save of a most rudimentary nature"; Communications with Admiral Doorman's flagship *De Ruyter* were "farsical"; "We had to reconcile two contradictory orders – one, the general directive to take station on the disengaged bow of the cruisers – the other, to remain astern of the Dutch destroyers, which were limited to a speed of 14 knots by the engine trouble"; "It was difficult to estimate the progress of the battle or to guess what the Admiral would do next"; "The crystal ball was our only method of anticipating the intention of Commander Combined Striking Force."

The most brutal, however, was this paragraph:

The Dutch fought with unfaltering courage and dogged determination. Admiral Doorman in the *De Ruyter* returning to the attack time after time in a literal obedience to the signal from ABDA Fleet on 26 February "You must continue attacks till enemy is destroyed". However, they had little else with which to fight, *Java* though badly outranged and with her speed reduced by old boilers endeavored to maintain her position throughout, firing steadily whenever her guns would range. The battle itself was a tragic commentary on the futility of attempting to oppose a powerful, determined, well equipped and organized enemy by the make shift improvisations that were used. It was evident that the Dutch had little tactical experience, their knowledge of communications was rudimentary and they went on the assumption that a hastily organized, uncoordinated force of ships from three navies could be assembled and taken into a major action after a one-hour conference. It is impossible for anyone who did not go to sea in the Striking Force to comprehend the utter lack, in the Dutch, of any knowledge of tactical organization and employment of a force as a unit. They were individual ship men and went to their deaths with grim foreknowledge. The Allied Force was little more than a column of strange task groups which entered the battle with a vague general directive and no specific missions.[11]

Commander Eccles would not be alone – far from it. Since the battle and the war, Admiral Doorman has been subject to severe criticism for his performance in the Netherlands East Indies campaign. Morison repeatedly criticized Doorman's "caution."[12] He also noted specifically that the US officers lacked confidence in Doorman.[13] John Prados called Doorman "aggressive to the point of recklessness."[14] Edwin Hoyt notes that Doorman was criticized as "misguided and stubborn."[15] British Eastern Fleet Admiral Sir Geoffrey Layton and First Sea Lord Sir Dudley Pound agreed that Doorman's handling of the ships was "deplorable."[16] Mike Carlton called Doorman "out of his depth."[17] Mike Coppock has probably been the most strident, borderline savage: "As he yelled 'Follow me!' in one of the most desperate and ill conceived sea battles in modern times, an ad hoc fleet of Allied warships was unnecessarily squandered in a do-or-die encounter that became the Armageddon of ego-driven Dutch Admiral Karel Doorman."[18]

The general opinion of Admiral Doorman outside of the Netherlands is that he was hapless, inept, and in over his head.

As noted earlier, there is reason to criticize Karel Doorman's performance in the Java Sea Campaign. His formation for transiting the Stolze Strait was unwieldy and may have contributed to the loss of the destroyer *Van Ghent*. His tactical plan for the Bali naval action was overly complicated. His reasons for not requesting the services of the *Houston*'s scout plane during the Battle of the Java Sea are unclear and the decision itself questionable.

However, while he did make mistakes, Doorman's actions in the campaign as a whole and in the Java Sea battle in particular were at worst defensible and generally tactically sound. That he was unsuccessful is not so much a reflection on his ability as it is on the situation that was forced upon him, in which among many, many other things, he was left with numerous judgment calls which had few clear correct answers.

Karel Doorman's fighting record may not show much in the way of success, but it must be pointed out that no other Allied commander in the Java Sea Campaign did much better. At Balikpapan, US destroyers sank four transports and a small combatant, taking no losses in return, in what was then and is now considered something of an underachievement. At Endau, the Royal Navy lost a destroyer for no loss to the Japanese. At Bantam Bay the *Perth* and *Houston* failed to sink any enemy vessels; the Japanese accidentally sank five of their own ships. Off Borneo, the *Exeter*, *Encounter*, and *Pope* also failed to sink any enemy ships. This is not to criticize the effort, the bravery, or the skill of the Americans, British, and Australians in these actions, which are beyond reproach, but only to point out the nature of the challenge they were facing.

Moreover, it becomes apparent from even a cursory glance at the often-contradictory criticisms above that Karel Doorman was always caught in a "damned if he did and damned if he did not" scenario. For instance, Doorman had taken his forces out in the Flores Sea and Banka Straits, only to turn them back as the result of air attack, which made him too "cautious." Yet when he took them out to battle in the Java Sea, he was "reckless."

By no means do the contradictions end there. Admiral Doorman was criticized for being "scared" of air attack, and he seems to have developed a belief after the Flores Sea action that the campaign was unwinnable without air power and that the fleet should probably retreat to Australia. This put him at odds with his superior Admiral Hart – who believed exactly the same thing. He was condemned for having only a short conference to prepare for the Battle of the Java Sea – when the enemy landing was believed to be imminent and where members of his task force arrived in port during the meeting. He was derided for having no battle experience nor the experience of leading a multinational force – by people who themselves had no experience of either.

It is said that he should have trained his force the morning of the Battle of the Java Sea – when it was expecting an imminent attack from sea and air. He was criticized for not quickly closing the range during the Java Sea battle, when if he had done he would likely have been cut off from his base and blasted to bits. He was condemned for fighting the Java Sea battle – a battle he did not even want to fight, a battle he thought was hopeless – to the bitter end – when those were his orders. It doesn't look as if it was even possible for Doorman to satisfy all these critiques. With the Java Sea Campaign, he was placed in a maze without a solution.

Though by no means a perfect naval commander – not a Togo or Nelson – Karel Doorman was hardly the mindless, incompetent coward many make him out to be. Losing an impossible battle or campaign does not make one incapable. It was probably put best in the work of noted British historian Arthur Marder: "No one could have tried harder in a more impossible situation than Doorman. Although his fleet was similar in numbers to the Japanese, it was doomed before a shot was fired."[19]

What is arguably the single defining thread for Karel Doorman is his concern for the men under his command, be they Dutch, British, Australians, or Americans. When his ships were battered in the Flores Sea, he withdrew rather than sacrificing his men needlessly. When the ships under his command were battered in the Banka Strait, he did the same. Believing he was facing a superior Japanese force in the Badoeng Strait, he developed a battle plan that, while flawed, limited their exposure in battle.

For the Java Sea action, the last chance to stop the Japanese invasion of Java, with orders to destroy that invasion fleet at all costs, Admiral Doorman gave orders that survivors of sunken and crippled ships were to be "left to the mercy of the enemy," because he simply could not spare the ships. Yet Doorman repeatedly did not follow his own orders, almost as if he had made a decision to save as many of the ships from this suicidal engagement as he could. He spent half the battle simply defending the crippled *Exeter* so the damaged British cruiser could withdraw, escorted by the damaged *Witte de With*. He allowed the US destroyers to go back to base when their torpedoes were expended. He ordered his one remaining destroyer *Encounter* to pick up survivors of the sunken *Kortenaer*. Then, with his own flagship mortally damaged, he ordered the last two ships in his force – two foreign ships – to save themselves and not stay on his account. Doorman then took great pains to make sure the flagship was evacuated of all crew, including the wounded.

These are the marks of a brave, humane, and honorable officer who gave his all in a losing fight. The Dutch consider the admiral a national hero, and have named several ships, including the Netherlands' first aircraft carrier, after him. It is time the English-speaking world history took a more positive view of Karel Willem Frederik Marie Doorman.

The Japanese would of course eventually lose the war in the Pacific. Their conquest of Singapore and the Netherlands East Indies would prove to be the high water mark of the Rising Sun. As the tide of war turned, their stars from the conquest of the "Southern Resources Area" would go to their inevitable fates.

Though Admiral Takagi had won the Java Sea battle, his tactics had impressed no one.[20] He was kicked upstairs, theoretically to run the attempted Japanese invasion of Port Moresby that resulted in the Battle of the Coral Sea in May. In reality, he had almost no tactical say in the battle. He would eventually head the Japanese submarine fleet, a position for which he was well suited. He died in 1944 on Saipan, possibly by suicide.

The luckless Admiral Nishimura would go on to his most famous role in World War II, leading a Japanese squadron of old battleships in counterattack against the US invasion of the Philippines in November 1944. It was to be a suicide mission to destroy the invasion beachheads.

Admiral Tanaka would become a nemesis to the US Navy, running the "Tokyo Express" convoys into Guadalcanal and, off that same island, cutting to pieces – literally – an attacking force of US cruisers, using only a few destroyers. The US Navy considered him perhaps the most brilliant Japanese admiral of World War II. The Japanese did not, perhaps because he was outspoken about Japan's conduct of the war, which eventually landed him in that center of naval glory: Burma.

The ineptitude in handling the *Perth* and *Houston* off the landing beaches in Bantam Bay would leave its participants scarred. It was Admiral Hara Kenzaburo whose forces were responsible for the defense of the beaches, and who ended up sinking more of his own ships than those of the enemy. Certainly Hara seems to have disappeared after that.[21] Admiral Kurita had bravely let two of his cruisers battle the two Allied fugitives while he personally watched the Battle of Soenda Strait from a distance. Some would say the desperate fight of the *Perth* and *Houston* deeply affected Kurita, an honorable man who cared about his men, but whose aggressiveness would be questioned. He once attacked Guadalcanal with two battleships, and allowed them to be chased off by a squadron of PT boats. His most famous action was off the American landing beaches in the Philippines. Like Admiral Nishimura, Kurita was leading in a force of battleships and cruisers in what was supposed to be a suicidal charge against the invasion beaches. Famously, he almost succeeded – but turned away with victory, albeit a temporary one, seemingly within his grasp. It was an incident that he was notably reticent to discuss.[22] It has been suggested that he did not want to go out the way the *Perth* and the *Houston* had.[23] In that respect, the *Perth* and *Houston* may have ultimately saved hundreds, even thousands, of lives during the Battle of Leyte Gulf.

Admiral Ozawa, considered the Imperial Japanese Navy's best tactician, would rise up high within the navy, becoming commander-in-chief of the Combined Fleet. However, this was 1945, by which time the Japanese had almost no ships.

After possibly sinking four of her own transports during the Battle of Soenda Strait, the *Mogami* would serve in the Battle of Midway with her faithful sister *Mikuma*. When a US submarine was spotted, the cruisers were ordered to take evasive maneuvers. The *Mikuma* fouled up the maneuver, causing the *Mogami* to plow into her port side. The damage enabled US carrier aircraft to find them and give them the day-long aerial battering the Japanese had perfected in the Java Sea Campaign. Five bomb hits detonated the *Mikuma*'s torpedo stowage, sinking her almost immediately. Six bomb hits left the *Mogami* so badly damaged she was out of action for almost a year.

When she returned to duty, the *Mogami* was literally not the same ship. While under repair, the Japanese had converted her to one of those heavy cruisers which also acted like a seaplane tender, in which she proved herself just as useless as the *Tone* and *Chikuma*. She was assigned to Admiral Nishimura's suicide squad night attack during the Battle of Leyte Gulf, but she was damaged so badly by gunfire that she had to turn back. Trying to crawl away from battle, burning and barely able to steer, she came across the *Nachi*. The *Nachi* then attempted to use the *Mogami* as cover to launch a torpedo attack, and turned in front of a cruiser barely able to steer. The result was yet another collision, again not the fault of the *Mogami*, who would be sunk by air attack that morning. The damage to *Nachi* would leave her, too, vulnerable to air attack, in which she was sunk in spectacular fashion in Manila Bay. By that time, the tables had been turned from the Java Sea Campaign and it was the Japanese who were under the falling skies.

The Allied nemesis *Ryujo* would meet her end in 1942, after being used as bait for air attack by a navy that could not afford to waste ships. *Naka* would be sunk by a submarine; *Jintsu* sunk in a night battle in the Solomon Islands in 1943. *Haguro* would actually be ambushed in May 1945 by the vanguard of a British-Dutch force that included the only major Royal Netherlands Navy warship to escape the East Indies, the light cruiser-destroyer-leader *Tromp*. The following month *Ashigara* would be ambushed in the Banka Strait by the British submarine *Trenchant* and sunk.

And the East Indies would never be the veritable well of oil that Japan had hoped it would. There was never enough oil to meet Japan's needs, and the tankers that transported that oil back to Japan were constantly attacked by US submarines. The vaunted Tarakan crude oil that was so light and sweet that it could be sprayed directly into a ship's furnaces would cause at least three Japanese ships – all aircraft carriers – to explode from the volatile fumes that the unrefined crude oil emitted.[24]

As for the East Indies and the Indonesian people, it was a case of be careful what you wish for. As much as they hated the Dutch, the Indonesians would find the Japanese worse. Capricious, incompetent, and brutal, the Japanese ran the Indies into the ground economically, and maintained the same policy of pillage and rape that had made the Imperial Japanese Army and the Kempeitai so hated in China.

Karel Doorman might be the biggest symbol – unfairly so – of the failures of ABDACOM, but even his most strident detractors would not claim he was the only problem.

As the eminent historian H. P. Willmott stated, "ABDA Command made mistakes, but the greater mistake was in being organized in days to rectify the errors and omissions of years."[25] That is the simple truth. The challenges it faced were the result of American isolationism and penury, Dutch pacifism, and British ambiguity.

Slapping together the naval forces of four countries in the matter of days is difficult enough, much more so when those countries cannot agree on what to defend – or how to defend them.

The inherent political problems with the ABDACOM structure were never solved, at least not until the Dutch assumed full command. Before then the intrigue among Admiral Hart, Admiral Helfrich, and Admiral Glassford had a negative impact on operations.

Admiral Hart was an excellent fleet admiral with formidable tactical abilities who cared about his men. He was also too honest, or, more accurately, too open, about ABDACOM's limited chances of success. That put him on a collision course with the Dutch, who considered his opinions defeatist and used it to leverage him out in favor of

Admiral Helfrich. Hart's efforts at keeping the political Admiral Glassford out of a tactical position backfired when Helfrich took over, for it meant that the US now did not have anyone in a position of leadership within the ABDA naval organization. The treatment of Admiral Hart by both ABDACOM and the US government was poor. The US Navy seems to have understood the crime done to Hart, and upon his return to the US placed him in charge of a commission investigating the attack on Pearl Harbor. Eventually, and ironically for a man with allegedly few political skills, Hart became a US senator.

The machinations of Conrad Helfrich and the Netherlands East Indies government, especially Deputy Governor General van Mook, to place one of their own in charge of ABDAFLOAT did not help the Allied cause in the Far East in the slightest. Admiral Hart's strategic sense had been accurate: the forces at his disposal were too small to be a counterweight to the Japanese onslaught. But if arranged correctly, they could have been a sword, more accurately a rapier, used to take quick stabs at the Japanese, to draw blood, to sting the Combined Fleet enough perhaps to buy some time.

Admiral Helfrich did not think that way. He treated the ABDA naval forces, that rapier, as a hammer. The result was inevitable: the rapier shattered. It is telling to note that between the two of them there were three planned operations to strike back at the Japanese. Hart had one – the Battle of Balikpapan – which resulted in significant, albeit not crippling, Japanese losses against no losses of his own. Helfrich had two – the battles of Badoeng Strait and Java Sea. The rapier was nicked at Badoeng Strait, which was an organizational mess, costing the Allies a destroyer against one destroyer merely damaged for the Japanese. At Java Sea the rapier shattered irreparably.

To restate, in some respects Conrad Emil Lambert Helfrich may seem like a villain – conniving, bullying, selfish, egotistical, mercurial, unreasonable, seeming to care little about those under his command, almost the opposite of Karel Doorman. And indeed much of what he did was not helpful to the Allied cause and even hurt it – witness the *Langley* and the *Willem van der Zaan*. But Helfrich was no villain. He did love the Netherlands and the Indies, and used his considerable tactical ability to try to defend them. Helfrich was most guilty of letting his ego get the better of him early in the campaign, and in letting his emotions get the better of him as the ABDA effort to defend Java worsened, his actions bordering on irrational until Admiral Palliser's withdrawal snapped him out of it. That emotion was understandable; in trying to defend the Indies, Helfrich was also trying to defend his home and family, whom he had to abandon, leaving with little more than the clothes on his back, when most of the remaining Dutch military fled to Ceylon during the fall of Java. He would accept the Japanese surrender on behalf of the Dutch government in 1945. Somewhat unsurprisingly, after the war he would write a self-serving memoir about the campaign.

ABDACOM and its naval component ABDAFLOAT might have had a chance to, if not successfully defend the Netherlands East Indies, then at least slow down the Japanese advance and cause significant losses. But that largely did not happen. Why?

This can be broken down into several major areas:

Initial dominoes – The first 72 hours of the Pacific War were an unmitigated disaster for the Allies in the Far East, leaving ABDACOM bereft of large military assets even before its formation. On December 8, Douglas MacArthur willfully disobeyed his orders from Washington and did not launch the required attack on Formosa, which resulted in the destruction of his Far East Air Force on the ground with almost no losses for the Japanese. This not only deprived ABDACOM of air assets but allowed the Japanese to transfer air groups to gain local air superiority at any point in the Indies they chose. The destruction of the *Prince of Wales* and *Repulse* on December 10 deprived ABDACOM of what would have been its largest, most powerful ships, the centerpiece for a significant naval force. The death of Admiral Sir Tom Phillips was the loss of a good, respected naval commander that ABDAFLOAT desperately needed.

Once the first dominoes fell, others followed, as dominoes tend to do. As the campaign continued, additional problems would reveal themselves, some of which in some way were related to the first.

Overstretched supply lines – The old anti-American credo might be paraphrased as "so far from the United States, so close to Japan." Supply lines from the United States and Great Britain to Singapore, Darwin, and Java were simply too long to overcome the almost criminal lack of preparation – getting supplies and assets on site – for the war that everyone knew was coming. Losses could not be replaced, ships could not be repaired or even maintained simply because of the distances involved.

Communications – Integrating sailors from four different countries and three different navies who spoke two different languages was never going to be easy. The additional pressures of a fast and relentless Japanese advance made it next to impossible. There was no time to develop a unified communications system or a unified code or tactical doctrine.

Almost total lack of air power – The loss of the US Far East Air Force and the British Malaya air force rippled throughout the campaign. As a result the overstretched ABDAIR was never able to get enough aircraft or experienced pilots to even contest control of the skies with the Japanese. The sailors of ABDAFLOAT were left constantly looking at the sky waiting for the bombs to fall from the next Japanese air attack.

Operational accidents and mechanical breakdowns – This last factor has been curiously absent of discussion in most histories. But it is difficult to find a naval campaign that has been more impacted by non-combat casualties. While groundings and collisions are not unheard of – for instance, during the Java Sea Campaign the Japanese carrier *Kaga* ran aground off Palau and the cruiser *Nagara* collided with the destroyer *Hatsuharu* at Kendari – the list of ABDAFLOAT ships lost temporarily or permanently to non-combat factors is truly striking:

1. Light cruiser USS *Boise* struck an uncharted reef in the Sape Strait and was lost to a planned ABDA counterlanding operation off Balikpapan and ultimately to the entire campaign;

2. Light cruiser USS *Marblehead* blew out a turbine and was lost to the same ABDA counterattack off Balikpapan;

3. Destroyer USS *Whipple* collided with the *De Ruyter* in a fog, the resulting damage left her unfit for combat;

4. Destroyer USS *Edsall* dropped a depth charge at too shallow a depth, the resulting damage left her unfit for combat;

5. Destroyer Hr. Ms. *Van Ghent* ran aground in the Stolze Strait and had to be scuttled;

6. Destroyer Hr. Ms. *Kortenaer* lost rudder control and ran aground off Tjilatjap and was thus lost to the ABDA counterattack off Bali;

7. Destroyer USS *Stewart* rolled over in drydock in Soerabaja and was ineffectually scuttled;

8. Destroyer USS *Pope* developed a leak in the hot well and was unavailable for the action in the Java Sea;

9. Destroyer Hr. Ms. *Witte de With* had one of her own depth charges detonate under her stern, the resulting damage caused her to go into the Soerabaja drydock where she would be scuttled; and

10. Destroyer HMS *Jupiter* was sunk after she apparently struck a discarded Dutch mine.

One might even count the HMS *Indomitable*, running aground off Jamaica and thus unable to join the *Prince of Wales* and *Repulse*, in this group. If one wants to include submarines, the figure gets even worse, with the USS *S-36* running aground off Makassar City.

Part of the issue here was the speed of the Japanese advance and the lack of Allied air protection, which denied ABDAFLOAT the necessary time and security for maintenance and repair of their ships and rest for the crews. A part was also played by the lack of charts for the Indies, for which the Dutch must bear some responsibility.

But how does one explain not one but two ships being damaged by their own depth charges? Such accidents can and do happen, but it is unusual for it to happen to two ships in such a short time period. Moreover the sinking of the *Jupiter* must stand as one of the most bizarre incidents of the war, for which neither the *Jupiter*'s skipper Commander Thew nor Admiral Doorman should be held responsible. The responsible party, it seems, would be the Dutch minelayer *Gouden Leeuw*. Why the *Leeuw* dumped the mines as she did is probably best left to the imagination.

For that matter, the *Gouden Leeuw* was hardly the only Royal Netherlands Navy ship to perform in a questionable manner. Commander de Vries of the *Evertsen* acted as if in a daze the night his ship was, in theory, supposed to go through the Soenda Strait with the *Perth* and *Houston*. And it remains hard to understand how the *Witte de With*'s Captain Schotel thought it a good idea, with the Japanese mere hours away from landing on Java and cutting off all the exits from the Java Sea, to give his crew shore leave in Soerabaja.

It may simply have been a symptom of the same affliction that gripped most of the Dutch establishment on Java – an inability to accept that they were about to lose. The only prominent Dutchman who could seem to understand that was Karel Doorman.

But that begs the question that has been central to the Allied effort in Southeast Asia: if the Dutch were going to lose the Indies, if the British were going to lose Singapore, if the Americans were going to lose the Philippines – if they were all indefensible – why fight? Why not just withdraw with all forces and supplies intact before returning to the fight at a better time?

The story of Leonidas and the 300 Spartans resonates again. They had a good idea they were going to lose at Thermopylae. They fought anyway. They wanted to buy time to create a defense line against the Persians in southern Greece. If that meant their lives, so be it. It would save many, many more.

And indeed, contrary to the conventional wisdom, the Allied effort in Indonesia did buy time for American wartime materiel production to catch and eventually surpass the Japanese and swamp them in the Pacific. While the Japanese plan of conquest of the Southern Resources Area was indeed not even delayed, let alone stopped, that is not the proper metric to use. ABDA resistance did not delay the Japanese *plan*, but it did delay the Japanese *themselves*. An early complete withdrawal from Southeast Asia might have preserved some military assets, but it would have allowed the Japanese to take over the area much more quickly and exploit it for their wartime needs. The subsequent war in the Pacific might not have turned out differently, but it might have – an early if largely uncontested withdrawal from the region by the Allies might have led to the political inertia the Emperor and his minions had hoped for; the impetus for liberation of the Pacific might simply not have been there. It is not inconceivable to imagine parts of Southeast Asia remaining enslaved by the Japanese for decades.

Even so, the Thermopylae analogy only goes so far. After the eventual Spartan defeat at Thermopylae, the Athenians abandoned their home in Athens and withdrew to more defensible positions in the Gulf of Salamis. Yet the Dutch, who now considered the East Indies their home with the Netherlands under Nazi occupation, would not withdraw. To them, it was unthinkable to not fight for their homes. They had buried that pacifist streak in a hurry.

So, why fight a hopeless battle? A battle you know you are going to lose?

Perhaps the words of the *Electra*'s T. J. Cain can provide insight:

[I]f an effective defence was quite impossible, why then was a hopeless defiance still attempted? Today, strangely enough, the answer seems far less clear cut than it did at the time; for the publication of official documents and so forth has actually confused the issue, or so I think. One sees merely the helplessness of Java, and the issue of whether to fight or not become[s], on the printed page, a problem of simple mathematics with only one solution. But at the time when one's own neck depended on the deliberations of Bandoeng – the Javan town that had become supreme H.Q. – the situation seemed to have its moral aspect, and this could not be ignored.

Cain continues:

> [D]espite such considerations, which look formidable enough when put down on paper, and detached, as it were, from their context … I don't think there was a man among us who would have opted for the sensible way out, which would, of course, have entailed our abandonment of Java.
>
> We knew we couldn't win, not in the ultimate. But at least we could fight, and fulfil our obligations. We knew that we couldn't stop an invasion, but we were still pretty confident that we'd take our toll of the invaders. We knew that the Nip was formidable, but we were sick of being chivvied around by him … British, Australian, American, Dutch, we were all in it together.[26]

It may sound unsophisticated, even childlike today, but it was really that simple.

NOTES

Chapter 1

1. Traditionally, Japanese surnames precede the given name; they are presented thus in this book.
2. While Japan consistently had emperors, she had not been effectively ruled by one in a thousand years. The emperor was practically Merovingian in his impotence, the real power being exercised by the emperor's shogun, who filled the role of Charles Martel and the "Mayor of the Palace" of medieval European fame.
3. The emperor at the time of Perry's visit to Tokyo Bay, Meiji's father and Hirohito's great-grandfather, had sworn an oath with his vassals that the "redheaded barbarians" must be driven from Japanese soil and Japan must "expand overseas" to prevent any further incursions. David Bergamini, *Japan's Imperial Conspiracy* (New York: William Morrow, 1971), p. 6.
4. "Combined Fleet" (*Rengo Kantai*) was the term for all the combined fleets of the "Imperial Japanese Navy" (*Dai Nippon Teikoku Kaigun*). Other Japanese terms of interest include "Japanese Navy" (*Nippon Kaigun* or *Nihon Kaigun*), "Imperial Navy" (*Teikoku Kaigun*), "Imperial Japanese Army" (*Dai Nippon Teikoku Rikugun*), and "Japanese Army" (*Nippon Rikugun* or *Nihon Rikugun*).
5. In 1904, when the Japanese attacked the Russians before the declaration of war, the Europeans considered it creative and bold. In 1941, when the Japanese attacked the Europeans and Americans before the declaration of war, they did not.
6. To clarify the 5:5:3:1.75:1.75 figures, the US was restricted to a total capital ship tonnage of 525,000 tons, Britain 525,000 tons, Japan 315,000 tons, France 175,000 tons, and Italy 175,000 tons. For aircraft carriers, the limitations were 135,000 tons; 135,000 tons; 81,000 tons; 60,000 tons; and 60,000 tons, respectively.
7. As a general rule, during this period, a "warship" or "man-of-war" meant any armed ocean-going vessel as large or larger than a destroyer intended for combat. A "destroyer" was a small, fast warship with 4in–5-in guns, torpedo tubes, and antisubmarine capability. A "cruiser" was larger and more heavily armed and armored than a destroyer but smaller than a capital ship. During this period "cruisers" came in two types: a "light" cruiser that carried 5in–6in guns and a "heavy" cruiser that carried 8in guns. Except for those of the US Navy, cruisers usually carried torpedo tubes. A "capital ship" meant a battleship or battlecruiser. A "battleship" was a large, heavily armored warship slower than a cruiser and carrying 14in–18in guns. A "battle cruiser" was something of a hybrid between a battleship and a cruiser, carrying the armament of a battleship but with the speed and armor of a cruiser.
8. David C. Evans and Mark R. Peattie, *Kaigun: Strategy, Tactics and Technology in the Imperial Japanese Navy 1887–1941* (Annapolis: Naval Institute Press, 1997), p. 275; Samuel Eliot Morison, *History of United States Naval Operations in World War II, Volume 3: The Rising Sun in the Pacific* (Edison, NJ: Castle, 1948), p. 28.
9. Evans and Peattie, pp. 220–221; Morison (1948), p. 22. Ultimately, a series of accidents would show that the *Fubuki*s were structurally unsound because of too much being placed on too small a displacement, but the design flaws were rectified before the Pacific War.
10. The emperor's given name of Hirohito is used here because of its familiarity to readers, but it should be noted that in Japan its use is considered improper. According to Japanese tradition, the name of the emperor was not referenced during his rule. Only in the West was the emperor called by his given name, Hirohito. With Hirohito's passing, Japanese tradition holds that he should be referenced by his posthumous name, Showa.
11. As an illustration of just how divided and chaotic China was during this time period, from 1912 to 1928, more than 1,300 Chinese had a personal army and a territorial base, meeting the minimum qualifications for a warlord. No fewer than six major wars were fought in China in the 1920s: the Zhili–Anhui War (1920), the First and Second Zhili–Fengtian Wars (1922, 1924), the Fengtian–Zhejiang War (1925), the Fengtian–Feng Yuxiang War (1925–26), and the Northern Expedition (1926–28). S.C.M. Paine, *The Wars for Asia, 1911–1949* (Cambridge: Cambridge University Press, 2012), pp. 18 and 26.
12. Also called the Kanto Army.
13. See, generally, Bergamini.

14. Bob Hackett and Sander Kingsepp, "Mogami-class Heavy Cruiser," *Imperial Japanese Navy Page*, www. combinedfleet.com, retrieved April 10, 2012.

15. The *Mogami* was constructed using extensive welding to save on weight and to help with the deception that she was in compliance with the London Treaty. Privately the Japanese laughed at the gullibility of the Allies. Later, when the *Mogami* went on her sea trials, it was discovered that firing her main guns caused the welded hull seams to split open. The Japanese stopped laughing; the cruisers had to be rebuilt. Four *Mogami*s subsequently fought in World War II and all were sunk.

16. Evans and Peattie, pp. 267–270.

17. The younger army officers often advanced their ideas through acts of *gekokujo*, a ritualized insubordination that was a tradition in the Japanese military going back to the samurai. Typically, a provincial lord would ignore the orders of the shogun, who would in turn ignore the wishes of the emperor. John Toland, *The Rising Sun: The Decline and Fall of the Japanese Empire, 1936–1945* (New York: Bantam, 1970), p. 3. How a military with a tradition of insubordination could function effectively remains rather vague.

18. Toland (1970), pp. 10–11; Bergamini, p. 571.

19. Among the incidents were the Manchurian Incident, the October Incident, the First and Second Tianjin Incidents, and the Shanghai Incident. Paine, p. 14.

20. Bergamini, p. 28.

21. Bergamini, p. 27, notes that Yamamoto Isoroku, then Navy Vice Minister, publicly accepted full responsibility for the *Panay* incident, but privately fumed that the army commander who had ordered the sinking was never disciplined.

22. Bergamini, p. 17.

23. Bergamini, p. 17, points out that Nakajima, a former chief of the Tokyo Kempeitai (the Imperial Japanese Army's military police that served as Japan's version of the Gestapo), was described as a "hard man of sadistic personality" and calls him, "a small Himmler of a man, a specialist in thought control, intimidation and torture." Iris Chang, *The Rape of Nanking: The Forgotten Holocaust of World War II* (New York: Penguin, 1998), p. 37, notes that Nakajima's own biographer called him "a beast," and "a violent man."

24. Bergamini, p. 44. Chang, p. 4, says the number of women who were raped was as high as 80,000.

25. Chang, p. 5.

26. Estimates of the number of dead vary between 100,000 and 300,000. Because so many were burned, buried in mass graves, or dumped into the Yangtze by the Japanese, the actual number will never be known. Figures listed here are from Chang, p. 4.

27. Toland (1970), p. 56. One of the Nazi officials, John Rabe, actually tried to protect the Chinese civilians. Rabe is still honored today in Nanjing.

28. H.P. Wilmott, *Empires in the Balance: Japanese and Allied Pacific Strategies to April 1942* (Annapolis: Naval Institute Press, 1982), p. 55; Paine, p. 185.

29. Bergamini, p. 698.

30. William H. Bartsch, *December 8, 1941: MacArthur's Pearl Harbor* (College Station, TX: Texas A&M University Press, 2003), pp. 21–23.

31. The typical Japanese pilot was not even issued a parachute, but instead a pistol and sword.

32. Japanese aircraft had a dual naming system that Allied observers found confusing. One name for an aircraft was the manufacturer's alphanumeric project code; the other was the official military designation, which consisted of a reference to the year the aircraft entered service according to the Japanese calendar plus a description of the aircraft. To use the Zero as an example, in "Mitsubishi A6M Type 00 Carrier Fighter," "Mitsubishi A6M" is the manufacturer's project code, Type 00 is a reference to the imperial year 2600, or 1940 in the Gregorian calendar, and "Carrier Fighter" describes the aircraft's function.

33. Bartsch (2003), pp. 28–29.

34. Okumiya Masatake, Horikoshi Jiro, and Martin Caidin, *Zero! The Story of Japan's Air War in the Pacific: 1941–45* (New York: E. P. Dutton, 1956), p. 61.

35. The figures come from Willmott, p. 55 and 63.

36. Willmott, pp. 61–62.

37. Paone, p. 176.

38. Bergamini, p. 726.

39. Bartsch (2008), p. 20.

40. Bergamini, p. 729.

41. Morison (1948), pp. 65–66.

42. Paine, p. 185.
43. In 1944 British Minister of Production Oliver Lyttelton even went so far as to say that the United States had "provoked" the Pacific by imposing the trade embargo. Such an opinion presumes a moral equivalency where none existed. It was not the US trade embargo against Japan that caused the problems in the Pacific. It was Japan's brutal, barbaric invasion of China, to which the American trade embargo was the final response, that ultimately precipitated the Pacific War. This view also fails to take into account Emperor Hirohito's *hakko ichiu* philosophy that called for Japanese dominance in East Asia, a hegemony that would include military intervention in any area that did not voluntarily become part of Prince Konoye's "New Order" in East Asia.
44. Bergamini, p. 733, quotes Yamamoto as gloomily saying, "I expect to die on the deck of my flagship, the battleship *Nagato*. In those evil days you will see Tokyo burnt to the ground at least three times. The result will be prolonged suffering for the people."
45. Bergamini, p. 739.
46. The Kingdom of Siam changed its name to Thailand in 1939, though it was temporarily renamed Siam again between 1945 and 1949.
47. The most extreme example of this doctrine of division was in the Second Naval Battle of Guadalcanal on November 14–15, 1942, when it divided a 14-ship force four ways. Samuel Eliot Morison, *The Two-Ocean War: A Short History of the United States Navy in the Second World War* (Boston: Little, Brown, 1963), p. 204.
48. Morison (1948), pp. 274–276; Bob Hackett, Sander Kingsepp, and Lars Ahlberg, "IJN KONGO: Tabular Record of Movement," *Imperial Japanese Navy Page,* www.combinedfleet.com, retrieved July 8, 2012.
49. Morison (1948), pp. 274–276; Bob Hackett and Sander Kingsepp, "IJN NATORI: Tabular Record of Movement," *Imperial Japanese Navy Page,* www.combinedfleet.com, retrieved April 10, 2012.
50. Morison (1948), pp. 274–276; Bob Hackett and Sander Kingsepp, tabular records of movement for IJN MOGAMI, HIJMS SENDAI, HIJMS YURA and HIJMS CHOKAI, *Imperial Japanese Navy Page,* www.combinedfleet.com, retrieved April–August, 2012.

Chapter 2

1. Stanley Weintraub, *Long Day's Journey Into War* (New York: Dutton, 1991), p. 181; and Edwin P. Hoyt, *The Lonely Ships: The Life and Death of the US Asiatic Fleet* (New York: David McKay, 1976), p. 141, have Hart playing golf with his chief of staff, Rear Admiral William R. Purnell. James Leutze, *A Different Kind of Victory: A Biography of Admiral Thomas C. Hart* (Annapolis: Naval Institute Press, 1981), p. 229, quotes from Hart's diary indicating that he planned to go to a movie. If so, it seems he never went.
2. Edwin P. Hoyt, *Japan's War: The Great Pacific Conflict* (New York: Cooper Square Press, 2001), pp. 7–8.
3. Hoyt (2001), p. 8.
4. John Gordon, *Fighting for MacArthur: The Navy and Marine Corps' Desperate Defense of the Philippines* (Annapolis: Naval Institute Press, 1984), pp. 5–7.
5. J. Gordon, p. 9.
6. Thomas C. Hart, Admiral, "Narrative of Events, Asiatic Fleet Leading up to War and From 8 December 1941 to 15 February 1942" (hereinafter "Hart Report"), pp. 7 and 14.
7. Hart Report, pp. 15–16.
8. Leutze, p. 164.
9. Leutze, p. 163.
10. Edward S. Miller, *War Plan Orange: The U.S. Strategy to Defeat Japan 1897–1945* (Annapolis: Naval Institute Press, 1991), pp. 61–62.
11. Miller, p. 60.
12. Willmott, p. 120.
13. F. C. van Oosten, *The Battle of the Java Sea* (Annapolis: Naval Institute Press, 1976), p. 10; Arthur J. Marder, *Old Friends, New Enemies: The Royal Navy and the Imperial Japanese Navy, Vol. 1: Strategic Illusions, 1936–1941* (Oxford: Clarendon Press, 1981), p. 206.
14. Marder (1981), p. 206.
15. Van Oosten, p. 10.
16. Marder (1981), p. 209, points out that of the 48 Royal Navy ships assigned to the Far East, under ADB-1 only three were to be in the vicinity of Singapore. The remainder were to be on escort and convoy duty.
17. Van Oosten, pp. 10–11.
18. Ronald H. Spector, *Eagle Against the Sun: The American War With Japan* (New York: Free Press, 1985), p. 86.

19. Hart Report, p. 14.
20. Bill Sloan, *Undefeated: America's Heroic Fight for Bataan and Corregidor* (New York: Simon & Schuster, 2012), p. 26. The P-35s in the Philippines were of a set that had originally been destined for Sweden. When American mechanics in the Philippines opened the crates to begin assembling the P-35s, they found the planes painted with Swedish markings and the instrumentation in Swedish.
21. The US version of the P-40, in its various iterations, was called the "Warhawk." Its export varieties were called the "Tomahawk" or the "Kittyhawk." For the sake of clarity, the term "Warhawk" will be used here for both domestic and export versions of the P-40. It should also be noted that "pursuit" was a term in the US Army Air Force, referencing the type of plane that others, including the US Navy, would call a "fighter."
22. John Burton, *Fortnight of Infamy: The Collapse of Allied Airpower West of Pearl Harbor* (Annapolis: Naval Institute Press, 2006), p. 54, 77; W. F. Craven and J. L. Cate (eds), *Army Air Forces in World War II. Vol 1: Plans and Early Operations, January 1939 to August 1942*, (Chicago Press, 1948), p. 203. It is frequently reported that the radar at Iba was the only radar in the Philippines, but that is not technically accurate. Craven and Cate, p. 186, state that seven radar sets had been shipped to the Philippines, but by the start of the war only two – the Iba radar and a set operated by the US Marines outside Manila, were operational. The Manila radar was not positioned to effectively warn of incoming aircraft from Formosa and did not figure in the air campaign.
23. Burton, p. 79.
24. Leutze, p. 218.
25. Leutze, p. 217.
26. Gordon, p. 22.
27. Bartsch (2003), p. 190.
28. Leutze, p. 247.
29. Leutze, p. 212.
30. Leutze, p. 212.
31. Craven and Cate p. 184.
32. Craven and Cate pp. 201–202; Sloan, p. 26. Burton, p. 54; and Bartsch (2003) give larger figures for aircraft, but those figures include spares.
33. Craven and Cate, pp. 182–183.
34. Craven and Cate, p. 188, 192.
35. Bartsch (2003), p. 192.
36. Leutze, p. 212.
37. Anthony P. Tully, "Naval Alamo: The Heroic Last Months of the Asiatic Fleet, December 1941–March 1942,", *US Asiatic Fleet*, www.asiaticfleet.com/javasea.html, retrieved January 18, 2005.
38. Leutze, p. 220; Morison (1948), pp. 158–160.
39. Morison (1948), pp. 158–160.
40. Hart Report, p. 34.
41. Except where noted otherwise, the accounts of the reconnaissance and contact incidents over Luzon come from Burton, pp. 71–75, 81–82.
42. Craven and Cate, p. 189, describe the efforts at Del Monte, which lacked natural cover, to camouflage the B-17s: "The one available spray gun was put to work night and day to change the shining silver color of the planes to an olive drab."
43. Craven and Cate, p. 188. Like many aspects of the Far East Air Force's performance in days leading up to the war and its first days, the order to move the B-17s is disputed. Both MacArthur and his chief of staff General Richard Sutherland claim that they ordered Brereton to move all of the B-17s to Del Monte. Craven and Cate's Official Army Air Force History has gone with Brereton's account, stating, "General Brereton's recollection fits so closely with readily established facts regarding the state of preparations at Del Monte [...] that it has been used as the basis of the account given here."
44. Burton, pp. 16–17.
45. Leutze, p. 218.
46. Bartsch (2003), p. 193.
47. On November 13, 1941, the aircraft carrier HMS *Ark Royal* was hit by one torpedo from the German submarine *U-81* and sank the next day within sight of Gibraltar. On November 25, 1941, the battleship HMS *Barham* was hit by three torpedoes from the German submarine *U-331*. Videocameras caught the battleship rolling over and exploding just before sinking. Both incidents occurred in the Mediterranean.
48. The widely respected British naval historian and analyst Arthur Marder called Singapore one of the "five

strategic keys" that "lock up the world." Richard Hough, *The Hunting of Force Z: The Sinking of the* Prince of Wales *and the* Repulse (London: Cassell, 1999), p. 77.

49. Hough, p. 77.
50. Willmott, pp. 102–103.
51. Miller, p. 264.
52. Christopher Shores, Brian Cull, and Yasuho Izawa, *Bloody Shambles, Volume One: The Drift to War to the Fall of Singapore* (London: Grub Street, 1992), p. 21. W. David McIntyre, *The Rise & Fall of the Singapore Naval Base, 1919–1942* (Hamden (CN): Archon, 1979), p. 121, discusses the positions of the guns. The exact capabilities of the guns defending Singapore remain disputed. See Marder (1981), p. 520 n. 56, and Karl Hack and Kevin Blackburn, *Did Singapore Have to Fall? Churchill and the Impregnable Fortress* (Kindle Edition) (London and New York: Routledge Curzon, 2004), ll. 2,504–3,180.
53. Morison (1948), p. 50 n. 3.
54. McIntyre, p. 153. The base was made operational but never fully completed.
55. In September 1939, *Admiral Graf Spee* began commerce raiding in the South Atlantic, ultimately engaging in a gun battle with the British cruisers *Exeter* and *Ajax* and the New Zealand cruiser *Achilles* off the Rio de la Plata in December 1939. The *Exeter* suffered heavy damage, but the *Graf Spee* was driven into neutral Montevideo, Uruguay, where her skipper was duped by the British into scuttling his ship and committing suicide.
56. Marder (1981), p. 216.
57. Arthur Nicholson, *Hostages to Fortune: Winston Churchill and the Loss of the* Prince of Wales *and* Repulse (Stroud, UK: Sutton, 2005), p. 45; Shores, Cull, and Izawa (1992), p. 28.
58. Weintraub, p. 64. The Buffalo required 27 modifications before it was considered safe or ready for combat. Hough, p. 82.
59. Hough, p. 95.
60. Shores, Cull, and Izawa (1992), pp. 40–41.
61. Hough, p. 95.
62. Leutze, pp. 195–196.
63. Warren, p. 43.
64. Leutze, p. 210.
65. Weintraub, pp. 64–65.
66. Sir John Collins, Vice Admiral, *As Luck Would Have It: The Reminiscences of an Australian Sailor* (Sydney, London, and Melbourne: Angus & Robertson, 1965), p. 100.
67. Burton, p. 68.
68. Burton, p. 68.
69. McIntyre, p. 211.
70. Ian Cowman, "Main Fleet to Singapore? Churchill, the Admiralty, and Force Z," *Journal of Strategic Studies*, 17:2 (1994), p. 83. The *Nelson* and *Rodney* were very distinctive for being the only battleships in the world to have all three of their main turrets (containing nine 16in guns) situated forward of the bridge structure.
71. Marder (1981), p. 227.
72. Marder (1981), p. 231.
73. Hough, p. 73.
74. Hough, pp. 73–74.
75. Martin Middlebrook and Patrick Mahoney, *The Sinking of the* Prince of Wales *&* Repulse: *The End of the Battleship Era* (Barnsley, UK: Leo Cooper, 2004), p. 46; Nicholson, pp. 173–176.
76. For a contrary opinion as to whether the *Prince of Wales* was sufficiently worked up, see Nicholson, pp. 172–173.
77. Marder (1981), p. 389.
78. Alan Matthews, *Force Z Survivors Association*, "The Sinking of HMS *Prince of Wales* and HMS *Repulse*: A series of personal accounts compiled from crew members," www.forcez-survivors.org.uk, retrieved February 22, 2012.
79. Middlebrook and Mahoney, p. 65. Roosevelt had met Churchill aboard the *Prince of Wales* for the conference that resulted in the Atlantic Charter.
80. The Royal Navy's official report on the loss of the *Prince of Wales* and *Repulse* (B. R. 1736 (8)/1955: *Naval Staff History Second World War*, "Battle Summary No. 14 (revised) Loss of H.M. Ships *Prince of Wales* and *Repulse*, 10th December 1941, hereinafter Admiralty Report"), p. 2, admits there is no record of the decision to send the *Prince of Wales* to Singapore.

81. For discussion of the continuing controversy and the relationship between Churchill and Pound, see, generally, Marder (1981), pp. 226–241. As naval analyst Ian Cowman summarized, "It has generally been presumed that Sir Dudley Pound succumbed to Churchill's pressure, resulting in the useless dispatch of an inadequately armed and insufficient number of vessels." Cowman, "Main fleet to Singapore? Churchill, the Admiralty, and Force Z," 17:2, 79–93, 79–80. See also Matthews, "The Sinking of HMS *Prince of Wales* and HMS *Repulse*"; Nicholson, pp. 33–35; and, generally, Christopher M. Bell, "The 'Singapore Strategy' and the Deterrence of Japan: Winston Churchill, the Admiralty and the Dispatch of Force Z," *The English Historical Review*, Vol. 116, No. 467 (June, 2001), pp. 604–634.

82. Marder (1981), p. 229 n. 28. In fairness, Middlebrooke and Mahoney, p. 54, question the accuracy of the charts for Kingston since the *Indomitable*'s escort, the corvette *Clarkia*, ran aground in the same spot.

83. Matthews, "The Sinking of HMS *Prince of Wales* and HMS *Repulse*."

84. Smuts' letter is widely quoted. This version comes from Middlebrooke and Mahoney, p. 68.

85. This fleet has also been called the Far East Fleet and the Far Eastern Fleet. The title of Eastern Fleet comes from B.R. 1736 (8)/1955: *Naval Staff History Second World War*, "Battle Summary No. 14 (revised) Loss of H.M. Ships *Prince of Wales* and *Repulse*," p. 2.

86. Marder (1981), p. 370.

87. Marder (1981), pp. 365–366, 370.

88. Marder (1981), p. 383.

89. Nicholson, p. 27.

90. Hart Report, p. 35.

91. Hart Report, p. 35.

92. Burton, pp. 84–85.

93. Burton, p. 85.

94. Burton, pp. 85–86.

95. Marder (1981), p. 398.

96. Shores, Cull, and Izawa (1992), p. 75.

97. Burton, p. 86; Shores, Cull, and Izawa (1992), pp. 75–77.

98. Burton, pp. 86–87. The Catalina was designated FV-V. Killed in this incident were Bedell, Flight Sergeant William Edward Webb, Sergeant Colin Burns Treloar (Royal Australian Air Force), Sergeant Edward Alexander Bailey, Sergeant Stanley Abram, Sergeant Peter Eaton, Leading Aircraftman Arthur Henry Chapman, and Aircraftman First Class William Thomas David Burnett; Shores, Cull, and Izawa (1992), pp. 75–77.

Chapter 3

1. Messimer (1985), p. 40.

2. Messimer (1985), p. 40; Anthony P. Tully and Gilbert Casse ("IJN Ryujo: Tabular Record of Movement," *Imperial Japanese Navy Page*, www.combinedfleet.com, retrieved April 10, 2012) says the *Ryujo* was equipped with Claudes and not Zeros as Messimer suggests.

3. Messimer (1985), p. 40.

4. Winslow (1982), p. 49.

5. Bartsch (2003), pp. 279–280.

6. Tully and Casse, "IJN Ryujo: Tabular Record of Movement," *Imperial Japanese Navy Page*.

7. Bartsch (2003), p. 280, identifies the pilot as Petty Officer 2nd Class Kawanishi Hiroshi.

8. The eight destroyers were Destroyer Division 15's *Hayashio*, *Natsushio*, *Oyashio*, and the *Kuroshio* and Destroyer Division 16's *Yukikaze*, *Tokitsukaze*, *Hatsukaze*, and *Amatsukaze*. Tully, "IJN Ryujo: Tabular Record of Movement," *Imperial Japanese Navy Page*, www.combinedfleet.com (retrieved April 10, 2012).

9. Bartsch (2003), p. 279.

10. Tully and Casse, "IJN Ryujo: Tabular Record of Movement," *Imperial Japanese Navy Page*.

11. Messimer (1985), p. 41.

12. Messimer (1985), p. 42.

13. Weintraub, p. 215; Hoyt (1976), p. 141.

14. Burton, pp. 120–121; Gordon W. Prange, *At Dawn We Slept: The Untold Story of Pearl Harbor* (New York: Penguin, 1981), p. 517.

15. Prange, p. 513. Ramsey's AIR RAID PEARL HARBOR, THIS IS NOT DRILL message has become perhaps the most famous message ever. It is understandably often confused with the similarly-worded ENEMY AIR

RAID PEARL HARBOR, THIS IS NOT A DRILL message that was sent some ten minutes later out of Pacific Fleet headquarters. Many histories have Clement informing Hart immediately after receiving Ramsey's message, but Burton, pp. 120–121, is very specific that Clement did not inform Hart until after receiving confirmation, which would have been the Pacific Fleet's later official message. Since this involved Hart sending his command to war, this would have been the proper procedure.

16. Walter Karig and Welbourn Kelley, *Battle Report: Pearl Harbor to Coral Sea (New York:* Farrar & Rinehart, 1944), pp. 111–112; Hoyt (1976), p. 141.
17. Morison (1948), p. 169 n. 6.
18. Messimer (1985), p. 37; J. Gordon, p. 34.
19. Hoyt (1976), p. 145.
20. Hoyt (1976), p. 146.
21. Messimer (1985), pp. 43–44.
22. Messimer (1985), pp. 43–44.
23. Morison (1963), p. 78.
24. William Manchester, *American Caesar: Douglas MacArthur 1880–1964* (Kindle Edition) (New York: Little, Brown and Company, 1978), l. 3,946.
25. Bartsch (2003), p. 60.
26. Louis Morton, *United States Army in World War II. The War in the Pacific* (Washington, DC: Center for Military History, United States Army, 1953), p. 80.
27. Weintraub, p. 256; Manchester, l. 3,933. Manchester, l. 3,296, claims Hart never told MacArthur or anyone in the Army of the attack on Pearl Harbor, which is seemingly contradicted by his later statement, l. 3,940, that Hart was with MacArthur. Admiral Hart's Report, p. 36, specifically states he told MacArthur's headquarters.
28. Bartsch (2003), p. 260.
29. Craven and Cate, p. 184.
30. William H. Bartsch, *Doomed at the Start: American Pursuit Pilots in the Philippines, 1941–1942* (College Station, TX: Texas A & M University Press, 1992), p. 52.
31. Bartsch (1992), p. 53.
32. Bartsch (2003), p. 281; Lewis H. Brereton; *The Brereton Diaries: The War in the Air in the Pacific, Middle East and Europe, 3 October 1941–8 May 1945* (New York: William Morrow and Company, 1946), p. 38; Burton, p. 122; Sloan, p. 28.
33. Bartsch (2003), p. 281.
34. Sloan, p. 28.
35. Bartsch (2003), p. 282.
36. Bartsch (2003), p. 414.
37. Sloan, p. 28.
38. Craven and Cate, p. 203. Much of this information seems to have been gleaned from reports by PBY and B-17 pilots who had discreetly flown close to Formosa in violation of MacArthur's orders.
39. Bartsch (2003), p. 260, supported by MichaelGough, "Failure and Destruction, Clark Field, the Philippines, December 8, 1941," *Military History Online*, www.militaryhistoryonline.com, 2007, retrieved July 7, 2012 gives the time of the phone call from Gerow as 8:00 am, but the time is disputed. Manchester, p. 230 and Weintraub, pp. 256–257, state that the call arrived earlier at about 3:40 am.
40. Bartsch (2003), p. 261; Manchester, p. 230; Weintraub, p. 257.
41. Bartsch (2003), p. 261. As Gough, "Failure and Destruction, Clark Field, the Philippines, December 8, 1941," points out, this statement is consistent with Bartsch's 8:00 am time for the phone call, as the earlier time for the call would have been under darkness when it would be extremely difficult to have "tails in the air."
42. Bartsch (2003), p. 284.
43. Burton, p. 128. Bartsch (2003), p. 287, says the Japanese struck Camp John Hay because their intelligence reports indicated that MacArthur was attending a retreat there.
44. Burton, p. 129. Burton cites as his source Walter D. Edmonds, *They Fought With What They Had: The Story of the Army Air Forces in the Southwest Pacific, 1941–1942* (Boston: Little, Brown and Company, 1951), p. 87. Edmonds, in turn, cites the official *Far East Air Force Diaries*, but he, pp. 91–93, goes on to question (though not totally discount) the authenticity of the *Diaries*. For his part, Brereton himself, p. 41, makes no mention of the phone call from MacArthur, only saying that he received a phone call from Sutherland at about 11:00 am authorizing the air strikes. MacArthur himself, in *Reminiscences* (Annapolis: Naval Institute Press,

1964), p. 120, says that, "Brereton never at any time recommended or suggested an attack on Formosa to me." He continues by saying the first he heard of it was in a newspaper report months later, then says that such a proposal should have been made to him in person.

45. Craven and Cate, p. 209.

46. Bartsch (1992), p. 444, notes that in his after-action report, Major Grover rather conveniently failed to mention his orders to the 3rd and the 21st. Not all of the aircraft of the 3rd and 21st heard Grover's orders; while ten Warhawks of the 3rd and 21 of the 21st heard the orders and proceeded to their new patrol areas, the remainder stayed on their original stations.

47. Burton, pp. 131–132. It should be pointed out that this analysis is in contravention with Bartsch, normally the gold standard in the study of the US Army Air Force in the Philippines. Bartsch says that Colonel George had been waiting until the incoming aircraft were some 15 minutes from Clark Field. I have gone with Burton because I find his explanation of George's dissatisfaction with Grover's deployments more plausible. As pursuit commander, George was aware of the limitations of the P-40 Warhawk, whose rate of climb was so slow that it could take 30 minutes to reach interception altitude. And even Bartsch acknowledges that George's waiting for so long to order Grover to intercept the incoming aircraft lacks a clear explanation.

48. Bartsch (1992), p. 445 n. 11, states, "It is assumed that this message reached Major Grover, though neither he nor his staff acknowledged receiving it."

49. Bartsch (1992), p. 69. Precisely who sent the message and under whose authority is unknown. Bartsch (1992), p. 445 n. 11, suspects that this message was motivated by the "KICKAPOO" order from Colonel George. But while staffers from the Clark Field radio room remember such a message going out, no one can say exactly who sent it.

50. Gough, "Failure and Destruction, Clark Field, the Philippines, December 8, 1941," (Table 4).

51. Craven and Cate, p. 234, n. 43.

52. Weintraub, pp. 518–519.

53. Bartsch (2003), pp. 72 and 314.

54. Walter D. Edmonds, *They Fought With What They Had: The Story of the Army Air Forces in the Southwest Pacific, 1941–1942* (Boston: Little, Brown and Company, 1951), p. 100.

55. Bartsch (2003), p. 311; Burton, p. 135.

56. Bartsch (2003), p. 312.

57. Burton, p. 135.

58. The Japanese Army Air Force and Naval Air Force were organized in ways that were not directly analogous to Western air forces, or, in fact, to each other, and trying to present their activities, particularly those of the army air force, for the English-speaking reader can be a challenge. The Japanese Army Air Force tried to use terminology consistent with the land army, with only limited success. During the time period of the Java Sea Campaign, the basic unit was the *shōtai* (flight or section) of three aircraft. Three or four *shōtai* formed a *chutai* (squadron or company). Two or more *chutai* formed a *sentai*, usually translated as "air group" (lit. "combat group"), which was the basic operating unit of the Japanese Army Air Force. Two or more *sentai* formed a *hikodan* (wing, flying brigade, or flying battalion; *hiko* meaning "flying"), two or more *hikodan* would form a *hikoshudan* (flying corps) or, later, a *hikoshidan* (flying division), and two or more *hikoshidan* would form a *kokogun* (air force). The land-based elements of the Japanese Naval Air Force similarly used *shotai* and *chutai*, but multiple *chutai* comprised a *kokutai* (sometimes shortened to "*ku*"), which is usually translated as "air group" or "air corps." Multiple *kokutai* would form an air flotilla. The *kokutai* was the basic unit of the land-based elements of the Japanese Naval Air Force. As such, their closest analogue in the Japanese Army Air Force was the *sentai*, but the navy *kokutai* were actually somewhat larger than the army *sentai*. To avoid overwhelming the reader with Japanese terminology, the term "air group" will be used for both the army *sentai* and the navy *kokutai*, with the caveat that they are not quite the same unit. Shores, Cull, and Izawa (1993), pp. 11–12; Mark Kaiser, "Unit Structure of IJA Air Force," *Japanese Aviation*, www.markkaiser.com/japaneseaviation/jaafstructure.html, retrieved March 17, 2013. The Japanese Naval Air Force's *kokutai* often operated using the name of their home base; for example, the home base of the Takao Air Group was at Takao, on Formosa.

59. Burton, p. 136.

60. The works include William Bartsch's excellent *December 8 1941: MacArthur's Pearl Harbor* and the aptly named *Doomed at the Start: American Pursuit Pilots in the Philippines* and John Burton's *Fortnight of Infamy: The Collapse of Allied Air Power West of Pearl Harbor*.

61. Burton, p. 132.

62. John Costello, *The Pacific War: 1941–45* (New York: Quill, 1982), p. 142.

63. Robert C. Daniels, "MacArthur's Failures in the Philippines, December 1941 – March 1942," *Military History Online*, www.militaryhistoryonline.com, published April 22, 2007, retrieved August 9, 2011.
64. Manchester, l. 4039, 3953.
65. Michael Gough, "Failure and Destruction, Clark Field, the Philippines, December 8, 1941 .
66. Weintraub, p. 454.
67. Craven and Cate, p. 205.
68. Manchester, l. 3,953, says Washington was "in a daze" at the Battle of Brandywine, Napoleon's "catatonic" state cost him the Battle of Waterloo, and Stonewall Jackson was in a similar state at the Battle of White Oak Swamp, "the low point in [his] military career."
69. Brereton, p. 44.
70. Roscoe (1949), p. 28.

Chapter 4

1. Burton, p. 90.
2. Burton, pp. 90–91.
3. Warren, p. 59.
4. Admiralty Report, p. 8.
5. Shores, Cull, and Izawa (1992), p. 80.
6. Burton, p. 92; James Leasor, *Singapore: The Battle that Changed the World* (Kindle Edition) (London: James Leasor, 2011), p. 170, has the order from his staff worded as, "Go for the transports, you bloody fools!"
7. The account of these attacks is taken from Burton, pp. 92–95.
8. Warren, p. 62; Burton, p. 95.
9. Shores, Cull, and Izawa (1992), pp. 83–84.
10. Shores, Cull, and Izawa (1992), pp. 90–91; Burton, p. 109.
11. Shores, Cull, and Izawa (1992), pp. 91–92; Burton, p. 110.
12. Shores, Cull, and Izawa (1992), p. 91; Burton, p. 110.
13. For a detailed discussion of the possibility that the *K-XII* sank the *Awagisan Maru*, see the entry on the *K-XII* at www.dutchsubmarines.com.
14. Shores, Cull, and Izawa, p. 82, claim that the *Awagisan Maru* took at least ten direct bomb hits.
15. Burton, p. 97.
16. Nicholson, pp. 60–61.
17. Marder (1981), pp. 406–412, describes the meeting in detail, but acknowledges that his account of the meeting is based on only a single source – Captain James W. McClelland – with almost no corroboration. McClelland was sent to observe the meeting at the direction of Admiral Sir Geoffrey Layton, who had been the head of the Royal Navy's China Station before its dissolution to become the Eastern Fleet. Layton was not happy about being passed over in favor of Phillips. Having been ordered by Phillips to set up the meeting before he left for Manila, and suspecting that the naval expedition would become a disaster, Layton sent McClelland effectively to spy on the meeting, which he did from an alcove in the darkened war room. This gives rise to the question of McClelland's impartiality; moreover much of his account comes from memory. Nicholson, pp. 61–63, lays out various reasons for questioning the accuracy of McClelland's account, including the aforementioned lack of corroboration, the nocturnal timing of this meeting and, perhaps most significantly, that no one in the room seems to have known of the Japanese attack on Kota Bharu three hours before. Nevertheless, there is no direct refutation of the idea that a meeting took place. In trying to give the most credence to McClelland's story, garbled and all, while stipulating that 3:30 am meetings are not standard operating procedure under most circumstances, we can surmise that: 1. Layton had arranged for the invitees to attend a meeting; 2. the Japanese attack on Kota Bharu was known, but perhaps not the extent of that attack; and 3. when that attack became known, this previously arranged meeting was moved up to deal with the emergency. Nevertheless, the reader should be advised that the facts and existence of this meeting are disputed and the scenario presented here is not the only possible one.
18. Most accounts state that the Japanese air attack began at around 4:00 am. Shores, Cull, and Izawa, p. 85, say the bombs started falling at "exactly" 4:15 am.
19. Shores, Cull, and Izawa, pp. 86–87; A. E. Percival, "*The War In Malaya (Extract from his official report to the government 1946),*" *FEPOW Community*, http://www.fepow-community.org.uk/, retrieved July 10, 2012.
20. Shores, Cull, and Izawa, pp. 85–86. Most of the bombs in this attack fell on the civilian area of Chinatown,

where 61 civilians, mainly Chinese and Sikhs, were killed and 133 injured. Somehow, the Chinese usually suffered disproportionately under Japanese aggression.

21. Shores, Cull, and Izawa, p. 87. Vigors threatened to take off on his own against orders, but abstained when he was threatened with court-martial.
22. Burton, pp. 96–97.
23. Marder (1981), pp. 411–412.
24. Nicholson, p. 64.
25. Admiralty Report, Appendix (D)(15), p. 30.
26. Marder (1981), pp. 412–413. Phillips' use of the word "intend" was deliberate and dispositive. According to Roskill (2004), p. 100, under British communications conventions, "[T]he originator of a signal using the word 'Intend' neither demanded nor expected an answer *unless the addressee disapproved of the intention expressed*" (emphasis in original).
27. Hough, p. 124.
28. Marder (1981), pp. 414–415. In actuality, the Japanese had two battleships – *Kongo* and her sister ship *Haruna* – ten cruisers, 24 destroyers, and 12 submarines; Marder (1981), p. 413.
29. The report on the submarines comes from Middlebrook and Mahoney, pp. 87–88.
30. Hough, p. 117.
31. Marder (1981), pp. 414–416. The British were using Ca Mau (Quan Long), located on the Ca Mau Peninsula about 150 miles southwest of Saigon and 40 miles northeast of Cape Cambodia, to determine distance because they wrongly believed the Japanese had an airbase there.
32. Hough, p. 124.
33. Marder (1981), p. 414.
34. Middlebrook and Mahoney, p. 105.
35. Hough, p. 115.
36. Middlebrook and Mahoney, p. 106.
37. Shores, Cull, and Izawa (1982), p. 125.
38. Morison (1948), p. 188.
39. Nicholson, p. 71.
40. Matthews, "The Sinking of HMS *Prince of Wales* and HMS *Repulse*."
41. Marder (1981), p. 423.
42. Middlebrook and Mahoney, p. 109; Marder (1981), p. 420.
43. Marder (1981), p. 423.
44. Marder (1981), p. 423.
45. Matthews, "The Sinking of HMS *Prince of Wales* and HMS *Repulse*." Matthews specifically mentions the "ultra modern surface scanning Radar" as being offline, but both Middlebrook and Mahoney and Nicholson make clear that the *Prince of Wales'* surface search radar was functional, if not entirely effective.
46. Marder (1981), p. 420.
47. This quotation by Captain Tennant is given in a number of histories of the action off Malaya, but the most detailed account of Tennant's full statement comes from Hough, p. 126.
48. Clay Blair, Jr., *Silent Victory: The US Submarine War Against Japan* (Annapolis: Naval Institute Press, 1975), p. 128.
49. Blair, p. 131.
50. Blair, p. 131.
51. Blair, p. 131.
52. By way of comparison, the legendary US submarine skipper Dudley "Mush" Morton, commanding the *Wahoo*, told his crew that their lives and their boat were expendable.
53. Blair, p. 131.
54. Blair, p. 131. Most histories refer to the "Mark 6 magnetic exploder" or some variation thereof, and this history will as well for the sake of simplicity, but it should be noted that technically the Mark 6 was not just the magnetic exploder, but the entire exploder assembly that included a magnetic exploder that could be deactivated and a contact exploder.
55. Winston S. Churchill, *The Grand Alliance* (electronic edition) (New York: Rosetta Books, 2002), p. 551.
56. Churchill, p. 552, admits that Phillips signaled his intentions before sailing, which strongly implies the prime minister knew about Force Z's planned counterattack. For a detailed discussion on the evidence that Churchill and Pound knew Force Z was at sea before this meeting, see Nicholson, pp. 76–81.

57. Nicholson, p. 77.
58. Churchill, p. 551.
59. Marder (1981), p. 405.
60. Nicholson, p. 26.
61. Middlebrook and Mahoney, p. 82; Statement of Lieutenant Iki Haruki in Matthews, "The Sinking of HMS *Prince of Wales* and HMS *Repulse*."
62. *Kongo* herself had been built in Great Britain, the last Japanese battleship to be constructed overseas. Her sister ships were simply copies constructed in Japan.
63. Shores, Cull and Izawa (1992), p. 54, 114; Marder (1981), p. 443. Middlebrook and Mahoney, p. 179, identify the Genzan Air Group commander as Nakanishi Niichi. Captain Sonokawa Kameo, in postwar interrogations (Interrogation of Captain Sonokawa Kameo, in Alan Matthews, *Force Z Survivors Association* "Pilot's Eye View," www.forcez-survivors.org.uk, retrieved July 18, 2012), had the Mihoro Air Group based "20 miles north of Saigon," an apparent reference to Thú Dâu Môt, and Kanoya based "60 miles southwest of Saigon." In fact, the Kanoya was based at Thú Dâu Môt. Okumiya, Horikoshi, and Caidin, p. 61, confirm the Mihoro at Thú Dâu Môt, but say a section of fighter and reconnaissance aircraft was based at an advance base at Soctrang, south of Saigon. This section was the Yamada Unit, so called because it was commanded by one Commander Yamada Yutaka. Shores, Cull and Izawa (1992), p. 54, 274; Marder (1981), p. 443. Sonokawa seems to have confused the Yamada with the Kanoya.
64. Marder (1981), pp. 443–444.
65. Middlebrook and Mahoney, p. 304, points to what they call "hearsay evidence" that Phillips' intelligence officer, upon his return to Singapore after the sinkings, found that "the naval staff ashore had known of the presence of Japanese torpedo bombers in Indo-China while Force Z had been at sea but had not thought it necessary to send a warning signal." This is apparently a reference to Marder (1981), p. 418, where after the destruction of Force Z, members of Phillips' staff discovered that accuate intelligence on the Nells' and Bettys' torpedo capabilities had been in Singapore but had not been shared with Phillips, either before or during Force Z's expedition, for reasons unknown. A far worse story comes from John Winton, *Ultra in the Pacific: How Breaking Japanese Codes & Ciphers Affected Naval Operations Against Japan* (London: Leo Cooper, 1993), p. 18. Captain Kenneth Harkness, head of the Far East Combined Bureau (British military intelligence in the Far East), returned to London in late 1942 to find that he was being blamed for a lack of intelligence for Force Z, despite the fact that he had regularly submitted reports. Upon his own investigation, he found that his reports had been "held up at a junior level, on the desk of a certain Commander," and had never reached the naval general staff.
66. Statement of Lieutenant Iki Haruki in Matthews, "The Sinking of HMS *Prince of Wales* and HMS *Repulse*."
67. Middlebrook and Mahoney, p. 83.
68. Admiralty Report, Appendix D(1), p. 31.
69. Admiralty Report, Appendix D(1), p. 31.
70. Middlebrook and Mahoney, pp. 119 and 122. They report that a PBY Catalina flew over Force Z and flashed a signal that the Japanese were landing north of Singora, but no record of the signal has been found. The term "degrees True" is a reference to a course or bearing with respect to True north. For instance, a ship on a course of 90 degrees True (or "90 degrees T" or "90° T" in shorthand) means a ship is headed due east. A course of 180 degrees True is due south. Otherwise, a report of a course or bearing is simply relative, with respect to the reporting party only.
71. Middlebrook and Mahoney, p. 123.
72. Middlebrook and Mahoney, pp. 127–128. Times are from Nicholson, p. 106.
73. Nicholson, p. 106, says Ozawa got the report at 3:40 pm.
74. Nicholson, p. 106.
75. Middlebrook and Mahoney, pp. 128–129, say that the reconnaissance aircraft was originally to have landed at "one of the outlying airfields at Saigon." The basing of the scout plane at Soctrang is a deduction based on Okumiya, Horikoshi, and Caidin, p. 61.
76. Interrogation of Captain Sonokawa Kameo, in Matthews, "Pilot's Eye View."
77. Nicholson, p. 107.
78. Middlebrook and Mahoney, p. 139.
79. Middlebrook and Mahoney, p. 139.
80. Middlebrook and Mahoney, p. 139.
81. Nicholson, p. 107 and Appendix, No. 56; Middlebrook and Mahoney, pp. 136–137. The narrative of the

Admiralty Report, p. 10, says the *Tenedos* was detached at 6:25 pm, but its own Appendix D(1) says the message was sent at 6:25 pm and the destroyer detached at 6:35 pm.

82. Middlebrook and Mahoney, p. 137.
83. Nicholson, pp. 107–108, speculates that Admiral Phillips had decided to return to Singapore long before his announcement, but kept up the pretense of still heading for Singora until darkness when the Japanese scout planes would be unable to report on any course change.
84. Nicholson, pp. 108–109.
85. Middlebrook and Mahoney, p. 141.
86. Middlebrook and Mahoney, p. 141.
87. Nicholson, p. 108.
88. Nicholson, pp. 108–109. Nicholson says the *Chokai* was outside the range of the *Prince of Wales'* Type 273 surface search radar, but Middlebrook and Mahoney, p. 142, point out that the radar had a theoretical range of 25 miles. Why it did not detect the *Chokai* remains a mystery, though Middlebrook and Mahoney, p. 120, also point out that during these early days of radar, "the sets did not always function satisfactorily."
89. Middlebrook and Mahoney, p. 145.
90. Middlebrook and Mahoney, p. 145.
91. Admiralty Report, p. 33.
92. Marder (1981), p. 369. Admiral Phillips had a habit of reaching into a particular desk drawer, taking out a tablet and swallowing it. This behavior caused many to conclude that Phillips was taking pills to stay awake, which might explain his haggard appearance and questionable decisions throughout the engagement. The tablets Phillips was taking were, in fact, chocolates, which occupied most of his desk and even his safe. The only energy-boosting substances Phillips took were vitamins.
93. Middlebrook and Mahoney, p. 152.
94. Nicholson, p. 115.
95. Nicholson, pp. 115–116.
96. Winton, p. 18.
97. Admiralty Report, p. 12.
98. Admiralty Report, p. 12, Note 4.
99. Shores, Cull and Izawa (1992), pp. 112–113.
100. Nicholson, p. 117.
101. Matthews, "The Sinking of HMS *Prince of Wales* and HMS *Repulse*."
102. Admiralty Report, p. 12. Precisely what prompted the inaccurate report of Japanese landings at Kuantan is disputed. Shores, Cull and Izawa (1992), pp. 111–112, state that during the night the coaster *Larut*, carrying RAF personnel, ran aground off Kuantan, which prompted a response from the coastal defenses. Collins, p. 103, shares a similar story about RAF ground crew in boats mistaken as Japanese. Leasor, p. 193, claims that water buffalos had wandered into a minefield, setting them off and convincing the local Indian troops Japanese were nearby. Marder (1981), pp. 437–438 n. 111, suggests the real explanation was a light Japanese reconnaissance that drew gunfire. Japanese boats were found in the area later on December 10.
103. Nicholson, pp. 117–18; Middlebrook and Mahoney, p. 166.
104. Nicholson, p. 118; Middlebrook and Mahoney, p. 168.
105. Nicholson, p. 117.
106. Middlebrook and Mahoney, p. 157.
107. Middlebrook and Mahoney, p. 167.
108. Middlebrook and Mahoney, p. 168.
109. Marder (1981), p. 438.
110. Middlebrook and Mahoney, p. 169.
111. Middlebrook and Mahoney, p. 173.
112. Admiralty Report, p. 13.
113. Middlebrook and Mahoney, p. 174.
114. G. Hermon Gill, *Australia in the War of 1939–1945, Series Two: Navy; Volume I: Royal Australian Navy 1939–1942* (Canberra: Australian War Memorial, 1957), p. 480.
115. Nicholson, p. 123.
116. Middlebrook and Mahoney, p. 181.
117. In postwar interrogations, Captain Sonokawa Kameo, who provided the Allies with a good part of their information about the Japanese side of the attack on Force Z, said the Genzan Air Group was the best unit in

the 11th Air Fleet. Captain Sonokawa was part of the Genzan Air Group.

118. Middlebrook and Mahoney, p. 181.
119. Nicholson, p. 124.
120. Matthews, "The Sinking of HMS *Prince of Wales* and HMS *Repulse*."
121. Middlebrook and Mahoney, pp. 179 and 181.
122. Middlebrook and Mahoney, p. 182.
123. Middlebrook and Mahoney, p. 183.
124. Middlebrook and Mahoney, p. 184. The Admiralty Report, p. 13, describes this attack as "very well executed and the enemy in no way perturbed by our gunfire."
125. Middlebrook and Mahoney, pp. 182–183.
126. Nicholson, p. 124.
127. Middlebrook and Mahoney, p. 183, 212.
128. Middlebrook and Mahoney, p. 186. The Japanese Official History says that after releasing his torpedo, Kawada realized he was going to crash and instead attempted a *kamikaze* run on the *Prince of Wales*, but could not make it and instead crashed after flying over the battleship. Kawada's plane crashed with no survivors, which begs the question of how the Japanese Official History knew what Kawada was thinking.
129. Matthews, "The Sinking of HMS *Prince of Wales* and HMS *Repulse*."
130. Middlebrook and Mahoney, p. 187.
131. William H. Garzke, Jr.; Robert O. Dulin, Jr.; and Kevin V. Denlay, *Death of a Battleship: The Loss of HMS Prince of Wales; December 10, 1941: A Marine Forensic Analysis of the Sinking* (2012 Update), pp. 14–16. The extent of the damage to the shaft itself is not known because dives to the wreck of the *Prince of Wales* have been unable to locate the stern segment of the propeller shaft.
132. Garzke, Dulin, and Denlay, pp. 16–17. Nicholson, p. 129 n. 23, explains the arrangement of the *Prince of Wales*' machinery. It was divided into four units – "A," "B," "X," and "Y" – each with a boiler room, an engine room, and an action machinery room. Each engine room drove a propeller shaft – respectively, starboard outer, port outer, starboard inner, and port inner.
133. Garzke, Dulin, and Denlay; p. 26.
134. Garzke, Dulin, and Denlay; p. 18.
135. Garzke, Dulin, and Denlay; p. 12, n. 6.
136. Nicholson, p. 125.
137. Middlebrook and Mahoney, p. 187.
138. Middlebrook and Mahoney, pp. 188–189. The misidentification is not as absurd as it sounds. The *Repulse* and the *Kongo* had similar masts and were both completed in Great Britain at about the same time.
139. I have gone with the Admiralty Report, p. 13, but it should be noted that Middlebrook and Mahoney, p. 190, has the attack coming from starboard.
140. Middlebrook and Mahoney, pp. 188–189.
141. Nicholson, p. 127. Marder (1981), p. 470, describes Tennant using a zigzag pattern in 30-degree increments to throw off the aim of the torpedo aircraft before they committed.
142. Garzke, Dulin, and Denlay; p. 19. "Voids" are empty spaces inside a ship that are often flooded to maintain ballast or counter lists.
143. Garzke, Dulin, and Denlay; p. 24.
144. Middlebrook and Mahoney, p. 208.
145. Admiralty Report, p. 38; Nicholson, pp. 125–126.
146. Hough, p. 143.
147. Nicholson, p. 127.
148. Admiralty Report, Appendix D(2), p. 34, has the signal reaching Kallang Naval Signal Station in Singapore at 12:04 pm. The time listed here from Middlebrook and Mahoney, p. 211, is when the signal reached Sembawang.
149. Middlebrook and Mahoney, pp. 211–212.
150. Shores, Cull, and Izawa (1992), p. 122.
151. Marder (1981), p. 469; Hough, p. 145.
152. Middlebrook and Mahoney, p. 216.
153. Shores, Cull and Izawa (1992), p. 116. Shores, Cull, and Izawa (1992) have Nabeta's given name as Miyoshi.
154. The following June, a Japanese destroyer rushing back to *Kido Butai* after trying to pin down the submarine USS *Nautilus* unwittingly led the fatal US airstrike straight to the Japanese carriers at the Battle of Midway.
155. Marder (1981), p. 470.

156. Except where noted otherwise, the account of the Kanoya Air Group's attack comes from Middlebrook and Mahoney, pp. 216–218, 221–223.

157. Garzke, Dulin, and Denlay; pp. 28–30.

158. Hough, p. 145.

159. Middlebrook and Mahoney, p. 223.

160. Admiralty Report, Appendix D(2), p. 34. The message is listed as having been sent at 12:20 pm, but based on the descriptions of damage this cannot be the case. Marder (1981), p. 471 n. 32, suspects that the first part of the message indicating position had been prepared but not sent when the next Japanese attack came. When that attack was over, the damage was appended and the message sent, but with the original time stamp.

161. Nicholson, p. 131.

162. Marder (1981), pp. 471 and 490.

163. Middlebrook and Mahoney, p. 235.

164. Nicholson, pp. 131–133.

165. Nicholson, p. 131.

166. Middlebrook and Mahoney, pp. 223–224; Marder (1981), p. 471.

167. Marder (1981), p. 471.

168. Middlebrook and Mahoney, pp. 224–225, give the details of the hits. Like most accounts, including the Admiralty Report, p. 16, they list five torpedo hits, not four, as is stated here. The fifth reported hit that is not included here is a portside hit hear the "Y" (aft) turret, which Australian naval archaeologist Kevin Denlay, who dove the wreck of the *Repulse*, "was simply *not* seen to be there" (emphasis in original). What is presented here is based on Denlay's report, *Expedition "Job 74": An overview of Expedition "Job 74" which carried Explorers Club Flag #118 to the wrecks of HMS* Prince of Wales *and HMS* Repulse, *South China Sea, May 13th – May 25th, 2007*, pp. 6–7. Interestingly, Tennant would only say there were "at least" four torpedo hits. William G. Tennant, "Initial Report by Captain W. G. Tennant, C.B., M.V.O., R.N." in "Loss of H.M. Ships Prince of Wales and Repulse," *Supplement to the London Gazette*, Thursday, 26 February 1948 (hereinafter "Tennant Report"), pp. 1,241–1,242.

169. Middlebrook and Mahoney, p. 235.

170. Tennant Report, p. 1,242.

171. Middlebrook and Mahoney, p. 244.

172. Nicholson, p. 133.

173. Nicholson, p. 133.

174. Middlebrook and Mahoney, p. 226.

175. Garzke, Dulin, and Denlay; p. 33.

176. Middlebrook and Mahoney, pp. 228–230.

177. Hough, p. 149.

178. Garzke, Dulin, and Denlay, pp. 32–33.

179. Middlebrook and Mahoney, p. 257; Costello, p. 158.

180. Matthews, "The Sinking of HMS *Prince of Wales* and HMS *Repulse*."

181. Admiralty Report, Appendix D(2), p. 34.

182. Middlebrook and Mahoney, pp. 231–232.

183. Admiralty Report, Appendix D(2), p. 34.

184. Admiralty Report, Appendix D(2), p. 34.

185. Except where noted otherwise, the capsize of the *Prince of Wales* and the near-capsize of the *Express* come from Middlebrook and Mahoney, p. 232, 248–49, 252–253; and Nicholson, pp. 134–135.

186. Garzke, Dulin, and Denlay, p. 34.

187. Shores, Cull and Izawa (1992), p. 123–124.

188. Admiralty Report, Appendix H, p. 39.

189. Middlebrook and Mahoney, p. 259.

190. Admiralty Report, Appendix D(2), p. 34.

191. Collins, p. 104.

192. Middlebrook and Mahoney, p. 305. Interestingly, after castigating Admiral Phillips for refusing to admit he was wrong on one issue (air cover), on the very next page they mention how he did, in fact, admit he was wrong on another (handling the ships under air attack).

193. Lieutenant Vigor's quote is often cited in short form but Shores, Cull, and Izawa (1992), p. 125, gives the full statement.

194. Figures come from Shores, Cull, and Izawa (1992), p. 123.

195. Henry Leach would later become First Sea Lord during the 1982 Falklands War, during which he made certain the Royal Navy had air cover from two aircraft carriers.

196. Shores, Cull, and Izawa (1992), pp. 124–125.

197. Shores, Cull, and Izawa (1992), p. 125.

198. Churchill, p. 555.

199. John Toland, *But Not In Shame: The Six Months After Pearl Harbor* (New York: Random House, 1961), p. 83.

200. Marder (1981), p. 508; Matthews, "The Sinking of HMS *Prince of Wales* and HMS *Repulse*."

Chapter 5

1. J. Gordon, p. 49.

2. Messimer (1985), p. 54.

3. The 1st had started out with 27 bombers, but one was forced to abort. J. Gordon, p. 49. Most sources indicate Cavite was bombed by both the 1st and Takao Air Groups, totaling 54 bombers. See, e.g., *The Official Chronology of the US Navy in World War II* (Chapter III: 1941). Shores, Cull, and Izawa (1992), pp. 177–178, with access to Japanese records, makes clear that it was only the 1st Air Group. J. Gordon, pp. 55–56, says the 1st Air Group bombed Cavite, but "at some point, possibly the last bombing run," 27 Betty bombers of the Takao Air Group joined in. According to Shores, Cull, and Izawa, during the attack on Cavite, the Takao Air Group was operating in two groups, bombing Nichols Field and parts of Manila, which may account for the confusion.

4. J. Gordon, p. 49.

5. J. Gordon, p. 49.

6. J. Gordon, p. 50; Burton, p. 188.

7. J. Gordon, p. 49, 60.

8. The precise dimension of that shortfall seems unclear. The figures here come from Gordon, p. 60. According to Gordon, the guns at Cavite could only reach 18,000ft; the guns at Sangley Point could theoretically reach 25,000ft, but that was dependent on a short horizontal range.

9. J. Gordon, p. 49.

10. J. Gordon, p. 50.

11. Messimer (1985), p. 54; Walter G. Winslow, *The Fleet the Gods Forgot* (Annapolis: Naval Institute Press, 1982), p. 258.

12. J. Gordon, pp. 50–51.

13. Ian W. Toll, *Pacific Crucible: War at Sea in the Pacific, 1941–1942* (New York: W. W. Norton, 2012), p. 52.

14. J. Gordon, p. 55; "Office of Naval Intelligence Combat Narrative: The Java Sea Campaign," U.S. Navy Office of Naval Intelligence, March 13, 1943 (hereinafter ONI Narrative) p. 6.

15. Blair, p. 132.

16. Blair, pp. 132–134.

17. Winslow (1982), p. 258; J. Gordon, pp. 54–55.

18. Roscoe (1953), p. 52.

19. J. Gordon, p. 54.

20. Leutze, p. 233.

21. Messimer (1985), p. 55.

22. Craven and Cate, p. 218 and p. 215; Shores, Cull, and Izawa (1992), pp. 176–177.

23. Messimer (1985), pp. 50–51; Hackett and Kingsepp, "HIJMS ASHIGARA: Tabular Record of Movement," *Imperial Japanese Navy Page*, www.combinedfleet.com, retrieved April 10, 2012.

24. Shores, Cull, and Izawa (1992), p. 177; *The Official Chronology of the US Navy in World War II* (Chapter III: 1941) Hackett and Kingsepp, "IJN NATORI: Tabular Record of Movement," *Imperial Japanese Navy Page*, www.combinedfleet.com, retrieved April 10, 2012.

25. Craven and Cate, p. 218.

26. Craven and Cate, p. 218, say the Japanese escort consisted of "an estimated 100 fighters." The figures used here of 56 from the 3rd and Tainan Air Groups come from Shores, Cull, and Izawa (1992), pp. 177–178.

27. J. Gordon, p. 50; Messimer (1985), p. 53; *The Official Chronology of the US Navy in World War II* (Chapter III: 1941).

28. Messimer (1985), pp. 52 and 56.

29. Shores, Cull, and Izawa (1992), p. 178.

30. Winslow (1982), p. 258.
31. Winslow (1982), p. 258: Morison (1948), p. 172.
32. J. Gordon, pp. 62–63. Blair, p. 134, says that 233 Mark 14 torpedoes were lost at Cavite. Gordon does not dispute the figure but says that most of the torpedoes lost were destroyer torpedoes, as most of the submarine torpedoes had been transferred to Corregidor before the war.
33. Messimer (1985), p. 55.
34. Blair, pp. 134–135.
35. Toll, p. 53.
36. *The Official Chronology of the US Navy in World War II,* (Chapter III: 1941) Leutze, p. 233.
37. J. Gordon, p. 59.
38. Manchester, ll. 4,089–4,096.
39. Shores, Cull, and Izawa (1992), p. 183; J. Gordon, p. 69; Hart Report, p. 41.
40. Shores, Cull, and Izawa (1992), p. 183; J. Gordon, p. 69.
41. Leutze, p. 234.
42. Walter G. Winslow, *The Ghost That Died At Sunda Strait* (Annapolis: Naval Institute Press, 1984), p. 33.
43. Winslow (1984), p. 33.
44. Winslow (1984), p. 33.
45. Duane Schultz, *The Last Battle Station: The Saga of the USS* Houston (New York: St. Martin's Press, 1985), p. 54.
46. Messimer (1990), pp. 19–20. As far as the lookouts could tell, Venus was not damaged.
47. Winslow (1984), pp. 36–37.
48. Schultz, p. 51.
49. Winslow (1984), p. 33.
50. Schultz, p. 55; Winslow (1984), p. 37.
51. Winslow (1984), p. 37.
52. Schultz, p. 56.
53. John Prados, *Combined Fleet Decoded* (Annapolis: Naval Institute Press, 1995) pp. 244–245.
54. Though unverifiable, there is a possibility that what they saw was in fact a mirage, perhaps a *Fata Morgana*, which many believe is the explanation behind the legend of the "Flying Dutchman."
55. Winslow (1984), pp. 38–39.
56. Blair, p. 136.
57. Blair, p. 137.
58. Theodore Roscoe, *United States Submarine Operations in World War II* (Annapolis: Naval Institute Press, 1949), p. 34; Ed Howard, "Instances of Circular-Running Torpedoes Reported by United States Submarines During World War II," www.subsowespac.org, retrieved October 20, 2012; Ed Howard, "USS *Perch* (SS-176) First War Patrol," www.subsowespac.org, retrieved February 18, 2013.
59. Blair, p. 148; Roscoe (1949), p. 38; Alden, p. 2.
60. Blair, pp. 147–48; Roscoe (1949), pp. 36–39.
61. Roscoe (1949), p. 38. Douglas MacArthur would later complain to Admiral Hart that "your people haven't sunk a single solitary ship"; Leutze, p. 243. In fact, they had sunk a single, solitary ship.
62. Blair, p. 149–151, Roscoe (1949), p. 36.
63. Roscoe (1949), p. 38.
64. Blair, p. 140.
65. Roscoe (1949), p. 33, credits *Sargo* with eight attacks.
66. Blair, p. 141.
67. Blair, p. 135.
68. Winslow (1982), p. 47.
69. Roscoe (1949), p. 28.
70. Winslow (1982), p. 88.
71. Hart Report, p. 41.
72. Messimer (1985), pp. 59–63; J. Gordon, p. 71.
73. Shores, Cull, and Izawa, p. 183, and J. Gordon, p. 71, mention this second attack. Curiously, Messimer (1985) does not.
74. Messimer (1985), pp. 62–64.
75. Leutze, p. 240.

76. Leutze, p. 234.
77. Leutze, pp. 240–244.
78. Glen Williford, *Racing the Sunrise: Reinforcing America's Pacific Outposts, 1941–1942* (Annapolis: Naval Institute Press, 2010), pp. 150–155.
79. Williford, p. 159. Williford does not specifically give the date of the final order directing the *Pensacola* Convoy to Brisbane, but his account indicates that it was given on or around December 12. Burton, p. 80, gives the date as December 12. For more details of the actions of the convoy and the controversy surrounding it, see, generally, Williford, pp. 143–175.
80. Manchester, l. 4,096; MacArthur, p. 121.
81. J. Gordon, pp. 78–80; Manchester, l. 4,096.
82. Leutze, p. 245. Some histories have Hart finding about the evacuation by civilian news, but Leutze makes clear MacArthur did in fact inform Hart directly, if belatedly.
83. Leutze, p. 244.
84. Roscoe (1949), p. 39; Blair, p. 153.
85. Leutze, p. 245; Hart Report, p. 45.
86. Brereton, pp. 61–62.
87. Hart Report, pp. 45 and 46.
88. Messimer (1985), pp. 102–105.

Chapter 6

1. Several histories place Admiral Hart's arrival on January 2, but Hart himself states it was the evening of January 1; Hart Report, p. 48. *The Official Chronology of the US Navy in World War II* (Chapter IV: 1942) also gives January 1.
2. Leutze, p. 252.
3. Leutze, p. 253.
4. Leutze, pp. 253–254.
5. Roscoe (1949), pp. 161–162.
6. Messimer (1985), p. 87.
7. Messimer (1985), pp. 87–88, 114, 126. Lionel Wigmore, *Australia in the War of 1939–1945, Series One: Army; Volume IV: The Japanese Thrust* (Canberra: Australian War Memorial, 1957), p. 418, 419 n. 3 identifies the Royal Australian Air Force unit initially at Ambon as No. 13 Squadron, but notes that it was replaced by a flight from No. 2 Squadron at the end of December.
8. Messimer (1985), p. 88.
9. The narrative of the meeting comes from Leutze, pp. 254–257.
10. Klemen L., "Vice-Admiral Conrad E.L. Helfrich," *Forgotten Campaign*, accessed June 1, 2012.
11. Prados, p. 249.
12. Messimer (1985), p. 114.
13. Messimer (1985), p. 114.
14. Messimer (1985), p. 114; Winslow (1982), pp. 120–121.
15. Messimer (1985), pp. 114–115.
16. Tom Womack, *The Dutch Naval Air Force Against Japan: The Defense of the Netherlands East Indies, 1941–1942* (Jefferson, NC and London: Macfarland, 2006), pp. 8–9, 70–71.
17. Roscoe (1949), p. 34; John D. Alden, *US Submarine Attacks During World War II* (Annapolis: Naval Institute Press, 1989), p. 2. There is a lot of uncertainty surrounding this attack. Alden indicates that the ship was also known as the *Nojima Maru*. *The Official Chronology of the US Navy in World War II* (Chapter III: 1941), "Dec 27 Sat." identifies the ship as the *Noshima*. Holmes, p. 20, identifies the ship as the *Nojima Maru* and says it was not heard from again. www.subsowespac.org *United States Submarine Losses During the Pacific War, 1941 to 1945* entry for "USS *Perch* (SS-176)" (accessed October 4, 2012) lists the *Perch*'s target as the *Nojima* and reports that the freighter was beached to prevent her sinking, but was eventually salvaged. *Japanese Naval and Merchant Shipping Losses During World War II By All Causes*, Joint Army–Navy Assessment Committee, published online at http://www.ibiblio.org/hyperwar/Japan/IJN/JANAC-Losses/JANAC-Losses-6.html (accessed October 19, 2012) lists no enemy ships sunk by the *Perch*.
18. Howard, "Circular Torpedo Runs."
19. The incident is detailed in Lodwick H. Alford, *Playing for Time: War on an Asiatic Fleet Destroyer* (Bennington, VT: Merriam Press, 2008), p. 70, with a slightly different version in J. Daniel Mullin, *Another Six-Hundred*

(Mt Pleasant, SC: J. Daniel Mullin, 1984), pp. 53–54.

20. Mullin, pp. 54–55.

21. Mullin, pp. 62–63; Alford, p. 72; Winslow (1982), p. 88.

22. Except where noted otherwise, the account of the *Peary*'s journey southward comes from Winslow (1982), pp. 88–92.

23. Mullin, pp. 62–63.

24. Messimer (1985), p. 125. Except where noted otherwise, the narrative of Patrol Wing 10's part in the accidental bombing of the *Peary*, and of her subsequent journey to Ambon, comes from Messimer (1985), pp. 126–138.

25. Messimer (1985), p. 129; *The Official Chronology of the US Navy in World War II* (Chapter III: 1941), "Dec 31 Wed."

26. The account of the attack on the *Heron* comes from Messimer (1985), pp. 129–131.

27. H. T. Lenton, *Navies of the Second World War: Royal Netherlands Navy* (New York: Doubleday, 1968), pp. 8–9; Jan Visser, *Royal Netherlands Navy Warships of World War II*, "Java-class Cruisers," http://www.netherlandsnavy. nl/Java-class cruisers.htm, retrieved June 10, 2012.

28. Lenton (1968), p. 7; Wilmott, p. 264; Lt Jurrien S. Noot, "Battlecruiser: Design Studies for the Royal Netherlands Navy 1939–40". *Warship International* (Toledo, Ohio: International Naval Research Organization) 3: 242–273 (1980), retrieved from Visser, *Royal Netherlands Navy Warships of World War II* (http://www.netherlandsnavy.nl), October 20, 2012.

29. Herman Theodore Bussemaker, "Paradise in Peril: The Netherlands, Great Britain and the Defence of the Netherlands East Indies, 1940–41," *Journal of Southeast Asian Studies*, Vol. 31, No. 1 (Mar. 2000), pp. 115–136, p. 120.

30. Jan Visser, "Naval Base Soerabaja," *Royal Netherlands Navy Warships of World War II*, http://www. netherlandsnavy.nl/Soerabaja.htm, retrieved June 10, 2012.

31. Jan Visser, "Tandjong Priok," *Royal Netherlands Navy Warships of World War II*, http://www.netherlandsnavy. nl/Priok.htm, retrieved June 10, 2012.

32. James D. Hornfischer, *Ship of Ghosts: The Story of the USS* Houston, *FDR's Legendary Lost Cruiser, and the Epic Saga of Her Survivors* (New York: Bantam, 2006), p. 7; Morison (1948), p. 298. Winslow (1982), p. 199, calls Tjilatjap "that stinking, fever-ridden little port on the south coast of Java." Schultz, p. 111, calls Tjilatjap "an uninviting native village."

33. Jan Visser, "Tjilatjap," *Royal Netherlands Navy Warships of World War II*, http://www.netherlandsnavy.nl/ Tjilatjap.htm, retrieved June 10, 2012.

34. Unfortunately, whatever effectiveness even these limited facilities could provide was compromised by an abject refusal of the Dutch to work on weekends. The Dutch explained this with words to the effect of, "Ja, Mynheer, the situation is serious but here things must go by custom, Roscoe. (1942), p. 62."

35. Middlebrook and Mahoney, p. 316. According to their account, the official British story is that a senior survivor of Force Z was sent to Batavia to work out the details, but found the ships in too poor a condition, which is certainly a possibility, especially in the case of the *Sumatra*. But that survivor, Commander R. J. R. Dendy, said that the deal was killed by Helfrich himself when he said he would not proceed without an order from Queen Wilhelmina, which is rather curious since Helfrich was allegedly the one who requested the deal, to which the British had given a high priority.

36. Van Oosten, p. 64; See Chapter 10.

37. Paul R. Yarnall, "Locations Of Warships Of 'Allied' Naval Units December 7 1941," *NavSource Naval History*, http://www.navsource.org/Naval/usfc.htm, last updated February 2005, retrieved March 25, 2013.

38. Hart Report, p. 55; ONI Narrative, p. 13 n. 11. Starting January 1, 1942, van Staveren had the rank of acting rear admiral. Jan Visser, "Rear-Admiral J. J. A. van Staveren," *Royal Netherlands Navy at War*, www.netherlandsnavy.nl, retrieved October 25, 2012.

39. Hart Report, pp. 58–59.

40. Hart Report, p. 59.

41. The details of these attacks are taken from pages "KXVII," "KXVII," "KXII," and "O 16," *The Submarines of the Royal Netherlands Navy 1906 – 2005*, http://www.dutchsubmarines.com/ retrieved October 4, 2012.

42. The account of the sinking of the *Shinonome* is from Jan Visser, "Who sank the Shinonome?" *Royal Netherlands Navy Warships of World War II*, http://www.netherlandsnavy.nl/Who sank the Shinonome.htm, retrieved June 10, 2012; Womack, *The Dutch Naval Air Force Against Japan*, pp. 55–56; Nevitt, "Fleeting Glory: The Fubukis of DesDiv 12," *Imperial Japanese Navy Page*, www.combinedfleet.com, retrieved July 8,

2012 and Nevitt "IJN Shinonome: Tabular Record of Movement," *Imperial Japanese Navy Page*, www.combinedfleet.com, retrieved August 8, 2012.

43. "K XIV," *The Submarines of the Royal Netherlands Navy 1906–2005*, http://www.dutchsubmarines.com/ retrieved June 10, 2012 notes disagreement as to whether the target was the *Nichiran Maru* or *Tonan Maru No. 3*.

44. "K XIV," *The Submarines of the Royal Netherlands Navy 1906–2005*; Womack, *The Dutch Naval Air Force Against Japan*, pp. 63–64. Most of the information included herein concerning the Royal Netherlands Naval Air Service comes from Womack's seminal work on the service, *The Dutch Naval Air Force Against Japan: The Defense of the Netherlands East Indies: 1941–1942*. Its efforts are included in these pages, to the extent allowed by considerations of space, in an attempt to help rectify what Womack justifiably believes has been an oversight among English-language authors in covering the actions of the Royal Netherlands Naval Air Service during the Java Sea Campaign.

45. "K XVI," *The Submarines of the Royal Netherlands Navy 1906–2005*, http://www.dutchsubmarines.com/ retrieved June 10, 2012; Nevitt, "IJN Sagiri: Tabular Record of Movement," *Imperial Japanese Navy Page*, www.combinedfleet.com, retrieved August 8, 2012.

46. Hackett and Cundall, "HIJMS Submarine I-166: Tabular Record of Movement," *Imperial Japanese Navy Page*, www.combinedfleet.com, retrieved March 21, 2013. I have gone with Hackett's and Kingsepp's date of December 24 over "K XVI," *The Submarines of the Royal Netherlands Navy 1906–2005*, which lists the *K-XVI*'s sinking as taking place the following day.

47. Hackett and Cundall, "IJN Minesweeper W-6: Tabular Record of Movement," *Imperial Japanese Navy Page*, www.combinedfleet.com, retrieved August 8, 2012.

48. Hart Report, p. 51; Jan Visser, "Admiral C. E. L. Helfrich, RNN," *Royal Netherlands Navy Warships of World War II*, "http://www.netherlandsnavy.nl/Admiral C_E_L_ Helfrich.htm," retrieved June 10, 2012.

49. The account of the *Sargo*'s torpedo testing comes from Blair, pp. 169–170.

50. Information on the activities of the *K-X* off Tarakan comes from "K X," *The Submarines of the Royal Netherlands Navy 1906–2005*, http://www.dutchsubmarines.com/ retrieved October 4, 2012.

51. Van Oosten, p. 18; Hackett, Kingsepp, and Cundall, "IJN Patrol Boat No. 38: Tabular Record of Movement," *Imperial Japanese Navy Page*, www.combinedfleet.com, retrieved October 25, 2012.

52. *The Official Chronology of the US Navy in World War II* (Chapter IV: 1942).

53. Why Wavell set up headquarters in Lembang as opposed to Bandoeng, where the Dutch had already set up command and control infrastructure, or Batavia, where the Dutch naval headquarters was located, has never been explained.

54. Alford, p. 116.

55. Alford, p. 119.

56. Mullin, p. 208.

57. Toland, p. 254.

58. Messimer (1985), p. 134.

59. Messimer (1985), p. 134.

60. *The Official Chronology of the US Navy in World War II* (Chapter IV: 1942), "January 11, Sun."

61. Donald. M. Kehn, Jr., *A Blue Sea of Blood: Deciphering the Mysterious Fate of the USS* Edsall (Minneapolis: Zenith, 2008), p. 101; Gill, p. 532; *The Official Chronology of the US Navy in World War II* (Chapter IV: 1942)"; Hackett and Kingsepp, "IJN Submarine I-123: Tabular Record of Movement," *Imperial Japanese Navy Page*, www.combinedfleet.com, retrieved October 27, 2012. The identity of the submarine involved in this attack is not generally reported; only Hackett and Kingsepp identify the submarine as *I-123*.

62. *The Official Chronology of the US Navy in World War II* (Chapter IV: 1942); Hackett and Kingsepp, "IJN Submarine I-124: Tabular Record of Movement," *Imperial Japanese Navy Page*, www.combinedfleet.com, retrieved April 10, 2012.

63. Kehn, pp. 103–104; Ugaki Matome, Chihaya Masataka (trans.), Donald M. Goldstein (ed.), and Katherine V. Dillon (ed.), *Fading Victory: The Diary of Admiral Matome Ugaki 1941–1945* (Pittsburgh: University of Pittsburgh Press, 1991), p. 80; Hackett and Kingsepp, "IJN Submarine I-124: Tabular Record of Movement." Interestingly, only Hackett and Kingsepp report that the *I-124*'s February 19 message was decoded by the Allies.

64. Hackett and Kingsepp, "IJN Submarine I-124: Tabular Record of Movement."

65. Hackett and Kingsepp, "IJN Submarine I-124: Tabular Record of Movement."

66. Kehn, p. 105; Hackett and Kingsepp, "IJN Submarine I-124: Tabular Record of Movement."

67. Hackett and Kingsepp, "IJN Submarine I-124: Tabular Record of Movement."
68. Gill, p. 533.
69. Kehn, pp. 104–106; Gill, pp. 532–533; Hackett and Kingsepp, "IJN Submarine I-124: Tabular Record of Movement."
70. Kehn, pp. 107 and 110. Most histories report that the *Edsall* either dropped a depth charge at too slow a speed or had one detonate under her stern. I have gone with Kehn, who in his history of the *Edsall* says the cause was a massive depth charge attack in the Howard Channel, whose shallow depth caused the concussions of the depth charges to rattle and crack the *Edsall*'s hull, as well as the hulls of the ships she was escorting.
71. Arthur J. Marder, Mark Jacobsen, and John Horsfield, *Old Friends, New Enemies: The Royal Navy and the Imperial Japanese Navy, Vol. 2: The Pacific War 1942–1945* (Oxford: Clarendon Press, 1990), pp. 13–14; Hackett and Kingsepp, "IJN Submarine I-60: Tabular Record of Movement," *Imperial Japanese Navy Page*, www.combinedfleet.com, retrieved April 10, 2012.
72. Peter Cannon, "The Battle of Endau, Malaya, 26–27 January 1942 – Part 1", *Journal of Australian Naval History*, Vol. 8, No. 2, 2011, pp. 66–98, p. 94, n. 55.
73. Hart Report, p. 70. He thought that the ship that might have been sunk was the *Trinity*.

Chapter 7

1. Celebes, the main island of the eponymous island group, consists almost entirely of peninsulas, with very little in the way of a central body. Roughly speaking, from a small land mass extend four peninsulas. Running due south is the South Peninsula, on which sits the island's largest city, Makassar (or Makassar City, to differentiate it from the many other iterations of Makassar in this area); the others are the Southeast Peninsula, the East Peninsula, and, to the north, the Minahassa Peninsula.
2. Hackett and Kingsepp, "HIJMS Jintsu: Tabular Record of Movement," *Imperial Japanese Navy Page*, www.combinedfleet.com, retrieved January 17, 2011.
3. Mullin, pp. 111–112.
4. Mullin, p. 115.
5. ONI Narrative, p. 16; Admiral Thomas Hart, "Events and Circumstances Concerning the 'Striking Force,'" dated February 6, 1942 (hereinafter "Striking Force Report"), p. 2.
6. Roscoe (1949), pp. 65–66.
7. Striking Force Report, p. 2.
8. Mullin, p. 116.
9. Winslow (1982), p. 151 and (1984), p. 61, seems confused as to the location of Kebola Bay, placing it on Soembawa (Sumbawa) Island. It is actually on Alor Island, in the Alor Archipelago north of Koepang (Kupang), Timor.
10. Winslow (1982), p. 151. The identities of six of the destroyers come from Mullin, p. 111. The presence of the *John D. Edwards* and *Whipple* is a deduction from Winslow (1984), pp. 61–62, confirmed by Kehn, p. 100. Winslow has eight destroyers planning to take part in the counterattack, suggesting that the *Houston*'s own two escorting destroyers (whom Winslow never identifies) were to take part, but Kehn, pp. 100–101, indicates that the *Alden* and *Edsall*, who had escorted the *Houston* into Kebola Bay, were never to be a part of the counterattack. The planned participation of the *Houston* in the Makassar Strait operation has received little attention; even Hart's own report and the ONI Narrative do not mention it. However, both Winslow (1982) and (1984) and the Reconstructed log of the *Houston* (*Report of the USS* Houston *dated 9 September 1945*, Enclosure (b), "Wartime Cruise of the *USS* Houston"; hereinafter "*Houston* log") make it clear that the cruiser was present with the other members of Task Force 5 at Kebola Bay on January 18.
11. Winslow (1984), p. 61; Hart Report, p. 2.
12. Winslow (1984), p. 61.
13. Winslow (1982), p. 152 and (1984), p. 61; Hart Report, p. 2. Sorting out the events leading up to the Battle of Balikpapan is a confusing task. Most versions agree that one aborted attempt was made to counterattack before the battle, but few can agree on the details. The reason seems to be that there were actually two aborted attempts at a counterattack, which Admiral Hart, though he is uncertain on the dates, makes clear in the Striking Force Report. The first ended on January 17 with the withdrawal of the *Boise* and *Marblehead* and their escorting destroyers, during the withdrawal from which the *Marblehead* suffered the initial turbine damage. The second attempt consisted solely of the rendezvous at Kebola Bay, which seems to have taken only a matter of hours. Irrespective of rank, few seem to have had a complete picture of the events. Hart and

Mullin place the refueling rendezvous at Koepang, and do not mention Kebola Bay; Mullin quotes a message showing the *Marblehead* was still en route to Koepang as of 3:36 am on January 18. Yet both Winslow and the *Houston*'s logs establish that the refueling rendezvous took place there on January 18 with the *Houston*, *Boise* and *Trinity* present. *The Dictionary of American Fighting Ships* entry for the *Trinity* (www.history.navy.mil/danfs/t8/trinity.htm, retrieved October 25, 2012) does have her at Kebola Bay, but leaving for Darwin on January 17. Winslow not only erroneously places Kebola Bay on Soembawa Island instead of Alor Island, but also has the mission cancelled because of the reports from the submarines *Pike* and *Permit*, which the ONI Narrative gives as the reason why the first mission was aborted. Admiral Hart seems to muddle the second attempt with the third (which resulted in the Battle of Balikpapan) by his ambiguity on the dates and by saying it was while returning from the second attempt that the *Boise* gashed her hull on the rock in Sape Strait. Morison (1948), p. 286, shows that the *Boise* actually struck the rock on the way to Balikpapan during the third counterattack attempt. Subsequently, the *Marblehead*'s turbine problems got worse and reduced her speed from 28 to 15 knots. What is presented here is an amalgamation of the Striking Force Report, the ONI Narrative, Mullin, Winslow, and Morison, as best as can be determined, with the acknowledgement that it does not comport with all the literal descriptions in all of the various versions of events.

14. Marder, Jacobson, and Horsfield (1990), p. 28.
15. ONI Narrative, p. 17.
16. *The Dictionary of American Fighting Ships, Trinity* (www.history.navy.mil/danfs/t8/trinity.htm, accessed October 25, 2012); Hackett and Kingsepp, "IJN Submarine I-124: Tabular Record of Movement"; Kehn, p. 101.
17. ONI Narrative, p. 16.
18. ONI Narrative, pp. 16–17; Dan Muir, "The Night Hawks of Balikpapan: The Balikpapan Raid, January 1942," *Forgotten Campaign: The Dutch East Indies Campaign 1941–1942*, retrieved June 1, 2012.
19. Mullin, p. 117.
20. Captain Robinson would be relieved, but not because of this incident, for which no fault was attached to him. On January 25, while the *Boise* was in Tjilatjap having her hull inspected for repairs, Robinson suffered what some believe was a heart attack. He returned to the US for treatment, and was replaced by his executive officer, Commander E. J. (Mike) Moran, who was promoted to captain. Vincent A. Langelo, *With All Our Might: The WWII History of the USS Boise (CL-47)* (Austin: Eakin, 2000), p. 45.
21. Hart Report, pp. 64–65.
22. Langelo, pp. 44–45, 48; Mullin, pp. 117–118.
23. Mullin, p. 117.
24. Langelo, p. 44; Mullin, p. 118.
25. Mullin, p. 116.
26. Leutze, p. 270.
27. Mullin, pp. 117–118.
28. ONI Narrative, p. 17.
29. Blair, p. 166.
30. Blair, pp. 166–167.
31. Mullin, p. 119.
32. John S. Slaughter, "Balikpapan 24 January 1942: First American Naval Offensive Since Spanish American War," *China Gunboatman Newsletter*, May 2000, p. 3.
33. Mullin, pp. 121–122.
34. Mullin, p. 120.
35. ONI Narrative p. 18; Mullin, pp. 122–123; Hoyt (1976), p. 197. Numerous sources state that the message was given by voice radio, but I have gone with Mullin as an eyewitness.
36. Mullin, p. 122.
37. Vincent P. O'Hara, *The U.S. Navy Against the Axis: Surface Combat 1941–1945* (Annapolis: Naval Institute Press, 2007), p. 22.
38. W. C. Blinn, "Night Destroyer Attack off Balikpapan, January 24, 1942," (hereinafter "Balikpapan Report"), Paragraph 2g.
39. The Samarinda airfield was not located in, or anywhere near, the town of Samarinda; Van Oosten, p. 19.
40. Winslow (1982), p. 145.
41. Klemen, "The Balikpapan Massacre, February 1942: 78 lost lifes [sic] for oilfields," *Forgotten Campaign*, retrieved June 1, 2012.

42. Benda, p. 541.

43. Klemen, "The Balikpapan Massacre, February 1942," states that anywhere from 64 to 78 Dutch were murdered by the Japanese at Balikpapan in the immediate aftermath of the invasion.

44. Mullin, p. 235.

45. Mullin, pp. 122–124.

46. The 4th Destroyer Flotilla consisted of the light cruiser *Naka* and the destroyers *Yudachi, Samidare, Harusame, Murasame, Minegumo, Natsugumo, Yamakaze, Suzukaze, Kawakaze,* and *Umikaze*.

47. On the other hand, Morison (1948), p. 288, says Admiral Nishimura "must have been one of the least competent Japanese flag officers."

48. Admiral Nishimura entered the Surigao Strait action of the Battle of Leyte Gulf sailing in one of his two battleships, then went right up to the main US battle line and opened fire without realizing that his other battleship, which had been steaming right behind him, had disappeared.

49. Hackett and Kingsepp, "HIJMS Naka: Tabular Record of Movement," *Imperial Japanese Navy Page*, www. combinedfleet.com, retrieved July 8, 2012; and "K XVIII." www.dutchsubmarines.com, credit the *K-XVIII* with actually sinking the *Tsuruga Maru*. American sources (see, e.g. *The Official Chronology of the US Navy in World War II* (Chapter IV: 1942)) credit the sinking to the *John D. Ford*. It was probably a combination of both. The truth will likely never be known.

50. O'Hara (2007) claims the *K-XVIII*'s torpedoes missed the *Naka* only to hit the *Tsuruga Maru* behind it in the anchorage. It makes sense; the *K-XVIII* was operating on the surface and would have likely gotten in only one attack before the Japanese counterattack. After the attack, Admiral Nishimura had his ships head east toward the K-XVIII and away from their transports.

51. Mullin, pp. 124–125.

52. The origins of the saying "Fortune favors the bold" are disputed. The villainous Turnus says it in Virgil's "*Aeneid*". He was killed shortly thereafter by the hero Aeneas. Pliny the Elder was quoted as saying it just before he sailed into Pompeii. He was killed shortly thereafter by the erupting Mount Vesuvius.

53. Morison (1948), p. 287.

54. The close escorts consisted of three World War I *Momi*-class destroyers that had been converted to patrol boats: *PB36* (ex-*Fuji*), *PB37* (ex-*Hishi*), and *PB38* (ex-*Yomogi*); four minesweepers: *W-15, W-16, W-17,* and *W-18*; and three sub-chasers: *CH-10, CH-11,* and *CH-12*.

55. O'Hara (2007), p. 22.

56. O'Hara (2007), pp. 22–23.

57. Blinn, "Balikpapan Report.

58. O'Hara (2007), p. 23.

59. Morison (1948), p. 287.

60. Morison (1948), p. 289.

61. O'Hara (2007), p. 23. A minority of histories, mostly Dutch, state that the *PB-37* was damaged by the *K-XVIII*'s earlier torpedo attack.

62. Roscoe (1953), p. 91.

63. O'Hara (2007), p. 24.

64. ONI Narrative, p. 22.

65. O'Hara (2007), pp. 24–25, Roscoe (1953), p. 91.

66. A "creeping barrage" is an artillery barrage in which the shells land in a pattern that slowly advances toward a target or position, usually used to cover advancing troops and to bombard an area in which the target has not been precisely located.

67. Mullin, pp. 137–138.

68. Roscoe (1953), p. 92.

69. Mullin, p. 139.

70. Mullin, p. 139.

71. Roscoe (1953), p. 92.

72. O'Hara (2007), p. 25.

73. O'Hara (2007), p. 25. Many of Nishimura's superiors were also convinced that the Battle of Balikpapan was only the work of submarines. Yamamoto's chief of staff Admiral Ugaki would say that the damage "must have been due to enemy submarines and planes which sneaked in there." Ugaki, p. 77.

74. Mullin, p. 142; ONI Narrative, p. 22.

75. Mullin, p. 142.

76. Roscoe (1953), p. 92.
77. Mullin, p. 143.
78. Alford, p. 98.
79. Mullin, p. 148.
80. Hoyt (1976), p. 210.

Chapter 8

1. Shores, Cull, and Izawa (1992), p. 324.
2. Gillison, p. 340.
3. Gillison, p. 339; Shores, Cull, and Izawa (1992), pp. 324–326. The air raid consisted of army Sallys of the 12th and 60th Army Air Groups, escorted by Nakajima Ki-43 "Oscar" fighters of the 64th Air Group, plus 26 navy Nells of the Mihoro Air Group and 18 Nells of the Genzan Air Group, escorted by 18 Zeros.
4. Shores, Cull, and Izawa (1992), pp. 325–326.
5. Gillison, pp. 339–340.
6. Yamashita Tomoyuki is also known as Yamashita Hobun. Richard Fuller, *Shokan: Hirohito's Samurai, Leaders of the Japanese Armed Forces, 1926–1945* (London: Arms and Armour, 1992), p. 236.
7. Marder, Jacobsen, and Horsfeld (1990), pp. 15–16.
8. Cannon (2011), p. 74; Shores, Cull, and Izawa, p. 346.
9. Cannon (2011), pp. 67–68.
10. Having based their Pearl Harbor attack on the attack by carrier-based British Swordfish torpedo-carrying biplanes on Italian warships at Taranto, the Japanese were very respectful of British biplane torpedo bombers.
11. Warren, p. 188.
12. Cannon (2011), pp. 70–72, 75. The *Canberra Maru* is sometimes called the *Kanbera Maru*.
13. Cannon (2011), p. 82, states, "The exact reasoning used to justify committing the last offensive air striking force as well as a weak surface force to attack the Endau landings does not appear in any of the primary or secondary source information researched by the author."
14. Warren, p. 118.
15. Cannon (2011), p. 76; Warren, p. 118.
16. Warren, p. 118.
17. Shores, Cull, and Izawa (1993), p. 20.
18. Cannon (2011), p. 83. I have gone with Cannon as the most recent scholarship on the engagement.
19. Cannon (2011), pp. 82–83; Shores, Cull, and Izawa (1993), p. 20. See p. 439, n.58 for details of the organization of the Japanese Army Air Force and Naval Air Force.
20. Cannon (2011), p. 83.
21. Shores, Cull, and Izawa (1993), p. 29.
22. Shores, Cull, and Izawa (1993), pp. 29–35.
23. Shores, Cull, and Izawa (1993), p. 36.
24. Cannon (2011), p. 83.
25. Shores, Cull, and Izawa (1993), p. 37.
26. Shores, Cull, and Izawa (1993), p. 39.
27. Warren, p. 189.
28. Shores, Cull, and Izawa (1993), p. 39.
29. Except where noted otherwise, the account of these ships and the account of their mission come from Cannon (2011), p. 77–81, and Peter Cannon, "The Battle of Endau, Malaya, 26–27 January 1942 – Part 2," *Journal of Australian Naval History*, Vol. 9, No. 1, 2012, pp. 7–42, pp. 11–12, pp. 21–22, pp. 15–16, p. 19, and pp. 30–31.
30. Cannon (2012), pp. 6–7. Hackett and Kingsepp, "IJN Minesweeper W-1: Tabular Record of Movement," *Imperial Japanese Navy Page*, www.combinedfleet.com, retrieved March 21, 2013, identify the ship as the minesweeper *W-1*.
31. Cannon (2012), p. 12; Gill, p. 559.
32. Deduction from Cannon (2012), p. 12, and Gill, p. 559.
33. Cannon (2011), p. 82.
34. Shores, Cull, and Izawa (1992), p. 160.
35. Shores, Cull, and Izawa (1993), p. 55.

Chapter 9

1. Kehn, p. 175.
2. Womack, *The Dutch Naval Air Force Against Japan*, p. 88; Kehn, p. 177.
3. Kehn, p. 175.
4. Messimer (1985), pp. 211–213.
5. Messimer (1985), pp. 213–216; Kehn, p. 69.
6. Gill, p. 536; Kehn, p. 68. The 1st Base Force consisted of the flagship light cruiser *Nagara*; destroyers *Natsushio*, *Kuroshio*, *Oyashio*, and *Hayashio*, comprising Destroyer Division 15; and the destroyers *Yukikaze*, *Tokitsukaze*, *Hatsukaze*, and *Amatsukaze*, comprising Destroyer Division 16.
7. USSBS, Interrogation Nav No. 7, USSBS No. 33 Interrogation of: Vice Admiral Shiraichi Kzutaka, October 15, 1945.
8. Kehn, p. 68.
9. Willmott, p. 289.
10. Shores, Cull, and Izawa (1992), p. 226.
11. Shores, Cull, and Izawa (1992), pp. 225–226; Hackett and Kingsepp, "HIJMS Nagara: Tabular Record of Movement," *Imperial Japanese Navy Page*, www.combinedfleet.com, retrieved April 10, 2012; Nevitt, "HIJMS Hatsuharu: Tabular Record of Movement," *Imperial Japanese Navy Page*, www.combinedfleet.com, retrieved September 21, 2012.
12. *The Official Chronology of the US Navy in World War II*, (Chapter IV: 1942).
13. Hackett and Kingsepp, "HIJMS Nagara: Tabular Record of Movement"; Nevitt, "HIJMS Hatsuharu: Tabular Record of Movement."
14. ATIS Doc. No. 4043 *Japanese Monograph No. 101: Naval Operations in the Invasion of the Netherlands East Indies Dec. 1941–Mar. 1942*, p. 23.
15. Klemen, "The Fall of Kendari, January 1942," *Forgotten Campaign*, retrieved October 18, 2012; *The Official Chronology of the US Navy in World War II* (Chapter IV: 1942); Kehn, p. 68; Shores, Cull, and Izawa (1992), p. 226.
16. Shores, Cull, and Izawa (1992), p. 226; ATIS Doc. No. 4043 *Japanese Monograph No. 101*, p. 24.
17. See Klemen, "The Carnage at Laha, February 1942 The Laha Airfield Executions," *Forgotten Campaign*, retrieved October 18, 2012; Russell, pp. 100–102; Mark Felton, *Slaughter at Sea: The Story of Japan's Naval War Crimes* (Barnsley, South Yorkshire, England: Pen & Sword, 2007), pp. 34–43.
18. Shores, Cull, and Izawa (1992), p. 227; Craven and Cate, p. 385.
19. Shores, Cull, and Izawa (1992), p. 227; Craven and Cate, p. 385.
20. Striking Force Report, pp. 3–4.
21. ONI Narrative, p. 26.
22. Mullin, p. 151.
23. Hoyt (1976), pp. 214–215.
24. Hornfischer, p. 42.
25. Jan Visser, "Rear-Admiral K.W.F.M. Doorman, RNN," *Royal Netherlands Navy at War*, www.netherlandsnavy.nl, retrieved June 10, 2012.
26. Jan Visser, "Rear-Admiral K.W.F.M. Doorman, RNN."
27. Jan Visser, "Rear-Admiral K.W.F.M. Doorman, RNN."
28. Marder, Jacobsen, and Horsfield, p. 47.
29. Klemen, "Rear-Admiral Karel W.F.M. Doorman," *Forgotten Campaign*, retrieved June 1, 2012.
30. Prados, p. 255.
31. The background information on Doorman's personality comes from Niek Koppen, *The Battle of the Java Sea*, DVD, 2006.
32. Striking Force Report, pp. 3–4; Hart Report, pp. 68–69.
33. Hart Report, p. 68.
34. Most sources, including Craven and Cate, pp. 383–384, and Edmunds, pp. 311–312, have the attack that shot down Major Straubel's B-18 occurring the following day, February 3. Many though not all of those same sources have Straubel succumbing to his injuries the day after the attack, which according to their timeline would have been February 4. I have gone with Shores, Cull, and Izawa (1993), p. 150, who consulted Japanese sources that show the attack on Straubel's B-18 was on February 2. The Wisconsin Aviation Hall of Fame (www.wisconsinaviationhalloffame.org/blog/p=1021) lists Straubel, a native of Green Bay and namesake of its airport, as having died on February 3, which is consistent with the timeline given by Shores, Cull, and Izawa.

35. ATIS Doc. No. 4043 *Japanese Monograph No. 101*, p. 24.
36. Shores, Cull, and Izawa (1993), p. 150; Messimer (1985), p. 216.
37. Shores, Cull, and Izawa (1993), p. 150.
38. Womack, *The Dutch Naval Air Force Against Japan*, pp. 33–34.
39. Craven and Cate, pp. 383–384; Bartsch (2010), p. 116.
40. Craven and Cate, p. 384; Bartsch (2010), pp. 116–117; Shores, Cull, and Izawa (1993), p. 155.
41. Womack, *The Dutch Naval Air Force Against Japan*, p. 98.
42. Shores, Cull, and Izawa (1993), pp. 154–155.
43. Craven and Cate, p. 383; Shores, Cull, and Izawa (1993), pp. 156–157.
44. Shores, Cull, and Izawa (1993), p. 155.
45. Shores, Cull, and Izawa (1993), p. 157.
46. Bartsch (2012), p. 120.
47. Lenton, pp. 10–11; Jan Visser, "De Ruyter-class cruiser," *Royal Netherlands Navy at War*, www. netherlandsnavy.nl, retrieved June 10, 2012.
48. Lenton, pp. 12–13.
49. Lenton, pp. 20–21.
50. Messimer (1985), pp. 232–233; Shores, Cull, and Izawa (1993), p. 156.
51. ATIS Doc. No. 4043 *Japanese Monograph No. 101*, p. 25.
52. ONI Narrative, p. 27.
53. See Gill, p. 555.
54. ONI Narrative, p. 27.
55. Hoyt (1976), p. 218.
56. Craig Chariton, "The Battle" (excerpts from the log of the *Marblehead*). USS *Marblehead & Dr. Wassell*, www.ussmarblehead.com/the_battle.html (hereinafter "*Marblehead* log"), retrieved March 27, 2012.
57. Shores, Cull, and Izawa (1993), p. 158.
58. Hoyt (1990), p. 101.
59. Hoyt (1976), p. 218.
60. Karig and Kelly, p. 189.
61. Winslow (1984), p. 93.
62. A "fire director" is a single, central location on a ship that controls the targeting of enemy ships or aircraft, picking a target and determining its course, speed, distance, and altitude in the case of aircraft and using that information to calculate firing solutions for the various guns on the ship. There can be primary and secondary directors, and usually separate directors for the main and secondary armament and heavy antiaircraft guns. If a director is disabled or contact with it lost, the guns switch to what is called "local control," and will make these determinations on their own.
63. Winslow (1984), pp. 88–89.
64. Schultz, p. 89.
65. Schultz, p. 15.
66. Winslow (1984), p. 90.
67. *Marblehead* log.
68. *Marblehead* log.
69. *Marblehead* log.
70. *Marblehead* log; Morison (1948), p. 300.
71. Hoyt (1976), p. 219; Schultz, p. 95.
72. Shores, Cull, and Izawa (1993), p. 158; Hoyt (1976), p. 219; Schultz, p. 95; *Marblehead* log.
73. Winslow (1984), pp. 88–89.
74. *Marblehead* log.
75. *Marblehead* log.
76. Hoyt (1976), p. 219; Winslow (1982), p. 160.
77. Winslow (1982), p. 160.
78. *Marblehead* log.
79. Winslow (1982), p. 161.
80. *Marblehead* log.
81. ONI Narrative, p. 30.
82. *Marblehead* log.

83. Winslow (1982), pp. 161–162.
84. *Marblehead* log.
85. *Marblehead* log.
86. Winslow (1982), pp. 160–161.
87. Hoyt (1976), p. 222.
88. ONI Narrative, p. 30.
89. Winslow (1982), p. 91.
90. Winslow (1982), p. 92; *Marblehead* log.
91. Hornfischer, p. 11.
92. Schultz, p. 98.
93. Schultz, p. 102.
94. Winslow (1984), pp. 92–93.
95. Winslow (1984), pp. 93–94.
96. Winslow (1984), p. 94. This plane was likely a C5M "Babs" scout plane. Shores, Cull, and Izawa (1993), p. 158.
97. ONI Narrative, p. 30.

Chapter 10

1. Mullin, pp. 163–164.
2. Mullin, p. 164.
3. ATIS Doc. No. 40431 *Japanese Monograph No. 101*, p. 25, describes "[taking] up the pursuit" and finding "the American ship 'Marblehead' fleeing 10 nautical miles south of Soembawa," with their attacks on the ship registering no hits.
4. Schultz, p. 112.
5. Winslow (1984), p. 96.
6. Schultz, p. 112; Mullin, p. 165.
7. Morison (1948), p. 298.
8. Hornfischer, p. 48.
9. David Thomas, *The Battle of the Java Sea* (New York: Stein and Day, 1969), pp. 125–126.
10. Schultz, p. 117.
11. Hoyt (1976), p. 224.
12. Leutze, p. 277.
13. Hart Report, p. 74.
14. Schultz, pp. 117–118.
15. Hart Report, p. 74.
16. Hoyt (1976), p. 226; Hart, Striking Force Report, p. 4.
17. Gill, p. 555.
18. Morison (1948), p. 299.
19. Gill, p. 555.
20. Gill, p. 555.
21. ATIS Doc. No. 40431, *Japanese Monograph No. 101*, p. 25.
22. Gill, p. 555.
23. Leutze, p. 277.
24. Hoyt (1990), p. 98.
25. Mullin, p. 255.
26. Hoyt (1990), p. 98.
27. Hart Report, p. 76.
28. Hart Report, p. 76.
29. Schultz, p. 119.
30. Hornfischer, p. 48.
31. Schultz, pp. 119–120. Winslow (1984), p. 100, has a slightly different version in which Rooks says, "A Jap cruiser will have one strike on us, but with two remaining we will try to break up his game."
32. Schultz, p. 119.
33. Winslow (1982), p. 19.

34. Schultz, pp. 118–119.
35. Nicholson, p. 163; Sir Geoffrey Layton, "EASTERN THEATRE OPERATIONS: the Diaries of Admiral Layton, C-in-C, China Station – November 1941 to March 1942," *Naval History*, http://www.naval-history. net/index.htm, retrieved January 12, 2013.
36. Anthony Newpower, *Iron Men and Tin Fish: The Race to Build a Better Torpedo During World War II* (Annapolis: Naval Institute Press, 2006), p. 108.
37. The Makassar Occupation Force consisted of IJN transports *Kinai, Nankai, Hokuroku, Matsue, Montevideo*, and *Yamashimo*, all *Marus*. The transports were accompanied by auxiliary oiler *San Clemente Maru*, acting as a replenishing vessel. Escort was provided by *Nagara*, Destroyer Division 8's *Asashio, Michishio, Arashio*, and *Oshio*, Destroyer Division 15's *Hayashio, Kuroshio, Oyashio* and *Natsushio*, Destroyer Division 21's *Wakaba, Hatsushimo*, and *Nenohi*, 21st Minesweeper Division's *W-7, W-8*, 2nd Subchaser Division's *CH-13, CH-14* and *CH-15*. Limited air support was provided by Carrier Divison 11's *Chitose, Mizuho*, and *Sanuki Maru*. The first echelon, with *Kinai, Nankai* and *Hokuroku Maru*s carried Captain Mori Kunizo's Makassar Occupation Force consisting of his Sasebo Combined Special Naval Landing Force. The second echelon, with *Matsue, Montevideo*, and *Yamashimo Maru*s carried the 5th and 6th Naval Construction Units.
38. Blair, p. 177; Hackett and Kingsepp, "HIJMS NAGARA: Tabular Record of Movement," *Imperial Japanese Navy Page*, www.combinedfleet.com, retrieved April 10, 2012.
39. Blair, p. 177.
40. Except where noted otherwise, the account of the *S-37*'s action off Makassar City comes from Roscoe (1949), pp. 73–74.
41. Range comes from Blair, p. 178.
42. Allyn D. Nevitt, "IJN Natsushio: Tabular Record of Movement," *Imperial Japanese Navy Page*, www. combinedfleet.com, retrieved April 10, 2012.
43. Klemen L., "Massacre of POWs, Dutch East Indies, 1941–1942," *Forgotten Campaign*, retrieved June 1, 2012.
44. Shores, Cull, and Izawa (1993), p. 172; Hackett and Kingsepp, "HIJMS CHITOSE: Tabular Record of Movement," *Imperial Japanese Navy Page*, www.combinedfleet.com, retrieved April 10, 2012.
45. Blair, p. 178.
46. Gill, p. 571; Hart Report, p. 78; C.E.L. Helfrich, *Memoires van C.E.L. Helfrich: Eerste Deel de Maleise Barrière* (Amsterdam: Elsevier, 1950), p. 345.
47. Alford, p. 114.
48. Schultz, p. 128.
49. ONI Narrative, p. 6; Mullin, p. 168.
50. Alford, p. 119.
51. Schultz, p. 119.
52. Schultz, p. 128.
53. Koppen, *The Battle of the Java Sea*, DVD.
54. Winton, p. 20; Mark Grimsley, "What If Singapore Had Not Fallen?" *Historynet.com*, http://www.historynet. com/what-if-singapore-had-not-fallen.htm (December 1, 2010), retrieved April 9, 2013; Willmott, pp. 333–334; Toll, p. 252.
55. Warren, pp. 213–214.
56. Willmott, pp. 329–331.
57. Hack and Blackburn, ll. 3,337–3,344.
58. James Leasor, *Singapore: The Battle that Changed the World* (Kindle Edition) (London: James Leasor, 2011), p. 244.
59. Willmott, p. 334.
60. Warren, pp. 278–279.
61. Ronald H. Spector, *In the Ruins of Empire: The Japanese Surrender and the Battle for Postwar Asia* (New York: Random House, 2007), p. 78.
62. Shores, Cull, and Izawa (1993), p. 80.
63. Roscoe (1949), p. 96, says that some of the refugees were Australian pilots who managed to jury-rig a transmitter that sent out an SOS signal. Shores, Cull, and Izawa (1993), p. 81, say the *ML310*'s skipper, British Lieutenant J. H. Bull, took two sailors and two Javanese fishermen in a native *prahu* into the Sumatra littoral and from there crossed the Soenda Strait into Merak on Java, where they flagged down a Royal Navy corvette. Given the timeframe of *S-39*'s rescue mission, the latter story seems more likely.
64. Roscoe (1949), p. 96.
65. Shores, Cull, and Izawa (1993), pp. 80–81.

66. Winston S. Churchill, *The Hinge of Fate* (electronic edition) (New York: Rosetta Books, 2002), l. 1,638.
67. Toll, p. 252.
68. Description of Sumatra is from Gill, pp. 563–564, Antonie Kroese, *The Dutch Navy at War* (London: George Allen and Unwin, 1945), p. 55; and Bob Hackett, "Oil Fields, Refineries and Storage Centers Under Imperial Japanese Army Control," *Imperial Japanese Navy Page*, www.combinedfleet.com, retrieved March 20, 2013.
69. Tully and Casse, "IJN Ryujo: Tabular Record of Movement."
70. Hackett and Kingsepp, "IJN Mogami: Tabular Record of Movement."
71. Womack, *The Dutch Naval Air Force Against Japan*, p. 106.
72. Gillison, p. 389.
73. Gill, p. 571.
74. Kehn, p. 110; Morison (1948), p. 308.
75. Kehn, p. 110.
76. Karig and Kelley, p. 199.
77. Gill, pp. 571 and 573.
78. Shores, Cull, and Izawa (1993), p. 92.
79. Tully and Casse, "IJN Ryujo: Tabular Record of Movement."
80. Gill, p. 573; Bob Hackett, Sander Kingsepp, and Peter Cundall, "IJN Patrol Boat No. 106," *Imperial Japanese Navy Page*, www.combinedfleet.com, retrieved April 10, 2012.
81. Gill, p. 573; Alford, p. 123; Hackett, Kingsepp, and Cundall, "IJN Patrol Boat No. 106"; Jan Visser, "Java," *Royal Netherlands Navy Warships of World War II*, www.netherlandsnavy.nl, retrieved August 19, 2012, and Hackett, Kingsepp, and Cundall give the time at about 4:30 am.
82. Jan Visser, "Java."
83. Gill, p. 573; Hackett, Kingsepp, and Cundall, "IJN Patrol Boat No. 106."
84. Gill, p. 573.
85. Gill, p. 573; Tully and Casse, "IJN Ryujo: Tabular Record of Movement." Shores, Cull, and Izawa (1993), p. 123, give the time as shortly before 8:00 am.
86. Shores, Cull, and Izawa (1993), p. 123.
87. Kroese, p. 56.
88. Shores, Cull, and Izawa (1993), p. 123; Tully and Casse, "IJN Ryujo: Tabular Record of Movement." Gill, p. 573, says the first attack took place at 11:50 am. Shores, Cull, and Izawa (1993) say the first attack took place at 10:30 am but consisted of seven Kates that had been launched at 8:05 am that took almost two and a half hours to reach the target, which seems rather implausible since the *Ryujo* was only some 100 miles away. They also say it was this first attack that disabled the *Exeter*'s Walrus floatplane. There were so many attacks that there is little agreement on their timing, sequence, damage, or even their number, with Gill listing 13 different attacks, but giving no details for any of them. The version of events presented here is an amalgamation of Shores, Cull, and Izawa (1993), pp. 123–124; Gill, pp. 573–574; and Tully and Casse, "IJN Ryujo: Tabular Record of Movement." The reader should be aware that based on the conflicting reports there are any number of possible scenarios for how the air attacks unfolded.
89. Shores, Cull, and Izawa (1993), p. 123; Tully and Casse, "IJN Ryujo: Tabular Record of Movement." Tully and Casse actually place the attack by the Genzan in midafternoon, but this is inconsistent with the timing of the attack by the Mihoro Air Group, based a similar distance away from the target, which they do not list at all.
90. Tully and Casse, "IJN Ryujo: Tabular Record of Movement." Shores, Cull, and Izawa (1993), p. 123, say this attack consisted of six Kates.
91. Shores, Cull, and Izawa (1993), pp. 123–124; Gill, p. 573.
92. Gill, p. 573.
93. Shores, Cull, and Izawa (1993), p. 124.
94. Kroese, p. 57.
95. Shores, Cull, and Izawa (1993), p. 124.
96. Tully and Casse, "IJN Ryujo: Tabular Record of Movement."
97. Tully and Casse, "IJN Ryujo: Tabular Record of Movement."
98. Shores, Cull, and Izawa (1993), p. 124, show four attacks by Kates from the *Ryujo*; Tully and Casse, "IJN Ryujo: Tabular Record of Movement," say the *Ryujo* launched four attacks but list five.
99. Shores, Cull, and Izawa (1993), p. 124.
100. Gill, p. 574.

101. Kroese, p. 57; Alford, p. 125.

102. Gill, p. 574.

103. Alford, p. 125.

104. Gill, p. 564; Womack, *The Dutch Naval Air Force Against Japan*, p. 105.

105. Gill, p. 564; Womack, *The Dutch Naval Air Force Against Japan*, p. 107.

106. Except where noted otherwise, the details of the sinking of the *Van Nes* and the *Sloet van de Beele* come from Womack, *The Dutch Naval Air Force Against Japan*, pp. 107–109.

107. Tully and Casse, "IJN Ryujo: Tabular Record of Movement."

108. Tully and Casse, "IJN Ryujo: Tabular Record of Movement."

109. Schultz, p. 121.

110. Winslow (1984), p. 100; Gill, pp. 580–581.

111. Schultz, pp. 121–122.

112. Shores, Cull, and Izawa (1993), p. 174.

113. Winslow (1984), pp. 100–101. Schultz, p. 122, has the time as 8:00 am.

114. The time comes from Gill, p. 585.

115. Shores, Cull, and Izawa (1993), p. 174.

116. Winslow (1984), p. 101. When the *Houston* returned to Darwin, crewmen were questioned as to the fate of the missing Buel and his P-40. After the survivors of the *Houston* were captured by the Japanese, they were questioned as to the fate of the missing Mavis. As it turned out, Buel's gunfire had set fire to the Mavis' fuel tanks, forcing it to ditch. Its survivors were later captured on Melville Island. In the process, Buel's P-40 had been badly shot up by the Mavis' gunners and crashed into the sea in flames. Shores, Cull, and Izawa (1993), p. 174.

117. Gill, p. 585.

118. Shores, Cull, and Izawa (1993), p. 175. Winslow (1984), p. 102, has 36 Bettys and nine Mavises.

119. Except where noted otherwise, the accounts of the *Houston*'s defense of the Timor convoy come from Winslow (1984), pp. 102–104; and Schultz, pp. 125–126.

120. Winslow (1982), p. 19.

121. Winslow (1984), p. 104. Destroyers were notoriously the thirstiest of warships. They were small and fast, but their small size meant they had little room for fuel, and their speed meant they used what little fuel they had very quickly.

122. Gill, p. 585, n. 3.

123. Shores, Cull, and Izawa (1993), p. 210; Sakai Saburo, Martin Caidin, and Fred Saito, *Samurai! The Rise and Fall of the Japanese Naval Air Force* (New York: iBooks, 2001), p. 90.

124. Shores, Cull, and Izawa (1993), pp. 200–201; Bartsch (2010), pp. 218–220.

125. "K-VII," *Dutch Submarines*, www.dutchsubmarines.com, retrieved October 4, 2012; Tom Womack, "Battle of Badoeng Strait: World War II Naval Duel off Bali," *World War II*, August 31, 2006, www.historynet.com, retrieved April 17, 2012; Kroese, p. 158.

126. I have gone with Shores, Cull, and Izawa (1993), p. 201; and Womack, *The Dutch Naval Air Force Against Japan*, p. 110, who say W-12 was shot down on February 18, even though Sakai himself, p. 95, says the floatplane was shot down on February 25.

127. Sakai, Caidin, and Saito, p. 91. Accounts of the February 19 air battle over Soerabaja are few, with both Craven and Cate, p. 392, and Edmonds, p. 346, making only vague references to the battle. What little information exists is fragmentary and conflicting, with the timeline especially problematic. Sakai says that he arrived over Soerabaja at 11:30 am to find the fighters waiting for him, but Bartsch (2010), p. 240, says that Mahoney only received the order to scramble "at about 1130." Meanwhile, Shores, Cull, and Izawa (1993), p. 210, say the Zeros left the bombers at 1:00 pm. Even assuming that Sakai is using Tokyo time, which the Japanese always did as a matter of standard practice, the reported times do not add up.

128. Sakai, Caidin, and Saito, p. 91, who twist the knife with the added comment "unlike the American fighters we encountered over Clark Field on December 8."

129. Sakai, Caidin, and Saito, p. 91, report that the pilots saw "[a]t least fifty Allied fighters." Shores, Cull, and Izawa (1993), p. 210, say the Japanese reported "engaging over 30 – possibly as many as 50 – P-36s and P-40s."

130. Bartsch (2010), p. 243.

131. Marder, Jacobsen, and Horsfield (1990), p. 38; Shores, Cull, and Izawa (1993), pp. 210–211; Bartsch (2010), p. 243. I have gone with Bartsch's figure of three P-40s shot down over the seven listed in Shores, Cull, and Izawa. Craven and Cate, p. 392, and Edmonds, p. 346, also list American fighter losses as three. Two of the

three pilots survived, the one who did not was Lieutenant Quanah P. "Chief" Fields, the first American Indian killed in World War II, who was machine gunned in his parachute after bailing from his fighter. Calculating from the three P-40s shot down and the 15 ABDAIR fighters shot down in Shores, Cull, and Izawa (1993) would leave 12 Dutch aircraft shot down. But given the uncertainty over just how many fighters were involved, and the veritable disappearance of ABDAIR after this point, it is likely the figure is higher. In the English-language media, information about the Dutch army air force units involved and their casualties in the February 19 air battle over Soerabaja is practically nonexistent. For these reasons, I have gone with Marder's figure of 40 Allied fighters shot down as more likely than the figure of 15 given in Shores, Cull, and Izawa (1993).

132. Sakai, Caidin, and Saito, p. 90.
133. Womack, *The Dutch Naval Air Force Against Japan*, p. 110.
134. Peter Grose, *An Awkward Truth: The Bombing of Darwin February 1942* (Crows Nest, NSW: Allen and Unwin, 2009), p. 23.
135. Gill, p. 586; Grose, pp. 23–24. This was actually Darwin's second wharf. The first had been eaten by termites.
136. Groese, p. 23.
137. Winslow (1984), p. 54.
138. Groese, p. 51.
139. Gill, p. 588.
140. Groese, pp. 72–73.
141. Gill, p. 589.
142. Messimer (1985), p. 249.
143. Shores, Cull, and Izawa (1993), p. 175.
144. Groese, p. 84.
145. Groese, pp. 5, 49, and 82.
146. Groese, pp. 82–83; Messimer (1985), p. 246.
147. Gill, p. 591; William H. Bartsch, *Every Day a Nightmare: American Pursuit Pilots in the Defense of Java, 1941–1942* (College Station, TX: Texas A & M University Press, 2010), pp. 224–225.
148. Groese, p. 86.
149. Groese, pp. 84–85; Shores, Cull, and Izawa (1993), pp. 176–177.
150. Messimer (1985), p. 248.
151. Messimer (1985), p. 248.
152. Anthony P. Tully, "IJN Kaga: Tabular Record of Movement," *Imperial Japanese Navy Page*, www.combinedfleet.com, retrieved April 10, 2012.
153. Groese, p. 81.
154. Groese, pp. 87–89.
155. Bartsch (2010), p. 226.
156. Groese, p. 91.
157. Bartsch (2010), pp. 230–234.
158. Gill, p. 592.
159. Messimer (1985), pp. 255 and 250–51.
160. Roscoe (1953), p. 96; Groese, pp. 105–06; Robert Sinclair Parkin. *Blood on the Sea: American Destroyers Lost in World War II* (Cambridge, MA: Da Capo Press, 2001), p. 21.
161. Gill, p. 593.
162. Roscoe (1953), p. 96. Winslow (1982), p. 95, says Catlett survived mostly because he was ashore in the hospital.
163. Gill, p. 594.
164. Messimer (1985), p. 252.
165. Groese, p. 111–114, discusses whether the attack on the *Manunda* was intentional or accidental.
166. Groese, p. 103.
167. Marder, Jacobsen, and Horsfield (1990), p. 39.
168. Messimer (1985), pp. 259–261; Gill, p. 594.
169. *The Official Chronology of the US Navy in World War II* (Chapter IV: 1942).
170. Shores, Cull, and Izawa (1993), pp. 181–182; Gill, pp. 594–595.
171. Hackett and Kingsepp, "HIJMS JINTSU: Tabular Record of Movement," *Imperial Japanese Navy Page*, www.combinedfleet.com, retrieved January 17, 2011.

Chapter 11

1. Morison (1963), p. 438.
2. Ugaki, Chihaya (trans.), Goldstein (ed.), and Dillon (ed.), p. 95.
3. ATIS Doc. No. 40431, *Japanese Monograph No. 101*, p. 28; Klemen L., "The Capture of Bali Island, February 1942," *Forgotten Campaign*, retrieved June 10, 2012.
4. ATIS Doc. No. 40431, *Japanese Monograph No. 101*, p. 13, which calls the Denpesar airfield "excellent."
5. Klemen, "The Capture of Bali Island, February 1942," *Forgotten Campaign*, retrieved June 1, 2012.
6. Hackett and Kingsepp, "HIJMS NAGARA: Tabular Record of Movement."
7. Gill, p. 582. Compare Morison (1948), p. 321, who claims ABDACOM "had ten days' warning of what was cooking."
8. Hackett and Kingsepp, "HIJMS NAGARA: Tabular Record of Movement."
9. Klemen, "The Capture of Bali Island, February 1942." *Forgotten Campaign: The Dutch East Indies Campaign 1941–1942* website currently offline.
10. O'Hara, p. 26.
11. Shores, Cull, and Izawa (1993), pp. 209–210.
12. Gill, p. 582.
13. Tom Womack, "Battle of Badoeng Strait."
14. Womack, "Battle of Badoeng Strait"; Blair, p. 180.
15. Womack, "Battle of Badoeng Strait."
16. C.E.L. Helfrich, *Memoires van C.E.L. Helfrich: Eerste Deel de Maleise Barrière* (Amsterdam: Elsevier, 1950), p. 363; Paul R. Yarnall, "Locations Of Warships Of 'Allied' Naval Units December 7 1941."
17. Helfrich, p. 363.
18. Bosscher, p. 263.
19. Gill, pp. 581–582; William Glassford, "Narrative of events in the South-West Pacific from 14 February to 5 April 1942" (hereinafter "Glassford Report"), pp. 19–20. Over the years, it has been disputed who came up with the operational plan; some histories say Admiral Doorman (see, e.g. Womack, "Battle of Badoeng Strait"), others say Admiral Helfrich (see, e.g. Winslow (1982), p. 41), still others say both (see, e.g. Bosscher, pp. 263–264). The issue may simply be a conflation of who came up with the operational plan versus the tactical plan. Both Gill and Glassford specifically state that Helfrich ordered Doorman to carry out the attack in this fashion. For his part, Helfrich, p. 362, says that Doorman came up with the plan but he supported it because there simply was no time to assemble the ships for a single attack.
20. Womack, "Battle of Badoeng Strait."
21. Gill, p. 582; Bosscher, p. 264. Helfrich, p. 362, says the idea for the motor torpedo boat attach came from his staff.
22. Womack, "Battle of Badoeng Strait."
23. Womack, "Battle of Badoeng Strait"; Thomas, pp. 140–141. Compare Morison (1948), p. 321, who makes an oblique criticism of Doorman with the statement, "[Al]though Admiral Doorman's Combined Striking Force was perfectly capable of meeting Kubo's Bali Occupation Force at sea with superior strength, he was unable to collect his ships in time to strike until the landing was completed."
24. Winslow (1982), pp. 40–41.
25. Gill, p. 584; Glassford, p. 22.
26. Glassford Report, p. 20.
27. Helfrich, p. 361.
28. Felipe C. Ramires, "The Fall of Bali." *SMMLonline*, http://smmlonline.com/articles/articles/badoeng.html, retrieved May 6, 2012, cites another similarity to the Balikpapan attack, "The attack plan improvised by Doorman followed practically the same strategy adopted by the American destroyers in the Battle of Balikpapan (24th of January of 1942), that is; the Allied strike forces should be positioned between the Japanese disembarkation lines."
29. Michel, p. 60; Morison (1948), p. 322; Thomas, p. 141.
30. By comparison, the Japanese ambush of Allied forces at the Battle of Savo Island off Guadalcanal in August 1942 may be instructive. In that engagement, the Japanese admiral, Mikawa Gunichi, led with torpedoes before gunfire as many believe Doorman should have done. Mikawa also led from the front in his flagship *Chokai*. This did not compromise Japanese tactics because the *Chokai*, unlike the *De Ruyter* and *Java*, carried torpedoes and used them to open the engagement.
31. Mullin, p. 170.

32. Womack, "Battle of Badoeng Strait"; Mullin, pp. 170–171.

33. Kroese, p. 60.

34. Mullin, p. 172.

35. Mullin, p. 172.

36. Most sources say the US destroyers were about 5,000yd behind the *Piet Hein* by the time the battle started, but Mullin, p. 172, based on survivor and eyewitness accounts, says the destroyers had actually been 2,000yd behind. I have tried to interpret these conflicting statements so that both are accurate.

37. Mullin, p. 172, allowing for his reported times being an hour behind the times in other reports. Ramires, "The Fall of Bali."

38. Paul S. Dull, *A Battle History of the Imperial Japanese Navy (1941–1945)* (Annapolis: Naval Institute Press, 1978), p. 56.

39. Womack, "Battle of Badoeng Strait."

40. O'Hara (2007), pp. 28–29; Womack, "Battle of Badoeng Strait."

41. Several sources (see, e.g. O'Hara, p. 29) say the *Asashio* was hit by the *Java*'s 40mm Bofors, with the searchlight destroyed, four killed and 11 wounded. But Dull, p. 356, says Japanese records do not mention a hit on the *Asashio* at this point in the battle, and O'Hara (2007), p. 31, later says Commander Abe signaled Admiral Kubo, "We did not receive any damage." The *Asashio* did in fact suffer searchlight destroyed, four killed and 11 wounded, but that was a result of damage inflicted by the 40mm Bofors of the Hr. Ms. *Tromp* of the Allied second wave attack.

42. O'Hara, p. 29.

43. It has been generally accepted that the *De Ruyter* did not get off a shot because her guns were facing the wrong way, but the respected Java Sea historian Tom Womack, "Battle of Badoeng Strait," says that the *De Ruyter* got "about the same number" of salvoes (nine) as the *Java*. Imperial Japanese Navy historian Paul Dull, p. 56, also says the *De Ruyter* got several shots off against the *Oshio*.

44. O'Hara (2007), p. 29.

45. Ramires, "The Fall of Bali."

46. Mullin, p. 173; Morison (1948), p. 324; Bosscher, p. 266; Ramires, "The Fall of Bali."

47. Mullin, p. 173.

48. Ramires, "The Fall of Bali."

49. Womack, "Battle of Badoeng Strait."

50. O'Hara (2007), p. 29.

51. Mullin, p. 174.

52. Mullin, p. 173.

53. O'Hara (2007), p. 29.

54. O'Hara (2007), p. 31; Mullin, p. 175.

55. Michel, p. 62.

56. Mullin, p. 175.

57. Morison (1948), p. 325.

58. Womack, "Battle of Badoeng Strait."

59. Mullin, pp. 174–175.

60. Michel, p. 61; ONI Narrative, p. 42.

61. See, e.g. Bosscher, p. 266; Winslow (1982), p. 41; Ramires, "The Fall of Bali."

62. Bosscher, p. 266.

63. See, e.g. Mullin, p. 173; Michel, pp. 61–62.

64. Prados, p. 256.

65. Bosscher, p. 266.

66. Mullin, p. 178.

67. ONI Narrative, p. 43.

68. Alford, p. 133.

69. O'Hara (2007), p. 31; ONI Narrative, p. 43.

70. Alford, pp. 133–134.

71. Alford, pp. 134–135.

72. O'Hara (2007), p. 31; Alford, pp. 135–136.

73. O'Hara (2007), p. 31.

74. O'Hara (2007), p. 31.

75. Morison (1948), p. 328; Hoyt (1976), p. 241.

76. Alford, pp. 135–136; Morison (1948), p. 328.

77. Dull, p. 58; O'Hara, p. 31.

78. Alford, p. 138.

79. Womack, "Battle of Badoeng Strait."

80. O'Hara, p. 32.

81. Ramires, "The Fall of Bali."

82. Womack, "Battle of Badoeng Strait"; Ramires, "The Fall of Bali."

83. Ramires, "The Fall of Bali."

84. Ramires, "The Fall of Bali."

85. Dull, p. 59.

86. Dull, p. 59.

87. O'Hara (2007), p. 32.

88. O'Hara (2007), p. 32; Alford, p. 139. Dull, p. 59, and Womack, "Battle of Badoeng Strait," say it was the *Stewart* who turned on her searchlight, but Alford, who was on the *Stewart* and makes a point of discussing the destroyer's use of the searchlight, makes no mention of it at this point, though he mentions the Japanese turning on theirs. He also suggests, p. 142, that the *Stewart* turned on her searchlight only once, that instance being her earlier illumination of the *Oshio*.

89. Mullin, pp. 180–181; ONI Narrative, p. 44. Mullin identifies the man as Chief Watertender R. E. Padgett of the forward repair party and ammunition passer. The ONI Narrative goes on to describe his fate, "During the engagement he floated around in the water, and the next day reached Bali. Joining up there with some isolated Dutch soldiers he finally succeeded in reaching Java and eventually regained his ship at Soerabaja."

90. O'Hara (2007), p. 32; Alford, p. 139.

91. O'Hara (2007), p. 32; Dull, p. 59.

92. Nevitt, "HIJMS Michishio: Tabular Record of Movement," *Imperial Japanese Navy Page*, www.combinedfleet. com, retrieved July 8, 2012; O'Hara (2007), p. 32.

93. Dull, p. 59.

94. Womack, "Battle of Badoeng Strait."

95. Womack, "Battle of Badoeng Strait."

96. Prados, p. 257.

Chapter 12

1.   Alford, p. 145.

2.   Alford, p. 177.

3.   Alford, p. 178.

4.   Alford, p. 178.

5.   Robert Sinclair Parkin, *Blood on the Sea: American Destroyers Lost in World War II* (Cambridge, MA: Da Capo Press, 2001), p. 47.

6.   Alford, pp. 178–179.

7.   Mullin, p. 185.

8.   Alford, p. 179.

9.   Alford, pp. 179–180.

10. Alford, p. 180.

11. Mullin, p. 184.

12. Mullin, p. 185.

13. Alford, pp. 184–185. Glassford, p. 22, says of the *Stewart*, "Every effort was made to save her ... [O]ur efforts to save her continued until the enemy had landed on the Island and was about to occupy the city." How this fits with *Stewart* crewman Alford's assertion that the announcement of the *Stewart*'s abandonment was made on February 22 is unclear. It may be that the February 22 announcement was made just to save her crew by getting them out of Java. Kale, quoted in Parkin, p. 47, says the crew was broken up on February 25, the day after the *Stewart* was struck by three Japanese bombs.

14. Marder, Jacobsen, and Horsfield, p. 43.

15. Toland (1961), p. 240.

16. There are multiple versions of this message, with differences due to editing. This version is an amalgamation of Toland (1961), p. 240, and Toll, p. 252.

17. Willmott, pp. 338–339.
18. Glassford Report, p. 26.
19. Thomas, p. 149.
20. Craven and Cate, p. 397.
21. Bartsch (2010), p. 276.
22. Alford, pp. 191–192.
23. Willmott, p. 338.
24. P. C. Boer, *The Loss of Java: The Final Battle for Possession of Java Fought by Allied Air, Naval and Land Forces in the Period of 18 February–7 March 1942* (Singapore: National University of Singapore Press, 2011), p. xxii. It is common belief that ABDACOM was "dissolved," with a specific time for dissolution given as 9:00 am February 25, 1942, by Willmott, p. 339. Gill, p. 603, is typical: "On [February 25] the ABDA Command was dissolved. On 22nd February Wavell discussed the withdrawal of his headquarters from Java with the Governor-General of the Netherlands East Indies, Jonkheer Dr van Starkenborgh Stachouwer, who thought that withdrawal after invasion would damage public morale, and that, as an alternative command organization was already in existence, it would be better that the ABDA Command should be dissolved, and not withdrawn. Wavell agreed, and in a message to the Chiefs of Staff advanced this view, pointing out that since the control of Burma had reverted to India, ABDA held little to command, and that the local defence of Java could be better exercised under the original Dutch organisation. The Chiefs of Staff concurred, and General Wavell accordingly dissolved his command at noon on the 25th February, and that night left by air for Ceylon[.]"
    However, Glassford, p. 27, is much more circumspect, stating, "The ABDA supreme command had ceased to exist. The direction of defense of JAVA was taken over directly by Dutch officers as follows – Navy, Vice Admiral Helfrich; Army Lieutenant General Ter Poorten; Air, Major General Van Oyen. The coordinating command reverted nominally to the Governor-General." The ONI Narrative, pp. 44–45, echoes Glassford's account, though it titles the act "Dissolution of the Supreme Command." Craven and Cate, p. 396, take the opposite tack, saying, "In Java, General Wavell closed his personal headquarters on 25 February, at which time the ABDA Command passed to the Dutch. The decision not to dissolve the command itself was in keeping with a purpose that Allied units in Java should continue to operate as long as it was possible." I have gone with Craven and Cate's interpretation. The term "dissolved" may simply be shorthand, because in practice it seems that only Wavell's supreme command level was dissolved. ABDACOM as an organization was not so much dissolved as no longer "ABDA," but just "D" – completely under Dutch control. The continued use of the terms "ABDA" and "ABDACOM" by historians (see, e.g. Bartsch (2010), p. 288) and, particularly, survivors of the campaign, with reference to events after the supposed "dissolution" of ABDACOM supports this interpretation, as do the references to "Unified Command" (see, e.g., Boer, p. xxii) or "Combined Headquarters" (see, e.g. Shores, Cull, and Izawa (1993), p. 245).
25. Bartsch (2010), p. 275.
26. Marder, Jacobsen, and Horsfield, pp. 43–44; Gill, p. 602.
27. Glassford Report, p. 36.
28. Glassford Report, pp. 36–37.
29. Glassford Report, p. 28–29.
30. Gill, p. 599.
31. Gill, p. 599.
32. O'Hara (2007), p. 33.
33. Mike Carlton, *Cruiser: The Life and Loss of HMAS* Perth *and Her Crew* (North Sydney, New South Wales, Australia: William Heinemann, 2010), p. 396.
34. Glassford Report, pp. 14–15.
35. Mullin, p. 209.
36. Collins, pp. 106–107.
37. Blair, p. 183.
38. Hackett, Kingsepp, and Cundall; "IJN Patrol Boat No. 106: Tabular Record of Movement," *Imperial Japanese Navy Page*, www.combinedfleet.com, retrieved April 10, 2012.
39. Thomas, p. 154.
40. Marder, Jacobsen, and Horsfield, p. 48.
41. Marder, Jacobsen, and Horsfield, p. 48, who call the move, "a bit of foresight on Gordon's part that has escaped notice in any published history." Including Gordon's own, which only states that when he received the

orders to head for Soerabaja, "Most of the shipping had been cleared from the port, with orders to make a get-away to the Indian Ocean." Oliver. Gordon, *Fight It Out: The Epic Story of HMS Exeter's Struggle Against Overwhelming Odds Told By Her Captain* (London: William Kimber and Co., 1957)

42. Mullin, pp. 201–202.
43. Winslow (1984), p. 108.
44. Hornfischer, p. 57.
45. Shores, Cull, and Izawa (1993), p. 226.
46. Winslow (1984), p. 109.
47. Michel, p. 61; Mullin, p. 166.
48. Hoyt (1976), p. 247.
49. Collins, p. 114.
50. Gill, p. 608.
51. Gill, p. 616, n. 8.
52. Glassford Report, pp. 37–38.
53. Gill, pp. 616–617. Collins, p. 114, is very coy about who gave these orders to the Western Striking Force.
54. Gill, p. 617; Willmott, p. 345.
55. Thomas, p. 151.
56. Shores, Cull, and Izawa (1993), p. 226.
57. Womack, *The Dutch Naval Air Force Against Japan*, p. 117.
58. Messimer (1985), p. 259.
59. Womack, *The Dutch Naval Air Force Against Japan*, p. 117.
60. ONI Narrative, p. 52. It should be pointed out that postwar journalist and former Imperial Japanese Navy officer Chihaya Masataka, writing in Donald M. Goldstein and Katherine V. Dillon (eds), *The Pacific War Papers: Japanese Documents of World War II* (Washington: Potomac, 2004), p. 270, says there was no landing on Bawean Island. Supporting Chihaya's position is *Japanese Monograph No. 101*, which does not mention the landing.
61. Winslow (1984), pp. 109–110.
62. Details of the conversation come from Koppen, *The Battle of the Java Sea*, DVD. Koppen has the meeting taking place in Lembang, but it likely took place in Bandoeng, to where Helfrich had relocated. Koppen also has the meeting taking place on February 26. Returning from the front, flying to Bandoeng or Lembang for a one-hour meeting, then flying back to Soerabaja again, then developing a battle plan, calling Helfrich again, arranging and holding a meeting to present that plan, supplying his ships, and leaving again makes for a full day, to say the least. This timeline leaves open the possibility that the meeting actually took place on February 25. If so, it would provide an alternative explanation of why Helfrich considered replacing Doorman.
63. ONI Narrative, p. 53, 87, Appendix II "Contact Reports Before and During the Battle of Java Sea."
64. There are multiple versions of the translation of this message. I have gone with ONI Narrative, p. 53. The Dutch version is in Helfrich, p. 398, which also gives the time the message was sent.
65. Frederick C. Sherman, *Combat Command* (New York: Bantam, 1982), p. 38.
66. Koppen, *The Battle of the Java Sea*, DVD.
67. Kroese, p. 71. Except where noted otherwise, the account of the conference comes from Kroese, pp. 71–74, who was in attendance.
68. Koppen, *The Battle of the Java Sea*, DVD.
69. Hornfischer, p. 61.
70. Oliver L. Gordon, "Appendix" in "Battle of the Java Sea, 27th February, 1942," *Supplement to the London Gazette*, Tuesday, July 6, 1948 (hereinafter "*Exeter* Report"), p. 3,942, who was in attendance. In his book, Gordon called the ride "a nightmare"; O. L. Gordon, pp. 42–43.
71. Michel, p. 70.
72. Kroese, p. 73.
73. ONI Narrative, p. 54.
74. Thomas, p. 158.
75. O. L. Gordon, p. 57.
76. Womack, *The Dutch Naval Air Force Against Japan*, p. 197 n. 23.
77. Winslow (1984), pp. 110–111.
78. Van Oosten, p. 39; Messimer (1985), p. 267.
79. H. E. Eccles, "Battle of Bawean Islands – Report of action; events prior and subsequent thereto," *U.S.S. John*

D. Edwards (216), DD216/A16-3/(CF 00020), March 4, 1942 (hereinafter "*Edwards* Report").

80. ONI Narrative, p. 52.
81. Gordon Report, p. 3,942.
82. Hart Report, pp. 71–72, says, "The tactical handling of the mixed forces was discussed. Since there would be little or no chance for training, there were bound to be difficulties but it was held that they would not be great because the force would be small and the tactics simple. The ship-to-ship communications were to be by short-range, high-frequency voice radio."
83. Glassford Report, p. 42.
84. Hornfischer, p. 62.
85. Thomas, p. 156.
86. Koppen, *The Battle of the Java Sea*, DVD.
87. Theo W. R. Doorman, "Commemoration of the Battle of the Java Sea 2012." Theo Doorman was Admiral Doorman's son by his second wife, both of whom were later evacuated from the Indies in dramatic fashion.
88. Koppen, *The Battle of the Java Sea*, DVD.
89. Winslow (1982), p. 111.
90. ONI Narrative, p. 54.
91. Except where noted otherwise, the text of the sighting reports sent to the Combined Striking Force comes from ONI Narrative, p. 55, 87.
92. Shores, Cull, and Izawa (1993), p. 238.
93. Mullin, p. 211.
94. ONI Narrative, p. 55.
95. ONI Narrative, p. 55.
96. Prados, p. 255; Winslow (1984), p. 113.
97. Shores, Cull, and Izawa, p. 238.
98. ONI Narrative, p. 88.
99. Mullin, p. 214.
100. ONI Narrative, p. 56. There are two versions of this message. The other version that is frequently quoted has Doorman signaling, FOLLOW ME. THE ENEMY IS NINETY MILES AWAY.
101. Mullin, p. 214.
102. Van Oosten, pp. 55–56, says the Japanese aircraft was just dumping its bombs before returning to base, as was standard operating procedure to guard against detonation of the bombs upon landing.
103. Marder, Jacobsen, and Horsfield, p. 55; Boer, p. 192.
104. Hornfischer, p. 69.

Chapter 13

1. Both *Proteus* and *Nereus* disappeared within a month of each other in late 1940, long after the Navy had sold them off. It is now theorized that both succumbed to catastrophic structural failure in stormy weather. The *Cyclops* left Barbados on March 4, 1918, supposedly headed for Norfolk, and was never seen again. Emerging during the subsequent investigation were allegations of incompetence and abuse – and even murder and treason – on the part of her skipper, but no solution. To this day the mysterious disappearance of the *Cyclops* remains the single largest loss of life in the history of the US Navy not directly involving combat. The US Navy's Naval History and Heritage Command maintains, "Her loss without a trace is one of the sea's unsolved mysteries." "Cyclops," *Dictionary of American Naval Fighting Ships*, US Naval History and Heritage Command, www.history.navy.mil/danfs, retrieved June 12, 2012.
2. Craven and Cate, p. 385.
3. Craven and Cate, p. 385.
4. Craven and Cate, pp. 385–386.
5. Messimer (1983), p. 25.
6. Grose, pp. 72–73.
7. ONI Narrative, p. 46.
8. Except where noted otherwise, information on the plan for the *Langley* and Convoy MS-5 comes from Dwight Messimer's seminal work on the *Langley* and the *Pecos*, *Pawns of War: The Loss of the USS* Langley *and the USS* Pecos (1983), pp. 26–28, 31–32, 34, 37.
9. Admiral Glassford, in his Narrative of Events, p. 30, said they left on February 21. Messimer (1983), p. 37, makes it clear that the *Langley* and Convoy MS-5 left at noon on February 22.

10. Messimer (1983), p. 37.
11. Messimer (1983), pp. 49–50.
12. Messimer (1983), p. 37.
13. Messimer (1983), p. 37.
14. Messimer (1983), pp. 37–38.
15. Glassford Report, p. 32.
16. Messimer (1983), p. 38.
17. See, e.g. Messimer, pp. 38–39.
18. Glassford Report, p. 30.
19. Messimer (1983), pp. 39–40.
20. Glassford Report, pp. 29–30.
21. ONI Narrative, p. 46; Glassford Report, p. 34.
22. Womack, *The Dutch Naval Air Force Against Japan*, p. 120, identifies the Catalinas as Y-65 and Y-71 from the Royal Netherlands Naval Air Service's 5th Aircraft Group.
23. Messimer (1983), p. 41.
24. The report "Operations, Action and Sinking of USS LANGLEY, period from February 22 to March 5, 1942" (hereinafter "*Langley* Report") p. 1, makes a common mistake in anglicizing the ship's name as the *William van der Zaan*. Frequently identified as a minesweeper, the *Willem van der Zaan* was actually a minelayer and training ship; Lenton, pp. 71, 76–77; Jan Visser, "Willem van der Zaan," *Royal Netherlands Navy Warships of World War II*, http://www.netherlandsnavy.nl, retrieved June 10, 2012.
25. Lenton (1968), pp. 71, 76–77.
26. Winslow (1982), p. 231; Visser, "Willem van der Zaan History."
27. Messimer (1983), p. 41; Winslow (1982), p. 231.
28. Messimer (1983), p. 42; Winslow (1982), pp. 231–232.
29. Messimer (1983), p. 42.
30. Glassford Report, p. 32. Admiral Helfrich's role in entangling the *Langley* with the *Willem van der Zaan* is minimized in official US sources. The ONI Narrative, p. 46, uses the passive voice to sidestep the issue: "As the *Langley* approached Tjilatjap she was met on the afternoon of the 26th by a Dutch mine layer and two Dutch Catalina flying boats. After some delay and confusion she left the slow Dutch boat …" Admiral Glassford's report, p. 31, ignores the matter entirely, saying, "It developed now that the LANGLEY […] was due TJILATJAP at 5:00 p.m. the 27th …"
31. Glassford Report, p. 32.
32. *Langley* Report, p. 2. Oddly, though Winslow (1982), p. 232, mentions this incident, Messimer's seminal work on the *Langley*, *Pawns of War* (1983), does not.
33. Messimer (1983), p. 44.
34. *Langley* Report, p. 2.
35. *Langley* Report, p. 2. The report "USS EDSALL record of known activities between 26 February 1942 and 1 March 1942" (hereinafter "*Edsall* Report"), p. 1, says the aircraft was sighted at bearing 190 degrees True, south southwest. Kehn, p. 116, says, "[T]he aircraft came from the east and departed in the same direction."
36. *Langley* Report, p. 2.
37. Messimer (1983), p. 43.
38. Messimer (1983), p. 50.
39. Glassford Report, p. 34.
40. ONI Narrative, p. 46.
41. See Anthony P. Tully, "Neglected Disaster: Nisshin," *Imperial Japanese Navy Page*, www.combinedfleet.com, retrieved April 10, 2012.
42. US investigators postwar examined the possibility that the *Langley*'s mission had been compromised in their interrogations of Japanese officers. Interrogation Nav No. 7 USSBS No. 33 Interrogation of: Vice Admiral Shiraishi, Kazutaka, IJN (Admiral Kondo's chief of staff), October 15, 1945, available at Hyperwar (http://www.ibiblio.org/hyperwar/AAF/USSBS/IJO/IJO-7.html) contains the following exchange:
Q. Did the Commander of the Second Fleet know that the LANGLEY was coming from AUSTRALIA to JAVA with aircraft reinforcements?
A. No.
43. Ugaki, p. 95, says that on February 26 a Japanese submarine reported a "carrier of the *Ranger* class" apparently headed for Tjilatjap. His entry for February 27 identifies the "carrier" as the *Langley*.
44. Hoyt (1976), p. 262, identifies the aircraft as "one of those lazy-looking Kawanishi flying boats." *The Official*

Chronology of the US Navy in World War II (Chapter IV: 1941) identifies the unit as the *Takao* Air Group.

45. Shore, Cull, and Izawa (1993), p. 241.
46. *Langley* Report, p. 2.
47. *Langley* Report, pp. 2–3.
48. Messimer (1983), p. 52.
49. Messimer (1983), p. 53.
50. Except where noted otherwise, the *Langley*'s wireless telegraph messages are taken from *Langley* Report, Enclosure (C).
51. Hoyt (1976), p. 262.
52. Messimer (1983), p. 56.
53. Messimer (1983), p. 57.
54. Messimer (1983), p. 59.
55. Messimer (1983), p. 59–60.
56. Messimer (1983), p. 61.
57. Messimer (1983), p. 62.
58. Messimer (1983), pp. 62–63.
59. Messimer (1983), p. 64.
60. Messimer (1983), p. 64.
61. ONI Narrative, p. 47. Edmonds, p. 418, paraphrases the ONI Narrative.
62. *Langley* Report, pp. 3–5.
63. Messimer (1983), pp. 66–67.
64. Messimer (1983), pp. 75–78. Shores, Cull and Izawa (1993), p. 241, appear to claim the second strafing run was by the Zeros of the Tainan Air Group led by Lieutenant Maki Yukio. I have gone with Messimer based on the *Langley* Report's claim, p. 4, that the strafing run was by six Zeros, which corresponds with Yokoyama's group.
65. Shores, Cull, and Izawa, p. 241, say the four-engine flying boat was a Qantas Airways Empire "C" boat called "Circe." Womack, *The Dutch Naval Air Force Against Japan*, p. 121, identifies her as a Qantas Airlines Empire "C" boat called "Corio."
66. *Langley* Report, p. 4.
67. *Langley* Report, pp. 4–5.
68. Messimer (1983), p. 79, 81.
69. Messimer (1983), pp. 86–87.
70. *Langley* Report, p. 4.
71. Messimer (1983), p. 82.
72. *Langley* Report, Enclosure (C).
73. *Langley* Report, p. 5.
74. Messimer (1983), p. 102.
75. *Langley* Report, Enclosure (C).
76. *Langley* Report, p. 5. Messimer (1983), p. 112, says the coding machines were smashed with a fire axe.
77. Winslow (1982), p. 235.
78. Winslow (1982), p. 237. *Langley* Report, p. 6, gives figures of six killed and five missing, but does not give a figure for wounded.
79. Messimer (1983), pp. 116–117.
80. Winslow (1982), p. 237.
81. *The Official Chronology of the US Navy in World War II* (Chapter IV: 1942).
82. Messimer (1983), p. 192.
83. Boer, pp. 182–183.
84. Bartsch (2010), pp. 275 and 277.

Chapter 14

1. Hara Tameichi, *Japanese Destroyer Captain* (Annapolis: Naval Institute Press, 1967), pp. 64–65.
2. Hara, p. 68.
3. Hara, p. 65.
4. The 2nd Destroyer Flotilla consisted of the flagship light cruiser *Jintsu*, destroyers *Yukikaze*, *Amatsukaze*,

Tokitsukaze, and *Hatsukaze* of Destroyer Division 16, and destroyers *Yamakaze* and *Kawakaze* of Destroyer Division 24. Destroyers *Ushio* and *Sazanami* of Destroyer Division 7, which had been operating as a screen for Cruiser Division 5, were attached to the 2nd Destroyer Flotilla for this battle; Van Oosten, p. 43. See Dull, pp. 76–77.

5. The 4th Destroyer Flotilla consisted of the flagship cruiser *Naka*, serving as a destroyer leader as most Japanese light cruisers did, destroyers *Asagumo* and *Minegumo*, of Destroyer Division 9, and destroyers *Murasame*, *Samidare*, *Harusame*, and *Yudachi* of Destroyer Division 2; Van Oosten, p. 42.

6. Toll, p. 257; Marder, Jacobsen, and Horsfield, p. 46.

7. Hara, p. 65.

8. Hornfischer, p. 68.

9. Hara, pp. 67–68.

10. Hara, p. 68.

11. Hara, p. 68.

12. Hara, p. 69.

13. Marder called Tanaka a "B admiral. Marder, Jacobsen and Horsfield, pp. 46–47."

14. Hara, p. 69.

15. Toland (1961), p. 248; Hara, p. 69.

16. Hara, p. 69.

17. Hornfischer, p. 72.

18. Hornfischer, p. 74.

19. Toland (1961), p. 244.

20. Morison (1948), p. 345.

21. ONI Narrative, p. 57; *Edwards* Report.

22. Counting everything from 5.5in to 6in guns as "6in."

23. Hara, p. 70.

24. Morison (1948), p. 343.

25. Winslow (1984), p. 113.

26. Dull, pp. 76–77.

27. O'Hara (2007), p. 38; Marder, Jacobsen, and Horsfield, p. 56; Winslow (1984), p. 114.

28. Thomas, p. 178; O. L. Gordon, p. 48; Marder, Jacobsen, and Horsfield, p. 56.

29. Marder, Jacobsen, and Horsfield, p. 56.

30. O'Hara (2007), p. 38; Morison (1948), p. 345.

31. Schultz, p. 149; Morison (1948), p. 345; Thomas, pp. 179–180.

32. Vincent P. O'Hara, "Battle of the Java Sea: 27 February 1942," *Thunder of the Guns: Battles of the Pacific War*, www.microworks.net/pacific/battles, retrieved March 29, 2012.

33. Toland (1961), p. 256.

34. Prados, p. 261.

35. Marder, Jacobsen, and Horsfield, p. 60; Van Oosten, p. 46.

36. Hara, p. 69.

37. Morison (1948), p. 345; Toland (1961), p. 250.

38. Hornfischer, pp. 78–79; Toland (1961), p. 249.

39. H. M. L. Waller, "Action Narrative – Day and Night Action Off Sourabaya, 27th February, 1942" in "Battle of the Java Sea, 27th February, 1942," *Supplement to the London Gazette*, Tuesday, July 6, 1948 (hereinafter "*Perth* Report"), p. 3,939.

40. Toland (1961), p. 250; Winslow (1984), p. 116.

41. Morison (1948), p. 345; O'Hara, "Battle of the Java Sea: 27 February 1942."

42. ONI Narrative, p. 64.

43. Schultz, p. 151.

44. Schultz, p. 150.

45. Winslow (1984), p. 115; Hoyt (1976), p. 251.

46. Oddly, the only history that has mentioned this consideration is Carlton, p. 417.

47. Mullin, p. 215.

48. Morison (1948), p. 345.

49. Marder, Jacobsen, and Horsfield, pp. 61–62, n. 15.

50. Hornfischer, p. 79.

51. Thomas, p. 182.
52. Prados, p. 263.
53. Thomas, p. 183; Hara, p. 70.
54. Shores, Cull, and Izawa (1993), p. 239; Bartsch (2010), p. 295.
55. Hara, p. 70; Boer, p. 195.
56. Bartsch (2010), p. 295–296.
57. Bartsch (2010), p. 296; Boer, pp. 195–196.
58. Bartsch (2010), p. 296.
59. Winslow (1984), p. 117.
60. Thomas, p. 184.
61. *Exeter* Report, p. 3,943.
62. Most sources credit the *Haguro* with the hit on the *Exeter*. See, e.g. Marder, Jacobsen, and Horsfield, p. 64; Morison (1948), pp. 346–347; Toland (1961), p. 253; Hackett and Kingsepp, "HIJMS Haguro: Tabular Record of Movement," *Imperial Japanese Navy Page*, www.combinedfleet.com, retrieved January 17, 2011. But Dull, p. 78; O'Hara (2007), p. 40; and Gill, p. 611, credit the *Nachi*.
63. *Exeter* Report, p. 3,943; Marder, Jacobsen, and Horsfield, p. 64. The time is from van Oosten, p. 47.
64. Gill, p. 611.
65. Koppen, *The Battle of the Java Sea*, DVD.
66. *Perth* Report, p. 3,940.
67. Toland (1961), p. 253.
68. Hornfischer, p. 83.
69. Hara p. 73.
70. ONI Narrative, p. 63.
71. ONI Narrative, p. 65.
72. Hornfischer, p. 84.
73. Tully, "Naval Alamo.
74. ONI Narrative, p. 65.
75. Toland (1961), p. 254.
76. Koppen, *The Battle of the Java Sea*, DVD.
77. Koppen, *The Battle of the Java Sea*, DVD.
78. Mullin, p. 215.
79. O'Hara (2007), p. 41.
80. Winslow (1984), p. 118.
81. Koppen, *The Battle of the Java Sea*, DVD.
82. Koppen, *The Battle of the Java Sea*, DVD.
83. I have gone with Dull, p. 78, who says that the time span between launch and hit and the distance covered "suggests that the torpedo came from the *Haguro*"; van Oosten, p. 49, who says "*Kortenaer* could have been hit by a torpedo launched from the *Haguro* and aimed at the *Houston*"; and *The Imperial Japanese Navy Page*, which says the torpedo definitely came from the *Haguro*. Thomas, pp. 187–191, credits the 2nd Destroyer Flotilla. Morison (1948), p. 347, says it was "probably" the *Jintsu*.
84. Marder, Jacobsen, and Horsfield, p. 65.
85. *Perth* Report, p. 3,940.
86. ONI Narrative, p. 65; *Edwards* Report.
87. ONI Narrative, p. 67.
88. Winslow (1984), p. 118.
89. For the pictures themselves, see Winslow (1984), pp. 226–227. Johnsen's photographs are blurry and vague, with ambiguities that have turned them into a sort of Rorschach Test for the Battle of the Java Sea. Winslow, in his persistent assertion that the Combined Striking Force inflicted considerable damage on the Japanese, cites one picture, showing a wake and a plume of black smoke far below the camera, as proof of a burning ship. This may be the case; Japanese records, however, suggest that a far more likely explanation is that the ship is laying a smokescreen. The picture does not provide nearly enough detail to identify the ship involved. In fairness to Winslow, it must be pointed out that after the Java Sea Campaign, the heavy cruiser *Nachi* was sent to Japan to be retrofitted for cold weather operations in the North Pacific and the Aleutians, which could have conceivably covered up repairs for damage received in the Battle of the Java Sea.
90. Dull, p. 78.
91. ONI Narrative, p. 68. Some versions state that the message was, BRITISH DESTROYERS

COUNTERATTACK. ONI Narrative, n. 56.

92. T. J. Cain, *HMS* Electra (London: Futura, 1959), p. 229.

93. Cain (1959), p. 229.

94. Toland (1961), p. 253. This quotation is normally associated with the earlier torpedo attack that sank the *Kortenaer*. But Dull, O'Hara, and van Oosten, who examined Japanese sources, make clear that while the *Jintsu* herself took part in the earlier attack, the sources do not mention the 2nd Flotilla's destroyers doing so. The figures from van Oosten, p. 116, suggest that Tanaka's destroyers launched far too late to have hit the *Kortenaer*. Dull credits the 2nd with two attacks, this one and a later one at around 7:36 pm. Van Oosten, p. 116, and O'Hara, p. 43, say the 7:36 pm attack was only made by the *Jintsu* herself. Morison (1948) says that the 2nd made the attack that sank the *Kortenaer* and the 7:36 pm attack, but that this attack was turned back before they could launch. Assuming they emptied their torpedo tubes on each attack, with one set of torpedo reloads the Japanese could have made only two attacks. Interestingly, Hara makes reference to his making only one torpedo attack, one that damaged the *Kortenaer*.

95. O'Hara (2007), pp. 41–42.

96. Cain (1959), p. 231.

97. T. J. Cain, "*H.M.S. Electra – Report of Action 27th February, 1942, by Senior Surviving Officer*" in "Battle of the Java Sea, 27th February, 1942," *Supplement to the London Gazette*, Tuesday, 6 July, 1948 (hereinafter "*Electra* Report"), p. 3,941.

98. Cain (1959), p. 221.

99. *Electra* Report, p. 3,941.

100. Cain (1959), pp. 232–233.

101. Cain (1959), p. 233.

102. Cain (1959), pp. 238–239; *Electra* Report, p. 3,941.

103. ONI Narrative, p. 69, 78; Bosscher, p. 607, n. 321. I'd like to thank Jan Visser for pointing me in the direction of this information.

104. Time is from J. E. Cooper, "Report of Battle of Java Sea, forwarding of," *U.S.S. John D. Ford* (228), DD228/ A16-3 (CF-8), April 8, 1942 (hereinafter "*Ford* Report"), Enclosure B – "Extracts from Radio Log 26 February – 1 March 1942," who paraphrases the signal as WHAT IS MATTER WITH YOU?

105. Thomas, p, 194; *Exeter* Report, p. 3,944.

106. Thomas, p. 194; *Ford* Report, Enclosure B – "Extracts from Radio Log 26 February – 1 March 1942."

107. O'Hara (2007), p. 42.

108. Morison (1948), p. 351; O'Hara, p. 42.

109. Thomas, p. 198; Hornfischer, pp. 85–86.

110. Schultz, p. 154.

111. Mullin, p. 219.

112. *Edwards* Report.

113. Time for sunset comes from Alford, p. 200.

114. Mullin, pp. 218–219; Alford, pp. 198–199.

115. ONI Narrative, p. 70.

116. Roscoe (1953), p. 105.

117. Alford, p. 199.

118. Mullin, p. 219.

119. Doorman's words are from Mullin, p. 226, but there is no close quote.

120. ONI Narrative, p. 70.

121. Morison (1948), p. 352.

122. Alford, p. 200; The ONI Narrative, p. 70, gives 6:22 pm as the time for the attack.

123. Alford, p. 200.

124. ONI Narrative, pp. 70–71.

125. Alford, p. 200.

126. Why he thought the Combined Striking Force would fight within its own minefield is unclear.

127. O'Hara (2007), p. 43.

128. Winslow (1984), pp. 120–121.

129. *Edwards* Report.

130. O'Hara (2007), p. 43.

131. Hara, pp. 74–75.

132. O'Hara (2007), p. 43.
133. Hara, p. 74.
134. Morison (1948), pp. 354–355.
135. Morison (1948), p. 355.
136. Schultz, p. 157.
137. *Ford* Report.
138. Winslow (1982), p. 121.
139. ONI Narrative, p. 73; Winslow (1982), p. 121; Hara, p. 75.
140. Marder, Jacobsen, and Horsfield, p. 68, which gives the time as 8:35 pm.
141. Toland (1961), p. 259.
142. ONI Narrative, p. 74.

Chapter 15

1. Bosscher, p. 610, n. 349.
2. Thomas, p. 203.
3. ONI Narrative, p. 72 and n. 65.
4. Van Oosten, p. 68. There is some dispute over whether Doorman was informed of the minefield and whether he informed his skippers. However, Parker (in Mullin, p. 209), who was at the February 26 conference in Soerabaja, specifically states they were told about the mines. Furthermore, given the speed with which the Allied sailors recognized the possibility of a mine mishap after the sinking of the *Jupiter* (see, e.g. Mullin, pp. 223 and 226), it seems obvious that they all knew about it. Van Oosten makes a point of saying that Doorman had been informed during the February 26 conference in Soerabaja, which also suggests that he informed his skippers.
5. USS *Houston*, EN3-11(CT) A8-21 Ser: 01139 September 9, 1945 (hereinafter "*Houston* log") Enclosure (a) (11) "Engagement Off Soerabaja February 27, 1942" says, "The Allied column of cruisers was zig-zagging but with no plan. All ships followed the motions of the *De Ruyter*, which was changing course without signal about 10 degrees to either side of the firing course about every ten or fifteen minutes."
6. Thomas, p. 207.
7. Hornfischer, p. 90.
8. Winslow (1984), p. 123.
9. O'Hara (2007), pp. 43–44; van Oosten, p. 53.
10. Schultz, p. 157.
11. *Perth* Report, p. 3,940.
12. Mullin, p. 226.
13. Winslow (1984), p. 121.
14. Winslow (1984), p. 121; Hornfischer, p. 89.
15. O'Hara (2007), p. 45.
16. Schultz, pp. 153–154.
17. O'Hara (2007), p. 45.
18. *Perth* Report, p. 3,940.
19. ONI Narrative, pp. 69–70.
20. Van Oosten, pp. 72–73, Womack, *The Dutch Naval Air Force Against Japan*, pp. 126–127.
21. One was to Helfrich asking for the location of the convoy. The second was in response to Binford's report that his destroyers had retired to Soerabaja.
22. Mullin, p. 226.
23. Van Oosten, pp. 72–73, Womack, *The Dutch Naval Air Force Against Japan*, pp. 126–127.
24. Collins Report, p. 138.
25. Schultz, p. 158.
26. Winslow (1982), p. 122: Winslow (1984), p. 208.
27. Morison (1948), p. 356, has one version of this signal. ONI Narrative, p. 74 has the other version as JUPITER TORPEDOED.
28. Mullin, p. 226.
29. ONI Narrative, p. 74.
30. Precisely how many were rescued remains disputed. Gill, p. 614, says, "About one-third of her complement

got ashore; one third were captured by the Japanese; and the remainder were lost." Gill notes that those captured were done so the following evening during a sweep by the *Ashigara* and *Myoko*. The ONI Narrative, pp. 74–75, n. 68 says, "A survivor says that 83 men, including 5 wounded, reached the beach, but in Soerabaja next day [Commander] Eccles heard that 214 survivors were at Toeban. This larger figure is probably correct, as under the circumstances most of the crew should have reached shore safely. Probably 83 landed at a single point."

31. One survivor of the *De Ruyter* said that the cruiser actually "stopped" to pick up the survivors of the *Jupiter*; Mullin, p. 226. I have not been able to corroborate this statement.

32. Mullin, pp. 223 and 226.

33. Van Oosten, p. 68.

34. Van Oosten, pp. 68–69; Womack, *The Dutch Naval Air Force Against Japan*, p. 197 n. 33.

35. Schultz, p. 158. His is the only source to give an exact course. Most sources say only that the column headed "north" or "in a northerly direction." The ONI Narrative seems to assume a course of due north but does not explicitly say so. Other sources dispute the course. Mullin, p. 226, says that the column turned northwest. Morison has the column headed north northwest for the remainder of the action, but does not give a course. Morison goes on to say that when Takagi's cruisers engaged Doorman later that night, they were "almost parallel," but all sources seem to agree that the Japanese were headed due north. Van Oosten has them turning due north then at some unspecified point in time turning slightly northwest, but again does not give a course. Dull, p. 85, uses van Oosten's figures. I am using Schultz's figures, backed up by the ONI Narrative, mostly for simplicity, but keep in mind that the column was also zigzagging. It is possible their zigzagging 10 degrees from the base course accounts for the reported differences in course. See *Houston* Log Enclosure (a)(11) "Engagement off Soerabaja, February 27, 1942."

36. Schultz, p. 157.

37. Schultz, p. 159.

38. Kroese, pp. 89–90.

39. The survivors of the *Houston*, disputing the survivors of all the other ships and even the ONI Narrative, have consistently maintained that the order of ships in the column was *De Ruyter*, *Houston*, *Perth*, and *Java*. See, e.g. *Houston* Log, Enclosure (a)(9) "Partial Log as Kept by Survivors"; Winslow (1984), p. 123. But Kroese's story would seem to conclusively show the order of the Allied cruisers as they passed by the survivors: "The Dutchman, the Australian, The American and at last another Dutchman." – i.e. in front-to-back order the *De Ruyter*, *Perth*, *Houston*, and *Java*. The survivors were in the perfect position to watch the ships as they passed by, one by one. It is possible that they were mistaken in the identities of the ships; Kroese's *The Dutch Navy at War* hints at this possibility, with one of his illustrations by J. H. Hoowij (reproduced in photographs section) showing the Allied cruisers passing by the *Kortenaer* survivors. The caption describes the order of ships as *De Ruyter*, *Perth*, *Houston*, and *Java*. Yet the picture appears to show the second cruiser in the column having a tall, tripod mast, which was a characteristic not of the *Perth* but of the *Houston*.

40. Morison (1948), p. 357.

41. Some, mainly English-speaking, sources say that the *Perth*'s Captain Waller ordered the *Encounter* to pick up the survivors. Other, mainly Dutch sources, assert that it was Admiral Doorman. The ONI Narrative, p. 75, sidesteps the issue by stating that the *Encounter* "was ordered" to pick them up. Hornfischer, p. 91, says the *Encounter* "stopped" to pick them up but adds "on whose authority is unclear." The most logical explanation is that both versions of events are true.

42. Waller's *Perth* Report makes no mention of such a signal from Doorman, but such a signal had to come.

43. The radio log of the *John D. Ford* paraphrases a voice message as " … pick up survivors we just passed in a boat." *Ford* Report, Enclosure (B) "Report of Battle of Java Sea, forwarding of: Extracts from radio log 26 February to 1 March 1942." The sender is unidentified; the intended recipients were listed as two British ships, which Bosscher identifies as, oddly, the *Electra* and the *Jupiter*; Bosscher, p. 612 n. 379. There was undoubtedly more to the message, giving at least the *Kortenaer* survivors' location. With the voice radios on the *De Ruyter* and the *Houston* out of commission and the *Java* at the other end of the column, this voice message could only have come from the *Perth*.

44. For reference, see *Houston* Log, Enclosure (a)(11) "Engagement off Soerabaja, February 27, 1942" stating the Japanese may have been marking the column's course by use of a "float light with battery and bulb."

45. Gill, p. 615; O'Hara. *The U.S. Navy Against the Axis: Surface Combat 1941–1945*, pp. 43–44.

46. Messimer (1985), p. 268.

47. Womack, *The Dutch Naval Air Force Against Japan*, p. 126; Messimer (1985), p. 268.

48. Womack, *The Dutch Naval Air Force Against Japan*, p. 126.
49. In Kroese's *The Dutch Navy at War*, J. H. Hoowij's illustration of the cruisers passing the *Kortenaer* survivors shows the forward guns of the *De Ruyter* trained to starboard.
50. ONI Narrative, p. 75.
51. ONI Narrative, p. 75. The radio log of the *John D. Ford* shows an almost identical message "BT target on port, four points, VA." *Ford* Report, Enclosure (B). The origin and intended recipients are unknown. This may have been the *Perth* providing a voice message for the *Java* and other ships in the vicinity.
52. Cooper Report, Enclosure (B). "Four points" is a reference to the 32-point compass rose, traditionally used in maritime navigation for both true and relative bearings. One point is equal to 11.25 degrees, thus four points equals 45 degrees and eight points equals 90 degrees.
53. Dull, p. 84; Tully, "Naval Alamo."
54. Hara, p. 76. It must be pointed out that Hara actually indicates that Takagi ordered the 5th Cruiser Division to slow down after it had reversed course and headed north. This does not make sense. Other reports give the impression of a running gun battle that lasted some 20 minutes, and the proposed torpedo firing solutions that the Japanese ultimately used involved a partial stern chase of the Allied cruisers. It was not an ideal solution and further suggests that Takagi had to catch up with the Allied column.
55. Winslow (1984), p. 123. Starshells are intended to reveal a target by backlighting it, but in order to silhouette a target a starshell needs to burst behind it.
56. *Perth* Report, p. 3,940. The evidence disagrees as to when the exchange of starshells occurred, whether it was before or after the 5th Cruiser Division reversed course. I have decided to go with before the reversal of course, on the logic that it was common practice when making first contact with the enemy at night to try to illuminate them.
57. Hornfischer, p. 91.
58. Hara, p. 74; Marder, Jacobsen, and Horsfield, p. 67.
59. *The Imperial Japanese Navy Page* www.combinedfleet.com lists the top speed of the *Myoko*-class cruisers as 34 knots. No specific speed is given for the ABDA cruisers, but Kroese, p. 89, quotes survivors of the *Kortenaer* as saying the cruiser column passed them at "top speed." Lenton, p. 11, lists the *De Ruyter*'s top speed as 32 knots and, p. 9, the *Java*'s top speed as 31 knots. "Top speed" in naval jargon does not necessarily always mean the fastest the engines can go, but given Doorman's warnings about the slowness of the *Kortenaer*, it is probably safe to assume the Combined Striking Force was running at a speed of at least 30 knots. If the 5th Cruiser Division was trying to catch up with the Combined Striking Force, the *Nachi* and *Haguro* had to be running at or near their top speed, likely 32–34 knots. The Japanese apparently pulled just about even with the Allied column after about 20 minutes. For a 20-minute chase the Japanese could have knocked more than a mile off the range.
60. I am indebted to a certain anonymous commenter who pointed me in the direction of the *Haguro*'s after-action report that stated she had been some 3,000–4,500yd behind the *Nachi*, which is much further than typical Japanese dispositions. Very few accounts mention the interval between the *Nachi* and *Haguro* at all, so I have only been able to partially confirm it, based on the differences in the firing solutions as described for both ships, which are discussed more fully below.
61. Toland (1961), p. 261; Gill, p. 615; Thomas, p. 211. Sources do not agree as to which direction the Japanese cruisers turned. I have gone with Dull, p. 85; and Gill, p. 615.
62. Australian diver and photojournalist Kevin Denlay, who dove the sunken wrecks of the *De Ruyter* and *Java* as part of an expedition from the Southeast Asian wreck-diving ship MV *Empress* in December 2002, found and photographed the *Java*'s portside guns pointing "defiantly upwards." This position strongly suggests that the *Java* continued to train her guns on the Japanese cruisers at her maximum range. Kevin Denlay, "Cruisers for Breakfast," *Sportdiving Magazine*, 2003, pp. 17–19.
63. "*Houston* Log," Enclosure (a)(11) "Engagement Off Soerabaja February 27, 1942."
64. ONI Narrative, p. 76.
65. Tully, "Naval Alamo."
66. Marvin Sholar, a US Navy signalman who had been assigned to the *De Ruyter* as a communications liaison, said that Doorman "suspected another torpedo attack and … turned away." Mullin, p. 227. There is no agreement as to the firing solution used by the Japanese. Waller's *Perth* Report says only that the Japanese ships were "a long way off." Morison (1948), p. 357, says the torpedoes were fired "when the two columns were almost parallel, 8,000 yards apart." Gill cites one Japanese report as saying 10,000m (10,936yd), adding that the torpedoes struck "after ten or fifteen minutes, the time estimated for them to reach their targets." Gill

also cites another, "more detailed Japanese report" as stating: "00.53 torpedoes started being fired (*Nachi* 8, *Haguro* 4) shooting angle 80 degrees, distance 9.5 kilometers" (10,389yd). Hara, p. 76, whose figures were later used by Hornfischer, says the solution was shooting angle 60 degrees at 10,000m. Though usually reliable, Hara's figures here must be questioned as he would have gotten this information secondhand because he himself was commanding the *Amatsukaze* during the battle. Additionally, 60-degree firing angle, while acceptable, would have had the torpedoes chasing the Allied ships northward somewhat. Thanks to the information provided by the anonymous commenter mentioned earlier, what seems to have happened is the *Nachi*, having apparently pulled even with the *De Ruyter* by this time, used the firing angle of 80 degrees and the *Haguro*, owing to her having dropped back, used the firing angle of 60 degrees. This is a supposition with only partial confirmation but it happens to fit the known facts. It would explain the varied reports on the Japanese side. Helfrich, p. 422, does not give the firing angle but lists two radically different (and ridiculously short) ranges for the *Nachi* (4,500m = 4,920yd) and *Haguro* (7,500m = 8,200yd). *The Maru Special: Japanese Naval Operations in WWII*, #95 (1985), p. 58, has a diagram of this last phase of the Battle of the Java Sea that shows two different torpedo firing angles that comport with the 60- and 80-degree solutions. Oddly, the detailed engagement report for the 5th Cruiser Division (listed as the "5th Squadron" in the records of the Japan Center for Asian Historical Records) shows a firing angle of approximately 135 degrees.

67. Takagi may not have had much choice due to his lavish use of his 8in ammunition. Hara, p. 78, states that at the end of the battle the *Nachi* had only 70 8in shells left. Eric Lacroix and Linton Wells II, *Japanese Cruisers of the Pacific War* (Annapolis: Naval Institute Press, 1997), p. 298, appear to disagree, noting that for the Battle of the Java Sea, the *Nachi* and *Haguro*, each with a supply of about 1,300 8in shells, fired 845 and 774 shells, respectively.

68. The 90-degree turn suggests that at least the *Nachi* had pulled even with the *De Ruyter* by this time.

69. Pretty much all histories, either in narrative or in map form, have the Combined Striking Force at this point remaining in column and executing a "column turn" or what Morison calls a "column movement" – basically a follow-the-leader move in which each ship turns at the same point on the water and into the same direction as the ship in front of it. The ONI's diagram illustrating this portion of the action follows this scenario. However, what actually seems to have happened is a "line turn," a "simultaneous turn," because ideally all the ships are supposed to turn simultaneously; an "echelon turn" as Jonathan Parshall and Anthony P. Tully, *Shattered Sword: The Untold Story of the Battle of Midway* (Washington, DC: Potomac, 2005), p. 346 describe such a maneuver; or what Morison (1948), p. 347, n. 11, simply calls a "turn" – each ship turning in the same direction simultaneously or as close to simultaneously as they can manage. Obviously, this represents a major change in the accepted narrative, but it fits both the known facts and tactical doctrine. The full explanation comes in my previous article on the subject, "A Turn Too Far: Reconstructing the End of the Battle of the Java Sea," *Military History Online*, www.militaryhistoryonline.com, April 3, 2011.

70. Winslow (1984), p. 124.

71. The ONI Narrative and most subsequent illustrations of this action show the *Java* turning separately from the other three cruisers. Why the *Java* would have turned separately has never been explained and on its face does not seem to make sense. It only makes sense if all four cruisers turned separately.

72. Tully, "Naval Alamo"; Van Oosten, p. 116, Bob Hackett and Sander Kingsepp, "IJN NACHI; Tabular Record of Movement," *Imperial Japanese Navy Page*, www.combinedfleet.com, retrieved November 18, 2013.

73. Mullin, p. 224.

74. Hornfischer, p. 92.

75. Hornfischer, p. 92.

76. Denlay, pp. 17 and 20.

77. Koppen, *The Battle of the Java Sea*, DVD.

78. Jan Visser, "Java."

79. Koppen, *The Battle of the Java Sea*, DVD.

80. Koppen, *The Battle of the Java Sea*, DVD.

81. Mullin, p. 226.

82. Winslow (1982), p. 210.

83. *Houston* Log, Enclosure (b): "The Wartime Cruise of the U.S.S. *Houston*."

84. ONI Narrative, p. 76; Tully, "Naval Alamo." Sholar said the *De Ruyter* was hit "as we were turning back"; Mullin, p. 227. The *De Ruyter*'s turn here is rarely even referenced, and I have not found a reason suggested for this turn. If one accepts the premise of a line turn, then a likely reason becomes apparent: to reform the column.

85. This is a supposition that happens to fit the facts and the scenario, but I must admit to finding no hard

evidence to support it. Doorman and his staff were well aware of torpedoes in the area and had a rough idea of their track. He would not have knowingly turned the *De Ruyter* into their firing track. The *Houston* had seen torpedoes pass her. The *De Ruyter* may have as well. For Doorman to have turned the cruiser in the very tight timeline provided by the known facts, they likely saw the *Nachi*'s torpedoes pass and guessed the *Haguro* had a similar firing solution with similar timing.

86. Mullin, pp. 226–227. Denlay, pp. 16 and 19, photographed and described the wreck of the *De Ruyter* with her forward guns pointing to starboard.

87. ONI Narrative, p. 76. This information makes it possible to calculate the *De Ruyter*'s heading when she was hit. If the Japanese report (quoted by Gill) of an 80-degree firing angle is used, the *De Ruyter* would have been heading 125 degrees True. If Hara's 60-degree figure, the solution likely used by the *Haguro*, is used, the *De Ruyter* was on a heading of 105 degrees True.

88. Klemen, "The Conquest of Java Island, March 1942," *Forgotten Campaign: The Dutch East Indies Campaign 1941–1942*, (offline but cached) http://www.dutcheastindies.webs.com/index.html, retrieved August 19, 2008.

89. Tully, "Naval Alamo." Denlay, p. 18, photographed the *De Ruyter*'s wheel still showing a starboard turn.

90. Klemen, "The Conquest of Java Island, March 1942."

91. Van Oosten, p. 116.

92. Mullin, p. 227.

93. Jan Visser, "De Ruyter (I) History."

94. Winslow (1984), p. 124, (1982), pp. 209–210.

95. Thomas, p. 212; Hoyt (1976), p. 256.

96. Koppen, *The Battle of the Java Sea*, DVD.

97. Klemen, "The Conquest of Java Island, March 1942."

98. Winslow (1984), p. 124, (1982), pp. 209–210. The *Houston* does not seem to have had a major problem avoiding the *De Ruyter*. The *Houston* Log, Enclosure (b), "The Wartime Cruise of the U.S.S. *Houston*", states that the *Houston* "had to swerve very sharply else we would have hit her." But aside from that blurb, none of the *Houston* survivors mention any particularly violent or sudden maneuvers to avoid the *De Ruyter*. The *Perth* Report, p. 3,940, says that the *Houston* headed out to starboard. Schultz, p. 160, quotes a survivor as saying, "The *De Ruyter* was ahead of us and slightly to our left" when she was hit. Schultz, p. 61, also quotes a survivor as saying, "We saw the tracks of torpedoes astern of us. They just went harmlessly on by." Both statements put the *Houston* to starboard of the *De Ruyter* and not in column. Winslow says that the *De Ruyter* had changed course to starboard and "[T]he *Houston* was about to follow when the flagship was hit." The ONI Narrative, p. 76, merely says the *Houston* "turned out of column to starboard." However, this version of events is contradicted by the ONI Narrative's own chart, which shows that neither the *Houston* nor the *Perth* had any reason for violent maneuvers to avoid the *De Ruyter* because the Dutch cruiser was not in their path. In fact, according to the ONI chart, the *Houston* would have had a more difficult turn to starboard. Notice here that none of these descriptions mentions where the *Perth* was when the *De Ruyter* was hit, even though if they were still in column the *Perth* would have been right ahead of the *Houston* and at least partially obstructing her view. Apparently, the *Houston* had an unobstructed view of the *De Ruyter* when the Dutch cruiser was hit, while the *Perth* was somewhere to port. The temporary loss of night vision due to the explosions of the *Java* and *De Ruyter* may have caused the *Houston* to lose track of the *Perth* in the darkness. Combine this with the near-collision later on as the *Perth* was passing the *Houston* and it is easy to see why the survivors of the *Houston* became convinced that they were immediately behind the *De Ruyter*.

99. *Perth* Report, p. 3,940. Waller's exact words are, "I just managed to miss her by the use of full helm and one engine stopped." In his own report, Collins, p. 3,938, clarifies by stating the *Perth* "avoided the blazing wreck by the use of full port rudder and one engine." The assumption seems to be that the *Perth* had to use these maneuvers to avoid plowing into the *De Ruyter*'s stern from the back, but neither Waller nor Collins actually says that. Accepting the premise of a line turn presents a much more believable scenario. The *De Ruyter* would have presented her stern jutting northwest toward the *Perth*. What seems to have happened is that the *Perth* was in danger of running into the *De Ruyter*'s stern from the side and, given her high rate of speed, possibly shearing it off. This required the *Perth* to make a very difficult turn to port, as Collins describes, which was northeast, as the ONI chart shows.

100. Hornfischer, p. 92.

101. Hara, p. 76.

102. Hara, p. 76.

103. This scenario is based on the circumstantial evidence of Takagi's northeast turn, but it is also deductive. If one accepts the premise of a line turn, the *Perth* turning northeast to avoid the *De Ruyter* would have been between the Dutch cruiser and the Japanese, and would have been silhouetted by the fires of the blazing wreck.

104. *De Ruyter* survivor Jaap Hodgeboom states, "In the distance we saw the Australian cruiser Perth turning around and disappear into the darkness." Elliot E. Coley, *Intelligence Operations at the Battle of the Java Sea* (Xlibris, 2009), p. 249.

105. Bosscher, p. 291.

106. One of the few historians to acknowledge it is Hoyt (1976), p. 258.

107. *Perth* Report, p. 3,940.

108. Morison (1948), p. 357. Morison states that the *Perth* and *Houston* had "separated, hoping to shake off the tracking enemy planes." But this is incorrect. By this time there were no Japanese aircraft aloft tracking the cruisers. Additionally, the cruisers were actually forced to separate by their maneuvers, especially those of the *Perth*, to avoid the *De Ruyter*.

109. Winslow (1984), p. 124–125; Schultz, p. 161, quotes a *Houston* survivor as saying, "We just barely missed her stern by about two feet." This incident is usually associated (as both Winslow and Schultz do) with the *Perth*'s maneuvers to avoid the *De Ruyter*, in part because Captain Rooks was trying to avoid torpedoes, but because that incident had the *Perth* ahead of the *Houston* while this incident had the *Perth* coming up from behind the *Houston*, this incident must have happened much later, after the *Houston* had passed the *Perth* as both cruisers had split up to avoid the *De Ruyter*. At this point in the battle, there were no Japanese torpedoes in the water. False sightings are not uncommon in war.

110. Koppen, *The Battle of the Java Sea*, DVD.

111. *Perth* Report, pp. 3,940–3,941.

112. Gill, p. 616. Helfrich would also add that "the decision of the captain of the Perth is even more regrettable as, after all, both cruisers did meet their end. Probably on the night of 27th–28th February they would have sold their lives at greater cost to the enemy." But these events are detailed in a later chapter.

113. Gill, p. 616.

114. O'Hara (2007), p. 44.

115. Hara, p. 78.

116. Hara, p. 78.

117. Lacroix and Wells, p. 298.

118. Winslow (1984), p. 125.

119. Winslow (1984), p. 125.

120. *Houston* Log, Enclosure (a)(9): "Partial log as kept by Survivors (of the USS *Houston*)."

121. Schultz, p. 203.

122. Adriaan Kannegieter, George Visser, and Jan Visser (trans.), "The Story of De Ruyter survivors, the flagship of Admiral Doorman, February 1942," *Forgotten Campaign: The Dutch East Indies Campaign 1941–1942* (offline but cached), http://www.dutcheastindies.webs.com/index.html, retrieved August 19, 2008.

123. Koppen, *The Battle of the Java Sea*, DVD.

124. Koppen, *The Battle of the Java Sea*, DVD.

125. Klemen, "The Conquest of Java Island, March 1942; Bernard Edwards, *Japan's Blitzkrieg: The Allied Collapse in the East 1941–42* (Barnsley, UK: Pen & Sword Maritime, 2006), p. 72.

126. Koppen, *The Battle of the Java Sea*, DVD.

127. Messimer (1985), p. 285.

128. Hornfischer, p. 94.

129. Hornfischer, p. 94.

130. Visser, "De Ruyter (I) History."

Chapter 16

1. Koppen, *The Battle of the Java Sea*, DVD.

2. *Ford* Report, Enclosure (B).

3. Toland (1961), p. 260.

4. Michel, pp. 71–72.

5. Toland (1961), p. 263. Binford's quote is inaccurate in that there were five ships, rather than the four he mentions.

6. J. A. Collins, "Report by Commodore Commanding China Force, 27th March, 1942," in "Battle of the Java Sea, 27th February, 1942," *Supplement to the London Gazette*, Tuesday, July 6, 1948 (hereinafter "Collins Report"), p. 3,939.
7. Schultz, p. 167.
8. Ronald McKie, *Proud Echo* (London: Robert Hale, 1953), p. 2.
9. Schultz, p. 165.
10. Winslow (1984), pp. 128–129.
11. Hornfischer, p. 99.
12. ONI Narrative, pp. 76–77; Gill, p. 615.
13. ONI Narrative, p. 77; Hara, pp. 66–67.
14. Collins Report, p. 3,939.
15. Shores, Cull, and Izawa (1993), p. 247.
16. Shores, Cull, and Izawa (1993), p. 249; Winslow (1984), pp. 131–132.
17. Winslow (1984), p. 129.
18. Schultz, pp. 167–168.
19. Mullin, pp. 229–230.
20. Hornfischer, p. 96; Carlton, p. 438.
21. McKie, p. 3.
22. Hornfischer, pp. 97–98.
23. Hornfischer, p. 98.
24. Winslow (1984), p. 130.
25. Schultz, p. 167.
26. Hornfischer, p. 98; Gill, p. 618.
27. Roscoe (1949), p. 83; Winslow (1984), p. 124.
28. Roscoe (1949), p. 83; Mullin, p. 227.
29. Gordon, p. 59.
30. Kroese, pp. 90–91.
31. Shores, Cull, and Izawa (1993), pp. 242–243; Sakai, Martin, and Saito, pp. 95–96.
32. Hackett, Kingsepp, and Cundall; "IJN Patrol Boat No. 106: Tabular Record of Movement."
33. Shores, Cull, and Izawa (1993), pp. 243–246
34. Toland (1961), pp. 263–264.
35. ONI Narrative, p. 78.
36. Toland (1961), p. 264.
37. Mullin, p. 230.
38. Mullin, p. 230.
39. ONI Narrative, p. 78, has Helfrich ordering the *Exeter* and her escorts to Tjilatjap, as does the Glassford Report, p. 55, one of the ONI Narrative's sources. But in his report, p. 3,944, Gordon says they were ordered to Colombo, Ceylon. Helfrich himself, p. 429, is emphatic that the *Exeter*'s loss of speed rendered her unfit for further combat operations and thus he ordered her to Colombo. He also says that the *Exeter* needed destroyer escort into the Indian Ocean. Interestingly, he does not say to where he directed the destroyers; Helfrich's comments hint that the destroyers had a separate destination once the *Exeter* was safely in the Indian Ocean. I have thus gone with Helfrich because of the corroboration by Gordon.
40. Mullin, p. 230.
41. ONI Narrative, p. 79.
42. Michel, p. 73.
43. Marder, Jacobsen, and Horsfield, p. 73.
44. Gordon, p. 60.
45. *Exeter* Report, pp. 3,944–3,945.
46. Mullin, p. 231.
47. Mullin, p. 231.
48. Gordon Report, pp. 3,944–3,945.
49. Marder, Jacobsen, and Horsfield, p. 73.
50. Quotations from Schultz, p. 171.
51. McKie, p. 5.
52. McKie, p. 5.

53. McKie, p. 4; Carlton, pp. 443–444.
54. Hornfischer, p. 102.
55. Winslow (1984), p. 132.
56. Carlton, p. 438.
57. Glassford Report, p. 53.
58. Carlton, p. 438.
59. Schultz, pp. 168–169; Winslow (1984), p. 131.
60. Winslow (1984), p. 132.
61. Schultz, p. 169.
62. Schultz, p. 169.
63. Schultz, p. 169.
64. Kathryn Spurling, *Cruel Conflict: The Triumph and Tragedy of HMAS* Perth (Kindle Edition) (Sydney, Auckland, London, and Cape Town: New Holland, 2008), l. 2,825.
65. Winslow (1984), p. 132.
66. Winslow (1984), p. 132.
67. Gill, pp. 618–619.
68. McKie, p. 5.
69. McKie, p. 6.
70. McKie, p. 14.
71. Carlton, p. 446.
72. McKie, pp. 20–23.
73. Winslow (1984), p. 133.

Chapter 17

1. Except where noted otherwise, the details of Dewey's sortie come from Carlton, pp. 439–441.
2. Winton, pp. 21–22.
3. Winslow (1984), pp. 131–132.
4. Shores, Cull, and Izawa (1993), pp. 246–247.
5. Sergeant Dewey is allegedly not the only one to have spotted the Western Invasion Convoy. Hornfischer, p. 112, says that on the afternoon of February 28, while the *Perth* and *Houston* were docked at Tanjoeng Priok, the *Hobart* of the Western Striking Force "had spotted the Western Attack Group idling to the north near Banka Island. But the Australian light cruiser's report never got past the Authorities in [Bandoeng]." It is difficult to reconcile this statement with Australia's official history, in which Gill, p. 617, says that the *Hobart* never spotted Japanese ships and in fact had exited the Soenda Strait into the Indian Ocean at around 9:00 am.
6. Winslow (1984), pp. 131–132; Hornfischer, pp. 112–113.
7. Carlton, p. 446.
8. Marder, Jacobsen, and Horsfield, p. 71; Jan Visser, "'Abandon Ship!' The Sunda Strait Battle, February–March 1942" *Forgotten Campaign: The Dutch East Indies Campaign 1941–1942* (website offline but cached), retrieved June 1, 2012; Helfrich, pp. 428–430.
9. Hornfischer, p. 106.
10. Carlton, p. 446.
11. Winslow (1984), p. 134.
12. McKie, p. 32.
13. There are several versions of this sequence, all with minor differences. This is amalgamated from Carlton, pp. 446–447, and McKie, p. 32. "Rattles" is a Royal Navy term for "alarm."
14. *Houston* Log, Enclosure (a)(9): "Partial Log as Kept by Survivors," Schultz, p. 174.
15. Winslow (1984), p. 135.
16. Winslow (1984), p. 134.
17. Spurling, l. 2,941; Hornfischer, p. 110.
18. O'Hara (2007), p. 50.
19. O'Hara, p. 50; Vincent P. O'Hara, "Battle of Sunda Strait 28 Feb.–1 March, 1942," *Thunder of the Guns: Battles of the Pacific War*, http://www.microworks.net/pacific/battles/, retrieved March 29, 2012.
20. Hara, p. 77, insists the *Perth* and *Houston* were somehow missed by the scout planes.
21. O'Hara (2007), p. 50.

22. Hornfischer, p. 110.
23. Carlton, p. 447.
24. O'Hara, "Battle of Sunda Strait 28 Feb.–1 March, 1942."
25. Morison (1948), p. 365.
26. *Houston* Log, Enclosure (a)(9): "Partial Log as Kept by Survivors."
27. Spurling, l. 2,941.
28. O'Hara (2007), p. 50.
29. O'Hara (2007), p. 51.
30. *Houston* Log, Enclosure (a)(9): "Partial Log as Kept by Survivors."
31. Hara, p. 77.
32. O'Hara, "Battle of Sunda Strait 28 Feb.–1 March, 1942."
33. O'Hara, p. 50.
34. O'Hara, p. 51.
35. Gill, p. 621.
36. *Houston* Log, Enclosure (a)(9): "Partial Log as Kept by Survivors."
37. O'Hara, p. 51.
38. O'Hara, pp. 51–52.
39. O'Hara, p. 52.
40. Winslow (1984), p. 136.
41. O'Hara (2007), p. 52.
42. O'Hara (2007), p. 53.
43. Tully, "Naval Alamo."
44. Winslow (1984), p. 138.
45. Morison (1948), p. 368; O'Hara (2007), p. 53.
46. Winslow (1984), p. 138.
47. Winslow (1984), p. 137.
48. O'Hara (2007), p. 53.
49. O'Hara, "Battle of Sunda Strait 28 Feb.–1 March, 1942."
50. McKie, p. 47;
51. Hornfischer, p. 123.
52. Carlton, p. 451.
53. O'Hara (2007), p. 53.
54. Shores, Cull, and Izawa (1992), p. 73. Inamura's transport was a specially designed army headquarters ship, and seems to have had a few aliases. As Gill, p. 620, n. 8, explains: "The real name of *Ryujo Maru* was *Akitsu Maru*. It was the practice of the Japanese to change the name of a ship for a particular operation as a security measure." But Hornfischer, p. 129, calls her the *Shinsu Maru*.
55. Gill, p. 620.
56. O'Hara (2007), p. 54.
57. O'Hara (2007), p. 54.
58. Gill, p. 621.
59. Toland (1961), p. 278, says a representative of the 5th Destroyer Flotilla was sent to apologize to General Inamura for torpedoing his transports.
60. Hara, p. 77.
61. Toland (1961), p. 268.
62. O'Hara (2007), p. 54.
63. Toland (1961), p. 278.
64. O'Hara, p. 55.
65. Hara, p. 77.
66. O'Hara, p. 54.
67. Hornfischer, p. 123.
68. Hornfischer, p. 114.
69. O'Hara, "Battle of Sunda Strait 28 Feb.–1 March, 1942."
70. Most versions of the *Perth*'s evacuation, based on McKie, p. 47, have Waller ordering abandon ship immediately after this torpedo hit. But the *Perth*'s senior survivor Lieutenant Commander J. A. Harper, in his report "Report on the Battle of Sunda Strait, 28 February – 1 March 1942" (dated October 1, 1945), also

found in McKie, p. 146 (Appendix II), insists this was *not* the case. Harper says that after yelling, "That's torn it," Waller "ordered to prepare to abandon ship," then "a few moments later" after another torpedo hit he "gave the order to abandon ship."

71. O'Hara, "Battle of Sunda Strait 28 Feb.–1 March, 1942."
72. Carlton, pp. 452–453.
73. Gill, p. 622.
74. Collins, p. 116.
75. Carlton, p. 459; Hornfischer, p. 127; Gill, p. 622.
76. O'Hara (2007), p. 54.
77. Winslow, p. 137.
78. Prados, p. 266.
79. Winslow, p. 138.
80. *Houston* Log, Enclosure (a)(9): "Partial Log as Kept by Survivors."
81. Winslow (1984), p. 138; Hornfischer, p. 136.
82. Hornfischer, p. 137.
83. O'Hara, "Battle of Sunda Strait 28 Feb.–1 March, 1942."
84. Hornfischer, p. 135.
85. Prados, p. 266; Hornfischer, p. 140.
86. Hornfischer, pp. 137–138.
87. Winslow (1984), p. 141; Schultz, pp. 189–190; Hornfischer, p. 138.
88. O'Hara (2007), p. 54.
89. See also *Houston* Log, Enclosure (a)(9): "Partial Log as Kept by Survivors."
90. O'Hara (2007), p. 55.
91. Gill, p. 621; Dull, p. 90.
92. Gill, p. 622.
93. Toland (1961), p. 271.

Chapter 18

1. Collins, p. 116; Carlton, p. 447.
2. Carlton, p. 447; Gill, p. 618.
3. Hornfischer, p. 108.
4. Van Oosten, p. 64, says the *Evertsen* had only been in commission since December 1, 1941 and that her crew had not had time for proper training. O'Hara, "Battle of Sunda Strait 28 Feb.–1 March, 1942" says of the *Evertsen*: "The Dutch captain didn't appear to fight very enthusiastically, beaching his command on Sebuku Besar. *Evertsen* had only been in commission since December, so her crew was not fully trained, for some reason had only two of her three boilers in operation and she certainly seemed – at best – an unlucky ship." Mackenzie J. Gregory, "Trying to stem the southward thrust of the Japanese threatening to engulf the Dutch East Indies in February/March of 1942. The Battle of Sunda Strait," Ahoy – Mac's Web Log, www.ahoy.tk-jk.net, retrieved April 22, 2013 says the *Evertsen* "seemed accident prone."
5. Dull, p. 73.
6. Gill, p. 617.
7. Winslow (1984), p. 132.
8. Van Oosten, p. 63.
9. ONI Narrative, p. 79; Hornfischer, p. 150.
10. Van Oosten, p. 63.
11. Van Oosten, pp. 63–64.
12. Van Oosten, p. 64.
13. MacKenzie, "Trying to Stem the Southward Thrust of the Japanese Threatening to Engulf the Dutch East Indies in February/March of 1942. The Battle of Sunda Strait."
14. ONI Narrative, p. 79.
15. "HNMS Evertsen (EV)," Uboat.net, www.uboat.net, retrieved June 10, 2012.
16. ONI Narrative, p. 81; Allyn Nevitt, "IJN Wakaba: Tabular Record of Movement," *Imperial Japanese Navy Page*," www.combinedfleet.com, retrieved September 21, 2012.
17. ONI Narrative, p. 80.
18. Alford, p. 216; Mullin, p. 241.

19. Mullin, p. 242.
20. Mullin, p. 244.
21. Alford, p. 216; Mullin, p. 241.
22. ONI Narrative, p. 80; Mullin, p. 241.
23. Mullin, p. 241. The ONI Narrative, p. 80, places the time the Japanese destroyer was sighted at 2:10 am, but both Alford and Mullin agree that 2:10 am was when the destroyer turned to parallel the Americans' course. The ONI Narrative has the range as 8,000yd but Alford, p. 216, gives a figure of 5,000yd. Alford seems to have misunderstood Mullin, from whom he draws part of his account of the destroyers' flight, as Mullin says the shooting started at a range of 5,000yd, a figure with which the ONI Narrative agrees.
24. ONI Narrative, p. 80; Alford, p. 216. Mullin, p. 241, has the time the two destroyers were sighted as 2:15 am and the time they formed the column as 2:20 am.
25. O'Hara (2007), p. 56; Nevitt, "IJN Wakaba: Tabular Record of Movement."
26. ONI Narrative, p. 80.
27. ONI Narrative, p. 80 and n. 75.
28. ONI Narrative, n. 75.
29. ONI Narrative, pp. 80–81.
30. Alford, p. 217; Mullin, p. 243.
31. Mullin, p. 243.
32. Mullin, p. 243.
33. ONI Narrative, p. 81.
34. Alford, p. 206.
35. O. L. Gordon, p. 61.
36. *Exeter* Report, p. 3,945.
37. O. L. Gordon, p. 60.
38. Michel, p. 73.
39. Welford C. Blinn, "Action Report – U.S.S. POPE (DD225), 1 March 1942," (hereinafter "*Pope* Report").
40. Mullin, p. 231.
41. *Exeter* Report, p. 3,947.
42. Mullin, p. 231.
43. Mullin, p. 231.
44. Mullin, p. 232; Exeter Report, p. 3,945.
45. *Exeter* Report, p. 3,945.
46. Gill, p. 622.
47. *Exeter* Report, p. 3,945.
48. This is a deduction based on the consistent positioning of the *Ashigara* and *Myoko* as north of the *Nachi* and *Haguro* and north of the *Exeter* during this action. Dull, p. 86; Gill, p. 623.
49. *Exeter Report, p. 3,945.*
50. *Exeter Report, p. 3,945.*
51. Dull, p. 87.
52. Dull, p. 87; *Exeter Report, p. 3,945.*
53. Dull, p. 86; O'Hara (2007), p. 59.
54. O. L. Gordon, p. 63.
55. *Exeter* Report, p. 3,945–3,946.
56. Michel, p. 75.
57. Koppen, *The Battle of the Java Sea*, DVD.
58. Hara, p. 78.
59. O'Hara (2007), p. 59.
60. Lacroix and Wells, p. 298.
61. O. L. Gordon, p. 65.
62. *Exeter Report, p. 3,945.*
63. *Exeter* Report, p. 3,945–3,946.
64. O. L. Gordon, p. 65.
65. O. L. Gordon, p. 63.
66. *Exeter* Report, p. 3,946.
67. O'Hara (2007), p. 60.

68. *Pope* Report.
69. O'Hara (2007), p. 60.
70. *Pope* Report.
71. O'Hara (2007), p. 60.
72. *Exeter* Report, p. 3,946.
73. *Exeter* Report, p. 3,946.
74. *Exeter* Report, p. 3,946.
75. O. L. Gordon, p. 67.
76. W. E. Johns and R. A. Kelly, *No Surrender* (London: W. H. Allen, 1989), p. 66.
77. Winslow (1982), p. 221.
78. *Exeter Report, p. 3,946.*
79. Gill, pp. 623–624; Allyn Nevitt, "IJN Inazuma: Tabular Record of Movement," *Imperial Japanese Navy Page* www.combinedfleet.com, retrieved August 8, 2012; Hackett and Kingsepp, "HIJMS Ashigara: Tabular Record of Movement," *Imperial Japanese Navy Page*, www.combinedfleet.com, retrieved April 10, 2012.
80. Tony Tully, "Loss of USS Pope" (statement of *Pope* survivor William Penninger), *WW2 Cruisers*, www.world-war.co.uk, retrieved March 2, 2012.
81. Tully, "Loss of USS Pope" (statement of Pope survivor William Penninger).
82. O. L. Gordon, p. 68.
83. Johns and Kelly, p. 68.
84. *Exeter* Report, p. 3,946; Nevitt, "IJN Inazuma: Tabular Record of Movement."
85. Gordon, p. 68. It would be more properly called mortal wounds, as naval archaeology has confirmed there were actually two torpedo hits on the cruiser, one amidships, another just forward of the "A" (forward) turret that nearly severed the bow, Nevitt, "IJN Inazuma: Tabular Record of Movement."
86. *Exeter* Report, p. 3,946.
87. Lacroix and Wells, p. 298.
88. Most histories give relatively short shrift to the sinking of the *Encounter* – often just a single sentence – so establishing precisely what happened to the destroyer from the few historians who have been thorough enough to delve into her fate is difficult. Winslow (1982), p. 223, mentions the ruptured suction lines but says they were to the fuel pumps. He also says that the rupture was just a mechanical breakdown and not due to battle damage. In fact, he mentions no hits from gunfire until Commander St. John Morgan ordered the *Encounter* abandoned and scuttled as "enemy shells pounded his stricken ship." Hackett and Kingsepp, "HIJMS Ashigara: Tabular Record of Movement," make no reference to blown suction lines and say that a near miss from an 8in salvo at an unspecified time caused unspecified damage to the *Encounter* that forced her scuttling. Vincent P. O'Hara ("Action South of Borneo: March 1, 1942," *Thunder of the Guns: Battles of the Pacific War*, www.microworks.net/pacific/battles/index.htm, retrieved March 29, 2012) says the *Encounter*'s suction line broke, which compromised her speed and maneuverability resulting in the 8in hit at 11:35 am. However, in his 2007 book *The U.S. Navy Against the Axis*, which is basically an update of his website *Thunder of the Guns*, O'Hara, p. 60, says that at 11:35 am "a [shell] splinter fractured a suction pipe … and disabled the forced lubrication system. Bearings overheated, and the ventilation system sucked smoke into the engine room, forcing its evacuation." I have gone with O'Hara's 2007 work as the most recent scholarship.
89. Hackett and Kingsepp, "HIJMS Ashigara: Tabular Record of Movement."
90. O'Hara (2007), p. 61.
91. Gill, p. 624; Nevitt, "IJN Inazuma: Tabular Record of Movement"; Hackett and Kingsepp, "HIJMS Ashigara: Tabular Record of Movement."
92. Mullin, p. 233.
93. *Pope* Report.
94. Winslow (1982), p. 223; Mullin, p. 233.
95. *Pope* Report.
96. *Pope* Report.
97. *Pope* Report; Winslow (1982), p. 223; Mullin, p. 233.
98. O'Hara, p. 61; Winslow (1982), p. 223.
99. Some sources indicate that a few of the Petes came from the seaplane tender *Mizuho*, but Hackett and Kingsepp, "IJN Seaplane Carrier Chitose: Tabular Record of Movement," *Imperial Japanese Navy Page*, www.combinedfleet.com, retrieved April 10, 2012, the latest scholarship on the matter, is specific that all ten came from the *Chitose*.

100. *Pope* Report.
101. Hackett and Kingsepp, "IJN Seaplane Carrier Chitose: Tabular Record of Movement."
102. Tully, "Loss of USS Pope" (statement of *Pope* survivor William Penninger).
103. *Pope* Report.
104. Mullin, p. 234.
105. *Pope* Report.
106. Tully and Casse, "IJN Ryujo: Tabular Record of Movement." Both the *Pope* Report and Mullin, p. 234, call the aircraft "Mitsubishi 97s." The Mitsubishi Type 97 was a land-based heavy bomber used by the Imperial Japanese Army. Their reference was intended for the Nakajima Type 97 Carrier Attack Plane, which was the "Kate" torpedo bomber.
107. Tully, "IJN Ryujo: Tabular Record of Movement."
108. Winslow (1982), p. 224.
109. *Pope* Report.
110. Alford, p. 209.
111. No one can seem to agree on precisely when the *Pope* sank. I have gone with O'Hara (2007), p. 61.
112. Alford, p. 211.
113. Alford, p. 211.

Chapter 19

1. Messimer (1983), p. 124.
2. Messimer (1983), pp. 123–124.
3. Glassford Report, p. 14.
4. Glassford Report, p. 31.
5. Glassford Report, p. 15.
6. Messimer (1983), p. 121; Paul Abernethy, "Action and Sinking of USS Pecos 1 March 1942" dated March 7, 1942 (hereinafter "*Pecos* Report"), p. 1. I have gone with Messimer and Abernethy over Glassford (Glassford Report, p. 16), who says the *Pecos* left Tjilatjap on February 25.
7. Glassford Report, p. 15.
8. Messimer (1983), pp. 121–122.
9. Messimer (1983), p. 122; Winslow (1982), pp. 165–166.
10. Messimer (1983), p. 122; *Pecos* Report, p. 3.
11. Messimer (1983), p. 122; *Pecos* Report, p. 1.
12. *Pecos* Report, p. 1; Messimer (1983), p. 125. Flying Fish Cove is sometimes called Fisherman's Cove.
13. Messimer (1983), pp. 122–123.
14. *Pecos* Report, p. 2. In his report Edwin M. Crouch ("USS EDSALL Record of Known Activities Between 26 February, 1942 and 1 March, 1942, dated May 21, 1942 (hereinafter "Crouch Report"), p. 7) says they came from the southeast.
15. *Pecos* Report, p. 2.
16. Messimer (1983), pp. 127–128.
17. Messimer (1983), p. 128.
18. Messimer (1983), pp. 128–129.
19. Crouch Report, p. 11. Kehn, p. 120, says the oil tanker was the *Belita*.
20. *Pecos* Report, p. 2.
21. Messimer (1983), p. 130.
22. *Pecos* Report, p. 2; Messimer (1983), p. 131.
23. Messimer (1983), pp. 131–132.
24. Messimer (1983), p. 132.
25. *Pecos* Report, p. 2.
26. Messimer (1983), p. 133.
27. Messimer (1983), p. 134; *Pecos* Report, p. 2.
28. Messimer (1983), p. 135.
29. Messimer (1983), p. 137.
30. Kehn, pp. 122–123; Hackett and Kingsepp, "IJN CHIKUMA: Tabular Record of Movement," *Imperial Japanese Navy Page*, www.combinedfleet.com, retrieved July 8, 2012.

31. Messimer (1983), p. 133; Kehn, pp. 122–123.
32. Messimer (1983), p. 137.
33. Messimer (1983), p. 133.
34. *Pecos* Report, p. 2.
35. Messimer (1983), p. 137.
36. Messimer (1983), p. 138. I have gone with Messimer over Abernethy (*Pecos* Report, p. 2), who says the first three bombs missed.
37. *Pecos* Report, p. 4.
38. Messimer (1983), p. 143.
39. *Pecos* Report, p. 2.
40. Messimer (1983), p. 142.
41. Messimer (1983), p. 144.
42. *Pecos* Report, Enclosure (B).
43. Messimer (1983), p. 145. Ikeda Masi is also known as Ikeda Masatake, Ikeda Masahiro, Ikeda Masayori, and, curiously, Ikeda Shoi. Kehn, p. 129.
44. Crouch Report, p. 12.
45. Messimer (1983), pp. 145–147; *Pecos* Report, p. 4.
46. Crouch Report, p. 12.
47. Messimer (1983), p. 141.
48. Messimer (1983), p. 144.
49. *Pecos* Report, p. 45; Messimer (1983), pp. 148–150; Kehn, p. 130.
50. Messimer (1983), pp. 151–153.
51. Messimer (1983), p. 154.
52. Messimer (1983), pp. 155–157.
53. Messimer (1983), pp. 157–159; Crouch Report, p. 5.
54. Messimer (1983), p. 159.
55. Messimer (1983), p. 159; Kehn, pp. 132–133.
56. Crouch Report, p. 12.
57. Messimer (1983), p. 160.
58. Abernethy Report, p. 4; Messimer (1983), p. 160.
59. Abernethy Report, pp. 3 and 5.
60. Messimer (1983), p. 163; Abernethy Report, Enclosure (B).
61. Kehn, pp. 132–133.
62. Messimer (1983), p. 163; *Pecos* Report, Enclosure (B).
63. Messimer (1983), pp. 168–169.
64. Messimer (1983), pp. 170–171; *Pecos* Report, p. 3.
65. Messimer (1983), pp. 177–178.
66. *Pecos* Report, p. 5.
67. Crouch Report, p. 16.
68. Messimer (1983), pp. 178–179; Crouch Report, p. 15.
69. Messimer (1983), pp. 157–159, 166; Crouch Report, pp. 11–12.
70. Messimer (1983), pp. 161 and 166.
71. Messimer (1983), p. 186; Crouch Report, p. 15.
72. Messimer (1983), p. 187; Crouch Report, p. 15.
73. Messimer (1983), p. 187.
74. Crouch Report, pp. 16–17.
75. Messimer (1983), pp. 190–191; ONI Narrative, p. 49.
76. Glassford Report, pp. 57–60.
77. Glassford Report, pp. 60–61; Collins, p. 117.
78. Glassford Report, p. 60.
79. Glassford Report, p. 61.
80. Shores, Cull, and Izawa (1993), p. 292.
81. Shores, Cull, and Izawa (1993), pp. 296–297. His last words allegedly were, "I'm going to change my socks"!
82. Shores, Cull, and Izawa (1993), pp. 295–302.
83. Craven and Cate, p. 398; Shores, Cull, and Izawa (1993), pp. 303–304.

84. Craven and Cate, p. 399.
85. Bartsch (2010), pp. 301–302.
86. Glassford Report, p. 34.
87. ONI Narrative, p. 50.
88. Glassford Report, p. 34.
89. Craven and Cate, p. 398.
90. Mullin, p. 249–250.
91. Bartsch (2010) pp. 286–287.
92. Bartsch (2010), p. 290.
93. Bartsch, p. 326, 425 n. 23; Jos Heyman, "NEI Aircraft in Australia," *ADF-SERIALS Australian & New Zealand Military Aircraft Serials & History*, http://www.adf-serials.com.au/research/nei.htm, retrieved May 23, 2013.
94. Lion Miles, Kelly Long, and Dixie Geary, "A Ship to Remember: USS Edsall (DD 219)," *USS Houston CA-30: The Galloping Ghost of the Java Coast*, www.usshouston.org, retrieved April 25, 2012.
95. Kehn, p. 236.
96. Kehn, p. 137; Hackett and Kingsepp, "IJN CHIKUMA: Tabular Record of Movement."
97. Kehn, p. 137; Miles, Long, and Geary, "A Ship to Remember: USS Edsall (DD 219)."
98. Messimer (1983), p. 123.
99. For full explanation of the evidence, see Kehn, pp. 139–143. The end of the *Edsall* is discussed in several sources, including O'Hara, pp. 62–63; Tully, "Naval Alamo"; Hackett and Kingsepp, "IJN CHIKUMA: Tabular Record of Movement"; and Miles, Long, and Geary, "A Ship to Remember: USS Edsall (DD 219)." Where there has been a direct conflict between these sources, I have gone with Kehn as the latest scholarship.
100. Kehn, pp. 143–144.
101. Kehn, p. 143 and 149.
102. Kehn, p. 144.
103. Kehn, p. 144.
104. Hackett and Kingsepp, "IJN CHIKUMA: Tabular Record of Movement." Miles, Long, and Geary, "A Ship to Remember: USS Edsall (DD 219)" say that a shell from the *Hiei* did hit the *Edsall* at 6:24 pm.
105. Kehn, pp. 144–145.
106. O'Hara (2007), p. 63.
107. Miles, Long, and Geary, "A Ship to Remember: USS Edsall (DD 219)."
108. Kehn, p. 145.
109. Kehn, pp. 145–47; 236.
110. Hackett and Kingsepp, "IJN CHIKUMA: Tabular Record of Movement."
111. Miles, Long, and Geary, "A Ship to Remember: USS Edsall (DD 219)."
112. Kehn, pp. 151–152.
113. Kehn, p. 147.
114. Kehn, pp. 150–151.
115. Kehn, p. 155; Miles, Long, and Geary, "A Ship to Remember: USS Edsall (DD 219)."
116. Miles, Long, and Geary, "A Ship to Remember: USS Edsall (DD 219)."
117. Kehn, p. 158.
118. Kehn, p. 157; Hackett and Kingsepp, "IJN CHIKUMA: Tabular Record of Movement."
119. Kehn, pp. 237–238.
120. Kehn, p. 158.
121. Kehn, p. 172.
122. Mullin, pp. 250–251, mentions the discovery of the graves. The remains were identified as F1 Sidney Amory, MM1 Horace Andrus, MM2 J. R. Cameron, MM3 Larry Vandiver, and F1 Donald Watters; Miles, Long, and Geary, "A Ship to Remember: USS Edsall (DD 219)." Kehn has subsequently speculated in his book *Blue Sea of Blood* that the execution was an organized effort to cover up the embarrassing ineptitude of *Kido Butai*. It has taken years of diligent research and effort by historians such as Kehn and family members of the crew to uncover the truth about the *Edsall*, her last stand, the heroic efforts of Joshua Nix and his crew, and their defiance in the face of certain death.
123. Blair, p. 186.
124. Holmes, p. 20.
125. Holmes, p. 20, "*Perch* (SS 176)," *United States Submarine Losses, World War II*, http://www.history.navy.mil/

library/online/sublosses/sublosses_main.htm, retrieved April 10, 2012; Hackett and Kingsepp, "Last Days of USS PERCH (SS-176)," *Imperial Japanese Navy Page*, www.combinedfleet.com, retrieved May 23, 2013.

126. Holmes, p. 20, "*Perch* (SS 176)."

127. Hackett and Kingsepp, "Last Days of USS PERCH (SS-176)" There has been some question as to the identity of the two destroyers that attacked the *Perch* on March 1. See, e.g. Allyn D. Nevitt, "IJN Amatsukaze: Tabular Record of Movement," *Imperial Japanese Navy Page*, www.combinedfleet.com, retrieved April 10, 2012; Allyn D. Nevitt, "IJN Hatsukaze: Tabular Record of Movement," *Imperial Japanese Navy Page*, www.combinedfleet. com, retrieved October 4, 2012; Allyn D. Nevitt, "IJN Minegumo: Tabular Record of Movement," *Imperial Japanese Navy Page*, www.combinedfleet.com, retrieved May 23, 2013; and Allyn D. Nevitt, "IJN Natsugumo: Tabular Record of Movement," *Imperial Japanese Navy Page*, www.combinedfleet.com, retrieved May 23, 2013. I have gone with Hackett and Kingsepp as the latest scholarship.

128. Blair, p. 188; Hackett and Kingsepp, "Last Days of USS PERCH (SS-176)."

129. Hackett and Kingsepp, "Last Days of USS PERCH (SS-176)."

130. Holmes, "*Perch* (SS 176)"; Hackett and Kingsepp, "Last Days of USS PERCH (SS-176)."

131. Holmes, "*Perch* (SS 176)"; Hackett and Kingsepp, "Last Days of USS PERCH (SS-176)."

132. Roscoe (1949), p. 98.

133. Holmes, "*Perch* (SS 176)"; Roscoe (1949), p. 98.

134. Holmes, "*Perch* (SS 176)"; Roscoe (1949), p. 98.

135. Holmes, "*Perch* (SS 176)"; Roscoe (1949), p. 99.

136. "K X."

137. Hackett and Kingsepp, "Last Days of USS PERCH (SS-176)"; Nevitt, tabular records of movement for IJN Amatsukaze, IJN Hatsukaze, IJN Minegumo, and IJN Natsugumo.

138. "K XVIII"; Hackett and Kingsepp, "IJN Patrol Boat No. 106: Tabular Record of Movement."

139. Hackett and Kingsepp, "IJN Patrol Boat No. 102: Tabular Record of Movement."

140. Lenton, p. 20.

141. "K X"; "K XIII"; "K XVIII"

142. "K XVIII"; "C.A.J. van Well Groeneveld."

143. Messimer (1985), p. 271.

144. Messimer (1985), p. 271.

145. Messimer (1985), p. 271; Glassford Report, p. 62.

146. Glassford Report, pp. 62–63.

147. Gill, p. 628.

148. Vincent P. O'Hara, "Other Engagements involving Forces fleeing Java: March 1–March 4, 1942," *Thunder of the Guns: Battles of the Pacific War*, http://www.microworks.net/pacific/battles/, retrieved March 29, 2012; Hackett and Kingsepp, "HIJMS ATAGO: Tabular Record of Movement," *Imperial Japanese Navy Page*, www.combinedfleet.com, retrieved July 8, 2012.

149. Hackett and Kingsepp, "HIJMS ATAGO: Tabular Record of Movement."

150. O'Hara, "Other Engagements involving Forces fleeing Java: March 1–March 4, 1942."

151. Tully, "Naval Alamo."

152. Details of the *Yarra's* last action come from Gill, pp. 629–630; and Stathi Paxinos, "The Mighty Minnow that Took on a Japanese Fleet," *The Age*, www.theage.com.au/articles/2004/04/22/1082616262661.html, April 23, 2004, retrieved October 13, 2012.

153. Figures for the *Yarra* come from H. T. Lenton, and J. J. Colledge, *British & Dominion Warships of World War II* (New York: Doubleday, 1968), p. 169. Figures for the *Kagero*-class destroyers *Arashi* and *Nowaki* come from Allyn Nevitt, "KAGERO Class Notes," Imperial Japanese Navy Page, www.combinedfleet.com, retrieved July 8, 2012.

154. Paxinos, "The Mighty Minnow that Took on a Japanese Fleet."

155. Gill, p. 632.

156. Glassford Report, pp. 11–12.

157. Winslow (1982), pp. 166–171.

158. Klemen, "The conquest of Java Island, March 1942."

Chapter 20

1. Messimer (1983), p. 190.

2.   Alford, pp. 239–240.
3.   Alford, p. 242.
4.   Alford, p. 242.
5.   Mullin, p. 254; Alford, p. 242–243.
6.   Mullin, p. 114.
7.   Alford, p. 243.
8.   1st endorsement, U.S. NAVAL FORCES SOUTHWEST PACIFIC, Operations, Action and Sinking of U.S.S. LANGLEY, period from February 22 to March 5, 1942 (CO LANGLEY File AP22/A16-3/gjp Serial C:01 of March 9, 1942).
9.   Messimer (1983), p. 193. Emphasis added.
10. Messimer (1983), p. 194.
11. *Edwards* Report.
12. Morison, (1948), pp. 310, 311 and 340.
13. Morison, (1948), p. 338.
14. Prados, 1995, p. 255.
15. Hoyt (1976), p. 258.
16. Marder, Jacobsen, and Horsfield, pp. 78–79.
17. Carlton, p. 423.
18. Mike Coppock, "The Battle of the Java Sea: A Fleet Wasted," *Sea Classics*, Sept. 2007.
19. Marder, Jacobsen, and Horsfield, p. 79.
20. Marder, Jacobsen, and Horsfield, pp. 77–78.
21. Fuller, p. 251.
22. Masanori Ito, Andrew Y. Kuroda (trans.), and Roger Pineau (trans.), *The End of the Imperial Japanese Navy*, Jove, 1984, pp. 177–179
23. Tully, "Naval Alamo."
24. The three carriers were the *Taiho*, *Shokaku*, and *Hiyo*, all sunk during the Battle of the Philippine Sea in June 1944.
25. Wilmott, p. 272.
26. May, pp. 206–207.

BIBLIOGRAPHY

Books

Alden, J., *US Submarine Attacks During World War II*, Naval Institute Press, 1989.

Alford, L., *Playing for Time: War on an Asiatic Fleet Destroyer*, Merriam Press, 2008.

Bartsch, W., *December 8, 1941: MacArthur's Pearl Harbor*, Texas A & M University Press, 2003.

Bartsch, W., *Doomed at the Start: American Pursuit Pilots in the Philippines, 1941–1942*, Texas A & M University Press, 1992.

Bartsch, W., *Every Day a Nightmare: American Pursuit Pilots in the Defense of Java, 1941–1942*, Texas A & M University Press, 2010.

Bell, C., *Churchill & Sea Power*, Oxford University Press, 2012.

Bergamini, D., *Japan's Imperial Conspiracy*, William Morrow & Co, 1971.

Bix, H., *Hirohito and the Making of Modern Japan*, Perennial, 2001.

Blair, C., *Silent Victory: The US Submarine War Against Japan*, Naval Institute Press, 1975.

Boer, P.C., *The Loss of Java*, National University of Singapore Press, 2011.

Bosscher, M., *De Koninklijke Marine in de Tweede Wereldoorlog*, Uitgeverij Van Wijnen, 1990.

Brereton, L., *The Brereton Diaries: The War in the Air in the Pacific, Middle East and Europe, 3 October 1941–8 May 1945*, William Morrow & Co, 1946.

Brown, D., *Warship Losses of World War Two*, Naval Institute Press, 1990.

Burton, J., *Fortnight of Infamy: The Collapse of Allied Airpower West of Pearl Harbor*, Naval Institute Press, 2006.

Cain, Lt Cdr T.J., *HMS Electra*, Futura, 1959.

Carlton, M., *Cruiser: The Life and Loss of HMAS* Perth *and Her Crew*, William Heinemann, 2010.

Chang, I., *The Rape of Nanking: The Forgotten Holocaust of World War II*, Penguin, 1998.

Churchill, W., *The Grand Alliance* (electronic edition), RosettaBooks, 2002.

Churchill, W., *The Hinge of Fate* (electronic edition), RosettaBooks, 2002.

Coley, E., Col., *Intelligence Operations at the Battle of the Java Sea*, Xlibris, 2009.

Colledge, J.J., *Ships of the Royal Navy: The Complete Record of all Fighting Ships of he Royal Navy From the Fifteenth Century to the Present*, Naval Institute Press, 1987.

Collins, V Adm Sir John, *As Luck Would Have It: The Reminiscences of an Australian Sailor*, Angus & Robertson, 1965.

Costello, J., *The Pacific War 1941–45*, Quill, 1982.

Craven, W.F., & Cate, J. L. *Army Air Forces in World War II: Vol. 1: Plans and Early Operations, January 1939 to August 1942*, University of Chicago Press, 1948.

Dull, P., *A Battle History of the Imperial Japanese Navy (1941–1945)*, Naval Institute Press, 1978.

Edmonds, W., *They Fought With What They Had: The Story of the Army Air Forces in the Southwest Pacific, 1941–1942*, Little, Brown & Co., 1951.

Edwards, B., *Japan's Blitzkrieg: The Allied Collapse in the East 1941–42*, Pen & Sword Maritime, 2006.

Evans, D., & Peattie, M., *Kaigun: Strategy, Tactics and Technology in the Imperial Japanese Navy 1887–1941*, Naval Institute Press, 1997.

Felton, M., *Slaughter at Sea: The Story of Japan's Naval War Crimes*, Pen & Sword, 2007.

Fuller, R., *Shokan: Hirohito's Samurai, Leaders of the Japanese Armed Forces, 1926–1945*, Arms & Armour, 1992.

Gill, G., *Australia in the War of 1939–1945, Series Two: Navy; Volume I: Royal Australian Navy 1939–1942*, Australian War Memorial, 1957.

Gillison, D., *Australia in the War of 1939–1945, Series Three: Air; Volume I: Royal Australian Air Force 1939–1942*, Australian War Memorial, 1962.

Gluck, C., & Graubard, S. (eds.), *Showa: The Japan of Hirohito*, Norton, 1992.

Goldstein, D. & Dillon, K. (eds.), *The Pacific War Papers: Japanese Documents of World War II*, Potomac, 2004.

Goldstein, D., & Dillon, K. (eds.), *The Pearl Harbor Papers: Inside the Japanese Plans*, Brassey's, 1993.

Gordon, J., *Fighting for MacArthur: The Navy and Marine Corps' Desperate Defense of the Philippines*, Naval Institute Press, 1984.

Gordon, O., *Fight It Out: The Epic Story of HMS Exeter's Struggle Against Overwhelming Odds Told By Her Captain*, William Kimber and Co., 1957.

Grose, P., *An Awkward Truth: The Bombing of Darwin February 1942*, Allen & Unwin, 2009.

Hack, K. & Blackburn, K. (eds.), *Did Singapore Have to Fall? Churchill and the Impregnable Fortress* (electronic edition), RoutledgeCurzon, 2004.

Hammond, J., *The Treaty Navy: The Story of the US Naval Service Between the World Wars*, Wesley/Trafford, 2001.

Hara, T., *Japanese Destroyer Captain*, Naval Institute Press, 1967

Helfrich, Lt Adm C.E.L., *Memoires van C.E.L. Helfrich: Eerste Deel de Maleise Barrière*, Elsevier, 1950.

Holmes, H., *The Last Patrol*, Wrens Park, 2001.

Hornfischer, J., *Ship of Ghosts: The Story of the USS* Houston, *FDR's Legendary Lost Cruiser, and the Epic Saga of Her Survivors*, Bantam, 2006.

Hough, R., *The Hunting of Force Z: The Sinking of the* Prince of Wales *and the* Repulse, Cassell, 1999.

Hoyt, E., *Japan's War: The Great Pacific Conflict*, Cooper Square Press, 2001.

Hoyt, E., *The Lonely Ships: The Life and Death of the US Asiatic Fleet*, David McKay, 1976.

Hoyt, E., *War in the Pacific, Volume I: The Triumph of Japan*, Avon, 1990.

Ito, M., Kuroda, A. (trans.) & Pineau, R. (trans.), *The End of the Imperial Japanese Navy*, Jove, 1984.

Johns, W.E., & Kelly, R.A., *No Surrender*, W.H. Allen, 1989.

Karig, Cdr W. & Kelley, Lt W., *Battle Report: Pearl Harbor to Coral Sea*, Farrarr & Rinehart, 1944.

Kehn, D.M. Jr., *A Blue Sea of Blood: Deciphering the Mysterious Fate of the USS* Edsall, Zenith, 2008.

Kroese, Lt. Cdr A., *The Dutch Navy at War*, Allen & Unwin, 1945.

Lacroix, E. & Wells, L., *Japanese Cruisers of the Pacific War*, Naval Institute Press, 1997.

Lamont-Brown, R., *Ships From Hell: Japanese War Crimes on the High Seas*, Sutton, 2002.

Langelo, Vincent A., *With All Our Might: The WWII History of the USS* Boise *(CL-47)*, Eakin, 2000.

Leasor, J., *Singapore: The Battle that changed the world* (electronic edition), James Leasor, 2011.

Lenton, H.T., *Navies of the Second World War: Royal Netherlands Navy*, Doubleday, 1968.

Lenton, H.T., & Colledge, J.J., *British & Dominion Warships of World War II*, Doubleday, 1968.

Leutze, J., *A Different Kind of Victory: A Biography of Admiral Thomas C. Hart*, Naval Institute Press, 1981.

Lundstrom, J.B., *The First South Pacific Campaign: Pacific Fleet Strategy December 1941–June 1942*, Naval Institute Press, 1976.

Lundstrom, J., *The First Team: Pacific Naval Air Combat from Pearl Harbor to Midway*, Naval Institute Press, 1990.

MacArthur, B., *Surviving the Sword: Prisoners of the Japanese in the Far East 1942–45*, Random House, 2005.

Manchester, W., *American Caesar: Douglas MacArthur 1880–1964* (electronic edition), Little, Brown & Co., 1978.

Marder, A., *Old Friends, New Enemies: The Royal Navy and the Imperial Japanese Navy, Vol. 1: Strategic Illusions, 1936–1941*, Clarendon Press, 1981.

Marder, A., Jacobsen, M. & Horsfield, J., *Old Friends, New Enemies: The Royal Navy and the Imperial Japanese Navy, Vol. 2: The Pacific War 1942–1945*, Clarendon Press, 1990.

Mawdsley, E., *December 1941: Twelve Days That Began a World War*, Yale University Press, 2011.

McIntyre, D., *The Rise & Fall of the Singapore Naval Base, 1919–1942*, Archon, 1979.

McKie, R., *Proud Echo*, Robert Hale, 1953.

Messimer, D., *In the Hands of Fate: The Story of Patrol Wing Ten: 8 December 1941–11 May 1942*, Naval Institute Press, 1985.

Messimer, D., *Pawns of War: The Loss of the USS* Langley *and the USS* Pecos, Naval Institute Press, 1983.

Michel, J., *Mr. Michel's War: From Manila to Mukden: An American Navy Officer's War With the Japanese*, Presidio Press, 1997.

Middlebrook, M., & Mahoney, P., *The Sinking of the* Prince of Wales *&* Repulse: *The End of the Battleship Era*, Leo Cooper, 2004.

Miller, E.S., *War Plan Orange: The U.S. Strategy to Defeat Japan 1897–1945*, Naval Institute Press, 1991.

Morison, S., *History of United States Naval Operations in World War II, Volume 3: The Rising Sun in the Pacific*, Castle, 1948.

Morison, S., *The Two-Ocean War: A Short History of the United States Navy in the Second World War*, Little, Brown; 1963.

Morton, L., *United States Army in World War II: The War in the Pacific – The Fall of the Philippines*, United States Army, 1953.

Mullin, J., *Another Six-Hundred*, J. Daniel Mullin, 1984.

Newpower, A., *Iron Men and Tin Fish: The Race to Build a Better Torpedo During World War II*, Naval Institute Press, 2006.

Nicholson, A., *Hostages to Fortune: Winston Churchill and the Loss of the* Prince of Wales *and* Repulse, Sutton, 2005.

O'Hara, V., *The U.S. Navy Against the Axis: Surface Combat 1941–1945*, Naval Institute Press, 2007.

Okumiya, M., Horikoshi, J., & Caidin, M., *Zero! The Story of Japan's Air War in the Pacific: 1941–45*, E.P. Dutton, 1956.

Paine, S.C.M., *The Wars For Asia 1911–1949*, Cambridge University Press, 2012.

Parkin, R., *Blood on the Sea: American Destroyers Lost in World War II*, Da Capo Press, 2001.

Peattie, M., *Sunburst: The Rise of Japanese Naval Air Power, 1909–1941*, Naval Institute Press, 2001.

Prados, J., *Combined Fleet Decoded*, Naval Institute Press, 1995.

Prange, G., *At Dawn We Slept: The Untold Story of Pearl Harbor*, Penguin, 1981.

Roscoe, T., *United States Destroyer Operations in World War II*, Naval Institute Press, 1953.

Roscoe, T., *United States Submarine Operations in World War II*, Naval Institute Press, 1949.

Roskill, S., *Churchill and the Admirals*, Pen & Sword, 2004.

Roskill, S., *The White Ensign: The British Navy at War, 1939–1945*, Naval Institute Press, 1960.

Russell of Liverpool, Baron E.F.L., *The Knights of Bushido: A History of Japanese War Crimes During World War II*, Skyhorse, 2008.

Sakai, S., Caidin, M., & Saito, F., *Samurai! The Rise and Fall of the Japanese Naval Air Force*, iBooks, 2001.

Schultz, D., *The Last Battle Station: the Saga of the USS* Houston, St. Martin's Press, 1985.

Sears, D., *Pacific Air: How Fearless Flyboys, Peerless Aircraft, and Fast Flattops Conquered the Skies and Won the War With Japan*, Da Capo Press, 2011.

Sherman, F., *Combat Command*, Bantam, 1982.

Shores, C., Cull, B., & Izawa, Y., *Bloody Shambles, Volumes I & II*, Grub Street, 1992/1993.

Sloan, B., *Undefeated: America's Heroic Fight for Bataan and Corregidor*, Simon & Schuster, 2012.

Spector, R., *Eagle Against the Sun: The American War With Japan*, Free Press, 1985.

Spector, R., *In the Ruins of Empire: The Japanese Surrender and the Battle for Postwar Asia*, Random House, 2007.

Spurling, K., *Cruel Conflict: The triumph and tragedy of* HMAS Perth (electronic edition), New Holland, 2008.

Thomas, D., *The Battle of the Java Sea*, Stein & Day, 1969.

Toland, J., *But Not In Shame: The Six Months After Pearl Harbor*, Random House, 1961.

Toland, J., *The Rising Sun: The Decline and Fall of the Japanese Empire 1936–1945*, Bantam, 1970.

Toll, I., *Pacific Crucible: War at Sea in the Pacific, 1941–1942*, W.W. Norton, 2012.

Ugaki, M, Chihaya, M. (trans.), Goldstein, D., & Dillon, K. (eds.), *Fading Victory: The Diary of Admiral Matome Ugaki 1941–1945*, University of Pittsburgh Press, 1991.

van Oosten, F.C., *The Battle of the Java Sea*, Naval Institute Press, 1976.

Warren, A.. *Singapore 1942: Britain's Greatest Defeat*, Hambledon and London, 2002.

Weintraub, S., *Long Day's Journey Into War*, Dutton, 1991.

Wigmore, L., *Australia in the War of 1939–1945, Series One: Army; Volume IV: The Japanese Thrust*, Australian War Memorial, 1957.

Williford, G., *Racing the Sunrise: Reinforcing America's Pacific Outposts, 1941–1942*, Naval Institute Press, 2010.

Wilmott, H.P., *Empires in the Balance: Japanese and Allied Pacific Strategies to April 1942*, Naval Institute Press, 1982.

Wilmott, H.P., *The Barrier and the Javelin: Japanese and Allied Pacific Strategies to February to June 1942*, Naval Institute Press, 1983.

Winslow, W., *The Fleet the Gods Forgot*, Naval Institute Press, 1982.

Winslow, W., *The Ghost That Died At Sunda Strait*, Naval Institute Press, 1984.

Winton, J., *Ultra in the Pacific: How Breaking Japanese Codes & Ciphers Affected Naval Operations Against Japan*, Leo Cooper, 1993.

Womack, T., *The Dutch Naval Air Force Against Japan: The Defense of the Netherlands East Indies, 1941–1942*, Macfarland, 2006.

Articles, Online articles and Monographs

Bell, C., "The 'Singapore Strategy' and the Deterrence of Japan: Winston Churchill, the Admiralty and the Dispatch of Force Z," *The English Historical Review*, 116:467, 604–634 (June 2001).

Benda, H., "The Beginnings of the Japanese Occupation of Java," *Far Eastern Quarterly*, Vol.15, No.4 (Aug. 1956), pp. 541–560.

Bussemaker, H., "Paradise in Peril: The Netherlands, Great Britain and the Defence of the Netherlands East Indies, 1940–41," *Journal of Southeast Asian Studies*, Vol.31, No.1 (Mar. 2000), pp. 115–136.

Cannon, P., "The Battle of Endau, Malaya, 26–27 January 1942 – Part 1," *Journal of Australian Naval History*, Vol.8, No.2 (2011), pp. 66–98.

Cannon, P.. "The Battle of Endau, Malaya, 26–27 January 1942 – Part 2," *Journal of Australian Naval History*, Vol.9, No.1 (2012), pp. 7–42.

Collins, J., "Report by Commodore Commanding China Force, 27th March, 1942" in "Battle of the Java Sea, 27th February, 1942," *Supplement to the London Gazette* (July 6, 1948), p. 3939.

Collins, Cdre J.A., "Reports on the Battle of the Java Sea," Ronald McKie, *Proud Echo*, Robert Hale (1953).

Coppock, M., "The Battle of the Java Sea: A Fleet Wasted," *Sea Classics* (Sept. 2007).

Cowman, I., "Main fleet to Singapore?" *Journal of Strategic Studies*, 17:2, 79–93 (1994).

Cox, J., "A Turn Too Far: Reconstructing the End of the Battle of the Java Sea," MilitaryHistoryOnline.com (April 3, 2011).

Daniels, R., "MacArthur's Failures in the Philippines, December 1941–March 1942," MilitaryHistoryOnline.com (April 22, 2007).

Denlay, K., "Cruisers for Breakfast," *Sportdiving Magazine* (2003), pp. 17–19.

Ford, D., "British Naval Policy and the War against Japan, 1937–1945," *International Journal of Naval History*, 4:1 (April 2005).

Glassford, W., "Narrative of Events in the South-West Pacific from 14 February to 5 April 1942," ONI Narrative.

Gordon, O., "Appendix" in "Battle of the Java Sea, 27th February, 1942," *Supplement to the London Gazette* (July 6, 1948).

Gough, M., "Failure and Destruction, Clark Field, the Philippines, December 8, 1941," MilitaryHistoryOnline.com (November 3, 2007).

Gregory, M., *Ahoy – Mac's Web Log* "Trying to stem the southward thrust of the Japanese threatening to engulf the Dutch East Indies in February/March of 1942. The Battle of Sunda Strait," ahoy.tk-jk.net (retrieved April 22, 2012).

Grimsley, M., "What If Singapore Had Not Fallen?" historynet.com/what-if-singapore-had-not-fallen.htm (retrieved April 9, 2013).

Hackett, B., & Kingsepp, S., "IJN MOGAMI: Tabular Record of Movement," CombinedFleet.com (retrieved April 10, 2012).

Hackett, B. & Kingsepp, S., "HIJMS ATAGO: Tabular Record of Movement," CombinedFleet.com (retrieved July 8, 2012).

Hackett, B. & Kingsepp, S., "HIJMS ASHIGARA: Tabular Record of Movement," CombinedFleet.com (retrieved April 10, 2012).

Hackett B. & Kingsepp, S., "HIJMS NACHI: Tabular Record of Movement," CombinedFleet.com (retrieved January 17, 2011).

Hackett, B. & Kingsepp, S., "HIJMS NAGARA: Tabular Record of Movement," CombinedFleet.com (retrieved April 10, 2012).

Hackett, B. & Kingsepp, S., "HIJMS HAGURO: Tabular Record of Movement," CombinedFleet.com (retrieved January 17, 2011).

Hackett, B., Kingsepp, S., & Cundall, P., "IJN Patrol Boat No. 102: Tabular Record of Movement," CombinedFleet.com (retrieved April 10, 2012).

Hackett, B., Kingsepp, S. & Cundall, P., "IJN Patrol Boat No. 106," CombinedFleet.com (retrieved April 10, 2012).

Hart, T., "Narrative of Events, Asiatic Fleet Leading up to War and From 8 December 1941 to 15 February 1942," ONI Narrative.

Hart, T., "Events and Circumstances Concerning the 'Striking Force,'" ONI Narrative (February 6, 1942).

Howard, E., "USS *Shark* (SS-174)," *United States Submarine Losses in World War II*, SubSoWesPac.org ((retrieved April 10, 2012).

Kannegieter, A., Visser, G., & Visser, J. (trans.), "The Story of De Ruyter survivors, the flagship of Admiral Doorman, February 1942," *Forgotten Campaign: The Dutch East Indies Campaign 1941–1942*, (offline but cached)

Klemen L., "The Capture of Bali Island, February 1942," *Forgotten Campaign: The Dutch East Indies Campaign 1941–1942* (website offline but cached) (retrieved June 10, 2012).

Klemen, L., "Massacre of POWs, Dutch East Indies, 1941–1942," *Forgotten Campaign: The Dutch East Indies Campaign 1941–1942* (website offline but cached) (retrieved June 1, 2012).

Klemen, L., "The Conquest of Java Island, March 1942," *Forgotten Campaign: The Dutch East Indies Campaign 1941–1942*, (website offline but cached.)

Layton, G., "EASTERN THEATRE OPERATIONS: the Diaries of Admiral Layton, C-in-C, China Station –

November 1941 to March 1942," naval-history.net/index.htm (retrieved January 12, 2013).

Leighton, R., "Allied Unity Of Command in the Second World War: A Study in Regional Military Organization," *Political Science Quarterly*, Vol.67, No.3 (Sept., 1952), pp. 399–425.

McConnell, R., "Operations, action and sinking of U.S.S. LANGLEY, period from February 22 to March 5, 1942," ONI Narrative.

Miles, Lion; Long; Geary, Dixie, "A Ship to Remember: USS *Edsall* (DD 219)," *USS Houston CA-30: The Galloping Ghost of the Java Coast*, USSHouston.org (retrieved April 25, 2012).

Nevitt, A., "KAGERO Class Notes," *Imperial Japanese Navy Page*, CombinedFleet.com (retrieved July 8, 2012).

Nevitt, A., "IJN Wakaba: Tabular Record of Movement," Imperial Japanese Navy Page "IJN Wakaba: Tabular Record of Movement," CombinedFleet.com (retrieved September 21, 2012).

Noot, Lt. J., "Battlecruiser: Design studies for the Royal Netherlands Navy 1939–40," *Warship International* (Toledo, Ohio: International Naval Research Organization) 3: 242–273.

O'Hara, V., "Action South of Borneo: March 1, 1942," *Thunder of the Guns: Battles of the Pacific War*, microworks. net/pacific/battles/index.htm (retrieved March 29, 2012).

O'Hara, V., "Other Engagements involving Forces fleeing Java: March 1–March 4, 1942," *Thunder of the Guns: Battles of the Pacific War*, microworks.net/pacific/battles/ (retrieved March 29, 2012).

O'Hara, V., "Battle of Sunda Strait 28 Feb. –1 March, 1942," *Thunder of the Guns: Battles of the Pacific War*, microworks.net/pacific/battles/ (retrieved March 29, 2012).

Paxinos, S., "The mighty minnow that took on a Japanese fleet," *The Age*, theage.com.au/ articles/2004/04/22/1082616262661.html (April 23, 2004) (retrieved October 13, 2012).

Percival, A E., "The War In Malaya (Extract from his official report to the government 1946)," FEPOW Community, fepow-community.org.uk/.

Ramires, F., "The fall of Bali and the naval battle of the Badoeng Strait 18–20 of February of 1942," smmlonline.com/ articles/articles/badoeng.html (retrieved May 6, 2012).

Sagan, S., "The Origins of the Pacific War," *Journal of Interdisciplinary History, 18:4, The Origin and Prevention of Major Wars*, 893–922 (Spring, 1988).

Sinfield, P., "Action off Endau," navyhistory.org.au/action-off-endau/

Tully, A., "Naval Alamo: The Heroic Last Months of the Asiatic Fleet: Dec 1941–March 1942," asiaticfleet.com/ javaseaAug02.html (retrieved January 13, 2005).

Tully, A., "Neglected Disaster: Nisshin," CombinedFleet.com (retrieved April 10, 2012).

Tully, A., "IJN Kaga: Tabular Record of Movement," CombinedFleet.com (retrieved April 10, 2012).

Tully, A., "Loss of USS Pope" (statement of Pope survivor William Penninger), world-war.co.uk (retrieved March 2, 2012).

Visser, J., *Royal Netherlands Navy Warships of World War II*, "Who sank the Shinonome?" netherlandsnavy.nl/Who sank the Shinonome.htm (retrieved June 10, 2012).

Womack, T., "Battle of Badoeng Strait: World War II Naval Duel off Bali," Historynet.com, August 31, 2006 (retrieved April 17, 2012).

Visser, J., "'Abandon Ship!' The Sunda Strait Battle, February–March 1942," *Forgotten Campaign: The Dutch East Indies Campaign 1941–1942* (website offline but cached) (retrieved June 1, 2012).

Visser, J., "Willem van der Zaan," *Royal Netherlands Navy Warships of World War II*, netherlandsnavy.nl (retrieved June 10, 2012).

Visser, J., "History of the Cruiser Tromp," *Royal Netherlands Navy Warships of World War II*, netherlandsnavy.nl (retrieved June 10, 2012).

Visser, J., "De Ruyter (I) History," *Royal Netherlands Navy Warships of World War II*, netherlandsnavy.nl/ (retrieved August 19, 2008).

Visser, J., "History of the Cruiser Java," *Royal Netherlands Navy Warships of World War II*, netherlandsnavy.nl (retrieved June 10, 2012).

Waller, H.M.L., "Action Narrative – Day and Night Action Off Sourabaya, 27th February, 1942" in "Battle of the Java Sea, 27th February, 1942," *Supplement to the London Gazette* (July 6, 1948), p. 3939.

Womack, T., "Battle of Badoeng Strait: World War II Naval Duel off Bali," *World War II* (August 31, 2006), HistoryNet.com (retrieved April 17, 2012), Kroese, p. 158.

Yarnall, P., "Locations Of Warships Of 'Allied' Naval Units December 7 1941," NavSource.org (retrieved March 25, 2013).

___, "Office of Naval Intelligence Combat Narrative: The Java Sea Campaign," Office of Naval Intelligence (March 13, 1943).

___, "Partial Log As Kept By Survivors, USS *Houston*," Enclosure (a)(11) "Engagement off Soerabaja February 27, 1942."

___, "Partial Log As Kept By Survivors, USS *Houston*," enclosure (a)(9) (September 9, 1945).

___, Report of *John D. Ford* (228): "Report of Battle of Java Sea, forwarding of: Extracts from radio log 26 February to 1 March 1942," Enclosure (B).

___, "Cyclops," *Dictionary of American Naval Fighting Ships*, history.navy.mil/danfs (retrieved June 12, 2012).

___, USS *Houston*, EN3-11(CT) A8-21 Ser: 01139 (September 9, 1945) Enclosure (a)(11) "Engagement Off Soerabaja February 27, 1942."

___, "*Shark I* (SS 174)," *United States Submarine Losses, World War II*, history.navy.mil/library/online/sublosses/sublosses_main.htm (retrieved April 10, 2012).

___, "K-VII," Dutch Submarines, DutchSubmarines.com (retrieved October 4, 2012).

___, Interrogation Nav No. 7 USSBS No. 33 Interrogation of: Vice Admiral ShiraichI, Kzutaka, IJN (Admiral Kondo's chief of staff) (October 15, 1945), available at Hyperwar.html

INDEX

Figures in **bold** refer to maps.

A-24 Banshee dive bomber 38, 123, 225, 267, 294
ABC-1: 35, 36, 50, 137
ABDA (American–British–Dutch–Australian) 4, 128, 129, 135, **136**, 140, 146, 148, 153, 156, 175, 176, 177, 178, 179, 182, 199, 208, 209, 210, 211, 212, 219, 224, 226, 239, 240, 244, 247, 252, 253, 255, 266, 281, 282, 284, 286, 287, 290, 292, 293, 295, 297, 298, 301, 316, 320, 332, 334, 336, 344, 355, 406, 410, 411, 412, 413, 414
ABDA Striking Force 175, 176, 177, 199, 208
ABDACOM (American–British–Dutch–Australian Command) 4, 8, 128, 134, 135, 137, 140, 144, 145, 146, 147, 148, 163, 175, 176, 181, 184, 191, 196, 199, 200, 202, 204, 206, 207, 209, 212, 214, 216, 224, 228, 229, 240, 243, 246, 247, 249, 260, 268, 269, 270, 271, 314, 339, 344, 369, 410, 411, 412
ABDAFLOAT (ABDA Navy Operational Command) 135, 140, 142, 148, 149, 152, 153, 156, 176, 177, 195, 197, 199, 203, 204, 208, 225, 226, 227, 228, 237, 243, 245, 247, 249, 250, 260, 261, 391, 392, 411, 412, 413
ABDAIR (ABDA Air Operational Command) 4, 135, 146, 180, 207, 215, 216, 225, 247, 248, 412
ABDARM (ABDA Army Operational Command) 4, 135, 140, 206, 247
Abernethy, Commander Elmer Paul 118, 370, 371, 372, 373, 374, 375, 377, 378, 379, 381
ADA (Anglo–Dutch–Australian) 35, 137
ADB (American–Dutch–British) 35, 36, 137
Admiral Graf Spee 44, 208
Aichi D3A carrier bombers 219, 373
Akebono 360, 361, 362
Alden, USS 33, 39, 51, 76, 109, 148, 149, 152, 176, 248, 250, 251, 254, 256, 287, 302, 303, 305, 325, 326, 332, 333, 355, 357, 358, 402
Allanson, Flight Lieutenant R. J. 166, 167
Amagiri 165, 169, 170, 342
Ambon 27, 128, 129, 130, 132, 133, 134, **136**, 137, 175, 176, 198, 200, 222

anti-aircraft weaponry
    3in guns 33, 113, 118, 134, 184, 185, 274, 276, 365, 373, 374, 375, 378
    5in guns 182, 184, 185, 188, 213, 214, 235, 254, 262, 274, 300, 301, 346, 350, 399
    5.25in guns 47, 93, 95, 96, 97, 101
    5in shells 71, 170, 185, 186, 197, 213, 234, 238, 300, 316, 346, 357, 399
    8in guns 18, 32, 39, 76, 84, 184, 208, 268, 283, 285, 287, 291, 292, 293, 301, 310, 316, 321, 346, 347, 350, 363, 387, 396, 397, 399
    8in shells 188, 290, 292, 296, 298, 310, 322, 325, 330, 342, 347, 350, 362, 363, 364, 366, 389, 399, 400
Ark Royal, HMS 41, 46, 187
Asagiri 165, 170, 342
Asahi Maru **157**, 160
Asashio 224, 231, 232, 233, 234, 235, 236, 237, 238, 239
asdic 4, 33, 86, 149, 201, 271
Ashigara 283, 360, 361, 362, 363, 364, 366, 367, 410
Asiatic Fleet 8, 29, 30, 31, 32, 33, 34, 36, 37, 39, 53, 54, 55, 56, 80, 82, 114, 117, 118, 119, 122, 123, 124, 125, 127, 128, 131, 143, 147, 148, 150, 174, 182, 193, 197, 200, 203, 204, 228, 247, 266, 370, 376, 392, 402
Atago 27, 51, 84, 248, 396, 397, 399
Awagisan Maru 70, 71, 72, 73, 141

B-24 Liberator heavy bomber 85, 258
Bali **136**, 137, 146, 148, 176, 183, 212, 223, 224, 225, 226, 227, 230, 231, 233, 238, 239, 240, 242, 243, 245, 249, 251, 256, 270, 274, 281, 286, 333, 334, 338, 357, 370, 372, 386, 396, 397, 406, 413
Bali Strait **136**, 139, 146, 224, 227, 228, 237, 245, 327, 333, 355, 356
Balikpapan 27, 39, 51, 119, **136**, 152, 153, 154, 155, 158, 160, 161, 165, 169, 175, 179, 181, 183, 196, 215, 229, 243, 245, 248, 254, 262, 281, 282, 295, 412, 413

Battle of 151, 157, 176, 194, 229, 230, 234, 243, 281, 407, 411

Banckert, Hr. Ms. 137, 182, 183, 207, 209, 211, 215, 226, 248, 250, 251, 332, 394

Banka Strait 149, 207, 208, 213, 226, 253, 259, 281, 288, 407, 408, 410

Bantam Bay 341, 342, 344, 345, 347, 348, 351, 352, 353, 407, 409

Barker, USS 33, 39, 118, 119, 176, 181, 183, 208, 210, 211, 226, 230, 249

Batavia 51, 128, 134, **136**, 139, 171, 194, 196, 204, 208, 212, 216, 245, 246, 251, 252, 253, 305, 314, 320, 321, 326, 328, 329, 336, 337, 339, 340, 344, 354, 384, 385, 395, 398, 400

Battle of the Java Sea 8, 241, 253, 281, **289**, 291, 292, 293, 298, 307, **309**, 310, **315**, 322, 326, 329, 331, 336, 337, 353, 357, 367, 396, 405, 406, 407

Bawean **136**, 253, 254, 262, 263, 307, 333, 359, 405

Bermingham, Lieutenant Commander John M. 123, 131, 132, 133, 220

Binford, Commander Thomas 236, 237, 241, 243, 256, 263, 297, 302, 305, 325, 326, 327, 332, 339, 356, 357

Bismarck 44, 46, 47, 48, 50, 83, 108, 181, 210, 299

Black Hawk, USS 33, 39, 51, 176, 249, 334, 402

Blinn, Lieutenant Commander Welford C. 333, 358, 359, 360, 364, 365, 366

Boeing B-17 Flying Fortress 36, 37, 38, 40, 60, 63, 64, 65, 66, 85, 86, 115, 116, 117, 122, 123, 144, 173, 174, 176, 180, 225, 246, 263, 267, 323, 332, 395

Boise, USS 39, 118, 119, 151, 152, 153, 154, 162, 176, 197, 198, 199, 213, 225, 243, 249, 254, 268, 412

Borneo 7, 14, 19, 24, 25, 27, 36, 39, 42, **136**, 137, 141, 142, 144, 145, 154, 161, 178, 180, 210, 215, 224, 255, 330, 334, 358, 359, 361, 363, 391, 392, 407

Brereton, General Lewis 38, 40, 59, 60, 61, 66, 67, 125, 176

Brett, Lieutenant General George H. 134, 176, 246, 268, 269, 402

Brewster Buffalos 45, 75, 100, 107, 129, 139, 163, 165, 216, 279, 295

Bristol Blenheim bombers 73, 165, 208, 339

British Eastern Fleet 8, 406

British Judge, HMS 370, 398

Brooke-Popham, Air Chief Marshal Robert 45, 46, 70, 74, 76, 163, 164

Browning Automatic Rifle (BAR) 274, 375

Bulmer, USS 33, 39, 151, 153, 154, 176, 181, 183, 203, 208, 210, 211, 226, 230, 249

C5M Babs reconnaissance craft 85, 86, 179

Cam Ranh Bay 27, 39, 82, 90, 141, 207, 248, 342

Campbell, Sub Lieutenant Gavin 51, 132, 133, 314, 323, 336

carley floats 103, 104, 106

Carrier Striking Force 26, 248, 282, 374, 390

Cartwright, Lieutenant Commander F. J. 91, 105, 106

Cavite Navy Yard 25, 32, 113, 114, 115, 116, 117, 326

Celebes 27, 132, 137, 145, 151, 155, 173, 182, 200, 203, 219, 357, 391

Celebes Sea 131, **136**

Centrifugal Offensive ("Strike South") 11, 24, 26, 84

Chennault, Claire Lee 22, 23, 40, 45

Chikuma 26, 248, 374, 387, 388, 389, 390, 391, 409

Childs, USS 34, 56, 128, 133, 174, 175, 179, 266, 395

Chokai 11, 27, 51, 70, **81**, 84, 88, 104, 207, 209, 248

Chömpf, Lieutenant Commander J. M. L. I. 232, 233, 236

Christmas Island **136**, 171, 249, 371, 372, 381, 388

Churchill, Prime Minister Winston 45, 46, 47, 48, 49, 50, 82, 83, 84, 85, 110, 137, 164, 203, 206, 244, 246

Clark Field 36, 37, 38, 39, 40, 57, 58, 60, 61, 62, 63, 64, 65, 80, 114, 117, **136**

Coley, Lieutenant Commander Lewis Elliot 256, 303, 357

Collins, Captain/Commodore John 46, 108, 168, 177, 248, 250, 252, 253, 331, 333, 336, 340, 350, 384, 398

Combined Chiefs of Staff 137, 244, 246, 266

Combined Striking Force 178, 180, 182, 183, 209, 210, 211, 212, 251, 252, 255, 256, **257**, 258, 260, 261, 262, 263, 264, 282, 284, 285, 286, 287, 288, 290, 291, 292, 293, 294, 295, 296, 297, 298, 301, 302, 303, 304, 305, 308, 310, 311, 312, 313, 314, 315, 316, 320, 321, 322, 323, 325, 326, 328, 331, 337, 345, 405

Cooper, Lieutenant Commander Jacob E. 161, 256, 356, 357

Coral Sea 223, 255, 408

Crouch, Commander Edwin M. 279, 372, 380, 381

Crozer, Petty Officer William J. T. 91, 100, 110

Curtiss P-40 Warhawk 22, 36, 180, 267

Darwin 51, 128, 134, 135, **136**, 148, 152, 176, 198, 208, 212, 213, 214, 215, 216, **217**, 218, 219, 220, 221, 222, 226, 266, 267, 268, 334, 353, 392, 412

Davao Gulf 57, 60, 144

De Back, Lieutenant Commander P. G. 144, 145, 394

De Meester, Captain 187, 194, 227, 236, 237, 238, 239, 261

De Ruyter 137, 176, 178, 181, 182, 183, 186, 188, 194, 195, 196, 207, 209, 210, 211, 215, 227, 228, 229, 230, 231, 232, 234, 243, 248, 249, 251, 254, 256, **257**, 258, 259, 260, 261, 263, 264, 284, 285, 287, **289**, 291, 292, 293, 295, 296, 299, 301, 302, 303, 304, 305, 307, 308, **309**, 310, 311, 312, 313, 314, **315**, 316, 317, 318, 319, 320, 321, 323, 326, 328, 330, 331, 345, 394, 405, 406, 413

De Vries, Lieutenant Commander Walburg Marius 337, 353, 354, 355, 413

Del Carmen 37, 38, 58, 61, 64, 116

Denpesar 176, 212, 224, 225, 227, 237, 240, 250, 251, 270, 271, 272, 274, 334, 357, 370, 371, 385

Doorman, Rear Admiral Karel Willem Frederik Marie 177, 178, 180, 181, 182, 183, 184, 185, 188, 189, 194, 195, 196, 199, 207, 208, 209, 210, 211, 227, 228, 229, 230, 231, 232, 235, 236, 237, 248, 252, 253, 254, 255, 256, 257, 258, 259, 260, 261, 262, 263, 264, 287, 288, 290, 291, 292, 293, 294, 295, 296, 297, 298, 301, 302, 303, 304, 305, 307, 308, 310, 311, 312, 313, 314, 316, 317, 318, 319, 320, 323, 325, 326, 330, 339, 345, 367, 370, 383, 400, 405, 406, 407, 408, 410, 411, 413, 414

Dornier Do-24 130, 141, 142, 144, 212

Eccles, Lieutenant Commander Henry Effingham 256, 259, 260, 264, 302, 303, 405, 406

Edsall, USS 33, 39, 51, 76, 109, 148, 149, 152, 176, 199, 243, 248, 249, 250, 271, 272, 273, 274, 277, 278, 279, 371, 372,

381, 384, 387, 388, 389, 390, 391, 393, 396, 400, 413

Electra, USS 48, 49, 76, 77, 80, 88, 92, 104, 106, 108, 248, 251, 256, 260, 285, 287, 288, 290, 291, 296, 299, 300, 302, 304, 305, **309**, 314, 331, 354, 414

Encounter, HMS 49, 76, 77, 248, 249, 251, 256, 260, 287, 291, 296, 299, 300, 301, 304, 308, **309**, 313, 314, 331, 332, 333, 334, 335, 354, 358, 359, 360, 361, 362, 364, 394, 396, 407, 408

Endau 164, 165, 166, 169, 171, 249, 407

Evertsen, Hr. Ms. 137, 140, 226, 248, 249, 252, 253, 327, 336, 337, 339, 353, 354, 355, 356, 413

Exeter, HMS 8, 76, 109, 208, 209, 210, 211, 226, 248, 249, 251, 256, 257, 259, 260, 264, 285, 286, 287, **289**, 290, 291, 293, 295, 296, 298, 299, 301, 305, 308, **309**, 325, 326, 327, 332, 333, 334, 335, 345, 354, 358, 359, 360, 361, 362, 363, 364, 394, 396, 407, 408

Express, HMS 48, 49, 76, 77, 80, 91, 94, 95, 105, 106, 109, 199, 249

Fairey Albacores 165, 166, 167, 332

Far East Air Force 8, 34, 36, 37, 38, 40, 57, 58, 59, 62, 64, 65, 115, 122, 123, 125, 176, 246, 266, 267, 412

Far East Command 69, 70, 73, 75, 89, 107, 163

Flores Sea **136**, 153, 182, 193, 194, 195, 196, 209, 210, 213, 214, 259, 281, 288, 371, 387, 407, 408

Formosa 13, 24, 27, 37, 40, 41, 59, 60, 61, 63, 65, 66, 67, 82, 85, 412

Fremantle 268, 269, 336, 372, 381, 384, 386, 391, 396, 398, 400, 401, 402, 403

Fubuki 141, 142, 165, 169, 170, 207, **343**, 344, 345, 346, 348,

Genzan Air Group **81**, 85, 90, 91, 92, 94, 171, 210, 211

Glassford, Admiral William A. 30, 32, 39, 57, 117, 118, 119, 127, 151, 152, 153, 154, 161, 162, 177, 195, 197, 204, 228, 229, 246, 247, 248, 252, 260, 269, 270, 271, 272, 273, 279, 327, 331, 332, 333, 336, 353, 365, 370, 380, 382, 383, 384, 386, 388, 395, 396, 397, 402, 403, 404, 405, 410, 411

Glenn Martin bombers 139, 141, 142, 145, 385

Goggins, Commander William B. 184, 186, 187, 193, 371, 400

Gordon, Captain Oliver Louden 208, 251, 256, 260, 290, 296, 301, 331, 333, 335, 358, 359, 360, 361, 362, 363, 364
Guadalcanal 223, 404, 409

Hachiro, Lieutenant Takeda 88, 104, 105
Haguro 27, 55, 222, 283, 284, 285, **289**, 290, 292, 293, 294, 296, 298, 299, 302, 303, 304, **309**, **315**, 316, 318, 319, 320, 325, 360, 361, 362, 363, 364, 410
Haruna 27, 51, 84, 396
hakko ichiu 20, 22, 23, 25
Hart, Admiral Thomas C. 29, 30, 32, 33, 34, 35, 36, 37, 38, 39, 40, 41, 45, 50, 51, 53, 54, 55, 56, 57, 58, 59, 67, 76, 79, 80, 113, 115, 117, 118, 120, 122, 123, 124, 125, 127, 128, 129, 130, 131, 135, 140, 141, 142, 143, 146, 147, 150, 151, 152, 153, 154, 161, 162, 176, 177, 178, 179, 182, 195, 196, 197, 198, 202, 203, 204, 207, 212, 214, 244, 260, 345, 391, 407, 410, 411
Harukaze 116, 286, **289**, 342, **343**, 344, 345, 346, 347, 348, 349
Hatakaze **343**, 344, 345, 346, 348, 349
Hatsuharu 175, 356, 412
Hatsuyuki 165, 170, 207, 342, **343**, 346
Hawker Hurricane 45, 50, 163, 165, 171, 205, 208, 268, 279, 328, 385
Helfrich, Vice Admiral Conrad Emil Lambert 128, 129, 139, 140, 141, 142, 143, 145, 147, 148, 153, 177, 178, 179, 195, 196, 203, 204, 208, 211, 214, 226, 227, 228, 240, 245, 246, 247, 248, 249, 250, 251, 252, 253, 254, 255, 257, 260, 261, 262, 263, 270, 271, 272, 273, 282, 290, 294, 295, 307, 308, 320, 321, 322, 323, 328, 330, 332, 333, 336, 340, 341, 345, 354, 382, 383, 384, 391, 392, 394, 400, 405, 410, 411
Heron, USS 34, 39, 128, 133, 134, 266
Hiei 26, 27, 248, 387, 389
Hoashi, Ensign **81**, 92, 100, 107, 108
Hobart, HMAS 208, 209, 210, 211, 226, 248, 251, 252, 253, 353, 354
Houston, USS 8, 30, 32, 33, 34, 38, 39, 117, 118, 119, 152, 153, 176, 181, 182, 183, 184, 185, 186, 187, 188, 189, 192, 193, 194, 197, 198, 199, 204, 208, 212, 213, 214, 215, 226, 228, 248, 249, 250, 251, 254, 256, **257**, 258, 259, 260, 262, 264, 268, 284, 285, 286, 287, 288, **289**, 290, 291, 292, 293, 296, 297, 298, 301, 303, 304, 305, 308, **309**, 310, 311, 312,

313, 314, **315**, 316, 317, 318, 319, 320, 321, 322, 327, 328, 329, 330, 331, 335, 336, 337, 338, 340, 341, 342, **343**, 344, 345, 346, 347, 348, 349, 350, 351, 352, 353, 354, 355, 358, 359, 371, 378, 379, 381, 382, 383, 384, 390, 394, 396, 397, 401, 402, 406, 407, 409, 413

Iba Field 38, 58, 61, 62, 64, 65, 80, 115
Iba radar 39, 59, 60, 61, 65
Ibo, Vice Admiral Takahashi 27, 200, 212, 222, 248, 283, 360, 361, 362, 367
Imperial Japanese Army 14, 21, 24, 27, 71, 144, 156, 164, 171, 248, 282, 348, 355, 410
Imperial Japanese Navy 4, 14, 15, 16, 18, 23, 24, 26, 77, 84, 111, 113, 119, 138, 143, 146, 149, 152, 162, 175, 188, 201, 229, 266, 281, 282, 304, 317, 340, 344, 348, 375, 387, 391, 409
Inazuma 360, 361, 364, 366
Indian Ocean 41, 47, 48, 50, 76, 110, 146, 171, 193, 196, 224, 240, 248, 270, 333, 334, 357, 371, 379, 396, 397, 402
Indochina 14, 22, 24, 25, 27, 77, 78, 79, 84, 86, **136**, 207, 248, 342
Indomitable, HMS 47, 49, 171, 268, 413
Isoroku, Admiral Yamamoto 18, 24, 25, 26, 85, 224, 248, 282, 284

Japanese Army Air Force 63, 115, 164, 166, 216, 339
Japanese Naval Air Force 18, 27, 54, 63, 65, 85, 95, 116, 180, 224, 275, 276, 373
Java Sea 7, 8, 9, 118, **136**, 138, 169, 177, 183, 195, 203, 213, 225, 227, 241, 243, 250, 253, 256
Jintsu 27, 55, 119, 222, 248, 283, 284, 285, 288, **289**, 290, 294, 299, 300, 304, 305, 308, **309**, 314, **315**, 357, 410
Jisaburo, Vice Admiral Ozawa 11, 27, 51, 52, 70, **81**, 84, 86, 87, 88, 111, 141, 207, 209, 210, 248, 252, 342, 367, 409
John D. Edwards 33, 39, 51, 76, 109, 152, 183, 189, 194, 211, 226, 227, 236, 237, 238, 239, 243, 248, 254, 256, 259, 287, 297, 298, 302, 303, 305, 325, 326, 332, 333, 355, 358, 402, 405
John D. Ford 33, 39, 113, 151, 153, 154, 156, 158, 159, 160, 161, 227, 230, 232, 233, 234, 235, 236, 237, 240, 248, 249, 250, 251, 254, 256, 263, 264, 287, 293, 297, 302, 305, 325, 326, 332, 333, 355, 356, 357, 358, 402

Johore Strait 43, 79, 80, 90, 167, 204, 205
Jolo 27, 125, 129, 130, 131, 132, 133, **136**, 144, 248
Jupiter, HMS 49, 76, 77, 149, 150, 248, 249, 251, 256, 260, 262, 263, 265, 273, 287, 290, 291, 296, 297, 299, 301, 303, 305, 308, **309**, 311, 312, 314, 321, 354, 413

K-X 144, 145, 250, 268, 394, 395
K-XI 400
K-XII 73, 141
K-XIII 395
K-XIV 142, 146, 153
K-XVI 142
K-XVII 141
K-XVIII 153, 156, 157, 158, 160, 161, 394, 395
Kaga 17, 26, 219, 248, 374, 375, 376, 387, 390, 412
Kai-shek, Chiang 17, 20, 21, 23
Kalijati airfield 339, 340
Kamikawa Maru 51, 52, 141, 142
Kamikaze 4, 290, 302, 320
Kanoya Air Group 63, 64, 85, 90, 100, 111, 184, 210, 263
Karpe, Lieutenant Commander Eugene S. 279, 380, 381
Kawakaze 360, 361, 363
Kendari 27, 136, 151, 173, 174, 175, 183, 196, 219, 224, 225, 245, 284, 286, 339, 391, 412
Kendari II airfield 173, 174, 175, 179, 180, 183, 184, 188, 191, 213, 215, 221, 224, 334, 357, 386
Kido Butai ("Striking Force") 4, 26, 55, 111, 219, 220, 221, 248, 262, 272, 357, 374, 375, 377, 382, 387, 388, 389, 390, 400, 402
Kinu 27, 84, 86, 87, 141
Koenraad, Admiral Pieter 227, 314, 322, 328
Koepang (Kupang) **136**, 151, 152, 153, 162, 198, 212, **217**, 219, 222
Kongo 27, 51, 77, 81, 84, 98, 248, 396
Kortenaer, Hr. Ms. 137, 147, 208, 211, 227, 230, 232, 243, 248, 249, 254, 256, **257**, 286, 287, 288, **289**, 290, 291, 294, 297, **309**, 312, 313, 314, 321, 331, 332, 354, 408, 413
Kota Bharu 50, 51, 69, 70, 71, 72, 73, 76, 77, **81**, 86, 87, 89, **136**, 141, 165
Kra Isthmus 70, 72, 73, 74
Kroese, Lieutenant Commander Antonie "Cruiser" 147, 211, 256, 297, 312, 331, 332
Kuantan 69, 72, **81**, 89, 90, 91, 92, **136**, 210

Kuching 26, 27, 142, 146, 210
Kumano 27, 51, 87, 141, 142, 342
Kwantung 13, 14, 20, 42
Kwantung Army 17, 18, 20
Kyuji, Admiral Kubo 174, 175, 224, 225, 226, 227, 231, 237, 239

Lacomblé, Eugene Edouard Bernard 188, 194, 253, 296, 319, 323
Langley, USS 34, 57, 118, 128, 144, 149, 176, 218, 247, 257, 265, 266, 268, 269, 270, 271, 272, 273, 274, 275, 276, 277, 278, 279, 295, 369, 370, 371, 372, 373, 375, 376, 377, 378, 379, 381, 385, 386, 388, 401, 402, 403, 404, 405, 411
Layton, Admiral Sir Geoffrey 75, 80, 167, 406
LB-30 Liberator 85, 176, 202, 221, 225, 246, 247, 258, 267, 330, 385
Leach, Captain John 47, 76, 94, 95, 96, 97, 98, 105, 106, 107, 109
Leyte Gulf 223, 404, 409
Liaotung Peninsula 13, 14, 18
Lingayen Gulf 31, 40, 61, 66, 82, 120, 121, 124, **136**, 391, 392
Lombok Strait **136**, 146, 148, 189, 202, 227, 231, 232, 240
Luzon 30, 31, 38, 39, 40, 57, 58, 60, 61, 65, 79, 82, 117, 120, 123, 124, **136**

MacArthur, General Douglas 32, 34, 35, 36, 37, 38, 40, 41, 50, 53, 57, 58, 59, 60, 61, 66, 67, 86, 122, 123, 124, 125, 143, 196, 203, 266, 412
Mack, Lieutenant William P. 158, 160, 293
Machina Wharf 114, 115
Madoera Strait 139, 181, 183, 333
Maher, Gunnery officer Arthur 119, 184, 188, 189, 204, 291, 296, 301, 327, 351
Makassar Strait 129, 131, 133, 145, 149, 150, 152, 153, 155, 176, 182, 196, 200, 254
Malay Barrier 146, 163, 198, 213, 214, 243, 250, 327, 355, 357, 358, 365, 367
Malay Peninsula 27, 41, 42, 43, 69, 73, 206
Marblehead, USS 30, 33, 34, 39, 151, 152, 153, 154, 161, 162, 176, 177, 181, 183, 184, 185, 186, 187, 188, 189, 192, 193, 194, 196, 197, 198, 199, 243, 249, 371, 378, 379, 381, 387, 388, 397, 400, 401, 402, 413
Marshall, US Army Chief of Staff General George C. 37, 58, 60
Marsman Building 32, 56, 113, 115, 117, 124

McConnell, Commander Robert P. 270, 271, 272, 273, 274, 275, 276, 277, 278, 279, 370, 373, 379, 381, 403, 404, 405

Mihoro Air Group 75, 85, 90, 93, 98, 104, 210

Mitsubishi G3M2 "Nell" bombers 23, 63, 64, 75, 85, 87, 92, 93, 94, 95, 96, 98, 104, 105, 107, 113, 114, 132, 134, 175, 179, 180, 184, 185, 186, 192, 199, 210, 211, 212, 240, 254, 373

Mitsubishi G4M "Betty" bombers 23, 63, 64, 85, 87, 100, 101, 103, 111, 175, 184, 185, 186, 192, 199, 210, 213, 215, 240, 254, 274, 275, 276, 332, 373

Mitsubishi Type 00 "Zero" fighter 23, 40, 45, 54, 63, 64, 72, 85, 113, 116, 123, 130, 163, 164, 179, 180, 215, 216, **217**, 219, 220, 221, 224, 225, 248, 254, 262, 274, 277, 295, 332, 385

Mogami 18, 27, 51, 84, 207, 211, 248, 342, **343**, 346, 347, 348, 349, 350, 409, 410

Morgan, Lieutenant Commander Eric St John 300, 314, 333, 360, 364

Morison, Samuel Eliot 19, 57, 79, 196, 223, 325, 345, 406

Myoko 27, 55, 144, 248, 283, 360, 361, 362, 363, 364, 366, 367

Nagumo, Admiral 114, 219, 221, 248, 374, 388, 390, 400

"nerks" 265, 274, 275, 276, 277, 278, 371, 375, 376, 377, 378, 388

Netherlands East Indies 11, 19, 23, 25, 35, 47, 118, 125, 128, 129, 137, 138, 140, 145, 146, 148, 173, 179, 247, 340, 395, 400, 406, 408, 411

Ngoro airfield 180, 199, 215, 216, 245, 267, 279, 332, 369, 385, 386, 395

Nobutake, Vice Admiral Kondo 26, 51, 55, **81**, 84, 248, 272, 396, 397, 398, 399, 400

Oosthaven 207, 208, 209, 211, 227

Palembang 27, **136**, 164, 165, 167, 206, 207, 208, 209, 211, 245, 246, 251, 339, 340

Palliser, Arthur F. E. 75, 79, 84, 86, 87, 91, 108, 109, 135, 204, 248, 252, 253, 294, 307, 332, 333, 334, 358, 359, 360, 361, 382, 383, 384, 395, 411

Parker, Lieutenant Commander Edward N. 229, 233, 234, 237, 256, 293, 294, 305

Parrott, USS 33, 39, 151, 153, 154, 157, 158, 159, 160, 161, 208, 211, 226, 227, 236, 237, 238, 239, 243, 249, 371, 384, 397

Patrol Wing 10: 8, 34, 39, 40, 51, 53, 54, 55, 56, 57, 113, 115, 116, 123, 128, 130, 131, 132, 144, 146, 147, 154, 155, 175, 219, 220, 251, 253, 314, 339, 395

Paul Jones, USS 33, 39, 118, 148, 151, 153, 154, **157**, 158, 159, 160, 161, 176, 181, 191, 192, 193, 248, 250, 251, 254, 256, 287, 302, 305, 325, 326, 332, 333, 355, 358, 402

Payne, Lieutenant Thomas 118, 214, 258, 259, 328, 329, 330, 336

PBY Catalina flying boat 7, 34, 39, 51, 52, 53, 54, 55, 56, 57, 69, 77, 113, 115, 116, 117, 122, 123, 125, 127, 128, 130, 131, 133, 149, 154, 180, 182, 211, 214, **217**, 218, 219, 221, 251, 253, 271, 272, 273, 277, 314, 323, 395, 396

Pearl Harbor 7, 8, 11, 17, 18, 23, 25, 26, 27, 29, 31, 35, 39, 52, 53, 55, 56, 57, 58, 59, 60, 63, 66, 67, 80, 83, 95, 110, 111, 114, 117, 118, 124, 139, 175, 176, 178, 212, 219, 221, 222, 242, 374, 377, 390, 402, 411

Peary, USS 33, 39, 114, 115, 123, 130, 131, 132, 133, 134, 174, 175, 199, 212, 214, **217**, 218, 220, 222, 243, 249

Pecos 34, 118, 181, 183, 331, 370, 371, 372, 373, 374, 375, 376, 377, 378, 379, 380, 381, 386, 387, 388, 390, 400, 401, 402

Pensacola, USS 38, 123, 124

Perak airfield 139, 179, 180

Percival, General Arthur 74, 75, 146, 164, 204, 205

Perry, Commodore Matthew 11, 13, 29, 30

Perth, HMAS 8, 248, 249, 251, 256, 259, 260, 287, **289**, 291, 292, 293, 296, 297, 298, 301, 302, 303, 304, 305, 308, **309**, 310, 314, **315**, 317, 319, 320, 321, 322, 327, 328, 329, 330, 331, 335, 336, 337, 338, 340, 341, 342, 343, 344, 345, 346, 347, 348, 349, 350, 353, 354, 355, 358, 359, 375, 382, 383, 384, 396, 407, 409, 413

Phillips, Admiral Sir Tom 41, 49, 50, 51, 74, 75, 76, 77, 78, 79, 80, 83, 84, 85, 86, 87, 88, 89, 90, 91, 92, 93, 94, 97, 99, 100, 102, 104, 105, 106, 107, 108, 109, 110, 117, 307, 323, 412

Phoenix, USS 198, 268, 269, 270, 384, 400, 401, 402, 403

Piet Hein 137, 182, 183, 194, 207, 211, 227, 230, 232, 233, 234, 235, 236, 249

Pillsbury, USS 33, 39, 114, 131, 151, 153, 154, 176, 181, 208, 210, 226, 227, 236, 237, 238, 239, 243, 249, 384, 397, 400

pom-poms 95, 96, 98, 101, 103, 298, 349
Pope, USS 33, 39, 151, 153, 154, **157**, 159, 160, 161, 227, 230, 232, 233, 234, 235, 236, 237, 240, 248, 249, 250, 251, 254, 256, 326, 332, 333, 334, 335, 358, 359, 360, 361, 362, 363, 364, 365, 366, 384, 394, 396, 407, 413
Pound, First Sea Lord Sir Dudley 47, 48, 82, 90, 110, 244, 406
Pownall, Major General Sir Henry R. 134, 147, 163
Prince of Wales, HMS 41, 44, 46, 47, 48, 49, 50, 74, 75, 76, 77, 79, 80, **81**, 82, 83, 84 85, 88, 89, 91, 92, 93, 94, 95, 96, 97, 98, 99, 100, 101, 102, 104, 105, 106, 107, 108, 109, 110, 111, 113, 117, 119, 139, 168, 171, 184, 186, 195, 199, 210, **256**, 261, 264, 295, 299, 323, 366, 412, 413
Pulford, Air Vice Marshal Conway 71, 74, 78, 79, 80, 109, 110, 206
Purnell, Admiral William R. 58, 182, 196, 197, 247, 384, 391
Pursuit Squadrons
  3rd 58, 64, 65
  17th 8, 61, 115, 116 176, 180, 199, 215, 216, 245, 267, 279, 295, 332, 369, 385, 395
  20th 38, 58, 61, 62, 65, 267
  21st 38, 58, 61, 62, 64, 116, 213
  33rd 217, 218, 219, 269, 369, 388, 391
  34th 38, 58, 65, 115, 116, 123

Rainbow 5: 34, 38, 58, 59, 60, 124
Raizo, Rear Admiral Tanaka 55, 119, 222, 281, 283, 284, 285, 290, 299, 304, 315, 361, 409
Repulse, HMS 47, 48, 49, 50, 51, 74, 75, 76, 77, 79, 80, **81**, 82, 83, 84, 85, 89, 90, 91, 92, 93, 94, 95, 98, 99, 100, 101, 102, 103, 104, 105, 108, 109, 110, 111, 113, 117, 119, 139, 168, 171, 184, 186, 195, 210, **256**, 261, 264, 300, 412, 413
Rooks, Captain Albert H. 33, 185, 186, 187, 188, 192, 193, 194, 198, 212, 213, 214, 251, 256, 286, 290, 291, 296, 311, 318, 319, 320, 321, 331, 336, 340, 341, 342, 345, 346, 347, 349, 350, 351, 354
Roosevelt, President Franklin 23, 30, 33, 34, 35, 48, 124, 137, 186, 203, 246
Royal Air Force 7, 45, 51, 52, 72, 73, 74, 75, 76, 79, 90, 100, 107, 135, 146, 164, 165, 167, 171, 206, 207, 208, 246, 252, 328, 339, 385
Royal Australian Air Force 50, 69, 71, 72, 73, 128, 130, 132, 164, 175

Royal Netherlands Naval Air Service 8, 138, 142, 146, 177, 211, 212, 339
Royal Netherlands Navy 4, 8, 129, 137, 138, 139, 140, 142, 146, 175, 177, 178, 181, 182, 194, 229, 250, 302, 395, 400, 410, 413
Ryujo 27, 55, 120, 207, 208, 209, 210, 211, 212, 215, 248, 282, 340, 342, 348, 352, 366, 410

Saburo, Lieutenant Sakai 63, 64, 215, 216, 332
Sadaichi, Admiral Matsunaga 85, 87, 88, 90
Sangley Point Naval Air Station 32, 56, 113, 114, 117, 118
Sendai 27, 51, 70, 71, 165, 166, 169, 170, 207, 248, 342
Shark, USS 34, 82, 127, 202, 203, 392
Shintaro, Rear Admiral Hashimoto 70, 72, 165, 169, 170
Shōji, Rear Admiral Nishimura 156, 157, 159, 161, 283, 288, 294, 299, 301, 304, 308, 322, 408, 409
Singapore Island 42, 46, 100, 164, 204, 205
Singapore Naval Base 41, 42, 43, 49, 50, 74, 79, 168, 171, 172, 199, 249, **256**
Soenda Strait 41, **136**, 146, 149, 194, 208, 226, 250, 251, 253, 327, 333, 334, 336, 337, 339, 340, 341, 342, **343**, 344, 345, 347, 354, 355, 358, 359, 394, 398, 409, 413
Soerabaja 36, 125, 127, 128, 129, 131, 132, **136**, 138, 139, 143, 145, 150, 154, 162, 174, 175, 176, 179, 180, 181, 182, 183, 188, 189, 196, 197, 199, 202, 212, 215, 216, 224, 225, 226, 227, 228, 230, 237, 240, 241, 243, 245, 248, 249, 250, 251, 252, 254, 255, 256, 257, 261, 262, 263, 267, 282, 284, 286, 287, 288, 290, 295, 301, 302, 303, 305, 308, 314, 321, 325, 326, 327, 328, 329, 331, 332, 333, 335, 338, 339, 354, 358, 370, 392, 394, 395, 400, 413
South China Sea 7, 11, 39, 41, 50, 52, 56, 64, 69, 71, 73, 80, **81**, 84, 86, 88, 93, 130, **136**, 168
Southern Expeditionary Force
  Eastern Force 26, 27, 55, 200, 208, 212, 222, 251
  Western Force 26, 27, 70, 84, 141, 222
Southern Resources Area 19, 25, 26, 173, 223, 281, 408, 414
Stewart, USS 33, 39, 131, 176, 181, 183, 189, 194, 203, 208, 211, 226, 227, 236, 237, 238, 239, 241, 242, 243, 244, 249, 251, 302, 378, 379, 381, 394, 401, 402, 413

Sumatra 7, 25, 27, 41, 43, 137, 138, 140, 146, 164, 165, 171, 178, 206, 207, 211, 212, 215, 223, 227, 240, 244, 251, 252, 330, 341, 353, 354, 355, 372

Tainan Air Group 63, 116, 123, 179, 215, 225, 254, 262, 274, 282, 332, 385
Takao Air Group 63, 64, 116, 180, 184, 186, 215, 274, 278
Takeo, Rear Admiral Takagi 55, 248, 283, 284, 285, 288, 290, 291, 292, 293, 294, 295, 298, 299, 302, 303, 304, 310, 314, 316, 317, 320, 322, 360, 361, 363, 364, 408
Talbot, Commander Paul H. 154, 155, 156, 158, 159, 160, 161, 162, 229
Tanjoeng Priok 167, 210, 211, 216, 245, 248, 249, 251, 252, 253, 257, 327, 330, 331, 335, 336, 337, 354, 396, 398
Task Force 5: 39, 57, 127, 131, 132, 151, 152, 153, 162
Ter Poorten, Lieutenant General Hein 135, 140, 206, 207, 211, 247, 279, 386
Tjilatjap 136, 139, 154, 176, 189, 191, 192, 193, 195, 197, 198, 199, 208, 212, 214, 224, 226, 227, 228, 230, 234, 236, 240, 243, 245, 248, 249, 250, 256, 269, 270, 271, 272, 273, 274, 277, 278, 279, 336, 337, 338, 340, 354, 369, 370, 371, 372, 381, 382, 384, 385, 386, 388, 395, 396, 397, 398, 400, 403, 404, 405, 413
Toshio, Captain Abe 231, 232, 233, 234, 237, 238, 239
Type 93 torpedo 18, 19, 283, 286, 294, 318, 321, 322, 345, 357, 363

US Army Air Force 8, 36, 179, 180, 245, 262, 263, 277, 369, 391
US Asiatic Fleet 8, 29, 30, 32, 33, 80, 119, 122
US Navy 4, 8, 11, 18, 21, 23, 26, 30, 31, 32, 33, 34, 35, 36, 38, 46, 56, 77, 82, 113, 114, 116, 117, 118, 119, 120, 123, 124, 127, 135, 139, 140, 141, 142, 143, 144, 147, 152, 154, 156, 159, 162, 181, 185, 187, 188, 192, 194, 197, 201, 202, 203, 204, 208, 220, 221, 229, 242, 246, 248, 250, 255, 265, 268, 274, 275, 285, 325, 331, 333, 334, 353, 357, 372, 379, 382, 384, 386, 390, 391, 392, 393, 394, 401, 404, 409, 411

Van Ghent, Hr. Ms. 137, 140, 148, 182, 183, 194, 207, 209, 211, 226, 243, 249, 256, 298, 301, 406, 413
Van Mook, Deputy Governor General Hubertus Johannes 128, 129, 196, 247, 400, 411
Van Well Groeneveld, Lieutenant Commander Carel Adrianus Johannes 142, 156, 157, 158, 161
Vickers Vildebeest 72, 165, 166, 167, 332
Vigors, Flight Lieutenant Tim 75, 79, 100, 107, 108, 109

Wagner, Captain Frank B. 56, 57, 113, 128, 130, 132, 133, 253, 314
Walrus floatplane 91, 100, 110, 210
Warder, Lieutenant Commander Frederick Burdette 120, 225, 226
Wavell, Lieutenant General Sir Archibald P. 128, 129, 134, 145, 146, 147, 176, 191, 197, 203, 204, 205, 206, 207, 211, 212, 215, 224, 240, 244, 245, 246, 247
Whipple, USS 33, 39, 51, 76, 109, 152, 176, 181, 207, 208, 243, 248, 249, 250, 271, 272, 273, 278, 279, 371, 372, 380, 381, 384, 388, 390, 401, 402, 413
Winslow, Lieutenant Walter 119, 152, 186, 188, 228, 251, 254, 295, 297, 298, 303, 308, 319, 322, 327, 336, 338, 342, 346, 350, 351, 352
Witte de With, Hr. Ms. 137, 140, 226, 248, 249, 254, 256, 287, 288, 291, 298, 299, 300, 301, 309, 325, 326, 333, 334, 335, 337, 339, 394, 408, 413

Yarnell, Admiral Harry 29, 30
Yura 27, 84, 87, 141, 142, 248, 342

7368